בס"ד

HASMONEAN HIGH SCHOOL

HASMONEAN

אל תקרי בניך אלא בוניך

**Boys' Prize Day 2015 Guest Speaker
With Our Gracious Thanks**

Thank you!

PRESENTED TO

Rabbi Dweck

Dweck

———————————————————

Headteacher

November 2015/Kislev 5776

War and Peace in the Jewish Tradition

THE ORTHODOX FORUM

The Orthodox Forum, initially convened by Dr. Norman Lamm, Chancellor of Yeshiva University, meets each year to consider major issues of concern to the Jewish community. Forum participants from throughout the world, including academicians in both Jewish and secular fields, rabbis, *rashei yeshivah*, Jewish educators, and Jewish communal professionals, gather in conference as a think tank to discuss and critique each other's original papers, examining different aspects of a central theme. The purpose of the Forum is to create and disseminate a new and vibrant Torah literature addressing the critical issues facing Jewry today.

The Orthodox Forum
gratefully acknowledges the support
of the Joseph J. and Bertha K. Green Memorial Fund
at the Rabbi Isaac Elchanan Theological Seminary
established by Morris L. Green, of blessed memory.

The Orthodox Forum Series
is a project of the Rabbi Isaac Elchanan Theological Seminary,
an affiliate of Yeshiva University

War and Peace in the Jewish Tradition

edited by
Lawrence Schiffman
and Joel B. Wolowelsky

Robert S. Hirt, Series Editor

THE MICHAEL SCHARF PUBLICATION TRUST
of the YESHIVA UNIVERSITY PRESS
New York

MY
S U

Library of Congress Cataloging-in-Publication Data

Orthodox Forum (16th : 2004 : New York, NY)
  War and peace in the Jewish tradition / edited by Lawrence Schiffman, Joel B.
Wolowelsky.
    p. cm. – (Orthodox forum series)
  ISBN 0-88125-945-4
  1. War – Religious aspects – Judaism. 2. War (Jewish law) 3. Just war doctrine.
  4. Peace – Religious aspects – Judaism. 5. Reconciliation – Religious aspects –
  Judaism. I. Schiffman, Lawrence H. II. Wolowelsky, Joel B. III. Title.
  BM538.P3O78 2004
  296.3'6242 – dc22
                                    2006038084

                              *   *   *

                            Distributed by
                      KTAV Publishing House, Inc.
                          930 Newark Avenue
                         Jersey City, NJ 07306
                          Tel. (201) 963-9524
                          Fax. (201) 963-0102
                             www.ktav.com
                           bernie@ktav.com

This book was typeset by Jerusalem Typesetting, www.jerusalemtype.com

Contents

About the Editors and Contributors

Judith Bleich is associate professor of Judaic Studies at Touro College in New York City. She has written extensively on modern Jewish history.

Michael Broyde is senior lecturer at Emoy University School of Law, where he is also director of the Project on Law, Religion, and the Family and a member of the Law and Religion Program. Ordained *yoreh yoreh v-yadin yadin*, he is author of *The Pursuit of Justice and Jewish Law: Halakhic Perspectives on the Legal Profession*, as well as numerous other works.

Shalom Carmy teaches Bible, Jewish thought, and philosophy at Yeshiva University and is editor of *Tradition*. He has published extensively and is the editor of two volumes in the Orthodox Forum series, most recently *Jewish Perspectives on the Experience of Suffering*.

Stuart A. Cohen is a professor Political Studies at Bar-Ilan University in Israel.

Robert S. Hirt is the senior advisor to the president of Yeshiva University and vice president emeritus of its affiliated Rabbi Isaac Elchanan Theological Seminary. He occupies the Rabbi Sidney Shoham Chair in Rabbinic and Community Leadership at RIETS.

Elie Holzer is Assistant Professor in the School of Education at Bar Ilan University and a Senior Research Associate at the Mandel Center for Studies in Jewish Education at Brandeis University, MA. His fields of research and publications are hermeneutics and the teaching and learning of Jewish texts, professional development in Jewish education, philosophy of Jewish education, and Religious Zionism.

Norman Lamm is the *Rosh ha-Yeshivah* of the Rabbi Isaac Elchanan

Theological Seminary and the Chancellor of Yeshiva University.

Herbert Leventer is an adjunct instructor of Philosophy at Yeshiva University.

Michla Pomerance is the Emilio von Hofmannsthal Professor of International Law at the Hebrew University of Jerusalem. Her areas of expertise include international adjudication, the principle of self-determination, and international legal aspects of the use of force.

Lawrence H. Schiffman is Chairman of New York University's Skirball Department of Hebrew and Judaic Studies and serves as Ethel and Irvin A. Edelman Professor of Hebrew and Judaic Studies. He is also a member of the University's Hagop Kevorkian Center for Near Eastern Studies and Center for Ancient Studies.

Yosefi Seltzer is an active duty Judge Advocate with the United States Army Legal Services Agency. He is also the founder and president of the American Association of Jewish Lawyers and Jurists Military Bar Committee.

David Shatz is professor of philosophy at Yeshiva University, editor of *The Torah u-Madda Journal*, and editor of the series MeOtzar Horav: Selected Writings of Rabbi Joseph B. Soloveitchik. He has published many books and articles relating to both general and Jewish philosophy.

Moshe Sokolow is the Fanya Gottesfeld-Heller Professor of Jewish Education at the Azrieli Graduate School of Professional Education and Administration and Editor of *Ten Da'at*.

Jeremy Wieder teaches at Yeshiva University, occupying the Joseph and Gwendolyn Straus Chair in Talmud at the Rabbi Isaac Elchanan Theological Seminary.

Joel B. Wolowelsky is Dean of the Faculty at the Yeshivah of Flatbush, where he teaches math and Jewish philosophy. He is associate editor of *Tradition, The Torah u-Madda Journal*, and the series *MeOtzar HoRav: Selected Writings of Rabbi Joseph B. Soloveitchik*.

Dov Zakheim is a consultant in McLean, va.

Series Editor's Preface

The Orthodox Forum is dedicated to addressing consequential issues currently confronting our community, while drawing upon the insights and wisdom contained in Jewish textual sources from the Biblical period to our own day.

After the six-day war, a sense of euphoria engulfed the Jewish world awaiting the onset of a Messianic era. Following the collapse of the Soviet Union, the world anticipated the end of global hostility. Yet, it wasn't too long before age old ethnic, religious and national conflicts resurfaced and hopes for peace gave way to cycles of violent conflicts in many regions of the world.

This volume, the fourteenth in the Orthodox Forum Series, War, Peace and the Jewish Tradition, brings together the thinking of a wide range of distinguished American and Israeli academicians and religious leaders from various disciplines, to shed light on the historical, philosophical, theological, legal and moral issues raised by military conflict and the search for peaceful resolution. We are grateful to Prof. Lawrence Schiffman, who capably chaired the conference, and to Dr. Joel B. Wolowelsky who skillfully took primary responsibility for editing the volume.

We trust that the scholar and lay person alike will find the analyses and ready access to primary sources in this volume to be challenging and rewarding and that the reader will gain valuable insights and appreciation of the relevance of Jewish sources in approaching contemporary challenges.

Robert S. Hirt

January 2007

Introduction

David Shatz

The choice of "War and Peace" as the topic of the sixteenth annual meeting of the Orthodox Forum in March 2004 was created by two catalysts: first, the United States' involvement in Iraq; second, Israel's ongoing war with terrorism.[1] The program committee of the conference felt that as the rest of the world was heatedly addressing these situations in countless forums, the Orthodox community needed to mobilize its intellectual and spiritual resources and develop perspectives on war informed by moral sensitivity, political wisdom, and above, all fidelity to the Biblical and rabbinic tradition. The committee was drawn, in the first instance, to two questions: when is it right, justified or obligatory to go to war – the *"jus ad bellum"* question; and how war, once justified or mandated, must be conducted – the *"jus in bello"* question. But in further deliberations other questions emerged, questions which cut to the very heart of the Jewish value system with regard to violence and peace.

The committee believed that discussions about how Judaism conceives the justification for war and the conduct of war should not be held in a vacuum; that is, they should not take place exclusively on the plane of halakhic and aggadic sources. Rather, religious explorations must engage secular ethical perspectives and secular legalities, as well as perspectives promulgated by Christianity in its quest for a definition of "just war." We need to place Jewish tradition in conversation with general moral sensibilities and international regulations. Accordingly, a few of the papers are strictly about secular ethics (Herbert Leventer's) or secular law (Michla Pomerance's and Yosefi Seltzer's). With regard to Jewish tradition, three topics are especially important: the ethics of entering and waging war (already referred to); the religious significance of having an army and of army service; and the value of peace.

JUS AD BELLUM: DECLARING WAR[2]

Whether a particular U.S. military action is justified according to Jewish law might seem more difficult to determine than whether a Jewish polity is justified in fighting wars. There is a developed literature on when a Jewish state can go to war, owing heavily to the founding of the State of Israel in the twentieth century and the questions to which that gave birth. The literature on non-Jewish wars is far more limited. Even so, we can outline two basic approaches to *jus ad bellum* in the case of non-Jews. One approach maintains that non-Jews may go to war in a situation of self-defense or of *rodef*. The latter refers to a case where a pursuer is seeking to kill someone else; a third party, Halakhah stipulates, may intervene to stop the pursuer.[3] On the analysis in question, then, we consider the situation of non-Jews who are in danger to be the situation of individual self-defense or *rodef* writ large – in other words, those justifications, it is suggested, apply to a group and not just an individual. The idea that an appeal to self-defense or *rodef* suffices to justify war is, however, problematic. Notably, Michael Broyde argues that Jewish law permits acts in war that cannot be justified via the self-defense or pursuer rationales. *Rodef* and self-defense, for instance, permit only the killing of a guilty party; they never permit killing innocent people, which sometimes is permissible in halakhically approved wars. Also, ordinarily people are not obligated (maybe not even permitted) to endanger their own lives to save others; they are so in war. In contrast to those who adduce the self-defense and pursuer model, R. Naftali Tzvi Yehudah Berlin (Netziv) and other authorities adopt a second approach, namely that there is a category of war in the Noahide laws that is far broader than these models.[4]

Turning from non-Jewish armies to the issue of how Jews may justify their own going to war, it is clear that for Jews there is a distinct category of *milhamah* that is not reducible to self-defense or *rodef*. We begin with the fact that Jewish law utilizes two main categories of war: *milhemet mitzvah* (mandatory war) and *milhemet reshut* (discretionary war, e.g. a war to expand territory; Broyde calls it "Authorized War").[5] *Milhemet reshut* may not be waged today because a declaration of such a war must be approved by the king, the Sanhedrin, and the *urim ve-tumim*, the oracular breastplate worn by the High Priest. Although arguably the requirement of a king is fulfilled by having a government that is not monarchic, including one democratically elected,[6] the other two institutions do not exist today. As for *milhemet mitzvah*, Maimonides understands this category as including the war against Amalek and the war against the Seven Nations. While these categories are not operative today, Maimonides adds another instance of mandatory war – one that would allow the State of Israel today to wage a *milhemet mitzvah*. He speaks of a war for the purpose of "saving Israel from an enemy that has taken aggressive action against them" – in other words, a defensive war (Laws of Kings 5:1).[7] Maimonides does not require approval by a Sanhedrin or *urim ve-tumim* for the waging of a mandatory war.[8] Even if Maimonides does require a "*melekh*,"[9] his view may be that a "king" is any Jewish government. Hence, if we follow Maimonides, Israel is justified in waging wars of self-defense in the full halakhic sense of "war." Indeed, Israel is obligated to wage those wars.

Many further questions arise. A particularly important one is whether a pre-emptive strike is justified in Jewish law, and if so, what actions on the part of the enemy justify the strike. The category of preemptive strike is mentioned in the Talmud in *Sotah* 44b (a war "to diminish the heathens so that they shall not come upon them").[10] There are different ways to understand this condition and to dissect the *gemara* that introduces it, but it has been argued that in the final analysis preemptive action is discretionary, a *milhemet reshut*, which would make it an inoperative category today due to the requirements of Sanhedrin and *urim ve-tumim*.[11] The pursuer and self-defense rationales would apply; but, again, these rationales are too narrow to trigger the full license associated with a *milhemet mitzvah*. That said, it is possible that Maimonides' formulation of one type of *milhemet mitzvah*, "helping Israel against an enemy that has taken aggressive action against them," will in certain circumstances justify preventive actions under the rubric of *milhemet mitzvah*. For instance, according to some, actions designed solely to prevent future attack are justified by reference to *milhemet mitzvah* when those actions are undertaken in response to previous armed attacks. This principle holds even if those enemy attacks were responses to earlier preemptive actions that could be justified only by reference to self-defense and not by reference to the conditions for bona fide *milhamah*.[12]

Finally, it bears mention that some authorities see entry into war by the State of Israel as deriving its justification from the same source as wars by non-Jewish governments, according to the opinion that recognizes a distinct category of *milhamah* for non-Jews. In that case, Broyde says, the rules of entering into and conducting war might follow those of international law and treaties.[13]

These are some of the issues surrounding Jewish views on *jus ad bellum*. Let us next turn to issues of *jus in bello*, the conduct of war.

JUS IN BELLO: THE CONDUCT OF WAR

Jewish sources present a view of *jus in bello* that is more permissive than many secular accounts. Broyde quotes the view of R. Eliezer Waldenberg, author of *Tzitz Eliezer*, as well as other authorities that in war the rules about what can and cannot be done are different than in normal contexts. Governments may take actions that individuals are prohibited to perform; and in war Halakhah allows killing human beings in circumstances where outside of the war context the killing would be prohibited. Examples include killing two comrades to rescue one (normally one must not take one life to save two) and imposing collective punishment on vast segments of an enemy society in response to the misconduct of a few, as could happen when terrorist perpetrators escape capture. After first seeking peace with the enemy, Broyde says, the Jewish polity may licitly embark on hostilities in a way that might involve causing civilian deaths, exerting "outrageous pressure" to obtain information, executing Hannibal orders by which a soldier is killed by his comrades to prevent a drawn out situation of a soldier in captivity, and seducing an opposing general with the aim of discovering war plans. If you can risk people's lives to go to war in the first place, the argument goes, surely you can take risks with enemy lives to win the war. In Broyde's words: "[O]nce 'killing' becomes permitted as a matter of Jewish law, much of the hierarchical values of Jewish law seem to be suspended as well, at least to the extent that the ones who are hurt are people who also may be killed." In war we have a type of *horaat sha'ah*, a temporary measure which partially suspends normal halakhic rules. Broyde adds, however, that while in general "Jewish law has few if any rules of battle," treaties and conventions bind combatants. Broyde also says that prudence may militate against these actions and that the exact circumstances may constrain what is permissible – a war for survival is different from a war for economic viability.

The basic thesis of Broyde's essay, then, is that the conduct of war is in fact the suspension of the normative ethics of Jewish law to prevent the eradication of Jewish society. Ethics in warfare are therefore fundamentally different from ethics in all other situations. Broyde goes on to note that this explains what he regards as the paucity of halakhic material on the conduct of war. Since Halakhah envisions war to entail the suspension of all violations – from the prohibition to kill downward – it permits the violation, as military need requires, of every prohibition with the single exception of *avodah zarah*. Assessing this need falls under the purview of military leaders, not rabbis or ethicists.

Broyde also raise the issue of who is a combatant. In his view, Halakhah maintains that anyone who materially contributes to the war effort is a combatant and thus a fair target. Of course, Jewish law sometimes demands overtures prior to declaring war to afford all who wish the opportunity to depart (known in Halakhah as the duty to surround on only three sides). Those who remain, however – including sympathetic civilians – are no longer innocents, and their death, when militarily necessary, is according to Broyde unfortunate but halakhically proper. Combatants, in Broyde's analysis, include as well players far from the battlefield who are directing or supplying enemy forces.

Herbert Leventer does three things in his paper. First, he presents a historical overview of the development of just war theory. He emphasizes that, though it originated within Christian theology, just war theory was radically revised in the seventeenth century to become a purely secular set of rules for the just conduct of war. It was this tradition that, from Grotius in the seventeenth century to Michael Walzer in the twentieth, has influenced governments and armies of the western world. The custom of nations observing these limitations has gradually evolved into a positive written international law, especially as codified in the various Hague and Geneva conventions. Walzer's 1976 book, *Just and Unjust Wars*, has become the classic modern statement of the following set of criteria for justice in war: aggression, actual or imminent, is the only just cause for going to war; there are limits to how badly you can treat your enemy, in recognition of his common humanity and of the ultimate goal of living in peace with him after the fighting ends; you must discriminate between combatants and civilians; and you must observe proportionality in all of the above.

Leventer next describes the method philosophers use to discuss the ethical issues raised by war. In their quest to ensure that the rules they elaborate are universal, philosophers are fond of abstracting from the specific details of actual wars or battles and describing ideal, often fantastic, cases. So, for example, to analyze the permissibility of killing innocent civilians in the course of a legitimate military operation, philosophers discuss the case of an aggressor who straps a baby on the front of his tank to shield himself from counterattack. They borrow from the rules of domestic law the requirement that "guilt" requires not just a bad action, but also a bad intention, and so defend the permissibility of killing the innocent shield because it was unintended collateral damage. This is a "secularization" of the Catholic doctrine of double effect, which maintains that if a single action produces two results – one good and intended, the other bad, not sought, and not the necessary means for achieving the desired effect – one is not morally liable for the unintended effect. One proves that killing the baby was unintended by one's willingness to fire on the tank even if it did not have a baby on it.

Finally, Leventer shows how contemporary philosophers have used these methods to analyze problems that have recently become important, such as preventive war, collective guilt (or at least, liability of civilians to share with uniformed soldiers the dangers of possible death), and situations – especially ones that involve fighting guerillas or terrorists – where it would be morally acceptable, and perhaps even required, to cause civilian deaths in order to save your own combatants.

Yosefi Seltzer describes the legal challenges facing the United States military and its allies in their prosecution of the Global War Against Terrorism. Seltzer details the Law of War and Geneva Convention doctrines and explores how they are being adapted to conflicts with aggressors who routinely violate these same principles. Because the terrorists are not lawful combatants when they conceal their arms and engage in unlawful attacks on civilian targets, they present very real challenges to the United States military. Using the broadest possible definitions of "self-defense," "lawful target," "combatants," "proportional response," and other key terms is critical to executing an effective response to unconventional and unlawful attacks while trying to abide by the various war conventions and customs. Because of the deceitful and treacherous tactics used by terrorists in the course of contemporary warfare, Seltzer suggests that the modern battlefield has been transformed from conventional warfare, similar to a two dimensional chessboard model, to one involving concealment and deception, more akin to the aura of the "Matrix" film trilogy.

The process of formulating and implementing evolving combat objectives and guidelines poses challenges to the entire chain of command. Consequently, revisions and "lessons learned" are being incorporated on a rolling basis into combat instruction and training. In some cases, the learning curve has resulted in unfortunate casualties, due to undisciplined excess and lax passivity. The scandals at the Abu Ghraib prison facility, Seltzer contends, should serve as a constant reminder of how the entire chain of command must constrain its conduct and train subordinates to follow the rule of law. Without explicit direction, discipline within the ranks, and accountability, chaos can ensue, ultimately destabilizing the mission. That said, it is feasible for soldiers to exercise good faith judgment and discipline as they apply the Rules of Engagement in situations involving imminent threats and to take measures that comply with the Law of War in the process of maintaining order and defending themselves, their units, and their nation's interests.

Moshe Sokolow's paper examines the concepts of spoils of war as it is treated in the Bible, Talmud, Midrash, and medieval exegesis. He then discusses the more general theme of militarism and morality in modern Jewish thought.

In the Bible, taking spoils is normally permitted, as implied by the imperative in Deut. 20:14 and amply illustrated in the wars against Midian, Og king of Bashan, and certain nations like Ammon and Moab. Yet in six instances, the Bible restricts or bans the taking of spoils, as in the case of the *ir ha-niddahat* (subverted city) and Saul's battle against Amalek. Sokolow explains that Biblical exceptions are made in the interests of eradicating infamy and taking care not to sully the name and reputation of Israel among the gentiles. In some instances, the Jews are simply refusing to participate in legitimate spoils (as in cases involving Abraham and the Jews of Shushan). The Midrash and medieval exegetes, in explaining the six cases where spoils were not taken or not permitted to be taken, stress the corrosive effects that taking spoils has on morality and halakhic behavior.

Sokolow then proceeds to assemble an array of figures in modern Jewish thought who stress the need to preserve purity in war. Among them are R. Samson Raphael Hirsch, Isaiah Leibowitz, and R. Aharon Soloveichik. Summing up their discussions, he writes that "[e]ven while engaged in morally defensible, even halakhically mandated activities, a Jew must be ever vigilant to maintain his singularity of purpose, and on constant guard against its adulteration or erosion."

In an epilogue, Sokolow points out the difference between pre-modern warfare, when soldiers owned their weapons, and modern warfare, when the state owns them. By dint of this distinction, modern soldiers may not be entitled to spoils, while pre-modern combatants were. In our day, the judgment of the Israeli Defense Forces is that looting is prohibited, as per the Hague and Geneva Conventions, but weapons, facilities, and property can be appropriated as spoils. Private property cannot be seized unless it serves an important military need.

As noted, the liberal secular viewpoint and the Jewish legal perspective conflict on many of these issues. It is interesting to ask what to make of this – is there any chance of reconciling general ethics and Halakhah in this regard? While we need not pursue this large issue here, it is worth noting Leventer's claim that occasional killing of innocents may be allowed even by non-Jewish "just war" theories.

AMALEK AND THE SEVEN NATIONS: THE MORAL PROBLEM

A powerful conflict between secular and Jewish perspectives, in the realm of both *jus ad bellum* and *jus in bello*, concerns the wars that Jews are commanded to wage against the Seven Nations and Amalek. On the surface, these commandments involve genocide. The moral unease that these commandments induce in religiously committed Jews may be mitigated by the fact these commandments do not apply today – the Seven Nations are no more and, according to Maimonides, we cannot identify Amalek. As Shalom Carmy notes, this impossibility of identification may be a providential way of avoiding the moral problem in practice. But even granted this inapplicability, the moral problem exists at the theoretical level – how could one justify the commandment to destroy another nation, even if the nation is not identifiable – as well as on the level of history (in the past the Jews had to carry out these commandments). Saying that

God is the one who fights the war against Amalek (as in Ex. 17:14–15) does not solve the problem. For God's ethics are still a problem – not, to be sure, His ethics in *prescribing* the battle, but rather His ethics in actually *waging* the battle.

According to Carmy, it is impossible to gain perspective on the radical commandments to extirpate the Canaanite nations and Amalek without viewing then in the context of Biblical and Talmudic teachings about war and peace: "Universal peace is the goal…Yet war is permitted, and success in waging war is extolled." He cites halakhic and aggadic statements hostile to war in principle, and the halakhic restrictions that surround elective war (*milhemet reshut*) are virtually impossible under contemporary conditions. Militant Zionists and their Orthodox opponents agreed about the peaceable orientation of traditional Judaism; R. Kook treated ancient warfare as a necessity of olden times.

The commandments referring to particular ethnic groups are inapplicable today because these nations no longer exist. Carmy argues that this is no accident of history. The practical fulfillment of these commandments is not part of God's plan for the post-ancient world, where individual moral choice may override ethnic identities and mores. As to the Canaanite inhabitants of the land of Israel, the explicit rationale for the command to eradicate is the threat of their religious influence. Moreover, R. Kook and several contemporary scholars and thinkers suggest that the primary application of these laws was limited to Joshua's generation, the initial era of conquest, and lapsed afterwards.

The struggle against Amalek, by contrast, is ongoing. Among the plethora of Amalekite vices detailed in homiletical literature, Carmy concentrates on factors implied by the Bible: the gratuitous nature of their hatred of Israel and its violation of the fraternal connection entailed by Amalek's descent from Edom. He rejects rationalization of the commandment based on belief in permanent, inherited viciousness as without scriptural or scientific warrant and conducive to the worst morality, and carefully draws on Hasidic approaches that spiritualize the present day prosecution of the age old struggle. An original analysis of Biblical prophecies against Edom leads him to conclude that Amalek's specific acts and motivations are symbols of perpetual temptations to violence and betrayal that will continue to infect the lives of nations until they are eradicated.

Ultimately Carmy remains dissatisfied with these justifications: the war against the Canaanites smacks of *realpolitik*; that against Amalek amounts to scapegoating. It is morally and religiously preferable to regard these commands as "laws without rationale, justifiable only from the standpoint of *Deus dixit*. Anything else either cheapens the word of God or degrades human moral judgment." Yet there is value in defining the mystery and the terror as precisely as possible in the light of the sources.

Norman Lamm, too, addresses the moral conflict. He first appeals to the practical solution – the impossibility of identifying Amalek in our time. In the course of sustaining this approach, he argues against the contention (one based on the wording of certain of Maimonides' rulings) that whereas the Seven Nations no longer exist, "Amalek" does, for the term denotes not simply biological Amalekites but any enemy of the Jewish people. Lamm notes that this thesis, if true, would mandate killing all members of enemy nations throughout the centuries, a consequence he regards as untenable; and he argues for a different understanding of Maimonides' view.

But even if Amalek does not exist today or cannot be identified, what about the theoretical moral problem – is it not problematic that in theory we should carry out the genocidal commandment, and that in Biblical times we did so in practice? At this juncture Lamm suggests that Halakhah is responsive to what he calls "developing morality." Certain practices that are Biblically permitted, such as polygamy, were later banned by rabbinic authorities, and certain Talmudic prescriptions (e.g., severe treatment of heretics) were declared by recent authorities to be inapplicable today. Moral sensitivities develop over time. The medieval source *Sefer Hasidim* endorses the idea of a continuing revelation "expressed in ever higher levels of morality." Lamm concludes that "the idea of refraining from harming civilian non-combatants," which is not explicit in the Torah, "should be looked upon as part of the 'continuing revelation.'" Likewise, " the reluctance to implement, even theoretically, the Torah's

draconian commandments concerning Amalek and the Seven Nations, bespeaks a later moral development, a kind of new application
of *lifnim mi-shurat ha-din* [supererogatory conduct]...," which is
part of Torah itself and that does not, therefore, look askance at the
Torah's original laws concerning the enemies of Israel.

INTERNATIONAL LAW

In the modern context the conduct of war and its aftermath is
governed by international law and treaties. Does Halakhah recognize the validity of international law? If so, is such law binding on
the Jewish state? What is the halakhic force of treaties such as the
Geneva Conventions? These questions, with regard to which there
is a paucity of literature, are addressed by Jeremy Wieder.

Wieder focuses first on finding a conceptual halakhic model
for international law, in particular as regards those cases where
certain actions are not explicitly addressed in halakhic sources but
are forbidden under international law. He examines two models:
first, the halakhic requirement that Noahides establish *dinim* – court
systems – and second, the principle of *dina de-malkhuta dina*, "the
law of the kingdom is law." Both of these relate to how individual
societies govern themselves, but perhaps the models can be extended
to international legal systems.

Maimonides held that *dinim* encompasses specifically the
enforcement by courts of the other six Noahide laws. The problem
with invoking the Maimonidean *dinim* model in connection with
international law, Wieder points out, is that it would not allow for
new regulations governing murder and theft that were not included
in *Hazal's* definitions of these categories. Nahmanides' view that
dinim encompasses a broader range of civil laws opens up the possibility of an expanded set of rules, but it might be that Nahmanides
included in *dinim* only those categories of civil laws that apply to
Jews. By contrast, those authorities who hold that Noahide laws
do not have to dovetail precisely with Halakhah might allow the
introduction of international laws into the Noahide system. At the
same time, in rabbinic teaching Noahide laws were given to Adam,
when there was no concept of boundaries between nations, and so it

is not clear that Halakhah would recognize separate nations bound to each other by *dinim*.

Turning next to "*dina de-malkhuta dina*," the appropriateness of this model depends on the rationale for *dina de-malkhuta dina*. Is the rationale that the king owns the land? That the people have consented to being governed? That society could not function without the principle? Wieder teases out the implications of each rationale for international law, arguing, for example, that the last rationale makes the principle applicable to the international scene. Wieder also inquires whether the two models (*dinim, dina de-malkhhuta*) mandate an enforcement mechanism. In the *dinim* model, establishing a legal system is mandatory. In the case of *dina de-malkhuta dina*, different rationales carry different consequences regarding mandatory status. The consent rationale, for example, does not imply a mandate, while the "social function" explanation does.

Do the models apply to make laws and treaties binding on the *Jewish* state? If Jews are obligated in the precept of *dinim*, this could mandate Jewish participation in the international enterprise. With regard to *dina de-malkhuta dina*, if the principle stems from consent of the people or the need for society to function (as opposed to the idea that the king owns the land), then it would apply to the Land of Israel.

Wieder next turns to the subject of treaties. Apparently, a treaty with an oath undertaken without deception is binding so long as it does not involve an "active" violation of Jewish law. However, *hillul Hashem* may be a factor as well in determining whether a treaty must be observed. For example (to cite one possible position), perhaps it would be obligatory to comply with a treaty that involves only "passive" violations of Halakhah if non-compliance would result in *hillul Hashem*. Wieder also suggests that if one side abrogates a treaty, such action would release the other party from its obligations unless expressly stipulated otherwise.

Finally, Wieder suggests that in some circumstances the State of Israel should participate in a system of international law even absent a theoretical model. For example, if it does not participate, Israel might become a pariah and be subject to danger, or *hillul Hashem* might occur. Of course a treaty that violates Halakhah requires further analysis.

Michla Pomerance's paper transports us from the realm of halakhic analysis to a close and detailed examination of international law as it bears on contemporary political situations. Her main thesis is that "Israel's present predicament has been tragically sharpened by some of the more worrisome trends in international law and international organizations." By distorting UN Charter tenets, and placing a so-called "right" of self-determination at the pinnacle, above the fundamental principle prohibiting the use of force, UN organs have tended to protect terrorist aggressors while condemning and delegitimizing the victims of aggression. In developing her thesis, Pomerance addresses first *jus ad bellum* and then *jus in bello* issues.

UN Charter provisions on the use of force, Pomerance notes, leave many questions unanswered, including the permissibility of anticipatory self-defense (preemptive strikes). On the basis of the drafting history of the relevant provisions, state practice, and considerations of logic, Pomerance concludes that a broad interpretation of the right of self-defense is warranted. However, a new "UN Law of Self-Determination" – a modern "just war" doctrine spawned by the UN General Assembly in 1960–61 and developed in an accelerated form thereafter – deformed and severely impinged upon existing legal rights. The beneficiaries of the new doctrine were peoples whom the Assembly deemed to be subject to "colonial exploitation and domination" or to be living under "racist regimes" or "alien occupation." Such "peoples" were increasingly granted exemption from obligations, while those who would "forcibly deprive" them of their "right to self-determination, freedom and independence" were to be denied their essential right to self-defense. The doctrine was repeatedly utilized to restrain and condemn Israel. Moreover, the new UN perspective also transformed the previous *jus in bello* edifice by significantly attenuating the conditions for receiving prisoner-of-war treatment and blurring the distinction between combatants and civilians in a manner conducive to unfettered violence.

In their attempt to diminish and ultimately expel Israel even from the pre-1967 borders and turn it into a pariah state, Palestinians and the Arab states found it useful to elicit the help of the International Court of Justice. The General Assembly's request for an advisory opinion of the Court on the legality of Israel's security fence led predictably to a joint exercise in political-judicial delegitimation of Israel's defensive measures. The very formulation of the question posed by the Assembly was, she says, biased against Israel; and in her opinion, the Court, which included outspoken critics of Israel, rubber-stamped the Assembly's pre-set conclusions. It ignored the terrorist context of the security fence and asserted that the "wall" was not necessary for attaining Israel's security objective. Significantly, the Court's perspective on the use of force has caused consternation to the United States as well, in cases in which it was involved. Among other Biblical verses Pomerance uses to capture the circumstances, she cites "in the place of justice, there is wickedness" (Eccl. 3:16).

Thus, Pomerance highlights the importance of understanding the asymmetries in the current assault against Israel; Israel's inability, morally and practically, to employ the full power of its weaponry against its enemies; and Israel's diplomatic isolation (which is aided and abetted by elements within Israel and the Jewish Diaspora). Above all, she emphasizes that for countering the attempts to delegitimize Israel's right to self-defense, it is necessary to recognize that the most baneful of the forces arrayed against Israel are "those that come dressed in the false garb of self-determination, human rights, and humanitarianism."

THE SIGNIFICANCE AND VALUE OF ARMY SERVICE

What is the significance of an army in Jewish thought? Who should serve in a Jewish army? Should Jews living in non-Jewish societies fight in wars waged by their host countries?

Let us begin with the question of who should serve in a Jewish army. During the long exile of the Jewish people, the claim was sometimes made that military exploits are inconsistent with Jewish spirituality. These claims may have arisen from the fact that Jews were living in the Diaspora and were politically and militarily powerless; the absence of those powers may have led to the thought that

they *ought* to be missing. Religious Zionism tried to change this conception and to invoke a Biblical model that portrayed great leaders
as both warriors and spiritual figures, on the model of Joshua and
David. In truth, such approaches were not altogether revolutionary.
Almost a millennium before Zionism, Maimonides had attributed
the Jews' loss of the Temple to their failure to learn "the art of war
and the conquest of lands."[14] In the Book of Deuteronomy, those
who are "fearful and faint of heart" do not serve (20:8),[15] but those
who abide by the priest's directive "do not let your heart go faint,
and do not fear" because God "walks with you," do serve (Deut.
20:3–4; note the similarity of the words in the priest's directive and
the formulation of the exemption). Thus the ideal army is an army
of the faithful. (This is how the Maccabees are presented in much of
traditional literature – a small army with God on their side.).

But nowadays, we encounter a different phenomenon and approach. Many ultra-Orthodox ("haredi") Israeli Jews (perhaps even
20,000 by some estimates) claim exemptions from military service,
citing the dangers of spiritual attrition and the loss of time for Torah
study. Stuart Cohen shows, however, that tensions between the IDF
and Orthodoxy are not exclusive to *haredim*. Soldiers of the *dati-
le'umi* ("religious-national") orientation also encounter challenges in
the army. To be sure, at first glance the IDF does appear to be quite
accommodating to observant soldiers. It provides the services of a
military rabbinate, arranges lectures on religious topics, organizes
Friday night meals and a seder attended by all troops, and conducts a
ceremony at which new recruits receive a copy of the *Tanakh* (many
times at the Western Wall). Moreover, soldiers now have access to
an abundance of works that deal with practical Halakhah in the
context of army service. Yet notwithstanding these elements of the
army experience, military service imposes pressures and tensions
on national-religious conscripts.

Only rarely do such challenges express themselves in the contradiction between military orders and rabbinic directives over
political issues, such as the military dismantlement of settlements.
More common are three other sets of difficulties.

The first arises from the fact that religious soldiers have contact with secularist comrades, whose comportment is foreign and perhaps threatening to their observant lifestyle. By way of response, some "national-religious" mentors propose segregating observant soldiers into their own groups. Others, however, adopt the strategy of "fortification" – preparing religious recruits to meet the experiences they will encounter in serving with secular Israelis, without arranging for assignment into their own groups.

Cohen next considers conflicts that fall into the category of "holiness." Soldiers face conflicts with regard to keeping Shabbat and *kashrut*, wearing *tzitzit* (when they must don camouflage), taking time out for prayer thrice daily, observing fast days, and serving in combat units with women. Interestingly, the military rabbinate is not often consulted on these matters; the soldiers prefer civilian rabbis from municipalities or *yeshivot*.

Finally, there is the basic conflict between service and study. *Haredim*, as noted, have used the duty to study Torah as the basis for exemption from military service. Religious Zionists have options such as *hesder* or *mekhinot*. The latter encourage observant Jews to climb the military ladder by enrolling in officer training programs, while the former do not. In recent years, only 18.2% of the male graduates of Israel's national-religious schools enroll in *hesder yeshivot*, while half the graduates declare the intention of enrolling in the IDF the normal way. This pattern signals the fact that young conscripts think in "either-or" terms and are not attracted by *hesder's* middle course.

Elie Holzer discusses how the army and military action, and to some extent political action, were viewed by four major figures or schools in ideologies of Religious Zionism. The first approach he analyzes is the "harmonistic-dialectical" model of R. Abraham Isaac Kook. Rav Kook considered such activities as a return to agricultural labors to be a harbinger of the "manifest redemption," a process by which the nation Israel would return to the political and historical stage – *but without need of military action*. In Rav Kook's vision, there will be no military confrontation between Israel and the other nations. Use of force is forbidden to the Jewish people and is not – or rather cannot be – a means to the messianic goal. The essence of that goal is the Torah state in which the Jewish people will become a moral and spiritual model for the rest of the world. Furthermore, it is precisely by living in Exile, bereft of political power, that Israel came to develop the moral sensitivity that they will exemplify in the era of redemption.

Holzer stresses another point as well. Rav Kook adopted the stance of "redemptive interpretation," a construal of events that places them within a harmonistic and teleological frame. From this harmonistic, teleological standpoint, secular Zionist activism, despite appearances, is nourished in sanctity. This method of redemptive interpretation, which often entails viewing the true reality as dramatically different from how things appear, becomes highly significant as Holzer turns to the view of Rav Kook's son, R. Tzvi Yehudah Kook.

R. Tzvi Yehudah Kook faced a different historical reality than his father did, a reality in which the State of Israel found itself involved in military confrontation within the redemptive process. Yet in his view military activism takes on great significance as it (like immigration to Israel) represents the revelation of the *Shekhinah* in the era of Redemption. The state is sacred and expresses God's presence in the world; likewise the state's army is sacred. The absence of a "kingdom of Israel," a militarily supreme Jewish polity, is nothing short of a *hilliul Hashem*, a desecration of God's name, while the successes of the IDF are a *kiddush Hashem* (sanctification of God's name). Holzer points out that R. Tzvi Yehudah's conception views not only self-defense but even aggression as imperative. "Redemptive interpretation," writes Holzer, "has become explicitly *prescriptive*." Such aggression fulfills the *mitzvah* of conquering the Land by military means. This *mitzvah* is absolute, and is in Holzer's words "not subordinate to any halakhic considerations, not even danger to life (*pikuah nefesh*)." Indeed, conquest represents a revitalization of Halakhah itself. Practical constraints are irrelevant, as God Himself is forcing the events.

In short, for R. Tzvi Yehudah Kook, the use of military force is a religious value. It is puzzling that he and his disciples saw this view as a continuation of his father's, given that his father taught that a national revival *without* force is the hallmark of redemption. To explain this phenomenon, Holzer suggests, *inter alia*, that R. Abraham Isaac's redemptive interpretation of events, for example, World War I (which represented for him the eradication of a religiously and morally corrupt culture and a herald of a new culture founded on religion and morality) served R. Tzvi Yehudah as a model for interpreting the later military events as well. The end result was an upheaval of his father's views on military activity.

R. Yitzhak Yaakov Reines, leader of Mizrahi, saw a need for political activities but rejected the claim that his times were messianic. He embraced two principles: the realistic principle, which mandates finding practical solutions to the plight of the Jewish people; and the ethical principle, that is, the commitment to religious and ethical principles binding on the Jew, which may set limits on political activism. Thus activism for R. Reines is not part of a redemptive process and must be balanced and informed by ethical principles. R. Reines meant in particular to exclude the use of force. As Holzer notes, R. Reines died in 1915 and had no need to reckon with the later reality in which Jewish survival necessitated the use of force. In those later days, religious Zionist figures recognized the value of using force in self-defense, while trying simultaneously to cultivate an ethical and religious aversion to bloodshed. Holzer traces this ethically-guided realistic approach through the writings of several later figures, including present day thinkers like Aviezer Ravitzky and R. Yehuda Amital.

Finally, R. Aharon Shmuel Tamares and R. Moshe Avigdor Amiel held that Torah is the antithesis of a power-centered, radical and total nationalist-political ideology. The latter – which these thinkers saw as idolatrous – leads to religious and moral corruption, the worship of physical force, and an abandonment of the religious-ethical mission of the Jewish people. Nationhood is not a matter of biology but of spiritual values by which a group shapes its life. R. Tamares saw the Zionist cries of "Homeland" as a call for a different Judaism. Even Mizrahi's effort to synthesize nationalism and Torah was subjected to harsh criticism because the relevant concept of "nationalism" was secular and derived from a secular source. The Jews' ethical sensitivity necessitates their divorce from national-political life. Notwithstanding their criticism of Zionism, both nonetheless desired a national Jewish polity – but of the right sort. The view of philosopher Yeshayahu Leibowitz is similar to that of Rabbis Tamares and Amiel, but it rejects the humanistic understanding of Judaism that their views imply and replaces humanism with submission to the divine will.

Turning from army service in Israel to army service in the Diaspora, Judith Bleich considers a question many college and post-college youth considered during the Vietnam war, and which many rabbinic figures pondered in previous centuries: should Jews have a positive attitude to joining the army of their host non-Jewish countries, or should "draft dodging" be permitted – or even encouraged? Over the centuries (including ancient times), there are instances of Jews serving as mercenaries or volunteers, and in 1806 Napoleon's Sanhedrin declared emphatically that Jews must serve in France's army. Post-Emancipation, large numbers of Jews were conscripted into non-Jewish armies. Nonetheless, Bleich shows that traditionalist authorities of the nineteenth and twentieth centuries viewed army service negatively, even though some wrote in a subtle and circumspect fashion designed not to displease government authorities. Serving in the army created problems in observing Jewish rituals and fulfilling religious obligations (e.g., Shabbat, *kashrut*, and dressing in a traditional manner). Furthermore, unless the service is during peacetime, Jews might be put in danger in a situation where such endangerment is not permitted by Halakhah. Also, Jews might impermissibly have to kill others, including fellow Jews. And, in general, Judaism allows wars of defense but not of aggression.

Many traditionalist authorities ruled that a person may not be "handed over" to fulfill a draft quota. Nevertheless, some authorities countenanced the use of a lottery by Jewish communal officials to fulfill draft quotas, provided that the lottery include all eligible conscripts. Hatam Sofer permitted pursuing exemptions or deferments and finding other ways of avoiding service, such as hiring a substitute. A later authority asserted that it is commendable to avoid army service at all costs, with the result that hiring a substitute even becomes a *mitzvah*. Danger to life was a salient consideration behind the foregoing rulings, so much so that authorities taught that it is preferable to accept employment involving Sabbath desecration than to place one's life in danger.

Even decisors who permitted army service did not do so because they thought army service was an ideal. There were exceptions to the negative trend, notably R. Samson Raphael Hirsch and R. Moshe Samuel Glasner of Klausenberg. Participation in World War II sometimes elicited a positive response to service because Jews were specifically targeted as victims in the war waged by the Nazis. Those qualifications aside, the dominant trend was negative. And since Jews did in fact serve, authorities had to grapple with challenges to observance and religious morality that arose in the army. Indeed, Hafetz Hayyim wrote a manual to guide Jewish soldiers through such challenges.

In contrast to the "negative" trend found among traditionalist authorities, liberal elements in the early Reform movement regarded army service as demonstrating patriotism as well as a means of achieving emancipation, enfranchisement, and equality. Jewish proponents of army service, however, needed to combat stereotypes of Jews held by non-Jews, stereotypes which called into question Jews' fitness for military service. These liberal proponents were not always successful in this effort; anti-Semitism flourished in the army, and Jews were accused of slacking and draft-dodging.

Bleich shows, in addition, that although liberal elements at one time espoused joining the military, and specifically denied that acceptance of the tenets of Judaism constitutes valid grounds for conscientious objections, prominent Reform rabbis changed their attitude after World War I, when pacifism and conscientious objection became part of the general culture. Later, however, when Hitler's forces came to power, such pacifism was modulated and the Central Conference of American Rabbis supported the United States' entry into the war. Two decades later, during the Vietnam era, anti-war sentiment again arose in the Reform movement. Bleich says that, ironically, liberal writers opposed to the Vietnam war ended up with a position close to the traditionalist view, but they misunderstood the latter and therefore saw themselves as breaking from it. The traditionalist position is that war is justified by, but only by, self-defense; wars of aggression are prohibited. Thus, Bleich contends that "neither patriotic enthusiasm that extols warfare nor absolute pacifism that precludes self-defense are reflective of the Jewish tradition."

THE VALUE OF PEACE

Is Judaism pacifistic? Militaristic? Something in between? Three papers deal with this extensively – Shalom Carmy's, Lawrence Schiffman's, and Dov Zakheim's. (Michael Broyde's has some relevant comments as well.)

All of us can quote the prophecy, "one nation shall not lift up a sword against another; they will no longer learn warfare" (Isaiah 2:4, Micah 4:3). Likewise it is well known that King David was not allowed to build the Temple because "you have shed much blood upon the earth…" (1 Chron. 22:8). But we can also cite the prophecy of the terrifying war at the "end of days," the war of Gog and Magog (Ezek. 38–39). Indeed Jewish eschatology is frequently militaristic, as Lawrence Schiffman's paper shows. The Bible itself portrays God as a warrior who fights with His armies and vanquishes the enemy. Thus it promotes the concept of a Holy War. Later in the Bible, Holy War gives way to battles waged by kings for national defense and, after destruction of the First Temple, to war as an instrument of rebellion against foreign conquerors. During the Second Temple, however, the eschatological war was taken as a Holy War against demonic powers that control the world, a war that will usher in the Davidic messianic era of world peace and the kingdom of God. Schiffman traces eschatological war themes through texts that include Apocalyptic literature and the Dead Sea Scrolls. He also explicates rabbinic texts and later apocalyptic material that focus on the war of Gog and Magog. Schiffman pays special attention to how these texts portray the fate of gentiles in the end of days. Whereas some of the texts maintain that all Gentiles will be killed in the Holy War to come, others (reminiscent of Isaiah's prophecies) assert that gentiles who recognize God and His Temple will be spared and will even participate in the Temple service. Maimonides, who adopts a naturalistic understanding of how the final redemption occurs, also believes that a great war will take place; and he makes waging the wars of the Lord a criterion for an individual's attaining *hezkat mashiah*, the status of a presumptive messiah. (This, I would add, even though the founding of the religion was based on Abraham's powers of rational persuasion [Laws of Idolatry 1:1]). In Maimonides' scenario, the messiah, not God, is the warrior. But the centrality of war to the redemptive process is common to all these texts.

Shalom Carmy, in his article on Amalek referred to earlier, argues that the mandated conquests of the Seven Nations and Amalek are exceptions rather than the rule. The larger context of Judaism, including prophecy and Halakhah, is primarily pacifistic, though not pacifist (opposed to war). "Universal peace is the goal. Ultimate sanctity, in the here and now, cannot coexist with the symbolism of the sword and even the righteous shedding of blood. Yet war is permitted, and success in waging war is extolled." In her article, likewise summarized earlier, Judith Bleich sees Judaism as fundamentally opposed to war although allowing it in certain circumstances – and (following a *midrash*) as replacing military warfare with the "war" waged in debates among Torah scholars.

In an essay that carries obvious contemporary relevance, Dov S. Zakheim considers the halakhic propriety of making peace with an enemy and asks what such a peace, if forged, would look like. Would it be it peace in the modern sense of peaceful coexistence and international reconciliation? Or something short of that?

At the outset Zakheim points out that, in the Talmud and rabbinic sources, peace "is seen more as a condition to be attained than as a practical policy objective;" that concepts like reconciliation and coexistence are as a rule applied to individuals rather than nations (including relations between Jews and non-Jews as in the concept of *darkei shalom*); and that generally coexistence with non-Jews "is framed in terms of dealing with the unpleasant reality that such people must be accommodated," so that "[r]econcilation with non-Jews is almost beside the point." Also, when the Torah discusses making peace with other nations, the terms of peace involve an agreement by the non-Jewish inhabitants to provide tribute and involuntary labor (albeit with Jews paying for the services) as well as to accept the seven Noahide laws. All in all, Biblical "peace" reflects a concept "markedly different from that which has come to be understood in modern times." It is harsher than unconditional surrender, and harsher too than a negotiated post-war treaty.

The Talmud does not fundamentally alter the Biblical notion and says little about the nature of a post-war peace. If anything, "[r]econcilation is unthinkable." The law prohibiting the sale of property in Israel to non-Jews, while not ruling out co-existence, nonetheless mandates permanent tension with them. Looking to post-Talmudic sources, Maimonides, according to one reading of a ruling of his, would in effect prohibit making peace with any non-Jewish people, whether in Israel or outside it; however, most decisors advocate a narrower reading that restricts the ban on peacemaking to the Seven Nations. Further, Zakheim maintains, the Talmudic text concerning "the three vows" (one of which limits aggressive political and military action on the part of the Jews) and the ruling that the prohibition against intermarrying with certain nations does not apply because we can no longer identify who is from the proscribed nations, suggests a measure of coexistence. In addition, despite all these severe limits on when the people Israel can make peace with non-Jews and what such a peace entails, some authorities do not impose the conditions for peace laid down in Deuteronomy. And when Jews are a minority, they may make arrangements with other nations by which they would serve as arms suppliers to the non-Jewish government. But this is not a treaty between equals.

What of the State of Israel today? It is clear that the conditional peace discussed in Biblical and rabbinic sources "is not applicable or attainable in current international affairs." Given this, is reconciliation or peaceful coexistence a halakhically viable objective? Zakheim argues that the State of Israel, although fully sovereign, must nevertheless function within the constraints of the international community within which it functions; it cannot become a hermit state. It is in this context that he invokes the principles of *mi-shum eivah* and *darkei shalom* ("because of enmity" and "the ways of peace") – which dictate keeping amicable relations with non-Jews – combined with a group of halakhic considerations (we can't identify descendants of the ancient nations, there is no requirement to convert Palestinians to the seven Noahide laws, not making peace could endanger Israel, and others). With these factors operating, "consideration must be given to the legitimate hopes of ordinary Palestinians..." Peace "is a religious, halakhic value that can, and should, color Israeli policy."

* * *

The issues surrounding war in Jewish tradition strike at the heart of vital and exciting issues in ethics, theology, law and philosophy of Halakhah. The essays that follow, we hope, will help readers think about contemporary dilemmas and Jewish tradition in a way that is sensitive, sophisticated, rigorous, and informed. The deliberations may well help us navigate through the urgent and terrifying circumstances of today's world.[16]

NOTES

1. To be sure, the war against terrorism does not fit the classical conception of war, insofar as it is not waged against an army and involves enemy combatants without uniforms.

2. Most of the points made in this section are found in Michael Broyde's article and/or in J. David Bleich, "Preemptive War in Jewish Law," *Contemporary Halakhic Problems* III (New York, 1989), 251–92. I outline here only the factors which could justify going to war, and omit further requirements (discussed in Broyde), such as extending an offer of peace or leaving room for people of the enemy population to flee before commencement of hostilities, which operate only once a war is recognized as proper. These additional requirements are discussed by Broyde.

3. See *Sanhedrin* 74a–b. A Jew is not only permitted but obligated to save the life of someone who is pursued. Whether a non-Jew is obligated to kill a pursuer or merely permitted to do so, which is a key question in our present context, is a matter of debate. For sources, see Broyde, 69, n. 29 and 30.

4. Netziv, *Ha'amek Davar*, Gen. 9:5; for references to others who held or opposed this view, see Broyde 46–47 and accompanying notes; Bleich 287–88.

5. See *Sotah* 44b. I leave to the side the term *milhemet hovah*, a term used by R. Yehudah, which R. Yohanan suggests is synonymous with the term *milhemet mitzvah* as used by the Rabbis. On further complications regarding the use of terms; see Bleich, "Preemptive War."

6. As per, for example, R. Abraham Isaac Kook, *Mishpat Kohen* (Jerusalem, 1985), #144, pp. 336–38.

7. The source of Maimonides' ruling is not clear, but good candidates are Jerusalem

Talmud, *Sotah* 8:10 and Babylonian Talmud *Eruvin* 45a. See Bleich, "Preemptive Wars in Jewish Law," 273–75.

8. This in contrast to Moses Nahmanides, addenda to Maimonides' *Sefer ha-Mitzvot*, negative prohibitions, no. 17. There Ramban requires consultation with *urim ve-tumim* even in a *milhemet mitzvah*.

9. While self-defense is obviously licensed without a *melekh*, only a king may conscript people to fight (see Bleich 283–84), and only if a battle is genuinely a "*milhamah*" must Jews endanger themselves to save others; likewise, only in *milhamah* may innocent life be taken, under certain conditions.

10. Maimonides does not mention this category in Laws of Kings, but does so in his commentary to Mishnah *Sotah* 8:7.

11. See Bleich, "Preemptive War." Bleich (p. 270) cites one authority, R. Yehiel Mikhel Epstein, author of *Arukh ha-Shulhan he-Atid* (*Hil. Melakhim* 74:3–4), who considers Maimonides' phraseology "to deliver Israel from an enemy *she-ba aleihem*" to apply even when the enemy is merely suspected of having aggressive intentions. However, Bleich notes that this view is not paralleled in any other commentary.

12. See Bleich, 289–91.

13. See Broyde's article, pp. 48–51 and accompanying notes. As Broyde notes, this position is of limited relevance to Israel in its conflict with an enemy who does not consent to restraining rules.

14. Maimonides, Letter on Astrology, trans. Ralph Lerner, in Isadore Twersky (ed.), *A Maimonides Reader* (New York, 1972), 465.

15. The Sages took the four exemptions in this chapter to apply only to discretionary wars (*Sotah* 44b).

16. I thank Rabbis Michael Broyde, Shalom Carmy, David Hertzberg and Jeremy Wieder for helpful comments and discussion.

Just Wars, Just Battles and Just Conduct in Jewish Law: Jewish Law Is Not a Suicide Pact!*

Michael J. Broyde

Rabbi Jose the Galilean states: "How meritorious is peace? Even in time of war Jewish law requires that one initiate discussions of peace." [1]

I. PREAMBLE

About ten years ago I wrote an article[2] on the halakhic issues raised by starting wars, fighting wars, and ending wars. Over the past five years, as I have spoken about the topic on various occasions,[3] the article has been updated, modified, and expanded and it forms the basis of some sections of this article.

Over the last five years, I have been privileged to serve as the *rosh kollel* (academic head) of the Atlanta Torah MiTzion Kollel, where I give a daily *shiur* (lecture) to its members. I have had numerous opportunities to speak with the Atlanta Torah MiTzion members about many different halakhic issues, and *halakhot* related to war is a regular topic of interest and discussion, as these members are in Atlanta having only recently completed five years of combined army service and serious Torah study in the course of their *hesder* yeshiva experience.[4]

Yet year after year, presentations of my article never interested any of these young men very much – they would listen politely (as such is *kavod ha-Torah*), but displayed no real enthusiasm for the theoretical topics put forward. What was of interest to these recent Israeli soldiers in *halakhot* of war? The answer is simple. As soldiers, they felt that they were not given enough real guidance to deal with the practical issues of battlefield ethics – actually fighting a war as a private, sergeant, or captain, with all of the moral ambiguities of the combat encounter. In fact, upon examination, I found that many of these halakhic issues are poorly addressed. The standard works that deal with Jewish law in the army omit these matters and provide no guidance at all as to basic issues related to fighting a war![5]

The conceptual reason behind this absence of discussion is pointed out by Rabbi Eliezer Yehudah Waldenberg in his responsa,[6] when he addresses the question of governmental policy concerning the obligation of rescuing captives (*pidyon shevuyim*). The basic rule, well known in Jewish law, is that one may not ransom captives for more than they are worth.[7] Rabbi Waldenberg was asked about a government's decision to send troops to rescue other captured soldiers, even when more soldiers might or will be killed during the mission than had been captured in the first place – which would seem to violate the Talmudic rule. Rabbi Waldenberg responds by positing two conceptual points. The first is that war is different from individual ethics and has a different set of rules. The second is that governmental decisions are different from individual decisions and also follow a separate set of rules. By this, Rabbi Waldenberg means that the basic *halakhot* of war allow the killing of human beings in circumstances that are otherwise prohibited. Furthermore, a government, by dint of serving the vast national interest of many people, is permitted – in situations of war – to consider diverse factors and reach results predicated on a vast national interest or consensus, even if it risks many lives for seemingly little real short-term gain. Thus, a government could conclude, he states, that it is proper to lose the lives of three soldiers to rescue one. (Of course, the reverse conclusion is also possible, although he does not dwell on that prospect.)

These two startling observations, which I believe to be correct and supported by many other sources in many different contexts related to war,[8] cause one to realize that Jewish law's view of combat conduct and battlefield ethics is, in fact, much simpler than one might think. If a government can choose as a matter of policy to engage in retaliatory military action that risks the lives of its own soldiers and civilians in a time of war, does it not follow that it may do so with enemy soldiers and civilians as well? Likewise, recognition of the responsibility of the government for such difficult wartime decisions would apply to the so-called Hannibal procedure, which refers to instructions in the case where a soldier has been kidnapped and the government realizes that it cannot rescue him. It then sets out to kill the soldier, so as to avoid the long, drawn out demoralizing situation of a soldier in enemy hands, when it concludes that such a policy best serves the nation.[9] While controversial as a matter of policy, it seems to be a valid option from the perspective of Jewish law. In wartime, Halakhah permits even the killing of innocent civilians as a side consequence of war. In this circumstance the government has decided that it must kill the terrorists who engage in the kidnapping of Israeli soldiers at any cost, and that cost might entail the death of the soldiers who are taken prisoner. The soldiers who are hostages are like innocent civilians, and their death by friendly fire is not an act of murder by those who have shot them. This would not be the case outside of the army setting.

Similarly, what might be otherwise considered outrageous pressure in extracting the information needed to save a soldier the government is seeking to rescue might well be permissible according to Jewish law, assuming that it would be effective in extracting the information, that less outrageous pressures would not be as effective, and assuming it is ordered by the army through a duly authorized military order following the "chain of command," and did not violate international treaties.

This view – that all conduct in war that is needed to win is permitted by *Halakhah* – was adopted by the late Rabbi Shaul Israeli, judge of Supreme Rabbinical Court in Jerusalem, in a famous essay.[10] Certainly there is a deep consensus that every violation of Jewish law other than *ervah* and idolatry would be permitted in the course of fulfilling valid military orders.[11] Moreover, it should seem quite reasonable to argue that if, for example, someone sent in to kill the enemy general – which we all agree is permitted in wartime – determines as a matter of strategy that it is tactically more effective to seduce the general, violating *ervah*, and steal the war plans than to kill him, that it should be allowed. (This approach, however, is not sufficient to explain the conduct of the heroine Yael in Judges 4:17–19, as she was not a combatant at all [as the text points out]; thus, the Talmudic rabbis resorted to a different rationale of *averah lishmah* to defend her *ma'aseh ervah*.[12])

Let me take it to the next step. If the government can rescue a soldier only by killing a dozen innocent infants in the enemy camp, may it do that? Are enemy civilians more or less sacred than one's own soldiers, and if they are not less sacred as a matter of technical *Halakhah*, might they be by dint of a presumptive *hora'at sha'ah* (temporary edict/suspension of law) that would permit such? Indeed, the basic thrust of this introductory section of the paper is that war has, by its very nature, an element of *hora'at sha'ah*, in which basic elements of "regular" Jewish law are suspended – once 'killing' becomes permitted as a matter of Jewish law, much of the hierarchical values of Jewish law seem to be suspended as well, at least to the extent that the ones who are hurt are people who also may be killed. Rabbi Abraham Isaac Kook,[13] for example, permits the sacrifice of oneself as a form of *hora'at sha'ah* that is allowed by Jewish law to save the community. While the voluntary act of heroic self-sacrifice and the killing of an unwilling victim are not parallel, I think that one who would permit a Jewish soldier to kill himself to save the community, would permit the killing of "less innocent" enemy solders or even civilians in such situations as well. In grave times of national war, every battle and every encounter rises to such a level, I suspect. Rabbi Joseph Karo in his commentary to Maimonides' Code explicitly notes that the power of a *beit din* (rabbinical court) includes the authority not only to kill people who are guilty of some violation of Jewish law but whose conviction otherwise lacks in technical proof, but also to kill people who are completely innocent, if in the judgment of the rabbinical court the exigencies of the times require such.[14] The authority for a *beit din* to make such a determination stems from its leadership role over the nation (*manhigei ha-kehillah*).[15] The same ability thus applies to duly authorized governments (secular and Jewish), and can be relegated to their structures of military command.

Indeed, the Israeli army assumes such a responsibility. Consider the following text from the Israel Defense Forces Code:

> Purity of Arms. The IDF serviceman will use force of arms only for the purpose of subduing the enemy to the *necessary* extent and will limit his use of force so as to prevent *unnecessary* harm to human life and limb, dignity and property. The IDF servicemen's purity of arms is their self control in use of armed force. They will use their arms only for the purpose of achieving their mission, without inflicting unnecessary injury to human life or limb, dignity or property, of both soldiers and civilians, with special consideration for the defenseless, whether in wartime, or during routine security operations, or in the absence of combat, or times of peace.[16]

The Talmud, in discussing why King David spared the life of Mephibosheth, son of Jonathan and grandson of Saul,[17] when the Gibeonites sought to have the remnants of King Saul's family killed, seems to recognize that in wartime the concept of *hillul Hashem* (avoiding the desecration of God's name) permits even the killing of otherwise innocent civilians. In this particular case, these killings were a naked act of retaliation, which the Talmud criticizes only as lacking in the proper morality for the Jewish people. The Talmud makes no mention of the fact that the underlying act – the murder of seven absolutely innocent people as an act of retaliation – violates the Jewish law rules of murder. The reason that is so is clear. This retaliatory conduct in wartime does not violate any such prohibition.[18] Indeed, this seems logical, as retaliation when done to teach a lesson is not a general violation of Jewish law,[19] and killing for a purpose is not prohibited in wartime: thus, retaliatory killing in war is permitted to the extent that it does not violate international treaties.

The same can be said for collective punishment of vast segments of society for the active misconduct of the few. The final obligation in the Noahide code – basic frameworks of commandments forming the universal law code that Jewish law believes to be binding on all humans – is *dinim*, commonly translated as "laws" or "justice." Two vastly different interpretations of this commandment are found among the early authorities, but they both share the basic approach of permitting collective punishment. Maimonides rules that the obligations of *dinim* require only that the enumerated Noahide laws be enforced within the system of justice to be established – but that absent such enforcement, all members of society may be punished. He states:

> How are all obligated by *dinim*? They must create courts and appoint judges in every province to enforce these six commandments and to warn the people about the need to obey the law. A person who violates any of these seven obligations (may be) (is)[20] killed with a sword. For this reason the inhabitants of Shekhem [the city] were liable to be killed[21] since Shekhem [the person] stole[22] [Dina], and the inhabitants saw and knew this and did nothing.[23]

Consequently, if one is in a situation where innocent people are being killed by terrorist acts that cannot be stopped by catching the perpetrators themselves, and those terrorists are supported by a civilian population that passively protects them and does not condemn them, collective punishment might well be permitted by Jewish law.[24] Nahmanides has a much more expansive conception of *dinim*, and would certainly permit regulations that include collective punishment.[25]

Admittedly, this lengthy preamble is terribly disquieting, and it heads in a direction that is deeply uncomfortable to me: Jewish law has no "real" restrictions on the conduct of the Jewish army during wartime, so long as the actions being performed are all authorized by the command structure of the military in order to fulfill a valid and authorized goal and do not violate international treaties. Sadly enough, it might turn out that most of these unpleasant activities we have considered might have to become tools in this quite gruesome *danse macabre* to which the long term consequences of defeat are too great to ponder. This is true both in the Jewish homeland and our beloved America.

Of course, this does not mean that there are no limits to the law of war. Rather, it means that the Jewish tradition does not impose upon its adherents any intrinsic limitations on the *Halakhah* of war except those that are derived from mutually agreed upon treaties or conventions agreed to by the combatants. Those limitations – external to Jewish law, but fully binding on all Jewish adherents – have the status either of treaties (which as explained below in section VI are fully binding) or international law accepted by the parties (which I explain elsewhere[26] are binding). Absent these mutually agreed upon limitations, Jewish law has few, if any, rules of battle. This makes the careful examination of proper guidelines especially important in light of both Halakhah's overriding commitment to general moral conduct and the stresses of a wartime situation.

II. INTRODUCTION

This article reviews Jewish law's attitude to an area of modern social behavior that "law" as an institution has shied away from regulating, and which "ethics" as a discipline has failed to successfully regulate: war. In this area, as in many others, the legal and the ethical are freely combined in the Jewish tradition. Unlike Jewish law's rules concerning "regular" war, regulations concerning those biblical wars as those against Amalek and the Seven Nations are not based on normative ethical values, but were designed to be used solely in the initial period of Jewish conquest of the land of Israel or solely in circumstances where God's direct divine commandment to the Jewish nation was clear. Thus, "Jewish law" as used in this article refers to that time period when direct visible divine direction in and interaction with the world has ceased; it is methodologically improper to discuss Jewish ethics in the presence of the active Divine with any other system of ethics, since the active (acknowledged) presence of the Divine changes the ground rules for ethical norms. Normative Jewish law confines itself to a discussion of what to do when the active divine presence is no longer in the world, and thus normative rules are in effect. This distinction, and the distinction between Old Testament Judaism and modern Jewish law, has been lost to some commentators.[27]

We will begin with a review of the legal or ethical issues raised that can justify the *starting* of war (*jus ad bellum*). This issue is crucial for any discussion of the ethics of the battlefield itself in the Jewish tradition. As developed below, there are numerous different theories as to why and when it is morally permissible to start a war which will kill people. What theory one adopts to justify a war, and what category of "war" any particular military activity is placed in, significantly affects what type of conduct is legally or morally permissible on the battlefield (*jus in bello*). The article continues by addressing various ethical issues raised by military activities in the order they would be encountered as hostilities advanced and then receded, including a discussion of the issues raised by peace treaties in the Jewish tradition.

This article demonstrates that the Jewish tradition has within it a moral license that permits war (and killing) that differs from the usual rules of self-defense for individuals. However, the permissibility to "wage war" is quite limited in the Jewish tradition and the requirement that one always seek a just peace is part and parcel of the process that one must exercise to initiate a legitimate war. The love of peace and the pursuit of peace, as well as the responsibility to eradicate evil, all co-exist in the Jewish tradition, each in its place and to be used in its proper time.

III. GROUNDS FOR STARTING WAR

A. Jewish Law's View of Secular Nations at War

Historically, Jews have been (and to a great extent, still are) a people living in a Diaspora, foreigners in and, later, citizens of countries where Jewish law was not the ethical or legal touchstone of moral conduct by the government. Even as citizens of a host country, it is necessary for adherents to the Jewish legal tradition to develop a method for determining whether that nation's military activity is indeed permissible according to Jewish law. Should the host country's military activities be deemed a violation of Jewish law, Jewish law would prohibit one from assisting that nation in its unlawful military activity and certainly would prohibit serving in its armed forces and killing soldiers who are members of the opposing army.[28]

Two distinctly different rationales are extant to justify the use of military force. The first is the general principle of self-defense, whose rules are as applicable to the defense of a group of people as they are to the defense of a single person. The Talmud[29] rules that a person is permitted to kill a pursuer to save his or her own life regardless of whether the person being pursued is a Jew or a non-Jew. While there is some dispute among modern Jewish law authorities as to whether Jewish law *mandates* or merely *permits* a non-Jew or bystander to take the life of one who is trying to kill another, nearly all authorities posit that such conduct is, at the least, permissible.[30]

It is obvious that the laws of pursuit are equally applicable to a group of individuals or a nation as they are to a single person. Military action thus becomes permissible, or more likely obligatory, when it is defensive in nature, or undertaken to aid the victim of aggression. However, using the pursuer paradigm to analyze "war" leads one to conclude that all of the restrictions related to this rationale apply as well.[31] War, if it is to exist legally as a morally sanctioned event, must permit some forms of killing other than those which are allowed through the self-defense rationale; the permissibility of the modern institution of "war" as a separate legal category by Jewish law standards cannot exist solely as a derivative of these self-defense rules.

There are a number of recent authorities who explicitly state that the institution of "war" is legally recognized as a distinct moral license (independent of the laws of pursuer and self-defense) to terminate life according to Jewish law, even for secular nations. R. Naftali Tzvi Yehudah Berlin[32] argues that the very verse that prohibits murder permits war. He claims that the term "At the hand of man, his brother"[33] prohibits killing only when it is proper to behave in a brotherly manner, but *at times of war, killing that would otherwise be prohibited is permitted.* Indeed, such an opinion can also be found in the medieval Talmudic commentary of Tosafot.[34] Rabbi Judah Loew (Maharal of Prague) in his commentary on Genesis 32, also states that war is permitted under Noahide Law. He claims that this is the justification for the actions of Simeon and Levi in the massacre of the inhabitants of Shechem. Furthermore, by this analysis even preemptive action, like the kind taken by Simeon and Levi, would be permitted. Also, Maharal at least implies that the killing of civilians who are not liable under the pursuer rationale is nonetheless permissible. It is worth noting that the dispute between Jacob on one side and Simeon and Levi on the other side as to the propriety of their conduct in Shechem is one of the few (maybe the only) incidents in the Torah where it is unclear who is ultimately correct. R. Shlomo Goren[35] posits that Jacob was correct, and thus Maharal of Prague is wrong.

Other authorities disagree. R. Moses Sofer[36] seemingly adopts a middle position and accepts that wars of aggression are never permitted to secular nations; however, he does appear to recognize the institution of "war" distinct from the pursuer rationale in the context of defensive wars. A number of other rabbinic authorities seem to accept this position as well.[37]

Indeed, the approach of R. Israel Meir Kagan to halakhic matters pertaining to Jewish soldiers in secular armies can only be explained if there is a basic halakhic legitimacy to war by secular (Noahide) nations, as R. Berlin claims. In his *Mishnah Berurah*, R. Kagan permits conscription into a secular nation's draft.[38] Although the central issues raised there regarding Sabbath violations (*hillul Shabbat*) of a soldier are beyond the scope of this article,

Rabbi Kagan's underlying view permits (and in some circumstances mandates) military service, and when called upon, killing people in the course of that duty: such can only be validated in a model of lawful war by secular nations. The same view is taken by R. Moses Feinstein as well as R. Yosef Eliyahu Henkin.[39]

One basic point needs to be made. It is not obvious to this writer that the military conduct of the State of Israel cannot be categorized under the rubric of "war" established by the above sources. Although there is a known tendency to seek to justify the conduct of the State of Israel in the context of "Jewish" wars (whose parameters are explained below), there is an equally clear trend among modern decisors of Jewish Law to seek to fit the conduct of the State of Israel into the general (universal) idea of war, and not the uniquely Jewish law model.[40] Among the halakhic authorities who advance arguments that can only stand if predicated on the correctness of the approach of R. Berlin and others are Rabbis Shaul Israeli, Yaakov Ariel, Dov Lior, Shlomo Goren and others.[41] The crux of this argument, often unstated, is that the government of Israel is not bound to uphold the obligations of war imposed on a "Jewish Kingdom" but merely must conduct itself in accordance with the international law norms that R. Berlin mentions. In this model, the rules discussed in the next section apply strictly to a Davidic dynasty, and the real rules of war simply follow international law norms as codified by treaties.

Of course, the approach of R. Berlin recognizes that treaties restrict the rights of combatants, but that exercise in self-restraint stems from a voluntary decision to agree to such rules and is thus beyond the scope of this paper and of limited applicability to the modern wars against terrorism fought by both America and Israel. As Captain Seltzer, formerly of the Judge Advocate General corps, notes:

> Members of the armed forces of a party to a conflict and members of militias or volunteer corps forming part of such armed forces lose their right to be treated as POWs whenever they deliberately conceal their status in order to pass behind the military lines of the enemy for the purpose of gathering

military information or for the purpose of waging war by destruction of life or property. Putting on civilian clothes or the
uniform of the enemy and engaging in combat are examples of
concealment of the status of a member of the armed forces and
qualify as a war crime. *Unprivileged belligerents – or unlawful
combatants – may include spies, saboteurs or civilians who are
participating in the hostilities or who otherwise engage in unauthorized attacks or other combatant acts. They are not entitled to*
POW *status, but merely "humane treatment," are prosecutable by
the captor, and may be executed or imprisoned. They are subject*
to the extreme penalty of death because of the danger inherent
in their conduct.[42]

Thus, conventions do not govern many of the unconventional techniques increasingly employed even by national entities, let alone
terrorist armies (such as Hezbollah or the Iraqi resistance).

B. A Jewish Nation Starting a War

The discussion among commentators and decisors concerning the
issues involved in a Jewish nation starting a war is far more detailed
and subject to much more extensive discussion than the Jewish law
view of secular nations going to war.

The Talmud[43] understands that a special category of permitted killing called "war" exists that is analytically different from
other permitted forms of killing, like the killing of a pursuer or a
home invader. The Talmud delimits two categories of permissible
war: Obligatory and Authorized.[44] It is crucial to determine which
category of "war" any particular type of conflict is. As explained
below, many of the restrictions placed by Jewish law on the type of
conduct permitted by war is frequently limited to Authorized rather
than Obligatory wars.[45]

Before examining the exact line drawn by the commentators
to differentiate between Obligatory and Authorized wars, a more
basic question must be addressed: by what license can the Jewish
tradition permit wars that are not obligatory, with all of the resulting carnage and destruction? Michael Waltzer, in his analysis of the

Jewish tradition, comes to the conclusion that optional or authorized wars are fundamentally improper, and merely tolerated by the Jewish tradition as an evil that cannot be abolished.[46] Noam Zohar rightly notes that such an answer is contrary to the basic thrust of the Jewish commandments, and proposes that optional or authorized wars are those wars whose moral license is clearly just, but whose fundamental obligation is not present, such as when the military costs of the war (at least in terms of casualties) are high enough that it is morally permissible to decline to fight.[47] As will be explained further below, I think this explanation is itself deeply incomplete, as the essential characterization of war entails risk, and declining to fight due to the cost would label all wars, other than those where the soldiers' lives are directly and immediately at stake, to be optional. A third answer is suggested by Rabbi Eliezer Waldenberg, who posits that even authorized or optional wars are limited by the duty to insure that all such wars have to be with the goal and intent to elevate true faith and to fill the world with righteousness, to break the strength of those who do evil, and to fight the battles of God.[48]

Rabbi Waldenberg's view, then, is that these wars are like all positive commandments that are not mandatory but are still considered good deeds. There is no obvious reason why all good deeds must be mandatory in the Jewish tradition – some good deeds, and some good wars, may be optional.[49]

c. Obligatory vs. Authorized Wars

According to the Talmud,[50] Obligatory wars are those wars started in direct fulfillment of a specific biblical commandment, such as the obligation to destroy the tribe of Amalek in biblical times. Authorized wars are wars undertaken to increase territory or "to diminish the heathens so that they shall not march" which is, as explained below, a category of military action given different parameters by different authorities.[51] Maimonides, in his codification of the law, writes that:

> The king must first wage only Obligatory wars. What is an
> Obligatory war? It is a war against the seven nations, the war

against Amalek, and a war to deliver Israel from an enemy who
has attacked them. Then he may wage Authorized wars, which
is a war against others in order to enlarge the borders of Israel
and to increase his greatness and prestige.[52]

Surprisingly enough, the category of "to deliver Israel from an
enemy…" is not found in the Talmud. In addition, the category of
preemptive war[53] is not mentioned in Maimonides' formulation of
the law even though it is found in the Talmud.

What was Maimonides' understanding of the Talmud and how
did he develop these categories? These questions are the key focus of
a discussion on the laws of starting wars. The classic rabbinic commentaries, both medieval and modern, grapple with the dividing line
between "a war to deliver Israel from an enemy who has attacked
them" and a war "to enlarge the borders of Israel and to increase [the
king's] greatness and prestige." Behind each of these approaches lies
a different understanding of when a war is obligatory, authorized, or
prohibited and the ethical duties associated with each category.

Judah ben Samuel al-Harizi's translation of Maimonides' commentary on the Mishnah suggests that Maimonides was of the
opinion that an Obligatory war does not start until one is actually
attacked by an army; Authorized wars include all defensive non-
obligatory wars and all military actions commenced for any reason
other than self-defense.[54] According to this definition, military action prior to the initial use of force by one's opponents can only be
justified through the "pursuer" or self-defense rationale. All other
military activity is prohibited.

R. Joseph Kapah, in his translation of the same commentary
of Maimonides, understands Maimonides to permit war against
nations that have previously fought with Israel and that are still
technically at war with the Jewish nation – even though no fighting
is now going on. An offensive war cannot be justified even as an
Authorized war unless a prior state of belligerency existed.[55]

R. Abraham diBoton, in his commentary on Maimonides'
Code (*Lehem Mishneh*),[56] posits that the phrase "to enhance the
king's greatness and prestige" includes all of the categories of au-

thorized war permitted in the Talmud. Once again, all wars other than purely defensive wars where military activity is initiated solely by one's opponents are classified as Authorized wars or illegal wars. Obligatory wars are limited to purely defensive wars.

R. Menahem ben Meir (Meiri), in his commentary on the Talmud,[57] states that an Authorized war is any attack which is commenced in order to prevent an attack in the future. Once hostilities begin, all military activity falls under the rubric of Obligatory. Similarly, R. Abraham Isaiah Karelitz (Hazon Ish) claims that Maimonides' definition of an Authorized war is referring to a use of force in a war of attrition situation.[58] In any circumstance in which prior "battle" has occurred and that battle was initiated by the enemy, the war that is being fought is an Obligatory one. According to this approach, the use of military force prior to the start of a war of attrition is prohibited (unless justified by the general rules of self-defense, in which case a "war" is not being fought according to Jewish law.)

R. Yehiel Mikhel Epstein, in his *Arukh ha-Shulhan he-Atid*, advances a unique explanation. He writes that the only difference between an Authorized and an Obligatory war is the status of those people exempt from being drafted – the categories mentioned in Deuteronomy 20.[59] In an Obligatory war, even those people must fight. However, he writes, the king is obligated to defend Israel "even when there is only suspicion that they may attack us." Thus the position he takes is that vis-à-vis the government there is only a slight difference between Authorized and Obligatory wars – the pool of draftable candidates. [60]

D. Summary

Jewish law regarding wars by secular governments thus can be divided into three categories:

(1) War to save the nation that is now, or soon to be, under attack. This is not technically war but is permitted because of the law of "pursuer" and is subject to all of the restrictions related to the law of pursuer and the rules of self-defense.

(2) War to aid an innocent third party who is under attack. This too, is not technically war, but most commentators mandate this, also under the "pursuer" rationale, while some rule this is merely permitted. In either case, it is subject to all of the restrictions related to the "pursuer" rationale.

(3) Wars of self defense and perhaps territorial expansion. A number of commentators permit "war" as an institution even in situations where non-combatants might be killed; most authorities limit this license to defensive wars.

So too, Jewish law regarding wars by the Jewish government can be divided into three (different) categories:

(1) Defending the people of Israel from attack by an aggressive neighbor. This is an Obligatory war.
(2) Fighting offensive wars against belligerent neighbors.
(3) Protecting individuals through the use of the laws of "pursuer" and self defense from aggressive neighbors. This is not a "war" according to the Jewish tradition.[61]

Finally, it is crucial to realize that there are situations where war is – in the Jewish tradition – simply not permitted. The killing that takes place in such wars, if not directly based on immediate self-defense needs,[62] is simply murder and participation in those wars is prohibited according to Jewish law. (How one categorizes each individual conflict can sometimes be a judgment about which reasonable scholars of Jewish law might differ; that does not, however, mean that such decisions are purely a function of individual choice. As with all such matters in Jewish law, there is a manner and matter for resolving such disagreements.[63]) This statement, of course, is incomplete. If Noahide law permits a war in situations that Jewish law does not, and Jewish law recognizes the use of Noahide law as a justification for such a war, then such wars cannot be a categorical violation of Jewish law (in the sense of being prohibited for Jews to engage in this conduct). I will leave that topic for another discussion, although the proper resolution of that matter has been hinted at elsewhere.[64]

IV. BATTLEFIELD ETHICS

A. Type of War

The initial question that needs to be addressed when discussing battlefield ethics is whether the rules for these situations differ from all other applications of Jewish ethics, or if "battlefield ethics" are merely an application of the general rules of Jewish ethics to the combat situation. This question is essentially a rephrasing of the question: What is the moral license according to the Jewish tradition that permits war to be waged? As explained above, the Jewish tradition divides "armed conflict" into three different categories: obligatory war, permissible war, and societal applications of the "pursuer" rationale.[65] Each of these situations comes with different licenses. The easiest one to address is the final one, the pursuer rationale: battlefield ethics based on the pursuer model are simply a generic application of the [general] field of Jewish ethics relating to stopping one who is an evildoer from harming (killing) an innocent person. While it is beyond the scope of this article to completely explain that detailed area of Jewish ethics, the touchstone rules of self-defense according to Jewish law are fourfold: Even when self-defense is mandatory or permissible and one may kill a person or group of people who are seeking to kill one who is innocent, one may not:

(1) Kill an innocent[66] third party to save a life;
(2) Compel a person to risk his or her life to save the life of another;
(3) Kill the pursuer after his or her evil act is over as a form of punishment.
(4) Use more force than minimally needed.[67]

These are generic rules of Jewish law derived form different Talmudic sources and methodologically unrelated to "war" as an institution.[68] Thus, the application of the rules of this type of "armed conflict" would resemble an activity by a police force rather than an activity by an army. Only the most genteel of modern armies can function in accordance with these rules.

On the other hand, both the situation of Obligatory war and Authorized war are not merely a further extrapolation of the principles of "self-defense" or "pursuer." There are ethical liberalities (and strictures) associated with the battlefield setting that have unique ethical and legal rules unrelated to other fields of Jewish law or ethics.[69] They permit the killing of a fellow human being in situations where that action – but for the permissibility of war – would be murder. In order to understand what precisely is the "license to kill," it is necessary to explain the preliminary steps required by Jewish law to actually fight a battle after war has been properly declared. It is through an understanding of these prescriptions (and proscriptions) that one grasps the limits on the license to kill one's opponents in military action according to Jewish law. Indeed, nearly all of the preliminary requirements to a permissible war are designed to remove non-combatants, civilians, and others who do not wish to fight from the battlefield.

B. Seeking Peace Prior to Starting War

Two basic texts form Jewish law's understanding of the duties society must undertake before a battle may be fought. The Biblical text states:

> When you approach a city to do battle with it, you shall call to it in peace. And if they respond in peace and they open the city to you, all the people in the city shall pay taxes to you and be subservient. And if they do not make peace with you, you shall wage war with them and you may besiege them.[70]

Thus the Bible clearly sets out the obligation to seek peace as a prelude to any offensive military activity; absent the seeking of peace, the use of force in a war violates Jewish law. Although unstated in the text, it is apparent that while one need not engage in negotiations over the legitimacy of one's goals, one must explain what one is seeking through this military action and what military goals are (and are not) sought.[71] Before this seeking of peace, battle is prohibited. The Tannaitic authority R. Jose the Galilean is quoted as stating, "How meritorious is peace? Even in a time of war one must initiate all activities with a request for peace."[72] This procedural requirement is quite significant: it prevents the escalation of hostilities and allows both sides to rationally plan the cost of war and the virtues of peace.

R. Shlomo Yitzhaki (Rashi), in his commentary on the Bible,[73] indicates that the obligation to seek peace prior to firing the first shot is limited to Authorized wars. However, in Obligatory or Compulsory wars there is no obligation to seek a peaceful solution. Indeed, such a position can be found in the Midrash Halakhah.[74] Maimonides, in his classic code of Jewish law disagrees. He states:

> One does not wage war with anyone in the world until one seeks peace with him. Thus is true both of Authorized and Obligatory wars, as it says [in the Torah], "When you approach a city to wage war, you shall [first] call to it in peace." If they respond positively and accept the seven Noahide commandments, one may not kill any of them and they shall pay tribute...[75]

Thus, according to Maimonides, the obligation to seek peace applies to all circumstances where war is to be waged. Such an approach is also agreed to in principle by Nahmanides.[76]

It is clear, however, according to both schools of thought, that in Authorized wars one must initially seek a negotiated settlement of the cause of the conflict (although, it is crucial to add, Jewish law does not require that each side compromise its claim so as to reach a peaceful solution).[77] Ancillary to this obligation is the need that the goal of the war be communicated to one's opponents. One must detail to one's enemies the basic goals of the war, and what one seeks as a victory in this conflict.[78] This allows one's opponents to evaluate the costs of fighting and to seek a rational peace. Peace must be genuinely sought before war may begin.

A fundamental and very important dispute exists with regard

to one facet of this obligation. Maimonides requires that the peaceful surrender terms offered must include an acknowledgment of and agreement to follow the seven Noahide laws, which (Jewish law asserts) govern all members of the world and form the basic groundwork for moral behavior;[79] *part and parcel of the peace must be the imposition of ethical values on the defeated society.* Nahmanides does not list that requirement as being necessary for the "peaceful" cessation of hostilities.[80] He indicates that it is the military goals alone which determine whether peace terms are acceptable. According to Nahmanides, Jewish law would compel the presumptive "victor" to accept peace terms that include all of the victors' initial demands save for the imposition of ethical values in the defeated society; Maimonides would reject that rule and permit war in those circumstances purely to impose ethical values in a non-ethical society.[81] To this writer this approach seems very logical and provides the basis for the comments of Rabbi Waldenberg that even Authorized wars have to be with the goal and intent to elevate true faith and fill the world with righteousness and fight the battles of God.[82]

c. The Civilian, the Siege,[83] and Standard of Conduct

The obligation to seek peace in the manner outlined above applies to battles between armies when no civilian population is involved. Jewish law requires an additional series of overtures for peace and surrender in situations where the military activity involves attacking cities populated by civilians. Maimonides states:

> Joshua, before he entered the land of Israel, sent three letters to its inhabitants. The first one said that those that wish to flee [the oncoming army] should flee. The second one said that those that wish to make peace should make peace. The third letter said that those that want to fight a war should prepare to fight a war.[84]

Nor was the general obligation to warn the civilian population enough to fulfill the obligation: Maimonides codifies a number of specific rules of military ethics, all based on Talmudic sources:

> When one surrounds a city to lay siege to it, it is prohibited to surround it from four sides; only three sides are permissible. One must leave a place for inhabitants to flee for all those who wish to abscond to save their life.[85]

Nahmanides elaborates on this obligation in a way that clearly explains the moral rationale by stating:

> God commanded us that when we lay siege to a city that we leave one of the sides without a siege so as to give them a place to flee to. *It is from this commandment that we learn to deal with compassion even with our enemies even at time of war;* in addition, by giving our enemies a place to flee to, they will not charge at us with as much force.[86]

Nahmanides believes that this obligation is so basic as to require that it be one of the 613 fundamental biblical commandments in Jewish law. However, Nahmanides clearly limits this ethical obligation to Authorized and not Obligatory wars, and this is agreed to by most other authorities.[87]

Essentially Jewish law completely rejects the notion of a "siege" as that term is understood by military tacticians and contemporary articulators of international law. Modern international law generally assumes that in a situation where "the commander of a besieged place expel[s] the non-combatants, in order to lessen the number of those who consume his stock of provisions, it is lawful, though an extreme measure to drive them back so as to hasten the surrender."[88] Secular law and morals allow the use of the civilians as pawns in the siege. *The Jewish tradition prohibited that and mandated that noncombatants who wished to flee must be allowed to flee the scene of the battle.* (I would add, however, that I do not understand Maimonides' words literally. It is not surrounding the city on all four sides that is prohibited – rather, it is the preventing of the *outflow of civilians or soldiers* who are seeking to flee. Of course, Jewish law would allow one to stop the *inflow of supplies* to a besieged city through this fourth side.[89])

This approach solves another difficult problem according to Jewish law: the role of the "innocent" civilian in combat. Since the Jewish tradition accepts that civilians (and soldiers who are surrendering) are always entitled to flee from the scene of the battle, it would logically follow that all who remain voluntarily are classified as combatants, since the opportunity to leave is continuously present. Particularly in combination with Joshua's practice of sending letters of warning in advance of combat, this legal approach limits greatly the role of the doctrine of "innocent civilian" in the Jewish tradition. Essentially, the Jewish tradition feels that innocent civilians should do their very best to remove themselves from the battlefield, and those who remain are not so innocent. If one voluntarily stays in a city that is under siege, one assumes the mantle of a combatant.[90]

An analysis that seeks to distinguish between combatants and civilians seems of value when one conceptualizes war in terms of a designated battlefield with confined corners that people can intentionally flee from if they wish to be civilians or run towards if they wish to do battle. However, this paradigm of war seems ill-suited to the majority of hostilities in the last century, and even more so of the last decade. When one is fighting a war in a civilian area, these rules seem to be the subject of a considerable amount of debate.

Not surprisingly, the contours of that debate have played out with considerable force in the pages of *Tehumin*, a contemporary periodical of the Religious Zionist community. Indeed, the earliest modern discussion of this topic was presented by R. Shaul Israeli in 1954 in response to the killing of civilians by Israel Defense Forces Unit 101 at Kibia (Qibya) in 1953.[91] R. Israeli argues that civilians who conspire to assist in the undertaking of military operations can be killed through the pursuer rationale, as they are materially aiding the murderers. (He notes that this is a basic distinction in Jewish law between judicial punishment, which can only be meted out to principals, and the pursuer rationale, which allows one to kill someone who has joined a conspiracy to kill an innocent person, if killing that conspirator will cause the end of the murderous act.[92]) Indeed, R. Israeli goes even further, and seems to adopt the view that those who simply extend support to terror – by encouraging acts of violence with mere words – can be labeled combatants as well. This is not, R. Israeli posits, any form of collective punishment, as only people who are guilty (whether of murder or conspiracy to commit murder) are actually being punished. However, as is obvious, this is a vast expansion of the simple understanding of the rules of *rodef*, or even the more complex statistical analysis of life-threatening activity put forward by some modern *aharonim* (latter-day decisors).[93]

This stands in sharp contrast with the approach taken by the late R. Hayyim Dovid Halevi (author of the *Aseh Lekha Rav* series), who categorically denies that the concept of pursuer can be applied in situations other than when the person is actually threatening the life of another person, and certainly may not be applied to cases where the person under discussion is 'merely' a political supporter of those who engage in such activities.[94]

The unintentional and undesired slaying of innocent civilians who involuntarily remain behind seems to this author to be the one "killing" activity which is permissible in Jewish law in war situations that would not be permissible in the pursuer/self-defense situations. Just like Jewish law permits one to send one's own soldiers out to combat (without their consent) to perhaps be killed, Jewish law would allow the unintentional killing of innocent civilians as a necessary (but undesired) byproduct of the moral license of war.[95]

In many ways, this provides guidance into the ethical issues associated with a modern airplane- (and long range artillery-) based war. Air warfare greatly expands the "kill zone" of combat and (at least in our current state of technology) tends to inevitably result in the death of civilians. The tactical aims of air warfare appear to be fourfold: to destroy specific enemy military targets, to destroy the economic base of the enemy's war-making capacity, to randomly terrorize civilian populations, and to retaliate for other atrocities by the enemy to one's own home base and thus deter such conduct in the future by the enemy.

The first of these goals is within the ambit of that which is permissible, since civilian deaths are unintentional. The same would appear to be true about the second, providing that the targets are genuine economic targets related to the economic base needed to

wage the war and the death of civilians are not directly desired. It
would appear that the third goal is not legitimate absent the designation of "Compulsory" or "Obligatory" war. The final goal raises a
whole series of issues beyond the scope of this article and could perhaps provide some sort of justification for certain types of conduct
in combat that would otherwise be prohibited, although its detailed
analysis in Jewish law is beyond the scope of this paper and relates to
circumstances where retaliation or specific deterrence might permit
that which is normally prohibited.

R. Yaakov Ariel advances one possible explanation for this
killing of 'innocent' civilians that places this exception in a different
light. R. Ariel posits that war is, at its core, societal in nature and
thus different from pursuer rationales in its basic model. War is the
collective battle of societies, R. Ariel posits, and thus there are no
innocent civilians; even babes in their mothers' arms are to be killed,
harsh as that sounds.[96]

The Jewish tradition mandated a number of other rules so as
to prevent certain types of tactics that violated the norms of ethical
behavior even in war. Maimonides recounts that it is prohibited to
remove fruit trees so as to induce suffering, famine, and unnecessary
waste in the camp of the enemy, and this is accepted as normative
in Jewish law.[97] In his enumeration of the commandments, Maimonides explicitly links this to the deliberate intention to expose the
enemy to undue suffering.[98] Nahmanides adds that the removal of
all trees is permissible if needed for the building of fortification; it is
only when done to deliberately induce unneeded suffering that it is
prohibited. However, Nahmanides still understands the Jewish tradition as requiring one to have mercy on one's enemy as one would
have mercy on one's own, and to not engage in unduly cruel activity.[99]
Even the greatest of scourges – exploitation of the female civilian
population of the enemy – was regulated under Jewish law.[100]

D. A Note on Nuclear War and Jewish Law
The use of nuclear technology as a weapon of mass destruction is
very problematic in Jewish law. In a situation resulting in Mutually

Assured Destruction if weapons are used, it is clear that the Jewish tradition would prohibit the actual use of such armaments if they were to cause the large scale destruction of human life on the earth as it currently exists. The Talmud[101] explicitly prohibits the waging of war in a situation where the casualty rate exceeds a sixth of the population. Lord Jakobovits, in an article written more than forty years ago, summarized the Jewish law on this topic in his eloquent manner:

> In view of this vital limitation of the law of self-defense, it would appear that a defensive war likely to endanger the survival of the attacking and the defending nations alike, if not indeed the entire human race, can never be justified. *On the assumption, then, that the choice posed by a threatened nuclear attack would be either complete destruction or surrender,* only the second may be morally vindicated.[102]

However, one caveat is needed: It is permissible to threaten to adopt a military strategy that one is in fact prohibited to implement in order to deter a war. While one injustice cannot ever justify another injustice, sometimes threatening to do a wrong can prevent the initial wrong from occurring. *Just because one cannot pull the nuclear trigger does not mean one cannot own a nuclear gun.*[103] It is important to understand the logical syllogism that permits this conduct. It is forbidden – because of the prohibition to lie – to threaten to use a weapon that one is prohibited from actually using. However, it can be clearly demonstrated that lying to save the life of an innocent person is permissible.[104] Thus, this lie becomes legally justifiable to save one's own life too. An example proves this point: If a person sought to kill an innocent party and one could not prevent that act by killing the potential murderer, one could threaten this person by saying, "If you kill this innocent person, I will kill your children." While, of course, one could not carry out the threat in response to the murder, the threat itself would be a permissible deterrent because lying to avoid a murder is permitted. This demonstrates that threatening to do that which one cannot actually do is generally permissible to save a life. The possession of nuclear weapons is simply an amplification of this logical analysis.

The overemphasis of the seriousness of the minor prohibition to tell an untruth at the expense of letting a person die is an example of an ethical valuation that is completely contrary to the Jewish ethical norm. In general, the underemphasis of the biblical ethical mandate of "not standing by while one's neighbor's blood is shed" is the hallmark of those who adopt a system of pacifistic ethics and explains why such an ethical direction is contrary to Jewish law. If one could save a life by telling a lie, such a lie would be mandatory in Jewish ethics.

The use of tactical (battlefield) nuclear weapons designed solely to be used on the field of battle (assuming that such weapons exist and have the stated limited effect), in circumstances where the complete destruction of the combatants would be permissible (such as after the proper warning and peace seeking), would be acceptable as well in Jewish law.

E. Summary
In sum, there clearly is a license to wage particular kinds of war and kill certain people in the Jewish tradition. However, in order to exercise this license, one must first seek peace; this peace must be sought prior to declaring war, prior to waging a battle, and prior to laying a siege. While war permits killing, it only permits the intentional killings of combatants. Innocent people must be given every opportunity to remove themselves from the field of combat.

V. FIGHTING ON THE SAME TEAM: ETHICS WITHIN THE ARMY

Judaism not only mandates a particular type of ethical behavior towards one's enemies, but compels one to adopt certain rules of conduct towards one's own soldiers as well. The Torah explicitly addresses the question of who shall be compelled to fight in a war. It states:

And when you approach the time for battle, the priest shall approach and speak to the people. He should say to them, "Listen Israel, today you are approaching war with your enemies; do not be faint in heart; do not be fearful and do not be alarmed; do not be frightened of them. Because God, your God, is going with you to battle your enemies and to save you." And the officers shall say to the people "Who is the person who has built a house and not yet dedicated it? He should return to his house lest he die in battle and another dedicate it. Who is the person who has planted a vineyard and never used the fruit? He should leave and return lest he die in battle and another use the fruit. Who is the person who is engaged to a woman and has not married her? He should leave and return home lest he die in battle and another marry her." *And the officers should add to this saying "Who is the person who is scared and frightened in his heart? He should leave and return lest his neighbor's heart grow weak as his has."*[105]

Two distinctly different exemptions are present in the Torah. The first is that of a person whose death will cause a clear incompleteness in an impending life cycle event. The second is a person whose conduct is deleterious to the morale of the army as a whole. While the position of Maimonides is unclear, Rabbi Abraham ben David of Posquières (*Ravad*) immediately notes that these two categories of exemptions are different in purpose and application.[106] *Ravad* states that the exemptions which relate to impending life cycle events apply only to an Authorized war; in an Obligatory war all must fight. However, he states that it is possible that the exemption for one who is fearful would apply even to an Obligatory war.[107]

The Talmud[108] explains this second exemption in two different ways. Rabbi Akiva states that it refers to a person who is lacking the moral courage to do battle and to see combat and watch people perish. Rabbi Yossi asserts that the fearfulness describes a person whose personal actions have been sinful (and who is thus afraid that in wartime he will be punished for his sins).[109] Most authorities maintain that one who is fearful of the war to such a degree that he classifies for such an exemption is compelled to take this deferral – it is not optional;[110] Jewish law prohibits one who is of such character from fighting.[111] While one could claim that this type of an exemption is a form of selective conscientious objection, such an understanding of the law would be in error. A person who "objects" is not given an exemption; certainly a person who is physically and psychologically capable – but who merely opposes this particular war – can be compelled to fight. It is only a form of psychological unfitness that earns one this type of exemption.

However, the most important limitation on this exemption is that it is limited to Authorized wars. In Obligatory wars, all who can, must fight.[112] Although one modern commentator seeks to argue that this is a basic model of a voluntary army,[113] I do not think that this argument is cogent. Rather, given the nature of a threat posed by a mandatory war, all – even those who are basically unfit – need to serve. Since the nation is in danger, the long term planning which allows those who have unfinished tasks to be exempt from fighting obviously is less relevant.

In addition to the question of who serves, Jewish law mandates certain ethical norms on the battlefield so as to ensure certain moral behavior. For example, the Torah requires, and it is quoted in the Midrash Halakhah and codes, that basic sanitary rules be observed while in military encampment.[114]

VI. PEACE TREATIES

The book of Joshua recounts that when the Gibeonites tricked the Jews into ratifying a treaty with them, they were not subsequently attacked because "We swore [not to attack them] by the name of the God of Israel and thus we cannot touch them."[115] Even though the treaty was entered into under fraudulent pretexts, the Jewish people maintained that the treaty was morally binding on them. Indeed, Maimonides in his classic medieval code of Jewish law, basing himself almost exclusively on this Biblical incident, codifies the central rule of treaties as follows:

It is prohibited to lie [or breach] in treaties and it is prohibited to make them [the defeated nation] suffer after they have settled and accepted the seven commandments.[116]

Rabbi David Ibn Zimra (*Radvaz*), in his commentary on Maimonides there, explains that "this is learned from the incident of the Gibeonites, since breaking one's treaties is a profanation of God's name."[117] According to this rationale, the reason why the Jewish nation felt compelled to honor its treaty with the Gibeonites – a treaty that in the very least was entered into under false pretenses – was that *others would not grasp the full circumstances under which the treaty was signed, and would have interpreted the breach of the treaty as a sign of moral laxity on the part of the Jewish people.* One could argue based on this rationale that in circumstances where the breach of a treaty would be considered reasonable by others, it would be permissible to breach.[118]

Rabbi Levi ben Gershon (*Ralbag*) understands the nature of the obligation to observe treaties differently; he claims that the reason the treaty with the Gibeonites had to be honored was that the Jewish nation "swore" to observe its obligation and the nations of the world would have otherwise thought that the Jewish people do not believe in a God and thus do not take their promises seriously (collectively and individually).[119]

Rabbi David ben Kimhi (*Radak*) advances an even more radical understanding of the nature of this obligation. Among the possible reasons he advances to explain why the treaty was honored – even though it was actually void because it was entered into based solely on the fraudulent assurances of the Gibeonites – is that others would not be aware that the treaty was really void and would (incorrectly) identify the Jewish nation as the breaker of the treaty. This fear, that the Jewish nation would be wrongly identified as a treaty breaker, he states, is enough to require that the Jewish nation keep all treaties duly entered into.[120]

Each of these theories, whatever the precise boundaries of the obligation to keep treaties is based on, presupposes that treaties are basically binding according to Jewish law.[121] It is only in the case of a visibly obvious breach of the treaty by one party that the second party may decline to honor it. Thus, Jewish law accepts that when a war is over, the peace that is agreed to is binding. Indeed, even in a situation where there is some unnoticed fraud in its enactment or ratification, such a treaty is still in force.

VII. CONCLUDING COMMENTS

When one reviews the rules found within Jewish law for waging war, one grasps a crucial reality of Jewish military ethics. The moral license that "war" grants a person or a country varies from situation to situation and event to event. The Jewish tradition treats different permissible wars differently. The battle for vital economic need carries with it much less of a moral license than the war waged to prevent an aggressive enemy from conquering an innocent nation. Jewish law recognized that some wars are simply completely immoral, some wars are morally permissible but grant a very limited license to kill, and some wars are a basic battle for good with an enemy that is evil. Each of these situations comes with a different moral response and a different right to wage war. In sum, it is crucially important to examine the justice of every cause. However, violence is the service of justice is not to be abhorred within the Jewish tradition.

Another point must be kept in mind. In the mid-1950s, President Dwight Eisenhower conducted a lengthy strategic review of the defensive options available to the United States during the Cold War. During the course of the review, it became clear that undertaking a conventional arms defense of Europe against the massive array of Warsaw Pact troops was a task that America (and Europe) was economically unprepared to do. It would require a tripling of the defense budget, the reinstitution of a near universal draft and the significant raising of taxes, all steps the American people would have been unprepared to take. Yet the defense of Europe was vital.

Eisenhower formulated the United States response with three defensive axioms. First, the U.S. would never start a war with the Warsaw Pact; second, the U.S. reserved the right to first use of nuclear weapons; and finally, such weapons would be targeted against civilian centers should war be initiated by the Soviets. [122] These policies prevented another world war from breaking out, as the Soviets were genuinely afraid of the massive destruction of their civilian populations.

We now know that President Eisenhower understood that these strategies were unethical if implemented in a war, but furthermore recognized that absent these policies, another world war would break out, and Europe might be overrun. Thus, he authorized these exact policies, notwithstanding his deep reservations about them (and perhaps even unwillingness to actually implement them in wartime). [123] Furthermore, to give these unethical policies 'teeth,' he promoted officers to be in command who provided a demeanor and mindset of being ready, willing and able to order a nuclear response without ethical reservations. [124] Such was needed to ensure that the policy – at its core, a bluff – would be effective.

And it was. *The Cold war was won on a bluff, with not a single shot fired between the superpowers.*

The articulation of the *halakhot* of war has an element of this type of public policy in it. War law is thus not an area where it is wise to actually articulate one's own ethical limits, as one must assume that both friend and foe read the literature. One should not expect candid statements of the limits of Halakhah (Jewish law), as such might be like Eisenhower announcing that the nuclear option is merely a bluff. Bluffs only work if others are uncertain that one is bluffing. [125]

We all pray for a time where the world will be different – but until that time, Jewish law directs the Jewish state and the American nation do what it takes (no more, but no less, either) to survive and prosper ethically in the crazy world in which we live.

NOTES

*Cf. *Terminiello v. City of Chicago*, 337 U.S. 1, 37 (1949) (Jackson, J., dissenting): "There is danger that, if the Court does not temper its doctrinaire logic with a little practical wisdom, it will convert the constitutional Bill of Rights into a suicide pact."
1. *Lev. Rabbah, Tzav*, 9.
2. Michael Broyde, "Fighting for Peace: Battlefield Ethics, Peace Talks, Treaties and Pacifism in the Jewish Tradition," in Patout Burns, ed., *War and its Discontents:*

Pacifism and Quietism in the Abrahamic Traditions (Georgetown University Press, 1996), 1–30.

3. See, e.g., Michael Broyde, "Battlefield Ethics in the Jewish Tradition," *95ᵗʰ Annual Proceedings of the American Society for International Law* (2001), 92–98 (published in 2002).

4. On the ideology of *hesder* yeshivot see e.g., R. Aharon Lichtenstein, "The Ideology of Hesder," *Tradition*, 19:3 (Fall 1981), 199–217.

5. Thus both R. Yitshak Kofman's *Ha-Tzava ke-Hilkhatah* (Kol Mevaser, 1992) and the more standard *Hilkhot Tzava* by R. Zekharyah Ben-Shelomoh (Yeshivat Sha'alvim, 1988) leave them out completely and focus exclusively on questions of ritual observance of Jewish law in the army setting. For an excellent review of *Hilkhot Tzava*, see Michael Berger, Book Review, *Tradition*, 25:3 (Spring 1991), pp. 98–100.

6. *Tzitz Eliezer* 12:57 and 13:100.

7. *Shulhan Arukh, Yoreh De'ah* 252:4.

8. The starting point for such a list is the thoughtful article by R. Shaul Israeli in *Amud ha-Yemini* 16, which has produced a wealth of intellectual progeny on parade in nearly every issue of *Tehumin* by such luminary authors as R. Yaakov Ariel, R. Shlomo Goren, R. Ovadya Yosef, and many others. There are no less than 64 articles dealing with war-related issues in the 23 volumes of *Tehumin*, the overwhelming number of which agree with the starting point of R. Israeli.

9. These Hannibal procedures have become a source of some controversy in Israel, where for nearly twenty years they have been standing orders in the case of a kidnapping. See Sara Leibovich-Dar, "Rescue by Death," *Ha-Aretz*, May 22, 2003 (article number 996968), which states that the three Israeli soldiers whose remains were recently returned where killed in such a fashion.

10. R. Shaul Israeli, "Military Activities of National Defense (Heb.)," first published in *Ha-Torah ve-ha-Medinah* 5/6 (1953–54): 71–113, reprinted in his *Amud ha-Yemini* (rev ed., Jerusalem, 1991) as Ch. 16, 168–205.

11. See e.g., R. Yaakov Ariel, "*Gezel ha-Goy be-Milhamah*," *Tehumin* 23:11–17 (5763). Although *yefat to'ar* requires discussion, this matter is different in that such conduct is not directly engaged in as part the pursuit of a valid military goal, but rather the law represents an attempt to address an issue that relates to troop morale and other such issues. See also note 100.

12. See *Yalkut Shim'oni, Shoftim* 247 and the comments of R. Moses Isserles, *Responsa of Rama* 11 and R. Jacob Reischer, *Shevut Yaakov* 2:117.

13. See *Mishpat Kohen* 143.

14. R. Joseph Karo, *Kessef Mishneh* on Maimonides, *Hilkhot Mamrim* (Laws of Rebels) 2:4–5 (see also notes of *Radvaz* there) as well as *Hilkhot Sanhedrin* (Laws of Courts) 24:4.

15. See R. Abraham Kahana-Shapiro, *Dvar Avraham* 1:1.

16. *The Spirit of the* IDF: *The Ethical Code of the Israel Defense Forces,* 1995 version, emphasis added. It is worth noting that when the code was rewritten in concise, bullet-point form in 2001, the language of the Purity of Arms clause was updated:

Purity of Arms – The IDF servicemen and women will use their weapons and force only for the purpose of their mission, only to the necessary extent and will maintain their humanity even during combat. IDF soldiers will not use their weapons and force to harm human beings who are not combatants or prisoners of war, and will do all in their power to avoid causing harm to their lives, bodies, dignity and property (The Spirit of the IDF, 2001 version, available online at www1.idf.il/DOVER/site/mainpage.asp?sl=EN&id=32).

Among other revisions (including decreased emphasis of the term 'unnecessary'), the newer version actually seems to maintain that the Israeli military reserves greater latitude to determine the extent that force – and collateral harm – is necessary and appropriate.

17. *Yevamot* 79a, but see Tosafot ad loc., s.v. *Armoni u-Mefiboshet.*

18. See e.g. the comments of Rashi, ad loc., s.v. *ve-al yithallel shem shamayim.*

19. For a recent, excellent work on this topic, see Tzvi H. Weinberger and Boruch Heifetz, *Sefer Limud le-Hilkhot Bein Adam la-Havero* (vol. 2): *Lo Tikom ve-Lo Titor* (Tsefat, 2003), which notes this point many times.

20. See R. Ahron Soloveitchik, "On Noachides," *Beit Yitzhak* 19:335–338 (5747), and see also R. Joab Joshua Weingarten, *Helkat Yo'av, Tanyana* 14 for the uncertainty of the translation.

21. See Genesis 34.

22. As to why Maimonides uses the word "stole" to describe abduction, see *Sanhedrin* 55a and R. Moses Sofer, *Hatam Sofer, Yoreh De'ah* 19.

23. Maimonides, *Hilkhot Melakhim* (Laws of Kings), 9:14.

24. And this is without any notion of *hora'at sha'ah*; See opinion of *Kessef Mishneh* supra, text accompanying note 14.

25. Commentary of Nahmanides, Genesis 34:14. For more on this dispute see Michael Broyde, "Jewish Law and the Obligation to Enforce Secular Law," in D. Shatz & C. Waxman eds., *The Orthodox Forum Proceedings VI: Jewish Responsibilities to Society* (1997), 103–143, which discusses the duties of citizenship from a Jewish law view. For more on Nahmanides' position, see R. Shlomo Goren, "Combat Morality and the Halakhah," *Crossroads* 1:211–231 (1987).

26. Michael J. Broyde, "A Jewish Law View of World Law," *Emory Law Journal* 54 (2005 Special Edition): 79–97.

27. See e.g., Maj. Guy B. Roberts, "Note: Judaic Sources of and Views on the Laws of War," *Naval Law Review* 37 (1988): 221.

28. For precisely such a determination in the context of the Vietnam war, see David Novak, "A Jewish View of War," in his *Law and Theology in Judaism* vol. 1 (New York, 1974), 125–135.

29. *Sanhedrin* 74a–b.

30. Jewish law compels a Jew to take the life of a pursuer (Jewish or otherwise) who is trying to take the life of a Jew; *Shulhan Arukh, Hoshen Mishpat* 425:1. *Minhat Hinnukh* says that this is permissible but not mandatory for a non-Jew; see R. Joseph Babad, *Minhat Hinnukh*, positive commandment 296. R. Shelomoh Zevin argues

with this position, claiming that it is an obligation; see R. Shelomoh Yosef Zevin, *Le-Or ha-Halakhah: Be'ayot u-Verurim* (2nd ed., Tel Aviv: Tziyoni 1957), pages 150–57. Other modern commentaries also disagree with the *Minhat Hinnukh*; for a summary of the discourse on this point, see R. Yehudah Shaviv, *Betzur Eviezer*, (Tzomet, 1990) pages 96–99, who appears to conclude that most authorities are in agreement with R. Zevin's ruling; see also R. Yitzhak Schmelks, *Beit Yitzhak, Yoreh De'ah* II, 162 and *Novellae of R. Hayyim Soloveitchik* on *Maimonides, Hilkhot Rotzeah* 1:9. For an excellent article on this topic, and on the general status of preemptive war in Jewish law, see R. J. David Bleich, "Preemptive War in Jewish Law," *Contemporary Halakhic Problems* IV (Ktav, 1989), 251.

31. What precisely these restrictions are, will be explained infra section III:A.

32. R. Naftali Tzvi Yehudah Berlin, *Ha'amek Davar*, Genesis 9:5.

33. Genesis 9:5; In Hebrew, *"Mi-yad ish ahiv."*

34. Tosafot *Shevu'ot* 35b, s.v. *katla had.*

35. R. Shlomo Goren, "Combat Morality and the Halakhah."

36. R. Moses Sofer, *Hatam Sofer, Yoreh De'ah* 1:19.

37. See e.g., R. Abraham Kahana-Shapiro, *Dvar Avraham*, 1:11; R. Menachem Zemba, *Zera Avraham* #24. The issue of selling weapons to non-Jewish nations is addressed in an essay of R. J. David Bleich, "Sale of Arms," in his *Contemporary Halakhic Problems* III, 10–13. In this essay, he demonstrates that the consensus opinion within Jewish law permits the sale of arms to governments that typically use these weapons to protect themselves from bandits.

38. R. Israel Meir Kagan, *Mishnah Berurah* 329:17.

39. Similar sentiments can be found in R. Samson Raphael Hirsch, who clearly enthusiastically endorses military service for one's own country; see *Horeb* at pp. 461–463. A similar but murkier view can be found in R. David Tzvi Hoffman, *Responsa Melamed le-Ho'il* 42–43. R. Joseph Elijah Henkin states in a letter written on December 23, 1941:

> On the matter to enlist to volunteer for the Army: In my opinion, there is a difference between the rules of the army which existed before now in America and England, and the obligation of the army now. Before, when the entire army consisted only of volunteers, and during wartime they called upon volunteers by appealing to sacrifice for one's own people and country, then certainly everyone was required to take on the burden; but now that there is obligatory service, and the obligations are changed and reorganized according to need and function, I see no reason why one should volunteer to go, so that someone else will be exempted, for there are boundaries to this – there needs to be a space, uniforms, and weapons for them…So now the correct way is a middle position: everyone should fulfill the obligation placed on him by the government and intend to improve his nation in every area and function he performs, not to show indifference nor get riled up against the Allies (reprinted in R. Yehudah H. Henkin, *Responsa Benei Banim* IV, pp. 93–94).

R. Moses Feinstein reaches a similar conclusion in *Iggerot Moshe Yoreh De'ah* 2:158, s.v. *u-be-davar* where he writes, "Even more so, when one is drafted into the army, where even more so one is obligated is serve in the Army under the principle of *din malkhut.*" On a personal note, I can attest to the prevalence of this practice in the Orthodox community of Germany during World War I, as my great uncle Jacob Buehler O.B.M. was killed in the battle of Verdun in 1916 fighting as a member of Kaiser Wilhelm's army.

40. See for example, a fine article (with whose conclusion I do not agree) by Ya'acov (Gerald) Blidstein, "The Treatment of Hostile Civilian Populations: The Contemporary Halakhic Discussion In Israel," *Israel Studies* 1:2 (1996): 27–44.

41. For R. Lior, see "*Gishat ha-Halakhah le-Sihot ha-Shalom bi-Zmanenu,*" *Shvilin* 33:35 (5745): 146–150. The others are referenced above, and yet others are cited in Blidstein's article, supra note 40. Many other contemporary Israeli poskim could be added to this list.

42. Captain Yosefi M. Seltzer, "How the Laws of Armed Conflict Have Changed," in this volume.

43. *Sotah* 44b.

44. The word *reshut* is sometimes translated as "permitted;" this is not correct, for reasons to be explained infra. R. Joseph Karo, in *Kessef Mishneh* (*Hilkhot Melakhim* 6:1) further divides the category of "Obligatory" into two categories, "Compulsory" and "Commanded." Thus, some modern commentaries divide the types of war into three. While this division is not incorrect, the legal differences between "Commanded" and "Compulsory" wars are not very significant; for this reason this article will continue to use the common bifurcation rather than any other type of division, as does the Mishnah and Maimonides.

45. Or perhaps on "Compulsory" wars according to those who accept a trifurcation of the categories; see note 44.

46. Michael Waltzer, "War and Peace in the Jewish Tradition," in *The Ethics of War*, ed. T. Nardin (Princeton, 1997).

47. Noam Zohar, "Can a War be Morally Optional?" *Journal of Political Philosophy* 4:3 (1996): 229–241.

48. *Tzitz Eliezer* 13:100.

49. From this it is clear that the Jewish tradition neither favors pacifism as a value superior to all other values nor incorporates it as a basic moral doctrine within Judaism. Judaism has long accepted a practical form of pacifism as appropriate in the "right" circumstances. For example, the Talmud recounts that in response to the persecutions of the second century (C.E.), the Jewish people agreed (literally: took an oath) that mandated pacifism in the process of seeking political independence or autonomy for the Jewish state (*Ketubot* 111a). This action is explained by noting that, frequently, pacifism is the best response to total political defeat; only through the complete abjuring of the right to use force can survival be insured. So too, the phenomena of martyrdom, even with the extreme example of killing one's own children rather than allowing them to be converted out of the faith, represents a

form of pacifism in the face of violence; See e.g., Haym Soloveitchik, "Religious Law and Change: The Medieval Ashkenazic Example," *AJS Review* 12:2 (1987): 205–223 and *Shulhan Arukh, Yoreh De'ah* 151 for a description of when such conduct is permissible.

However, it is impossible to assert that a pacifistic tradition is based on a deeply rooted Jewish tradition to abstain from violence even in response to violence. It is true that there was a tradition rejecting the violent response to anti-Semitism and pogrom; yet it is clear that this tradition was based on the futility of such a response rather than on its moral impropriety. Even a casual survey of the Jewish law material on the appropriateness of an aggressive response to violence leads one to conclude that neither Jewish law nor rabbinic ethics frowned on aggression in all circumstances as a response to violence. See e.g. *Shulhan Arukh, Hoshen Mishpat* 421:13 and 426:1 which mandate aggression as a response to violence. That is, of course, not to say that pacifism as a tactic is frowned on. Civil disobedience as a tactic to gain sympathy or as a military tactic of resort in a time of weakness is quite permissible.

R. Maurice Lamm in his seminal essay on pacifism and selective conscientious objection in the Jewish tradition concludes by stating:

> It must be affirmed that Judaism rejected total pacifism, but that it believed strongly in pragmatic pacifism as a higher morally more noteworthy religious position. Nonetheless, this selective pacifism is only a public, national decision, and not a personal one. (Maurice Lamm, "After the War – Another Look at Pacifism and Selective Conscientious Objection," in *Contemporary Jewish Ethics*, M. Kellner, ed. [New York, 1978], 221–238).

50. *Sotah* 44b.

51. The Talmud additionally recounts that there are three ritual requirements for an Authorized war to commence. The details of the ritual requirements for such a war are beyond the scope of this paper; see generally, Bleich, supra note 30 and Zevin, "*Ha-milhamah*" in his *Le-Or ha-Halakhah*.

52. Maimonides, *Hilkhot Melakhim* 5:1.

53. "To diminish…," supra text accompanying notes.

54. See Maimonides' commentary to *Sotah* 8:7. Maimonides' commentary to Mishnah was originally written in Arabic. This version, printed in the commentary section appended to the Vilna edition of the Talmud, is the most common translation.

55. See Translation of R. Joseph Kapah, *Mishnah Sotah* 8:7. This is generally considered the better translation. For more on the distinction between the two translations of Maimonides' *Commentary on the Mishnah*, see R. J. David Bleich, "Preemptive War in Jewish Law," *Tradition* 21:1 (Spring 1983): 3–41, pp. 9–11.

56. Commenting on Maimonides, *id.* R. David bar Naftali Hirsch, *Korban ha-Edah* (in his addendum, *Shiurei Korban*, to the Palestinian Talmud, 8:10) has a slightly narrower definition, which is very similar to diBoton. An authorized war may be undertaken "against neighbors in the fear that with the passage of time they will wage war. Thus, Israel may attack them in order to destroy them." Thus, an

authorized war is permitted as a preemptive attack against *militaristic* neighbors. However, war cannot occur without evidence of bellicose activity.

57. R. Menahem ben Meir, Commentary of *Meiri* to *Sotah* 43b.

58. See R. Abraham Isaiah Karelitz, *Hazon Ish, Mo'ed* 114:2. He writes, "they kill Israel intermittently, but do not engage in battle."

59. See infra, Section v.

60. See R. Yehiel Mikhel Epstein, *Arukh ha-Shulhan he-Atid, Melakhim* 74:3–4. The thesis of Noam Zohar (at note 47 above) is buttressed by the approach of the *Arukh ha-Shulhan*.

61. In addition, the varying types of wars are flexible, not rigid. Armed aggression can begin as being permissible because of "pursuer" and then, due to a massive unwarranted counter-attack by the enemy, can turn into an Obligatory war; after the battlefield has stabilized the war can become an Authorized war.

62. See R. Joseph Karo, *Beit Yosef, Hoshen Mishpat* 425:6–7 (uncensored version).

63. For further discussion of this issue, see *Shulhan Arukh, Yoreh De'ah* 242 and commentaries *ad locum*.

64. See R. Shaul Israeli, *Amud ha-Yemini* 16. For an example of this type of discussion, see Michael Broyde and Michael Hecht, "The Return of Lost Property According to Jewish & Common Law: A Comparison," *The Journal of Law and Religion* 13 (1996): 225–254, Michael Broyde and Michael Hecht, "The Gentile and Returning Lost Property According to Jewish Law: A Theory of Reciprocity," *Jewish Law Annual* XIII (2000): 31–45.

65. And prohibited wars. Perhaps the most pressing ethical dilemma is what to do in a situation where society is waging a prohibited war and severely penalizes (perhaps even executes) citizens who do not cooperate with the war effort. This question is beyond the scope of the paper, as the primary focus of such a paper would be the ethical liberalities one may take to protect one's own life, limb, or property in times of great duress; see e.g., R. Mordecai Winkler, *Levushei Mordekhai* 2:174 (permitting Sabbath violation to avoid fighting in unjust wars); but see R. Meir Eisenstadt, *Imrei Eish, Yoreh De'ah* 52.

66. The question of who is "innocent" in this context is difficult to quantify precisely. One can be a pursuer in situations where the law does not label one a "murderer" in Jewish law; thus a minor (*Sanhedrin* 74b) and, according to most authorities, an unintentional murderer both may be killed to prevent the loss of life of another. So, too, it would appear reasonable to derive from Maimonides' rule that one who directs the murder, even though he does not directly participate in it, is a murderer, and may be killed. So, too, it appears that one who assists in the murder, even if he is not actually participating in it directly, is not "innocent;" see comments of *Maharal* of Prague on Genesis 32. From this *Maharal* one could derive that any who encourage this activity fall within the rubric of one who is a combatant. Thus, typically all soldiers would be defined as "combatants." It would appear difficult, however, to define "combatant" as opposed to "innocent" in all combat situations with a general rule; each military activity requires its own assessment of what is

needed to wage this war and what is not. (For example, sometimes the role of medical personnel is to repair injured troops so that they can return to the front as soon as possible and sometimes medical personnel's role is to heal soldiers who are returning home, so as to allow these soldiers a normal civilian life.) See also the discussion below.

67. This last rule has been subject to a considerable amount of renewed examination in light of the analysis of R. Yitzhak Ze'ev Soloveitchik that one may, as a matter of right, kill a *rodef* (pursuer) as he is a *gavra bar katila* (someone deserving to be put to death who has the status of "living dead"). While Blidstein, supra n. 40, notes that it is surprising how quickly that theoretical analysis has moved into practical *halakhah*, I am not surprised at all, and this is part (I suspect) of the dramatic impact conceptual *lamdut* has had on normative *halakhah*, a topic worthy of an article in its own right.

68. For a discussion of these rules generally, as well as various applications, see R. Joseph Karo, *Shulhan Arukh, Hoshen Mishpat* 425 (and commentaries). In addition, R. Jacob ben Asher, *Tur, Hoshen Mishpat* 425 contains many crucial insights into the law. (However, the standard text of this section of the *Tur* has been heavily censored, and is not nearly as valuable a reference as the less widely available uncensored version.)

69. See Section I.

70. Deuteronomy 20:10–12.

71. See e.g., Numbers 21:21–24, where the Jewish people clearly promised to limit their goals in return for a peaceful passage through the lands belonging to Sihon and the Amorites.

72. *Lev. Rabbah, Tzav,* 9.

73. Rashi, commentary to Deuteronomy 20:10.

74. *Sifri* 199, commenting on *id.* One could distinguish in this context between Obligatory wars and Commanded wars in this regard, and limit the license only to wars that are Obligatory, rather than merely Commanded. It would appear that such a position is also accepted by *Ravad*; see *Ravad* commenting on *Hilkhot Melakhim* 6:1 and Commentary of *Malbim* on Deuteronomy 20:10.

75. Maimonides, *Hilkhot Melakhim* 6:1.

76. See his commentary on *id.*

77. I would, however, note that such is clearly permissible as a function of prudent planning. Thus, the Jewish nation offered to avoid an authorized war with the Amorites if that nation would agree to a lesser violation of its sovereignty; see Numbers 21:21.

78. Of course, there is no obligation to do so with specificity as to detailed battle plans; however, a clear assertion of the goals of the war are needed.

79. *Hilkhot Melakhim* 6:1. These seven commandments are: acknowledging God; prohibiting idol worship; prohibition of murder; prohibition of theft; prohibition of incest and adultery; prohibition of eating the flesh of still living animals; and the obligation to enforce these (and others, perhaps) laws. For a discussion of these laws in context, see *Arukh ha-Shulhan he-Atid, Hilkhot Melakhim* 78–80.

80. Commentary of Nahmanides on Deuteronomy 20:1; of course, if after the surrender, a Jewish government were to rule that society, such a government would enforce these seven laws; however, it is not a condition of surrender according to Nahmanides.

81. This is just one facet in the debate between Maimonides and most other authorities as to whether Jewish law requires the imposition of the Noahide code on secular society. Elsewhere (*Hilkhot Melakhim* 8:10), Maimonides explains that in his opinion there is a general obligation on all (Jews and non-Jews) to compel enforcement of these basic ethical rules even through force in all circumstances; see also *Hilkhot Melakhim* 9:14 for a similar sentiment by Maimonides. Nahmanides disagrees with this conception of the obligation and seems to understand that the obligation to enforce the seven laws is limited to the non-Jewish rulers of the nation, and is of a totally different scope; for a general discussion of this, see R. Yehudah Gershuni, *Mishpetei Melukhah* 165–167. It is worth noting that a strong claim can be made that Tosafot agrees with Nahmanides in this area; see Tosafot, *Avodah Zarah* 26b, s.v. *ve-lo moredim*.

82. *Tzitz Eliezer* 13:100, supra at note 48.

83. Or naval blockade.

84. *Hilkhot Melakhim* 6:5. Maimonides understands the Jerusalem Talmud's discussion of this topic to require three different letters. If one examines *Shevi'it* 6:1 closely, one could conclude that one can send only one letter with all three texts; see *Arukh ha-Shulhan he-Atid, Hilkhot Melakhim* 75:6–7.

85. *Hilkhot Melakhim* 6:7.

86. *Supplement of Nahmanides to Maimonides' Book of Commandments*, Positive Commandment #4 (emphasis added).

87. *Id.* See also *Minhat Hinukh* 527. R. Gershuni indicates that the commandment is limited to Compulsory wars, rather than Commanded wars. His insight would seem correct; *Mishpetei Melukhah* commenting on *id.* It is only in a situation where total victory is the aim that such conduct is not obligatory.

88. Charles C. Hyde, *International Law* (Boston, 1922), §656; for an article on this topic from the Jewish perspective, see Bradley Shavit Artson, "The Siege and the Civilian," *Judaism* 36:1 (Winter 1987): 54–65. A number of the points made by R. Artson are incorporated into this article, although the theme of the purpose of the Jewish tradition in the two articles differs somewhat.

89. See R. Yehiel Mikhel Epstein, *Arukh ha-Shulhan he-Atid, Hilkhot Melakhim* 76:12.

90. Although I have seen no modern Jewish law authorities who state this, I would apply this rule in modern combat situations to all civilians who remain voluntarily in the locale of the war in a way which facilitates combat.

91. R. Shaul Israeli, "Military Activities of National Defense (Heb.)," first published in *Ha-Torah ve-ha-Medinah* 5/6 (1953–54): 71–113, reprinted in his *Amud ha-Yemini* (rev ed., Jerusalem, 1991) as Ch. 16, 168–205.

92. To the best of my knowledge, this principle is first cogently noted by R. Meir Simha of Dvinsk in *Or Sameah, Hilkhot Rotzeah* 1:8.

93. For examples of this, see R. Abraham Isaiah Karelitz, *Hazon Ish, Ohalot* 22:32 and R. Isser Yehudah Unterman, *Shevet mi-Yehudah* 1:8. (See also R. Unterman's analysis of heart transplantation, *"Be'ayat Hashtalat Lev me-Nekudat Halakhah,"* in *Torah she-be-al Peh* 11 (1969):11–18 and *Noam* 13:4 (1971):1–9). Both of these authorities employ statistical analysis to delimit Jewish law status. Regarding the rules of pursuit – one may kill a person as a pursuer only in a situation where the likelihood that such a person is not a pursuer is so statistically unlikely as to be considered a *mi'ut she-eino matzui.*

94. See R. Hayyim Dovid Halevi, *"Din ha-Ba le-Hargekha Hashkem le-Hargo be-Hayyenu ha-Tzeboryim,"* *Tehumin* 1:343–348 (5740). This approach stands in sharp contrast with the insight of the *Maharatz Hayot,* who adopts the view that the King's ability to punish (kill) those who rebel is grounded in the rules of *rodef* and not the *dinei melekh.* See R. Tzvi Hirsch Chajes, *Kol Kitvai Marahatz Hayot* 1:48. The most difficult and harsh example of this view, in this writer's opinion, is taken by R. Itamar Warhaftig, who writes (*halakha le-m a'aseh,* to the Israeli police) that one may intentionally kill non-violent demonstrators in a violent demonstration as the public safety is threatened by their mere presence. See Dr. Itmar Warhaftig, *"Haganah Atzmit be-Averot Retzah ve-Havalah,"* *Sinai* 81 (1977): 48–78.

95. See R. Shaul Israeli, *Amud ha-Yemini* 16:5 and R. Joseph Babad, *Minhat Hinnukh,* Commandment 425 who discusses "death" in war in a way which perhaps indicates that this approach is correct. See also Bleich, supra note 30, at 277 who states, "To this writer's knowledge, there exists no discussion in classical rabbinical sources that takes cognizance of the likelihood of causing civilian casualties in the course of hostilities..."

96. R. Yaakov Ariel, *"Haganah Atzmit (ha-intifada ba-halakhah),"* *Tehumin* 10: 62–75 (1991). He bases his view on the famous comments of the *Maharal* on the biblical incident of Shekhem, which defend the killing of the innocent civilians in that conflict along such a rationale. R. Shlomo Goren, "Combat Morality and the Halakhah," *Crossroads* 1:211–231 (1987) comes to the opposite conclusion. See also the article of R. Yoezer Ariel (brother of Yaakov Ariel), who also reaches a different conclusion; R. Yoezer Ariel, *"Ha'onashat Nokhrim,"* *Tehumin* 5:350–363 (1979). In this writer's view, R. Yoezer Ariel's paper correctly distinguishes between individual and national goals in these matters.

97. *Hilkhot Melakhim* 6:8.

98. *Sefer ha-Mitzvot (Book of Commandments),* Negative Commandment #57.

99. In his supplement to Maimonides, *Sefer ha-Mitzvot* (Positive Commandment 6).

100. The rules related to sexuality in combat are unique in Jewish law because the Talmud (*Kidushin* 21b) explicitly states that even that which is permissible was only allowed because of the moral weakness of men in combat. While the details of these regulations are beyond the scope of this paper (See Zevin, supra note 30, at 52–54 for a detailed description of these various laws), it is clear that the Bible chose to permit (but discourage) in very narrow situations in wartime so as to inject some realistic notion of morality into what could otherwise be a completely

immoral situation. The rules explicitly prohibited multiple rapes, encouraged marrying such women, and limited the time period where this was permitted to the immediate battlefield. A number of liberalities in ritual law were also allowed, reflecting the unique aspects of war. Why these particular laws did not apply in wartime, but others did, is also a topic beyond the scope of this paper.

101. *Shevu'ot* 35b. Tosafot notes that this applies even to a Jewish government fighting an authorized war; See generally, R. J. David Bleich, "Nuclear Warfare," *Tradition* 21:3 (Fall 1984): 84–88; (reprinted in *Confronting Omnicide: Jewish Reflections on Weapons of Mass Destruction*, D. Landes, ed. (1991), p.209 as well as in R. Bleich's own *Contemporary Halakhic Problems* III, 4–10).

102. R. Immanuel Jakobovits, "Rejoinders," *Tradition* 4:2 (Spring 1962): 202 (emphasis in original); (reprinted in *Confronting Omnicide: Jewish Reflections on Weapons of Mass Destruction*, D. Landes, ed. (1991), p. 199). See also Walter Wurzberger, "Nuclear Deterrence and Nuclear War," in *Confronting Omnicide*, p. 224 and Maj. Guy B. Roberts, "Note: Judaic Sources of and Views on the Laws of War," *Naval Law Review* 37 (1988): 221.

103. R. J. David Bleich, "Nuclear Warfare," supra n. 101. Although this author finds this logically persuasive, it is difficult to find a clear source in the Jewish tradition which permits one to threaten to do that which is prohibited to do; see e.g. R. Moses Isserles, *Hoshen Mishpat* 28:2.

104. See e.g., R. Aharon Zakai, *ha-Bayit ha-Yehudi* (Jerusalem, 1986) vol. 7 ch. 3.

105. Deuteronomy 20:2–9 (emphasis added).

106. See *Hilkhot Melakhim* 7:1–4 and comments of *Kessef Mishneh*, *Radvaz*, and *Lehem Mishneh ad locum*, all of whom interpret Maimonides as agreeing with *Ravad* on this issue. Maimonides in his *Sefer ha-Mitzvot* appears to adopt the position of *Ravad* in total; see *Sefer ha-Mitzvot*, Commandment 191.

107. Compare *Lehem Mishneh* commenting on *id.* and *Arukh ha-Shulhan he-Atid*, *Hilkhot Melakhim* 76:3 for an analysis of Maimonides' position.

108. *Sotah* 44a.

109. There is some dispute over how a person would prove his acceptability for any one of these exemptions; see R. Yehudah Gershuni, *Mishpetei Melukhah* 7:15 for a detailed discussion of this issue and R. Zevin, supra note 30, at 31–32.

110. See commentaries on Maimonides.

111. Maimonides accepts the opinion of Rabbi Akiva as normative (*Hilkhot Melakhim* 7:3); while *Hinukh* accepts the opinion of Rabbi Yossi (*Sefer ha-Hinukh*, Commandment 526). Most authorities accept Rabbi Akiva's opinion as normative; see *Arukh ha-Shulhan he-Atid*, *Melakhim* 76:22; see also R. Aryeh Leib Gunzberg, *Sha'agat Aryeh ha-Hadashot* 14:2 for more on this dispute.

112. *Sifri* 198.

113. Noam Zohar, "Can a War be Morally Optional?" supra n. 239.

114. See Deuteronomy 23:10–15; *Sifri* 257; Maimonides, *Hilkhot Melakhim* 6:13–14; see also *Arukh ha-Shulhan he-Atid*, *Melakhim* 75:18.

115. Joshua 9:19.

116. Maimonides, *Hilkhot Melakhim* (Laws of Kings and Their Kingdoms) 6:3. As explained above, it seems intuitive that those who argue with Maimonides' requirement of acceptance of the seven Noahide laws as explained above would disagree with its application here too; see e.g., R. Yehudah Gershuni, *Mishpetei Melukhah* p. 173.

117. Commentary of *Radvaz ad loc.* Such can also be implied from Maimonides' own comments of *Hilkhot Melakhim* 6:5.

118. In Judaism, the term "*hillul Hashem*" (desecration of God's name) denotes a prohibition whose parameters are fixed not by objective legal determinations, but by the perceptions of observers in the moral sphere. This is a very atypical prohibition in the Jewish legal system.

119. Commentary of *Ralbag* to Joshua 9:15.

120. Commentary of Radak to Joshua 9:7. This theory would have relevance to a duly entered into treaty that was breached by one side in a non-public manner and which the other side now wishes to abandon based on the private breach of the other side. Radak would state that this is not allowed because most people would think that the second breaker is actually the first one and is not taking the treaty seriously.

121. This is also the unstated assumption of the Babylonian Talmud, *Gittin* 45b–46a, which seeks to explain why treaties made in error might still be binding.

122. See "Statement of Policy by the National Security Council on Basic National Security Policy, October 30, 1953," in *The Pentagon Papers* (Gravel ed.), vol. 1, doc. 18, 412–429.

123. There is a great deal of debate among scholars and historians as to Eisenhower's true private feelings on the actual use of nuclear weapons in "massive retaliation." See e.g., Richard H. Immerman, "Confessions of an Eisenhower Revisionist: An Agonizing Reappraisal," *Diplomatic History* 14:3 (Summer 1990), p. 326, who felt that "Eisenhower never considered the nuclear option viable, except in the sense one considers suicide viable;" and Frederick W. Marks III, *Power and Peace: The Diplomacy of John Foster Dulles* (Praeger, 1993), pp. 108–09, who, though acknowledging Immerman's view as plausible, represents the consensus view of military and nuclear experts as holding that Eisenhower was clearly willing to "go nuclear." See also George H. Quester, "Was Eisenhower a Genius?" *International Security* 4 (Fall 1979): 159–79.

124. One of the contentions of Immerman's "Confessions" is that Eisenhower shrewdly used Secretary of State John Foster Dulles in a similar civilian role as a spokesperson and ambassador of these ends. Of course, there was the danger that even if Eisenhower himself would not have used nuclear weapons, at least some of his successors might have.

125. For an example of bluffing in Jewish law (whose truth ultimately cannot be determined), see the comments of R. Yehiel Mikhel Epstein regarding informing (*mesira*), *Arukh ha-Shulhan* 388:7; See also, Michael Broyde, "Informing on Others for Violating American Law: A Jewish Law View," *Journal of Halacha and*

Contemporary Society 41 (2002):5–49; Justice Menachem Elon, "Extradition in Jewish Law," *Tehumin* 8 (1988):263–86, 304–09; R. J. David Bleich, "Extradition," *Tehumin* 8 (1988): 297–303; and R. Shaul Israeli, "Extradition," *Tehumin* 8 (1988): 287–96. See also R. Yehudah Herzl Henkin, *Responsa Benei Banim* III, p. 146.

Philosophical Perspectives on Just War

Herb Leventer

Imagine that a spaceship lands on another planet. It seems to be uninhabited except for lots of alien chicken-like creatures. The crew sets up camp where the alien nests had been, and even takes a few of the eggs to make an omelet. When some bigger aliens see this, they scurry over and peck away at the astronaut. He kicks them away, killing one.

Was any wrong done in this scenario? From the astronauts' point of view, clearly not. But suppose the government had been enlightened enough to include in the crew a philosopher. He might see things differently, especially when a later ship arrives to establish a permanent base, settling in many areas previously filled with "chicken" nests, relying on regular forays to gather eggs, and causing frequent fighting off and killing of the "roosters" who protested. The philosopher might say that his crew had done wrong in taking over the planet, since it was not empty and ownerless, but already inhabited by the chicken-aliens; that the eggs, like the land, were the chickens' property and so it was theft to take them; that the crew had committed murder in killing the roosters who protested; that we were not justified in assuming that simply because the aliens looked like chickens, they were mere animals with no rights. Perhaps they are simply a different type of life form. We would have to study them to see if they had reason, created institutions like marriage and government, engaged in complex behavior – for if they did, they would have the same rights as we humans do. And by violating those rights, we would have committed an act of aggression, and have started an unjust war.

A situation like this actually did occur five hundred years ago, with the Spanish discovery, conquest, and settlement of South America. And King Ferdinand of Spain did send philosophers along with the warrior-explorers.

In 1514, when an early Spanish expedition landed on the mainland of South America, the conquistadors, before entering a village, would stop a few hundred feet away and read a declaration.[1] The first part was a brief capitulation of world history leading up to the papacy of Alexander VI and his donation of the New World to the king of Spain. The second part, which gave the declaration its name, required the Indians to accept the king as their lord and to allow the faith to be preached. If they accepted immediately, they would be peaceful subjects. If not, they would be subjugated by force and we "shall take you and your wives and children, and shall make slaves of them…and we shall take away your goods…and we protest that the deaths and losses which shall accrue from this are your fault…. And that we have said this to you and made this Requirement, we request the notary here present to give us his testimony in writing." This declaration was dutifully read thousands of times over the next few years as Mexico, Peru, and the rest of the New World were conquered. Often, it would be read to the wind from the deck of the ship before it landed, or to the empty forest, or to passing peasants who had no power, and almost always it would be read to people who, not knowing Spanish, would have no idea what was being said. It certainly looked like an empty charade – and many contemporaries made predictable fun of it. Why, then was it read? And does it deserve its reputation as an example of the silliness of mandating rules to govern the conduct of soldiers on campaign?

Soon after the discovery of the Americas in 1492, priests and friars were sent to convert the natives to Christianity. Many of the Dominicans who went were outraged at the treatment of their potential converts – the massacres, enslavement, expropriation of land and property, and use of force to convert – and saw themselves as the protectors of their new charges. They raised these issues with their superiors in Spain, and even petitioned King Ferdinand himself. As a sincere Christian, concerned with acting justly, he was troubled by these protestations. To answer them, and provide a defense of the justness of the conquest, he convened a forum of leading clergy and professors of philosophy to discuss the issue.[2] The issues were the legitimacy of the existing government of the natives, their right to own property, whether they had the same human rights as Europeans or were "natural slaves," and just what wrong they had done that would justify using force against them.

The answer given by the forum was a defense of the justness of the conquest, but with several provisos, the main one being that it would be unjust to attack without giving the Indians a chance to peacefully accept Spanish sovereignty. A document, the "Requirement," was written to provide a means to make such an offer, after which warfare would be justified.

Of course, this was a legalistic sham, which ignored most of the real issues raised by the Dominican friars. But the debate continued, and Ferdinand and his successor Charles convened many other forums to discuss them. The issue was also the subject of several courses of lectures at the universities, and our knowledge of the debates comes from the student notes of courses given by the leading theologian at the University of Salamanca, the Dominican Francesco de Vitoria. In the 1530s, he gave lectures on the American Indians and on the laws of war.[3]

Vitoria starts by asking by what right the Spaniards claimed dominion over the Indians' lands. He rejects the reliance on the 1493 grant by Pope Alexander. Vitoria was a conciliarist, who rejected the idea that the Pope had any temporal authority, much less the power to make gifts like the 1493 Bull of Donation of the New World to King Ferdinand. So the right could only come if the Indians, who *seemed* to own their land, were actually incapable of exerting true dominion, or if they were the equivalent of children, who in law could not yet control their property but needed a guardian. Four possible grounds for such a denial of dominion had been suggested: that they were sinners, non-Christians, madmen, or irrational. Vitoria rejects the first two as simply mistaken in law,[4] and the last two as mistaken in fact, since all evidence shows that the Indians were both sane and rational, as evidenced by their creation of an ordered society with laws, governing bodies, and commerce. The fact that the Indians were clearly not as educated, and their civilization not as advanced, as Europeans' might put them in the position of immature children, in which case Spain could, perhaps, act as their guardian, but this would clearly be a temporary situation of control. The Indians clearly owned their land, and Spanish conquest would seem to be theft, unless the land had been acquired in a just war, after which, according to the customary law of nations, it would be just to enslave the vanquished and expropriate their property.[5]

A just war, then, is the only way to secure a just title to the land. Vitoria quickly rejects three reasons that had commonly been given: difference of religion, enlargement of empire, and glory and wealth "cannot be a cause of just war." Rather, "the sole and only cause for waging war is when harm has been inflicted…. The cause of the just war is to redress and avenge an offence…. If the barbarians deny the Spaniards what is theirs by the law of nations, they commit an offense against them. Hence, if war is necessary to obtain their rights, they may lawfully go to war." The strongest claims of rights violated by the Indians are axiomatically asserted to be the right that all men have to travel and settle freely in any country and the right to preach. A derivative right is the right to intervene to protect the new converts from persecution. Finally, if the stories of cannibalism and human sacrifice turned out to be true, the Spaniards would have the right to intervene to protect the innocent victims from egregious violations of natural law. But, "*not every or any injury gives sufficient ground for waging war"* because "the effects of war are cruel and horrible – slaughter, fire, devastation." This is a plea for proportionality: it is wrong to respond to "trivial offenses" with war. There is an obvious problem here of defining "triviality" – each prince is prone to exaggerate the degree of "harm" he has suffered. "It is possible that they act in vincible error, or under the influence of some passion." The solution is not to trust any *one* man; the prince should consult other wise men, and he should especially "listen to the arguments of the opponent" as part of a careful examination of the "justice and causes of war…. One must consult reliable and wise men who can speak with freedom and without anger or hate or greed. This is obvious."

Vitoria concludes with a series of apodictic statements about "what and how much may be done in the just war?" The overall tone is permissive; basically, if the war is just, *"one may do everything necessary for the defence of the public good."* It is lawful to seize the goods of the enemy to pay for the costs of the war; not only to destroy their fortresses, but also to "set up garrisons in his territory, if that is necessary" and to occupy them to ensure future security; and to "teach the enemy a lesson by punishing them for the damage they have done." But what of the "innocent" – the civilians, the non-soldiers, the women, and children? Here, Vitoria is basically permissive, but suggests voluntary moderation: "it is occasionally lawful to kill the innocent not by mistake, but with full knowledge…if this is an accidental effect," for example, in storming a city, where you know you will be "burning the innocent along with the combatants" because "it would otherwise be impossible to wage war against the guilty." But we must retain a sense of proportionality – if the garrison is "not of great importance for eventual victory," or if you would have to kill a "large number of innocents…in order to defeat a small number of enemy combatants," such killing is not permissible. What of people who are currently innocent, "but may pose a threat in the future," like the children of Saracens, who are likely to fight us when they grow up? It would be "utterly wrong" to kill them, because they have not yet committed a crime. We can also confiscate property, impose tribute, enslave the people, and reorganize the government.

In general, one should aim "not for the destruction of his opponents" but for the establishment of peace, and therefore be moderate in both fighting and ending the war.

How did Vitoria know all of this? He relied on a thousand-year tradition of discussion of the criteria of justice in fighting wars and of reconciling the political imperatives of killing in war with the religious teachings of Christianity, which would seem to condemn killing as immoral. This had started in the fifth century with Augustine and reached its height in the thirteenth century with Aquinas.

THE HISTORICAL BACKGROUND
TO JUST WAR THEORY

Augustine was the first figure in the newly triumphant Christian church to reverse the early literal interpretations of Jesus's teaching, which would seem to make all killing, even in war, a sin. For instance, when Jesus says "resist not evil, but if any one strike thee on the right cheek, turn to him the left also," Augustine explains that "what is required here is *not* a bodily action, but an inward disposition."[6]

But the permission to kill in warfare is based mainly on God's granting to kings of the right and obligation to ensure the "peace and safety of the community." Given this divine origin, the people must obey even an "ungodly king," even if he gives an "unrighteous command." Also, the killing they do at his command is guiltless, because "actions in battle were not murderous, but authorized by law." Further, the evil in warfare is not that people are killed (there is nothing intrinsically evil in "the death of some who will soon die in any case"). Rather, "the real evils in war are love of violence, revengeful cruelty…lust of power, and such like."

Augustine distinguishes the social good from one's personal good, public from private morality, selfishness from altruism. He is skeptical that killing in self-defense is justified. In his dialogue, *On Free Will*,[7] he admits that civil law does not punish and even "gives the wayfarer the right to kill a robber to save his own life," but sees this as a concession to human weakness. It "permits the people that it governs to commit lesser wrongs to prevent the commission of greater. For the death of one who lies in wait to kill another is a much slighter thing than that of one who would merely save his own life." But he goes on to say "I do not see how these men, though blameless under the law, can be altogether blameless; for the law does not compel them to kill, but leaves it in their power." In a very stoic twist, Augustine asserts that it is a sign of "concupiscence" to put such high value on something that is transient, not really central to who you are, i.e., on your mere body as opposed to your soul. For your soul cannot "be taken away by killing the body," and if it could, it would be of small value and not worth killing for. "Wherefore, while I do not condemn the law that permits such people to be killed, I do not see how to defend those who kill them." In short, to kill in self-defense is wrong, because it puts too high a value on (one's own) physical life in this world, as opposed to life in the world to come, but to kill in war involves no wrong, because "soldiers do not thus avenge *themselves*, but defend the public safety."[8] So, killing in war is precisely the one exception to the normal Christian rule condemning the taking of life.

Eight centuries later, Aquinas made two additions to this Christian justification of war: the doctrine of double effect[9] and the list of three criteria that make a war just.

Aquinas defends killing in self-defense. While agreeing with Augustine that "killing is only allowed by action of public authority for the common good," he posits that one can perform an act that has two different effects ("saving one's own life," and "killing the attacker") while only intending one of those. The morality of the action is determined only on the basis of what one intended, not what incidentally also happened. Thus, in the case of self-defense, if one's intent is only to save one's own life, but the act also has the secondary effect of killing the attacker, the act remains justified. Moderation is required – if you can save yourself from the attacker without killing him, that is, of course, preferable; if you use more force than necessary, even intending only to save yourself, your action becomes illicit because of the lack of proportionality. This "doctrine of double effect" is the classic defense of "collateral damage" and killing of the innocent in siege situations (or, in modern warfare, bombing where it is not possible to avoid hitting non-combatants along with the military target.)

Aquinas specifies "three conditions for a just war:" (1) the ruler must have proper authority, (2) "a just cause is required," that is, the enemy must "deserve such a response because of some offense on their part," and (3) you must have "right intention…[that is] not out of greed or cruelty, but for the sake of peace, to restrain evildoers and assist the good." He concludes that "even if the war is initiated by a legitimate authority and its cause is just, it can become unjust because of evil intentions." This formulation became particularly influential after Aquinas' "code," the *Summa Theologiae*, became the standard textbook of church doctrine after about 1500. Christian writers from Vitoria to our own day cite it as unquestioned authority.

PRINCIPLES OF JUST WAR THEORY

Just war theory is a secularization of the Christian defense of the morality of war codified by Aquinas.[10] The expansion and secularization of just war theory occurred in the 17th century, especially in the writings of Grotius. The wars of the Protestant Reformation of the 16th century showed that a religious justification was not satisfactory, since the warring parties differed precisely on what the Christian texts meant. The wide spread of warfare, both in space and in time, made the issue of justification of more immediate concern than ever before. The end of feudalism reduced the effectiveness of the informal constraints of the "chivalric ethic," as did the mass, popular nature of religious wars. The need for an alternative to religious theory coincided with (and perhaps helped to make popular) the growth of neo-stoic philosophy, which included an expansion of the concept of "natural law." This based morality on the innate ideas, discoverable by reason and introspection, a process available to any rational man, and not requiring or dependent on any divine revelation. Much of modern political theory (like ideas about a social contract and human rights) derived from the same movement.

Hugo Grotius, a Dutch jurist, wrote *The Law of War and Peace*[11] in 1625, in the midst of the Thirty Years War. One of his main concerns was to limit the bloodshed of war. The 17th century saw a major change in the way wars were fought (this has been called the "military revolution").[12] The most obvious change was the perfection of guns and artillery, which made it possible to aim more accurately and thus kill more effectively. This also made the problem of collateral civilian casualties (during sieges) more common than it had previously been. The second was the expansion in size of armies by more than an order of magnitude (most battles of the 15th century "Hundred Years War" were between armies of less than a thousand – there were only a thousand British soldiers at Agincourt, for instance), whereas in the Thirty Years War, the figure was usually in the tens of thousands. The third change was the professionalization of the armies – they were now trained and drilled to act in unison, obey orders, allowing for complex strategies, and insuring that most of the men in the field actually fought (the wearing of uniforms, and the printing of training manuals, were 17th century innovations).

Grotius's task was to elaborate a set of rules and constraints on the conduct of war that could win general assent. How can one discover what "reason" requires? Grotius saw that appealing to any contemporaries, or to himself, would not find acceptance – the Catholic would distrust a Protestant, the Baptist a Calvinist, and so on. Rather, all could agree on the wisdom of the ancients, the Greek and Roman writers. Most of the examples given to justify his points (that poisoning wells of the enemy is wrong, that killing a soldier holding a flag of surrender is wrong…) are taken from ancient texts. Grotius demonstrates a certain ambiguity on just what he is proving with his citations. Sometimes he refers to them as examples of the "law of nations," sometimes as "natural law," sometimes the "custom of peoples." But, whatever the goal, History, it seems, is the best teacher.

Grotius notes that there is sometimes a difference between the law of nations and the law of nature. His main example is poisoning. "If you are permitted to kill a man, it makes no difference from the standpoint of the law of nature whether you kill him with a sword or by poison…[for he] has deserved to die. But the law of nations – if not of all nations, undoubtedly of the better kind – has now for a long time forbidden the killing of an enemy by poison. The agreement was reached out of consideration for the general welfare, to keep the dangers of war…from spreading too far." Contrariwise, the law of nations had from ancient times to his day allowed the killing of prisoners and hostages, while the law of nature forbids it. Grotius uses examples like this to emphasize that the international law that his book is creating is different from and superior to either of its two sources[13]

Of course, the publication of a philosopher's defense of limits on the conduct of war had no direct effect on the way military leaders or politicians actually fought. Yet it did help to create a climate of opinion among the leaders of society. The book was reprinted and translated many times over the next few hundred years, and it became part of the accepted wisdom of enlightenment intellectuals (much like Beccaria's *Crimes and Punishments*, which was concerned with the domestic equivalent of war). When the nations of Europe began formally to create an international law in the mid-19th century, Grotius' insights were incorporated in the several Geneva and Hague conventions from 1857 to 1907, which in turn were influential in the programs of the League of Nations after World War I and the United Nations after World War II. Concurrently, many individual states wrote rules of military conduct for their own armed forces, the most influential being Lieber's code for the Union forces during the Civil War, which was copied by the Prussian Army, among many others, and incorporated wholesale into the 1899 Hague Convention II, on the Laws and Customs of War On Land.[14]

A significant change occurred in the nature of just war theory in the period from Grotius to the First World War. There was a shift away from concern with justice in the initiation of war to concern with justness in the fighting itself. The main reason for this was the development of the theory of sovereignty of the territorial state, which developed after the Peace of Westphalia ended the Thirty Years War. The assumption now was that every sovereign nation had an inherent right to start a war for whatever reason it chose, in whatever it defined as its own self-interest. This was the doctrine of "reason of state." This combined with the jealous guarding of self-interest by maneuvers to maintain a "balance of power" in Europe, and, as imperial expansion grew in the 19ᵗʰ century, throughout the colonial world as well. War was simply a political tool to maintain and fine-tune this strategic balance. Clausewitz's *On War* (1822) is the reflection of this: war is simply a continuation of politics, in need of no justification, and subject to no limits. For the Christian just war theorists, the main limit on war was at the first step, the initiation of hostilities; for the 18–19ᵗʰ century politicians who believed in *raison d'etat*, it was only in the course of fighting that limits could be thought of. This is why most of modern discussion and legislation about just war focuses mainly on the conduct of armies during war.

In our times, "just war theory" is usually defined as a set of half a dozen criteria for justifiably starting a war and for the kind of killing that can be done in the course of the fighting. For most thinkers, *all* of the criteria must be met for the war to be considered just:

1. Formal declaration by the proper authority in that particular state.
2. Just cause, usually aggression, along with a list of clearly unjust causes, like economic benefit; expansion of your ideology, religion, or political system; territorial expansion, etc. There is an ongoing debate on whether humanitarian intervention, supporting one side in a civil war, or preventive action are possible just causes.
3. Right intention; the goal must be not just to resist the aggression or right the wrong, but also to live with the perpetrator afterwards, i.e., to achieve peace. From this derives the obligation to rebuild the defeated enemy's economic and political structure after the fighting ends and the obligation to restrain the viciousness of the actual fighting, so as not to preclude the possibility of both sides living together in peace afterwards.
4. Last resort, or, more accurately, resort to arms should not be one of your *first* responses to the wrong.[15]

5. Recognition that the enemy is still a human, thus limiting what you can do to him during the battle, as well as when he is captured or defeated.
6. Civilian immunity, or, more accurately, discrimination in the fighting between Combatants and noncombatants.

A background condition, which is relevant to many of these six conditions, is proportionality. Since war always involves killing, and frequently escalates out of control to even more horrible acts, one should calculate whether this enormous cost is worth bearing to start a war to right a relatively trivial wrong or, during the war, whether a particular battle is worth fighting to gain a small tactical advantage. An otherwise just war can become unjust if it fails either of these tests of proportionality.

Let us see how this tradition treats some of the topics of this symposium.

The obligation of the soldier to fight is usually assumed, and rarely discussed. Grotius is typical: "what a slave is in a household, a subject is in a state, and hence…by nature undoubtedly all subjects may be taken to serve in war."[16] The historical fact that most societies have given exemptions (to clergy, for example) is just an example of where the law of nations goes beyond what is required by natural law. In cases where the justness of the war is itself in doubt, the citizen is obligated to defer to the authorities, if only for the sake of civil peace and to reinforce the general rule that everyone is better off if everyone obeys the laws. However, when you are certain that the war is wrong, then both Aquinas and Vitoria, but not Grotius, agree that you should refuse to fight, rather than rely on the defense of obedience to superior order; since *you* are sure that the war is unjust, you personally no longer have a right to kill. All the 19th and 20th century codes, from Lieber to the Hague and Geneva Conventions, agree that a soldier can be punished for obeying an order which itself is a violation of the laws of war, but it was only in the aftermath of World War II that a formal recognition was given, with the creation of tribunals like the one at Nuremberg, and the explicit elaboration of the legal category "war crimes." This specifically included the provision that "the fact that any person acted pursuant to the order of his Government or of a superior does not free him from responsibility for a crime."[17] This legal jeopardy created an implicit right (and perhaps obligation) for the soldier to refuse certain orders, and thus, arguably, to refuse to fight at all if the entire war were unjust.

One of the greatest changes in the just war tradition has been increasing protection to prisoners of war. Everyone up to Grotius and his 18th century simplifiers agreed that they could be killed, and they could certainly be enslaved. Thus, Grotius's discussion of POWs takes the form of a discussion of the "humanity and kindliness" with which we should treat any slave.[18] The later codes specify more and more details on just what this humanity and kindliness requires. For Lieber, it is a simple list: "prisoners of war shall be fed upon plain and wholesome food, whenever practicable, and treated with humanity. They may be required to work for the benefit of the captor's government." They must be given medical treatment. No violence may be used to extort information. The Hague Convention of 1899 added a specification that "food, quarters, and clothing" be "on the same footing as the troops" who captured them, that prisoners had to give only "name and rank," that they be paid for any labor they performed, and that they be allowed to practice their religion. After World War II, an extremely detailed[19] convention was written, specifying, for example that food "be sufficient in quantity, quality and variety to keep prisoners in good health and to prevent loss of weight or the development of nutritional deficiencies. Account shall also be taken of the habitual diet of the prisoners." Canteens must be provided where they may buy extra food "soap and tobacco and articles in daily use [at]…local market prices." Latrines "shall be maintained in a constant state of cleanliness." "Adequate premises and necessary equipment" must be provided for them to engage in sports and games, and on, and on…. [20] This is typical of the post-war expansion in the concept of "human rights" beyond the minimums that Grotius identified as basic.

The most influential attempt to update just war theory in our time is Michael Walzer's book *Just and Unjust Wars*.[21] While accepting most of what had by then become the classic Grotian analysis, Walzer shifts the focus in four ways. He uses examples from modern and contemporary history and wars, and he expands on the discussion of "just cause" by including borderline cases, like pre-emptive strikes, counter-interventions in civil wars, and humanitarian interventions (precisely the types of cases that have replaced outright defense against invasion as the main cause of wars in our time). Walzer expands a minor criterion of justness into a major one: probability of success. He also allows for the possibility of "justified wrongdoing" in extreme emergency – i.e., he gives some rules for breaking the rules of conduct during war.

Walzer describes the just war tradition as having evolved into two sets of rules: the rules for justly starting a war, which he calls the "theory of aggression" or the "legalist paradigm," and the rules for justly fighting in the war (which he sees as an account of individual rights, "how they are retained, lost, exchanged [for war rights] and recovered" in conditions of war), the most important of which, he claims, is the distinction between combatant and noncombatant.

"Nothing but aggression can justify war," according to Walzer's understanding of the legalist paradigm.[22] Aggression is defined as "any use of force or imminent threat of force by one state against the political sovereignty or territorial integrity of another." Also, "once the aggressor state has been militarily repulsed, it can also be punished." Walzer then devotes several chapters to modifying this, and offering five "revisions" of the legalist paradigm. (1) Preemptive[23] war is sometimes acceptable, if the threat is real and imminent enough (like Israel in 1967), (2) territorial integrity can be breached in cases of secession or "national liberation," (3) counterintervention is just, when someone else has already intervened in a civil war, (4) humanitarian intervention to correct such egregious[24] violations of human rights as enslavement or massacre is permitted, and (5) punishment after the war ends is very rarely acceptable, and only in cases of Nazi-like states, the reason being the traditional one that "the object in war is to achieve a better state of peace."

The rules for fighting in a war are much less absolute; they change over time, and with social change (countries get more civilized over time) and technological change. Their general aim is to limit the intensity and suffering in combat, to call for moderation and proportionality in the use of deadly force, in order to distinguish war from mere massacre by setting *some* limits. These rules are closely related with basic human rights, and assume that all soldiers are in a certain sense equal, on both sides, and that noncombatants have a much greater claim than combatants not to have their rights overridden. In a controversial revision of just war theory, Walzer claims that these rules, too, are subject to a major revision – they can be overridden in cases of "supreme emergency."

"Supreme emergency" is a case when the very existence of the community is at stake, not simply some tactical advantage in the course of normal battle. The example Walzer gives is the strategic terror bombing of German cities in World War ii, whose explicit purpose was to destroy civilian morale by targeting residential areas, not military targets. This was a clear violation of the war convention. The justification was that no other path was available to Britain to slow down the German advance, which would have destroyed liberal democracy in Europe. Walzer says this may well have been the correct thing to do, but only if Churchill acknowledged that he was doing something wrong.

Walzer has developed this argument at length in his essay[25] on "dirty hands," i.e., the necessity for politicians sometimes to do immoral things in the course of fulfilling their public responsibilities. The example he gives there is the "ticking bomb" that a terrorist has hidden in the big city. To prevent massive destruction of innocent lives, the political leader *should* approve torturing the terrorist to discover the location of the bomb. Torture is a clear violation of a basic human right and is wrong, but in this case, it is right to do the immoral thing.[26] The fact that you should override the prohibition does not let you off the hook. Walzer insists that you must acknowledge responsibility so that you will feel the gravity of your action (and so be very careful not to appeal to supreme emergency too easily), and also because to be moral, you should do *something* to balance the moral equation of the evil thing you were forced to do. He compares this to civil disobedience – if you violate a law in order to do good, you should appear in court and accept the punishment (he does not go so far as to say that you should also drink the hemlock).

In a way, this is just a version of the classical idea of the tragic: sometimes you might be forced to kill your daughter to allow the ships to sail to fight a just war.[27] Life can place you in a situation where the perfectly rational action is clearly morally wrong; this must leave a "blemish on one's life." Not that you should be subject to punishment. But there are other types of consequences that would seem to fulfill the same function: "a duty to show regret, to apologize, to make restitution, to provide reparation."[28] The example Walzer himself cites is the refusal to give a medal or any other recognition after the war to the head of British Bomber Command, who planned the killing of so many German civilians in the "terror-bombing" campaign.[29]

Until the 20th century, most discussion assumed that the rules of just war were a moral requirement, but not a legal one. At best, they were part of natural law, discoverable by any rational human, but not enforced. It was mainly after World War I that there were attempts to create a written positive law of war for the world community. The main impetus was the revulsion felt at the enormous destructiveness of the war, and the combined feeling that the war ought not to have been fought at all (it was a big accident, either caused by the alliance system, which supposedly forced one nation after another to blindly go to war to fulfill its treaty promise to do so if its ally were attacked, or caused by the romantic underestimation of the brutality and deaths normal to war). This was exacerbated by the inhumanity of new weapons like poison gas and aerial bombardment. And so, the League of Nations sought to limit war, and created several groups which produced a series of Conventions that limited the actions that states could take while fighting even a justified war. This codification of limits did not clarify very much the conditions under which it would be acceptable to start a war. The assumption of a priority and sanctity to sovereign states and to territorial boundaries led to an assumption that boundary crossing was the major act that would justify a military response, and the major definition of the crime of "aggression." The UN continued this approach after WWII. The key document here is article 51 of the UN Charter, which specifies "the inherent right of individual or collective self defense if an armed attack occurs," but outlaws war in all other cases.

How important is this switch in international law from the unwritten laws of nature and laws of nations to written positive law?[30] It is often assumed that the change is one of greater obligation to obey. J.L. Brierly, the author of the standard textbook of international law (first edition, 1928, fifth edition, 1955), argued that this assumption was incorrect, and based on a false dichotomy: international law is really either "natural law" derived from the very nature of states and societies, or positive law, derived from the written rules and treaties that states have consented to obey. In fact,

> there need be no mystery about the source of the obligation to obey international law. The same problem arises in any system of law.... The international lawyer then is under no special obligation to explain why the law with which he is concerned should be binding.... We cannot avoid some such assumption as...natural law. The ultimate explanation of the binding force of all law is that man...is constrained, in so far as he is a reasonable being, to believe that order and not chaos is the governing principle of the world.

Brierly goes on to specify the sources of twentieth century international law as fourfold: 1) written treaties and conventions, 2) general practices accepted as binding, i.e., custom, 3) general principles of law recognized by civilized nations, and 4) the writings of the most highly qualified publicists of various nations, which are evidence of 2 and 3.[31]

But, even if we grant that international law is binding in the secular world, we must still ask about its status in the Halakhah. David Novak makes a convincing case that it is equally binding, both as the *din* of Noahide law, and also because natural law is independently recognized in *Humash* as existing prior to (and being a precondition of) the giving of the Torah. What other law could

Moshe have been judging the people by when Yitro visited him, before the giving of the Torah on Sinai?[32]

Is it a good thing that international society has converted moral standards and customary behavior into legal requirements? In the absence of an executive branch capable of enforcing the rules, it would seem that nothing has been gained. No less an authority than Kant was cynical about the self-serving use that the powerful would make of just war theory, claiming that Grotius would be cited only as justification, never as a restraint, by those marching off to war.[33] The main benefits are the same teaching function, and declaration of desirable goals, as already existed when just war was mere natural law. It shames the indifferent and it educates the realist by framing the analysis of war so as to show the benefits to both sides of adherence to the rules.

It has been suggested that such "education of the realist" is more effectively done by a written than by an unwritten law.[34] The context is one of the strangest incidents in the history of realist analysis of war: the first two decades of the cold war. The existence of nuclear weapons, which could in theory annihilate the whole planet, raised the stakes significantly. It was thought that mathematical analysis, especially in the form of "game theory," might help both predict what the other superpower would do and decide how best to respond. This was the heyday of talk of "first strikes" and "preventive wars": why not use our nuclear superiority to destroy the USSR before it grew strong enough to threaten us with the same fate? John von Neumann invented various "prisoners' dilemma" situations to explore the best ways of resolving conflict in a bipolar nuclear world. The surprising conclusion was that even when each side made perfectly rational decisions, it would necessarily produce a bad result in some situations.

Take the "dollar auction." You offer a dollar bill to the highest bidder, under the condition that the second-highest bidder must pay his bid yet get nothing; the result is bad for both bidders. A bids a nickel, B bids 25 cents, A counters with 50 cents; B would lose his 25 if he stopped, so he bids 51 cents. When the bidding gets to 99 cents, the 98 cent low bidder would lose all unless he outbid his opponent again. It is "rational" for the low bidder to continue up to $1.99 – but that is clearly (and paradoxically) irrational. The psychological ease of getting caught up in such a "tit for tat" situation seems similar to escalations in pre-war situations (or, for that matter, in actions during the fighting itself). The best way of avoiding the paradoxical result seems to be creating laws defining such a "game" as "wrong" in itself. This is precisely the type of "law" that just war theory creates.

PHILOSOPHICAL PERSPECTIVES

What is special about the way a philosopher reflects on the problem of justice in war? How does it differ from the way a politician, general, historian, or political scientist examines war? According to Rawls, "the politician looks to the next election, the statesman to the next generation," while it is "the task of the student of philosophy to articulate and express the permanent conditions and the real interests" of society.[35]

Since Kant, philosophers have used the concept "universalizability" as the central feature of justice. In Kant's original formulation, it is a "categorical imperative" to "act only on that maxim that you can at the same time will to be a universal law." This reflects our basic ideas of fairness: what is good, right, and just for one to do should be also good for everyone else to do; conversely, we can recognize an immoral act by our recoil from the thought: "what if everyone else did that?" In some ways, this captures the difference between short and long-term views of our actions to which Rawls refers. It also provides a method of examining moral issues by stepping back from the specific and always richly complex issue before us and looking instead at a simpler form of the same act. If, to be right and good, an act must be universalizable, we can discover what to do in complex situations by examining simplified abstract ones. We can be like a mathematician – as long as we assume that the rules of, say, geometry, are universally true, we can discover the correct facts about geometric forms without even looking at any actual forms. In fact, if you want to know how many degrees the angles of a triangle add up to, it would be misleading to take a protractor to an actual triangle; better to construct an ideal triangle in your head, and discover the proof that the angles *must* total 180°.[36]

The problem in war that has attracted most interest among philosophers is the basic one of killing. Precisely who can and who cannot justly be killed? Precisely why are you allowed to kill him? Is it necessary that he be "guilty"? That he "forfeited" his right to life? That he be a "threat" to your life? That he have even taken any positive action at all? If you might (or even would surely) accidentally kill a bystander while killing someone you are allowed to kill, what should you do? To avoid *ad hoc* (much less *ad hominem*) distortions in our analysis of such questions, philosophers invent abstract examples to illustrate the possible distinctions. By varying the conditions in these examples, and noticing how our intuitions about the rightness of an action change, we can discover problems in our original assumptions, and clarify what the right action really is. A handful of these invented cases, like the Trolley and Transplant cases,[37] have become standard shorthand ways of noting certain distinctions.

A trolley is heading down a track. The conductor notices five people on the track; he slams on the brakes, but they don't work. He then notices that there is a spur ahead leading off to a side track. He is about to switch onto it when he notices that one person is walking on that track. If he does nothing, five will be killed; if he switches to the spur, one will be killed. Our intuition is that he *may* (and probably *should*) kill the one rather than the five. It would seem that we are all "consequentialists," i.e., we think that the action that produces the best (often numerical) overall consequences is the moral one. But what about a surgeon, who has five terminally ill patients – one will die without a kidney transplant, the others need a heart, a liver, etc. – and all have the same rare blood type. A new patient who is perfectly healthy, but needs a minor surgical procedure, walks into his office; he has that same rare blood type. If the doctor kills the new patient, he will then have five organs he can transplant to save the five others. Our intuition is that it would definitely be wrong for him to do this, even though the resulting situation will produce the best overall result, i.e., five rather than just one patient alive. It seems that some things are morally wrong, even if they produce the better result. Varying the trolley situation can also make the point. Suppose there is no side spur in the track, but there is an overpass ahead, on which a fat man is leaning over the railing. The conductor happens to have a gun. Can he shoot the fat man, causing him to fall in front of the trolley, in which case the trolley will stop on impact with his large body, thereby saving the five? Again, our intuition is that this would be wrong. But why is it wrong? The final result, after all, will be the same one dead and five saved as in switching tracks. The usual answer is to appeal to the doctrine of double effect, with an addition to Aquinas' definition. If one action has two effects, one good and one evil, but you intend only the good, you are not liable for the evil side effect, *but only with the further proviso* that the good effect not be the direct result of the evil effect. So, by switching tracks, you save the five whether or not there is anyone on the side track, while in the fat man case, it is only if the body of the fat man brings the train to a stop that the five will be saved; that is, his death is the direct and necessary means of saving the five.

The strategy of thought in the above example is to show that a seemingly plausible rule for deciding what killing is morally acceptable in one situation ("do what saves the most people") leads to an unacceptable conclusion when applied to a seemingly similar situation, and *therefore* must be incorrect. Most philosophers who discuss just war (and international law in general) reject consequentialist/utilitarian justifications for the same reason. Of course, in the guise of prudential reasoning, it still plays a role as *an additional* reason for doing or refraining from doing some act in war. For example, one reason for obeying any "rule" of war (like the requirement that you not shoot prisoners of war or use poison gas) is that you wish to gain the benefit of having the other side treat *your* soldiers in the same way. But if this justification by reason of reciprocity were the main reason, it would not make sense to continue to abide by the rule if the other side rejected it first. Just war theorists wish their restrictions to be stronger than that; they want the rules to be binding even if one side ignores them (and we do not think that *we* should have shot German hostages in World War II just because the Germans did).

Another reason for rejecting consequentialist reasoning as unacceptable for crudely "counting the numbers" is that it leads to unacceptable views of proportionality. For instance, if the enemy captures one of your pilots, should you risk ten other pilots or soldiers by mounting a rescue operation? In almost all cases, you would save more of your own soldiers by *not* trying to save the one. But there is universal (and intuitive) agreement that we should mount the rescue. Or, at a more global level, if we were to simplify the stakes in World War II to "saving" six million Jews from death, would it have been right to fight it if you knew that the cost in total lives lost would be the fifty million that it turned out to be?

Philosophers make one more assumption, which Walzer calls the "domestic analogy:" that we can understand actions and what the rules should be in inter-state war by analogy to similar actions (like homicide) within a state, i.e., in criminal law. So, states are to international relations as individuals are to the domestic realm.[38]

PROBLEMS IN JUST WAR THEORY AND
SOME POSSIBLE NEW SOLUTIONS

Just causes of war

What is a just cause? "Self-defense" is the usual answer, the goal being not merely to end the threat to the self, but also to "vindicate" (*vindicar* meaning to seek vengeance, punish, restore to the previous state). The analogy here is to the domestic criminal who says, "your money or your life." Simply to disarm him is clearly not enough. Ending the immediate threat would leave open the possibility that he might come back tomorrow with the same demand. We want to protect the potential victim in the future and restore to him or indemnify him for the loss he has suffered [his wallet, his self-esteem and trust, his fearlessness]. Punishment after the crime is taken to be an effective means of accomplishing these goals.

So, there are significant implications for the breadth of the war, and the actions that will define it, in the very definition of "self-defense." In 1991, it would seem that the justice of war against Iraq lay not merely in forcing Iraq to withdraw from Kuwait, but also in insuring that it did not invade again and also in compensating the victim for its losses – by destroying the aggressor's armed forces and weaponry, occupying the country, changing the government, seeking reparations, etc. There is not as clear a distinction as one might think between justification for starting a war (*jus ad bellum*) and justice in fighting that war (*jus in bello*).[39]

Self defense against what? Most obviously, against aggression. But what kind of aggression?

Do we mean only armed military invasion? This is the definition given in the UN charter as the only excuse for resorting to war.

Or perhaps we mean even unarmed incursion into your sovereign territory? If one country chases out its ethnic minority into its neighbor's country, is that neighbor harmed?

Or the threat of invasion, as opposed to an actual border crossing? If Egypt proclaims its intent to push the Jews into the sea, does Israel have to wait until the first tanks roll across its border? Given the speed of modern warfare, and the possibility of planes and missiles winning a decisive advantage in the first hours, it might be suicidal to allow this advantage to the aggressor, and Israel's preemptive strike in the 1967 Six Day War is generally taken to be one of the few examples of justified preemptive war.

Or the preparation for an attack even without an explicit threat? But military buildups are always proclaimed as defensive. Surely, every state has the right to prepare for its own defense, and it is difficult to establish a difference between offensive and defensive arms. It makes no sense to leave the decision to the state which fears being the victim – that would give the advantage of "justness" to the most fearful and distrustful state. Every other country in the world could say, in justice, that they felt threatened by, for instance, American military might, and so have a just cause to attack us for threatening them. Why should North Korea or Iraq be any different? We might be tempted to make the nature of the state the deciding factor – if it is a state that has in the past acted aggressively, it would seem rational to interpret its present ambiguous "self-defense" actions as preparation for aggression. But that would be to punish someone for what he *is* rather than for what he *does*. It now seems, for instance, that Saddam Hussein *did* change after his defeat in 1991 – he was still an obnoxious leader, but was no longer a threat to his neighbors. There are so many obnoxious, evil, selfish leaders in the world who do not value the interests of their own countries, much less the interests of the global community, that there would be constant war if outside powers were justified in intervening just to replace them with better people.

What about humanitarian intervention? Where the threat is only very indirectly to us – i.e., the threat is to world peace or global justice – the Serbs are killing off Moslem civilians or the Hutus the Tutsis in an attempt at genocide. Or where the legal sovereign is mistreating his own subjects (Saddam Hussein in Iraq, or Hitler and the German Jews before 1939, or Stalin during the purges of the 1930s, or the Southern states of the United States during the worst of the Jim Crow era, or the Khmer Rouge in Cambodia killing a third of its own population) but is not seeking to impose his unjust internal policy on others outside of his borders. To justify most interventions of this sort would be to condemn the world to constant wars.

Buchanan and Koehane have recently defended preventive war in the above two situations. Their argument is unusual for combining a defense of preventive war against both weapons of mass destruction (and other massive threats to the state) and against genocides (and other massive violations of human rights of peoples), while refusing to justify preventive war against incrementally increasing, but relatively low level, violence (as in the former Yugoslavia). It has three steps:

1. There is a prima facie justification for using force to prevent a situation if you would be justified in using force after the situation occurred and if the situation would be almost impossible to stop after it had started. Consider two scenarios: first, a group is *already* releasing a lethal virus into a major city; surely we could use force to stop them from releasing more. Second, you learn that a terrorist group has a lethal virus it is

planning to release; you know that the virus is now in the lab, and after it leaves the lab, you do not know which city it will be sent to. Isn't it as certain that you can destroy that lab (and not just to protect your own city, but also if it is a city in some other country)?

2. The assumption among just war theorists that those who have not attacked you have a "right not to be attacked" is false for two reasons. First, you do *not* necessarily violate someone's rights when you kill him before he has done something wrong. "At common law, an individual may use deadly force in self-defense if a reasonable person would judge that he is in danger of death...even If the target has not yet caused harm." In the international arena, where the stakes are higher (millions might die) and there is no effective police to intervene, there is even less requirement that the harm be imminent than in the domestic case. Secondly, "it is incorrect to say that the group has done nothing. It has *wrongfully imposed an especially high risk of serious harm on others.*" Analogizing to the law of conspiracy, the group's "specific intention" and "agreed plan of action" *are* "acts," and satisfy the condition that "a crime must include an act, not merely a guilty mind."

3. Relying on Security Council approval for military intervention has moral flaws, most importantly that there is no accountability mechanism to insure that moral justness rather than political self-interest will guide its decisions. Buchanan and Koehane suggest such a mechanism. "Prior to taking preventive action, states will be required to enter into a contingent contract" to present the evidence for their case to the Security Council and to agree "to submit to an evaluation by an impartial body after the" action. If that evaluation undermines the justification, the intervening state would be liable to sanctions (compensation for those who suffered, financial support for rebuilding the invaded country). "If states know *ex ante* that these rules are in place, incentives for opportunistic interventions...will be diminished." On the other hand, if the later evaluation proves that the assessment by the invading country was accurate, then

"the attacking states would indeed have performed a public service for the world by eliminating…the threat that weapons of mass destruction would be used or that large-scale violations of basic human rights would be inflicted." Therefore, "those states that had not shouldered the risk of preventive military action would bear special responsibility for financial support in rebuilding …[and] also bear responsibility for peace enforcement. That is…would be sanctioned as 'free riders,' who were informed about the threat but refused to act."[40]

David Luban also attempts to justify at least some preventive wars. After recognizing the problems with any broad permission (he cites Kissinger's caution against making preventive war a "universal principle available to every nation," which would create endless wars), he justifies a single exception – rogue states. These are states like Hitler's Germany or Saddam Hussein's Iraq, which are "militaristic…[have] a track-record of violence…and a buildup in capacity to pose a genuine threat." These three criteria "make it overwhelmingly likely that it is arming with belligerent intentions." Luban's innovation is to notice that, with a rogue state, the difference between preemptive and preventive war disappears, because the "trajectory of the rogue state makes it an 'imminent' attacker, *provided that we recharacterize imminence in probabilistic rather than temporal terms.*" If we do, then "the moral basis for permitting preemptive war – to defend against an enemy attack that is all but certain – applies" to preventive war as well. But this permission is only for cases when the threat is direct; if the fear were merely that the state supports, tolerates, or fails to repress terrorists, it would be unacceptable to allow a preventive war because of the requirement of "universalizability."

It would make dozens of states legitimate targets…. Moreover… on pain of incoherence, [it would] permit wars against states that harbor…organized crime, or even the release of toxic wastes across borders…. After all, for someone responding to a mortal threat, death is death whether it results from a terrorist attack that a state is sponsoring or an environmental toxin that it won't stop its factories from releasing.

In short, this leads to a counterintuitive result.[41]

Other situations are questionable as just causes. Are all borders equally sacrosanct? Does it matter that the border was only recently established? Or was imposed by outsiders? Or was never accepted by the inhabitants? Or is rejected by the people who actually live there, like Kashmir? Or are a few miles of uninhabited desert on a border where shifting sand obliterates all markers? Does it make any sense to say that every inch matters, as Egypt did in Sinai and Syria in the Golan? Is a threat, like propaganda, without any overt acts preparatory to an invasion, a just cause? Do we mean to include not simply "border crossing," but also economic threats in the form of blockades, sanctions, boycotts? How about discriminatory economic policies, like imposition of tariffs or violations of patent rights? I lump these economic policies together to make clear the mischief to international peace that would result if any one of them were to be considered "aggression."

What about a country that produces something we ban as illicit, like opium? And is it relevant that more Americans are killed by opium than were killed in all of al Qaeda's terrorist attacks? Weren't Afghanistan's opium exports also a just *casus belli*? Or a country – like several Caribbean islands – that provides a service to our enemies, like money laundering, which facilitates criminal activity in our country?

What about granting asylum to our enemies? But if Afghanistan wronged the U.S. by harboring al Qaeda, do we wrong Cuba by offering asylum to anti-Castroites who wish to overthrow him?

The requirement of universalizability for any rule to be just would seem to require a "no" answer to all of these expansions of the concept of "aggression."

Tort law might help clarify some of these issues. There are actions which are inherently dangerous or nuisances – like playing with fire on your own property, raising pigs, operating a tannery or noisome factory. It is lawful for you to do them, but you are also liable at law if that operation damages your neighbor. (This is the concept of "strict" liability – i.e., even though you did not directly do or even intend a damage, you are liable for it if it is a [not necessarily "the"] foreseeable consequence of what you did do or intend.) The damage does not have to be as severe as the flames from the leaves burning in your backyard igniting the garage next door; even if it is only the predictable, necessary stench of the pig manure, you have wronged your neighbor and he has recourse at law against you. There is obviously a continuum here – burning leaves occasionally, burning garbage every day, experimenting with explosives...Each case has to be judged separately, and it is difficult to compose a useful absolute rule. We might heed Joel Feinberg's cautions[42] about not seeking to correct every offense we are faced with. Living in a society means tolerating others, even when they are obnoxious. There is a rule of proportionality – forcing an offender to cease is usually more trouble than it is worth, and it is possible that your normal lifestyle is equally offensive to him. This is as true in international as in domestic society. Perhaps we do not even want an absolute rule or definition. The model of judicial discretion, as opposed to mandatory sentences, or, more generally, the model of common law as opposed to codified law, might be more conducive to justice, not to mention peace.

Innocent aggressors

Walzer, and all codes of international law, put "aggression" at the center of the justification for war. The aggressor, by his very action, forfeits his "right to life," which is why you are blameless when you kill him in self-defense; he *deserves* the harm you do to him. But the concept of losing your right or deserving punishment is problematic. Judith Jarvis Thomson illustrates this with a series of fantastic scenarios.[43]

Evil Aggressor threatens a Victim. He tells Victim that if he gets a tank, he is going to run Victim down. He does get the tank, and heads towards Victim. Fortunately, Victim has an anti-tank gun. Surely, he can use it to blow up the tank and permissibly kill the man who is trying to kill him, because the aggressor has forfeited his right not to be killed.

Now consider a different scenario. Evil Aggressor is about to climb into the tank after threatening Victim, who is just raising his anti-tank gun to fire; suddenly Aggressor falls off the steps of the tank and breaks both legs. He can no longer drive the tank, and so is no longer a threat. It does not seem that that Victim can now go ahead and kill him. But why not? Hasn't he already forfeited his right not to be killed? And he is still Evil and so deserves punishment. But since he is no longer a threat, he regains his right not to be killed, even though he remains deserving of *some* punishment.

Consider scenario three. Innocent Aggressor is hallucinating, and thinks the Victim is getting into a tank to attack him, and so climbs into his tank to destroy Victim first. Surely Victim is in the same danger as in case one, and can defend himself by killing Innocent Aggressor. But this Aggressor is clearly not evil, so how can he have forfeited his right not to be killed? But since he *is* a threat, his "innocence" does not reverse his forfeit of his right not to be killed.

Scenario four is Innocent Shield of Aggressor. Evil Aggressor is moving the tank by remote control towards Victim. To prevent Victim from destroying the tank, he has strapped an innocent baby to the front of the tank. Can Victim destroy the tank even though that will kill the innocent baby? Thomson thinks "yes." The baby is the victim of bad luck, to have been caught by the Evil Aggressor, but this is not the Victim's problem, certainly not to the extent that he must give up his right to self-defense.

But if you can kill an innocent shield to save your own life, why not kill an innocent fellow passenger in the lifeboat by eating him to keep from starving to death?

Thomson finds the distinctions difficult to justify. Her conclusion is that clearly we can be unlucky enough to find ourselves in situations where "something other than ourselves...has made us cease to have rights we formerly had." It is not our own evil or forfeit that has done this. Presumably, some version of the doctrine of double effect is at work. Aggression justifies self-defense even against the innocent, if that is the only way to save yourself. You intend to destroy only the tank; you can do that only by also killing the shield or the crazy innocent behind the wheel.

This approach distances innocence from immunity to harm, and so clarifies the justification for killing in self-defense in situations where the enemy soldiers (or terrorists) place themselves in the midst of civilians before they fire. The innocence of the "shields" creates no restriction on your right to fire back.

Innocence can also be compromised by sovereignty. The reason aggression is the supreme international crime, and an all-but automatic justification for defensive war, is that our international system respects the sovereign independence and immunity of all states. Some realists have claimed that this is an unwarranted "worship" of the state. The answer has usually been that each state derives its legitimacy from the assent (even if often non-democratic) of its population. It is the human condition to gather into societies; states are the contemporary form of such societies. People have often shown that they would rather by ruled by their *own* ruler, no matter how corrupt, than have a better outsider or better form of government forced on them. This reasoning leads to an uncomfortable conclusion: if the people's consent to their state is what justifies the ban on starting wars even with "bad" states, then aren't the people also responsible for their government's *own* aggressions? So, doesn't every citizen bear responsibility for the unjust actions of his state? We might want to modify this by accepting a sliding scale of degrees of responsibility, but only after recognizing that *every* citizen (except those who join the "resistance") bears *some* responsibility, and therefore is at best an "Innocent Aggressor," not even an "Innocent Shield;" we therefore, need be less concerned with killing him.

Francis Kamm seems to have something like this reasoning in mind in her suggestion of thinking in terms of "discount ratios" and "violability ratios" when balancing civilian deaths. The scenario she imagines is a bombing raid against a military factory on the border between Victim and Aggressor. If the collateral damage in one type of raid would be ten civilians on Victim's side and a hundred on Aggressor's side, we would be justified in choosing that over another type of raid in which the deaths would be, say, twenty and twenty – by factoring in the "lack of innocence" of the Aggressor civilians. Actually, Kamm's revision of traditional just war theory is even more radical, for she would introduce a "discount ratio" even for combatants. If Aggressor has two possible routes, one of which would kill one Victim noncombatant, the other of which would kill a hundred Victim combatants, Victim would be *wrong* to encourage the second route.[44]

Jeff McMahan takes a different tack in rejecting the traditional requirement of "discrimination" between combatants and noncombatants. He suggests that liability to be murdered in war should not be an "all-or-nothing" criterion. Rather, a truer view would be to calculate three variables to establish proportional moral responsibility: quantity of the threat, amount of the harm, and "degree of the potential target's moral responsibility."

So, the computer researcher with a grant from the Defense Department and the doctor who patches up wounded soldiers "in order that they may return to combat" deserve to be targets as much as soldiers do. Yet, McMahan recoils from his own conclusions, because "opening such a door…is profoundly dangerous." He concludes that although "the traditional requirement of discrimination is false as a criterion of moral liability…in war…it ought nevertheless to be upheld as a convention to which all combatants are bound…because it would be worse for everyone were the [morally incorrect] taboo to be breached." Why does McMahan bother to make his argument, distinguishing, as he says, between the "deep morality" of war and the "laws of war," if he rejects its applicability in practice? He is unclear, but it seems that a major reason is to avoid the "dirty hands" problem. If, in an emergency, you engage in the occasional assassination, terror (rather than mere strategic) bombing, killing of civilian shields – you do no wrong, and have no reason even to feel regret. Moral clarity, it seems, does not always lead to greater humanity.[45]

Trans-state Actors and Piracy[46]
One area that was mentioned by Grotius and most other early writers, but has not been elaborated on by them or by Walzer, is piracy.

Grotius simply notes that none of his rules of war apply to military actions against pirates (where, presumably, "anything goes"). But what is it that we do when we commit violence against pirates? It is not "police action," nor "war," but is clearly related to both. Since much of the military action of the last few years has been in response to "terrorism," this has become an important question to answer. For, clearly, the terrorist has much in common with the pirate – he is a non-governmental agent, perpetrating violence against civilians, outside his own country (where his own local police would be responsible for stopping him), seemingly no one state's problem, but clearly everyone's problem. Perhaps we should re-examine the rules that were elaborated by the civilized states of the 18th and 19th centuries to justify and regulate their actions against pirates.

The ancient Roman terminology was revived: the pirate was "an enemy of all mankind [*hostis humani generis*]" who, having placed himself beyond the protection of any state, is no longer a national, and therefore "any nation may, in the interest of all capture and punish" him (by summary execution at sea, or by hanging, with or without a trial, in the next town).[47] Of course, pirates were distinguished from privateers, who engaged in the exact same activities as pirates but under license from some state and in the service of the political goals of that state. Captain Kidd, for example, switched back and forth from outlaw pirate to privateer holder of a license from William III to attack French shipping in 1695. Similarly, a British court in 1909 declared that a Bolivian band of pirate-rebels who attacked British ships off Bolivia were *not* pirates, because their lawless attack was directed against the sovereignty of a single country, Bolivia, and so was lacking the "spirit and intention of *universal* hostility" that would define real "piracy."[48] This suggests that the key distinguishing feature of "piracy" from legal "privateering-style" attacks is not private gain versus political end, but rather, focused hostility to one state versus universal hostility. From this perspective, those groups who are neither insurgents nor plunderers, but whose terrorist actions exhibit a "universal hostility" – like al Qaeda, whose suicide bombs target New York buildings and Spanish trains, American soldiers and Kenyan office workers – are the real "pirates" of our time, and, perhaps for that reason, might be dealt with outside the law. But, you cannot have it both ways. If you treat them as a quasi-sovereign entity by "declaring war" on them, then you are not relieved of following the rules of war.

Grotius notes that there is a big difference between pirates and states that engage in illegal acts. Even a bad state has to be treated with moderation and according to law, because it "does not cease to be a state...[since the citizens have] associated to live by law and render justice...A sick body is still a body; and a state, though seriously diseased, is still a state as long as it still has laws and courts." On the other hand, "pirates and robbers band together to commit crime" and so do not have the benefits of lawful warriors. Grotius says it is unlikely, but possible, that such groups, "by choosing another way of life, may become a state." Until then, they can be killed or robbed with impunity.[49]

Justice in Ending Wars

The aftermath of war is another area that both Grotius and Walzer slight, though they both agree that the justness of the ending of the war is part of the justness of the conduct of the war, and so is a key feature in deciding on the justness of the war *per se*. Lieber was the theorist who most explicitly noted that the purpose of war is to achieve peace (and not to win, *per se*).[50] The complexities of achieving peace have become evident in several modern wars, certainly Vietnam, Yugoslavia, many African conflicts, Afghanistan and Iraq. The war is clearly not over until some reconciliation has been achieved. But what are the components? Restitution? War crimes trials? Punishment of the perpetrators of the war, or of the war crimes? Repatriation of the expelled? General amnesty and proclamation of a clean slate? Non-punitive "peace and reconciliation" show trials? The general problem seems to be the conflict between peace and justice. Justice seems to require that the "guilty" be somehow punished; but there are usually so many of them that it would be impossible to restore peace while excluding them. Perhaps the solution is the recognition by most just war theorists that the "justice" of the war requires that the main intention of the war be to restore peace.

Since this often requires that the "guilt" of the other side be ignored, "justice" can be seen as requiring that the "guilty" *not* be "brought to justice."[51] "The duty of peace must outweigh the duty of justice – although this is an excruciating tradeoff," Gary Bass cautions. We must always keep in mind that legal justice "is only one political good among many – like peace, stability and democracy."[52]

Walzer has recently modified his views to include a recognition that a just ending is a requirement for the initiation and conduct of a war worthy of being considered "just."[53] But he has also complicated the idea of an end by raising the possibility that two countries might be fighting several different wars simultaneously, some just, some unjust. The example he gives is contemporary Israel. There is a Palestinian war to destroy Israel, a second Palestinian war to create an independent state. An Israeli war for security; and a fourth war by Israel to expand its territory. Walzer considers only the second and third to be "just" wars. Furthermore, they can be ended only by renouncing the first and fourth wars.[54] As if to emphasize the tentative nature of these suggestions, Walzer has recently suggested another variation on the theme of justice in ending wars. While a war cannot be considered just if its ending is unjust, the ending of a war might be just in itself, even though the war itself was unjust. "Democratic political theory, which plays a relatively small part in our arguments about *jus ad bellum* and *in bello*, provides the central principles of this account. They include self-determination, popular legitimacy, civil rights, and the idea of the common good."[55]

Occupation

Grotius deals with the rules to which the occupying army is subject, but he envisaged a situation where the occupation would last only while the fighting was still going on, and would cease when a treaty ending the war was signed, after which sovereignty would revert to the defeated government. But what about modern wars, where one of the goals of the war is precisely to remove the existing government? Is the occupying power really an "army?" Is its activity really best described as "war?" What are its obligations to create a civilian government to replace itself? If humanitarian intervention is ever justified, it is clear that the major part of its activity will not involve killing, i.e., traditional military activity. Perhaps it is time to revive the Cold War concept of "police action," not in its original form (as Truman's cynical way of starting the Korean War without asking congressional approval by artfully claiming that the military would be involved in mere "police [i.e., minor] action" rather than a *real* war), but as a really new style of non-aggressive large scale use of force; not to kill, but to restrain, disarm, protect the persecuted, and create new political structures in a failed or grossly unjust state. This would, of course, require the creation of a stronger international police force than the UN or the U.S. have been willing to do (as they demonstrated in the former Yugoslavia).

Proportionality

Proportionality implies that you do not resort to war for a small wrong and that you do not resort to a war unless you have a reasonable expectation of winning, because the goal of war is to restore peace. This refers only to the start, since surely there will be many small battles in the course of the war in which the odds of success might be slim, but you take a chance anyway. It is only when *all* the battles are predicted to end in defeat that the war ceases to be just. This seems counter-intuitive in some cases. At first glance, it simply means you can't commit suicide; so, seemingly, after the blitzkrieg in Poland, Belgium was right to surrender without much of a fight to Germany. And, conversely, had we known of the widespread guerilla resistance in Vietnam, it would have been wrong to have started a war with the Vietcong – you are not allowed to destroy a country to save it.

Some troubling problems have been raised about the measurement of proportionality. At its crudest, the concept requires weighing the number of people you kill during the war against the number of people you save from being killed (or whose previous deaths you go to war to avenge). So, "in 2001 many watched the death toll of Afghan civilians with the hope that it would not exceed the 3,000 Americans killed on September 11." But this is surely *not* the relevant number; rather, it is "the number of additional lives that

would have been lost to terrorism had the war not been fought."[56]
Similarly with the Israeli response to suicide bombers: it is irrelevant
that more Palestinians may be killed by the Israeli retaliation than
Israelis were killed in the original bombings; the comparison should
rather be to the *additional* victims there might have been without
the counterattacks.

A more significant and troubling aspect of the proportionality
requirement has to do with the number of people you can justifiably kill during the war. It is assumed that you are not required to
give equal valuation to every person. So, in a battle, if there are two
possible tactics, one of which will cause you 100 casualties, and the
enemy 200, and another, in which you will lose only 50, but the enemy will lose 400, you can save half of your own men at the cost of
twice the losses of enemy soldiers. But is there *any* ratio that would
not be moral? Would saving one of your men be worth increasing the
enemy's casualties by 1,000? If certain battles should not be fought
where the gain in military advantage is relatively small, but the loss
of life is great, it would seem that there is a level to which it would be
unjust to raise enemy losses for a tiny saving in your own losses.

This requirement militates against waging war on an amor-
phous enemy – that is why a "war against evil" is unjust. By definition,
you can never eradicate evil from the world, and therefore it is wrong
to try. This is very different from trying to eradicate one particular
instance of evil, which, of course, is a possible, and therefore, just,
goal. Similarly, it is both irrational and unjust to declare war on an
ideology, like communism, or militant Islam, or on a type of action,
like terrorism.

This is similar to the criticisms often made against the supposed "war" on drugs, or cancer, or organized crime. In general,
there is great popular confusion about the varieties of defensive actions available to a state or society. The major divisions are between
"military" and "police" activity, and between acute and chronic
problems. The first of each set participates in the aura of heroism,
valor, bravery; the second is more humdrum. There is pressure to
wrap the cloak of heroism over dutiful performance of endless tasks,
but this misleads us about the criteria of success, which are very dif-

ferent for each. Wars do not last forever – there are discrete battles, which add up to produce clear winners and losers. Police work, on the other hand, is endless. No matter how many robbers are caught, there are sure to be more next week; no one expects the police to eradicate robbery or murder. No one considers it a failure of policing if crime continues; success is defined as reducing or controlling crime, not ending it. Susan Sontag makes similar comments on the use of military metaphors in relation to cancer and AIDS.[57]

Recently, there have been discussions in the field of medicine about the distortions caused by the use of "military" metaphors in thinking about disease.[58] George Annas blames the military metaphor for leading people to "over mobilize…Military thinking concentrates on the physical, sees control as central, and encourages the expenditure of massive resources to achieve dominance."[59] Yet the very idea of eradicating, "defeating," or "conquering" disease is incoherent. Many diseases are really chronic conditions for which "cure" is the wrong goal. Containment, palliation, and management of normal functioning outside the diseased area are more appropriate.[60] The rhetoric of a "war on cancer" sets unrealistically high goals of "winning." But what could it mean to win? Often to destroy every cancer cell requires destroying a large number of healthy cells. Would living with the slight risk of recurrence, monitoring to minimize it, not be saner? Isn't the desire to live risk-free irrational?[61] There have been some calls for restraint, pointing out that there are dangers and unexpected side effects of attempting to vanquish, rather than merely contain, disease, and pointing out that it is just as much a part of the practice of medicine to know when *not* to act, as when to intervene. This call for "statesmanship" is as appropriate in the field of war as in medicine.

If we learn nothing else from just war theory, we learn that sometimes the most just action is not to make war at all, but to settle for an uncertain and risky peace.

NOTES

1. The "requirimento." Louis Hanke, *The Spanish Struggle for Justice in the Conquest of America* (Boston: Little, Brown and Company, 1949), quote on 33.

2. Spanish *junta*, which met for close to a year at Burgos, a leading financial and in-
    tellectual center of Spain. Only in our fantasies would the President of the U.S. or
    the Prime Minister of Israel convene an "orthodox forum" to discuss the justice of
    their conduct of an ongoing war, much less halt further deployments while await-
    ing its conclusions. A major expedition with two thousand men under the new
    governor, Pedrarias, was about to set sail in the summer of 1513; Ferdinand made it
    wait for almost a year while the *junta* deliberated, and wrote up the "Requirement,"
    which they were ordered to read before engaging in military action in America.
    Technically, the Indians' failure to respond affirmatively to the "Requirement" was
    the *casus belli*, that is, the excuse that "legalized" subsequent military actions.

3. *Political Writings*, ed. by Anthony Pagden and Jeremy Lawrence (Cambridge:
    Cambridge University Press, 1991), 231–327; I paraphrase part of Pagden's introduc-
    tion, xxiv–xxviii.

4. Vitoria had elaborated on this point in a lecture "On Dietary Laws" (Pagden,
    Political Writings, 205–230, esp. 225), a discussion of cannibalism, which he declared
    wrong even in a lifeboat situation, much less as a ritual practice. Although he
    doubted the stories of Indian cannibalism and human sacrifice, he still examined
    whether, if this *were* the case, it would be a just cause for declaring war on them.
    He answered with a "yes" that was surprisingly qualified. "The reason why the
    barbarians can be conquered is *not* that their anthropophagy and human sacrifices
    are against natural law, but because they involve injustice (*iniuria*) to other men."
    The injustice is that "the victims of these practices are often unwilling, for example
    children" and it is "therefore lawful to defend them…and wage war on them to force
    them to give up these rituals." He is careful to deny that violation of natural law in
    itself would justify war, because that would lead to an even worse result of constant
    war – the example he gives, perhaps tongue in cheek, is that he would not want
    to justify France, say, invading one of the Italian states, by citing the well known
    "fact" that Italians are sodomites. John Rawls comes to the opposite conclusion in
    The Law of Peoples (Cambridge: Harvard University Press, 1999), 94. Defending
    wars of humanitarian intervention, he says, "if the offenses against human rights
    are egregious, and the society does not respond to the imposition of sanctions,
    such intervention in the defense of human rights would be acceptable *and would
    be called for* [emphasis added]." The example he gives is a "society like the Aztecs,"
    which is not aggressive to other countries, but "which holds its own lower classes
    as slaves…available for human sacrifice."

5. "It is the general law of nations (*ius gentium*) that everything captured in war be-
    longs to the victor…even to the extent that their people become our slaves." Pagden,
    Political Writings, 283.

6. Augustine, *Reply to Faustus, the Manichaen*, XXII, 76, emphasis added. The quotes in
    the next paragraph are from XXII, 74–5. Augustine touched on war only peripherally
    in several other works, the most significant being the dialog *On Free Will*. See also
    Richard Shelly Hartigan, "Saint Augustine on War and Killing: The Problem of the
    Innocent," *Journal of the History of Ideas* 27, no. 2 (April–June 1966): 195–205; Robert

L. Holmes, *On War and Morality* (Princeton, New Jersey: Princeton University Press, 1989), chap. 4; and R.A. Marcus, "Saint Augustine's Views on the 'Just War'," in *The Church and Just War*, ed W.J. Sheils (Cambridge, Mass.: Blackwell, 1983).

7. De Libero Arbitrio, I, 5, 11–13

8. *Reply to Faustus*, xxii, 74, emphasis added. Notice how different this is from the Talmud's reason for not obeying a tyrant's order: you kill him or I will kill you – "how do you know that your blood is redder?" – where the point is the equality of each human, rather than the fact that neither's physical humanity is particularly valuable (*Sanhedrin*, 74a).

9. *Summa Theologiae*, ii–ii, Question 63 (Homicide), section 7 (Is it permissible to kill in self-defense?). J. David Bleich notes that the concept of double effect is similar to the *halakhah* of unintended acts (*daver she-eino mitkaven*), which do not engender even the minimal culpability that inadvertent transgressions (*shogeg*) entail, citing R. Shimon's opinion in *Beitzah* 22b. But, he emphasizes, this is limited to violations of Sabbath restrictions and to cases where the "unintended" act is not *certain* to occur. In the Halakhah, "a necessary effect cannot be regarded as unintended. Accordingly, military action which of necessity will result in civilian casualties cannot be justified on the contention that the killing of innocent victims is unintended." "Nuclear War through the Prism of Jewish Law: The Nature of Man and War," in Daniel Landes, ed., *Confronting Omnicide. Jewish Reflections of Weapons of Mass Destruction* (Northvale, New Jersey: Jason Aronson, 1991) 209–223. Philosophers have spilled much ink teasing out the moral relevance of distinguishing between intending and merely foreseeing. See, for example, Suzanne Uniacke, *Permissible Killing. The Self-defense Justification of Homicide*, (Cambridge: Cambridge University Press, 1994), Chapter 4: "The Double Effect Justification;" Shelly Kagan, *The Limits of Morality*. (Oxford: Clarendon Press, 1989), Chapter 4: "Intending Harm"; Alison McIntyre, "Doing Away with Double Effect," *Ethics* 111 (January 2001): 219–255; F.M. Kamm, "Toward the Essence of Nonconsequentialism," in Alex Byrne, *et al*, editors, *Fact and Value. Essays on Ethics and Metaphysics for Judith Jarvis Thomson*, (Cambridge, Mass.: MIT Press, 2001), 155–181, and especially her "Failures of Just War Theory: Terror, Harm, and Justice," *Ethics* 114 (July 2004): 650–692 for a revision of the doctrine of double effect in order to permit intentional harm to noncombatants.

10. *Summa Theologiae*, ii–ii, Question 40 (War) for the three criteria of just war.

11. I follow the historiography of James Turner Johnson, in his books: *Ideology, Reason, and the Limitation of War: Religious and Secular Concepts 1200–1740* (Princeton: Princeton University Press, 1975) and *Just War Tradition and the Restraint of War* (Princeton: Princeton University Press, 1981), and article "Grotius' Use of History and Charity in the Modern Transformation of the Just War Idea," Grotiana IV (1983), 21–34. Johnson's main point is that what began as a purely religious doctrine was transformed in the 17th century by the incorporation of Roman ideas of the law of nations (*jus gentium*) and stoic ideas of natural law into a modern, secular, historically-based intellectual tradition, which reflected and helped create a "developing moral consensus in western culture about two perennial issues: under what condi-

tions force is justified in the protection of societal values, and what limits ought to be observed in even such justified use of force" ["Grotius' Use of History," 22]. Turner notes that there was no significant religious contribution to the development and discussion of just war from the late 16th century until the 1950's debate on the use of nuclear weapons, when Protestant theologians like Paul Ramsey (*War and the Christian Conscience* [Durham, NC: Duke University Press, 1961]) endeavored to "recapture just war theory as a base for constructive Christian thought" on the morality of war. Incidentally, the prominence of Ramsey is significant in another way – he was also one of the creators of modern medical ethics, where a similar set of issues (the nature of justified killing, of a fetus or brain-dead person, for instance) for long set the tone of the debate. The comparison of these two areas of applied ethics has not been noted before, but surely it is no coincidence that two of the most prominent scholars in medical ethics today are working on issues of just war right now (F.M. Kamm and Jeff McMahan).

12. When the Carnegie Endowment for International Peace published a new translation in 1925, the editor listed seventy-seven editions and translations, two-thirds of them before 1750, so it was clearly a very popular book. Interest waned, though – only twelve reprints from 1750 to World War I. Presumably this is because most of the ideas in its 900 pages were incorporated in shorter, more popularly written handbooks, especially those of Christian Wolff and Emmerich Vattel (both mid-18th century). The best translation is by Louise R. Loomis, in her slightly abridged version for the Classics Club: Hugo Grotius, *The Law of War and Peace* [De Jure Belli ac Pacis] (New York: Walter J. Black, 1949).

13. Geoffrey Parker, *The Military Revolution. Military Innovation and the Rise of the West 1500–1800* (Cambridge: Cambridge University Press, 1988).

14. Grotius, *Law of War*, Book III, iv, 15–18. Grotius makes the same point later, where he seems to denigrate "law" as being too minimal a guide to just conduct: "When I first started to explain this part of the law of *nations* [emphasis added], I declared that many things are said to be lawful or permissible…that either are far from the rule of right…or at least, with more piety and more applause from good men, they should be left undone." He then quotes Seneca: "How much broader the rule of duty than the rule of law! How numerous are the demands of religion, humanity, generosity, justice, good faith, all of which lie outside the tables of the law!" For Grotius, his new "international law" should reflect the "rule of duty," which requires more than the previously existing laws (of nature or of nations). And so, he says, "I must now retrace my steps and deprive the warmakers of almost all the privileges I may seem to have conferred, but did not confer, on them." Grotius, *Law of War*, Book III, x, 1.

15. A handy collection of most of these codes is Leon Friedman, ed., *The Law of War. A Documentary History.* Volume I (New York: Random House, 1972).

16. There is no such thing as "lastness," for one can always imagine another diplomatic note, mediation attempt, or possible concession after the previous one. So, insistence that war be the literal last resort would be to condemn politics to a version

of Zeno's paradox of Achilles and the tortoise. Supposedly, if the tortoise is given a head start in the race, Achilles can never overtake it: when Achilles runs half the distance between the two, the tortoise advances an inch, when Achilles runs half of the remaining distance, the tortoise advances a half inch.... Since there are an infinite number of halfway points between the two, it seems that the swift runner can never overtake the slow tortoise. The error, of course, is to assume that it takes an infinite amount of time to pass an infinite number of points, which is wrong because there is no need to actually stop at each point to in order pass it.

17. Grotius, *Law of War*, Book I, vi. 3.

18. Control Council Law No 10, Berlin, 1945, entitled *Punishment of persons guilty of war crimes, crimes against peace and against humanity*, cited in Friedman, 909. Since it is war itself, that is the "crime against peace," it would seem that this implies a right to refuse to fight at all in an unjust war.

19. Grotius, *Law of War*, Book III, xiv. 6, where he comments "here we should praise the mercifulness of the Jewish law, which ordained that a Jewish slave, after a fixed time had elapsed, should be set completely free, with gifts." Typically, this is cited along with a series of quotations from Plutarch, Cicero, and Tacitus, on the treatment of slaves as well as tenants or servants, i.e., the Bible is just one of many other historical examples of the custom of nations, which with the passage of time has become the "law of nations," and is evidence for what must be the universal "law of nature."

20. Geneva Convention III (1949) *Convention relative to the treatment of prisoners of war*, in Friedman, 589–640.

21. My students, on reading this, often comment that this sounds more like summer camp than a POW camp. Sadly, the U.S. is currently reversing this history of ever more humane treatment of POWs, mainly by redefining the qualifications for being treated as a POW. Lieber provided a very different model when his code insisted on treating captured Confederate soldiers with all the deference due to soldiers of a sovereign state, simply noting that that such treatment "neither proves nor establishes an acknowledgment of the rebellious people...as a public or sovereign power," nor would it prevent "the legitimate government from trying the leaders of the rebellion...for high treason." (Lieber *Code*, Art. 153, 154). They are treated well only in recognition of their common humanity. Perhaps the fact that Lieber had one son fighting in the Confederate Army and two in the Union Army made it easier for him to recognize the common humanity even of an "illegal" and "treasonous" rebel.

22. *Just and Unjust Wars. A Moral Argument with Historical Illustrations* (New York: Basic Books, 1977). The later editions of 1992 and 2000 are identical except for different introductions. There is a sympathetic study by Brian Orend, *Michael Walzer on War and Justice* (Montreal: McGill-Queen's University Press, 2000). There is a large and still-growing critical literature. Among the best of the early articles is C.A.J. Coady, "The Leaders and the Led: Problems of Just War Theory," *Inquiry* 23 (1980): 279–291; and, of the recent articles, Igor Primoratz, "Michael Walzer's Just

War Theory: Some Issues of Responsibility," *Ethical Theory and Moral Practice* 5 (2002): 221–243.

23. Walzer, *Just and Unjust Wars*, 61–63.

24. But not *preventive* war. In the aftermath of the Sept. 11, 2001 terrorist attack on the United States, the Bush administration asserted a new "Bush Doctrine," defining the right of self-defense as including the right to initiate preventive wars ("National Security Strategy of the United States of America, September 2002," 6, in www.whitehouse.gov/nsc/nss.pdf). For a qualified philosophical defense, see Allen Buchanan and Robert O. Koehane, "The Preventive Use of Force: A Cosmopolitan Institutional Proposal," *Ethics & International Affairs* (2004): 18:1, 1–22.

25. The massacre of a third of the Cambodian population by the Khmer Rouge in the 1970s, and the vicious Balkan wars and the Rwandan massacre of the Tutsis in the 1990s, led to much discussion of just how badly governments had to act to justify humanitarian intervention. See Samantha Power, *"A Problem From Hell." America and the Age of Genocide* (New York: Basic Books, 2002). A good introduction to the philosophical literature is Deen K. Chatterjee and Don E. Scheid, editors, *Ethics and Foreign Intervention,* (Cambridge: Cambridge University Press, 2003). See Walzer's reluctant defense of such intervention, "The Politics of Rescue," in his *Arguing About War* (New Haven: Yale University Press, 2004), 67–81.

26. "Political Action: The Problem of Dirty Hands," *Philosophy and Public Affairs* (1972/3), 160–181. Walzer does not take the obvious step of distinguishing *prima facie* moral rightness from moral rightness "all things considered" (as W.D. Ross did in The *Right and the Good* (Oxford: Clarendon Press, 1930), 19 ff). This would have avoided the awkward contradiction of claiming, "it is the right thing to do the immoral action." Presumably, Walzer avoided this way out in order to emphasize the gravity of doing the immoral act as a way to restrain its use. Christopher W. Gowans, in *Innocence Lost. An Examination of Inescapable Moral Wrongdoing* (New York: Oxford University Press, 1994), criticizes Walzer for assuming that the problem of dirty hands is peculiar to political life; he insists that a "domestic analogy" is relevant here. The politician's problem is not different in kind from any individual's problem when faced with inescapable moral wrongdoing. For his discussion, and references to what he calls the "dirty hands literature," see 228–236.

27. The morality of using torture in wartime became a practical issue when the Bush administration wrote several legal justifications of the practice to deal with al Qaeda terrorists. The discussion became more heated after it was graphically revealed that crude torture was being used to interrogate POWs captured in the Iraq war in 2003. It is surprising how quickly that prohibition, long considered a basic human right, could be disregarded, and the idea not merely of practicing, but openly legalizing, it became a legitimate topic of discussion. Many of the best articles in this debate, including Walzer's, are collected in Sanford Levinson, ed., *Torture. A Collection* (New York: Oxford University Press, 2004).

28. Nussbaum's comments on Aeschylus' *Agamemnon* are similar to Walzer's point. Agamemnon is fighting a just war (i.e., one commanded by the gods) against the

Trojans. When he is told that the only way to get the wind to blow to allow his ships to sail is to propitiate one of the gods by sacrificing his daughter, Iphigenia, he obeys, knowing that it is an immoral act. The Chorus criticizes him, not for the act, but for the enthusiasm with which he performs it (he says, "it is right and holy that I should desire with exceedingly impassioned passion the sacrifice...[of] the maiden's blood.") As Nussbaum summarizes the criticism: "this does not mean that in no circumstances is it the best available course to kill; it does mean that even such rationally justifiable killings violate a moral claim and *demand emotions and thoughts appropriate to a situation of violation* [emphasis added]." Martha C. Nussbaum *The Fragility of Goodness. Luck and Ethics in Greek Tragedy and Philosophy* (New York, NY: Cambridge University Press, 1986), quotes on 35 and 48. Notice the other interpretation possible in such a situation: the commentators *praise* Abraham for eagerly arising early and saddling the donkey himself in his rush to obey God's command that he sacrifice *his* child.

29. From the discussion of this issue by the legal philosopher John Gardner, "In Defense of Defenses," in the *Festschrift for Nils Jareborg* (Uppsala, 2002). An example of another form that such a "blemish" can take is the case of God's refusal to allow King David to build the Temple "because thou hast shed much blood upon the earth in My sight." But this blood was shed at God's command in divinely sanctioned wars, so why should it entail punishment? Radak explains, "among the blood of the gentiles that he spilled, it is possible that among those who were not combatants there were good and pious people [i.e., innocent noncombatants]." R. J. David Bleich comments that David's "accountability is assuredly solely in the form of *lifnim mishurat ha-din*...nevertheless, a degree of moral culpability exists despite halakhic sanction." ("Response to Noam Zohar" in Daniel H. Frank, ed., *Commandment and Community: New Essays in Jewish Legal and Political Philosophy* (Albany: State University of New York Press, 1995) 264–265.

30. This tension over "justified wrongdoing" is reflected in the Halakhah. Note our approach to the case of medically mandated eating on Yom Kippur. Clearly, the rules of the fast are overridden by *pikuah nefesh*, but we still make an effort to reduce the violation to the minimum: "whenever such people are obliged to break the fast, the amount...consumed should not constitute the volume whose consumption normally carries the penalty of excision." And yet, the sick person should *bentch* before and after eating, and even add the festival *ya'aleh ve-yavo* because, according to Maimonides, "to him the Day of Atonement is as ordinary festivals are to us, seeing that he is...religiously obliged to break the fast." Immanual Jakobovits, *Jewish Medical Ethics* (New York: Bloch Publishing House, 1959), 51, 69 and notes.

31. Concurrently, the idea developed that it was not even necessary that the "law" be ratified in normal treaties, or written by states themselves. Most current international law is really made by the authors of articles in the journals of international law, "not by states, but by 'silly' professors writing books" (in Louis Sohn's trenchant phrase). The concept of "customary international law" has arisen to assert the binding nature of such law. "But it is not clear what is added by laying the mantle of

CIL over what is essentially a campaign against the morality of other states…Even
if there were some incremental benefit in calling 'illegal' the 'immoral' conduct of
other states…this…is outweighed by the costs to state sovereignty…of authorizing
a system whereby a form of non-treaty 'law' could be created without the consent
of affected states." Samuel Estreicher, "Rethinking the Binding Effect of Customary
International Law," *Virginia Journal of International Law*, 44 (2003–2004) 5–17,
quotes on 15 and 11.

32. J.L. Brierly, *The Law of Nations. An Introduction to the International Law of Peace*,
6th ed. (New York: Oxford University Press, 1963), 49–56. This approach is repeated
by the contemporary successor to Brierly's text: Ian Brownlie, *Principles of Public
International Law* (Oxford: Oxford University Press, 1998). Before giving the same
list of the sources of obligation, Brownlie notes that whereas "a statute is binding in
the United Kingdom by reason of the principle of the supremacy of Parliament…no
such machinery exists for the creation of rules of international law.… All [decisions
of the UN, general treaties, decisions of the International Court, etc.] are lacking
the quality to bind states…in the same way that Acts of Parliament bind the people
of the United Kingdom. In a sense, 'formal sources' do not exist in international
law. As a substitute, and perhaps an equivalent, there is the principle that the general consent of states creates rules.… What matters then is the…*evidences* of the
existence of consensus among states concerning particular rules or practices." 1–2.
Treaties and UN resolutions are certainly such evidence, but so also are unratified
treaties, textbooks of international law, from the first one (Grotius's) to Brownlie's
own, and the practice of states. It is as if, *merely by talking* of the laws of war, proper
treatment of prisoners of war, acceptable methods of interrogation, etc., states
create an international law that they are then obliged to follow, *even if they did not
actually ratify* that particular Geneva Convention. This becomes important in cases
like Additional Protocol I on the Protection of Victims of International Armed
Conflict, added to the 1949 Geneva Conventions in 1977. This is the first major
effort to specify "proportionality," i.e., what collateral civilian damage is excessive.
The U.S. (along with two-thirds of those countries that *did* ratify the 1949 Geneva
Conventions) has not ratified it, but, if the above definition of international law is
correct, we are still bound by its provisions.

33. David Novak *Natural Law in Judaism* (Cambridge: Cambridge University Press,
1998), esp. chapter 2. "Scriptural foundations." For a defense of the binding nature
of the one of the main areas of natural law, see Haim H. Cohn, *Human Rights in
the Bible and Talmud* (Tel Aviv: MOD Books-Broadcast University Series, Tel Aviv
University, 1989).

34. "Grotius, Pufendorf, Vattel, and the like…although their code…has not the slightest
lawful force and cannot even have such force (since states as such are not subject to
a common external constraint) – are always duly cited in *justification* of an offensive
war, though there is no instance of a state ever having been moved to desist from
its plan by arguments armed with the testimony of such men." But Kant was not
as cynical and hopeless as this sounds, for he continues: "this homage that every

state pays to the concept of right (at least verbally) nevertheless proves that there is to be found in the human being a still greater, though at present dormant, moral predisposition to eventually become master of the evil principle within him…and also to hope for this from others." "Toward perpetual peace [1795]," in Immanuel Kant, *Practical Philosophy*, translated and edited by Mary J. Gregor (Cambridge: Cambridge University Press, 1996) 326–7. Kant was much opposed to the very idea of "just war." He thought mankind had evolved enough to work toward putting all relations between states on a legal footing, in accord with Reason, rather than settling for the lesser goal of merely reducing the horrors of existing wars. His proposal was that the most advanced European states take the first step by pledging to solve their disputes non-violently; this would be a model for other states to follow. This is similar to the approach of the League of Nations, and to John Rawls' suggestions in *The Law of Peoples* (44) that a "psychological process" of "moral learning" at the international level, similar to the civic education in lawful behavior learned within liberal states, is the way to achieve international peace. The best discussion of Kant's essay is W.B. Gallie, *Philosophers of Peace and War. Kant, Clausewitz, Marx, Engels and Tolstoy* (Cambridge: Cambridge University Press, 1978).

35. See the article "Prisoners' Dilemma" in Ted Honderich, ed., *Oxford Companion to Philosophy* (Oxford: Oxford University Press, 1995) for the suggestion that the need for the moral rules based on duty is one of the main conclusions from the paradoxes such puzzles generate. A good general discussion is William Poundstone, *Prisoner's Dilemma: John von Neumann, Game Theory, and the Puzzle of the Bomb* (New York: Doubleday, 1992).

36. John Rawls, *The Law of Peoples* (Cambridge: Harvard University Press, 1999), 97.

37. Grotius paints himself in just such colors: "I have refrained from taking up topics that belong to another treatise, such as showing what course of action is practically advantageous. For those matters have their own special science, which is politics…. As mathematicians view their figures abstracted from bodies, so I in my treatment of law have held my mind aloof from all particular events." Grotius, *Law of War*, Preface, paragraphs 57, 58.

38. Philippa Foot invented the trolley problem in her article "Abortion and the Problem of Double Effect" *Oxford Review 5* (1967); Judith Jarvis Thomson elaborated on it in "Killing, Letting Die and the Trolley Problem" (1976), reprinted in her *Rights, Restitution & Risk. Essays in Moral Theory* (Cambridge: Harvard University Press, 1986), 78–93. There is a large literature, with ever more baroque variations; see, for a recent example, the exchange between Frances M. Kamm and John Harris "The Doctrine of Triple Effect and Why a Rational Agent Need Not Intend the Means to His End" in *The Proceedings of the Aristotelian Society* (2000) 21–57. Harris (unlike most other philosophers) ridicules such use of "artificial" and "implausible" examples to discern the moral permissibility of different types of killing: he sarcastically entitles his section "the moral difference between throwing a trolley at a person and throwing a person at a trolley."

39. Chiara Bottici, "The Domestic Analogy and the Kantian Project of *Perpetual Peace*,"

Journal of Political Philosophy 11:4 (2003), 392–410. Only a few modern writers reject this analogy. Hedley Bull does, claiming that a unique set of rules (and not the same rules that govern domestic actions) govern international society. Charles R. Beitz also rejects the analogy, mainly to deny that states have a right to self-defense, or any other rights modeled on individual rights (*Political Theory and International Relations* [Princeton: Princeton University Press, 1979], 51–53).

40. I have avoided using these Latin terms, because they are misleading. The concepts, of course, existed; but the use of Latin phrases to describe them was an invention of Austrian lawyers of the 1920s – presumably to increase the prestige of their proposed treaties limiting war by claiming a spurious antiquity for the phrases. See Robert Kolb, "Origin of the twin terms *jus ad bellum/jus in bello*," *International Review of the Red Cross* (1997) 320: 553–562.

41. Buchanan and Koehane, "The Preventive Use of Force," quotes at 5 and 14

42. David Luban, "Preventive War," *Philosophy and Public Affairs* 32:3 (2004) 207–248. quotes on 226 and 230, emphasis added.

43. *Offense to Others. The Moral Limits of the Criminal Law* (New York: Oxford University Press, 1985).

44. I have conflated her slightly different versions from *Rights, Restitution and Risk*, 33 ff and *The Realm of Rights* (Cambridge: Harvard University Press, 1990) ch. 14 "Ceasing to Have a Right."

45. F.M. Kamm, "Failures of Just War Theory: Terror, Harm, and Justice," *Ethics* 114 (2004): 650–692, esp. 679. This article attacks the doctrine of double effect, for incorrectly forbidding intentional attacks on civilians (does it really matter that the pilot of the plane bombing the factory is really a "baby killer," who enlisted only because this would give him the chance to kill civilian children as a "side effect?"). It also attacks the concept of discriminating between civilians and soldiers (who is more "guilty," the soldier asleep in the rear, or a politician or cleric actively inciting the unjust war?).

46. Jeff McMahan, "The Ethics of Killing in War," *Ethics* 114 (2004): 693–733, esp. 722–730.

47. See Gerry Simpson's book *Rebellious Subjects: War, Law and Crime* (London: Polity Press, 2005) for a good discussion of the ambiguities of "piracy" and how a terrorist like bin Laden fits that category, especially given the fluid line between pirates and government-licensed privateers (which is how bin Laden started, when the U.S. supported his guerilla war against the Russians in Afghanistan), and Peter Watson Huggins, *Trans-state Actors and the Law of War: A Just War Argument*, Ph.D. Dissertation submitted to Dept. of Government of Georgetown University, May, 2003; but for some skeptical comments on the pirate analogy, see Eugene Kontorovich, "The Piracy Analogy: Modern Universal Jurisdiction's Hollow Foundation," *Harvard International Law Journal* 45:1 (Winter 2004), pp. 183–237.

48. Brownlie, *Principles of Public International Law*, 235.

49. *Republic of Bolivia v. Indemnity Mutual Marine Assurance Co.* (1909) 1 KB 785, and its citation in *Re Piracy Jure Gentium* (1934) AC 586; both cases discussed in Simpson *Rebellious Subjects*. In the Court's words, the Bolivian rebels were "not only not the

enemy of the human race" but, since they were rather "the enemy of a particular state," they were therefore not pirates at all.

50. Grotius, *Law of War*, Book III, iii.2 and xix.3.

51. Lieber Code, Article XVI, where he says the reason that "military necessity does not admit of cruelty...maiming...torture...use of poison...wanton devastation" is because such acts would make "the return to peace unnecessarily difficult." XXIX: "The ultimate object of all modern war is a renewed state of peace."

52. This seems to be the conclusion of Lon Fuller, in the invented case he gives discussing the morality of post-1945 prosecution of citizens who had used Nazi-era laws during World War II against their fellow citizens. See "The Problem of the Grudge Informer," in his *The Morality of Law* (New Haven: Yale University Press, 1969), appendix.

53. Gary J. Bass, "Jus Post Bellum," *Philosophy and Public Affairs* 32:4 (2004) 384–412, quote at 405. See also Brian Orend, "Justice after War," *Ethics & International Affairs* 16:1 (2000): 43–56.

54. Walzer, "The Triumph of Just War Theory (And the Dangers of Success)," in *Arguing About War* (New Haven: Yale University Press, 2004), 3–22.

55. Walzer, "The Four Wars of Israel/Palestine," in *Arguing About War*, 113–129.

56. Michael Walzer, "Just and Unjust Occupations," *Dissent Magazine* (Winter, 2004), editorial.

57. Thomas Hurka, "Proportionality in the Morality of War," *Philosophy and Public Affairs* 33:1 (2005), 34–66; quote at 59. For historical surveys see Judith Gail Gardam, "Proportionality and Force in International Law," *American Journal of International Law* 87 (1993) 391–413, and William J. Fenrick, "The Rule of Proportionality and Protocol I in Conventional Warfare," *Military Law Review*, 98 (1982) 91–127.

58. "The transformation of war-making into an occasion for mass ideological mobilization has made the notion of war useful as a metaphor for all sorts of ameliorative campaigns whose goals are cast as the defeat of an 'enemy.' We have had wars against poverty, now replaced by the 'war on drugs,' as well as wars against specific diseases, such as cancer. Abuse of the military metaphor may be inevitable in...a society that increasingly restricts the scope and credibility of appeals to ethical principle.... War making is one of the few activities that people are not supposed to view 'realistically'; that is, with an eye to expense and practical outcome. In all-out war, expenditure is all-out, unprudent – war being defined as an emergency in which no sacrifice is excessive." Susan Sontag, *AIDS and its Metaphors* (New York: Farrar, Strauss & Giroux, 1989), 11.

59. Bruce Arrigo, "Martial Metaphors and Medical Justice: Implications for Law, Crime, and Deviance," *Journal of Political and Military Sociology* 27 (1999): 307–322.

60. G.J. Annas, "Reframing the Debate on Health Care Reform by Replacing our Metaphors," *New England Journal of Medicine* 332 (1995): 744–747.

61. This would be equivalent in the international arena to negotiation, compromise, containment, partial solutions, defensive strategies, learning to live with threats, and accepting that tragic imperfections and injustices will always exist.

62. Grotius recognized this in his own call for restraint: "Quite inadmissible is the

doctrine proposed by some, that by the law of nations it is right to take up arms in order to weaken a rising power, which, if it grew too strong, might do us harm.... That the bare possibility that violence may be some day turned on us gives us the right to inflict violence on others is a doctrine repugnant to every principle of justice. Human life is something that can never give us absolute security. The only protection against uncertainty and fear must be sought, not in violence, but in divine providence and harmless precautions." Grotius, *Law of War,* Book II, i.17.

From a Chessboard to the Matrix: The Challenge of Applying the Laws of Armed Conflict in the Asymmetric Warfare Era

Yosefi M. Seltzer

HOW THE FIELD OF BATTLE HAS CHANGED

The battlefield has changed primarily because it is no longer a traditional chessboard scenario, having transformed from a conventional front to an asymmetric,[1] or multifaceted, one. Assets that must be defended are no longer just military but civilian as well. Not only was the World Trade Center destroyed on September 11, 2001, but nightclubs, vacation resorts, subways, civilian aircraft, places of worship, and embassies have been the subject of attacks in such diverse locales as England, France, Argentina, Russia, Spain, Kenya, Tanzania, Jordan, Japan, Indonesia, and Turkey. The terrorists are intent on maximizing the number of indiscriminate civilian casualties. In the attacks on the World Trade Center and the Pentagon, they murdered thousands of citizens from approximately 80 countries. Thus, the terrorists seem to be intent upon upsetting the world order, weakening democratic states into appeasement and capitulation, and instigating chaos by any means necessary while ignoring international customs and conventions, most notably by not distinguishing between military and civilian targets.

Moreover, the terrorists frequently utilize unconventional means and tactics. They frequently disguise themselves in civilian attire, use concealed explosives, and exploit women[2] and medical personnel to surreptitiously transport weapons and launch sneak attacks. The recruitment and dispatch of children as young as age 12 to serve as snipers, arms couriers and suicide bombers is now disturbingly commonplace.[3] Further, the enemy has been known to conceal weapons stashes and seek refuge near or inside of schools, hospitals, religious facilities, and antiquities.

Because these abhorrent targeting decisions and tactics demonstrate a blatant disregard for the Law of War and a brazen attempt to exploit the protected status of civilians and non-military facilities, the United States must graduate its strategy and tactics beyond historically accepted principles and adapt accordingly in order to defend itself and its allies.

The United States is attempting to respond to these unlawful practices by working within the constraints of the evolving Law of War. This policy includes putting the world on notice that any nation that harbors or supports terrorism will be regarded as a hostile regime, particularly those rogue nations that agree to provide terrorists with weapons of mass destruction.[4] President George W. Bush's administration has spearheaded the worldwide coalition against terrorism by employing all available diplomatic, financial, law enforcement, intelligence, and military means and creating the Department of Homeland Security and the Homeland Security Council. Congress has supported these endeavors by passing a flurry of legislation including authorizing the use of self-defensive action in Afghanistan and Iraq and passing the U.S.A. Patriot Act.

The need to utilize the broadest possible definitions of "self defense," "lawful target," "combatants," "proportional response" and other key terms are critical to executing an effective response to unconventional – indeed unlawful – attacks while trying to abide by the various war conventions and customs. For example, the legal basis for use of force in Afghanistan in response to al-Qaeda and the Taliban for their attacks on the World Trade Center and the Pentagon was self-defense under Article 51 of the United Nations' (UN) Charter. Although neither UN Security Council Resolution (UNSCR) 1368, dated Sept. 12, 2001, nor UNSCR 1373, dated Sept. 28, 2001, expressly authorized the use of force against the terrorists, both resolutions recognize the United States' "inherent right of self-defense."

The process of formulating and implementing evolving combat objectives and guidelines poses challenges to the entire chain of command. It begins with the creation of policy by the Commander in Chief, Secretary of Defense, and their advisors and culminates with the execution of the Rules of Engagement (ROE) and war protocols by combat commanders and lower enlisted infantry, artillery, and aviation soldiers, many of whom are too young to legally drink alcohol.

Consequently, revisions and "lessons learned" are being incorporated on a rolling basis into combat instruction and training. The internet has proved quite valuable in this regard: companycommand. army.mil and platoonleader.army.mil among other sites enable combat-tested soldiers to share their experiences with those who are about to deploy.

That said, however, changing a soldier's mental approach in order to modify his/her defensive instincts to the nefariously evolving threats is more gradual. For example, a soldier on guard duty outside a military compound will not always make the appropriate defensive response in a matter of seconds when a taxi driver in civilian clothing coasts in his car towards the gate, stops, requests assistance and upon the sentry's approach, detonates a concealed explosive. Unfortunately, such tragedies have jolted some soldiers to become reflexively defensive, such as when a van full of Iraqi civilian women and children was riddled with bullets because they failed to slow down while approaching a security checkpoint. In response, the military has begun to utilize new weapons and tactics such as the use of robots to check for explosives, remote-controlled road tire spikes and nets, instant oil slicks, paint-ball guns that coat windshields, and other non-lethal devices that will help soldiers proportionally respond to potential threats in their confrontations with locals while reducing the number of unnecessary casualties.[5]

In some cases, the learning curve has resulted in unfortunate casualties, due to undisciplined excess and lax passivity. The scandals at the Abu Ghraib prison facility should serve as a constant reminder of how the entire chain of command must constrain its conduct and train subordinates to the rule of law. The compulsory humiliation inflicted upon detainees at the prison undermined the human rights aspiration of Operations Iraqi Freedom and Anaconda, dampened the fledgling admiration the local inhabitants were developing for the United States, provoked international condemnation, and instigated retaliatory attacks on U.S. citizens in theater. It is evident that without explicit direction, discipline within the ranks and accountability, chaos can ensue, which ultimately destabilizes the mission.

That said, it is feasible for soldiers to exercise good faith judgment and discipline as they apply the ROE when they face imminent threats, and take measures that comply with the Law of War in the process of maintaining order and defending themselves, their units, and their nation's interests.

REVISED COMBAT ETHICS: THE ADOPTION OF THE PREEMPTION DOCTRINE

It is generally agreed that two types of action legitimately fall within the ambit of international law: (1) actions authorized by the UN Security Council under Chapter VII of the UN Charter, and (2) actions that constitute a legitimate act of individual or collective self-defense pursuant to Article 51 of the UN Charter and/or customary international law.[6] Chapter VII puts forth the parameters in which the Security Council may confront acts of aggression or other threats to international peace or security.[7] After identifying a threat, then exhausting other tactics short of force to compel compliance, the Security Council can authorize a member state or group of states to use force in accordance with Article 42.[8]

Under the second theory, States possess an inherent right to protect their national borders, airspace and territorial seas from attack.[9] Article 51 of the UN Charter authorizes "…the inherent right of individual or collective self defense if an armed attack occurs against a member of the UN until the Security Council has taken measures necessary to maintain international peace and security."[10] Further, many States, including the United States, embrace an interpretation of the UN Charter that extends beyond the black letter language of Article 51, embracing the customary law principle of "anticipatory self defense" that justifies the use of force to repel not just actual armed attacks but also "imminent" armed attacks.[11] Under this concept, a State is not required to absorb the "first hit" before it can resort to the use of force in self-defense to repel an imminent attack.[12]

Anticipatory self defense finds its roots in the 1842 *Caroline* case and a pronouncement by then-U.S. Secretary of State Daniel Webster that a State need not suffer an actual armed attack before taking defensive action, but may engage in anticipatory self defense if the circumstances leading to the use of force are instantaneous, overwhelming and leave no choice of means and no time for deliberation.[13] Anticipatory self-defense also serves as a foundational element as embodied in the concept of "hostile intent," which makes it clear to commanders that they do not and should not have to absorb the first hit before their right and obligation to exercise self-defense arises.[14] As with any form of self-defense, the principles of necessity and proportionality constrain the actions of the offended State.[15] These concepts will be discussed shortly.

For almost two hundred years, the right of anticipatory self-defense was predicated upon knowing, with a reasonable level of certainty, the time and place of an enemy's forthcoming attack. However, in this age of terrorism where warnings may not be easily observed and anticipated, President George W. Bush has determined that the United States will not wait because the consequences could be catastrophic: "The greater the threat, the greater is the risk of inaction – and the more compelling the case for taking anticipatory action to defend ourselves, even if uncertainty remains as to the time and place of the enemy's attack."[16]

In "The National Security Strategy of the United States of America" published in September 2002, the U.S. government has graduated the use of force doctrine from anticipatory self-defense to preemption:

> We must be prepared to stop rogue states and their terror-ist clients before they are able to threaten or use weapons of mass destruction against the United States and our allies and friends. Our response must take full advantage of strengthened alliances, the establishment of new partnerships with former adversaries, innovation in the use of military forces, modern technologies…. It has taken almost a decade for us to com-prehend the true nature of this new threat. Given the goals of rogue states and terrorists, the United States can no longer solely rely on a reactive posture as we have in the past. The in-ability to deter a potential attacker, the immediacy of today's threats, and the magnitude of potential harm that could be caused by our adversaries' choice of weapons, do not permit that option. We cannot let our enemies strike first.[17]

President Bush justified the change in response to the unconven-tional, more aggressive nature of contemporary terrorist threats, in large part because the gradual, observable massing of enemy forces on a nation's borders is no longer the means by which an attack can be anticipated:

> We must adapt the concept of imminent threat to the capa-bilities and objectives of today's adversaries. Rogue states and terrorists do not seek to attack us using conventional means. They know such attacks would fail. Instead, they rely on acts of terror and, potentially, the use of weapons of mass destruc-

tion – weapons that can be easily concealed, delivered covertly, and used without warning.[18]

Thus, the doctrine of preemptive self-defense will be relied upon in future instances where the President concludes that an enemy has been identified, the risk of attack by that enemy is real and imminent, and a delayed response would enable the enemy to inflict significant harm upon the United States, its allies, or interests.

THE LAW OF WAR

The Law of War, often referred to as the law of armed conflict, is defined as the part of international law that regulates the conduct of armed hostilities.[19] It derived from the Law of The Hague, the Geneva Conventions of 1949, the 1954 Hague Cultural Property Convention, the 1972 Biological Weapons Convention, the 1977 Geneva Protocols,[20] the 1980 Conventional Weapons Treaty, and the Chemical Weapons Convention of 1997.[21]

The Law of War consists of four principles. The first is the principle of military necessity, or military objective, which prohibits a belligerent from destroying or seizing the enemy's property unless required by the necessities of war.[22] The second principle forbids the use of arms, projectiles, or materiel calculated to cause unnecessary suffering.[23] The third principle of discrimination, or distinction, requires that Parties to a conflict must direct their operations only against combatants and military objectives, as distinguished from protected property, persons, or places.[24] The final principle states that the anticipated loss of life and damage to property incidental to attacks must be proportional, not excessive, in relation to the concrete and direct military advantage expected to be gained.[25]

The principle of military necessity authorizes the use of force needed to accomplish the mission but does not authorize acts otherwise prohibited by the Law of War.[26] Attacks are limited to objects by their **nature** (e.g., combatants, armored fighting vehicles, weapons, forts, combat aircraft and helicopters, supply depots of ammunition, and petroleum tanks), **location** (e.g., a narrow passage through which the enemy formation must pass, bridge along the enemy's main supply route), **purpose** (e.g., civilian buses or trucks that move soldiers from point A to B, a military munitions factory) or **use** (e.g., an enemy headquarters located in a school, an enemy supply dump located in a residence, a hotel that is used to house enemy troops) that make an effective contribution to military action and whose total or partial destruction, capture or neutralization, in the circumstances ruling at the time, would make for a definite military advantage.[27] The distinction between **purpose** and **use** is that **purpose** is concerned with the intended, suspected, or possible future use of an object whereas **use** is determined by the present function of the object.[28]

The second principle forbids combatants from using arms that are *per se* calculated to cause unnecessary suffering, sometimes referred to as superfluous injury (e.g., projectiles filled with glass, irregularly shaped bullets, lances with barbed heads).[29] A weapon would be deemed to cause unnecessary suffering only if the employment of a weapon for its normal or expected use would inevitably cause injury or suffering significantly disproportionate to its military effectiveness.[30] Clearly, necessary suffering is permitted in war because objectives are achieved by combatants through the infliction of severe injury or loss of life.[31] Thus, scrutiny cannot be conducted in a vacuum: a weapon's effects must be considered in the context of comparable, lawful weapons or munitions in use on the modern battlefield.[32] Moreover, a State is not required to foresee or anticipate all possible uses or misuses of a weapon because almost any weapon can be misused. For example, a knife could be properly used to slit the throat of an enemy combatant or improperly if the same knife is misused by gouging eyes or severing limbs in such a manner as to cause the victim to slowly bleed to death while writhing in agony. Further discussion regarding permitted weapons follows below.

The principle of discrimination or distinction forbids indiscriminate attacks that are not directed at a specific military objective (e.g., Iraqi SCUD missile attacks on Israeli and Saudi cities during the Persian Gulf War).[33] It also requires that military objectives be distinguished from protected persons or places.[34] Distinction obligates the clashing parties to engage only in military operations that distinguish the civilian population (or individual civilians not taking a direct part in the hostilities) by directing force exclusively against combatants and military objects.[35] A textbook violation is one in which a suicide bomber detonates the explosive in a crowded marketplace that includes one or two soldiers but thousands of civilians.

The final principle of proportionality is concerned with un-avoidable and unplanned collateral damage inflicted upon civilian personnel and property while attacking a military objective. Not all collateral damage is a violation of the Law of War: for the attack to be deemed unlawful, the collateral or incidental damage to non-combatants or civilian objects must be excessive to the attempted military advantage to be gained by the attack.[36] In the course of conducting an evaluation, "military advantage" should not be re-stricted to tactical gains or even the isolated attack but should be viewed within the full context of the war strategy. Thus, dropping a bomb on a motor pool of 100 parked enemy Humvees even though a handful of civilians may be injured or killed may be permissible, whereas dropping a bomb on a single soldier traveling through a city street crowded with civilians may be impermissible.

In general, the Law of War applies in international armed con-flict, that is, conflict between two or more of the High Contracting Parties, even if the state of war is not recognized by one of them.[37] Although the U.S. has not adopted all of the various conventions and protocols in their entirety, the Department of Defense (DoD)'s policy is to comply with the Law of War during the conduct of mili-tary operations and related armed conflict activities,[38] although all other operations need only comply with the principles and spirit of the Law of War.[39] Thus, in peacekeeping operations such as Haiti, Bosnia and Somalia, the U.S. adopted the principles and spirit of the Law of War.

Historically, a member of the U.S. military who commits an offense that may be regarded as a "war crime" will be charged under a specific article of the Uniform Code of Military Justice (UCMJ).[40] Commanders are legally responsible for war crimes committed by their subordinates when they either ordered the commission of the act, knew about the act, either before or during its commission, but did nothing to prevent or stop it, or should have known that the acts would be committed or were committed and failed to take the necessary and reasonable steps to insure compliance with the Law of War and to punish violators.[41] The commanders must therefore investigate and report suspected war crimes, as appropriate.

In the case of other persons subject to trial by general courts-martial for violating the Law of War, the charge will be "Violation of the Law of War" rather than a specific UCMJ article.[42] Another prosecutorial tool is the War Crimes Act of 1997 (U.S. Code Title 18, Section 2441) that provides U.S. federal courts with jurisdiction to prosecute any person inside or outside the U.S. for war crimes where a U.S. national or member of the armed forces is involved as an accused or as a victim.[43]

In the twentieth century, there has been a concerted, yet controversial, effort to apply the Law of War to internal armed conflicts for humanitarian reasons. The 1977 Geneva Protocol I Additional to the 1949 Geneva Conventions (hereafter AP I) attempted to expand the application of the Law of War to include certain wars of "national liberation" for States that are parties to that convention.[44] The U.S. is not a party to AP I and does not recognize this extension of the Law of War.[45]

It should be noted that during internal armed conflict, Geneva Convention Common Article III imposes limited humanitarian protections and domestic laws apply, which means that guerillas will not receive immunity for their actions. Notwithstanding Common Article III, the application of domestic laws enables the state to punish those subject to its jurisdiction for committing crimes, whether they are state actors or insurgents.[46] As well, if the rebels lack international legal status, another state's right to intervene in the rebel's host state's domestic affairs is minimal.[47]

Finally, violations of the Law of War may also be prosecuted under the auspices of international tribunals, such as the Nuremberg and Tokyo tribunals established by the Allies to prosecute German and Japanese war criminals after World War II.[48] The creation of the United Nations also resulted in the exercise of criminal jurisdiction over war crimes by the international community, with the Security Council's establishment of the International Tribunal to Adjudicate War Crimes Committed in the Former Yugoslavia as well as the International Criminal Court.[49]

RULES OF ENGAGEMENT (ROE)

ROE are directives issued by competent military authorities that characterize the circumstances and limitations under which U.S. forces will initiate and continue combat.[50] ROE are drafted with the Law of War, national policy, public opinion, and military operational constraints in mind and are routinely more restrictive than what the Law of War permits. An origin of ROE is the seminal writings on military strategy by Karl Von Clausewitz, who opined that war is but a means of achieving political ends.[51] This theory has been understood as a precedent to the modern understanding that ROE promotes the linkage of military operations with the underlying political objectives.[52]

The ROE are formulated by the President and the Secretary of Defense or their designees, with assistance from the Judge Advocate General or his designee, in order to provide concise guidance to commanders and soldiers as to what criteria they should consider when identifying combatants and military objectives, determining which weapons are permissible, and defining the scope of the mission.

ROE also ensure that national policy and objectives are reflected in the action of commanders in the field, particularly under circumstances in which communication with higher authority is difficult.[53] For example, the ROE may prohibit the engagement of certain targets or the use of particular weapons systems out of a desire not to incite the enemy, inflame world opinion, or unnecessarily escalate hostilities.[54] Political concerns include the influence of international public opinion through media coverage, the effect of host country law, and the Status Of Forces Agreements (SOFAs) with the United States.[55]

In multinational operations, the UN Security Council will often serve as the ROE proponent by drafting resolutions that define the permissible scope of force authorized to accomplish the mission that may include weapons collection, public security, or the arrest and detention of individuals subject to an International Tribunal (e.g., UNSCR 940 in Haiti, UNSCR 1031 in Bosnia).[56] The Commander may issue ROE to specify particular Law of War principles that apply to the particular mission, such as restrictions on the destruction of cultural, civilian, or religious property and minimizing the infliction of injuries on civilians.[57]

In all cases, U.S. forces retain the right to use necessary and proportional force for unit and individual self-defense in response to a "hostile act" or "hostile intent."[58] A "hostile act" exists when an enemy launches an attack or other use of force against the United States, U.S. forces and, in some cases, U.S. nationals, their property, U.S. commercial assets or other designated non-U.S. forces, foreign nationals, and their property.[59] A "hostile act" is also one in which force is used to directly obstruct or curtail the execution of duties or a mission, including the retrieval of U.S. personnel or vital U.S. Government property.[60] A "hostile act" activates the right to utilize proportional force in self-defense to deter, neutralize, or destroy the threat.[61] "Hostile intent" occurs when the threat of imminent use of force against the United States, U.S. forces, or other designated persons and property is evident.[62] It is also the threat of force used directly to obstruct or curtail the execution of duties or a mission including the retrieval of U.S. personnel or vital U.S. Government property.[63] The existence of a "hostile act" or "hostile intent" activates the right to utilize proportional force in self-defense to deter, neutralize, or destroy the threat.[64]

U.S. forces are also permitted to respond to a "hostile force." A "hostile force" is one in which any civilian, terrorist, paramilitary, or military force, with or without national designation, has committed a "hostile act," exhibited "hostile intent," or has been declared hostile by appropriate U.S. authority.[65] Once a force is declared "hostile," U.S. forces do not need to witness a "hostile act" or "hostile intent" in order to engage.[66] Thus, a soldier dressed in enemy attire that is asleep or eating may be attacked.

As circumstances require, revisions to the ROE may be requested by appealing up the chain of command or may be dictated *sua sponte* from the top of the chain of command.

TARGETING DECISIONS: LAWFUL AND UNLAWFUL COMBATANTS, CIVILIANS, HUMAN SHIELDS, HISTORIC, CULTURAL AND RELIGIOUS SITES, PUBLIC WORKS, HOSPITALS

Military objectives, otherwise known as lawful targets, are defined as objects that, by their nature, use, location, or purpose make an effective contribution to military action and whose total or partial destruction, capture or neutralization, in the circumstances ruling at the time, offers a definite military advantage.[67] Military personnel, equipment, units, and bases are always military objectives – regardless of their location – while other objects may become military objectives. The provision deals only with intentional attack; a collateral damage assessment must be simultaneously made prior to the attack.

Combatants are lawful targets unless "out of combat," meaning, they are captured or wounded, sick or shipwrecked and no longer resisting.[68] Combatants are military personnel engaged in hostility during an armed conflict on behalf of a party to the conflict, aside from medical personnel and chaplains, although even such individuals can lose their protected status if they express a hostile act or intent.[69] Combatants include: the regular armed forces of a State Party to the conflict, militia, volunteer corps, and organized resistance movements belonging to a State Party to the conflict that are under responsible command, wear a fixed distinctive sign recognizable at a distance, carry their arms openly, and abide by the Law of War.[70]

A combatant is entitled to carry out attacks on enemy military personnel and equipment and bears no criminal responsibility for killing or injuring enemy military personnel or civilians taking an active part in hostilities or for causing damage or destruction to property, provided his or her acts are in compliance with the Law of War.[71] If captured, a combatant is entitled to Prisoner Of War (POW) status.[72] A combatant may be tried for breaches of the Law of War, but may only be punished for such breaches after a fair and regular trial.[73] The Law of War prohibits intentional attacks on non-combatants such as civilians who are not taking an active part in hostilities, medical personnel, chaplains, and those out of combat – including POWs, the wounded, sick and shipwrecked.[74]

The use of human shields presents moral and legal concerns. When combatants surround themselves with civilians or hide in population centers during combat, the civilians that provide the "armor" are referred to as human shields. If they are willing and actively conduct surveillance, transport weapons, or generally assist with combat planning or operations, their status as non-combatants is in doubt. They may be deemed collaborators because they are assisting with the objectives of those they harbor and, therefore, appear to be aligned in spirit and purpose. However, if the civilian simply serves as an immovable intermediary between the attacker and the shielded combatant or is held as a hostage, prior to launching an attack, the Law of War concerns regarding proportionality, necessity, and discrimination must be more carefully contemplated than in the first example, in addition to drawing a conclusion as to whether the greater target is a military objective.

An argument can be made that in anti-terror operations in which house to house fighting in an urban area is necessary and prior evacuation warnings have been issued to civilians, those individuals that choose to remain with the intention of making it more difficult for the Law of War abiding force to target terrorists are actively resisting and therefore cannot be distinguished from combatants.[75] The consequence of declining to evacuate means that the non-evacuating civilians assume the risk that they will be treated the same way as combatants, to include the risk of injury or death; the moral and legal duty to protect the lives of the Law of War abiding force will override.[76] More eloquently stated:

> ...a person may be liable to suffer harm if, through his own culpable action, he has made it inevitable that someone must suffer harm. In such a case, it is permissible, and sometimes even obligatory, to harm the morally guilty person [complicit

human shield] rather than to allow his morally culpable action to cause harm to the morally innocent. The interests of the innocent [Law of War abiding force] have priority as a matter of justice.[77]

Thus, forces that embrace the Law of War should not be forced to incur self-inflicting wounds when terrorists use women, children, the sick, or elderly as willing human shields.

Hiring assassins, putting a price on the enemy's head, and offering rewards for an enemy "dead or alive" is prohibited.[78] It does not, however, preclude attacks on individual soldiers or officers or targeting military command and control of the enemy, whether in the zone of hostilities, occupied territory or elsewhere, so long as the attack is not treacherous.[79] Treachery is the killing, wounding or capture via acts that invite the confidence of an adversary to lead him to believe that he is entitled to, or is obliged to accord, protection under the rules of international law applicable in armed conflict – with the intent to betray that confidence.[80] Assuming no false confidence is solicited and a proper Law of War analysis adequately contemplates military necessity, proportionality, and humanity in concluding that someone is a proper military objective, that individual is a lawful target and is, therefore, not killed treacherously. Thus, it will not matter whether the attack was planned several months in advance or that morning, whether it was executed by a Special Forces unit in hand-to-hand combat, a robotic drone glider, a sniper, or a bomb dropped from 10,000 feet. Further discussion of treachery is discussed in the Tactics section below.

Regarding civilian property, there is a presumption that it is not a military objective if it is an object that is traditionally associated with civilian use (dwellings, schools, etc.).[81] However, if civilians are located within a military objective, such as a weapons factory or petroleum plant, the objective remains a military one and thus a lawful target, subject to military necessity and proportionality constraints. Moreover, if enemy forces have taken up position in buildings that otherwise would be regarded as civilian objects, such as a school, retail store, museum, or house of worship, the building transforms

into a military objective, subject to military necessity and proportionality constraints.[82] The circumstances ruling at the time – the
combatant's use of a building – permit an attack if it would offer a
definite military advantage.[83]

Hospital or safety zones may be established by agreement between the warring parties on behalf of the wounded, sick, and civilians.[84] As well, fixed or mobile medical units and medical transports
shall be respected and protected and cannot be intentionally attacked
unless they are used to commit "acts harmful to the enemy."[85] If individuals commit "acts harmful to the enemy" from a medical unit
or hospital, a warning must be given along with a reasonable time to
comply before the attack may commence.[86] However, when receiving
fire from a hospital, there is no duty to warn before returning fire
in self-defense, such as in the Richmond Hills Hospital scenario in
Grenada.[87] Moreover, incidental damage to medical facilities situ-
ated near military objectives is not a *per se* violation of the Law of
War, assuming proportionality considerations are contemplated.

If the combatants are defending a city or town, they may be
attacked if their defensive positions are indivisible from the city or
town.[88] However, if enemy forces abandon the building or their
defensive positions and permit the approaching ground forces to
occupy the territory, the change of circumstance eliminates the
building or town's "military objective" status.[89] Thus, attacking or
bombarding towns or villages that are undefended is prohibited.[90]
There is a general requirement to warn before a bombardment, but
it only applies if civilians are present and when the assault is not a
surprise attack.[91] Warnings do not need to be specific as to time and
location and may be published through broadcasts or leaflets.[92]

Cultural property, which includes buildings dedicated to religion, art, and historic qualities, is protected from intentional attack
so long as it is not being used for military purposes or otherwise is
regarded as a military objective.[93] Thus, a palace that is used solely
as a museum to house artifacts is not a military objective whereas
the same palace used as a command and control center by the enemy is. The party seeking protected status of the property should
place distinctive and visible signs to warn the enemy in advance,[94]

although the U.S. traditionally relies upon intelligence to identify such protected facilities.[95] Attempts to conduct operations from or store weapons or troops in such facilities will eliminate the facility's protected status.

Turning to public utilities and works, the rules are not U.S. law but should be considered because of the pervasive world-wide acceptance of international protocols.[96] Under Amended Protocol I, dams, dikes, and nuclear electrical generating stations should not be attacked – even if they are lawful targets – if it causes the release of dangerous forces and inflicts "severe losses" upon the civilian population.[97] The U.S.'s objection is to the use of the "severe loss" term that suggests a different standard than the well-established proportionality test. Military objectives that are adjacent to potentially dangerous forces are also immune from attack if the attack may release the forces, although parties have a duty to avoid locating military objectives near such locations.[98] Works and installations containing dangerous forces may be attacked only if they provide "significant and direct support" to military operations and attack is the only feasible way to terminate the support.[99] Parties may construct defensive weapons systems to protect works and installations containing dangerous forces; however, these weapons systems may not be attacked unless they are used for purposes other than protecting the installation. This rule can easily become ambiguous to apply; the enemy may fire from beside a power plant because it is defending the power plant or, more deviously, utilizing the power plant's protected status as it attempts to thwart the enemy's advancing forces. In such cases, the specific circumstances relevant to the particular situation must be carefully evaluated by commanders in the field.

Tactics

Certain deceptive tactics are permitted if they abide by the Law of War and the actions are conducted in good faith.[100] Examples include the creation of fictitious units by planting false information, putting up dummy installations, false radio transmissions, or using a small force to simulate a large unit.[101] In the 1991 Gulf War, coalition forces used deception cells to create the impression that they were going to attack near the Kuwaiti boot heel as opposed to the "left hook" strategy that was actually implemented. The massing of forces was simulated using smoke generators, inflatable Humvees and helicopters, artificial radio traffic that was broadcast through portable radio equipment, and loudspeakers that played recorded tank and truck noises.[102]

As well, combatants may wear enemy uniforms but cannot fight in them with the intent to deceive, although a POW escapee may wear an enemy uniform or civilian clothing to enable his getaway.[103] Regarding captured equipment and state-owned supplies, the capturing party may use it but must first remove all enemy insignia in order to fight with it.[104] Private transportation, arms, and ammunition may be seized, but must be returned with compensation after peace is secured.[105]

Treachery and perfidy are prohibited under the law of war.[106] Some examples include suicide bombers costumed in civilian attire as they approach U.S. forces or civilians,[107] feigning incapacitation by wounds/sickness,[108] simulating surrender,[109] or misusing the Red Cross, Red Crescent, or other cultural property symbol while organizing or executing combat tactics or operations.[110] However, for the prohibited act to be considered a violation of the Law of War, it must occur during an international armed conflict and be a proximate cause in the killing of enemy combatants.[111] Consequently, because of the high threshold, the U.S. and other countries routinely exercise extreme caution when confronting an adversary that is known to utilize treacherous tactics. As an example, if the enemy is notorious for using ambulances or taxis to smuggle enemy combatants or weapons, those vehicles will be subjected to greater scrutiny and the operators may lose their protected status, depending upon the specific circumstances of the confrontation.

Permitted Weapons

All U.S. weapons, weapons systems, and munitions must be reviewed for legality under the Law of War by the service Judge Advocate General before the engineering and manufacturing development contract is awarded and before the award of the initial production contract.[112] The test is whether a weapon or munitions acquisition or use is consistent with Law of War and arms control treaties to which the United States is a party or customary international law to which the U.S. subscribes.[113] An analysis must be conducted in order to evaluate "military necessity" – meaning, the purpose for the weapon or munition – as compared to the prohibition of weapons or munitions intended to cause unnecessary suffering.[114] Although combatants may incur "necessary" suffering, which clearly includes the possibility of severe injury or loss of life, the weapon is problematic if its normal or anticipated use would cause unnecessary suffering that is disproportionate to the military advantage or necessity to be gained.[115]

Regarding land mines, the United States generally regards land mines (anti-personnel and anti-vehicle) as a lawful weapon, subject to the restrictions contained in national policy and the Amended Protocol II, United Nations Convention on Certain Conventional Weapons (UNCCW).[116] On February 27, 2004, a new U.S. landmine policy was announced. Until 2010, anti-vehicle landmines that are non-self-destructing can only be used outside of Korea with the President's permission.[117] After 2010, non-self-destructing anti-personnel and anti-vehicle landmines cannot be used anywhere.[118]

Turning to Chemical Weapons, the Chemical Weapons Convention (CWC) was ratified by the U.S. and came into force in April 1997 wherein the signatories agreed to never develop, produce, stockpile, transfer, use or engage in military preparations to use chemical weapons.[119] Retaliatory use is not allowed, and chemical stockpiles must be declared, subjected to on-site inspection, and subsequently destroyed.[120] Signatories also agreed not to use Riot Control Agents (RCAs such as tear gas or pepper spray) as a "method of warfare."[121] The U.S. has renounced the first use of RCAs in armed conflicts except in defensive military modes to save lives such as: controlling riots in areas under direct and distinct U.S. military control, to include rioting POWs; dispersing civilians where the enemy uses them to mask or screen an attack; rescue missions for downed pilots/passengers and escaping POWs in remotely isolated areas and in rear echelon areas outside the immediate combat zone; and to protect convoys from civil disturbances, terrorists and paramilitary organizations.[122] In such cases, presidential approval is a prerequisite.[123] Moreover, the Senate insisted upon the exception that permits the use of RCAS against "combatants" when the U.S. is not a party to the conflict and when participating in UN Charter peacekeeping operations.[124] Bacteriological and biological warfare are prohibited by the Biological Weapons Convention, ratified by the U.S. in 1975 and its precursor, the 1925 Geneva Protocol.

POWS AND DETAINEES; PROPER TREATMENT, MILITARY TRIBUNALS

The status of individuals who are captured during combat must be determined in order to decide what protections they deserve. The U.S. applies a broad interpretation to the term "international armed conflict," set forth in Common Article 2 of the Conventions, which means that judge advocates are encouraged to advise commanders that, regardless of the nature of the conflict,[125] all enemy personnel should initially be accorded the protections of the Geneva Convention Relative to the Treatment of Prisoners of War Convention (GPW), at least until their status may be determined.[126] When doubt exists as to whether captured enemy personnel are entitled to continued POW status, Article 5 (GPW) Tribunals must be convened to determine the prisoner's status.[127] Civilians captured along with combatants also receive POW status.[128] The most beneficial aspect to POW status is "combatant immunity," that is, so long as the combatant complies with the Law of War, he or she will not be prosecuted for any casualties he/she inflicts during international armed conflict.[129]

The legal obligation to provide adequate food, facilities, and medical aid to all POWs can pose significant logistical problems in fast-moving tactical situations.[130] POWs must be transported from the combat zone as quickly as circumstances permit and, subject to valid security reasons, POWs must be allowed to retain their personal property, protective gear, valuables, and money; these items cannot be seized unless properly receipted for and recorded as required by the GPW.[131]

No physical or mental torture, nor any other form of coercion, may be inflicted on POWs to secure information of any kind.[132] POWs who refuse to answer may not be threatened, insulted, or exposed to unpleasant treatment of any kind.[133] They are entitled to food, clothing, shelter, medical attention, and hygiene.[134] The Detaining Power may utilize the labor of POWs who are physically fit, taking into account their age, gender, rank, and physical aptitude, and with the goal of maintaining adequate physical and mental health.[135] Non-commissioned officers who are POWs shall only be required to do supervisory work.[136] If officers or persons of equivalent status ask for suitable work, reasonable effort should be made to find it for them, but they may not be forced to work.[137]

Regarding medical treatment, captured wounded and sick prisoners must be treated the same way that the capturing army would treat its own injured soldiers.[138] The order of treatment is determined solely by urgent medical needs such that no adverse distinctions may be established because of gender, race, nationality, religion, political opinions, or any other similar criteria.[139] If compelled to abandon the wounded and sick to the enemy, commanders must leave medical personnel and material to assist in their care, as far as military considerations permit.[140] As conditions allow, parties are obligated to search for the wounded and sick, particularly after combat.[141] Subject to essential security needs, mission requirements and other legitimate, practical limitations, the International Committee of the Red Cross (ICRC) must be permitted to visit POWs and provide them with certain types of relief.[142] Typically, the U.S. Department of State, in coordination with the Department of Defense, will invite the ICRC to observe POW, civilian internee, or detainee conditions as soon as circumstances permit.[143]

In Military Operations Other Than War (MOOTW) (e.g., Somalia, Haiti, Bosnia), persons who commit hostile or serious criminal acts against U.S. forces and are captured are not entitled to POW protection as provided by the GPW because MOOTW do not involve an international armed conflict that the U.S. has ratified.[144] These persons may be termed "detainees" instead of POWs, although the GPW still provides a template for detainee care.[145] They are entitled to "humane treatment," which is an undefined term but may include basic rights such as not being physically abused, humiliated, or harassed and an entitlement to food, clothing, shelter, and medical attention.[146]

Members of the armed forces of a party to a conflict and members of militias or volunteer corps forming part of such armed forces lose their right to be treated as POWs whenever they deliberately conceal their status in order to pass behind enemy lines for the purpose of gathering military information or for the purpose of waging war by destruction of life or property.[147] Putting on civilian clothes or the uniform of the enemy and engaging in combat are examples of concealment of the status of a member of the armed forces and qualifies as a war crime.[148]

One recent notable distinction worth mentioning occurred when U.S. Special Operations Forces donned indigenous attire when accompanying Northern Alliance indigenous forces in Afghanistan in 2001 in order to avoid being singled out and targeted as U.S. service members.[149] In the process, they wore distinctive hats and scarves, as opposed to civilian attire, in order to blend in, but still demonstrate a distinctive sign.[150]

Unprivileged belligerents, also known as unlawful combatants, may include spies, saboteurs, or civilians who are participating in the hostilities or who otherwise engage in unauthorized attacks or other combatant acts.[151] These individuals are not entitled to POW status, but merely "humane treatment," are prosecutable by the captor, and may be imprisoned or executed, depending upon their actions.[152] They are subject to the extreme penalty of death because of the danger inherent in their conduct.[153]

For example, the President determined that the Taliban and al-Qaeda are unlawful combatants because they lack some, if not all, of the four attributes that characterize lawful combatants.[154] The President declared that because al-Qaeda is not a state party to the Geneva Convention, it is a foreign terrorist group, and its members are therefore not entitled to the protections of the Geneva Convention.[155] At the time of publication, litigation is pending that contests the treatment and reduced legal protections such detainees have received, whether they are U.S. citizens or foreign born.

As for the Taliban, although Afghanistan is a party to the Geneva Convention and the Geneva Conventions apply to the Taliban detainees, they are not entitled to POW status because they have not effectively distinguished themselves from the civilian population of Afghanistan nor conducted their operations in accordance with the laws and customs of war.[156] Instead, they knowingly adopted and provided support to the unlawful terrorist objectives of al-Qaeda.[157] Thus, the President concluded that although the Geneva Conventions apply to Taliban but not al-Qaeda detainees, neither Taliban nor al-Qaeda detainees are entitled to POW status.

Moreover, there is a distinction between the U.S. and allied interpretations of the protocols of war in the area of identifying unconventional lawful combatants for POW status purposes, which can present a challenge to U.S. forces during multinational operations. The Geneva Protocol Additional I (AP I) of 1977 states that combatants who carry arms openly, are commanded by a responsible person, comply with the Law of War, and have an internal discipline system are entitled to POW status if captured while engaging in combat.[158] Although this protocol was ratified by 147 nations, the U.S. has not ratified it because it does not reflect international law that requires the four criteria including that combatants wear a fixed distinctive sign recognizable at a distance. The U.S. contends that combatants that only meet the GP I standard are not formally holding themselves out as combatants and therefore do not comply with the Law of War principle of distinction.[159] The consequence of this is that more civilians will be attacked because it will be harder to identify proper combatants if they are not required to wear distinctive insignia or outfits that are recognizable at a distance. The U.S. believes that combatants must behave – and appear – like lawful combatants in order to be entitled to POW status if captured. To avoid a conflict during multinational operations between the U.S. and nations that ratified GP I, the various participants allocate sectors in the theater of operations with each exclusively managing the individuals they capture.

On November 13, 2001, the President signed an order authorizing the creation of military commissions to try individuals, including members of al-Qaeda, who have engaged in, aided, abetted, or conspired to commit acts of international terrorism that have caused, threaten to cause, or have as their aim to cause injury to or adverse effects on the United States or its citizens or to have knowingly harbored such individuals.[160] These military commissions have the authority to mete out punishment, including life imprisonment or death.[161] The President will decide who is subject to the order on a case-by-case basis. On August 31, 2005, the Secretary of Defense (SECDEF) issued Military Commission Order No. 1, which contains the rules and procedures for the military commissions.[162] Most basic military court martial rights will be implemented; however, most notably, the Rules for Courts-Martial and the Military Rules of Evidence do not apply and a two-thirds vote is required for a finding of guilty beyond a reasonable doubt and determination of sentence, although a sentence of death requires a unanimous vote.[163] On November 8, 2005, the U.S. Supreme Court agreed to hear a case that challenges the legality of the military commissions.[164]

THE DEBACLE AT ABU GHRAIB: INTERROGATION AND CUSTODIAL HARASSMENT

The harassment and torture of prisoners held at Abu Ghraib prison in Iraq, as well as recent disclosures of prisoner maltreatment in Afghanistan and Guantanamo Bay, Cuba, were not only violations of U.S. military doctrine but also undermined the U.S.'s diplomatic objectives. Reports indicated that naked prisoners were forced into humiliating positions, at least one prisoner was sodomized, beatings and electric shocks were inflicted, head blows rendered detainees unconscious, dogs were used for intimidation, and other prohibited acts were employed by the Abu Ghraib staff.[165] The Military Police (MP) also forced prisoners to run naked through the hallway, handcuffing them to each other and forcing them to strip and form a human pyramid.[166] These acts incited an already skeptical international community and Arab world while simultaneously sending the message to the native Iraqis that in fact the U.S. is willing to commit acts that are similar to those committed by Saddam Hussein's regime.

This is not the first time such techniques have been used by the U.S. A Central Intelligence Agency training manual on coercive interrogation methods that was produced during the Vietnam War describes techniques such as those used in Iraq, Afghanistan and Guantanamo Bay, Cuba, suggesting that they have a long history with U.S. intelligence and were based on research and field experience.[167]

At the time of writing, the extent of awareness and endorsement by the chain of command – both civilian and uniform – of the unlawful tactics was just beginning to come to light.[168] It was reported in June 2004 that in August 2002, the Justice Department advised the White House that torturing al-Qaeda terrorists in captivity abroad "may be justified" and that international laws against torture "may be unconstitutional if applied to interrogations conducted in the war on terrorism."[169] Moreover, an American officer at Abu Ghraib said Lt. Gen. Ricardo Sanchez, the highest-ranking U.S. military officer in Iraq, was present during some interrogations and/or allegations of prisoner abuse.[170] In early 2003, three top military lawyers lodged complaints about the Justice Department's definition of torture and how it would be applied to interrogations, to no apparent avail.[171]

There are multiple theories that explain why the Abu Ghraib incidents occurred. Reports indicated that intensified pressure to produce actionable information prompted Army interrogators to implement tactics that exceed what Army interrogation rules allow.[172] In addition, there was a scramble for personnel immediately after Saddam Hussein's army was crushed. Abu Ghraib was staffed with reserve MPs – who lacked Army prison guard training – and substitute interrogators from an amalgam of units and private contractors.[173] The chaos that ensued can also be attributed to the fact that inadequately trained MPs, who were serving as guards, followed instructions from military intelligence officials to "rough up" the prisoners in order to "get answers."[174]

The lack of accountability for the actions of private contractors contributed to the chaos. It was proposed by White House Administration lawyers that government agents who might torture prisoners at the President's direction could not be prosecuted by the Justice Department.[175] Private contractors served as interrogators at Abu Ghraib and did not participate in the military chain of command, which meant they were not subject to military codes of conduct and not held to the same rules as government workers, including the Geneva Conventions.[176]

Crimes committed by contractors in a combat zone may be prosecutable under the Military Extraterritorial Jurisdiction Act (MEJA),[177] but it has yet to be determined whether contractors that were not operating under a Department of Defense contract at the time the offenses were committed can be prosecuted under the MEJA.[178] The test cases referred to the Justice Department for prosecution may be those of six civilian contract employees from CACI International Inc. and Titan Corp. who are alleged to have participated in torturous acts at Abu Ghraib.[179]

In an Army investigative report, Maj. Gen. George R. Fay and Lt. Gen. Anthony R. Jones concluded that at least 35 military intelligence personnel and civilian contractors and 13 military police were responsible for a minimum of 44 instances of abuse of Iraqi prisoners.[180] The investigation found that U.S. military intelligence officials conspired to hide at least eight Iraqis detained by U.S. Forces from delegation of the International Committee of the Red Cross, amounting to a clear violation of Defense Department rules and the Geneva Conventions.[181]

In a separate inquiry, headed by former defense secretary James R. Schlesinger, it was determined that actions by Secretary of Defense Donald H. Rumsfeld contributed to confusion over what techniques were permissible for interrogating prisoners in Iraq and faulted the Joint Staff for not recognizing that military police officers at Abu Ghraib were overwhelmed by an influx of detainees.[182] The independent panel concluded that Lt. Gen. Sanchez and his deputy, Maj. Gen. Walter Wojdakowski, did not ensure proper staff oversight of detention and interrogation operations.[183]

Finally, the Army report on conditions at the Abu Ghraib

prison, authored by Maj. Gen. Antonio M. Taguba, concluded that soldiers were poorly prepared and inadequately trained to conduct Internment and Resettlement (I/R) operations prior to deployment, at the mobilization site, upon arrival in theater, and throughout their mission.[184] The Taguba report also found that MP units were directed by Army intelligence officers, CIA agents, and private contractors to implement physical and mental conditions that would lay the groundwork for favorable military intelligence interrogations.[185] It has been reported that military intelligence officers, contract interpreters, CIA officers, and other operatives wore civilian clothes in order to conceal their identities from prison officials when they confronted prisoners.[186] Moreover, top military intelligence officials and the CIA agreed to hide as many as 100 "ghost" detainees without officially registering them, in part, to keep them from international human rights organizations.[187]

In October 2005, the Department of Defense clarified that contingency contractor personnel who accompany U.S. military forces remain subject to U.S. laws and regulations, including Law of War constraints.[188] Moreover, at the time of this publication, Congress was in the process of approving legislation that would require all Defense Department interrogation techniques to be standardized and contained within the Army Field Manual.[189]

Another growing area of concern is that as early as the 1990s, the U.S. has handed over captives to authoritarian Muslim regimes that routinely employ torture in order to elicit information, which enables the U.S. to publicly distance itself from the infliction of torture while benefiting from the extracted information.[190] This technique, known as "extraordinary rendition," is a topic for another time.

As a result of the excesses inflicted upon the prisoners, the Pentagon announced in June 2004 that it opened 30 investigations into 34 deaths at detention facilities in Iraq and Afghanistan.[191] Staff Sergeant Ivan Frederick, Corporal Charles Graner, and Private First Class Lynddie England were convicted and sentenced to prison along with others for their roles in the mistreatment of the detainees, although officers have largely escaped punishment.[192] Although the scandal generated condemnation internationally and uproar in the Arab world, the full impact of the excesses committed at Abu Ghraib have yet to be revealed. One general fear is that Americans taken captive during future combat operations may expect harsher treatment than they could otherwise be subjected to under the Geneva Conventions. On June 18, 2004, Paul Johnson Jr., a Lockheed Martin contractor, was beheaded by Islamic radicals in Saudi Arabia who vowed to treat him as Muslim detainees were treated in Iraq's Abu Ghraib prison.[193] One month before, Nick Berg, an American small business operator, was beheaded at the hands of militants in Iraq who claimed it was done to avenge the Abu Ghraib scandal.[194] The Abu Ghraib incidents may have also inflamed local and regional resistance in Iraq, manifesting itself through suicide bombers who have flocked to Iraq in order to participate in Jihad against the U.S. and its allies.

OCCUPATION FORCE ISSUES

Territory is considered occupied when it is under the authority of the hostile armed force, but only extends to territory where authority has been established and can effectively be exercised.[195] However, military occupation (commonly referred to as belligerent occupation) is not conquest; it does not involve the transfer of sovereignty to the occupying force because it is unlawful for an occupant to annex occupied territory or to create a new state while hostilities continue.[196] It is also forbidden to compel the inhabitants of occupied territory to swear allegiance to the hostile occupier.[197] Occupation is temporary and will cease when the occupying power is expelled or withdraws.

Occupied territory is administered by a military government due to the inability, or undesirability, of allowing the host government to exercise its functions.[198] The occupying power has a legal duty to restore and maintain public order while respecting the laws of the occupied nation, unless resistance is overwhelming.[199] The occupying power may allow the local authorities to exercise some or all of their governmental functions, subject to the authority of the occupier.[200] If the occupant considers it necessary, as a matter of immediate security needs, it may assign protected persons to specific residences or internment camps and may enact penal laws, provided it informs the populace.[201] If an accused person is prosecuted under the penal laws, he is entitled to a fair trial, right to counsel, present evidence, call witnesses, and appeal a conviction.[202]

Subject to security precautions, the civilian population in occupied territory is entitled to important fundamental protections and benefits such as adequate food, medical supplies and treatment, hygiene, public health measures, family honor, life, property, and religious practice privileges.[203] Individual or mass forcible deportations of protected persons from the occupied territory are prohibited.[204] Moreover, children must be granted special protection and care, particularly with respect to their education, food, medical care, and protection against the impacts of war.[205]

The occupying power may not compel protected persons to serve in its armed forces, nor to work unless they are over eighteen years old, and then only on work that is necessary for the needs of the occupying force, for public utility services, or for the feeding, sheltering, clothing, transportation or health of the occupied country's citizenry.[206] The occupying power is specifically prohibited from forcing inhabitants to participate in military operations against their own country, and this prohibition includes work that directly promotes the military efforts of the occupying force, such as construction of fortifications, entrenchments, and military airfields.[207] Voluntary employment is permissible.

SEIZURE OF PROPERTY, DEMOLISHING BUILDINGS AND COLLECTIVE PUNISHMENT

Enemy military state-owned property and private property abandoned on the battlefield, such as cash, arms depots, means of transport, stores and supplies and all moveable property, becomes U.S. property and its confiscation is permitted.[208] However, personal retention of a war trophy by an individual soldier is restricted under U.S. law because confiscated enemy military property becomes U.S. property. The destruction or seizure of enemy property is prohibited unless such action is "imperatively demanded by the necessities of war"[209] or "rendered absolutely necessary by military operations."[210] Real estate may be used for marches, camp sites, and construction of field fortifications, while buildings may be destroyed for sanitary purposes or used for shelter for troops, the wounded and sick, vehicles, and for reconnaissance, cover and defense.[211] Fences, woods, crops and buildings may be demolished, cut down, and removed in order to clear a field of fire, to clear the ground for a landing field, or to furnish building materials or fuel if imperatively needed for the army.[212]

Pillaging, which is the unauthorized taking of private or personal property for personal gain or use, is expressly prohibited,[213] although the occupying power may requisition goods and services from the local populace to sustain the needs of the occupying force in proportion to the resources of the country and of such a nature as not to involve the population in the obligation of taking part in operations of the war against their country.[214] The occupying power must subsequently pay cash for such requisitions or provide a receipt and make payment as soon as possible.[215]

Collective punishment for individual acts, corporal punishment, imprisonment in premises without daylight and, in general, any form of torture or cruelty, may not be imposed upon POWs.[216] With regard to the demolition of facilities, installations or materiel, it is prohibited unless such action is "imperatively demanded by the necessities of war"[217] or "rendered absolutely necessary by military operations."[218] Of course, it is not difficult to envision a scenario where a strategically located barn, house, or other structure may be destroyed because it has served as a hideout for enemy combatants or storage site for munitions and therefore must be destroyed to prevent the enemy from returning to the site.

CONCLUSION

In the face of asymmetric warfare, the United States has been forced to confront the Laws of Armed Conflict in a profoundly novel manner. Because its enemies often resort to indiscriminate attacks on civilians, acts of treachery, utilize human and humanitarian shields, and intentionally defy the rules that govern combat, the United States has been forced to invoke a broader interpretation of self-defense in order to preserve itself, its allies, and the historically evolved framework that governs international conflict. In the process, the United States has generally exhibited a steadfast commitment to the principles and policies incorporated within the Law of War, even as its adversaries disregard it. It has been assertive and uncompromising in its national security posture while at the same time mostly maintaining humanitarian standards, including in targeting decisions, respecting places of worship and cultural norms, preserving historic antiquities, and treating the local populations in a civilized manner.

The United States is in the midst of modifying its practices, but not without sustaining further casualties or controversy. Hundreds of U.S. soldiers, civilians, and relief workers have been murdered by suicide bombers, indiscriminate roadside bombs, and other heinous acts. Since September 11, 2001, President Bush implemented overt and covert procedures to confront asymmetric warfare and has consequentially begun to face legal challenges in the courts and mounting Congressional scrutiny. The impulse to secure actionable intelligence in order to accelerate the war on terrorism was a motivating factor that led to the Abu Ghraib scandal, whose long-term impact is, to date, uncertain. In the short term, the excesses incited criticism of the U.S's presence in Iraq and even resulted in sporadic retaliatory acts of vengeance, as demonstrated by the beheading of two American civilians, and an emboldened insurgency. Will the scandal unfairly tarnish the U.S. for years to come, as the atrocities in Vietnam did for decades after the U.S. withdrew? On the bright side, perhaps the cost-benefit analysis in the aftermath of Abu Ghraib will serve as an unambiguous reminder of how hasty, excessive acts can actually set back the mission rather than advance it. Time will tell.

Nonetheless, in the face of grave threats posed by unrelenting terrorists who exploit every tactic, target, and civilian shield, it is reassuring, even inspiring, to know that the United States military has made a concerted effort to defend and promote the Law of War

principles due to the ingrained conviction that maintaining decorum in the world order – even during combat – secures an enduring
benchmark for all of humanity.

NOTES

*The opinions expressed herein are entirely the author's and should not be attributed to the
United States Department of Defense, its Army, or the Judge Advocate General's Corps. The
2006* Army Operational Law Handbook *(visit:* http://jagcnet.army.mil/, CLAMO *public
document area), was routinely consulted in the course of preparing this analysis.*

*I would like to thank my wife, Michelle, for her encouragement as well as for introduc-
ing me to Rabbi Michael Broyde (Emory Law School, Young Israel of Atlanta), who has
been a noble role model, mentor, teacher and friend. I also dedicate this work to all past,
present and future Jewish soldiers who serve, whether in the American Armed Forces or
those of other nations. What you are accomplishing is a* kiddush Hashem.

1. An opponent (a state, transnational group such as an international terrorist or-
    ganization, or a drug cartel, or various other types of players) seeks to counter
    the superior technology or firepower of a superpower or regional power with
    unconventional means. Susan W. Brenner, Marc D. Goodman, *In Defense Of
    Cyberterrorism: An Argument For Anticipating Cyber-Attacks*, 2002 U. Ill. J.L. Tech.
    & Pol'y (Spring, 2002): 1,2 n.2. Asymmetric combat is a version of not fighting
    within the Law of War that may include the use of surprise in all its operational
    and strategic dimensions and the use of weapons in ways unplanned by the United
    States. *Id.* Not fighting fair includes the concept that an opponent will utilize a
    strategy that alters the terrain on which a conflict is fought, such as using urban
    areas, places of worship and medical facilities as bunkers, targeting civilians and
    employing unlawful weapons such as concealed suicide belt explosives.
2. Farhana Ali, *The Bomber Behind the Veil*, Balt. Sun, December 13, 2005, at 19A.
3. Peter W. Singer, *Terrorists Must Be Denied Child Recruits*, Brookings Institution,
    January 25, 2005.
4. White House, *National Strategy to Combat Weapons of Mass Destruction*, 3 (Dec.
    2002).
5. Steven Komarow, *Pentagon Deploys Array of Non-Lethal Weapons*, USA Today, July
    25, 2005 at 14A.
6. *Army Operational Law Handbook 2006*, at 2 (Major Derek I. Grimes, ed., 2006)
    [Hereinafter: *OpLaw Handbook*]. Article 51 of the Charter states: "Nothing in the
    present Chapter shall impair the inherent right of individual or collective self
    defense if an armed attack occurs against a member of the UN until the Security
    Council has taken measures necessary to maintain international peace and secu-
    rity...."
7. *OpLaw Handbook*, at 2.
8. *OpLaw Handbook*, at 2.
9. *OpLaw Handbook*, at 5.

10. UN Charter, Art. 51 quoted in *OpLaw Handbook*, at 4.

11. *OpLaw Handbook*, at 5.

12. *OpLaw Handbook*, at 5.

13. *See* Letter from Daniel Webster, U.S. Secretary of State, to Henry Fox, British Minister in Washington (Apr. 24, 1841), *in* 29 British And Foreign State Papers 1840–1841, *at* 1138 (1857) cited in John Yoo, *Agora: Future Implication Of The Iraq Conflict: International Law And The War In Iraq*, 97 American Journal International Law 563, 572 (July 2003); *OpLaw Handbook*, at 6.

14. *OpLaw Handbook*, at 6.

15. *OpLaw Handbook*, at 6.

16. The White House, *The National Security Strategy of the United States of America*, 15 (2002).

17. The White House, *The National Security Strategy of the United States of America*, 14, 15 (2002).

18. The White House, *The National Security Strategy of the United States of America*, 15 (2002).

19. *OpLaw Handbook*, at 12.

20. *OpLaw Handbook*, at 15 (Although the U.S. has not ratified AP I and II, 155 nations have ratified AP I).

21. *OpLaw Handbook*, at 15–16.

22. Art. 23, para. (g) of the Annex to Hague IV.

23. Art. 23, para. (e) of the Annex to Hague IV.

24. Protocol Additional to the Geneva Conventions of 12 Aug 49 and relating to the Protection of Victims of International Armed Conflicts (Protocol I), 8 June 1977, [hereinafter AP I] Art. 48.

25. FM 27–10, para. 41, change 1.

26. Art. 23, para. (g) of the Annex to Hague IV.

27. AP I Art. 52(2) cited in *OpLaw Handbook*, at 21–22.

28. Commentary on the Additional Protocols of 8 June 1977 to the Geneva Conventions of 1949, para. 2022 (Y. Sandoz, et al. eds., 1998) cited in Maj. Eric Talbot Jensen, *Unexpected Consequences From Knock-On Effects: A Different Standard for Computer Network Operations?* 18 Am. U. Int'l L. Rev. 1145, 1155 n30 (2003).

29. Art. 23, para. (e) of the Annex to Hague IV; FM 27–10, para. 34.

30. Memorandum, Office of The Judge Advocate General of the Army, International and Operational Law Division, to US Army Armament Research, Development and Engineering Center, subject: Legal Review, Mk 211, MOD O, Cal. .50 Multipurpose Projectile, at 17 (14 Jan. 2000) cited in Maj. Donna Marie Verchio, *Just Say No! The SIRUS Project: Well-Intentioned, But Unnecessary and Superfluous*, 51 A.F. L. REV. 183, 226 n222 (2001).

31. *OpLaw Handbook*, at 17.

32. Memorandum, Office of The Judge Advocate General of the Army, International and Operational Law Division, to U.S. Army Armament Research, Development and Engineering Center, subject: Legal Review, Mk 211, MOD O, Cal. .50 Multipurpose

Projectile, at 17 (14 Jan. 2000) cited in Maj. Donna Marie Verchio, *Just Say No! The* SIRUS *Project: Well-Intentioned, But Unnecessary and Superfluous*, 51 A.F. L. REV. 183, 226 n222 (2001); *OpLaw Handbook*, at 18.

33. AP I Art. 51, para. 4.
34. *OpLaw Handbook*, at 13.
35. AP I Art. 51, para. 2 cited in *OpLaw Handbook*, at 14.
36. AP I Art. 51, para. 5(b).
37. Art. 2, common to all 4 Geneva Conventions; *OpLaw Handbook*, at 14.
38. DoD Directive 5100.77, para. 5.3.1.
39. Chairman of the Joint Chiefs of Staff Instruction 5810.01, para. 4.a., *OpLaw Handbook*, at 15.
40. FM 27–10, para. 507b.
41. FM 27–10, para. 501.
42. UCMJ Art. 18 states: General courts-martial have jurisdiction to try any person who by the Law of War is subject to trial by a military tribunal.
43. "War Crimes" are defined as (1) a grave breach in any of the international conventions signed at Geneva 12 August 1949, or any protocol to such convention to which the United States is a party; (2) prohibited by Article 23, 25, 27, or 28 of the Annex to the Hague Convention IV, Respecting the Laws and Customs of War on Land, signed 18 October 1907; (3) which constitutes a violation of Common Article 3 of the international conventions signed at Geneva, 12 August 1949, or any protocol to such convention to which the United States is a party and which deals with non-international armed conflict; or (4) of a person who, in relation to an armed conflict and contrary to the provisions of the Protocol on Prohibitions or Restrictions on the Use of Mines, Booby-Traps and Other Devices as amended at Geneva on 3 May 1996 (Protocol II as amended on 3 May 1996), when the United States is a party to such Protocol, willfully kills or causes serious injury to civilians.
44. See generally W. Hays Parks, *Book Review: The International Law Of Armed Conflict: Personal And Material Fields Of Application*, by Edward K. Kwakwa. Dordrecht, 26 GW J. INT'L L. & ECON. 675, 686 (1993); *OpLaw Handbook*, at 14.
45. See generally W. Hays Parks, *Book Review: The International Law Of Armed Conflict: Personal And Material Fields Of Application*, by Edward K. Kwakwa. Dordrecht, 26 GW J. INT'L L. & ECON. 675, 676 (1993); *OpLaw Handbook*, at 14.
46. Maj. Alex G. Peterson, *Order Out of Chaos: Domestic Enforcement of the Law of Internal Armed Conflict*, 171 Military Law Review, 1, 19–20 (March 2002).
47. Maj. Alex G. Peterson, *Order Out of Chaos: Domestic Enforcement of the Law of Internal Armed Conflict*, 171 Military Law Review, 1, 20 (March 2002).
48. *OpLaw Handbook*, at 36.
49. *OpLaw Handbook*, at 36.
50. DoD Dictionary, http://www.dtic.mil/doctrine/jel/doddict/data/r/index.html.
51. Karl Von Clausewitz, *On War* 87 (Michael Howard & Peter Paret eds. & trans., Princeton Univ. Press 1976) (1832) cited in Maj. Mark S. Martins, *Rules of Engagement for Land Forces: A Matter of Training, Not Lawyering*, 143 MIL L.R. 1, 34 (1994).

52. Dep't of Air Force, Project Contemporary Historical Evaluation For Combat Operations (CHECO) Report Rules Of Engagement 1 January 1966 1 November 1969 (1969), Reprinted In 131 Cong. Rec. 5248, 5249 (1986) [Hereinafter CHECO Report 1969]; Maj. Michael A. Burtin, United States Army Command And General Staff College, School Of Advanced Military Studies, Defense Technical Information File No. AD–A184 917, Rules Of Engagement: What Is The Relationship Between Rules Of Engagement And The Design Of Operations? 8 (1987); Morris, Supra Note 15, at 12–13 cited in Maj. Mark S. Martins, *Rules of Engagement for Land Forces: A Matter of Training, Not Lawyering*, 143 MIL L.R. 1, 34 (1994).
53. *OpLaw Handbook*, at 90.
54. *OpLaw Handbook*, at 90.
55. *OpLaw Handbook*, at 90.
56. *OpLaw Handbook*, at 90.
57. *OpLaw Handbook*, at 90.
58. *OpLaw Handbook*, at 93.
59. *OpLaw Handbook*, at 91.
60. *OpLaw Handbook*, at 91.
61. *OpLaw Handbook*, at 91.
62. *OpLaw Handbook*, at 91.
63. *OpLaw Handbook*, at 91–92.
64. *OpLaw Handbook*, at 92.
65. *OpLaw Handbook*, at 92; LTC Pamela Stahl et al, *Legal Lessons Learned from Afghanistan and Iraq, Vol. 1*, Center for Law and Military Operations, 1 Aug. 2004, at 97.
66. *OpLaw Handbook*, at 92.
67. AP I. Art. 52.
68. *OpLaw Handbook*, at 16.
69. *OpLaw Handbook*, at 16.
70. Geneva Convention III, Art. 4; Geneva Convention I, Art. 13; *OpLaw Handbook*, at 16.
71. *OpLaw Handbook*, at 16.
72. *OpLaw Handbook*, at 16.
73. *OpLaw Handbook*, at 16.
74. Geneva Convention I, Articles 12, 24; Geneva Convention II, Art. 12; AP I, Art. 51; *OpLaw Handbook*, at 17.
75. Emmanuel Gross, *Use of Civilians as a Human Shield: What Legal and Moral Restrictions Pertain to a War Waged by a Democratic State Against Terrorism?*, 33 Justice, 3, 9 (Autumn 2002).
76. Emmanuel Gross, *Use of Civilians as a Human Shield: What Legal and Moral Restrictions Pertain to a War Waged by a Democratic State Against Terrorism?*, 33 Justice, 3, 10 (Autumn 2002).
77. Jeff McMaHan, *Innocence, Self-Defense and Killing in War*, 3(3) The Journal of Philosophy, 193, 204 (1994) quoted in Emmanuel Gross, *Use of Civilians as a*

Human Shield: What Legal and Moral Restrictions Pertain to a War Waged by a Democratic State Against Terrorism?, 33 Justice, 3, 10 (Autumn 2002).

78. FM 27–10, para. 31 and Executive Order 12333, para. 2.11.
79. W. Hays Parks, *Memorandum of Law: Executive Order 12333 and Assassination*, Army Lawyer, 1, 4 (Dec. 1989); FM 27–10, para. 31, at 17; Maj. Tyler J. Harder, *Time to Repeal the Assassination Ban of Executive Order 12,333: A Small Step in Clarifying Current Law*, 172 Military Law Review, 1, 25 (June 2002).
80. AP I Art. 37(1).
81. AP I Art. 52(3).
82. *OpLaw Handbook*, at 22.
83. *OpLaw Handbook*, at 22.
84. Geneva Convention I, Art. 23 and 35.
85. FM 27–10, para. 257 and 258 and Geneva Convention I, Art. 19.
86. FM 27–10, para. 258.
87. *OpLaw Handbook*, at 23.
88. FM 27–10, para. 39 and 40, change 1.
89. *OpLaw Handbook*, at 22.
90. FM 27–10, para. 39.
91. FM 27–10, para. 43.
92. *OpLaw Handbook*, at 22.
93. HR Art. 27.
94. HR Art. 27.
95. *OpLaw Handbook*, at 23.
96. *OpLaw Handbook*, at 23.
97. AP I, Art. 56.
98. *OpLaw Handbook*, at 23.
99. AP I, Art. 56.
100. FM 27–10, para. 48.
101. FM 27–10, para. 51.
102. Rick Atkinson, *Crusade: The Untold Story of the Persian Gulf War* 331–33 (Houghton Mifflin 1993).
103. *OpLaw Handbook*, at 24 citing Geneva Convention III, Art. 93.
104. *OpLaw Handbook*, at 24.
105. Hague Convention IV, Annex Art. 53.
106. HR Art. 23(b); FM 27–10, para. 50.
107. Robert J. Bunker and John P. Sullivan, *Suicide Bombings in Operation Iraqi Freedom*, Institute of Land Warfare of the Association of the United States Army, Sept. 2004, at 12.
108. AP I Art. 37(1)(b).
109. FM 27–10, para. 50.
110. *OpLaw Handbook*, at 24.
111. *OpLaw Handbook*, at 25.
112. Army Regulation 27–53, Air Force Instruction 51–402 and SECNAVINST 5711.8A.

113. Army Regulation 27–53, Air Force Instruction 51–402 and SECNAVINST 5711.8A.
114. *OpLaw Handbook*, at 17.
115. *OpLaw Handbook*, at 17–18.
116. *OpLaw Handbook*, at 19.
117. http://www.state.gov/t/pm/wra/c11735.htm.
118. http://www.state.gov/t/pm/wra/c11735.htm.
119. Chemical Weapons Convention, Art. 1.
120. Chemical Weapons Convention, Art. 3–5.
121. Chemical Weapons Convention, Art. 1.
122. Executive Order 11850.
123. Executive Order 11850.
124. S. Exec. Res. 75 – Senate Report, s-3373 of 24 April 1997, section 2 – conditions, (26) – riot control agents cited in *OpLaw Handbook*, at 19.
125. DoD Directive 5100.77, para. 5.3.1.
126. *OpLaw Handbook*, at 27.
127. *OpLaw Handbook*, at 28.
128. Geneva Convention III, Art. 4(A)(4).
129. Geneva Convention III, Art. 4(A)(2)(d).
130. *OpLaw Handbook*, at 28.
131. *OpLaw Handbook*, at 28.
132. FM 27–10 para. 93.
133. FM 27–10 para. 93.
134. Geneva Convention III, Art. 25–32.
135. FM 27–10 para. 125.
136. FM 27–10 para. 125.
137. Geneva Convention III, Art. 49.
138. Geneva Convention III, Art. 13.
139. Geneva Convention III, Art. 16.
140. Geneva Convention III, Art. 15.
141. Geneva Convention III, Art. 3.
142. Geneva Convention III, Art. 81.
143. *OpLaw Handbook*, at 33.
144. Geneva Convention III, Art. 2.
145. *OpLaw Handbook*, at 28.
146. Presidential Military Order entitled: "Detention, Treatment and Trial of Certain Non-Citizens in the War Against Terrorism," Sec. 3 (November 13, 2001).
147. FM 27–10 para. 74.
148. FM 27–10 para. 74 and 504.
149. LTC Pamela Stahl et al, *Legal Lessons Learned from Afghanistan and Iraq, Vol. 1*, Center for Law and Military Operations, 1 Aug. 2004, at 64.
150. LTC Pamela Stahl et al, *Legal Lessons Learned from Afghanistan and Iraq, Vol. 1*, Center for Law and Military Operations, 1 Aug. 2004, at 64.
151. *OpLaw Handbook*, at 17.

130 *Yosefi M. Seltzer*

152. FM 27–10 para. 82.

153. FM 27–10 para. 82.

154. *See* January 22, 2002 NSC statement of U.S. policy regarding al-Qaeda and Taliban detainees referring to GC III Art. 4.

155. Statement by the Press Secretary on the Geneva Convention, Feb 7, 2002.

156. Statement by the Press Secretary on the Geneva Convention, Feb 7, 2002.

157. Statement by the Press Secretary on the Geneva Convention, Feb 7, 2002.

158. AP I, Articles 43 and 44.

159. *OpLaw Handbook*, at 472–473.

160. Presidential Military Order entitled: "Detention, Treatment and Trial of Certain Non-Citizens in the War Against Terrorism," Section 2(a)(1) (November 13, 2001).

161. Presidential Military Order entitled: "Detention, Treatment and Trial of Certain Non-Citizens in the War Against Terrorism," Section 4(a) (November 13, 2001).

162. DoD Military Commission Order (MCO) No. 1, August 31, 2005 superseded previous Military Commission Orders. More information can be found at: http://www.defenselink.mil/news/commissions.html.

163. DoD MCO No. 1, Aug. 31, 2005.

164. Charles Lane, *High Court to Hear Case on War Powers: Use of Military Panels For Detainees Is Tested*, Wash. Post, Nov. 8, 2005, at A1.

165. Josh White, *Abuse* Report Widens Scope of Culpability, Wash. Post, August 26, 2004, at A1, A16; Josh White and Thomas E. Ricks, Iraqi Teens Abused at Abu Ghraib, Report Finds, Wash. Post, August 24, 2004, at A1, A4; Sewell Chan, 2 Marines Guilty of Abusing Prisoner, Wash. Post, June 4, 2004, at A18; Rajiv Chandrasekaran and Scott Wilson, *Mistreatment Of Detainees Went Beyond Guards' Abuse*, Wash. Post, May 11, 2004, at A1, A13.

166. Christian Davenport, *England's Testimony; MPs Were Told To "Rough Them Up,"* Wash. Post, May 23, 2004, at A21.

167. Walter Pincus, *Iraq Tactics Have Long History With U.S. Interrogators*, Wash. Post, June 13, 2004, at A8.

168. For ample discussion, see Dana Priest and Bradley Graham, *U.S. Struggled Over How Far to Push Tactics*, Wash. Post, June 24, 2004, at A1, A6.

169. Dana Priest and R. Jeffrey Smith, *Memo Offered Justification for Use of Torture*, Wash. Post, June 8, 2004, at A1, A20.

170. Scott Higham, Joe Stephens and Josh White, *Prison Visits By General Reported In Hearing*, Wash. Post, May 23, 2004, at A1, A21.

171. Josh White, *Military Lawyers Fought Policy on Interrogations*, Wash. Post, July 15, 2005, at A1, A6.

172. R. Jeffrey Smith, *Documents Helped Sow Abuse, Army Report Finds*, Wash. Post, August 30, 2004, at A1, A17; Seymour M. Hersh, *Chain of Command*, New Yorker, May 17, 2004, 38–43.

173. Dave Moniz and Peter Eisler, *U.S. Missed Need for Prison Personnel in War Plans*, USA Today, June 15, 2004, at 8A (Of an active-duty force of roughly 500,000 sol-

diers, only about 1,000 are certified for prison guard duty with the vast majority posted in U.S. military prisons).

174. Christian Davenport, *England's Testimony; MPs Were Told To "Rough Them Up,"* Wash. Post, May 23, 2004, at A21.

175. Jess Bravin, *Pentagon Report Set Framework For Use of Torture,* Wall Street Journal, June 7, 2004, at A1, A17.

176. Ariana Eunjung Cha and Renae Merle, *Line Increasingly Blurred Between Soldiers and Civilian Contractors,* Wash. Post, May 13, 2004, at A1, A16.

177. The Military Extraterritorial Jurisdiction Act, (18 U.S.C. Sec. 3261) states in relevant part:

> Whoever engages in conduct outside the United States that would constitute an offense punishable by imprisonment for more than 1 year if the conduct had been engaged in within the special maritime and territorial jurisdiction of the United States – while employed by or accompanying the Armed Forces outside the United States; or while a member of the Armed Forces subject to chapter 47 of title 10 (the Uniform Code of Military Justice), shall be punished as provided for that offense.

178. Ellen McCarthy and Renae Merle, *Contractors and the Law; Prison Abuse Cases Renew Debate,* Wash. Post, Aug. 27, 2004, at E1, E4.

179. Renae Merle and Ellen McCarthy, *6 Employees From CACI International, Titan Referred for Prosecution,* Wash. Post, Aug. 26, 2004, at A18.

180. R. Jeffrey Smith, *Intelligence Personnel Are Implicated; Army Inquiry on Abuse Is Separate From Review By Schlesinger Panel,* Wash. Post, Aug. 25, 2004, at A13.

181. R. Jeffrey Smith, *Intelligence Personnel Are Implicated; Army Inquiry on Abuse Is Separate From Review By Schlesinger Panel,* Wash. Post, Aug. 25, 2004, at A13.

182. Bradley Graham and Josh White, *Top Pentagon Leaders Faulted in Prison Abuse; Oversight by Rumsfeld and Others Inadequate, Panel Says,* Wash. Post, Aug. 25, 2004, at A1, A12; Eric Schmitt, *Defense Leaders Faulted by Panel in Prison Abuse,* N.Y. Times, Aug. 24, 2004.

183. *Excerpts From the Schlesinger Report,* Wash. Post, Aug. 25, 2004, at A13.

184. Jackie Spinner, *Soldier: Unit's Role Was to Break Down Prisoners; Reservist Tells of Orders From Intelligence Officers,* Wash. Post, May 8, 2004, at A1, A16.

185. Seymour M. Hersh, *Torture at Abu Ghraib,* New Yorker, May 10, 2004, at 45; Seymour M. Hersh, *Chain of Command,* New Yorker, May 17, 2004, at 42–43.

186. Seymour M. Hersh, *The Gray Zone,* New Yorker, May 24, 2004, at 41.

187. Josh White, *Army, CIA Agreed on "Ghost" Prisoners,* Wash. Post, Mar. 11, 2005, at A16.

188. DoD Instruction 3020.41, Sec. 6.1.3.

189. Lindsey Graham, *Rules for Our War,* Wash. Post, Dec. 6, 2005, at A29.

190. Jane Mayer, *Outsourcing Torture,* New Yorker, Feb. 14 & 21, 2005, at 106–123; Dana Priest and Joe Stephens, *Secret World of U.S. Interrogation; Long History of Tactics in Overseas Prisons Is Coming to Light,* Wash. Post, May 11, 2004, at A1, A12; Peter Beinart, *TRB From Washington; Outsourcing,* The New Republic, May 31, 2004, at

6; Daniel Byman, *Reject the Abuses, Retain the Tactic*, Wash. Post, Apr. 17, 2005, at B1, B5.

191. Sewell Chan, *Pentagon Reinforces Policy for Reporting Deaths of Detainees*, Wash. Post, June 11, 2004, at A18.

192. Josh White, *Reservist Sentenced to 3 Years for Abu Ghraib Abuse*, Wash. Post, Sept. 28, 2005, at A12; Jennifer McMenamin, *England given 3 years in abuse at Iraq prison*, Balt. Sun, Sept. 28, 2005.

193. Craig Whitlock, *Islamic Radicals Behead American; In Saudi Arabia Kidnap Victim's Body Is Found Near Capital*, Wash. Post, June 19, 2004, at A1.

194. www.Foxnews.com, *Militants Behead American Hostage in Iraq*, (Fox News, May 11, 2004).

195. Hague Convention IV Art. 42.

196. Geneva Convention IV, Art. 47.

197. Hague Convention IV, Art. 45.

198. *OpLaw Handbook*, at 30.

199. Hague Convention IV, Art. 43.

200. *OpLaw Handbook*, at 30.

201. Geneva Convention IV, Art. 78.

202. Geneva Convention IV, Art. 72 and 73.

203. Geneva Convention IV, Art. 46–63.

204. Geneva Convention IV, Art. 49.

205. Geneva Convention IV, Art. 50.

206. Geneva Convention IV, Art. 51.

207. Geneva Convention IV, Art. 51.

208. FM 27–10, para. 59 and 396; Hague Convention IV, Annex Art. 53; U.S. Constitution Art. I, Sec. 8, Clause 11.

209. Hague Convention IV, Art. 23(g).

210. Geneva Convention IV, Art. 53.

211. FM 27–10 para. 56.

212. *See* Geneva Convention IV, Art. 53 concerning the permissible extent of destruction in occupied areas, cited in FM 27–10 para. 56.

213. Annex to Hague Convention IV Art. 47; Geneva Convention I, Art. 15; Geneva Convention II, Art. 18 and Geneva Convention IV, Art. 33.

214. FM 27–10, para. 412.

215. FM 27–10, para. 412; Annex to Hague Convention IV, Art. 52.

216. FM 27–10, para. 163.

217. Hague Convention IV, Art. 23(g).

218. Geneva Convention IV, Art. 53.

"What is this Bleeting of Sheep in My Ears": Spoils of War / Wars that Spoil

Moshe Sokolow

PREFACE:[1]

The title of this essay comprises the challenge that the prophet Shemuel issued to King Shaul (1 Samuel 15:14) to justify his actions in sparing the life of Agag, King of Amalek, and helping himself to the spoils of Amalek. The permission or prohibition of spoils of war serves in this essay as a code word for the concern of ancient, medieval, and contemporary Jewish law and ethics with the often irreversible and irremediable consequences of the force of martial arms.

The essay focuses, in a series of parallel inquiries, on: the Biblical textual evidence and its straightforward, contextual,

Interpretation; the subsequent development of these texts in Talmud, Midrash, and medieval *parshanut* (exegesis); and the treatment
of militarism and morality in modern and contemporary Jewish
thought.

A. ARE SPOILS OF WAR PERMISSIBLE?
THE BIBLICAL EVIDENCE[2]

Taking spoils is generally permitted by the Torah. Indeed, we are
enjoined to "enjoy the spoils of your enemy which the Lord your
God gives you" (Deut. 20:14).[3] This principle was practiced by the
Israelites throughout the Biblical period. After the battle against
Midian, the Israelites plundered, "all their animals, and all their
livestock, and all their wealth" (Numbers 31:9), and after defeating
Og, King of the Bashan, they "retained as booty all the cattle and
the spoil of the towns" (Deut. 3:7).[4] During the time of Yehoshua,
"the Israelites took the cattle and the spoil of the city [Ai] as their
booty, in accordance with the instructions that the Lord had given
Yehoshua" (Joshua 8:27). King David and his officers "dedicated
some of the booty of the wars to maintain the house of the Lord"
(1 Chr. 26:27),[5] after a rout of the Cushites during the reign of King
Asa "very much spoil was taken" (2 Chr. 14:12), and following King
Yehoshafat's great victory over Ammon, Moab, and Se'ir, we are told
that "for three days they were taking booty, there was so much of
it" (ibid., 20:25).[6]

    In practice, soldiers and noncombatants shared the spoils.
After the battle against Midian, God instructed Moshe to "take an
accounting of the spoils" and to divide them equally between the
soldiers and the rest of the community (Numbers 31:25 ff).[7] King
David subsequently made it an official policy, declaring: "The share
of those who took to battle and the share of those who remained in
the rear will be equal" (1 Samuel 30:24). The only exceptions were
the Levites, who received no share at all.[8]

*　*　*

On the other hand, six specific incidents in the Bible restrict or
denounce the enjoyment of spoils.

(1) When Abraham returned from his successful pursuit of the four Mesopotamian kings, the King of Sedom offered him the property of Sedom and Amorah in exchange for the people whom he had rescued. Abraham issued a flat refusal, declining to accept even a token of his victory, saying: "I swear to the Lord, God Most High, Creator of heaven and earth, that I will not take so much as a thread[9] or a sandal strap, lest you say, 'It is I who made Avram rich,'" "*im mi-hut ve-ad serokh na'al ve-im ekah mi-kol asher lakh*" (Gen. 14:22–23).

(2) After Shimon and Levi avenged their sister Dinah's honor by slaying the men of Shekhem, they plundered the town ("*Benei Yaakov ba'u al ha-halalim va-yavozu ha-ir asher tim'u et ahotam,*" Gen. 34:27).[10] Yaakov was incensed by their behavior and condemned his sons for dishonoring and endangering him: "You have brought trouble on me (*akhartem oti*), making me odious among the inhabitants of the land" (Gen. 34:30). He promptly demanded of his household to get rid of the spoils and undergo ritual purification (35:2).

(3) The punishment of a subverted city (*ir niddahat*) is extremely harsh. The guilty inhabitants, along with their cattle, are put to the sword and all that is inside the city is "proscribed" ("*herem,*" Deut. 13:16). We must "burn the town and all its spoil" (ibid., 17), and beware "let nothing that has been proscribed stick to your hand" (ibid., 18).

(4) Just before the walls of Yeriho are toppled, Yehoshua orders the people, on the pain of death, to "beware of that which is proscribed" ("*herem,*" Joshua 6:18), lest "you will cause the camp of Israel to be proscribed and bring calamity (*akhartem*) upon it" ibid.).[11]

(5) On the eve of Shaul's battle against Agag, Shemuel orders the proscription of everything Amalekite. "Spare no one, but kill alike men and women, infants and suckling, oxen and sheep, camels and asses" (2 Samuel 15:3).[12] And when he rebukes Shaul for his "defiance of the Lord's will" (ibid., 19), Shemuel levels the specific accusation of "why did you swoop down on the spoil?" ("*va-ta'at el ha-shalal,*" ibid.).

(6) Finally, the Jews of Persia declined to plunder their enemies (Esther 8:11). While they exercised their right of self-defense, the Jews "did not lay hands on the spoil" (*bizzah*) neither in Shushan proper (ibid., 9:10), nor in the provinces (ibid., 16).

From all of the above cases, it appears that while sharing spoils is essentially sanctioned, the exercise of that right is frequently curtailed and even denounced. Twice (*ir niddahat* and Amalek) we find looting called "evil in God's eyes" (i.e., defiance of His will), and refraining from looting is called "correct in God's eyes." Twice (Abraham and Mordekhai-Esther), an individual and a community are cited approvingly for declining to benefit from spoils which were rightfully theirs,[13] and in two additional cases (Shekhem and Yeriho), the illegal or dubious acquisition of spoils is denounced as defiling and calamitous.

B. AN EXPLANATION

Why were these exceptions made to the rule of spoils?

(1) The treatments of both Amalek and the *ir niddahat* are sufficiently alike[14] to allow an explanation in common: An effective way to eradicate infamy is to obliterate everything with which it was associated. The mere relationship of possession to possessor suffices, in such cases, to transfer the stigma that attached to one onto the other. To belong to an Amalekite, or to a subverted city, is, axiomatically, to suffer its fate and its consequences.

(2) Yaakov's vilification of his sons over despoiling Shekhem and Yehoshua's excoriation of Akhan for looting Yeriho (Joshua 7:19 ff.), also share an explanation: sullying the name and reputation of Israel among the gentiles. Yaakov was concerned with the impression the incident would leave on the neighboring Canaanites and Perizites, and feared that the righteous justification for the execution of the town's males, "Should our sister be treated like a whore?" (Gen. 34:31) – would be compromised if it were to become known that his sons had seemingly turned noble revenge into personal profit.[15]

Yeriho, like Shekhem before it, marked the Israelites' first contact with the indigenous population of their land. God had originally promised that "all the peoples of the earth shall see that the Lord's name is proclaimed over you, and they shall stand in fear of you" (Deut. 28:10). Yehoshua, like Yaakov, conscious of first impressions, decreed that "all the silver and gold and objects of copper and iron are consecrated (*kodesh*) to the Lord" (Joshua 6:19). Were even one Israelite to realize personal gain therefrom, the gentile nations would lose their awe of Israel's aura of divinely ordained purpose, making the task of the conquest all the more arduous and costly, a premonition realized all too well at the Ai.[16]

A significant linguistic link between Yaakov and Yehoshua consists of the verb *akhar* (cf. c2), to cause calamity, which features prominently in both episodes.[17]

(3) The antithesis of taking spoils illegally is declining to share in legitimate spoils, and that is the counterpoint provided by the examples of Abraham and Mordekhai-Esther to the incidents of Shekhem, Yeriho, and Amalek.

Abraham spurns a share of the wealth he recovered. He says gallantly: "For me, nothing but what my servants have used up" (Gen. 14:24), deferring entirely to his allies. "As for the share of the men who went with me – Aner, Eshkol, and Mamre – let them take their share" (ibid.).[18] While virtue is, proverbially, its own reward, the Torah hastens to point out in the very next verse that "some time later the word of the Lord came to Abram in a vision, saying, "Fear not, Abram...Your reward shall be very great" (ibid., 15:1).

The Megillah of Esther emphasizes reversals, one of which is the matter of the spoils.[19] The king's original instructions regarding the 13th of Adar massacre of "all the Jews, young and old, children and women" (3:13) included the provision, "to plunder their possessions" (*u-shelalam la-voz*; ibid.), and so it was proclaimed as law (3:14). When the tables are turned, a law, identical in every detail, is again promulgated, now empowering the Jews to massacre and exterminate their attackers "together with women and children" (8:11), and

providing the right "to plunder their possessions" (*u-shelalam la-voz*;
ibid.). The Jews of Persia and Media, like their forefather Abraham,
repudiate the right and spurn the spoils. They content themselves
with "light and gladness, happiness and honor" (8:16).[20]

C. MIDRASH AND PARSHANUT

The denunciation of plunder is sharpened in the Midrash and in
medieval Biblical exegesis. In each of these six cases, the point is
made and reiterated that spoils of war have a corruptive and corrosive influence on ethical, moral, and, ultimately, halakhic behavior.
Concomitantly, the sources expand the approbation awarded for
restraint from rightful spoils.

(1) Abraham's marshalling his forces prior to pursuing the four kings
is referred to by the Torah as "*va-yarek et hanikhav*" (Gen. 14:14;
JPS: "he mustered his retainers"), on which the Midrash elaborates
by focusing on the antonymic meanings of *va-yarek*: to fill and to
empty: "Rabbi Simeon ben Lakish says: He filled them up with precious stones and pearls."[21] For what purpose, ask the Tosafot? "So
that they would not be motivated by money, but concerned [only]
with rescuing lives."[22]

(2) Yaakov's condemnation of his sons (*akhartem oti*) is interpreted
in one Midrash as "the barrel contained clear water and you sullied
it,"[23] and another Midrash, extending the metaphor, adds that "the
essence of *akhar* is a kind of confusion; something that complicates
the peace and restores strife."[24]

Yaakov feared the danger to his sons from within themselves as
much as he feared the danger that now threatened his family from
the neighboring tribes; he was aware of the potentially disruptive and
contaminating effect which morally dubious behavior has on those
whose practice it. As a third Midrash comments on this selfsame
process of moral deterioration: "He who spills gentile blood will
eventually shed Jewish blood, while the Torah was given to sanctify
His great name."[25]

As we shall discuss below (D7), the strife which was initiated by the brothers' act of *akhar* was fraternal, and its disastrous consequence was these same brothers' subsequent attempt to murder Yosef.[26]

(3) The spoils of the *ir niddahat*, as noted above, were to be utterly destroyed. "Let nothing which has been doomed stick to your hand…in order that the Lord may turn from His blazing anger and show you compassion…for you will be heeding the Lord your God" (Deut. 13:18–13). The Mishnah (*Sanhedrin* 10:6) comments: "For as long as evildoers exist (God's) anger exists. Once the evildoers perish, the anger disappears."

And the Gemara (*Sanhedrin* 113b) adds: "Who are these evildoers? Rav Yosef says: thieves."

Difficult as it may be to imagine, it was suspected that there were unscrupulous people who would even stoop to steal the spoils of an *ir niddahat*. Such infamy, it was feared, would reignite God's indignation, which would remain kindled until the thieves were caught and punished.

In the context of our suggestion that righteousness is undermined by ungainly personal profit (b2, c6), it pays to note the continuation of the Mishnah, which instructs:

> Property held by the righteous who reside within that city is to be destroyed, while that held by those who reside outside the city is to be spared.[27]

The Gemara asks:

> Why does the Torah require that property held within the city by righteous residents must be destroyed? Since their money motivated them to live there in the first place, let it be destroyed.[28]

According to this Gemara, even the righteous suffer on account of their association with the city. While they are personally spared the fate of its guilty inhabitants, they must pay a price for having allowed monetary considerations to override their moral sensibilities. To own property within a corrupt and potentially subverted society is not, by itself, actionable; to reside within that city in order to oversee that property and enhance its value, however, is an offense which requires retribution.

(4) When Israel suffers a reversal at Ai, God's message to Yehoshua is that it is the consequence of sin. "They have stolen; they have broken faith! …I will not be with you any more unless you root out from among you what is proscribed" (Joshua 7:11–12). Yehoshua casts lots among all the tribes, clans, and houses, eventually singling out Akhan as the perpetrator. "Tell me," he says to Akhan, "what you have done" (v. 19). According to the Midrash, Akhan confesses:

> "It is true; I have sinned against the Lord" (v. 20). Not this alone, but I have trespassed (*ma'al*) against other (spoils) before. Yehoshua said: "Do not hold anything back from me" (v. 19). Akhan replied: "I saw among the spoil…" (v. 21); I saw what was written in the Torah: "And enjoy the spoil of your enemy" (Deut. 20:14). And do not think that I acted out of poverty for I am the richest man in my tribe. Right away, "Yehoshua sent messengers…to the tent…and displayed (the spoils) before the Lord" (vs. 22–23). Yehoshua said before God: 'Master of the universe. These are the things that prompted Your anger against Your children. Here they are'! Yehoshua acted on his own initiative and God concurred, and His anger was removed from Israel.[29]

Akhan failed to understand that Yehoshua's specific ban on the spoils of Yeriho[30] superseded the Torah's general sanction of plunder and for this he, and all of Israel, were punished. Only when Akhan is put to death, "and all Israel pelted him with stones" (v. 25), is the situation remedied and, as promised by the Mishnah cited above, "the anger of the Lord subsided" (v. 26).

(5) Citing Yaakov's blessing to Shaul's ancestor, Binyamin, the Mi-

drash equates "In the evening he divides the spoil" (*yehallek shalal*; Gen. 49:7), with "Shaul died for the trespass (*ma'al*) that he had committed against the Lord in not having fulfilled the command of the Lord" (1 Chr. 10:13).[31] Of that trespass, another Midrash notes:

> Rabbi Eliezer ha-Moda'i says: God swore upon His throne not to leave a single descendant of Amalek beneath heaven, in order that people should never say "this camel is Amalekite, this sheep is Amalekite."[32]

Assuming God's oath is a metaphor for sacrosanctity, Rabbi Eliezer's interpretation is clearly aligned with the Biblical text in which Shemuel's denunciation of Shaul for plundering Amalek[33] is described as "defiance of the Lord's will" (*ha-ra be-einei Hashem*; 1 Samuel 15:19).

Medieval *parshanut* expands upon the Midrash. Abrabanel, for one, comments:

> The verse: "the memory (*zekher*) of Amalek" (Deut. 25:19) indicates that nothing shall remain of them, nor should their spoils be taken, so that the name of Amalek should no longer be remembered…This [verse] is truly whence Shemuel derived [his order to Shaul], "proscribe all that is theirs" (1 Samuel 15:3), as clearly as though God had expressly commanded him in this respect[34]…in order that no one should think that this war was like all others in which spoils, booty, and slaves were to be taken. He commanded the proscription of everything so that anyone hearing how the Israelites enjoyed none of the spoils would recognize and understand that their only intention was proscription on account of what Amalek did to Israel upon their exodus from Egypt.[35]

(6) The Talmud saw Mordekhai and Esther's confrontation with Haman as compensation and atonement for Shaul's mishandling of Agag and Amalek:

What did the Judean (*Yehudi*) do to me, and how did the
Benjaminite (*Yemini*) repay me?…David declined to kill Shim'i
[ben Gera], from whom Mordekhai was descended…Shaul
failed to kill Agag, from whom Haman, the oppressor of Israel,
was descended.[36]

Medieval exegesis extends this comparison a step further. Ralbag [Gersonides] writes:

It appears that the intention behind proscribing Amalek, as
per God's command to Israel not to benefit from any of their
possessions, was to underscore the fact that the divine intention was only revenge for what Amalek did to Israel upon their
exodus from Egypt…to deter others from committing the same
evil…But when Shaul and Israel took the spoils, they demonstrated that their intention was not revenge but selfish gain (*le-
ho'il le-atzmam*), and this contradicted the divine will. It would
appear that it was precisely for this reason that the Jews, during
the time of Mordekhai and Esther, restrained themselves from
taking any of the spoils of their enemies. [37]

Similarly, Rabbi Bahya:

The straightforward meaning of "hand upon the throne of
the Lord" (Exodus 17:19) is that God requires every reigning
king of Israel to take an oath to wage the Lord's war against
Amalek. This means that all the spoils of this war are forbidden
to be enjoyed (*asur be-hana'ah*); they all belong to God and
not to man. This is why Shaul was punished…and this is why
Mordekhai took care not to enjoy the spoils of Haman, who
was a descendant of Amalek.[38]

In Partial Summary:
Abraham pays his soldiers in advance lest the desire for booty become an obstacle to the rescue operation. Yaakov condemns the

looting of Shekhem for the dangerous precedent it established of adulterating moral rectitude with monetary gain. Thieves were not beyond looting even an *ir niddahat* after its population was executed, incurring a divine wrath which subsided only with their elimination[39] – as further attested by the kindred case of Akhan at Yeriho. Finally, Shaul's error in allowing the plunder of Amalek leads to his downfall, and requires a compensatory act of restraint on the part of his descendants, Mordekhai and Esther.

D. MODERN JEWISH THOUGHT:
PURITY OF ARMS, PURITY OF PURPOSE

The following Midrash provides a fascinating, albeit problematic, precedent for the modern and contemporary clarification of the moral dilemmas occasioned by the various calls to arms in Jewish history:

> "Don't overdo goodness and don't act the wise man to excess" (Eccl. 7:16). This applies to Shaul when he "advanced as far as the city of Amalek" (1 Sam. 15:5). Rav Huna and Rav Benaya said that (Shaul) began to debate with his Creator, saying: God said, "Now go and attack Amalek" (op. cit., v.3). [Shaul countered:] Even if the men (of Amalek) sinned, did the women sin? Did the children? Did the cattle, oxen, and donkeys sin? A heavenly voice came out and said: "Don't overdo goodness" beyond your Creator.[40]

Since none of the preceding soliloquy is explicit in the Biblical text – and little else is even implicit – it would appear that the moral reservations it expresses are more likely those of the *darshanim* than of Shaul. Caught on the horns of a moral dilemma of their own making, they introduce the notions of absolute and relative morality in order to resolve the conflict they have themselves created between Shaul's ostensibly laudable moral stance and the immutable historical fact of his chastisement and punishment. Shaul, they submit, was "*overly* righteous." In other circumstances, questioning the morality of slaying women, children, and animals, would be commendable;[41] in the face of an absolute divine imperative, however, it becomes an unpardonable act of hubris.

Moreover, from the conclusion drawn in the continuation of this Midrash, it appears that misplaced moralizing becomes, paradoxically, demoralizing:[42]

> Rabbi Simeon ben Lakish says: Whoever acts compassionately where cruelty is called for will eventually act cruelly when compassion is required. And where did [Shaul] act cruelly instead of compassionately? To wit: "And he [Shaul] put Nob, city of priests, to the sword" (1 Sam. 22:19), and Nob should not have been treated like the seed of Amalek.[43]

The Sages add: Whoever acts compassionately where cruelty is called for, will eventually be called to account. To wit: "And Shaul and his three sons died" (1 Sam. 31:6).

*   *   *

In the last section of this essay we shall examine several modern and contemporary analogues to the deliberation imputed to Shaul by the Talmud and Midrash. Based upon some of the same episodes and proof texts cited in the previous sections, these writers display similar moral sensitivity and exhibit similar despair over the contamination of moral rectitude through the wanton lust for spoils and the exercise of power.

(1) Samson Raphael Hirsch comments:

> The contrast with Amalek is necessary for the education of Israel and the development of its own identity until it reaches perfection.[44]

The nature of that perfection lies in the eventual triumph of divinely ordained morality over the situational ethic imposed by the force of arms. He continues:

Not Amalek, per se, but the memory and legend of Amalek, betoken evil to the moral future of humanity. As long as mankind's annals sing the praises of military heroes; as long as those who stifle and destroy human satisfaction are not doomed to oblivion; untold generations will look admiringly upon those warriors and encourage their emulation in praise of violent deeds.

Amalek's reign in this world will come to an eventual and final end only when divine morality becomes the sole criterion for deeds large and small, and the recognition of morality increases in the world in equal, not opposite, proportion to greatness and strength. As man's greatness and valor increase, so shall the guilt he will bear for transgressing the laws of morality, and the crimes of mighty nations will be detested the more their perpetrators grow powerful.

In effect, this is the ultimate purpose of God's supervision of history.[45]

(2) On Abraham's "arming" of his men (c1) the Talmud noted:

Rav Abahu said in the name of Rav Elazar: Why was our patriarch Abraham punished and his descendants oppressed by Egypt for 210 years? Because he impressed [Torah] scholars (*talmidei hakhamim*) into military service (*angaria*).[46]

Andre Neher elaborates:

In arming his disciples, he was necessarily emptying them of the content of the Torah in which he had for years been educating (training, initiating) them.[47]

And of the *amora* Shemuel's view: "He filled them with gold" (*horikan be-zahav*), he adds:

He overlaid them with precious stones in order that their objective should be disembarrassed (purged, emptied) of every spirit of booty hunting, and might find its one and only proper motivation in the will to rescue those in danger. That is to say, Abraham was at pains to eliminate all lure of economic advantage – the factor that constitutes an accessory inducement to go to war, as potent as it is criminal.[48]

(3) The Midrash explains that the "tools of lawlessness" (*kelei hamas*; Gen. 49:5), for which Yaakov excoriates Shimon and Levi, refer to implements of war "stolen" from Esav,[49] and it metaphorically transforms the sword and bow with which Yaakov "took" the city of Shekhem from the Amorites (Gen, 48:22) into *mitzvot* and "good deeds" (*maʿasim tovim*).[50] Neher adds:

> What they (Targum, Midrash, and Talmud) are concerned is to avoid the ethically embarrassing association of Yaakov's name and Yaakov's achievements with an enterprise that was, from start to finish, one of violence…. And so, by dint of weeding the episode of Shekhem right out of the text, there is achieved one of the finest pieces of pacifist transmutation effected by Jewish exegetical alchemy. [51]

(4) The condemnation of "the hands of Esav" is echoed by Yeshayahu Leibowitz:

> Therefore in our moral-religious soul searching, we neither justify nor apologize for wartime bloodshed, per se (in which our own blood was shed more than our enemies'). The great problem arises in the manner of the conduct of the war – which continues unabated to this day – and of what follows it. The problem is great and complex. Since permission has been granted us for the "profession of Esav" (*umanuto shel Esav*), the distinction between permitted and forbidden, justifiable and unconscionable, has become very fine…and it is incumbent upon us to check and examine whether we have crossed the line or not.[52]

(5) In this same vein, Irving Greenberg has written:

> The bitter Jewish experience (of the Diaspora, in general, and
> the Holocaust, in particular) taught that while it is true that
> "power corrupts, and absolute power corrupts absolutely," ab-
> solute powerlessness corrupts even more...
>
> On the other hand, given the corrupting effects of power,
> Jews cannot be given a blank check in that exercise any more
> than any other group. It is racism to believe that Jews are
> congenitally incapable of doing evil to others.... If memories
> of the Holocaust are only used to justify Jewish behavior and
> never to challenge and judge it, then it will be dismissed as
> propaganda.
>
> The memory of our past torment must lead us to greater
> efforts to treat others with consideration and ethical sensitiv-
> ity.[53]

(6) R. Ahron Soloveichik discusses several moral and halakhic
ramifications of the episode involving Shaul and Agag. Among
them is the matter of the *kal va-homer* (*a fortiori* inference) from
the law of the broken-necked heifer (*eglah arufah*: Deut. 21:1ff),
which is imputed to Shaul by both the Talmud and Midrash:[54] "If
in the case of a single victim [of homicide] the Torah requires an
eglah arufah, how much more so must all those [Amalekite] lives
[require atonement]?"

Rav Ahron asks:

> It appears strange that Shaul had to resort to the Halakhah of
> *eglah arufah* to prove that murder is to be abhorred. Why could
> he not have proven his point from "do not murder" (*lo tirtzah*)
> or "do not stand [idly] upon the blood of your neighbor" (Lev.
> 19:16)?[55]

His answer is based upon the Talmudic interpretation of the "confession" of the city elders (Deut. 22:7):

We do not assume that the slain person was killed illegally. We assume that he was starving and attempted armed robbery in order to obtain food. The one attacked could have surrendered his money and prevented [the] killing. The Torah, however, took into account human frailty and anticipated that a person would defend his own money. Since a burglar shows himself capable of murder in case his intended victim offers resistance, the Torah permits killing a robber. Such a killing is suspected when an *eglah arufah* is brought. The killing was not forbidden, but it would have been better for a man not to kill in defense of property. *Kapparah* (atonement) through *eglah arufah* is required.

Thus Shaul saw from *eglah arufah* that killing, even where permitted, is better avoided.[56]

(7) On the occasion of the discovery of the Jewish "underground" (*mahteret*) in 1984, Rabbi Yehudah Shaviv wrote in *Nekudah*, the organ of the settlements in Judea, Samaria, and Gaza:

It is surprising to find Yaakov first offering piercing moral criticism of Shimon and Levi (Gen. 49:5–7) only many years after the fact…Why didn't he react at the time of the incident? Why, at that time, did he raise only pragmatic concerns (i.e., Gen. 34:30)?

The answer can be found in both the text and its exegesis. It is written: "For in anger they slew men (*hargu ish*) and at their pleasure they maimed oxen (*ikkru shor*)" (Gen. 49:6), on which Rashi, following the Sages, comments: "'Men' refers to Hamor and the people of Shekhem; 'Oxen' means that they sought to maim Yosef, who was called 'Ox' (cf. Deut. 33:17)."

Not for naught did Yaakov combine these two different and distant events, for he saw a line leading directly from the slaying of the men of Shekhem to the desire to kill Yosef. True, the men of Shekhem deserved to die; but that was not why Shimon and Levi slew them. They were seeking a release for their rage and anger.

Whoever feels free to let his anger out even on guilty gentiles will ultimately try to commit fratricide, for rage has no bounds and no limits. Whoever breaches the walls of morality in an all-consuming rage will ultimately breach it entirely, and something which began in rage and in anger will turn into deliberate action; to, God forbid, an accepted norm of life.

One who kills a gentile in anger, will eventually try to kill a Jew, deliberately.[57]

E. AMALEK AS THE EVIL WITHIN US

R. Shaviv's focus on the pernicious effects which unregulated violence ultimately unleashes on its own perpetrators leads us to the contemplation of a final theme: Amalek, the evil within us. The proposition embodied in this theme is that the externalization of evil is but an immature and preliminary step to the eventual, mature, recognition that the real source of evil resides within us and that it is evil internalized that most sorely needs extirpation.[58]

Nowhere is this theme developed with greater pathos and poignancy than in the sermon delivered in the Warsaw Ghetto on *Shabbat Zakhor*, 1942, by R. Kalonymos Shapira. Basing himself on the text of the *Mekhilta*: "Neither the name nor the throne [of God] is complete until the seed (*zera*) of Amalek is destroyed,"[59] he asks:

It should have stated: "Until Amalek is destroyed." [The seed of Amalek] implies until we destroy what Amalek implants (*zorea*) in us, because those seeds remain even after Amalek itself is destroyed.

The Sabbath, profaned by so many of Israel, God forbid, under the duress of Amalek's persecution, will remain profaned by many of them, and its sanctity violated, for a long time to come...The abstention from forbidden foods will not be observed so scrupulously by so many of them if, God forbid, they fail in its observance in the time of Amalek. And will those youngsters who are forced to miss Torah study, who don't know whether they are still alive because of their anguish and persecution, God forbid, will they ever return to their prior preoccupation with the Torah?[60]

Afterword:

The contemporary significance of the sources and interpretations we have cited is abundantly clear. Even while engaged in morally defensible, even halakhically mandated activities, a Jew must be ever vigilant to maintain his singularity of purpose, and on constant guard against its adulteration or erosion.[61] The eradication of Amalek from without must always be accompanied by the extirpation of the Amalek within. As the martyred R. Shapira concluded his sermon:

> Even after Amalek is destroyed, neither His name nor His throne is complete until the seed of Amalek, the seeds it implants in us, are destroyed. Therefore He said: "I shall surely destroy" (*mahoh emheh*; Ex. 17:14) because the doubling of the verb indicates immediacy…"I shall surely destroy," speedily, so that not many seeds will remain behind.[62]

An Ethico-Halakhic Epilogue:

What justifies the taking of spoils in the first place? Granted that it is practiced universally, but what legal and moral grounds sanction spoils of war rather than proscribe them as grand larceny?[63]

Rapaport (op. cit.) cites a responsum[64] which justifies the royal practice of granting charters (fiefdoms?) on the grounds that "it is the right of kings (*hok ha-melakhim*) upon forcibly conquering a country in war, that all houses, fields and vineyards belong to [the king] and the people become his tributaries," linking this to a provision made by Rambam (*Gezeilah* 5:13), which exempts royal expropriation from the category of larceny (*einah gezel*). Accordingly, Rapaport writes:

> Two principles underlie acquisition by acts of war. (A) brute force (*ha-koah ve-ha-alimut*), in which the victor overcomes the vanquished by "force of arms" (*ba-koah ha-milhamah*);

(B) the fact that the force is exercised by a king, rather than by a private individual, constituting "the right of kings." Clearly, the king, in this context, represents the entire public...and personifies it...There is, therefore, a fundamental partnership of two principals in the acquisition of spoils. (A) the public, by means of the king; (B) the soldiers and their camp who constitute the source of the "force of arms." [65]

Based on the last stated principle, the sanction and division of spoils of war in the contemporary period would follow historical precedent in some respects and diverge in others. With the state, rather than the king, representing and personifying the public, a constitutionally declared war would entitle the exercise of "the right of kings" and the expropriation of spoils, in general, would therefore be sanctioned.

The division of the spoils, however, would present a novel twist. In the pre-modern period, soldiers were entitled to their personal share in half of the spoils because they fought with private, personal weapons and therefore constituted an independent element in the sanctioning equation called "the force of arms." With all weapons of war today – including side arms! – being the property of the state, soldiers must be regarded as agents of the state – rather than "independent contractors" – and their automatic entitlement to spoils would be questionable.

While the state – like the king – has the option of awarding spoils to individual soldiers, "there would, in any event, be a prohibition of larceny on any soldier who helped himself to any spoils or plunder."[66]

TOHAR HA-NESHEK: SPOILS OF WAR AND THE PURITY OF ARMS

The following is the operative definition of looting and spoils of war that is in current force in the Israel Defense Forces.[67]

Looting

Looting is the theft of enemy property (private or public) by individual soldiers for private purposes. In ancient times, conflicting conceptions were held. On the one hand, the Bible presents an approach that sees looting as a negative act, as, for instance, in the Akhan Affair (Joshua, 7), in which Akhan was put to death because he had taken of the consecrated spoils. On the other hand, looting was permitted in other civilizations, and even served as a means for the ruler to generate motivation among the soldiers to fight, as they looked forward to the looting.

Today, at any rate, looting is absolutely prohibited. The Hague Conventions forbid looting in the course of battle as well as in occupied territory. The Geneva Conventions contain provisions banning the looting of the wounded, sick, shipwrecked, civilians, and cultural property. Looting is regarded as a despicable act that tarnishes both the soldier and the IDF, leaving a serious moral blot. Section 74 of the Military Jurisdiction Law forbids looting, prescribing a punishment of ten years' imprisonment in respect thereof. During the Galilee War, there were unfortunately cases of looting of civilians in Lebanon, including a case where even officers – a major and captain – were demoted to the rank of private and given a long prison term.

Spoils of War:

Over the years, the weapons arsenal of the IDF has grown as a result of capturing spoils courtesy of the Arab armies. Some of them, such as the RPG and Kalashnikov, the T-54, "Ziel" trucks, and 130 mm guns were even introduced into operational use in the IDF.

Other interesting items include an Iraqi MIG 21 plane, whose pilot defected to Israel, and guns captured in the Yom Kippur War and subsequently directed against the Egyptians. The crowning achievement was the case involving the capture of an Egyptian radar coach in the War of Attrition, brought intact to Israel.

One must distinguish between looting and taking spoils of war. Seized weapons, facilities, and property belonging to the enemy's army or state become the property of the seizing state. Private property that does not belong to the state is immune to seizure and conversion to booty. Nevertheless, a military commander is allowed to seize private property if this serves an important military need.

For example, a commander may commandeer a civilian vehicle to evacuate wounded urgently or take possession of a house porch if this is necessary for carrying out surveillance.

NOTES

1. An earlier, partial version of this essay appeared in *Maʾayanot* vol. XI, "On Teaching *Tanakh*" (1985; Hebrew), 194 ff.
2. We will concern ourselves only with "spoils of war," i.e., booty taken from Israel's vanquished enemies after battle, and not with such treasures as may have come into Israelite possession by default, such as the Egyptian loot that surfaced after the drowning in the sea (*bizzat ha-yam*) and the hidden "Amorite" treasures they were destined to discover, unaided, in the homes of the conquered peoples. See Deut. 6:10–11, *Hullin* 17a, and *Bava Metz'ia* 25b.
3. Radbaz (Responsa, vol. 4, #205), in an attempt to rehabilitate – as witnesses for a bill of divorce – people who commit larceny against gentiles (*geneivat ha-akum*) suggests that this verse may be interpreted as granting license to such action. It is difficult to tell whether he accepts this argument judicially or only rhetorically. Cf. Yaakov Ariel: "Theft from a Non-Jew in War" (Heb.), *Tehumin* 23 (5763/2003): 11 ff.
4. According to Ramban (Numbers 31:23), the war against Sihon and Og was distinct from the one conducted against Midian. Since the land occupied by Sihon and Og was part of the "promised" land, their victory entitled them to all the spoils, without reservation, including – according to the Talmud (*Hullin* 17a) – such prohibited items as pork loins. The battle against Midian, however, was waged primarily to exact vengeance for the episode at Shittim – and not for the acquisition of territory – therefore they refrained from plundering things that were prohibited to them, including all Midianite vessels, *kelei Midian*. See the responsa of Radbaz (vol. 6 #2205), and *Sho'el u-Meishiv* (vol. 1 #246) who elaborate on the theme considerably. For a thorough halakhic discussion of spoils, cf. R. Shabbetai Rapaport: "The Division of Spoils of War," (Heb.) *Arakhim be-Mivhan Milhamah* (1985), 199–207.

    The *Sifrei* to an adjacent verse (31:11) grants the Midianite spoils yet another distinction: "They brought all the spoils and booty, human and animal, to Moshe and to Elazar the Kohen:" This indicates that they were righteous men of probity who were not suspected of larceny. Unlike the situation wherein "the Israelites violated the proscription" (*herem*; Joshua 7:1), here they brought all the spoils to Moshe. (Cf. Ariel, *op. cit.*, 13 #1.)
5. According to *Sifrei* (*Shoftim* #161), "all the people would place their plunder before [the king] and he would select first." This parallels the *Mekhilta's* observation – apropos of Pharaoh (*Beshalah, Va-Yehi* 1; ed. Horovitz-Rabin p. 89) – that: "It is generally customary for a king (*derekh melakhim*; later [*Shirah* 7, p. 140]: *nimusei malkhut*) that the people gather up all the spoils and place them before him, and he gets first pickings." David's conduct in the matter of spoils is adduced to his virtue. In *Sefer*

ha-Ikkarim (4:26), R. Yosef Albo creates a contrast between Shaul, who "fell upon" the spoils, and David, who first offered the people their share (1 Sam. 30:26).

Rambam (*Hilkhot Melakhim* 4:9) codifies the division of spoils, awarding the king half, up front (*mahatzeh be-rosh*), with the balance divided between the soldiers and civilians. Rapaport (*op. cit.*), 201, suggests that the king's share was intended to cover the expense of maintaining the army and the sanctuary and, as such, were exempted from the prohibition of "he shall not accumulate too much silver and gold" (Deut. 17:17).

According to 1 Chr. 18:11, David also dedicated spoils taken from the Amalekites. Since, as we shall shortly see (A5), it was forbidden to take Amalekite spoils – even to dedicate them to the Lord! – it may be that the reference here is to the spoils of Tziklag that David recovered from the Amalekites. To wit: "David rescued everything the Amalekites had taken...Nothing of theirs (Tziklag) was missing... spoil or anything else...David recovered everything" (1 Sam. 30:18–19).

Similarly, Mordekhai and Esther's possession of "the house of Haman" (Esther 8:2) can be justified on the grounds that it was first expropriated by King Ahashverosh (8:7), thereby annulling its (presumed) Amalekite provenance. Cf. S.Y. Zevin: *Le-Or ha-Halakhah* (Jerusalem, 1957), 43.

6. The victories of Asa and Yehoshafat came to be regarded as two of four "classic" illustrations of divine military intervention. See *Lam. Rabbah* (*Petihta* #30; ed. Buber p. 32).

7. *Ba'al Halakhot Gedolot* maintained that the war against Midian sets precedent while *Noda be-Yehudah* (II, *Yoreh De'ah* #201) regards it as *sui generis*. Further re: distribution, cf. *Iggerot Moshe Yoreh De'ah* I, #216.

The subsequent stipulation that "soldiers took their own plunder" (vs. 53) is interpreted by Rashi (vs. 32.) to indicate that moveable goods (*metaltelin*) were kept individually and not subject to communal division. See Rapaport, "The Division of Spoils," 200. American law defines spoils of war as: "enemy movable property lawfully captured, seized, confiscated, or found, which has become United States property in accordance with the laws of war" (*United States Code*, Title 50: War and National Defense; Chapter 39: Spoils of War).

8. Rambam associates this prohibition – along with the one which forbids the Levites landed estates (*Sefer ha-Mitzvot*, prohibition #170, and *Hilkhot Shemittah ve-Yovel* 13:10) – with Deut. 18:1: "neither *kohanim* nor *leviyyim*, the entire tribe of Levi, shall have either a share (*helek*) or a portion (*nahalah*) among Israel." As pointed out by Yoel bin Nun: "*Spoils of War in Israel*" (Heb.), *Alon Shevut* 5/10, the frequent use of the word "share" (*helek*) to signify spoils of war, may be behind this association.

9. Abraham's use of *im...ad* ("from...to") implies a contrast between *hut* and *serokh na'al* that the words "thread" and "shoelace" fail to convey. It is likely in this case that *hut* refers not to just any thread, but the cord that held the traditional Middle-Eastern headdress in place, providing a clear contrast to the strap that was used to bind the sandals and implying all-inclusivity. Their equivalent usage in conventional English would be akin to "from head to toe."

10. The use of *Benei Yaakov* in v. 27, as opposed to Shimon ve-Levi in v. 25, has the

exegetes split on which sons participated in the plundering (see, *inter. alia.*, Ibn Ezra, Rashbam, Ramban). Whether the *"elohei ha-nekhar"* could have had their idolatrous associations nullified, or Yaakov acted with stringency (*hihmir*), is discussed in responsa *Kol Mevasser* (1:23).

11. Whether Yehoshua acted rashly in imposing a unilateral ban on the spoils of Yeriho (*Sanhedrin* 43b–44a, Rashi s.v. *ata garamta lahem*) is moot. (Cf. responsa *Be-Tzel he-Hokhmah* 1:27, who distinguishes between this proscription and the voluntary foregoing of spoils in Numbers 21:2–3.) The sacrosanctity of *herem* is also discussed by the Netziv in his commentary on *Shir ha-Shirim* (4:1) – which, by the way, also contains several of his opinions on how Israelite armies were organized and administered.

12. The appearance here of camels is consistent with the desert origins of Amalek. Rambam (*Guide* 3:39), explaining the laws of redemption of the first-born, cites the spoils of Midian – which included only sheep, cattle and donkeys – as more representative of those times, since camels and horses "are generally found only among individuals and only in a few places."

13. A kindred episode is narrated in 2 Chronicles 28, apropos of a smashing victory that Pekah ben Remaliah, king of Israel, obtained over Ahaz, king of Judah. After a battle that saw 120,000 (!) Judeans killed – including the king's son, chamberlain and viceroy – and 200,000 women and children (!) taken captive, "they also took a large amount of booty from them and brought the booty to Samaria" (vs. 8). On their return, they were met by the prophet, Oded, and several Samarian notables, who persuaded them to release their captives, "for the wrath of the Lord is upon you" (vs. 11), and "it would mean offending the Lord" (vs. 13). The soldiers relinquished their captives and booty, and the Samarian notables used the booty to clothe the captives whom they conducted to the city of Yeriho, where they released them.

    It is noteworthy that the phrase *haron af* [*Hashem*], ("the wrath of the Lord," vss. 11 and 13) appears in two subsequent episodes (2 Chronicles 29:10, 30:8), both of which also focus on the fate of captives. As noted below, it also features prominently in the consequences of an *ir niddahat* (c3) as well as in story of Akhan (c4).

14. Compare, in particular, Deut. 13:16 and 1 Samuel 15:3.

15. Malbim (1 Samuel 15:19) cites the "profit motive" as the cause for Shaul's plunder of Amalek: "*ki yetzer hemdat ha-rekhush hittah libbekha mi-mitzvat Hashem.*" On its further dangers, see c3.

16. The idea that dubious moral behavior, let alone outright sin, makes Israel vulnerable to attack and defeat, is explicit in the Midrashic treatment of the proximity of "Amalek came and fought with Israel" (Ex. 17:8) to "The Israelites quarreled and …tried the Lord, saying, 'Is the Lord present among us or not'?" (v. 7). Cf., *inter. alia.*, *Pesikta Rabbati* (cpt. 13), *Pirkei de-Rabbi Eliezer* (cpt. 44), and *Mekhilta* (Ex. 17:8). The latter stipulates that "enemies attack only in the wake of sin and transgression" "*she-ein ha-soneh ba elah al ha-het ve-al ha-aveirah*"), and offers the additional opinion that the location of the Amalekite attack, Refidim, symbolizes that "the Israelites relinquished their grasp on the Torah" (*rafu yedeihem min ha-Torah*).

    The penetration of the Israelite aura of invincibility is similarly treated by the

Midrash *Tanhuma*, apropos of the ambiguous verb *"karkha"* (Deut. 25:18; JPS: "surprised you") that is used to describe the Amalekite attack:

> The Sages say: *"karkha,"* he cooled you off before others. Rabbi Hunia said: This resembles a boiling hot bath that no one could enter. Along came a scoundrel and jumped in. While he got scalded, he cooled it off for others. Here, too: When Israel left Egypt, God split the sea before them and drowned the Egyptians, frightening all the other nations, to wit: "Now are the clans of Edom dismayed" (Ex. 15:15). Once Amalek came and attacked them, despite getting what they deserved they cooled Israel off before the nations of the world.

17. While acknowledging that Israel had to wage a war of conquest on account of sin, R. Kook assigns the blame to a different sin (*Orot*, p. 14):

> Were it not for the sin of the golden calf, the gentile inhabitants of Israel would have made peace with Israel.... No wars would have ensued. Instead, the inclination would have been toward peace, as in the Messianic era. But sin interfered and this has been delayed for thousands of years.

> See, also, Yehoshua 7:25 and 1 Chr. 2:7 where Akhan's name is actually given as Akhar. A related use of *akhar* appears in 1 Sam. 14. Shaul had adjured his men not to eat until nightfall (v. 24), but Jonathan, who was absent, tasted some honey (v. 27). Upon being rebuked, he blames Shaul for having weakened his troops, saying "My father has brought calamity on the people (*akhar avi et ha-aretz*)...If only the troops had eaten today of the spoils captured from the enemy, the defeat of the Philistines would have been greater still" (vs. 29–30).

18. According to the Midrash (*Gen. Rabbah* cpt. 43), David's division of spoils (cited earlier) was patterned after this precedent: "... and so it was from that day and above" (1 Samuel 30:25; cf. Rashi *ad. loc.*). R. Yudan said: The verse (in Samuel) doesn't state "[from that day] forward" *ve-hala'ah*, but "above" *le-ma'alah*. From whom did [David] learn? From his ancestor, Avraham, who said, "Save only that which the young men have eaten and the portion (*helek*) of the men who accompanied me" (Genesis 14:24).

19. Other "reversals" include the manifold ways in which Haman, the viceroy, is humbled, while Mordekhai, the relative unknown, is elevated. Mordekhai, who sought no reward for saving the king's life, was made viceroy (10:3) and dressed in regal finery (8:15), while Haman – who thought that no one was more deserving of honor than he (6:5) – while not exactly hoist on his own petard, is surely impaled on his own stake, just as he had prepared to do to Mordekhai (7:10). Given this emphasis on "tit for tat," it would befit the symmetry of the plot for Haman to be disheveled as the antithesis of Mordekhai's sartorial upgrading. Although no such reference is made explicitly in the text, Talmudic Aggadah provides one. According to *Megillah* 16a, Haman's daughter is reported to have thrown a chamber pot on her father's head – thinking he was Mordekhai – hence his return home "hiding his head" (6:12).

20. Invisible in the Biblical text, but not lost from aggadic sight, is the identification

of Haman "the Agagi" (Esther 3:1) with the Amalekite king, Agag. Assuming the identification is historical and was known to the Jews of Persia, it could explain their reluctance to enjoy the spoils that fell to them on account of his instigation. Cf. the commentary of Rabbi Bahya ben Asher cited below (c6).

21. Gen. Rabbah 43:2.
22. *Sukkah* 31b, s.v. *yarok*. Also cf. Tosafot, *Hullin* 47b, s.v. *elah yerukah*.
23. Gen. Rabbah 80:10 *"tzelulah haytah he-havit ve-akhartem otah"*.
24. *Midrash Sekhel Tov*, Gen. 34:30 (ed. Solomon Buber [Berlin, 1900], 195).
25. *Seder Eliyahu Rabbah* cpt. 28. Also cf. D8, infra.
26. Midrash *Gen. Rabbah* (cpt. 99) and *Tanhuma* (*Va-Yehi*, 9), identify Simeon and Levi, the perpetrators of the massacre at Shekhem, as the brothers who first schemed to do Yosef in. This identification is both textual and logical. Gen. 37:19 speaks of "brothers" (*ish el ahiv*), as do 34:25 (*ahei Dinah*) and 49:5 (*ahim*) – both of which refer explicitly to just those two. Logically, ten brothers, maximum, could fall under suspicion. The four sons of the concubines were Yosef's friends (37:2) and are therefore excluded. Reuben (37:21 and 42:22) and Judah (37:26) were principally and openly opposed to the murder; Issachar and Zevulun, it may be reasoned, would hardly have spoken first in the presence of their older brothers. That leaves just Simeon and Levi to take the blame.
27. *Sanhedrin, op. cit.*
28. *Sanhedrin* 112a.
29. *Num. Rabbah* 23:6. According to this Midrash, Yehoshua had prohibited the spoils of Yeriho on his own initiative – on the analogy between the "first" of the spoils and the "first" of the dough (*hallah*), which is consecrated to God – and God concurred. Indeed, Yerushalmi *Berakhot* (9:5) refers to this as one of three things that were enacted by a "lower" court (*beit din shel mattah*) and ratified by the "supreme" court (*hiskim Ha-Kadosh Barukh Hu imahem*).
30. R. David Kimhi (Radak, ad. loc.) cites an alternative Midrashic tradition (*Tanhuma Mas'ei* 5), according to which the spoils of Yeriho were prohibited – at Yehoshua's initiative, with divine acquiescence – because the conquest took place on Shabbat. [*Tzitz Eliezer*, citing Radak, concludes, "We should derive a beneficial practice (*hanhagah tovah*) from this case and consecrate to God any booty that falls into our hands as the result of a conquest that may take place on Shabbat" (vol. 3, sec. 9, chapter 2, #12).]

Gersonides (Ralbag, *ad. loc.*) offers an alternative consideration, suggesting that the spoils were prohibited in order to forestall the possibility that the Israelites would relate any future financial success to the wealth obtained from Yeriho, which, in turn, could conceivably lead to their positive reevaluation of idolatry. This very reason, he adds, also accounts for the prohibition against rebuilding Yeriho.

Malbim (*ad. loc.*) cites the miraculous nature of the victory as the core reason for the prohibition ("Since the conquest was through a divine miracle, it was appropriate that its booty be sanctified to God, Who conquered") and specifically exempts the property of Rahav – who is cited in the continuation of the verse – from the confiscation of the city's spoils in general.

(On the question of whether the battle for Yeriho was fought on Shabbat, cf. Yehudah Eisenberg: *"The Conquest of Yeriho"* [Heb.] data.ac.il/data/tanach/melech/8.htm.)

31. *Gen. Rabbah* 99:3. Regarding *m aʾal* (trespass), see section c4.

32. *Mekhilta*, Exodus 17:16.

33. Samuel's caustic use of "swooping" to plunder (1 Samuel 15:19; *va-taʾat el ha-shalal*) is identified by Nahmanides (Ramban, Lev. 19:26) with the prohibition against eating blood: "Because of the abundance of spoil of cattle, as soon as their blood was spilled on the ground, they tore off their limbs and ate them before life had entirely left the animals." The phrase is also treated as opprobrium by R. Yosef Albo (*Sefer ha-Ikkarim* 4:26) in creating a contrast between Shaul, who "fell upon" the spoils [personally], and David, who, unselfishly, first offered the people their share, as noted above (n. 5).

34. Abrabanel's emphasis on the divine origin or, at least, divine status of Shemuel's instructions, appears to be aimed at Maimonides who, in the Introduction to his Commentary on the Mishnah, gives these instructions as an example of a prophetic, i.e., non-divine, initiative, *Divrei Soferim*.

35. Abrabanel, 1 Samuel 15:3.

36. *Megillah* 12b–13a.

37. Ralbag, 1 Samuel 15:6.

38. R. Bahya, Exodus 17:19. Also cf. n. 17, above.

39. Compare *Torah Temimah* (Deut. 13:18, #61): "According to *Semahot* (2:9), 'stealing from *herem* is comparable to murder or idolatry,' which accounts for these thieves being called 'evildoers.'" Cf. n. 24, above.

40. I have followed the text of the Midrash *Eccl. Rabbah* 7:16, rather than the Talmudic text in *Yoma* 22b. Cf. Moshe Sokolow: "Autonomy versus Heteronomy in Moral Reasoning, The Pedagogic Coefficient," *Hazon Nahum* (NY, 1997), 659 ff.

41. Neither the Midrash nor medieval exegesis was oblivious to the moral dilemmas that inhere in the Biblically mandated treatment of Amalek and the seven nations occupying Canaan, of whom it was commanded "You shall not let a soul remain alive" (Deut. 20:16). Maimonides (Guide 1:54) says: "Do not think that this deed is an atrocity or an act of vengeance; rather it is rationally compelling…to eliminate all obstacles that would prevent the attainment of perfection, i.e., (knowledge) of God."

    [Elsewhere in the Guide (3:11), Maimonides lists irrationality and ignorance as the cause of war and violence, stating: "Just as a blind man who cannot see, stumbles, injures himself, and causes harm to others…Groups of people, due to their stupidity, grievously harm themselves and others…Through knowledge of truth – enmity and strife are averted and people will no longer harm each other. The reason for the disappearance of hatreds, hostility and struggles is people's awareness, at that time, of the Divine truth."]

    Bahya ben Asher (Deut. 20:16) argues: "If your heart urges you to suggest that we are acting cruelly towards innocent children…in fact, it is not cruelty but a righteous act of self-preservation."

In several Midrashim (eg., *Pesikta Rabbati* and *Pesikta de-Rav Kahana* to *Parashat Zakhor*), we find the ostensible cruelty towards Amalek juxtaposed with the Torah's demand for cordial relations with others who have harmed Israel, particularly Egyptians and Edomites. Maimonides, too, as though anticipating the charge of racism towards the "seed of Amalek," points out (Guide 3:50) that the commandment of eradication applies to Amalek only as a consequence of his historical activities, and doesn't even extend to other ethnic/racial Edomites.

42. *Eccl. Rabbah*, 7:16.
43. Cf., in particular, 1 Samuel 15:3 and 1 Samuel 22:19.
44. S.R. Hirsch, Exodus 17:13.
45. Ibid., v. 14.
46. *Nedarim* 32a.
47. Andre Neher: "Rabbinic Adumbrations of Non-Violence: Israel and Canaan," *Studies in Rationalism, Judaism, and Universalism* (London, 1966), 184. In contrast to the opinion of Rav: "He emptied them of Torah" (*horikan be-Torah*), Rashi (*Nedarim, ad. loc.*) says: "(Abraham) taught them Torah"
48. Ibid., 183.
49. *Gen. Rabbah* 98:9.
50. Ibid., 97:6. Targum Onkelos, similarly, renders: "My prayers and supplication," and likewise *Baba Batra* 123a.
51. Neher, "Rabbinic Adumbrations," 196. Rabbinic tradition, however, is not monolithically pacifistic. As demonstrated by the alternative view presented in this Midrash (*Gen. Rabbah* 98:9 and 80:10), violent military action in defense of life – and even property, as we shall shortly see – is not only condoned, it is imputed to Yaakov himself:

> R. Nehemiah says: Yaakov wished that his sons had not committed that deed…but once it was done he said: "Am I to abandon my sons to the gentile nations?" What did he do? He took up sword and bow and stood at the entrance to Shekhem, saying: "If they come to attack my sons I shall defend them."

> Rashi comments, in the same vein: "When Shimon and Levi slew the men of Shekhem, all the surrounding nations came to attack them, so Yaakov armed himself to oppose them."

52. Yeshayahu Leibowitz: "After Kibiya" (Hebrew), in *Torah u-Mitzvot ba-Zeman ha-Zeh* (Tel Aviv, 1954), 170. [Kibiya was the site of an IDF reprisal for an Arab terrorist attack on Israel.] The passage is translated somewhat differently – but to the identical effect – in *Judaism, Human Values and the Jewish State* (Cambridge MA, 1992), 187–188.
53. Irving Greenberg. *The Ethics of Jewish Power* (National Jewish Resource Center, 1984), 1–3. I have found no more striking application of this "ethical sensitivity" than the following sentiment expressed by Rabbi Immanuel Jacobovits ("The Morality of Warfare," *Leylah* vol. 2 no. 4 (1983):

> A medieval Jewish source movingly tells us that the one hundred shofar sounds at our New Year's services corresponds to the one hundred groans by the

mother of Sisera (Judges 5:28) when she saw her son killed in his battle against the Israelites.

Sisera was a brutal tyrant, wreaking terror on our people. His death was our salvation. Yet, he had a mother, and to this day we hear her cries and recall her grief over the death of her child.

Even terrorists have mothers, and we must not be indifferent to their anguish. This is but one of the remarkable features of Judaism in an effort to ensure that even war does not harden us to the point of not caring for the loss and suffering of our enemies.

[In our context, it is worth noting that the concern of Sisera's mother for her son's tarrying at the battle is deflected by her servants, who suggest that he is preoccupied with "dividing up the spoil" (*yehalleku shalal*; Judges 5:30).]

54. *Yoma* 22b and *Eccl. Rabbah* 7:16, cf. n. 40, above.

55. R. Ahron Soloveichik: "The Mitzvah of Destroying Amalek" (compiled by Lee H. Michaelson) *Ha-Mevaser* (Student Organization of Yeshiva University, March 9, 1967). [The question is raised, in a somewhat different context, in his *Logic of the Heart, Logic of the Mind* (Jerusalem, 1991), 171.]

56. Ibid. The answer is based upon the Talmudic discussion of *eglah arufah* in *Sotah* 43b. Deut. 21: 7 states: "And [the elders of the nearest town] shall pronounce this declaration, 'Our hands did not shed this blood...'" The Talmud asks: "Would it ever occur to us that the elders of the court are murderers? Rather, 'Our hands did not shed' means that they did not send the stranger on his way without provisions." The reference to armed robbery is an allusion to Exodus 22:1: "If the thief is tunneling (*ba-mahteret*) and he is beaten to death, there is no bloodguilt in his case."

57. "*Ha-horeg goy be-harono, sofo mevakesh le-harog Yehudi be-ratzon.*" Yehudah Shaviv: "The Lost Honor of Dinah, the Daughter of Leah," *Nekudah* 81 (14 December, 1984), 23. Shaviv relies, in part, on the Midrash cited above (C2), and, in part, on the commentary of Ramban on Yaakov's blessing.

58. Tzvi Kurzweil notes that according to R. Yisrael Salanter, "transformation" is preferable to "extirpation:"

It is also worth noting that R. Yisrael distinguishes between the sublimation (*kibbush*) of the inclination to evil and its repair (*tikkun*), i.e., transforming evil into good. He emphasizes that transformation (*hafeikhah*) is preferable because "it is impossible at all times to reach the quality of heroism of conquest that makes it insufferable." Also, "the sublimated qualities are capable of poisoning the intellect."

The poison that sublimation injects into man's spiritual forces is reminiscent of the pejorative results of the "delay of gratification."

"The Psychological Roots and Educational Significance of the Mussar Movement. Based on the Writings of Rabbi Israel Salanter," (Heb.), in *Hinnukh ha-Adam ve-Ye'udo* (Jerusalem, 1978), 217–228 (especially 223).

"Transforming the impulse of man, which was evil from his youth" (cf. Ramban,

Deut. 30:6, 28:42, *et. passim.*), is also the basis for the view of R. Avraham bar Hiyya on how to overcome "the factors that produce war and killing in this world;" *Hegyon ha-Nefesh, Shàar* 4). See Aviezer Ravitzky: "Peace," in Arthur A. Cohen, Pierre Mendes-Flohr (eds.): *Contemporary Jewish Religious Thought* (NY, 1987), 695.

59. *"Ein Hashem shalem ve-ein ha-kise shalem ad she-yimheh zarò shel Amalek;"* Interestingly, a variant reading in the Midrash *Lekah Tov* substitutes "evildoers" (*reshà'im*) for "the seed of Amalek" [based, perhaps, upon 1 Samuel 15:8: "Go and utterly destroy the evildoers, the Amalekites" (*et ha-hattà'im et Amalek*), thus adding force to the identification of Amalek as the personification of evil.

60. Kalonymos Kalman Shapira, *Esh Kodesh* (Jerusalem, 1960), 169–170.

61. This point is also made by the *Sefat Emet* in a homily on *Parashat Toledot* (Petrokov, 1905; 105–106):

> The Sages attributed the verse "save me from treacherous lips" (Ps. 120:2) to Yaakov at the time he was required to say, "I am Esau, your firstborn" (Gen. 27:19). The righteous man, who adheres to the truth even as he is obliged, on occasion, to use untruth… needs divine assistance not to become a willing adherent of treachery, (God) forbid. By saying "save me," Yaakov sought not to become attached to the untruths he was about to utter.

62. Shapira, *Esh Kodesh*, p. 170.

63. This question is dealt with in an essay by Yoel bin Nun (cf. n. 8, supra.), which he composed (remarkably!) in December 1973 during his IDF service in the city of Suez.

64. Radbaz, vol. 3, #968 (533).

65. Ibid., 203 ff.

66. Ibid., 207. Hugo Grotius: *On the Laws of War and Peace*; Chapter Six, #10, writes in a similar vein:

> A distinction must be made between actions in war, that are really of a PUBLIC NATURE, and the acts of INDIVIDUALS occasioned by public war: by the latter, individuals acquire an absolute and direct property, in the things which they take, and by the former, the state makes those acquisitions.

67. *Laws of War in the Battlefield*: Israel Defense Forces, Department of International Law, Military Law School (1998; Unclassified), Chapter 6: Acts Prohibited On the Battlefield; Looting and Spoils of War (69–70).

> http://www.idf.il/hebrew/organization/patzar/atar1/mls1/pirsumim/warfare/warfare_e.pdf

> Also cf. Ehud Luz: *Wrestling with an Angel: Power, Morality, and Jewish Identity* (Yale University Press, 2003) on the influence Jewish tradition has had on military affairs and kindred issues in the Zionist movement and the State of Israel.

The Origin of Nations and the Shadow of Violence: Theological Perspectives on Canaan and Amalek

Shalom Carmy

First of nations Amalek; his end is perdition.

(*Numbers* 24:20)

God of the people who conquered Canaan by storm
And they bound him with straps of *tefillin*.
(*Shaul Tchernichovsky*, "Before the Statue of Apollo")

Such as we were we gave ourselves outright
(The deed of gift was many deeds of war)
(*Robert Frost*, "The Gift Outright")

God said to [Moses]: "I told you to make war against [Sihon] but you offered him peace. By your life I will fulfill your ordinance. Whenever they go to war they must begin by offering peace.

(*Deuteronomy Rabbah* 5:13)

On a steamy afternoon late in the premiership of Menachem Begin, I was accosted in the subway by a Hasidic rabbi-Ph.D. Casting about for an appropriate subject, he asked me what's new in *Tradition*. Searching for an uncontroversial answer, I mentioned R. Ahron Soloveichik's forthcoming article justifying Israel's operations in Lebanon. He was astonished that we would waste space justifying the invasion. I suggested that since war entails killing people, and killing is ordinarily subject to strict prohibition, waging war is not something that a scrupulous individual would treat lightly. To my interlocutor this made no sense. If even a war initiated for economic aggrandizement comes under the halakhic category of *milhemet mitzvah* (an obligatory war), he argued, how much more so a preemptive strike against terrorist bases? He was incredulous when I informed him that the Gemara specifically excluded economically motivated war from *milhemet mitzvah*.[68]

Twenty years later, an Israeli religious Zionist professor lectured on the Biblical view of warfare. His thesis was that Biblical morality in this area marked a great advance over the ethic prevalent in the Ancient Near East. Nothing in his presentation could provoke disagreement. When the lecture concluded, an earnest young man wearing a backpack came forward. Why, he wanted to know, if Judaism was so progressive in the past, does our people not take the lead in making sacrifices in order to inaugurate the reign of peace. The professor reiterated his points, but failed to connect to the uncompromising energy behind the question.

These two anecdotes represent, for me, two extremes of intuitive feeling about the normative Jewish attitude to war. The tolerant attitude towards war is that of most non-Jewish political thought throughout history. It does not regard war as an inherent evil, justified only under extraordinary circumstances. Accordingly, one can derive neutral or even positive teachings about war from normative

Jewish sources. When a person inclined in this direction falls into ignorance, he is most likely to err in the direction of interpreting Halakhah as more friendly to war than it is.

The pacific outlook, longingly expressed by the young man with the backpack, conforms to the contemporary liberal view of war. As stated by the British military historian Michael Howard, writing late in the Cold War period: "It regards war as an unnecessary aberration…and believes that in a rational, orderly world wars would not exist: that they can be abolished, as slavery was abolished, by a collective effort of the conscience of mankind. On the other hand it accepts that wars may have to be fought…"[69] When war becomes necessary, from this perspective, it is only as an act of self-defense or to defeat or prevent the infliction of some terrible injustice.

My assignment is to discuss the two examples of obligatory war that violate the liberal conscience, at least *prima facie*: the war of conquest, and possibly annihilation, against the seven nations of Canaan, and the commandment to obliterate Amalek. Yet it is impossible to discuss them in a vacuum, without reference to the question of war in general. Do the teachings of Judaism cohere, overall, with the promptings of the liberal conscience? In that case the Canaanite and Amalekite wars are "local" exceptions to the ethical-religious rule. Or is Judaism indifferent to the liberal ethic, in which case the Jewish theology of war and contemporary "enlightened" morality are incommensurate, and the two obligatory wars are part of a general pattern? If we adopt the former alternative, the problem is why these two cases diverge from the norm. If we are convinced of the latter, it may still be worthwhile to investigate the special imperatives attached to these two conflicts, but no apologetic will succeed in bringing normative Judaism closer to the ethical intuitions of the young man with the backpack.

In the next section I will adumbrate my reasons for believing that the main thrust of Judaism is pacific rather than bellicose. This introductory discussion will provide the essential background for the more detailed analysis of the seven nations and Amalek. Even a brief sketch, however, cannot overlook the intricacy of the textual material. The sharp disputes within our community regarding the

Jewish view of war result from this complexity in the Biblical and Rabbinic witness, though they are intensified by the ideological disorders and political upheavals of the 20th century.

I

"Joshua vs. Isaiah?" Modern Jews Read the Bible

The casual modern reader of the Bible is struck by the ubiquity of war in its pages. Violence is as Biblical as milk and honey. "Possessing the gate of one's enemies" (Genesis 22:17), pursuing them until they "fall before you by the sword" (Lev. 26:7–8) are divine blessings for the righteous. Prophecies of consolation to Israel, including those of eschatological intent, often contain references to the smiting of her enemies.[70] Conquest and slaughter are memorable features of the book of Joshua, which has thus become a synecdoche for the bellicose theme in Biblical narrative. The last example, of course, pertains to the Canaanite nations, not to ordinary warfare. Yet it is understandable that readers who are not inclined to distinguish among wars, and who are influenced by other Biblical texts implying a positive view of warfare, are liable to prejudge the issue, and lump all the wars of Israel together as ingredients of a thoroughly bloody vision.

For an alternative assessment of the place of war in Biblical religion it is essential to situate the texts we have just alluded to in their total theological context. An outline of the alternative vision draws on sources proclaiming peace as an ideal and on halakhic constraints on waging war, while also taking into account historical-anthropological factors.

The Torah's hostility to war as an ideal is encapsulated in the prohibition against constructing the altar using hewn stones: "for you have passed your sword over it and profaned it" (Exodus 20:22). God does not allow the great David to build the Temple because he was "a man of war" who "spilled blood"; this task devolved upon Solomon, whose name is derived from the root *shalom* (1 Chronicles 28:3). The Messianic period is marked by the abolition of war: "one nation will not raise the sword against another, and they will study war no more" (Isaiah 2:4; Micah 4:3). The significance of these laws and verses for Biblical theology cannot be ignored.

Among the *halakhot* governing the prosecution of war – and for the moment we are concerned only with non-obligatory war; we will return to the seven nations and Amalek later – the most important constraint is the requirement that the sovereign solicit the approbation of the Sanhedrin, and consult the Urim and Thummim.[71] Where this is practicable, the war-making power is subject to the veto of the religious elite. For the past two millennia, in the absence of Sanhedrin and other conditions, the effective result is to outlaw all elective wars. R. Ahron Soloveichik, in the article mentioned above, went further. He argued that even wars of self-defense may require ratification by the Sanhedrin and so forth, so that justified acts of self-defense would not count as halakhic war but merely as collective self-preservation, as police actions, so to speak.[72] This innovation may appear to be little more than a matter of terminology, and is based, in any event, on a questionable reading of Rambam's *Sefer ha-Mitzvot*, but it indicates the extent to which halakhic restrictions have, in effect, imposed a pacific agenda.

For us, living at the beginning of the 21st century, when Orthodox Jewry has become popularly identified with a militant nationalistic ethos, it is difficult to imagine the contempt exhibited by champions of "muscular Judaism" towards the pacific tendencies found in the Halakhah. Tchernichovsky's neo-pagan lament of 1901 for the "god of the people who conquered Canaan by storm," only to be bridled and pacified by the straps of *tefillin*, is a radical, but characteristic, reaction. In the late mandatory Jerusalem depicted in Agnon's *Shira*, even the laws of *kashrut* are despised by one character as contributing to Jewish passivity and aversion to violence: "The entire exile is the consequence of kosher meat. Had the Jews not appointed a special person to slaughter, all would slaughter, and they would not fear a gob of blood and would not avoid defending themselves and the Gentiles would not dare to kill them."[73]

This animus towards traditional Judaism forms the backdrop to a Yiddish newspaper article published fifty years ago by R. Eliyahu

Henkin.[74] R. Henkin simultaneously confronts a double challenge. On the one hand, "adversaries accuse us of not acting in the war of the seven nations, and especially that of Amalek, in the manner of contemporary enlightened nations." On the other hand, there are "the freethinkers who study Bible as history…and admire aggression and vengeance, and derive support from the Bible." While the challenge is directed against the two exceptional wars rather than the entire institution of war in the Bible, it would naturally extend to any manifestation of excessive bellicosity in Jewish tradition. R. Henkin's immediate concern, in this article, is that the accusation promotes anti-Semitism, implying that the harsh behavior described is indicative of the nature of the Jewish people. R. Henkin's simple response to this charge is that the Jewish people did not act on their own in prosecuting these wars: they were commanded by God.

R. Henkin goes on to deal with another set of problems. Although the problematic commandments were fulfilled only because the command came from God, how can we be certain that the behavior they prescribe does not become paradigmatic? With the passage of time the horror inflicted only for the sake of God can become acceptable even when not commanded by Him. R. Henkin answers:

> To prevent the stories told in the Bible from influencing our nature and spirit, the study of Bible comes with a *sacred melody*, and matters are stated as if in a *different world*. The nations we were commanded to make war against, according to Hazal, have become mingled with *others* and no longer exist. One cannot make inferences to others, for there is no commandment and no prophet.

Here he is making two distinct points. One is legal, pertaining to the applicability of the specific *halakhot* concerning the Canaanites and Amalek in our times, and will be considered below. The other is philosophical and pedagogical. R. Henkin boldly asserts that proper education alienates these Biblical narratives from their original historical context. The opposition, formulated in the title of his essay, between the sacred study of the Bible and "Bible as history," constitutes an outright rejection of the secular Zionist project of reclaiming the Bible as history rather than as the ahistorical word of God.

Superficially, R. Henkin's position is reminiscent of the approach frequently taken by Conservative Jewish scholars with a humanistic orientation. They will concede that a particular Biblical passage or constellation of ideas is unacceptable to them, only to happily eliminate the embarrassment by suggesting that the Rabbis, with their more advanced moral sensibilities, interpreted away the "original" meaning of the text.[75] This kind of reasoning is out of bounds from an Orthodox viewpoint, which treats both *Torah she-be-al peh* and *Torah she-bi-khtav* as true, and regards the former as the authentic frame of reference for our understanding of the latter. Hence for R. Henkin, and for us, the theological reading that hovers over the text's historicity at a low altitude cannot displace the historical reality of the *mitzvah* as progressive notions replace primitive ideas. The *peshat* of the Halakhah, so to speak, cannot be detached from its significance. In his newspaper article, R. Henkin is too busy combating the sinful bluster of militant nationalism to work out the precise interaction between these different levels of understanding. If, however, there is merit in R. Henkin's contention that our interpretation of these commandments, and perhaps of other features of Biblical war, ascribes them to a "different world" – and I believe there is – we are not exempt from that task.

If R. Henkin preached a contemporary message of Judaism liberated from the vivid presence of real Canaanites and Amalekites, R. Kook commented on that bygone world. In a famous letter to Moshe Seidel, R. Kook states that pacifism, in Biblical times, was not a live option:

> Regarding war: It would have been impossible, at a time when all the neighbors were literal wolves of the night, that only Israel refrain from war. For then they would have gathered and eradicated them, God forbid. Moreover, it was necessary for them to cast their fear on the barbarians through harsh conduct, albeit

with the hope of bringing humanity to the state that it ought
to reach, but without prematurely anticipating it.[76]

This formulation explains not only why war is treated as a normal part of life, but can even serve as a rationalization of the special
ferocity required for the conquest of Canaan.

For many of you, R. Kook's observation appears self-evident.
Isaiah's vision (ch. 11) of the lion and the lamb lying down together
is an ideal. Whether we take the prophecy literally, like Ravad, or
figuratively, like Rambam, we believe that human nature can become
surprisingly different, for the better, from what it has been in the
past.[77] Yet I suspect that how we understand Jewish teaching about
war depends not only on our hope for the future and on our analysis
of the scriptural record and its context. It also depends on how we
read the present. How close are we to the Messianic age?[78]

The positive creed of those who spurned the tradition's "straps
of *tefillin*" in favor of reanimating their ancient tribal version of a
primeval Nietzschean self-assertion was less the glorification of
war than resentment of the fact that, in a world driven by violence,
Jews were condemned to play the eternal victim. Individuals like
R. Soloveitchik, who are "liberal" in the sense that they do not glory
in war, who have little respect for the ideas of secular nationalism,
and even less desire to adopt them as a way of rejecting Halakhah,
remain deeply suspicious of fashionable schemes and scenarios for
peace in our time.[79] Militant nationalists of the secularist and neo-
pagan stripe, like many others who did not adopt a consciously ir-
religious outlook, were convinced that the "wolves of the night" were
not vestiges of the past but continuing threats. Their only reason for
optimism was the hope that next time around, the Jews would be
as emancipated from their moral inhibitions as our oppressors. If
the scholar I encountered in the subway was careless about his use
of Torah sources, it's probably because, to his mind, accuracy about
these *halakhot* doesn't really matter.[80] The world is a dangerous
place, especially for Jews. Halakhic delicacy and theological idealism
in this field are excess baggage. If one must talk (and talking is, of
course, what many of us do for a living) it is more in our interest to

embrace overheated rhetoric and exhortation rather than to be invaded by the cowardice of conscience. If ever a people had an excuse to think this way, it is the Jewish people in the 20th century.

The young man with the backpack, too, comes to the Bible with his own set of expectations and assumptions. He thinks that he has seen the future and that it is good. As a contemporary German social theorist puts it: "In the modernization theory of the postwar period the non-violent resolution of conflict even became a defining feature of modernity." The theorist immediately adds: "[t]his blunt rejection of violence was accompanied by a certain tendency to underestimate its importance in the present. It allowed an optimistic gaze firmly fixed on the future to view the bad old world in its death-throes with impatience and without genuine interest."[81]

The young man is impatient to realize Isaiah's vision of peace. Not coincidentally, it is an ideal that he can share with non-Orthodox and non-Jewish members of his socio-economic class, the modern liberals for whom violence is an aberration from the normal course of life, acceptable only in faraway countries of whom we know nothing, attractive only to people utterly different than ourselves. His is an attitude rooted in what Judith Shklar dubbed "the liberalism of putting cruelty first," the aversion to the infliction of pain and devastation above all other evils. It is reinforced by vestiges of real or ersatz Christian pacifism, which includes the conviction that the Messianic age has already, in a significant manner, arrived: in the acute phrasing of the outspoken Christian pacifist Stanley Hauerwas, the point is not so much what Jesus would do, as how to live in a world transformed by his cross and resurrection.[82] It is especially cherished among spiritual people who do not respond to other religious ideas, to whom eschatology beckons like a solitary star in a vacant sky. It is an attitude that diametrically counters the liberal dogma that religion bears prime responsibility for the evils of war.[83]

Moving back to the sources, we may venture a tentative hypothesis about the place of war in the Bible that does at least approximate justice to the variety of themes. Universal peace is the goal. Ultimate sanctity, in the here and now, cannot coexist with the symbolism of the sword and even the righteous shedding of blood. Yet war is permitted, and success in waging war is extolled. In addition to the two categories of obligatory war (*milhemet mitzvah*) to which we shall turn momentarily, and the category of defensive war, there are also discretionary wars (*milhemet reshut*). These wars are subject to halakhic and moral constraints, but they are not outlawed in principle. David could not build the Temple, but it was he who prepared the way for its construction.

One Halakhah captures the tension between the ideal and the real in the Jewish conception of war. The Halakhah teaches that it is permissible to carry adornments in public on Shabbat. What is the law regarding weapons? "A man may not go out wearing a sword, or with a bow, or a shield, or a club, or a spear." R. Eliezer disagrees on the grounds that weapons adorn the man. To which the Sages respond: "They are a disgrace (*genai*)," and prove their point by quoting Isaiah 2:4. For R. Eliezer, martial skills and weaponry are valued in the world we inhabit; arms adorn the man. According to the Sages, necessity does not translate into value. What deserves admiration is what is useful from the standpoint of the eschaton: on that day, the tools of war will have no use and no allure. The normative Halakhah follows the Sages; R. Eliezer is incorporated as a minority opinion.[84]

II
Why Are There No Obligatory Aggressive Wars Today?

The war against the seven nations of Canaan and the war against Amalek have one obvious common denominator: as a practical matter, neither is applicable today. From a theological perspective, however, it is important to investigate why that is so in each case. The crucial question is whether the barrier to conducting such a war is a consequence of (regrettable?) historical accident, or whether we should regard it as a fortunate situation, reflecting the will of God.

In addition to the Canaanites and Amalek, the Torah contains one section that singles out a particular ethnic group for negative discrimination. Deuteronomy 23:4–7 promulgates a variety of restrictions on marriage to Edomite, Egyptian, Ammonite and Moabite converts to Judaism and their descendants; regarding Ammon and Moab, we are also commanded not to initiate peace negotiations before engaging them in battle.[85]

Do these groups still exist as distinct nations? The discussion in Mishnah *Yadayim* 4:4 implies that Ammon no longer exists. Sennacherib's policy of forced resettlement "mingled all the nations," thus obliterating original ethnic identities. There is further discussion in Rabbinic literature, continued by the medieval authorities, regarding the extent of this mingling: does it apply to Ammon alone, to all the nations, or to all of them excepting Egypt. The discussion implies that the Assyrians are not responsible for all the "mingling;" subsequent dislocations accomplished or completed what the Assyrians began. Maimonides rules that none of these nations survives today.[86]

No classical rabbinic sources define the contemporary status of the Canaanites and Amalekites. There is no reason to assume that the confusion of nations affecting other groups failed to affect these groups. Maimonides, however, seems to distinguish between the Canaanites, about whom he explicitly states that they no longer exist as a recognizable nation and the Amalekites, about whom he is silent.[87] In practice, of course, neither Maimonides nor any other medieval authority can identify contemporary Amalekites.

The commandment to eradicate the seven Canaanite nations does not apply today. According to Maimonides, Amalek is alive and the *mitzvah* is in force, at least theoretically. What exactly does this mean? One option is that the commandment indeed applies at the theoretical level. The other nations do not exist anymore; for that reason it is logically impossible to identify their constituent members. Amalek is different: if we could identify a contemporary Amalekite (which we can't) we would be obligated to pursue fulfillment of the commandment.[88] A much-publicized alternative approach to Rambam's view is associated with the Soloveitchik family. This view maintains that the historical Amalek no longer exists, but that the role of Amalek as a group dedicated, as a national principle, to the persecution and destruction of the Jewish people, persists. Nazi Germany, for example, had the status of Amalek.[89] We shall return to this question below.

For now, let us turn to the theological significance of Sennacherib's policy. Maimonides holds that discrimination against Amalek and other ethnic groups is justified because a nation, like an individual, is responsible for its actions and thus may be punished collectively.[90] One might hold that our inability to observe these commandments today is an accident of history: there are no more Moabites or Canaanites, so the objects of discrimination are now defunct. Alternatively, one might ascribe the historical change to the workings of divine providence: if these nations no longer exist, it is because the practical fulfillment of these commandments is not part of God's plan for the post-Assyrian world.

The rationale for the last suggestion would run as follows: The commandment to limit marriage with Moabites, Edomites and so forth, even after their conversion, makes sense when members of ethnic groups can be expected to identify totally with the mores of their respective nations. The residue of one's original identity may thus remain a factor in present life, even down to the tenth generation. The rise of empires – Assyria, Babylonia, and their successors – and the policy of mixing populations, destroys these identities and also undercuts the automatic equation of ethnic identity and individual character.

This suggestion should be borne in mind. If valid, it may be pertinent to the two cases before us. As we shall see, however, the particular circumstances of the laws regarding the Canaanites may present an entirely different set of considerations. The same may be true with respect to Amalek, whether one treats them as extinct, like the other nations, or, following Maimonides, grants Amalek a contemporary ethnic or ideological role.

III

Laws Concerning War Against the Canaanites

Deuteronomy 20 differentiates between the obligatory war of conquest against the seven nations of Canaan and other wars. Once hostilities commence, "you shall not let a living soul survive." According to Maimonides and Nahmanides, this is the only difference: the laws concerning the obligation to offer peace before entering into war (verses 10–14) apply equally to the Canaanites and to other nations.[91] Rashi appears to hold that the obligation of offering peace applies only to discretionary war but not to the war against Canaan in verses 15 ff.[92]

Several Rabbinic statements seem to support Maimonides and Nahmanides. The key text (*Gittin* 46a and Yerushalmi *Shevi'it* 6:1) recounts Joshua's peace overtures to the Canaanites before Israel crossed the Jordan. The simple meaning of Joshua 11:19, that no city agreed to peace with Israel except for Gibeon, implies that this option was available to the Canaanites. The most plausible defense of Rashi is that he accepts the possibility of peace with the Canaanites but maintains that they must negotiate before the onset of hostilities; once the war with them begins, according to Rashi, it must be carried on to the bitter end.[93] Needless to say, the views of Maimonides and Nahmanides strike the modern sensibility as more humane, and the modified interpretation of Rashi is welcome.

The rationale for the commandment is fairly explicit: "that they not teach you to do the abominations they performed for their gods" (Deut. 20:18). *Sefer ha-Hinnukh* discerns a dual emphasis: the Torah wishes to prevent their negative example and also to inculcate, through the harsh punishment meted out, a horror of idolatry.[94] The former option, more explicit in the Bible, implies that the prohibition pertains in the land of Israel, the divinely ordained dwelling place of the Jewish people. The latter could be extended to all places where idolatry exists and Jewish power extends. According to Nahmanides, the law applies to Canaanites in the land of Israel: this is in keeping with the first rationale cited and also fits his general emphasis on the centrality of the land. Maimonides imposes the obligation with respect to Canaanites outside the land of Israel, when Jewish conquest expands the bounds of Jewish control. This view would be consistent with both proposals of the *Hinnukh*.[95]

R. Henkin's blunt assertion that the applicability of these *halakhot* is strictly limited to the divinely ordained Biblical injunctions is a crucial move in attempting to narrow the gap between an honest Jewish self-understanding and the promptings of the liberal conscience. Despite Kahanist distortions, it applies only to the ancient Canaanites, not to their putative modern successors. This protestation, however, carries conviction insofar as it successfully explains not only that the laws in question are exceptional from a technical legal standpoint, but that they also do not lend themselves to theological generalization. Our discussion in the previous paragraph may be helpful in two ways:

1) The liberal outlook is, in principle, opposed to ideologically motivated aggression (though in practice it is often tolerant of violence in the service of "progressive" ideals). Yet it is not without significance whether the laws regarding the ancient Canaanites are motivated, not by "secular" national ambitions, but by the spiritual imperative of eliminating idolatry.

2) The argument that this obligatory war is localized in the land of Israel constitutes a further modification. According to this approach, the Torah does not advocate imposing its monotheism on all mankind, ready or not, but insists only on creating a space in which Israel can pursue her own spiritual destiny. Something of this idea can be maintained according to the more expansive view of Maimonides, as we have seen.

Theory and Practice – the Biblical Record

The Biblical record stands at an angle to the codified law we have just surveyed. The Jews are warned repeatedly of dire consequences should they fail to eradicate the Canaanites, who will then become "pins in your eyes and thorns in your sides" (Numbers 33:55; see also Joshua 23:13). Yet the fulfillment of the commandment was evidently neglected, even in the time of Joshua, and more so after his death. To be sure, there are lovers of the Jewish people with a humanistic orientation who might be pleased at this deficiency. Thus R. Kook, who surely deplored disobedience towards God, takes comfort in the fact that they sinned by too much humanity rather than too much brutality: "Even in sin its eye was not evil towards the entire human race...for they did not annihilate the nations," thus exhibiting "an inner tendency to seek the welfare of all human beings, which was excessive."[96] The unadulterated Biblical text is less charitable.

Despite severe chastisement (see Judges 2) the war against the seven nations is not rekindled, even in periods of repentance. It is as if the opportunity, once squandered, could not be recovered. The last war against the Canaanites, that of Deborah and Barak against Yavin and Sisera (Judges 4–5), is provoked by enemy oppression rather than by zeal to resume the original war of conquest.[97] Is it possible that the obligation indeed lapsed after the first generations to enter the land?

Some modern scholars have toyed with such a position. It is compatible with Moshe Greenberg's "empathetic reading" of the law, grounded in three assumptions: that eradicating enemies was acceptable in ancient Israel's milieu; that the success and survival of Israel, in the opinion of the Biblical authors, depended on the exclusive worship of God; and, first and foremost, that a relatively small nation, at the beginning of its path, was liable to succumb to the idolatrous culture that surrounded it.[98] These factors mitigate the wrongness of the law, in Greenberg's opinion. As Israel becomes more rooted in the land, the security concern becomes weaker, and the law falls into desuetude.

Uriel Simon proposes to deny the historical concreteness of the "ideal" account, viewing it as an allegory that renders palpable, for this one-time conquest, that "God makes war for Israel" (Joshua 10:14), and to express through the total *herem* the aspiration that Israel preserve itself from the bad influence of its neighbors by being "a people that dwells alone and is not counted among the nations."[99]

The primary intent of Simon's allegorization is to eliminate the perceived discrepancy between the conquest by storm narrated in Joshua and the slow infiltration implied by the lack of archaeological evidence for rapid conquest. Leaving aside the question of whether such desperate remedies are needed,[100] Simon acknowledges another motive: by denying the literal sense of the Biblical account (and presumably the command in Deuteronomy as well) he can avoid the "the moral distress that mass slaughter causes to anyone who is not a Kahanist fundamentalist." Greenberg condemns the Bible but forgives its authors; Simon makes peace with the Bible, while erasing the Halakhah. For Simon, too, the failure to persist in the policy of mass slaughter (assuming it ever commenced) is unproblematic.

The views of the aforementioned academicians provide background for three solutions posited by Orthodox thinkers:

R. Bin-Nun, in effect taking up R. Kook's remarks, believes that the Jewish mentality is deeply averse to war. For that reason, it was necessary for God to command the prosecution of the conquest with ferocity. Allowing any room for mercy would risk a collective loss of nerve. This approach is similar to Greenberg's in appealing to the pressures of circumstance.[101] From this perspective we can also understand why the commandment is suitable to the initial period of settlement and not to later generations.[102] R. Bin-Nun's article does not, however, offer a halakhic justification for the lack of impetus to renew the war after it comes to a standstill.

Some years ago I attempted to develop such a justification. My point of departure was the question of *keri'ah le-shalom* – the initial invitation to negotiate peace. As noted above, both Maimonides and Nahmanides apply this obligation to the war against the seven nations. Even Rashi, forced to account for the Talmudic story about Joshua's messengers of peace, cannot deny some role for this concept, and therefore must concede that peace was possible at least before the Jews crossed the Jordan and was ruled out only afterwards. I therefore suggested that once the war was abandoned it could not be started up again without offering conditions of peace. What had begun as failure to obey God's command had become the inertia of an unsatisfactory *de facto* peace.

A bold approach emerges from a newly published passage by R. Kook:

> If it were an absolute duty for every Jewish king to conquer all the seven nations, how would David have refrained from doing so? Therefore, in my humble opinion, the primary obligation rested only on Joshua and his generation. Afterwards it was

only a commandment to realize the inheritance of the land promised to the patriarchs.[103]

These words provide a far more robust explanation of the disappearance of the war against the Canaanites, after the rebuke in Judges 2, than R. Bin-Nun's proposal or mine. That is because it takes someone of R. Kook's stature to challenge the consensus, according to which this law is eternal. R. Kook himself immediately notes that his view appears to contradict Maimonides' decision to count this *mitzvah* in his *Sefer ha-Mitzvot*.[104]

Let us recapitulate the last two sections: The explicit rationale for the command to eradicate the Canaanite inhabitants of the land of Israel is the threat of their religious influence. The *Hinnukh* added that the fate of the Canaanites also manifests horror at idolatry. The command was not fully executed and there is some evidence that its primary historical (and perhaps, according to R. Kook, halakhic) application was limited to the first generations of conquest. These ideas, and the detailed lines of reasoning we presented, tend to decrease the distance between the Torah and contemporary liberal reasoning on this question, without annulling it.

The Pitfall of Rationalization

It is common to think that bringing *mitzvot* closer to human considerations is a good thing in itself, and that it makes Judaism more palatable to people who are uncomfortable with mystery or appalled by commandments that offend their sensibilities. If this is always true, then our previous discussion, in addition to its possible value in understanding the Biblical text, also strengthens the appeal of Judaism. In our case, I am not sure that this is so. Hence the ideas developed so far cannot be used as apologetic, at least not without further deliberation.

The problem is that rationalization often means explaining *mitzvot* in terms of human needs and desires. Doing this makes it easier to generalize to other situations. The more successful one is in promoting a rationale that makes sense, the greater the danger that the commanded war will be assimilated to the model of the ordinary aggressive war of conquest. Such a war, if it can be excused at all, is surely devoid of any religious merit.

Western expansion abounds with stories of the displacement and extermination of aboriginal peoples. The 19th century historian Theodore Roosevelt, later to achieve political prominence, wrote: "Every such submersion or displacement of an inferior race, every such armed settlement or conquest by a superior race, means the infliction and suffering of hideous woe and misery." Though he defended the displacement of American Indians on the grounds that they held tenuous title to the land in the first place and that white men made better use of the land, Roosevelt insisted: "It was our manifest destiny to swallow up the land of all adjoining nations that were too weak to withstand us."[105] Most of us would judge his recognition of the horror more honest than the reasons adduced in justification.

Once we start talking this way, cynicism is not far behind. Consider a high-powered Israeli intellectual, quite liberal theologically though nominally Orthodox, who strikes the "bad boy" pose endearing to his admirers, returns the gaze of the camera and announces: "The Jewish God is stingy. His land only has room for one people, His own." (One reviewer, under the impression that Orthodox rabbis can be expected to refer to God approvingly, complained that PBS chose a Kahanist to speak for Torah!) As it is, the opinion-maker is refuted by the text: Abraham was willing to divide the land with Lot (Genesis 13); Moses pleaded with Hobab to join Israel's quest and to share in the benefits thereof (Numbers 11). If his "explanation" still resonates with an audience, it is because he offers a reason that conforms to ordinary realistic calculation.

Professor Greenberg's empathetic reading is surely not lacking in moral gravity. Yet one factor in his analysis is the conviction that ancient Israel was driven by the belief that the exclusive worship of God is essential for national welfare. The implication is that obeying the Biblical command is a matter of enlightened self-interest, rather than a commitment to God or even revulsion towards idolatry for its own sake, and not as a means to collective security. Ultimately, this formulation makes the eradication of the Canaanites nothing more or less than an exhibition of *raison d'état*, albeit a misguided one not to be repeated. Of course, Greenberg is not writing from an Orthodox perspective: his goal is extenuating the Bible's wrongness, not justifying it. Orthodox thinkers who would learn guardedly from his suggestions should beware of the unintended implications.

The Orthodox approaches we noted are rooted in the Halakhah and posit, in varying degrees, a difference between the initial stage of conquest and later periods. To the skeptical mind, this view, too, is suspiciously close to the pressure of a nationalistic manifest destiny that pursues expansion until territorial satiation is attained, and war of conquest is no longer necessary. R. Bin-Nun's approach, which is congruent with R. Kook's statements, also presupposes a psychological thesis about early Israel, namely an initial aversion to slaughter that must be overcome for the sake of survival. Naturally, we do not wish to treat these factors as equivalent to secular motivations and rationalizations. We are speaking of divine command, not human invention. The moment we become glib about the various rationales, however well grounded in the sources, we risk falsifying them. We shall return to this problem at the end of our discussion of Amalek.

IV

Eternal Amalek

The offense of Amalek is mentioned twice in the Torah. Their attack is narrated in Exodus (17:8–16), after which Moses inscribes and teaches Joshua, on divine instruction, that God will blot out the memory of Amalek "from under the heavens," and make war against Amalek "from generation to generation." Deuteronomy (25:17–19) commands Jews to remember what Amalek did and places upon them the onus of effacing Amalek's memory.

Among the multitude of vices and transgressions ascribed to Amalek in Aggadic and homiletic literature, two have a basis in the Bible.[106] One flows from Deuteronomy, which speaks of Amalek "happening upon you on the way, when you were weary." This implies that the attack was uncalled for; it was not the outcome of conventional calculations of self-interest. This idea is behind the notion that Amalek is the enemy who values destruction of the Jew as an end in itself. The other is cognizant of Amalek's descent from Esau (Genesis 36:12), the brother of Jacob, which injects the theme of fratricide. Both elements are stated by Nahmanides: "Amalek came from afar, as if striving to overcome God...Also he is the offspring of Esau and our kinsman intruding in a quarrel not his."[107]

We focus on reasons for enmity towards Amalek that are somewhat grounded in the Bible because these elements will be important later on. We are not surveying the plethora of later discussions on this subject because our task is less to explain why Amalek deserves destruction than why Israel is commanded to become the agent of that destruction and what that means to us today.

Some writers seize upon the idea of an inherently and eternally evil nation, independent of their actions at a particular time, and therefore calling for extermination. The politically moderate professor of law George Fletcher finds this explanation plausible: "It is not clear whether this means that the guilt of the tribe passes from generation to generation, but that would at least provide an account of the peculiar Jewish obligation to continue the war against Amalek." His moral verdict follows inexorably: "From the story of Amalek to the doctrine of original sin, to the birth of anti-Semitism, to the problem of German guilt, we see one baleful and pernicious line of argument. This is surely one of the most regrettable chapters in the history of Western thought. Ezekiel could rail against it, but he could not defeat it."[108] Such a rationale can be applied equally to other cases of discrimination, but its employment is particularly sensitive regarding Amalek. Unlike the marriage restrictions applying to Moab *et al*, the law of Amalek entails physical extermination. And as the *Avnei Nezer* pointed out, the fate of Amalek, unlike that of the seven nations, is perpetual and does not depend on its present actions.[109]

The *Hinnukh*, assuming a version of this theory, asks why nations are created if their fate is perdition, and stresses that their wickedness was not inevitable, given free will, adding that at some point in history these groups, or members thereof, served a positive purpose. Thus, descendants of Amalek became great Torah scholars.[110] R. Henkin is not atypical when he rejects the Jewish pedigree of Nazi racism by stressing that Jews cannot arrive at such decisions on our own but only through divine command, because only an omniscient being can deliver such a judgment about an entire group.

Despite such qualifications and apologetics, the view that any group possesses an inherently evil identity that is transmitted infinitely from generation to generation cannot be recommended. Fletcher considers it a reasonable explanation for an ancient law, but there is absolutely nothing in the Bible itself that would lead one to accept it. From a contemporary moral perspective it is not an acceptable rationale. Nothing in our science tends to confirm the idea that groups of human beings differ so radically in their genetic endowment as to justify their extermination.[111] And *pace* R. Henkin, thinking that such distinctions exist, even if the thought bears no practical fruit, engenders a state of mind hospitable to homicidal racism. Why accept a rationale that is not rooted in Scripture, does not suit our science, and is conducive to the worst morality? Far better to say nothing.

A second strand of thought denies the contemporary obligation to wage war against Amalek. Professor Avi Sagi adduces Hasidic sources implying that the battle against Amalek is a spiritual one.[112] Again, it is not our interest here to examine the ideologies and vices with which Amalek is identified. Sagi, in effect, allegorizes the commandment. This approach cannot resolve our problem, inasmuch as the commandment to wipe out Amalek remains a real one, not a figurative one. R. Yaakov Medan, however, distinguishes among the Hasidic texts. Some, such as the *Noam Elimelekh*, in keeping with their homiletic agenda, indeed sidestep the fulfillment of the *mitzvah*. Others, such as *Sefat Emet*, spiritualize the commandment rather than allegorize it. In other words, they speak of wiping out the memory of Amalek as a commandment that is literally fulfilled today through overcoming the "spirit of Amalek." The imposition of physical force, under contemporary conditions, is left to God, but requires some degree of human participation, which is not limited to physical warfare.[113] This approach is rooted in the Biblical accounts:

Exodus 17 presents the obliteration of Amalek as an act of God; only in Deuteronomy 25 is the commandment given to Israel.[114] It would also fit Maimonides' implicit view that the commandment has not lapsed with the disappearance of identifiable Amalek.

The flavor of the spiritualized approach to eradicating Amalek can be conveyed in the words of R. Avigdor Amiel's sermon for *Parashat Zakhor*. He contrasts Amalek, the paragon of militarism, with Israel, whose weapon is the book in which the story of Amalek is inscribed.[115] Alluding to the hopes that World War I – "the war to end war" – would spell the end of militarism, the author argues the futility of fighting evil with evil: "When Judaism declared war against militarism it was not through militarism. God said to Moses: 'Write this as a memorial in the *book*'" (134). For R. Amiel the spiritual over-coming of Amalek is not accomplished passively, nor is it achieved by countering violence with an undifferentiated conception of love: "whoever would be merciful, must first be just, and if he would begin with mercy, he will ultimately lack it and instead display cruelty" (135). Contrasting, in effect, the Christian gospel of love with the Torah's ideal of exorcising the culture of violence, R. Amiel's pacific interpretation of the commandment to destroy Amalek yet holds fast to the original vigor of the divine word.

The idea of a war fought by God with minimal human in-volvement resonates through several Biblical texts. I omitted these sources from our prior discussion about the Biblical attitude to war because they do not play a large role in contemporary Jewish thought. Christian pacifists, however, have exploited this theme in arguing that the Hebrew Bible anticipates their position.[116] The first evidence for this theme is Moses' promise, before the parting of the sea: "God will make war for you, and you will be silent" (Exodus 14:14). On other occasions the outcome of a war is determined by divine agency, without significant human intervention, such is the war of Jehoshaphat against Moab and Ammon (II Chronicles 20). The famous paradigm of such a victory is Hezekiah's defense of Jerusalem against the Assyrians (II Kings 18–19; Isaiah 36–37).[117] The same is true of the eschatological "Gog and Magog" prophecies. Here the great foe, representing an assemblage of nations not otherwise associated with enmity towards Israel, invades after the people are restored to their land. The extensive examples of this type of prophecy (Ezekiel 38–39, whence the names God and Magog derive; Zachariah 14; Joel 4) depict God Himself as the agent of destruction. Interestingly, while Ezekiel and Zachariah describe a gory battleground, in Joel the projected war does not actually occur: God "roars from Zion" and the response is silent submission.[118] Thus, we have one irenic eschatological scenario in which ultimate bloodshed is finally averted.

At first blush, this model of divinely initiated warfare has affinities with the inward war against Amalek suggested by the Hasidic texts. As we shall see, the story is a bit more complicated.

Uncovering the Amalek in Edom

In this section I wish to present a hitherto unnoticed theological aspect of Amalek. As already observed, Amalek is descended from Esau. Insofar as the nomadic Amalekites dwelt separately from Edom, the Bible does not refer explicitly to this kinship: the only geographical coincidence of the two groups is the battle at Mount Seir during the time of Hezekiah (1 Chronicles 4:43 ff).[119] Later Jewish literature, of course, frequently connects them. The later literature also identifies Edom with Rome, and Amalek with the Roman Empire and its successors. To the historical factors proposed by scholars to explain this development, one might add the nature of the prophecies, which seem excessive if applied to a minor regional kingdom.[120] I submit that the severity with which Edom is judged in some narratives and prophecies has to do with the genealogy of Amalek. If this is true, then certain unique characteristics of the prophecies against Edom may offer a clue about the theological role of Amalek.

The first text where Edom exhibits extraordinary hostility towards the Jewish people is Numbers 20. Here the Israelites, on their journey to Canaan, request passage through the land of their brother Edom. The king of Edom responds with threats of war backed by full mobilization. R. Soloveitchik once suggested that the extreme hostility of the king of Edom is symptomatic of Edom's symbolic function as a "metaphysical" opponent of Israel. That is to say, Edom here fills the role ordinarily served by Amalek.[121]

Some of the prophecies concerning Edom are not unlike those regarding its neighbors, though some of these castigate Edom especially for betraying its fraternal relation to Jacob or for exploiting the destruction of Judah to expand its territory.[122] Our current interest is in two unusual prophecies, Isaiah 34 and Obadiah. The placement of Isaiah 34 is distinctive. It does not appear in the portion of the book devoted to prophecies concerning the nations (chapters 13–23), but together with the prophecies of redemption that follow Isaiah's last series of prophecies about the Assyrian attack and precede the narrative part of the book.[123] The brief book of Obadiah is dedicated in its entirety to the theme of Edom.

Isaiah 34 and Obadiah share one remarkable characteristic. In both prophecies it appears that all nations are summoned to render judgment on Edom. At the same time, it is unclear whether Edom is judged separately or as part of a larger congeries of nations. Thus, Isaiah 34 invites all the nations to witness the divine indignation against all the nations. Only in verse 5 does attention shift to Edom: "For my sword is satiated in heaven; it descends upon Edom." From this point on, Edom is the exclusive object of God's wrath. Obadiah presents a similar profile. The first verse calls the nations to rise up against Edom,[124] while the last section (verse 16 ff) includes the other nations in the punishment: "As you have drunk upon my holy mountain so shall all the nations drink perpetually; they shall drink, and swallow, and become as though they had never been."[125]

Approaching these prophecies with the equation Edom=Amalek in hand, we face two problems. One pertains to the spiritualization question that arose in the previous section. Obadiah's prophecy definitely insists upon Israel's agency in vanquishing Edom and establishing the kingdom of God: "Then saviors shall arise on mount Zion to judge the mount of Esau; and the kingdom shall be God's" (v. 21). In Isaiah 63:1–6, God marches alone against Edom; in an echo of the prophecies just cited, He complains about the lack of help: "I have trodden the winepress alone, and of the peoples none was with

Me…And I looked about, and there was no helper, and wondered there was none to uphold." This fits the Amalek-model set down in Deuteronomy, where obliterating Amalek is a commandment upon Israel. It differs from the "Gog and Magog" model, which is compatible with human passivity, and stands in sharp contrast to the Hezekiah-Jehoshaphat model, where God is the sole agent of war.[126] Again, we are forced to conclude, on halakhic grounds and now on literary grounds as well, that the final triumph over Amalek cannot take place without human activity, even if the primary victory is God's.

Let us now confront the paradoxical content of these prophecies: the simultaneous sense that Edom-Amalek is the object of judgment, with the nations of the world serving as either spectators or partners in the "coalition of the willing," on the one hand, and the implication that these prophecies target for punishment that very collection of nations, on the other hand. The simplest solution to this paradox, in my opinion, is that the nations as a whole deserve the unmitigated measure of the divine fury, but that in actuality it is only Edom-Amalek that absorbs the full blow. In the language of Isaiah 34, God's indignation is directed at all the nations, His sword is satiated with blood, but the sword descends only on Edom, the people subjected to "my *herem*" (34:5).

Against this background, the story of Amalek is more than an ancient episode inexplicably magnified and amplified so that its evil reverberates down through the corridors of recorded time, an evil never to be silenced until its perpetrators are extinguished. The original offense of Amalek, the particular nature of which we only glimpse through a fog of exegesis and homiletic, stands for a fundamental and radical enmity between God and the entire social-political world of the nations. It is an estrangement that would justify, in principle, the universal *herem*, which the last of the prophets, in the closing moments of prophetic utterance, offers as the dread alternative to eschatological reconciliation (Malachi 3:24). The divine wrath is not expended on the whole of violent, rebellious humanity, but only upon Amalek.

The approach adumbrated here, on the basis of our reading

of these prophecies, does not dispense with the classic discussions about the exact nature of Amalek's transgression. These attempts at interpretation and rationalization remain untouched. However, our approach tackles the problem of proportionality: why long ago wickedness remains such a central part of our consciousness and a presence, albeit a shadowy one, in the halakhic corpus. Our answer is that the specific acts and motivations of Amalek are symbols of perpetual temptations to violence and betrayal that will continue to infect the lives of nations until they are eradicated.

As a genuine solution to the problem of Amalek this answer is unsatisfactory, whatever its coherence with the prophetic themes we excavated. It fails on moral grounds. A moment's reflection reveals that the process whereby general guilt is transferred to an individual or group within the collective has a name. The object of this process is called a scapegoat.[127] The psychological equilibrium achieved by denominating a scapegoat often makes it a necessary process if the collective is to survive its burden of well-deserved guilt. All things being equal, it is best that the scapegoat be the member of the community most deserving of the stigma and the penalty. Nonetheless, the institution is morally reprehensible. If our discussion has merely replaced Fletcher's specter of racially transmitted guilt with that of a sociologically sanctioned disproportion, have we gained anything morally?

My revered teacher R. Aharon Lichtenstein once wrote that the obligation to destroy Amalek, in its full scope, "cannot be explained or justified by any standard of natural ethics. It can be legitimated only by being anchored in divine command and obedience." This brought a rebuke from an eminent Jerusalem rabbi. As quoted by R. Lichtenstein, the critic insisted that the extermination is indeed ethical, insofar as it required by the norms and considerations of a divine morality transcending our feeble understanding. Granting the cogency of this formulation, R. Lichtenstein persisted, was not the gap between them a mere matter of semantics. And his critic replied that from an educational standpoint terminological variations are highly significant.[128] In this exchange the primary concern was apparently ensuring respect for the moral integrity of God's word.

The present essay awakens deeper worries than those that motivated R. Lichtenstein's reflections. For we have advanced partial explanations and justifications in full knowledge of their unsatisfactory quality. This is true of suggestions regarding the war against the Canaanites that smack of *realpolitik*; it is even more so with respect to an analysis of Amalek that ascribes to the mitzvah an orientation that would deter emulation if attributed to a human agent. In the final analysis it is hard to avoid the conclusion that it is morally and religiously preferable to regard the command to eradicate Amalek, and perhaps the commandment regarding the seven nations, as laws without rationale, justifiable only from the standpoint of *Deus dixit*. Anything else either cheapens the word of God or degrades human moral judgment. It is not my intention to dispel the mystery – nay the terror – which we experience in confronting these halakhot. My only extenuation is the hope that our long discussion helps us to define the mystery and the terror as precisely as possible in the light of the sources.

V

The Full Harshness of the Terrifying

Over thirty years ago, Professor Eliezer Schweid published an article that deserves more attention than it has received.[129] Meditating on the challenge earlier posed in the name of George Fletcher, Schweid denies any relationship between the Torah's teachings with regard to Amalek and the Canaanites, on the one hand, and Nazi theories of race, on the other hand. Although rabbinic sources ascribe moral qualms to Saul, and Martin Buber made of the deposed king a fount of moral protest against the Halakhah, there is no hint of such criticism in the Bible itself. In the Biblical view, there is nothing wrong with the kind of comprehensive punishment meted out to these nations. That is because the Bible grants God the untrammeled and unqualified moral authority to dispose of nations according to their deserts, even to their destruction. Amalek and the seven nations of Canaan are "sinners in the hand of the Almighty God," but so is Israel. In the aftermath of the Golden Calf, God decrees the destruction of the Jewish people, and if they disobey Him in His land, they too will be swept away, "as [the land] vomited the people who were there before you" (Leviticus 18).

Exonerating Judaism from the charge of racism and genocide, says Schweid, does not guarantee a comforting message. He writes:

> Surely this does not make the commands and the acts that derive from them less terrifying or less problematic in contemporary eyes. To the contrary, perhaps it is precisely thus that we finally confront the full harshness of the terrifying, and the exact nature of the problem.[130]

If our analysis so far has done so little to alleviate our profound moral discomfort with the Halakhah, it is because we have evaded the full pressure of Schweid's problem. We must therefore confront the terrifying nature of God's claim on man, within the context of these laws. Only then can we attempt a provisional reconciliation with the teachings of Judaism.

The conflict between the norms of Judaism is stark and terrifying. On one side, God claims everything. There is no place hidden from His authority. Over against this lies not only the humanistic demand for autonomy, but the theological principle, deeply embedded in the same Torah, which proclaims divine mercy. The tension between these great experiences is as familiar as Rashi's commentary to the first verse of the Torah: God wished to create the world in accordance the attribute of judgment; knowing that the world could not withstand it, He employed the attribute of mercy as well. As religious individuals, we experience the two opposing attributes of God, *middat ha-din* and *middat ha-rahamim* (judgment and mercy) not only in the pages of books, but also in the most intense moments of our lives.

Schweid's article emphasizes the attribute of judgment because it is the absolute severity of God that is most troubling to us and that comes to expression in the laws of obligatory war. Further analysis uncovers a pattern in the interaction of *din* and *rahamim*. Just as creation is inaugurated with *din* (through the divine name *Elokim*) and continues in the mingling of *din* and *rahamim* (the combination of the Tetragrammaton and *Elokim* in chapters 2–3 of Genesis), so the history of God's interaction with His world is marked by the thunderclap of judgment, modified by the tidings of mercy. The first ten generations of humanity culminate in a divine judgment of virtual extermination, followed by God's promise never again to visit humanity with such all-consuming punishment. As the Rav *z"l* observed more than once, total commitment to God entails the legitimacy of human sacrifice. God demands this seemingly absurd cruelty of Abraham. After the *akedah*, the severe claim of divine judgment is not transcended – the absoluteness of the divine imperative is not done away with – yet the practice of human sacrifice is banished from the cult. Moses, too, is confronted on his way back from Midian (Exodus 4:21 ff) by the wild charismatic numinous presence, a terrifying crisis almost incomprehensible to our later perspective.[131] After Moses' intercession, God reveals to him the thirteen attributes of mercy (Exodus 34), with their promise of forgiveness that has remained the cornerstone of our pleas ever since.

All beginnings are mysterious, and the most intimate origins are the most mysterious of all. *Hazal* (*Hagigah* chapter 2) designated the study of such matters esoteric. We commonly subsume under this category the mystical study of cosmological origins and ontological foundations. However, the Yerushalmi includes *arayot*, defined as the mystery of incest at the root of human reproduction. A sense of horror and fascination underlies our repressed awareness of the intimate secret at the heart of our human origins, whether it is expressed in terms of the practical necessity of allowing the first man's children to cohabit with one another, lest the race perish, or in terms of the Freudian family romance. We do not plumb the depths of these matters in public, out of concern for the honor of God and in order to draw a veil of concealment around the necessities of our own history.

The commandments to which this essay is devoted, the war of conquest in ancient Canaan and the eternal war against Amalek, touch upon the hidden mysteries of our religious and social existence. The two great horrors: idolatry, the betrayal of our Creator, and the ideology of violence and fratricide. The war to conquer Canaan is the war to construct a Jewish society, in the land allocated to us by God, free of the presence of idolatry. Amalek, as we have seen, represents gratuitous violence ("happening upon you on the way"), the primeval rebellion against the divine order of history. Let us not forget the other Biblical theme marked by Nahmanides: Amalek's attack on Israel was an attack against his brother. It is worth noting that the primal act of murder in the Bible was Cain killing Abel; only after the Flood does the Torah condemn homicide as a universal offense against the image of God in man. To this very day, when the full horror of murder strikes us, we are haunted by the blood of Abel: murder is of the brother, not the other.[132]

God's "original" plan, as it were, was to create the world under the attribute of judgment. Judgment is not withdrawn; it is only tempered by mercy. The conquest of Canaan by storm was not repeated. The second conquest of the land, the one that was never annulled, occurred through settlement: "not by arms and not by force, but through My Spirit, says the Lord of Hosts" (Zachariah 4:6). The struggle against an Amalek who is no longer permanently identifiable with any ethnic group is conducted primarily through the book.

To achieve, as individuals and as a community, an authentic and faithful balance between the commandments of harshness and the life of loving kindness is a frightening but unavoidable task. Without the constant awareness of *middat ha-din*, without faithfulness to the real and frightening demand it imposes upon us, our commitment to the worship of the one holy God and His ethics of life deteriorates into sentimentalism and wishful thinking about our own spiritual state and that of the world. Absent the knowledge of *middat ha-rahamim*, the "sweetening" of the original imperative, cloaked in all its numinous fascination and terror, our purported obedience is corrupted into a feral willfulness. According to the Midrash I cited as an epigraph to this essay, Moses took the initiative in offering Sihon peace. God went beyond commending him for it and inscribed his practice as the eternal *halakhah*.[133] *Hazal* had a lesson to teach here, though, despite all the good will in the world, it is one that cannot be applied by rote.

The intellectual task of fully understanding these components of Judaism is even more forbidding than the practical aspects. To gaze upon the hidden wellsprings of these *halakhot*, and contemplate unblinking the mysteries they encapsulate, is not an enterprise for the faint of spirit. Singing of "the gift outright," Robert Frost rhapsodizes about America's possession of, and by, the land. He is not oblivious to the moral and existential cost: But Frost makes his acknowledgement *sotto voce*, placing the telltale line "The deed of gift was many deeds of war" in parentheses. There is wisdom in his choice. For us, pursuing not the secular vision of occidental "manifest destiny" but the possession of God, the shadow side of our battle against evil must be bracketed even as it is recognized. It must be bracketed because the risk of giving one subsidiary element undue importance in our religious life and thinking is too great. At the same time it must be acknowledged, first of all because otherwise we would be suppressing a real ingredient of our religious outlook, but also because we would be evading the work of *heshbon ha-nefesh*, our responsibility to engage in self-examination.

R. Yehudah Halevi (*Kuzari* ii, 36 ff) wrote that Israel among the nations is like the heart among the human organs, the most sensitive and therefore the hardiest. Battered by the feral willfulness of radical national self-assertion and lured by the oppressor's face disguised behind the mask of piety, we are commanded to avoid emulating the nations of Canaan whom God expelled from the land, and to remember Amalek, for the disappearance of whose legacy we must strive. Thus we are to live waiting for that day when "God will be One and His Name will be One" (Zechariah 14:9).

NOTES

1. See *Sanhedrin* 16 and *Berakhot* 3b. I had no Gemara with me in the subway, but recalled that the *Ya'arot Devash*, a copy of which happened to be in my bag, cites it. My interlocutor, however, declined to look in the book. With an air of embarrassed reticence he reminded me that the author of *Ya'arot Devash*, R. Yonatan Eyebeschuetz, had been the subject of various accusations and therefore (!!) his Talmudic quotations could not be relied on. Perhaps this was just as well: the volume I pressed on him skips the crucial line I wanted.
2. Michael Howard, *War and the Liberal Conscience* (New Brunswick, 1986), 3. Howard

distinguishes the liberal view from conservatism, which regards war as inevitable, and Marxism, which maintains that it can be eliminated only after the destruction of the established social order (11). One may be a liberal in the normative sense of condemning unnecessary military action, without being a liberal in Howard's political sense, which has to do with human nature and institutions. The young man with the backpack is a liberal in this sense too. This may be why his conversation with the lecturer was unsatisfactory. My use of the adjective "liberal" in this essay varies with context, and usually refers to both concepts of liberalism.

3. See *inter alia* Isaiah 13–14; 47; Ezekiel 25 ff; 38–39; Nahum; Zechariah 14.

4. Mishnah *Sanhedrin* 1:5; Bavli *Sanhedrin* 16a; Rambam, *Hilkhot Sanhedrin* 5:1.

5. R. Ahron Soloveichik, "Waging War on Shabbat," *Tradition* 20:3 (Fall 1982) 179–187; 181–183.

6. S.Y. Agnon, *Shira* (Tel Aviv, 1974), 306.

7. "Study of Bible in Sanctity and Bible as History," in *Kitvei ha-GRYE Henkin* Volume 1 (1980), 211–213. Citations on 211.

8. See, for example, Moshe Greenberg, "The Use of Rabbinic Midrash as an Educational Resource in Studying the Book of Joshua," in *Ha-Segullah ve-ha-Koah* (Haifa, 1985), 11–27. As I note below, Greenberg's approach is subtler than my reference here implies.

9. R. Avraham Y. Kook, *Iggerot ha-Reiyah* I (Jerusalem, 1943) § 99, p. 100. See also the letter published in his *Ma'amrei ha-Reiyah* (Jerusalem 1984) 508. Bernard Stahl called to my attention the passage in *Shemonah Kevatzim* II (Jer., 1999), 280–1 (Notebook 5, section 177).

10. *Hilkhot Melakhim* 12:1.

11. R. Kook himself can be mobilized on both sides. On the one hand, he fervently believes in the imminence of redemption and considers his age to be one of progressive social consciousness. On the other hand, in his well-known essay "War" (in *Orot*) he regards World War I as an engine of eschatological progress and accepts participation in future wars as a natural corollary of Israel's return to political life. Among R. Kook's proclaimed spiritual progeny, the messianic message can also be inverted, as proximity to the pinnacle of history justifies the militarism consummating it. See, on all these issues, Elie Holtzer's paper for this conference.

12. Tzvi Zohar, *He'iru Penei ha-Mizrah: Halakhah ve-Hagut Etzel Hakhmei Yisrael ba-Mizrah ha-Tikhon* (Jerusalem, 2001), 309 and 426 n 26, awards a gold star to R. Hayyim David Halevi for citing the existence of the UN as a sign that the world is edging closer to the Messianic ideal of international peace. Zohar deems it interesting that R. Soloveitchik, in *Kol Dodi Dofek*, implies that the only good the UN has done is to preside over the foundation of the Israeli state. It is indeed an instructive contrast.

13. On some egregious misreadings of sources in the name of militant Zionism, see Yitzchak Blau, "Ploughshares into Swords: Contemporary Religious Zionism and Moral Constraints," *Tradition* 34, 4 (2000), 39–60.

14. Hans Joas, *War and Modernity* (Blackwell, 2003), 31. Later in the book (112) Joas maintains that Americans prefer to imagine bloodless wars because of the over-

whelming traumatic memory of the Civil War. This seems odd to me, as 20th century Europe bears a much heavier and more recent burden of mass slaughter. Is it not possible that the purported American inclination to see wars in antiseptic terms derives precisely from the fact that, except for the Civil War, this country has been unaccustomed to mass victimization?

15. "Stanley Hauerwas and the Editors on 'In the Time of War,'" *First Things* (February 2002), 11–15.

16. On the contemporary attractions of pacifism, see my "Reading Gandhi at Yeshiva" (*Torah U-Madda Journal* 10); on contemporary images of religion vs. secularism with respect to war, see my "Is Religion Responsible for War?" (*Torah U-Madda Journal* 11); Note that the view I am describing here is *not* pacifist (rejecting war) but pacific, placing a high value on peace and advocating exceptional effort and risk in the hope of attaining it.

17. Mishnah *Shabbat* 6:4. See R. Kook's commentary *Ein Ayah* to *Shabbat* chapter 6 §§ 43–45.

18. Whether the law about offering these nations peace applies after the generation of Moses is discussed by Ramban, at the end of his objections to Rambam's *Sefer ha-Mitzvot, Negative Commandments*.

19. See Tosefta *Yadayim* 2:8 and analysis of *Tosafot* to *Megillah* 12b s.v. *zil* and to *Yevamot* 76b s.v. *minyamin, inter alia*. Maimonides is at *Hilkhot Issurei Bi'ah* 12:25. For exhaustive documentation on this subject, see *Otzar ha-Poskim, Even ha-Ezer* 4. Assyrian exchange of population was intended to weaken ethnic cohesion. This could be achieved by partial resettlement. On this policy, see M. Cogan, *Imperialism and Religion: Assyria, Judah and Israel in the Eighth and Seventh centuries* B.C.E. (Missoula, 1974).

20. *Hilkhot Melakhim* 5:4. In *Sefer ha-Mitzvot, Positive Commandments*, he explains at length why the non-existence of Canaanites does not undercut the eternal status of the commandment, explicitly making a contrast with Amalek. *Sefer ha-Hinnukh* 528 (end of *Parashat Shoftim*) rules, against Maimonides, that the obligation applies today to any identifiable remnants of the Canaanite nations.

21. See R. Moshe Sternbuch, *Mo'adim u-Zemanim* 11 § 164. See also Elliott Horowitz, "From the Generation of Moses to the Generation of Messiah: Jews Confront 'Amalek' and His Incarnations," *Zion* 64:4 : 425–454.

22. See, for example, *maran ha-Rav* Yosef Dov Soloveitchik, *Kol Dodi Dofek* in *Be-Sod ha-Yahid ve-ha-Yahad*, 392.

23. *Guide* III, 41. The deterrent element in Maimonides' formulation is in keeping with the general tenor of his theory of punishment as presented in this chapter.

24. *Hilkhot Melakhim* 6:1; Nahmanides, Commentary to Deuteronomy 20:10 and to Numbers 21:21.

25. Rashi to Deuteronomy 20:10. Rashbam to 20:16 rules out a peace initiative but allows Israel to respond positively to Canaanite overtures as in the case of Gibeon.

26. The large literature on Rashi's position includes Mizrahi and *Gur Aryeh ad. loc, Lehem Mishneh, Hilkhot Melakhim* 6:1, *Hazon Ish Yoreh De'ah* 157:2.

27. *Hinnukh* 425 (*Va-Ethannan*).

28. See *Hilkhot Melakhim* and *Hazon Ish*. See also commentary in *Rambam la-Am*, 380. Compare *Hilkhot Avodah Zarah* 7:1.
29. *Ein Ayah* 2:300, §115.
30. Rashi interprets as a reference to Deuteronomy's law about the seven nations Deborah's statement to Barak that God has commanded him to fight (Judges 4:6). Malbim says that she is conveying her own prophecy, not Moses', regarding God's will for the present situation. Either there would be no need for a prophetic word to remind Barak of an ongoing halakhic duty or there was no such immediate obligation.
31. Greenberg, *Ha-Segullah ve-ha-Koah*, 19.
32. Simon: "Post-Biblical and Post-Zionist Archaeology," in Israel L. Levine and Amichai Mazar: *Ha-Pulmus al ha-Emet ha-Historit ba-Mikra* (2001), 135–140; (reprinted in Simon's *Bakkesh Shalom ve-Rodfehu*).
33. In his essay "The Bible in Historical Perspective and Israelite Settlement in Canaan" in the same volume (ibid., 3–16), R. Yoel Bin-Nun observes the obvious: two versions of Israel's conquest of Canaan are already evident in the Bible itself – Joshua depicts a chain of almost unbroken victory, while Judges testifies to the very limited success achieved. He suggests that conquest is often punctuated by initial, sweeping triumphs, followed by a long, frustrating period of protracted resistance. A glance at the daily newspaper confirms the plausibility of his view.
34. Y. Bin-Nun, "The Book of Joshua: *Peshat* and Rabbinic Statements," in *Musar, Milhamah ve-Kibbush* (Alon Shevut, 1993), 31–40. See also Joshua A. Berman, *Narrative Analogy in the Hebrew Bible: Battle Stories and their Equivalent Non-battle Narratives* (Leiden; Boston: Brill, 2004), 47–48. According to Berman, with the exception of chapter 8, which he attempts to explain on other grounds, the narrative of the conquest in Joshua avoids presenting the perspective of the Canaanites in order to "objectify" them and deny them humanity. This insight is consistent with the view that participation in the enemy's subjective experience would undermine the will to war.
35. The notion that rugged extraordinary measures are appropriate at the inception of the conquest may be reflected in the injunction of *herem*, the total destruction of property, after the first campaign at Jericho (Joshua 6). I believe that this idea can shed light on the strange position taken by Nahmanides regarding the destruction of Arad (Numbers 21:1 ff). He maintains that the Arad mentioned in the Torah is identical with the Tzefat mentioned in Judges 1. Both towns are destroyed by the Israelites and renamed Horma. Offhand, there is insufficient reason to make the equation. After all, the original names are different, the interval between the time of Moses and that of Judges is substantial, and the name Horma, meaning a place totally destroyed, would fit any site subjected to such devastation. In my opinion, Nahmanides found troubling the savagery of Israel razing the city to the ground. The case of Jericho, of course, could be justified as the opening campaign, which would warrant self-denial on the part of the warring nation. The vow to subject Arad to the *herem*, according to Nahmanides, resulted from Israel's inability to

respond immediately to the attack launched by the Canaanite king of Arad: for that reason they vow to treat the capture of Arad, when that occurs, as a religious sacrificial war and not as an ordinary conquest. The *herem* of Tzefat, however, has no apparent rationale. Hence Nahmanides may have been impelled to conflate it with the story previously narrated in the Torah. In a recent conversation (6/25/03), R. Bin-Nun concurred with my proposal. For a complementary perspective see R. Tzvi Schachter, "Pearls of Our Master," *Bet Yizhak*, 37, 43 f.

36. R. Kook, *Tov Ro'i, Sotah* (Jerusalem, 5760), §8, p. 22.

37. One could resolve this difficulty by suggesting that the eternal commandment, according to Maimonides harmonized with R. Kook, is to inhabit and govern the land of Israel. Only in the first generations would this entail the eradication of the Canaanites. My suggestion would find a place for *yishuv Eretz Yisrael* according to Maimonides, an omission that has troubled many commentators. Unfortunately, it really doesn't fit Maimonides' language.

38. The discussion of Roosevelt and quotations from his works are derived from Warren Zimmermann, *First Great Triumph: How Five Americans Made Their Country a World Power* (New York, 2002), 219 ff.

39. For the range of vices symbolized by Amalek, see R. Yaakov Medan, "Amalek," in *Al Derekh ha-Avot*, 316–397.

40. Nahmanides, Commentary to Exodus 17:16.

41. George Fletcher, *Romantics at War: Glory and Guilt in the Age of Terrorism* (Princeton, 2002), quotes from pages 144 and 147.

42. *Avnei Nezer, Yoreh De'ah* 11 § 508.

43. According to *Mekhilta*, end of *Beshallah*, we do not accept Amalekite converts. Nonetheless, the rabbinic statement cited above implies that such converts existed. In any event Maimonides omits this prohibition (see Rambam, *Hilkhot Issurei Bi'ah* 12:17). *Avnei Nezer* argues that Amalekites must be allowed to convert, since even the Canaanites, who are guilty of widespread idolatry, have that opportunity. For later discussion of the *Mekhilta* passage, see Sagi, cited below, nt. 45, 338 n. 49.

44. On this issue, see, for example, Stephen Jay Gould's *The Mismeasure of Man*. C. Turnbull, in *The Mountain People*, imputed to the African group he studied, the Ik, such moral insensitivity (which he ascribed to relocation followed by ecological disasters inculcating, over generations, an irreversible and thorough selfishness) that they must be dispersed forever. His work, once popular among philosophers, is now considered highly unreliable. See most recently, R. Grinker, *In the Arms of Africa: a Life of Colin M. Turnbull* (University of Chicago, 2001).

45. Avi Sagi, "The Punishment of Amalek in Jewish Tradition: Coping with the Moral Problem" (*Harvard Theological Review* 87:3, July 1994), 323–346.

46. See Medan, "Amalek," *Al Derekh ha-Avot* (2001), 317–396, n. 40 for his extended discussion of this point *contra* Sagi.

47. It is revealing that Sagi (323), remarks on the fact that "even" God is occupied with the obliteration of Amalek, while a consecutive reading of the Torah starts out with God's oath and then promulgates a human obligation.

48. Citations are from R. Avigdor Amiel, *Derashot el Ammi*, III, chapter 14: "Sword and Scripture" (132–143).

49. See, for example, John Howard Yoder, *The Politics of Jesus*.

50. See also *Lam. Rabbah*, Proem 30 and R. Eliyahu Dessler, *Mikhtav me-Eliyahu*, I 201.

51. On the imagery of Joel 4:15–16 see Meir Weiss, "On One Biblical Metaphor," in *Mikra'ot ke-Kavvanatam* (Jerusalem, 1987), 27–86; original appearance *Tarbiz* 34. I have dealt with this entire issue in greater detail in my lectures on Joel.

52. We are not concerned here with the exclusion of Amalek from the halakhic category of the "children of Esau." See Nahmanides to Genesis 36:12 and R. Yehudah Gershuni, "On the *Mitzvah* of Eradicating Amalek," in *Kol Tzofayikh* (Jerusalem, 1980), 437–438.

53. A standard article is G. Cohen, "Edom and Rome," in A. Altmann, *Biblical and Other Studies* (1964). E. Horowitz's article in *Zion* 64:4 contains updated material on these identifications. Louis Feldman, "Josephus' Portrait of Jacob," *JQR* 79, 130–133 maintains that the identification of Edom and Rome is as early as Josephus.

54. My allusion is based on the Rav's annotated manuscript of this lecture on *Parashat Hukkat*. In support of his thesis, one may note the radical contrast between the bellicosity expressed in Numbers and the command in Deuteronomy 2 to avoid provoking "your brothers the children of Esau who dwell in Seir." The two narratives can be harmonized in a variety of ways, most plausibly perhaps, following Rashbam's view distinguishing the kingdom of Edom from the inhabitants of Seir. Whichever explanation is adopted, the difference in tone is remarkable. It appears that Numbers and Deuteronomy have different goals in narrating these episodes. In Deuteronomy, the point is either that God has provided a homeland for the neighbors of Israel as He has for us, or that the reason Israel did not conquer their territory was a specific prohibition rather than divine weakness, as it were (see Nahmanides and Seforno *ad loc.*). In Numbers, according to the Rav, we confront the eternal hostility of Edom = Amalek.

55. See, for example, Amos 1; Jeremiah 49:7 ff; Ezekiel 25 and 35; Malachi 1.

56. In this, Isaiah 34 is similar to the second, more specialized prophecy against Edom in Ezekiel. Chapter 25 is placed within the prophecies concerning the nations section (chapters 25–32). Chapter 35 is among the prophecies of redemption (34–48).

57. Cf. Jeremiah 49:14 and note slight differences.

58. The second person probably refers to Edom, who had celebrated the destruction (Targum; Rashi; Radak). The punishment is that their merry intoxication will become a drunken stupor. According to Ibn Ezra, the prophet is addressing Israel: as they had drained the bitter cup (see Jeremiah 25:27 ff and 49:12), so will those who rejoiced at their plight.

59. On the fundamental difference between "Gog and Magog" and Amalek, see R. Kook, *Olat Reiyah* I, 232.

60. Though I have arrived at this analysis independently, there are obvious parallels to the work of René Girard, e.g. *Violence and the Sacred* (Baltimore, 1977).

61. R. Aharon Lichtenstein, "Halakhah and Conduct as Foundations of Ethics: Theoretical and Educational Reflections," in *Arakhim be-Mivhan Milhamah: Ethics and War in the Light of Judaism: Essays in Memory of Ram Mizrahi* (Yeshivat Har-Etzion, 1985), 13–24; quote 23 f.
62. Schweid, "The Annihilation of Amalek and Eradication of the Amorite," *Moznayim* 33 (1971): 201–209.
63. Ibid., 206.
64. In the Rav's work, this idea is most lucidly expressed in his manuscript *The Emergence of Ethical Man*, edited by Michael Berger (Hoboken, 2005).
65. See Genesis chapters 4 and 9. That fratricide ("the voice of the blood of your brother") rather than the "Kantian" transgression against humanity, is central to the original murder, was pointed out by students in my Honors "Genesis and Literature" course Yeshiva College, Fall 2003.
66. Commentators on *Midrash Rabbah* were troubled by the nature of Moses' initiative. If his action was in conformity with Deuteronomy 20, he was simply following the law. If not, how is his initiative justified? In the narrative order of the Torah, the law of Deuteronomy 20 had not yet been promulgated at the time when Moses encountered the Amorites (Deut. 2–Numbers 21).

Amalek and the Seven Nations: A Case of Law vs. Morality

Norman Lamm

I offer no apologies for this exercise in apologetics. The Torah's injunctions against the people of Amalek and the seven Canaanite nations are enshrined in the Halakhah and, although they have not been put into practice since the Biblical period, they do present today's believers with thorny moral problems that call for understanding and, thus, apologetics. Without any claim to a comprehensive treatment of the issue, this paper will endeavor to analyze the Halakhah on these commandments and attempt to resolve, or at least mitigate, the moral and ethical problems they engender within the confines of Orthodox Judaism.[1]

SOME SCENARIOS

Not long ago, the press reported that a devout young Moslem in England belongs to al-Muhajiroun, a group of dedicated Islamists, and was invited to a conference that will honor the "Magnificent 19" hijackers who perpetrated the September 11, 2001 terrorist attacks on the United States. The group leader told him, "The actions of these 19 are completely justified in the light of Sharia [Islamic law]…I don't believe any Muslim who believes in Islam, and believes in his Lord, would disagree with that." He turned to his Imam to resolve his conflict between his faith and his own moral doubts about this course of action. Assuming the Imam was moderate and humane, but a convinced Muslim, what should he say?

Imagine now this unlikely but theoretically possible occurrence: a young Orthodox Jew who is totally committed to Halakhah but is morally sensitive, turns to his Rabbi with a painful dilemma. He has befriended a Gentile and learned by sophisticated DNA testing that the man is unquestionably of Amalekite or Canaanite descent, someone whom the Torah commands be destroyed. What should the Rabbi say?

The parallels are obvious. The first scenario is *halakhah lema'aseh* for Moslems. The second, while not of immediate practical significance, is morally troubling for religious Jews. It is now our task to turn to the sources and consult our conscience in order to develop an answer to our theoretical inquirer.

THE BIBLICAL RECORD

In the Torah's record of the relations of ancient Israel with the surrounding nations, certain of them stand out as implacable enemies deserving of special treatment. They are Amalek, a tribe that attacked the stragglers of Israel with notorious cruelty, and the "seven" indigenous or aboriginal "nations" which occupied what was to become *Eretz Israel*. The Biblical verses are as follows:

Amalek: There are two major passages in the Pentateuch that concern Amalek, the first enemy that Israel encountered after the crossing of the Red Sea.

a. Exodus 17:8–16 – Amalek came and fought with Israel at Rephidim. Moses said to Joshua, "Pick some men for us, and go out and do battle with Amalek".… Joshua did as Moses told him and fought with Amalek…And Joshua overwhelmed the people of Amalek with the sword. Then the Lord said to Moses, "Inscribe this in a document as a reminder, and read it aloud to Joshua: I will utterly blot out the memory of Amalek from under heaven!" And Moses built an altar and named it *Adonai nissi*. He said, "It means, 'Hand upon the throne of the Lord!' The Lord will be at war with Amalek from generation to generation."

b. Deuteronomy 25:17–19 – Remember what Amalek did to you on your journey, after you left Egypt – how, undeterred by fear of God, he surprised you on the march, when you were famished and weary, and cut down all the stragglers in your rear. Therefore, when the Lord your God grants you safety from all your enemies around you, in the land that the Lord your God is giving you as a hereditary portion, blot out the memory of Amalek from under heaven. Do not forget!

There are several passages in the Early Prophets that speak of the way these charges were or were not carried out. Chief among them is the story of the prophet Samuel and King Saul (1 Samuel 15:1–9):

Samuel said to Saul, "I am the one the Lord sent to anoint you king over His people Israel. Therefore, listen to the Lord's command. Thus said the Lord of Hosts: I am exacting the penalty for what Amalek did to Israel, for the assault he made upon them on the road, on their way up from Egypt. Now go, attack Amalek, and utterly destroy all that belongs to him. Spare no one, but kill alike men and women, infants and sucklings, oxen and sheep, camels and asses!"…Saul destroyed Amalek from Havilah all the way to Shur, which is close to Egypt, and he captured King Agag of Amalek alive. He utterly destroyed all the people, putting them to the sword; but Saul and the troops spared Agag and the best of the sheep, the oxen, the second-born, the lambs, and all else that was of value. They would not destroy them; they destroyed only what was cheap and worthless.[2]

The prophet was furious at the king for failing to obey the divine instructions, and informed him that he would lose his throne as a result. Samuel summoned the troops to bring Agag to him, whereupon he proclaimed to Agag, "As your sword has bereaved women, so shall your mother be bereaved among women," and he executed him.

Towards the end of the Biblical period, in the Scroll of Esther, we read of the classical anti-Semite, Haman, that he was the son of Hamdatha the Agagite. Agag himself, as we learned from the Samuel incident, was an Amalekite, and Haman thus reenacted his notorious ancestor's genocidal intentions concerning Jews.[3]

The Seven Nations[4]: The Torah distinguishes between other ("distant") nations and the much closer "seven nations" in the following passage from Deuteronomy 20: 9–18:

> When you approach a town to attack it, you shall offer it terms of peace. If it responds peaceably and lets you in, all the people present there shall serve you as forced labor. If it does not surrender to you, but would join battle with you, you shall lay siege to it; and when the Lord your God delivers it into your hand, you shall put all its males to the sword. You may, however, take as your booty the women, the children, the livestock, and everything in the town – all its spoil – and enjoy the use of the spoil of your enemy, which the Lord your God gives you. Thus you shall deal with all towns that lie very far from you, towns that do not belong to nations hereabout. In the towns of the latter peoples, however, which the Lord your God is giving you as a heritage, you shall not let a soul remain alive. No, you must utterly destroy them – the Hittites and the Amorites, the Canaanites and the Perizzites, the Hivites and the Jebusites – as the Lord your God has commanded you, lest they lead you into doing all the abhorrent things that they have done for their gods and you stand guilty before the Lord your God.

The stricter attitude towards nations bordering the Land of Israel obviously has to do with the greater danger of assimilation of the idolatrous cultures. The farther away the offending nations, the less of a danger do they present.

Earlier in Deuteronomy (7:1, 2), the Torah is more explicit in its abhorrence of the Seven Nations: "When the Lord your God delivers them to you and you defeat them, you must utterly destroy them: grant them no terms and give them no quarter."[5]

THE PROBLEM

The moral issues raised by the by these Biblical commandments center on the total war against these ancient enemies of Israel. Even enlightened modern countries engage in wars in which innocent bystanders are killed and maimed in the course of battle. But that is not the same as specifying that, as a matter of military or diplomatic policy, non-combatant men, women, and children are to be killed, and that these acts of vengeance are to be visited upon their descendants forever.

For contemporary men and women, the moral issue is exacerbated because of our experience with and therefore abhorrence of genocide – although it is uncertain that the term is properly applicable to the commandments concerning Amalek and the Seven Nations. This pejorative characterization of an ancient policy on the basis of a relatively new legal concept is at least open to question. The official legal definition of genocide, according to the Convention on the Prevention and Punishment of Genocide, is the killing or maiming of a *national, ethnic, racial,* or *religious* group. A *national* group is defined as a set of individuals whose identity is defined by a common country or nationality or national origin. An *ethnic* group is one of common cultural traditions, language, or heritage. A *racial* group is one defined by physical characteristics. A *religious* group is a set of people of common religious creeds, beliefs, doctrines, practices, or rituals.

The question is whether the entities that incurred the Biblical wrath fit it into any of these categories. It is certainly not religious, because most or all other groups of the ancient Near East were equally polytheistic. It is not a racial category, because to our knowledge there is no evidence that Amalek differed physically from any of the other contemporary groups. Moreover, if it was racial in nature, no exceptions would be countenanced, yet (as we shall see presently), Maimonides and others allowed for exceptions if the enemy groups accepted a peace offer by Israel. The acceptance by Amalek or the Seven "Nations" of the Noahide Laws or the offering of peace by the Israelites thus spares them from the draconian Biblical punishment. The genocides of recent history, most especially the Holocaust, left no escape for Jews or Gypsies. It should not be considered an ethnic matter, for we know nothing, or almost nothing, of distinct cultures or languages that were peculiar to Amalek or the hapless seven. Further, Maimonides (*Guide of the Perplexed* III:50) makes the point that Amalek, alone among the children of Esau, was singled out for horrific punishment. For this reason, the most significant possibility is that of nationhood. Can any group of a thousand or five thousand individuals who unify themselves under one leader reasonably be considered a "nation?" Or are they a "tribe?" Is the third Assembly District of Springfield, MA, a nation? Is Staten Island a nation – and would it be a nation if it declared its independence from the United States? The moral question remains despite categorization of the commanded acts, but the use of a specific pejorative nomenclature – "genocide" – is emotionally laden and understandingly complicates clear thinking about the issue.

There are, basically, two elements of moral concern. One is the Amalek commandment, whereby the descendants of Amalek are forever condemned to death, apparently without regard to their own conduct. The Torah's explanation implies a genetic defect in the Amalekites. The other is the Seven Nations commandment, whereby the seven indigenous Canaanite tribes are to be wiped out – "you shall not let a soul remain alive" – and the reason is their abominable culture and religion which threaten to corrupt the incoming Israelites.

Neither of these stands up well under mortal scrutiny. Here is a blatant case of Law versus Morality. How should a Jew loyal to Halakhah respond?

A first response is to deny any separate and independent value to morality. What the Law says, that is what is good. Hence, by definition, the Torah's commandments concerning Amalek and the Seven Nations are good and not open to moral objection. This essentially Platonic idea (as developed in his *Republic* and *The Laws*) is translated into Jewish terms by one of the most outstanding rabbinic authorities of the twentieth century, R. Avraham Yeshayahu Karelitz, known by the title of his major work, the *Hazon Ish*.

For the Hazon Ish, it is inconceivable that humans can devise a moral code that, in any way, is more noble or demanding than the laws of the Torah. Nothing that came after the Sinaitic revelation can lay claim to improving on the Torah's legislation. Morality is whatever the Halakhah says. Law trumps conscience; conscience, morality, ethics can never be the source or have the power of *mitzvah*. The sole function of ethics and conscience is to inspire one to observe the Halakhah as the Word of the Almighty.[6]

The Hazon Ish subscribes to the conventional view of the Talmudic tradition, that of the declining generations: "If the earlier generations were like angels, we are like humans; if they were like humans, we are like donkeys" (*Shabbat* 112b). It would appear, then, that succeeding generations are utterly powerless to solve their moral dilemmas by positing a more stringent code of practice in the name of a more developed moral intuition.

Yet that is not the rule in all cases, and while it holds for the proximity to or distance from Sinai – any oral tradition suffers diminution in time, thus making the reports by the earlier generations more reliable than those of the later ones – the process of deterioration need not be considered universal.[7]

Proof of this thesis is the fact that in certain important cases, the Rabbis had the right – which they exercised – of suspending Biblical law passively when they regarded it as counter-productive, as in the case of the Scroll of the Suspected Adulteress (the *sotah*), or the abandonment on technical grounds of the death penalty, or the gradual abolition of slavery, or when they wished to protect another halakhic commandment (such as banning the sounding of the *shofar* on Rosh Hashanah which falls on a Saturday). In the first half of the third century CE, the *amora* Rav ordered punishment by flogging for one who officially married a woman by sexual intercourse, even though a marriage so consummated is technically valid according to Biblical law. Similarly, polygamy was widely practiced in the Biblical period, but was formally banned for Ashkenazi communities by Rabbenu Gershon, "the Light of the Exile," in the 11th century. The Talmud's severe treatment of heretics – at times the heretic should be thrown into a pit, at others he at least must not be rescued from the pit – is suspended nowadays, according to the Hazon Ish himself, because it is inoperative in times of "the hiding of God's face," i.e., when the society no longer feels itself bound by the strictures of faith, and because it is counter-productive.[8]

If anyone harbors serious doubts about inevitable changes in the moral climate in favor of heightened sensitivity, consider how we would react if in our own times someone would stipulate as the *nadan* for his daughter the equivalent of the one hundred Philistine foreskins which Saul demanded of David (1 Samuel 18:25) and which dowry David later offered to him for his daughter Michal's hand in marriage (II Samuel 3:14)…The difference in perspective is not only a matter of esthetics and taste but also of morals.

The relation of law and morality in secular philosophy is quite complex, and has a long and distinguished history. The question of whether they are rivals or whether law is that part of the moral code which is enforceable, was famously debated in the latter part of the 19th century between the philosophers John Stuart Mill and James F. Stephen.[9] The overwhelming number of authoritative classical Jewish scholars in general favors the latter over the former. The late Prof. Yeshayahu Leibowitz has over many years denied passionately that Halakhah contains an ethical system. But neither passion nor brilliance can change the facts of the Torah's and Talmud's profound commitment to the moral content of Judaism. I do not believe that the denial by Hazon Ish of any independent value to ethics or conscience is necessarily the only authentic voice of Torah Judaism on this subject. In an article I co-authored with Prof. Aaron Kirschenbaum, I argued that Judaism recognizes Natural Law, and this constitutes a system of morality that chronologically (but not axiologically) precedes the Halakhah.[10] Separating Halakhah from morality does violence to both, turning Halakhah into a codex of rigid and sometimes heartless rules and morality into a kind of unstructured and emotionally driven method, as imprecise as it is subjective, of deciding upon one's conduct.[11] Note that the Torah goes out of its way to explain and justify the harsh commandments against both Amalek and the Canaanite aborigines. *That very explanation implies that the Torah itself recognized the moral problem* of the harshness of the edict, especially against the innocent children of the reprobates. This offends the modern aversion to vengeance[12] in general and to genocide in particular and, more important, seems to go against the grain of the Torah's own principle not to punish the children for the sins of the fathers (Deut. 4:16). Thus, the Talmud in *Yoma* 22b has King Saul protesting the divine command to exterminate all of Amalek: if the Torah is so concerned with the life of one individual – as in the rite of the *eglah arufah* – certainly it should be concerned with so large a number as Amalek. And if humans sinned, why punish the animals? And if adults sinned, why harm the children?[13] To which a divine voice replied: Do not be overly righteous.[14]

We are thus presented with a special case of the larger problem of the conflict between certain Biblical and halakhic imperatives that are *prima facie* morally questionable. The issue of Amalek and the Canaanites is especially dramatic, and we shall attempt to deal with this specific case as an example of other such dilemmas.

Before dealing with this special case, it should be noted that the Jewish tradition recognized that, whereas the Torah's commandments are almost always morally edifying, there are specific instances where the consequences of the *mitzvot* can prove morally undesirable.

Thus, the Sages offer a poignant comment on the verse in Koheleth (Eccl. 4:1): "I returned and considered all the oppressions that are done under the sun; and behold the tears of the oppressed who have no comforter; the oppressors have power, but they [the victims] have no power."

The Midrash (*Lev. Rabbah* 32:8), applies Koheleth's pained cry

of the powerless victims of oppression to the case of *mamzerim,*
illegitimate offspring of adulterous or incestuous liaisons, who are
forbidden to marry other Jewish people:

> Daniel the Tailor applied to *mamzerim* the verse "behold
> the tears of the oppressed": their parents sinned, and these
> wretched ones – what did they do to deserve this? So, the father
> of this one had illicit relations with a woman; but what sin did
> the son commit? "Who have no comforter but the oppressors
> have power" – [this refers to] the Great Sanhedrin of Israel who
> confront [the *mamzerim*] with the power of Torah and exclude
> them [as the Torah says,] "a *mamzer* shall not come into the
> community of Israel" [i.e., not marry into the community].
> "They (the victims) have no power" – so the Holy One said,
> "It is, then, incumbent upon Me to comfort them, for in this
> world they have [halakhic] defects (of illegitimacy), but in the
> world-to-come, as [the Prophet] Zechariah said, 'I have seen
> [the people of Israel] and they are as the pure as the purest gold'"
> (i.e., the entire people, including those regarded in this world
> as *mamzerim,* will be considered as without blemish and thus
> all will be able to intermarry with each other).

The Halakhah was meant for the welfare of the entire community, and the laws concerning illegitimacy certainly have a powerful
deterrent effect on those who would otherwise casually sink into
moral turpitude; yet it inevitably disadvantages certain innocent
individuals. That is the nature of all law, sacred or profane – a
phenomenon already noticed by Plato, and later by Maimonides.
And herein lies a problem, or a group of problems. How should the
disadvantaged few look upon the law that effectively discriminates
against them? Is there not a moral objection to being victimized by
the law? Is not the community obligated to ameliorate the situation?
Or, more directly, is the law – the Halakhah– identical or even just
compatible with moral standards?

We face not dissimilar problems with regard to the Biblical
commandments concerning Amalek and the Canaanite Nations.

The tradition grappled with them, directly or indirectly, going back to the Mishnah[15] and the Talmud. They were discussed by the medieval authorities, and have been treated by contemporary halakhic scholars, philosophically oriented thinkers, and historians.

In the following pages I shall make use of the classical sources on Amalek and the Canaanite nations from the Bible through later Talmudic authorities and, as well, contemporary scholars. With regard to the latter, I am indebted to all of them but, of course, I take responsibility for developing the theme in my own way.

THE HALAKHAH

In order better to understand how the Jewish tradition grappled with this dilemma, it is important to note the fact that the Sages were not unaware of moral concerns as well as other problems in the plain reading of Scripture, and were willing – albeit in a highly disciplined manner – to act to bring Jewish law to consider ethical and moral as well as other legal issues. They were prepared to identify the limitations that the Halakhah placed upon the implementation of the Biblical commands.

The Mishnah itself hardly mentions Amalek. In one case (*Megillah* 3:6) it merely includes the public reading of the Amalek passage in Exodus (17:8) on Purim, and in the other (*Kiddushin* 4:14) as one of a series of popular maxims, namely, that the best of ritual slaughterers is "a partner of Amalek."

The Torah's "rules of war," as filtered through the prism of the Jewish tradition, offer a context that makes the Biblical mandate appear far less cruel than it seems from initial confrontation with the text itself. To begin with, the Torah divides the gentile world (the Noahides) into two categories: those who observe the Seven Noahide Commandments and those who do not; the former are considered civilized, the latter as uncivilized because of the unredeemable degeneracy of their cultures, religions, and legal codes – or their cruelty in warfare. Even the Amalekites and Canaanites, singled out in the above verses for especially harsh treatment, could save themselves by accepting the Seven Commandments. The following summarizes much of the halakhic legislation:

- Before undertaking the siege of a hostile city, offers of peace must be undertaken. The terms are subservience and tribute.
- The peace proposals must be made to all, even Canaanites and Amalekites.[16]
- If they accept upon themselves the Seven Noahide Commandments, they are considered as citizens and treated as equals before the law. [17]
- Ammonites and Moabites, because they mistreated the Israelites in their long trek from Egypt, could not be accepted as proselytes,[18] forever; but it was forbidden to wage war against them.
- All treaties must be solemnly observed by both parties – Israel and the enemy.
- A siege may be laid against a "city" – a term which excludes a village or a metropolis.
- It is forbidden to lay a siege merely for the purpose of destroying a city or taking its inhabitants as slaves.
- The peace terms must be offered by Israel *before* any attack against a city by a blockade of hunger, thirst, or disease.
- The peace terms must be offered to a hostile city for three consecutive days, and even if the terms are rejected, a siege may not be undertaken before the enemy has commenced hostilities.
- No direct cruelties may be inflicted even when the city is under siege.
- No city may be totally blockaded; an opening must be left for people to leave the city.
- Soldiers of Israel were expected to act with exemplary behavior; even slander and gossip were not to be tolerated.
- Those of the enemy condemned to death (i.e., those who rejected the offer of observing the Seven Commandments) were to be killed as painlessly as possible.
- Enemy dead were to be buried honorably.[19]
- A city was not be razed needlessly.
- Women, children, the old, and the sick were not to be harmed.
- Captives of war were to be treated humanely.

Most significant of the above items is the one regarding the offer of peace proposals *even* to the Amalekites and the Canaanites. The source for this law is a bold ruling by Maimonides (*Hilkhot Melakhim* 6:1), for which I can find no clear precedent in earlier Talmudic literature. The Talmud (*Sotah* 35b) accepts the repentance of the condemned tribes. Rashi limits this dispensation to those groups living outside the borders of the Holy Land. Tosafot (*ad loc.*) maintain that the mitigation obtains even for the tribes bordering the Holy Land, provided they sue for peace before the beginning of hostilities. Maimonides extends it even to local tribes who sued for peace even after war breaks out, but insists that they accept upon themselves the Noahide laws as non-negotiable.[20] Maimonides further rules that the Biblical commandment to pursue and destroy Amalek "from generation to generation" was limited to those descendants of Amalek who persisted in their barbaric ways. If they do not continue the abominable practices of the Biblical Amalek, the sentence of death is not applicable. But if they do follow the same Amalekite policies, the severe judgment holds sway and is considered a legitimate act of self-defense. Accordingly, the Amalek commandment cannot be considered racial or ethnic but is, rather, behavioral.

DO THE AMALEKITES EXIST ANY LONGER?

So much for the basic outline of the halakhic theory of wars. Even more relevant is the issue of history. We read a record of a court session headed by some of the most significant and authoritative sages during the early Tannaitic period. This deals with tribes other than Amalek, yet is most germane to our thesis. The Mishnah (*Yadayim* 2:17) discusses the case of Judah, an Ammonite proselyte, who appeared before a venerable court in the latter part of the first century c.e. and asked permission to marry a Jewess. The Torah explicitly forbade Ammonites and Moabites from marrying within the Jewish people (Deut. 23:4–5). On this basis, Rabban Gamliel opined that the request not be granted. However, R. Yehoshua ruled that the petitioner be permitted to marry a Jewess. His reasoning: both Moabites and Ammonites no longer populate the same areas as in Biblical days, because the Assyrian King Sennacherib enforced massive population transfers so that it is impossible to identify individual Ammonites and Moabites. After further dialogue, the Mishnah ruled that the man may marry the Jewess.[21] This important decision means that today it is impossible to identify the descendants of Amalek, the seven Canaanite nations, Ammonites, etc., and hence the Biblical injunctions, mentioned above, are impossible to implement. Thus, halakhically, these commandments are no longer operative and have not been invoked since the Biblical period.

However, the question is whether this dispensation for members of the inhabitants of Ammon and Moab extends to descendants of the Seven Nations and Amalek. Here is how Maimonides (*Hilkhot Melakhim* 5:4, 5) codifies the Halakhah:

> *Halakhah* 4: It is a positive commandment to destroy the Seven Nations, as it is said, "you must utterly destroy them" (Deut. 20:17). If one has the opportunity and fails to kill one of them, he transgresses a negative commandment, as it is said, "you shall not let a soul remain alive" (Deut. 20:16). But their memory has long since perished.

> *Halakhah* 5: Similarly (*ve-khen*), it is a positive commandment to destroy the remembrance of Amalek, as it is said, "you shall blot out the memory of Amalek" (Deut. 25:19). It is also a positive commandment to remember always his evil deeds and the waylaying [he resorted to], so that we keep fresh the hatred he manifested, as it is said, "Remember what Amalek did to you" (Deut. 25:17). The traditional interpretation of this injunction is: "Remember – by word of mouth; do not forget – out of mind, that it is forbidden to forget his hatred and enmity."

Note that Maimonides, in *halakhah* 5, when discussing Amalek, fails to add the last clause in *halakhah* 4 concerning the Seven Nations, namely, "But their memory has long since perished." This would imply an inequality between the halakhic treatment of the Seven Nations and of Amalek. Indeed, our teacher, Rabbi Joseph B. Soloveitchik ("the Rav") o.b.m., concludes from this omission that,

"It would appear from Maimonides' statements that Amalek is still in existence, while the Seven Nations have descended into the abyss of oblivion."[22] Only the Seven Nations are obsolete and only they were identified by R. Joshua as having lost their identity because of the enforced co-mingling by the two kings. It follows that Amalekite descendents live on with us, and therefore the law to destroy them is still in force. And since "The Lord will be at war with Amalek from generation to generation," as the Exodus verse relates, they will not be obliterated until the coming of the Messiah.

The question then arises: If Amalek still survives, where is Amalek today? The Rav's answer is that "Amalek" undergoes a metamorphosis "from generation to generation." The Rav quotes his father, Rabbi Moshe Soloveitchik, o.b.m., who expands the injunction against Amalek to include any nation that seeks to destroy the Jewish people. His father then proceeds to discern two separate commandments concerning Amalek: the Deuteronomic obligation to extirpate Amalek's memory devolves upon every Jew with reference to individual Amalekites, and the Exodus verse, "I will utterly blot out the memory of Amalek from under heaven," implies the readiness of the entire community to do battle against the whole people of Amalek as a "just war," a *milhemet mitzvah*. The first of these two commandments applies to all the genealogical descendants of Amalek. The second applies to the peoples of Israel and Amalek as a whole, and concerns not specifically Amalek as such, but *any* entity that seeks to destroy the people of Israel and which thereby becomes the "Amalek" of that generation.

According to this analysis, our moral problem is exacerbated: even today we are commanded to destroy individuals who may lay claim to such unsavory genealogy, innocent individual descendants of evil people who flourished three thousand years ago; and the moral issue of genocide[23] – destroying a whole nation that is anti-Semitic. Emotionally, the latter is a policy that may be gratifying and may certainly be well deserved. But the political and human consequences are stark and overwhelming.

But even aside from the natural reluctance even to imagine ourselves engaging in such morally problematic activities, there are several reasons to question the whole schema just described. I find it enormously difficult to disagree, especially for the record, with my own revered master. I am acutely aware of the halakhic ethic that *ein meshivin et ha-ari le-ahar mittah*, "one does not refute the lion after he has died" (*Gittin* 33a). But I also feel bound by the maxim of R. Akiva, that "This is Torah, hence I must study it," i.e., without bowing to authority (*Berakhot* 62a).[24] Surely, the Rav himself would have recommended intellectual honesty. In that spirit, I offer the following critique.

First, I believe that the reason for Maimonides failing to mention "But their memory has long since perished," is the word *ve-khen*, "similarly," at the beginning of *halakhah* 5. Maimonides thereby implies that the Seven Nations, the subject of *halakhah* 5, is subject to the same terms as Seven Nations, the subject of *halakhah* 4. This would lead one to conclude that just as the law requiring the utter destruction of the Seven Nations is no longer relevant because of the Mesopotamian and Babylonian policy of intermingling all subjugated peoples, so too is it impossible nowadays to identify with any degree of certainty who is and who is not a descendant of Amalek. Hence, it was unnecessary for Maimonides to repeat the clause in question. Moreover, it is important to note that in *halakhah* 1 of the self-same chapter 5, Maimonides exemplifies "obligatory wars" as the wars against the Seven Nations, against Amalek, and in self-defense. The implication is that the wars against the Seven Nations and against Amalek are treated as equal to each other, without any distinction made between them as to the intermingling of peoples.[25]

Moreover, it is clear from the words of the *Hinnukh*, who usually follows Maimonides, that the Amalekites and Canaanites alike have long since disappeared from the scene of history and whatever stragglers who survived have been assimilated to other peoples.[26]

Second, as a practical matter, the policy of intermingling was applied to *all* victims of these two ancient tyrants. True, the Jewish people was spared for a variety of historic reasons which are not relevant to other ancient peoples. It is hardly imaginable that the Assyrian and Babylonian chieftains kept Amalek intact solely to befuddle the descendants of their Jewish subjects centuries later. Why, then, should we assume that the Seven Nations were assimilated, but the Amalekites were not?

Third, the conclusion of the Rabbis Soloveitchik, father and son, weighs heavily on one's conscience. It would demand of us to act decisively in the second scenario at the beginning of this paper, telling the innocent young enquirer that it his duty to murder his friend whom DNA testing has positively been identified as an Amalekite, who thus by his very presence proves that the two ancient kings were unsuccessful in wiping out Amalek either by mingling or murder. And we would have to offer our understanding and sympathetic justification to the Imam of the young Moslem who, in the first scenario, is being solicited to join an Islamist terrorist group. Both acts simply violate our deepest moral sentiments as Jews, especially Torah Jews, and would vitiate all reasons proffered by eminent halakhic authorities to soften the impact of the commandments. But even more than conscience is involved here: enlarging the scope of the commandment to destroy nations that are blood-thirsty, etc., places us on a slippery slope. If enlargement is in order, why not include self-hating Jews in the Amalek category? And why not, thereafter, Jews who are not observant? Or Jews who are observant but in a different way or who do not agree with my beliefs or principles? After the Rabin assassination and the current murmurings of a repeat act of regicide, such a bizarre and absurd conclusion is not unthinkable. (I have heard of such terribly dangerous inanity uttered in casual seriousness.)

Fourth is a matter of consistency. If the commandment to destroy the very memory of Amalek applies to any national group that seeks to extirpate every living Jew, then we must treat this as a halakhic matter, and perforce apply this with all the stringency that the Torah makes clear, i.e., the verdict of death must be pronounced on every last member of that nation *and all its descendants* – forever. So, for instance, Nazi Germany would have to be totally destroyed, *including* those Germans who revolted against Hitler, those who attempted at the risk of death to save Jews, those who rebuilt a democratic state on the ruins of the Third Reich, and those who chose to throw in their lot with the State of Israel. Clearly, that is impractical and unacceptable.

Fifth, the idea that we have the right or even the duty to expand the *mitzvah* of exterminating Amalek beyond the limits of its ethnic-genetic identity, turning a real community into an expanding metaphor, runs into serious difficulties. It is true that in the course of time, this tendency to turn *Amalek* into *Amalekism* became so deeply rooted in Jewish thinking, that many important enemies of Israel were identified halakhically as direct descendants of Amalek. Thus, a tannaitic *aggadah* of the First Century identifies Rome as Amalek.[27] But a free-wheeling tendency, if taken literally, faces even greater problems from the perspective of history, including our contemporary times. Following is a list drawn up by Daniel Jonah Goldhagen[28]:

> All over Europe, Gentiles have expelled Jews, sometimes for hundreds of years: Crimea in 1016, Paris in 1182, England in 1290, France in 1306, Switzerland in 1348, Hungary in 1349, Provence in 1394, Austria in 1421, Krakow in 1494, Lithuania in 1495, Portugal in 1497, and most of Germany during the 14–16 centuries. From the 15th century until 1722 Russia forbade Jews to enter its soil. Most infamously, Spain expelled its Jews in 1492…Mass-murdering of Jews began in 414 when the people of newly Christianized Roman Alexandria annihilated the city's Jewish community. The mass slaughter of Jews reached an especially momentous frenzy during the First Crusade in 1096. The crusaders killed the Jews of one community after another in Northern France and Germany…Between 1348 and 1350, during the black plague, ordinary Germans slaughtered the Jews of roughly 350 communities, virtually every city and town, rendering Germany almost *judenrein*. During the Chmielnicki massacres of 1648–1656, ordinary Ukrainians slaughtered more than 100,000 Jews in cities and towns across Poland. The Russian pogroms from 1871 to 1906, though they

claimed a fraction of the victims of earlier atrocities, shocked the Western world.

And we have not even mentioned the Holocaust…Thus, if we legitimize the identification of Amalek with any people who are viciously anti-Semitic, many of whom sought not only to persecute but to wipe us out completely, we would have to apply the biblical command to extirpate every anti-Semitic entity as "Amalek," including Crimea, France, England, Switzerland, Hungary, Provence, Austria, Poland, Lithuania, Portugal, Spain, Ukraine, Russia, certainly Germany, and nowadays many, if not most, of the Islamic countries. And if indeed they be classified as *Amalekim*, how about their descendants whom we are bidden to annihilate "from generation to generation?" How many non-Jews would then remain to populate the planet? Such an ambitious program of wholesale vengeance might solve the problem of anti-Semitism as well as that of the earth's overpopulation, but it offends one's moral sensitivity and is simply beyond moral comprehension and would therefore constitute a massive *hillul Hashem*.

Sixth, the apparent reason for expanding Exodus verse to all anti-Semitic nations is to make sure that the Biblical passages remain relevant even if Amalek as such disappears. But that requires a kind of halakhic legerdemain; the simple (*peshat*) of the verses specifies Amalek. Others among the aboriginal inhabitants of Canaan might have qualified for divine vengeance, but the Torah specifically and explicitly says, "Amalek." Making the second commandment relevant by an expansion to include all enemies of Israel appears more homiletic than halakhic. Is it not preferable to keep the technical *halakhah* close to simple *peshat,* the literal meaning of the verses, and utilize the power of *derush* to caution against Amalek-types that may arise in the future? Furthermore, while the aim is commendable – to keep the law as relevant as possible – these commandments would certainly not be the only ones that are now defunct as a result of the development of history. One need only mention the many laws relating to the sacrifices in the Temple, the incense, the law of the Rebellious Son, the Scroll of the Adulteress, capital punishment, etc., etc.

Seventh, if the Rav and R. Moshe are right, why haven't any halakhic decisors throughout the ages recorded the *mitzvah* to destroy any vicious and genocidal anti-Semitic nation as part of the 613 commandments? Other than this admittedly sophisticated halakhic inference from the Maimonides text, we find no such law or assertion in our literature. Further, if the Halakhah intended that the Biblical enmity towards Amalek is meant to apply to all enemies of Israel, why was it not so codified *explicitly* by Maimonides – not only by inference – or by any other of the Talmudic giants throughout the ages?[29]

Finally, the Rav and R. Moshe assert that the final destruction of Amalek will not take place until or about the time of the coming of the Messiah. The author of the earlier *Sefer Yere'im*, and contemporary Talmudists as well, clearly reserve that commandment to the reigning Israelite king, representing the entire Jewish nation – a situation that no longer prevails, and will not until the Messianic restoration of the monarchy.[30] But that does not necessarily mean that in order for the Biblical commandment to retain its relevance and validity it is imperative to posit the continued existence of Amalek until Messianic times. It must be established, of course, that a time will come when the divine anger, His oath of punishment for the Amalekites, will be appeased. At one point in history, God has to win His war unconditionally. Otherwise the Exodus verse, "I will utterly blot out the memory of Amalek from under heaven," will always remain unfulfilled – and that is unthinkable. But what happens afterwards, when the Messiah and redemption have come and Amalek is finally banished from the world? Does the verse become obsolete? And if that is acceptable, why is it not acceptable to say that Amalek disappeared for good under the two pagan kings, as did the Seven Nations, and is therefore obsolete in our times, and forever after? Deferring the fulfillment of the commandment to eschatological times does not solve the problem.

Hence, with most respectful apologies to the revered Rabbis Soloveitchik, father and son, I find it difficult to accept their thesis.

Indeed, there are distinguished Talmudists who maintain that the author of *Semag* held that the commandment to read from the

Torah those passages relating to the injunction to remember the vile deeds of Amalek is *not* Biblically mandated, and that *Maimonides apparently agrees* that this is so.[31] If this is correct, then Maimonides in all probability held that the entire matter of Amalek is no longer applicable. Yet the lesson we derive from the Amalek episode remains one that we must learn and re-learn in every generation even if we do not carry out the Biblical mandate in practice: there *is* such a thing as absolute, radical evil; there are people and groups that have lent themselves to becoming the agents of all that is demonic and have remained unrepentant. It is not possible to coexist with unreconstructed barbarians who have forfeited their right to our sympathy and who make us feel embarrassed to be members of the same human race. No amount of psychologizing can remove from an immoral reprobate the onus of paying for his crimes as a way of protecting society. This is how we "remember" Amalek for all times – remember, not murder; expound, not execute.

At the risk of getting involved in a family dispute, I note the opinion of R. Yitzchak Ze'ev Soloveitchik o.b.m. (=Reb Velvel), brother of R. Moses and uncle of R. Joseph, who maintains that there never was a commandment to individual Jews to destroy individual Amalekites; this action was incumbent only upon the people of Israel as a whole, through the king, and as an act of war. The Prophet Samuel did not slay Agag because Agag was an Amalekite, but because Agag was a murderer; his parting words to Agag – "As your sword has bereaved women, so shall your mother be bereaved among women" – substantiate that assertion. Maimonides himself (*Sefer ha-Mitzvot*, end of Pos. Com. #248) explicitly states that the commandment to destroy Amalek devolves upon the *tzibbur,* the entire people, and not upon individual Jews.[32] Furthermore, it is not only the king of the reconstituted People of Israel who decides when and where to fulfill the Torah's commandment concerning Amalek; he must do so only at the urging of the prophet who will arise in the Messianic era.[33]

I humbly suggest that we focus on the difference between the verses in Exodus and in Deuteronomy cited at the beginning of this essay. Exodus has God Himself threatening Amalek: "I will utterly

blot out the memory of Amalek from under heaven." This verse
contains no commandment or obligation upon humans. It is God's
oath, and it His duty, as it were, to destroy Amalek. We have no right
to impose limitations on God's freedom, and it is entirely reasonable
to say that the Almighty, in His own time and way, will deal with all
people of extreme cruelty and consider them as the Amalekites of
that generation if He so wishes. We leave it to the Almighty to deal
with the new Amalekites of every era. It is He who will revive His
people and redeem Israel and the world – and deal appropriately
with the wicked of the earth. The Master of the World is free to
adopt the interpretation of R. Moshe Soloveitchik and expand the
content of "Amalek."

The passage in Deuteronomy, however, places the responsibility in the hands of humans, of Jews: "*you* shall blot out the memory
of Amalek from under heaven. Do not forget." This verse yields
two commandments, namely, the duty laid upon Israel to destroy
Amalek, and the injunction to remember and not forget the cruelty
of Amalek. If we now follow the teaching of R. Yehoshua, that after
Sennacherib we can no longer identify the ancient peoples with
any certainty, this leads us to conclude that individual Jews are now
exempt from the command to do away with individual Amalekites.
We are under no obligation to harm any vicious anti-Semite and
we must not utterly destroy any miserable country that adopts anti-
Semitism as national policy (except, of course, in self-defense or in
war), but we must "remember and not forget" the cruelty of Amalek,
thus refining our own sensibilities and re-learning the Psalmist's
teaching that to love God is to hate evil (Ps. 97:10). The decision not
to destroy a group or nation does not imply passivity and tolerance
of evil. Hence, the fulfillment of the commandment to remember
does not require the continued existence of Amalek upon whom we
can wreak vengeance. Here we may accept the expansion of "Amalek" proposed by R. Moshe; it is only in the fulfillment of the strict
halakhah of destroying Amalek that we must remain content with
the literal understanding of the term. It is easier and textually more
parsimonious to canonize the disgust at Amalek-like cruelty in the

"remember" verse than to "homileticize" what R. Moshe considers the second commandment.

Rabbinic authorities closer to our days also dealt with these issues, which they considered most troublesome. Thus, an unusual explanation of the Amalek verses that reveals sensitivity to the problem is offered by Rabbi Yonatan Eibuschutz (1690–1764) in his *Ya'arot Devash* (Part 2:9). He refers to Proverbs (25:21), "If your enemy is hungry, feed him; if he is thirsty, give him water." From this, he writes, we learn the attitude of the Torah that one ought to act nobly and not with vengeance towards an enemy. Hence, lest we extend this ethical principle to Amalek as well and forget its brutality towards us, the Torah explicitly excluded Amalek from this general attitude, because "the divine Throne is incomplete" as long as Amalek survives. Paraphrasing a passage in the Talmud (*Megillah* 7b), he declares that the Sages of Israel proclaimed, "You are causing us to arouse the enmity of the (other) nations who will consider us people of bad character who are vindictive and harbor hatred towards them." By limiting the severe Biblical judgment on Amalek to Amalek alone, he attempts to remove it as a model for relations to other enemies of the Jewish people. He concludes with a novel interpretation of the well known passage (*Megillah* 7a) that one ought drink (wine) on Purim to the point that he cannot distinguish between "blessed is Mordecai" and "cursed be Haman." His insight: Under the influence of liquor one might forget that by our very nature we ought be kind even to an enemy, and that Haman (a descendant of Amalek) is an exception.

Mention should be made as well of Rabbi Yaakov Tzvi Meklenburg[34] (1785–1865), who wrestles with the problem of the divine commandment not to allow any Canaanite soul to live, and quotes the opinions of Maimonides and Nahmanides. He avers that the Torah's law concerning the Canaanites must not be regarded as cruel, because it was directed only against idol worshippers, but if the Canaanites rejected idolatry they were indeed welcomed as citizens in the Land of Israel. He is mostly concerned about the assumption that this harsh commandment is directed not only against mature males (who may presumed to be, for the most part, warriors), but also against women and minors. He refuses to accept the fact that such a cruel law could possibly be the correct interpretation of a divine text, and clearly sees the need for an authentic apologetic. He then proceeds to re-interpret and re-translate the words *lo tehayeh* as "You are not required to provide" food, without which life is unthinkable, and other forms of support to such people, rather than, "you shall not allow them to live." It is inconceivable to him to imagine that such a law could possibly issue from a merciful Deity.

There are several strategies that we must consider in order to solve or at least mitigate this apparent conflict between Halakhah and morality.

A DEVELOPING (HALAKHIC) MORALITY

First, we must turn to the question of a developing morality, i.e., new moral notions that surpass those of the past. The notion of a moral development in Judaism should not be confused with the "New Morality" of the middle to late 1900's. The latter did not seek to improve on and elevate accepted individual moral principles, but attempted an entire overhaul of conventional morality in order to make it conform to new practices, such that mores were now blessed as morals. We entertain no such notions. What we are discussing here is the troubling awareness, by those fully located within the halakhic tradition, of moral or legal injunctions that engender consequences that are either themselves immoral or that injure innocent parties.

That later Rabbinical authorities can generate stringencies that go beyond certain Biblical laws is not an altogether unknown idea in Jewish life. Thus, a principle of Halakhah accepted in practice is this: "The Sages established their views in the place of contrary Torah legislation where the action they forbade is passive."[35] While an extensive review of this principle is beyond the scope of this paper, it should be pointed out that the Sages imposed their rulings even in the face of opposition to Biblical law for a number of reasons, including the protection of workers from losing their pay, to spare certain types of *mamzerim* from the taint of bastardy, to enhance sexual morality, and many other such cases.[36] A significant case in point is that of the law of the levirate marriage (*yibbum*), which is Biblical in origin: If a man dies childless, it is the responsibility of his brother to marry his widow; should he refuse, he must undergo the ceremony of *halitzah*, which exposes him to a degree of opprobrium. The Ashkenazic *rishonim* decreed, on the basis of a debate in the Talmud (*Yevamot* 39b), that *yibbum* be proscribed and only *halitzah* be performed. Their reason: if the surviving brother does not have purity of intentions, i.e., if he engages in relations with his erstwhile sister-in-law for reasons of sexual gratification rather than the fulfillment of a *mitzvah*, he is committing incest. Hence, it is best that *yibbum* be banned altogether.[37]

Similarly, albeit of lesser cause for astonishment, it is an acknowledged principle amongst *posekim* that non-Jews should not appear holier than the people of Israel, and that Jews should therefore accept upon themselves additional stringencies if such strictures are adopted by non-Jews. Hence, Maharsham promulgated a ban on publicly smoking on Tishah be-Av. In the same spirit, one of the greatest of Hasidic masters, known as the Hiddushei ha-Rim, maintained that the only source he could find for applying the *mitzvah* of appointing judges in the Diaspora derives from this same reason: because otherwise it would appear that non-Jews are more respectful of their religion than Jews are of theirs.

Should not the same reasoning apply to the commandments concerning Amalek and the Seven Nations? The fact that the civilized world had begun to abhor genocide ever since the beginning of World War II is unquestionably a major contribution to morality – even if this particular aversion is honored more in the breach than in the practice.

But if we accept the concept of a developing morality in Judaism, annoying and disconcerting problems persist. Thus, on the one hand, does not the assertion of a developing moral sensibility imply that the original position was immoral by our newer standards and nevertheless was sanctified by Torah law, which we profess to be eternal and indisputably sacred? On the other hand, is it possible that the Torah would deny to any generation the right to abide by a "stricter moral code" even if this latter is not itself explicitly located within the classic texts of Judaism? Is there no room in Judaism for autonomous moral judgment, especially when it is derived, as in our case, from bitter historic experience?

I do not accept the notion that contemporary concepts of morality and the ideal of exclusive moral autonomy are sufficient to override a Biblical commandment or for declaring Halakhah – or an individual *halakhah* – superfluous by dubbing it "optional."

The contemporary scene offers illustrations aplenty of trendiness triumphant, often wrapped in the mantle of prophetic modernity. We are acquainted with the tendency to invest contemporary political doctrines or sociological theories with the sanctity or at least prestige of a "higher morality." But not every politically correct policy or theory – or fad – can be allowed to override the commandments first heard at Sinai. Many popular ideas have proved to be ephemeral, or culturally conditioned, and do not deserve to be considered sufficiently weighty as to present a problem for believers in the Halakhah.

However, the concept of "developing morality" can prove acceptable and helpful if it is based upon Torah laws and Torah morality. The moral reasoning for which we attempt to circumvent a Biblical mandate must itself issue from or be compatible with Torah and *mitzvot*, a reasoning based upon a profound belief that the Torah is the source and confirmation of moral excellence, and that – to quote an oft repeated teaching of the Rav – the thirteenth *Ani Maʾamin* (of Maimonides' twelve Articles of Faith) is the belief that Torah is viable and applicable to each individual generation. Hence, in each of the cases mentioned above, the "new" standard we seek to implement and which apparently conflicts with previously recognized Torah law, has roots in the Torah and is "new" only in the sense that it has only recently emerged into our own moral awareness and gained traction in our consciousness. It is not, therefore, a matter of judging the Torah from the vantage of our newly acquired "superior" morality. It is not a genuinely novel, historic moral conception that we pit against the Biblical moral tradition, but it is the evolving contemporary consciousness that has encouraged us to rediscover what was always there in the inner folds of the Biblical texts and halakhic traditions. Our moral sensitivity leads us to find warrant in the Torah heritage.

There is no justification for a totally independent and autonomous moral doctrine to cancel out a Biblical commandment. No matter how hard and earnestly we try to force Halakhah into the Promethean bed of our subjective conception of morality, the conclusion has the ring of inauthenticity. But we are not merely spiritual technicians who have no moral compass to guide us. That is, whereas we cannot create a new morality to oppose the Biblical one, we most certainly are free to exercise our judgment and experience in searching out authority in the Biblical and Rabbinic traditions to identify elements in Judaism that support a limitation of or alternative to the original doctrine.

Our goal must be the attainment of moral propriety, in the name of which we seek to revise the formal halakhic ruling, *which is itself derived from halakhic principles or clear Jewish teachings.* We are not free to arrogate to ourselves the right to invent new ethical or moral doctrines in opposition to Torah, but we are free, indeed compelled, to use our creative moral and halakhic reasoning to reveal the latent moral judgments of the Torah that may contradict what we have previously accepted as the only doctrine in Torah.

Rabbi Nahum Eliezer Rabinovitch of Ma'ale Adumim, the author of a thoughtful essay on the Torah as the catalyst for the evolution of moral values in history,[38] offers illustrations of the gradual mitigation of the institution of slavery, aiming at its total abolition, the acceptance of warfare as a temporary measure until universal peace is achieved, and other such major issues, all of which are grounded in Torah itself.

For instance, in the case of slavery, the opposing principle is *ki avadai hem*, that all humans are servants of the Creator, and hence we must discourage slavery to a human master. There is sufficient halakhic data to support the abolition of the institution of slavery. In the case of capital punishment, the opposing principle is the sanctity of life (*ve-hai ba-hem*) and the creation of man in the Image of God. The choice before us, in such cases, is the tension between the

Torah's explicit legislation vs. the Torah's implicit value system. (This distinction is not unlike Prof. Gerald Dworkin's famous formulation that apart from rules in a legal system, there are also "principles" and "policies." A "rule" is equivalent to our *halakhah*, and a "principle" is "a requirement of justice or fairness or some other dimension of morality" – a value that is expressed in our *lifnim mi-shurat ha-din* and inheres in the body of law we call the Torah.)

By the same token, the idea of refraining from harming civilian non-combatants, although it has no explicit origin in Torah,[39] reflects the Torah value of "Thou shalt not kill" (Ex. 20:13) and "The fathers shall not put to death for the [sins of the] children, neither shall the children be put to death for [sins of the] the fathers; every man shall be put to death for his own sin" (Deut. 24:16.) Likewise, the reluctance to implement, even theoretically, the Torah's stern commandments concerning Amalek and the Seven Nations, bespeaks a later development that always inhered latently in Torah itself. This may be looked upon as a non-technical kind of *lifnim mi-shurat ha-din* which supererogatory nature is part of Torah itself.

Mention should be made of "Situational Ethics" that in recent decades has been much discussed, a movement that rejects code-morality and its generalizations in favor of moral judgments made for particular and usually non-replicable situations. Some aspects of it may be legitimately useful for solving our problem.

Situational or Contextual Morality need not be identified with moral relativism. While in its original formulation it argued for very few general rules – primarily "love" – and manifold specific details of the individual enough to regard him and his situation as unique, we are not obliged to accept this as indivisible doctrine. We may well prefer to judge the qualities of our conduct by a far larger number of rules, namely, those of the Halakhah, and yet allow the individual situation to be examined and judged in its uniqueness.

Rabbi Aharon Lichtenstein has demonstrated that Judaism rejects contextualism (another name for "situational ethics") as a self-sufficient ethic, but nevertheless "has embraced it as the modus operandi of large tracts of human experience. These lie in the realm of *lifnim mi-shurat ha-din*. In this area, the halakhic norm is itself situational."[40] He invokes the Ramban in identifying morality as supererogatory (*lifnim mi-shurat ha-din*), thus keeping morality within the bounds of the halakhic tradition: "If…we recognize that Halakhah is multiplanar and many dimensional; that, properly conceived, it includes much more than is explicitly required or permitted by specific rules, we shall realize that the ethical moment we are seeking *is in itself an aspect of Halakhah*" (my emphasis).

A corollary of this elevated aspiration is the stricter criterion of conduct expected of people of higher station. This allowed the tradition to imply the violation of unstated superior standards where the Biblical text appeared overly harsh. Thus, there are a number of examples where the Sages confronted a Scriptural text describing punishment ordained for a transgression, a punishment puzzled them by its severity, and which they attempted to mitigate by reading more grave infractions into the bare text. For example, Nadav and Avihu, sons of Aaron, were consumed by fire (apparently meaning that they were struck by lightning) during the service in the Tabernacle because, the Torah, tells us, they offered up a "strange fire" in the course of offering the incense (Lev. 10: 1–3). So severe a penalty for so slight a transgression certainly appears unjust, so the Rabbis speculated that the two sons of Aaron were guilty of far more serious conduct that indeed merited Draconian punishment. Thus, they were arrogant in making legal decisions in the presence of their elders, specifically Moses (JT *Shevi'it* 16a); they were overweening in their ambitions, entertaining hopes that the two elders – their father Aaron and uncle Moses – would die so they could take over the reins of leadership (*Tanhuma, Aharei Mot* 6); they were flippant in the course of the Sinaiitic revelation (*Tanhuma, Be-Ha'alotekha* 16). Yet other sources speak of other defects of character warranting harsh punishment (*Yalkut Shimoni*, Lev. 10 no. 524 and Lev. 16, no. 571). What obviously drove the Sages to offer these and similar reasons is the genuinely Jewish teaching of *middah ke-negged middah*, that the punishment must fit the crime. The solution thus came internally, from the Halakhah itself.

Another illustration of apparent injustice and consequent efforts by the Sages to suggest internal reasons whereby the Biblical

narrative satisfies significant moral considerations is the story of
the Ark of the Covenant in 1 Samuel Chapter 6. The Philistines
had captured the Ark and suffered deadly plague. They therefore
returned the Ark to the Israelites in Beit Shemesh, and the latter
rejoiced and offered sacrifices to mark the occasion. Then, inexplicably, the Almighty brought a plague upon the Jews – killing seven
or fifty thousand (the text is ambiguous) Jews of Beit Shemesh,
who then sought to send the Ark elsewhere. Here the Midrashim
speak of the lack of respect (*derekh eretz*) by the Jews towards the
Ark, and especially so in comparison with the heathen Philistines
(*Tanna de-Bei Eliyahu Rabbah* 11; Gen. R. 54:4). The *Yalkut* accuses
the Beit Shemeshites of irreverent behavior (*Yalkut Shimoni* no.
103); other sources have them addressing the Ark contemptuously.
Yet other sources, including some of the major medieval exegetes,
add that they gazed brazenly into the Ark, violating major Biblical
transgressions, flippancy in failing to retrieve the Ark when it could
and should have been done, etc.

What we learn from the above, and other such cases, is that the
Sages were troubled by misgivings about what they perceived are
questionable moral judgments in the narrative – all this although
there is no hint of this in the text – and they could not reconcile
themselves to what appeared to be unjust or apparently arbitrary
conduct by the Creator Himself. Therefore, they suggested halakhically appropriate rationales for the punishment of the "transgressors."
The moral problem was thus solved without recourse to external,
non-halakhic sources.[41]

Prof. Haym Soloveitchik maintains that according to the medieval classic *Sefer Hasidim*, there is place in Judaism for ever higher
levels of morality. "We find in the Torah that anyone who is capable
of understanding [a demand] even though he was not [explicitly]
commanded is punished for not realizing [the requirement] on
his own." And, "The will of God, the *retzon ha-Bore*, has not been
cabined or confined within the overt dictates of the Torah, written
or oral." These newly discovered norms of the author, Rabbi Judah
and his fellow Pietists of medieval Germany, allow for newer and
greater forms of morality, and certainly should not be dismissed

simply because they have no *explicit* recognition in either the Written or Oral Torah. Further, again in the words of Soloveitchik, "They [the Pietists] had discovered God's will in its plenitude and, surely, obedience to this was not optional." Thus there were two sources of authority for the Hasid. "And these two revelations – the explicit and the implicit – should hardly be conceived of as competing poles of allegiance, but as concentric circles emanating from a unitary (and ever expanding) Divine Will, the outer perimeter of which takes on meaning only because of the wide ambience of the inner." The creativity of *Sefer Hasidim* lies not in imposing moral considerations that arise independently of Torah, but in tapping the wellsprings of Torah and locating *implicit* in them ideas and values that constitute more sublime moral ideals. [42]

It is interesting to note that a strikingly similar idea is expressed by one of the later and most creative Zaddikim of Beshtian Hasidism, R. Tzadok ha-Kohen of Lublin, who distinguishes *ratzon* from *mitzvah*.[43] The *mitzvah* is the inviolable halakhic command. The *ratzon*, the divine Will, goes beyond the legal and represents a supererogatory, higher form of religious aspiration.

This approach does not derogate the value of society's evolving moral sense, but seeks to avoid moral fashionableness from establishing itself as the ultimate criterion of right and wrong, undercutting the Biblical-Talmudic tradition which is the cornerstone of Judaism, as well as Western civilization, and which has served us so well for three millennia.

Exactly how to determine what is a serious latent Biblical-halakhic moral stance, and what is an ephemeral illusion issuing from one's subjective conscience or from the moral *Zeitgeist* of the environing culture and then grafted upon Torah, is a legitimate and important question, lest the doors be opened wide to well-meaning but irresponsible amateurs.

We must at all times remember that we are dealing with Halakhah, in its full legal capacity, not with vague homiletics or simplistic evocation of generalized, "feel good" notions. The ability to discriminate between such vague appeals to fuzzy religious preachments on one hand, and sound and solid halakhic data on the other, is critical and emphasizes the need for such questions to be adjudicated by mature and responsible halakhic authorities who are, at the same time, sensitive to the currents of contemporary moral philosophy. A responsible religious Jew must step back and consider what is truly the will of God and what is mores masquerading as morals, homiletics parading as Halakhah, and taste disguised as Torah.

These caveats are especially applicable to the area of sexual mores. For instance, no amount of earnest moralizing can convert homosexual relations, which the Torah considers an abomination, into a form of an acceptable alternative morality. "Thou shalt love thy neighbor as thyself" does not trump the ban on illicit love, whether homosexual or heterosexual or incestuous.

Hence we must seek to preserve the integrity of our moral conscience and yet avoid exploitation that results from insufficient sensitivity to or respect for that tradition. The opposing principle that we seek to enshrine as the more morally attuned to our generation is, in some significant way, an extension of a genuine halakhic datum – such as a *lifnim mi-shurat ha-din* growing out of a *din*. The "morality" under consideration must itself issue autochthonously from within the halakhic tradition, although it was latent, concealed until we have turned to it, pressed on by our consciences.

None of the above proposals imply any negative moral judgment on the Torah's original laws concerning the mentioned enemies of Israel which, prevailing during the earlier period, were quite acceptable morally in their time.[44] The moral validity of the Biblical law is based upon the principle of reciprocity: it is an appropriate response to a brutal attack by Amalek, which opened the door to later attacks by other enemies. Not to do so would have been to expose the Israelites to further savage actions by their surrounding tribes. Compassion of this sort, in the context of that period of history, would be a "compassion of fools" as it was termed by Ramban (to Deut. 7:15 and 19:13) and "compassion for murderers is comparable to the spilling blood" – reminiscent of contemporary pacifists whose lack of realism makes it possible for the most heinous of people or nations to remain unopposed. It is worth mentioning a tradition that the intended victims of the Amalek attack on Israel consisted primarily of the non-Hebrews who left Egypt with Israel, and *gerim*, foreigners who were determined to join the faith of Judaism.

The conclusion we may draw from this review of the halakhic record is that the commandments are not as merciless as one would imagine without recourse to the relevant post-Biblical material on the subject. For pious Jews, the Bible is authoritative only as interpreted by the Oral tradition, with its astonishing diversity of opinions and the limitations teased out of the bare verses of the Scriptural text by the Oral Law. The considerable leeway given to civilian bystanders,[45] the preference for peace over hostilities, and the postponement to eschatological times of the fulfillment of the Biblical commands – all these point to a remarkably humane attitude. One might say that only the most radical pacifist is entitled to complain about the classical Jewish views of warfare. And only those nations that have unblemished records in their history have the moral right to raise moral objections to the Torah.

Most assuredly, our discussion of the Halakhah on Amalek and the Seven Nations has not solved all the moral problems to our satisfaction as believing Jews. And it is believing Jews most of all – those whose commitments have been shaped by Torah in its fullest sense, and whose moral expectations of Torah are higher because of their exposure to its ethical norms – who must be satisfied both as to the way the Torah's rules of engagement have been understood and used, and to what we may anticipate for the future. That is, we can "solve" the problem for contemporary times and the future in the practical sense, based upon the factual disappearance of the last vestiges of the Amalekites and Canaanites – the second "scenario" at the beginning of this paper can come to a satisfactory solution – but we must also be able to justify the implementation of the harsh commandments in Biblical times from a theological and moral point of view.

In sum, one must respect the Rabbis' reluctance to acknowledge a conflict between morality and law because to do so would jeopardize the integrity of the Halakhah and would impute moral insensitivity to their predecessors.[46] If the countervailing moral theme itself can be derived from authentic halakhic or aggadic sources, as here proposed, the distance between the purely formal and the moral is lessened, our moral sensitivity is salvaged and acknowledged, and the danger of a moralistic antinomianism is diminished.

That is what we have attempted in this paper, however partial or limited our success has been. It is not an easy task for a generation of a people that survived the most devastating genocidal attack in its history.

NOTES

1. Among the many secondary sources consulted in preparation of this paper, mention should be made of David S. Shapiro's *Studies in Jewish Thought* (New York: Yeshiva University Press, 1975,) vol. 1, especially pp. 345–346, a work important primarily for the context of the Halakhah's treatment of war in general. An analytic paper by Avi Sagi in *The Harvard Theological Review* (1994) is notable for its strength both in comprehensiveness and in organization of the material. Sagi has a philosophical agenda: that morality is not dependent upon religion, and that the Torah's commands must accord with moral considerations. I accept this view, especially because I consider man's moral impulses as God-given and implicit in man's creation in the Divine Image; see below, n. 9. Maimonides (*Guide* III:17) already polemicized against the deterministic Islamic sect, the Ash'ariyya, who denied human initiative and therefore identified the good as the spoken word of God. However, Sagi tends to overstate his argument at times, ignoring important Talmudic and post-Talmudic data which are contrary to his view. For instance, on p. 324 he states categorically that all authorities agree that morality is independent of the Torah's commandments, yet the Talmud (*Berakhot* 33b, based on the Mishnah 5:3) records a respectable amoraic opinion that the halakhic rules are always meant to be disciplinary and a test of man's loyalty and are not intended as moral or ethical commandments. Later, R. Isaac Arama, one of the most important medieval Bible exegetes, clearly places the revealed laws as higher than human moral intuition; see his *Akedat Yitzhak*, 42. More recently, an excellent review and thorough-going analysis of the sources in exploring the moral problems presented by the Amalek commandments and their application is that of Yaakov Medan in "Amalek" in *Al Derekh ha-Avot*, ed. Bazak, Vigoda, and Monitz (Alon Shevut: Machon Herzog, 2001). Between Sagi and Medan, many of our relevant sources are covered.

2. On the basis of textual analysis, Medan (371–373) suggests that Samuel's harsh exhortations were a *hora'at sha'ah*, a temporary suspension of the Halakhah, one permitted to a bona fide prophet, and not the original *mitzvah* of God; it therefore does not obligate future generations. R. Moshe Sternbuch (*Mo'adim u-Zemanim* vol. 6, no. 99) maintains on casuistic halakhic grounds that Samuel's role was not part of the general *mitzvah* of destroying Amalek. He follows *Hagahot Maimuniyot* to *Hilkhot Melakhim* 5 in stating that the true fulfillment of the Amalek command-

ment will occur only after the arrival of the Messiah. However, the problem with postponing this commandment to eschatological times is that, as will be seen, the descendants of Amalek no longer exist – or, at best, are no longer identifiable.

3. The first mention of Haman's Amalekite lineage is in Targum Jonathan to Esther 3:1.

4. The exact number is problematical. The maximum number is seven: Canaanites, Hittites, Perizzites, Amorites, Jebusites, Hivites, and Girgashites. Most often, the last group is omitted; see Rashi to Exodus 33:2. Sometimes the Perizzites are not mentioned. See Exodus 3:8, 17; 13:5; Deut. 20:17. *Sifre* to Deut. 26:9 states that the five basic ones are those whose land was "flowing with milk and honey." Ibn Ezra to Gen. 15:20 maintains that all were related and their generic term was Canaanites. To avoid confusion, and because the difference in numbers does not affect this essay, we shall refer to them as the Seven Nations, or simply as Canaanites.

5. In the following pages, we shall generally treat Amalek and the Seven Nations as a unit. However, see *Responsa Avnei Nezer* no. 508, who maintains that the Seven Nations were more culpable because of their abominable conduct, whereas the Amalekites were condemned not because of their own misdeeds but because of their nefarious ancestors.

6. *Sefer Emunah u-Bitahon*, chapter 3.

7. See my *Torah Umadda*, pp. 86–109 on the theme of the degeneration of the genera-tions. See, too, Rav Kook's *Iggerot ha-Reiyah*, 369 and R. Tzadok Hakohen's *Peri Zaddik to Bereshit (Va-Yehi)* p.109, in the name of the Tzaddik of Pershischa, all of whom accept the principle reluctantly and declare that inwardly, in the sense of growing saintliness, the later the generation, the greater.

8. *Hazon Ish* to *Yoreh De'ah, Hilkhot Shehitah* 2:16.

9. For a summary of the sources in greater detail, see Jacob J. Ross, "Morality and the Law," in *Tradition* vol. 10, no. 2 (Winter 1968):5–16.

10. In "Freedom and Constraint in the Jewish Judicial Process," the *Cardozo Law Review* vol. 1 (Spring 1979). The late Prof. Marvin Fox later wrote against the idea of a Natural Law in Judaism, but it did not convince me to change my mind.

11. The late Rabbi Walter S. Wurzburger has written wisely of the "inevitable evolution of the notions of moral propriety in the wake of ever-changing social, economic, and cultural conditions." See his "Law as the Basis of a Moral Society," in *Tradition* (Spring 1981):40–41.

12. In contemporary society, vengeance is considered morally objectionable. Recently, however, scientists have discovered that revenge can be quite "normal" and often plays a positive role in human relations. See "Payback Time: Why Revenge Tastes So Sweet," by Benedict Carey, in *The New York Times* (July 27, 2004), Science Section, p. 1.

13. Saul's actions were not motivated by moral considerations; after all, he did kill all the women and children and spared only Agag and the captured booty. Politically, it was an understandable move. He needed Agag as an ally against his traditional enemy, the Philistines. It is possible that he put a moral face on a political move – a

tactic not unknown in history, even in our times. See Yoel Bin-Nun, "*Massa Agag*," in *Megadim* 17 (1989) and Medan, 376–378. I prefer to interpret the "do not be overly righteous" not as an ordinary reprimand, but as a sarcastic retort by the Almighty to Saul, as if to say, "don't try to deceive Me with your *tzidkut* when I know very well that you are guilty."

14. This point is elaborated in Responsa *Avnei Nezer* 508:3. He suggests that the Almighty knew that the demonic nature of Amalek was ingrained in them as a sort of genetic endowment. However, this assertion is refuted by the Talmud (*Gittin* 57b), which avers that descendants of Haman (an Amalekite) taught Torah in Bnei Brak, descendants of Sisera taught children in Jerusalem, and descendants of Sennacherib – Shemaya and Avtalyon – taught Torah publicly.

15. In the early part of the Mishnaic period, there was concern that the divine command to wipe out a whole people would confirm Gentile assertions that Jews were hostile to the rest of humanity. See Louis H. Feldman, "Josephus' Portrait of Moses, Part Two," *Jewish Quarterly Review* 83 (1992):35–41.

16. The significance of this law lies in the lack of distinction between Amalek and the Seven on one side and all other nations on the other. See further, below.

17. Medan concludes that Samuel's insistence that the Amalekites were to be annihilated whether or not they changed their conduct and became civilized was a temporary ruling, an action reserved for a prophet. See above, n. 2.

18. There is an opinion that according to the *Mekhilta*, Ammonites and Moabites were permitted to convert to Judaism but they were forbidden to marry a Jewess. See *Megillat Sefer* to *Semag*, Neg. Com. 115; and R. Meshulam Roth, Responsa *Kol Mevasser* II, 42. p. 84b.

19. *Mekhilta* 181.

20. Rabbi Shlomo Goren, *Meshiv Milhamah* V, p.244, asserts that according to R. Meir Simhah of Dvinsk in his *Or Sameah*, Nahmanides also agrees with Maimonides that the injunction to destroy all enemy humans of Amalek and the Seven Nations is suspended if they accept the offer of peace terms by Israel. Maimonides appears to have carried the day in this opinion; most *rishonim* agree with him. See, too, Rabbi Y.Y. Weinberg, Responsa *Seridei Esh* II, 73, who holds that according to Maimonides, while Amalek and the Seven Nations as well as other hostile entities are to be offered the option of peace, there is a difference between other ("distant") nations, who may opt for peace even after hostilities begin, whereas with Amalek and the Seven Nations no peace can be negotiated once they have undertaken military action. Cf. *Hazon Ish* to Rambam, *Hilkhot Melakhim* 5, and see Medan, 363–366.

21. Tosafot (*Yevamot* 76b) maintains that historically there were two such incidents. Sennacherib moved the populations of defeated nations to different areas, so as to weaken their resistance to his rule, but the people returned to their original homes; later, Nebuchadnezzar, the Mesopotamian monarch, "mixed up the world," i.e., moved whole peoples to other areas, commingling individuals such that in the course of time no one knew for sure his lineage and ancestry. Moreover, he later exterminated many of the tribes. Hence, the acts of population transfer plus

genocide made it highly unlikely that any individual of these peoples in succeeding generations could be sure of his ancestry. It is on this basis that the *tanna'im* declared that the strictures against marrying Ammonites and Moabites no longer obtained.

22. This article appeared originally in Hebrew as *"Kol Dodi Dofek"* in *Divrei Hagut ve-Ha'arakha* (Jerusalem: World Zionist Organization, 1982), 9–55. It first appeared in English as "Fate and Destiny" in *Theological and Halachic Reflections on the Holocaust* (New York: Ktav, 1992), pp. 51–117.

23. See above, n. 5.

24. See too *Shulhan Arukh Yoreh De'ah* 242: 3 and 7, and Rema to 3. Also, R. Hayyim of Volozhin, *Ruah Hayyim* to *Avot* 1:5 (p. 17).

25. R. Abraham, the son of Maimonides, lumps Amalek and the Seven Nations together in his response to the queries of R. Daniel ha-Bavli; see his Responsa in the Frankel edition of Maimonides' *Sefer ha-Mitzvot* (Bnei Brak, 1995), 543b.

26. *Hinnukh, Mitzvah* 425.

27. See L. Ginzberg, *Legends of the Jews* vol. 2, p. 25, n. 147. It is popularly held that it was Josephus who identified Rome as Amalek: see Bacher Tann, 1 (1930), 146 (but one must first clarify if this was meant in a halakhic or a midrashic sense); Louis H. Feldman, "Josephus' Portrait of Daniel," *Henoch* 14 (1992), 37–96, 65–71; Christopher Begg, "Israel's Battle with Amalek according to Josephus," *Jewish Quarterly Review* vol. 4 (1997), 201–216, especially p. 215.

28. *The New Republic* of January 21, 2002, page 21.

29. See *Guide for the Perplexed* III:50, where Maimonides himself implies that *only* Amalek was condemned and not other peoples.

30. Ridvaz (*Hilkhot Melakhim* 5:5) and others hold that the commandment to destroy Amalek applies only to the Messianic age. See too the article *Shituf Nashim be-Milhamah* by R. Shelomo Min-haHar in *Tehumin* vol. IV, p. 75 f.

31. See R. Ovadiah Yosef, *Responsa Yabi'a Omer*, Part 8, 54, who cites an authority who maintains that the *Shulhan Arukh* (*Orah Hayyim* 685) sides with this opinion, because he, R. Joseph Karo, declares that *some say* that the reading is Biblically mandated (referring to Rosh and Tosafot), implying that others (Maimonides and *Semag*) disagree, and that he sides with the latter.

32. The author of *Hinnukh* also speaks of the Amalek commandment as one that is incumbent upon the *tzibbur* but, unlike Maimonides, he means by this that every member of the public is under this command, not the nation as a whole.

33. The material on R. Yitzchak Ze'ev Soloveitchik can be found in *Be-Din Mehiyyat Amalek* by the late R. Shmuel Dickman, in *Kovetz ha-Mo'adim*, ed. R. Joseph Buksbaum (Jerusalem: Moriah, 2002), pp. 311–322. See too above, n. 21.

34. *Ha-Ketav ve-ha-Kabbalah to* Deurotonomy (13:12, 20:10, 16.)

35. In an illuminating passage, Ritva to *Rosh ha-Shanah*. 32b cites "a gem from Ramban" that while an individual *shevut* has only Rabbinic force, when it had some foundation in Biblical legislation, the Sages in many places allowed it to override a Biblical prohibition.

36. In the order presented in the text above, the sources are: Tosafot, *Berakhot* 15a s.v. *afilu*; *Sefer ha-Makneh* to *Kiddushin.* 76a; *Tosefot Yom Tov* to Mishnah *Nedarim* 11:12. However, when the Biblical law is explicit, the Rabbis did not impose their views; see *Turei Zahav* to *Yoreh De'ah* 117, and Rabbi Yeshoshua Baumol, *Responsa Emek Halakhah* vol. II, 1.

37. An elaborate discussion of the views of the Ashkenazic authorities as opposed to Sephardic and Yemenite traditions may be found in R. Ovadiah Yosef, *Responsa Yabi'a Omer* 6, *Even ha-Ezer* 14.

38. "The Way of Torah" appeared in Hebrew in the author's *Darkah Shel Torah* in 1999. The somewhat condensed English version was published in *The Edah Journal* 3:1, (Tevet 5763=2003).

39. Indeed, there has been some recent revisionist thinking on this subject, especially in the light of significantly higher casualties among Israeli troops as a result of the "purity of arms doctrine" that has heretofore guided Israeli military policy. To use the Talmudic phraseology, is the blood of Israeli soldiers any less red than that of enemy Arab civilians? See the article by my son, Shalom E. Lamm, "Purity of Arms: A Critical Evaluation," in the *Journal of International Security Affairs* No. 8 (Spring 2005), 37–47.

40. "Does Jewish Tradition Recognize an Ethic Independent of Halakhah?" in *Contemporary Jewish Ethics*, ed. Menachem Marc Kellner (Sanhedrin Press, 1978), pp. 102–123. Rabbi Eugene Korn's "Legal Floors and Moral Ceilings: a Jewish Understanding of Law and Ethics," in *The Edah Journal* 2:2 (Tevet 5762 = 2002) deals with the author's conception of the relationship between Halakhah and morality, and contains a summary of the leading cases of *lifnim mi-shurat ha-din.*

41. See Meiri to *Avot* 4:25, "turn it (Torah) over and turn it over, for all is contained within it." Meiri implies that (unlike the conventional interpretation) one should seek within Torah for the solution to problems that arise in Torah.

42. Haym Soloveitchik, "Three Themes in the *Sefer Hasidim*," in AJS Review, volume I (1976): pages 311–356.

43. *Tzidkat ha-Tzaddik* 224.

44. See *Sifre* to *Be-Ha'alotekha* 27, and R. Meir Simhah of Dvinsk, *Meshekh Hokhmah* to *Be-Ha'alotekha* (Numbers 11:1) and R. Naftali Tzvi Yehudah Berlin, (Netziv), *ad loc.*

45. This holds for all wars, whether obligatory or permissible, except for Amalek and the Seven Nations. The rationale for these exceptions is that the practice of these two groups was exceedingly cruel, and the response therefore was correspondingly cruel. Maimonides seems to indicate that even in the event of a war between Israel and other countries (other than Amalek and the Seven Nations) it was forbidden to harm non-combatants, if the other side did not constitute an immediate danger. See Goren, *op. cit.* I, 14, 16.

46. Or even to God Himself; see David Weiss Halivni, "Can a Religious Law be Immoral?" in *Perspective on Jews and Judaism: Essays in Honor of Wolfe Kelman*, (The Rabbinical Assembly, 1978), pp. 165–170.

International Law and Halakhah

Jeremy Wieder

"It is a people that shall dwell alone, and shall not be reckoned among the nations."

(Numbers 23:9)

"In that day shall Israel be the third with Egypt and with Assyria, a blessing in the midst of the earth; for that the Lord of Hosts has blessed him, saying: 'Blessed be Egypt My people and Assyria the work of My hands, and Israel My inheritance.'"

(Isaiah 19:24–25)

In the current international arena there exists a body of law that governs the relationships between nations as pertain to war and its aftermath. This law exists in two forms: (1) laws that are codified in treaties such as the Geneva Conventions and (2) customary law. The origins of contemporary international law date back to the nineteenth century, when various groups of citizens in Europe organized and began to push their governments into adopting norms that would lessen the severe impact of war, both on the combatants and civilian population.[1] The question addressed in this paper is to what extent, if any, Halakhah might recognize the validity of such a system of law and its binding nature upon the State of Israel.

Clearly, there are norms of war that are prescribed, or at least alluded to, in Scripture that are halakhically binding. However, there are certainly many actions that are not addressed explicitly or implicitly in the classic sources of Halakhah and are forbidden under international law. The discussion here concerns these actions. It focuses not on the individual conventions and specific laws, but rather on the broader notion that international law should have any meaning within a halakhic framework, other than for pragmatic considerations.[2]

Engaging this topic presents two difficulties. First, little has been written on the topic. The topic of Halakhah that governs conduct in war has been written about[3] but only from an internal perspective, i.e., exploring the halakhic norms that bind us irrespective of what international law might permit. Second, *Hazal* had little or nothing to say about this topic. This lack of discussion can be attributed to two causes. First, the basic formulations of Halakhah as we possess them were laid down in a period in which Jews lacked a sovereign state; the paucity of material in the Mishnah, Bavli and Yerushalmi is a reflection of this reality. Second, the concept of international law, as mentioned above, did not exist in the period of *Hazal*; while there certainly were norms and expectations of war and its aftermath, adherence to these was subject to the whim of the parties involved, and there was no body of nations that claimed jurisdiction over their enforcement. Moreover, any laws governing relations between nations were conceived as the subject of understanding between two nations, not among humanity as a whole.

The discussion here will focus on three issues:

1. Are there any halakhic sources that might serve as a conceptual model for international law?

2. How does Halakhah relate to treaties signed by the halakhic state? If these treaties contravene Halakhah, to what extent are they binding?
3. What pragmatic halakhic considerations might be brought to bear on the question?

I. THE CONCEPT OF INTERNATIONAL LAW IN HALAKAH

Considering rules of war in an international context within a halakhic framework assumes that Halakhah recognizes war as a valid action among Noahides. The historical existence of war among gentile nations is biblically reflected from the prototypical "father of warfare," *Tuval-Kayin*, in Genesis (4:22) to Daniel's vision of the wars between the superpowers at the close of the Biblical period. The ubiquity of warfare in human history is perhaps best articulated in Chronicles (II 15:5–6):

> At those times, no wayfarer was safe, for there was much tumult among all the inhabitants of the lands. Nation was crushed by nation and city by city, for God threw them into panic with every kind of trouble.

Reality, however, does not automatically confer legitimacy.[4] With respect to a halakhic state there are clearly delineated categories of war: *hovah*, *mitzvah* and *reshut*.[5] Presumably, a nation has a right to defend itself from attack by another nation, but is there ever a circumstance in which a nation of Noahides may initiate a war? Even if there is not, there may still be rules that govern the way a nation, attacked in violation of Halakhah, defends itself. It would seem, however, that a war fought for survival would allow the threatened nation to do almost anything necessary to protect itself.[6] If, however, it is permissible for a gentile nation to initiate a war, it is more likely that there would also be rules that would govern the conduct of defensive warfare.[7]

The Talmud (*Gittin* 38a) cites the dictum of R. Papa that "*Ammon u-Moav taharu be-Sihon*," i.e., the land that *Sihon* conquered from the Ammonites and Moabites was no longer subsumed under the prohibition, found in Deuteronomy (2:9, 19), of conquering territory from those two nations. The Bavli here speaks of the notion of *kinyan kibbush*, acquisition by conquest, as distinct from other modes of acquisition. The notion that territory may be acquired through one nation's conquest of another and that the territory is not considered "stolen" or "occupied" does not in itself imply that the actions are legitimate, nor anything about the existence of an international law. It may well be that just as a thief can, under certain circumstances, acquire property illegitimately and yet still be the rightful owner, so too, a nation that conquers territory in war, even illicitly, may acquire legal title to the territory.[8] This position was adopted by a number of relatively recent *Aharonim*.[9]

Maimonides, however, suggests otherwise. He writes (emphasis mine):

> If a heathen king wages war and brings captives for sale, or if he gives permission to anyone who wishes to take captives *from among the people against whom he is warring* and to sell the captives, and also if his law is that he who does not pay the tax shall be sold into slavery or that anyone who does such-and-such or fails to do so shall be sold into slavery, then his law is law, and a slave who is bought according to that law has the status of a heathen slave (*eved kena'ani*) in every respect (*Hilkhot Avadim* 9:4).

Maimonides, basing himself on the above passage in *Gittin* regarding Ammon and Moab, states that a king who captures prisoners in war or in a war-action by proxy acquires legal title to the people enslaved by such actions. Similarly, when a king's laws dictate that a tax delinquent may be sold into slavery, the enslavement is valid. By implication, however, if the enslavement were not in accordance with his laws, *dinav*, the enslaved individual would not be regarded halakhically as an *eved kena'ani*. Maimonides' presentation suggests that he sees the principle of conquest as falling under the rubric of *dina de-malkhuta*, expanded to fit an international context.

The reason that the king's actions would be invalid during a time of peace or when not following *dinav* is that we draw a distinction between *dina de-malkhuta*, which is valid and binding, and *hamsanuta de-malkhuta*,[10] which is not.[11] This analysis yields at least two significant principles:

1. War between two nations, according to Maimonides, is regarded (at least in some circumstances)[12] as legitimate – if Sihon's war on Moab had been illegal, the land would still have been considered the property of Moab and off-limits to the Jews.
2. There are rules that govern the status of property conquered in war and, perhaps by extension, the conduct of war itself.[13]

In a most basic sense then, Halakhah clearly envisions war between gentile nations as a legitimate enterprise, with laws that govern its conduct.[14] The details of these laws, however, remain unclear.

In this vein, the *Netziv*, (*Ha-Emek Davar*, Genesis 9:5) comments (emphasis mine):

> "At the hand of a man's brother:" God explained: when is one penalized [for murder]? When he ought to have acted with brotherly love. As opposed to wartime, a time of hatred and a time to kill – there is no penalty for that at all. *For thus was the world established*. As it says in *Shavu'ot* 35: "A regime which kills one-sixth is not penalized." And even a king of Israel is permitted to wage a *milhemet reshut*, even though Jews will be killed thereby.

While the above Talmudic passage, according to Maimonides' reading, implies the existence of the concept of "international law" in the conduct of warfare, it does not in any way suggest what the conceptual underpinnings of such a system are. Put differently, the Talmud speaks of one specific rule, which we would classify as a detail of a larger concept of international law of warfare. Is this simply an isolated detail, or is there a larger halakhic category that might encompass all kinds of rules governing warfare, this detail being just one of them?

Two models that could serve as a framework for international law come to mind: 1) *dina de-malkhuta dina*[15] and 2) the precept of *dinim*[16] found among the Noahide laws. While each of these models could potentially serve as the basis, each may have certain limitations. With respect to each it would be necessary to examine three issues:

1. Both of these categories, at first glance, address how individual societies govern themselves internally. Can the scope of either category be expanded beyond national boundaries?
2. Would it mandate a system of international law, or merely suggest it as a possibility, which the nations of the world might choose to adopt?
3. Specifically from the perspective of the Jewish state, would it be applicable to a halakhic state, i.e., does the precept of *dinim* apply to Jews as well (or was the precept of *dinim* supplanted by *Parashat Mishpatim*), and is *dina de-malkhuta* applicable in a Jewish national context?

1. Scope

The principle of the Noahide *dinim* receives limited attention in Rabbinic literature. The Talmud itself says nothing other than that gentiles are commanded to establish courts, without discussing over what matters those courts have jurisdiction. Maimonides assumes that the precept of *dinim* is limited to the enforcement of the other six Noahide laws.[17] Nahmanides, on the other hand, understands that the precept includes not only a judicial function, but also a broader set of rules of civil law (beyond the prohibitions of murder and theft, which exist explicitly in the Noahide code) that a society must have.[18]

According to Maimonides' view, the rules of international engagement, if they exist, would have to be subsumed not under *dinim*, but under the categories of two of the other seven Noahide laws – murder and theft. Conceivably, restrictions on killing in war could be included within the prohibition of murder, and restrictions on treatment of property could fall under the prohibition of theft. The commandment of *dinim* might mandate an attempt to create an international enforcement agency, since Maimonides understands *dinim* as an obligation to enforce the other six Noahide laws. Upon further consideration, however, this model is inadequate for the creation of a full body of international law. According to both opinions (Maimonides and Nahmanides), the other six Noahide laws are divinely legislated laws with specific details located in *Torah she-be-al peh*. One cannot add details or requirements to specific commandments. If they are not included within *Hazal*'s description of murder or theft, Halakhah would not recognize the international community's authority to impose any restrictions on unwilling nations. Since Maimonides himself does not see *dinim* as anything beyond the enforcement of the other six Noahide laws, there is no basis for expanding it to include practices accepted as customary by the international community.

Nahmanides' position, on the other hand, allows for the possibility that the international community might be able, from the standpoint of Halakhah, to expand upon those restrictions that are already inherent in the Noahide code. This possibility is dependent on one's understanding of Nahmanides' position. Some argue that his notion of *dinim* includes only those categories of civil law that are found in Halakhah, and therefore apply to Jews, i.e., *Hoshen Mishpat*.[19] Should this be the case, *dinim* would, as in the Maimonidean position, be of limited applicability to the concept of international law. Those strictures that govern behavior of Jews towards enemy combatants and civilians during war would govern Noahide behavior as well, but there would no room for the international community to legislate further without the agreement of all of its constituents.

The second approach assumes that Noahides are commanded to have a system of laws, but those do not necessarily have to dovetail precisely with Halakhah.[20] In the formulation of the *Rema*:

A Noahide is commanded only to adhere to his societal norms, and to judge "between a man and his brother and the stranger"

[Deut. 1:16] justly, but not to follow the Jewish laws Moses transmitted to us at Sinai; it is merely customary law. [21]

If this is the case, then the specific laws of a Noahide society derive from logic and custom, not revelation. And thus, it is possible to posit that these laws that Noahides are required to observe need govern not only internal issues but relations with other political entities, as well. This approach, *per se*, does not prove that the requirement of *dinim* transcends political boundaries, but it allows for the possibility. Nonetheless it should be noted that since, within the halakhic conception, the law of *dinim* was given to mankind (Adam and his family) at a time in which there was no concept of boundaries between nations, it is not clear why Halakhah should recognize the later concept of separate nations that are not collectively bound to each other by *dinim*.

The concept of *dina de-malkhuta dina* suggests greater possibilities for a halakhic conception of a dynamic system of customary international law. Drawing on this concept to formulate a halakhic category for international law would require one of two conceptual adjustments. Either we would need to posit that what defines a *malkhut* can be expanded at times to encompass all of the citizens of the world or to claim that just as there exists a principle that internal matters must, as a demand of the Noahide laws, be governed by some kind of "*din*," so too, there exists a similar principle with respect to the world as a whole.

There are multiple ways of understanding *dina de-malkhuta dina,* and not all them lend themselves to such expansions. *Ran,* for example, asserts that the premise of *dina de-malkhuta* is that a king owns the land, as evidenced by the fact that he can expel inhabitants at will, and, as a result, his commands must be obeyed.[22] This notion cannot be expanded to the international arena unless we were to construe international law as rooted in the principle that "might makes right," meaning that if a country were powerful enough to destroy the citizens of another country, its law would be binding for the other country.[23] Extrapolating from this model, international laws would apply only to those nations in the world where the ability to force compliance exists; in nations where no such possibility exists, international law would not be, halakhically speaking, binding.[24]

There are, however, several formulations of *dina de-malkhuta* that might lend themselves to expansion to the international arena. Two stand out in this context.

1) Beginning with the *Rashbam*,[25] there are a number of *Rishonim* who find the underpinnings of *dina de-malkhuta* in the consent of the citizens of the country to the rule of the king. If the citizens would refuse to accept the authority of the ruler, his law would not be treated as binding. According to this position we must ask: what exactly is it that makes one country distinct from another? That is, if one works with the accepted assumption that the consent of every individual is not needed to validate *dina de-malkhuta*, but rather that some type of majority suffices, how does one draw the boundaries? After all, it cannot be simply a question of the domain controlled by the king, since it is not his rulership over a domain that creates law, but the acceptance by a defined group of people of his authority and his laws. What is it, then, that defines the "group of people" as being distinct from another group of people who are not bound by these laws? And what is it that allows a group of nearby citizens in an adjoining country to opt out and not be bound by the law?[26] One approach would be to argue that, as a matter of halakhic principle, the world consists of one large country whose inhabitants have agreed to divide it into different areas, each of which may govern itself as it sees fit. If this is the case, situations entailing interaction between two of these "areas" might once again be subject to the collective will of the entire world. Thus, *dina de-malkhuta* might begin with the *malkhut* being the entire world and only subsequently divided into individual countries, which govern themselves internally. The will of the collective entity, however, would remain as a system of law governing the relationships between countries.

This position is adopted by R. Shaul Yisraeli.[27] He writes (emphasis mine):

We can therefore conclude that international law (*dina de-malkhuta she-bein medinah u-medinah*) derives from the consent of the nations' citizens, and even though it relates to matters of life and death, their consent suffices. *This is the basis for the laws of war.* And indeed, if each and every nation would agree to outlaw war, in such a way that war would cease to be practiced among the nations,[28] neither war nor conquest would be legal, and a nation which engaged in warfare would be judged murderous. However, as long the practice of warfare is accepted among the nations, war is not prohibited to me, and for this reason even the Jewish people can engage in a *milhemet reshut.*

2) A number of *Aharonim*[29] have suggested that the basis for *dina de-malkhuta* can be found in the need for society to be able to function, an argument that suggests some kind of natural law. In the words of the *Maharshal*, "if not for it, the world would not endure but be destroyed." Logically speaking, the same principle applies to the international arena. This is certainly the case in a world where rapid transportation and communication has effectively reduced the size of the world so that frequently events in one place have immediate and powerful ramifications thousands of miles away.[30]

There is one caveat to the entire discussion of *dina de-malkhuta* and international law. That is, the law can only be considered halakhically binding in situations where it is applied consistently. If it is applied inconsistently it could be construed as *hamsanuta de-malkhuta*, robbery by the government, and not as *dina de-malkhuta*, the law of the government. One of the requirements that the *Rishonim* and *Aharonim* assume to be a *sina qua non* of *dina de-malkhuta* is a "*davar she-yesh lo kitzvah*," a tax that has a limit, i.e., not subject to whim, but fixed by law.[31] Were the king to apply his law to one city or province and not another, it would not be considered valid. What if international law were applied to some countries and not others? It seems obvious to me that such a distinction would constitute a *davar she-ein lo kitzvah*.[32]

2. Mandatory Nature

As we have suggested earlier, if the basis for international law were the Noahide precept of *dinim*, there would be a mandate upon all nations to create, if possible, a system of enforcement for whatever laws exist. The debate between Maimonides and Nahmanides in their understanding of the obligation relates only to the culpability of the parties involved. Both agree that, when possible, Noahides are obligated to set up courts to enforce the Noahide code. In the international context (as opposed to the context of the Biblical Shekhem), it is probable that Maimonides would acknowledge that no one party could be held culpable for not enforcing *dinim* due to the difficulty in actually doing so. Ideally, however, all would agree that the international community should create such a system.

If one adopts *dina de-malkhuta* as the basis for a system of international law, the mandatory nature of enforcement would depend on which specific model of *dina de-malkhuta* chosen. Of the two theories mentioned above, the theory of consent of the citizens would not mandate an enforcement mechanism. After all, there is no specific obligation that there be *dina de-malkhuta*. Presumably, if the inhabitants of a country decided that they are not interested in having a king or his laws and would prefer to confine themselves to the seven Noahide laws, they would be permitted to do so. The same would hold true for the larger world. If, however, one chooses the model that focuses on the need of the world to function, it is logical that, since people are granted the right to legislate primarily so that society can function, they are also obligated to take advantage of that right. In a sense, it is part of the obligation of "He did not create it a waste, but formed it for habitation" (Isaiah 45:18), and this would apply both in the national and international contexts.

3. Applicability to the Jewish State

With regard to the applicability of *dinim*, there are a number of sources that assume that the precept applies to Jews as well. In its discussion of the Noahide laws, the Talmud (*Sanhedrin* 56b) states:

> "Social laws:" Were then the children of Noah bidden to observe these? Surely it has been taught: The Israelites were given ten

precepts at Marah, seven of which had already been accepted by the children of Noah, to which were added at Marah social laws, the Sabbath, and honoring one's parents. "Social laws:" for it is written, "There [at Marah] he made them a statute and an ordinance" [Ex. 15]...But Raba answered thus: the author of this *Baraita* [which states that the social laws were added at Marah] is a *tanna* of the the School of Manassah, who omitted social laws and blasphemy [from the list of Noahian precepts] and substituted emasculation and the forbidden mixture. For a *tanna* of the School of Manassah taught: The sons of Noah were given seven precepts, viz., [prohibition of] idolatry, adultery, murder, robbery, flesh cut from a living animal, emasculation and forbidden mixtures.

The assumption of the Talmud is that the seven Noahide precepts were repeated to the Jews shortly before their arrival at Mount Sinai and that the precept of *dinim* applies to the Jews. Maimonides' presentation is also quite clear:

Six precepts were given to Adam: prohibition of idolatry, of blasphemy, of murder, of adultery, of robbery, and the command to establish courts of justice. Although there is a tradition to this effect – a tradition dating back to Moses, our teacher, and human reason approves of these precepts – it is evident from the general tenor of the Scriptures that he (Adam) was bidden to observe these commandments. An additional commandment was given to Noah: prohibition of eating a limb from a living animal, as it is said: "Only flesh with the life thereof, which is the blood thereof, you shall not eat" (Gen. 9:4). Thus we have seven commandments. So it was not until Abraham appeared who, in addition to the aforementioned commandments, was charged to practice circumcision. Moreover, Abraham instituted the Morning Service. Isaac set apart tithes and instituted the Afternoon Service. Jacob added to the preceding law (prohibiting) the sinew that shrank, and inaugurated the Evening Service. In Egypt Amram was charged to observe other precepts, until Moses came and the law was completed through him (*Hilkhot Melakhim* 9:1).

It is by no means necessary that the laws that govern the Jewish state internally be identical in all respects to those that may govern other nations (if one adopts the position of the *Netziv* above). But if one assumes that the precept of *dinim* mandates that the other nations of the world create and enforce a body of law to govern international relations, there is no reason that the commandment of *dinim* given to the Jews should not mandate Jewish participation in the said international enterprise, at least as it relates to its international conduct, even if at the same time, rules that govern the Jewish state internally may differ from those in the rest of the world.

With respect to *dina de-malkhuta*, there is long history of debate as to whether or not it applies to Jewish kings in the Land of Israel.[33] The dominant view, that of R. Eliezer of Metz, is that it does not apply. His view stems from the notion that *dina de-malkhuta* is based upon the king's ownership of his land, and since the Land of Israel is owned by the Jewish people, it cannot be owned by a king and hence is not subject to *dina de-malkhuta*. As we noted earlier, if one adopts this view of *dina de-malkhuta*, it cannot serve as the basis for a system of international law anywhere. If, however, one adopts the view that *dina de-malkhuta* stems from the consent of the inhabitants, there is no reason to assume that it should not apply to the Land of Israel, as well.[34] Moreover, even if one rejects the applicability of *dina de-malkhuta* within Land of Israel, it would be because it has been supplanted either by *dinei Yisrael* or by the *mishpat ha-melukhah*. To the extent, however, that those may not be applicable outside of the Land of Israel, there is no reason to assume that *dina de-malkhuta* has been supplanted.

Finally, if one assumes that *dina de-malkhuta* is based upon the need for the world to function, it would be intuitive that in the international arena there is no reason that the halakhic state should *a priori* be exempted from being bound by international law.

II. TREATIES IN HALAKAH

As one might expect, *Hazal* do not discuss the issue of treaties, *per se*. There are numerous Biblical examples of *beritot* (treaties) and alliances between nations (although all of them are bilateral), but *Hazal* show little, if any, interest in them. There is only one discussion of a treaty between the Jews and another nation that is discussed, albeit briefly, in the literature of *Hazal*. That is the treaty with the Gibonites found in the book of Joshua. The Gibonites, one of the seven Canaanite nations, approached the Jews and presented themselves as members of a foreign nation who wished to conclude a treaty with the Jews. They successfully deceived the leaders of the Jewish nation, who failed to seek divine counsel, and, as a result, we read in Joshua 9:15:

> Joshua established friendship with them; he made a pact with them to spare their lives, and the chieftains of the community gave them their oath.

When the people later discovered the deception they wished to renege on their agreement, but the leadership refused to go along. Scripture continues:

> But the Israelites did not attack them, *since the chieftains of the community had sworn to them by the Lord, the God of Israel*. The whole community muttered against the chieftains, but all the chieftains answered the whole community, "*We swore to them by the Lord, the God of Israel; therefore we cannot touch them. This is what we will do to them: We will spare their lives, so that there may be no wrath against us because of the oath that we swore to them.*" And the chieftains declared concerning them, "They shall live!" And they became hewers of wood and drawers of water for the whole community, as the chieftains had decreed concerning them. Joshua summoned them and spoke to them thus: "Why did you deceive us and tell us you lived very far from us, when in fact you live among us? Therefore, be accursed! Never shall your descendants cease to be slaves,

hewers of wood, and drawers of water for the House of my God." But they replied to Joshua, "You see, your servants had heard that the Lord your God had promised His servant Moses to give you the whole land and to wipe out all the inhabitants of the country on your account; so we were in great fear for our lives on your account. That is why we did this thing. And now we are at your mercy; do with us what you consider right and proper." *And he did so; he saved them from being killed by the Israelites.*

Although we know from other places in scripture that a *berit* typically entailed a ceremonial passing (Genesis 15:9–18, Jeremiah 34:10–11, 19, Deuteronomy 29:31), no such ceremony is recorded here in Joshua. The emphasis appears to be on the oath that accompanied the treaty.[35]

The discussion in *Hazal* regarding the Gibonite treaty revolves around one question: why was the oath binding if it was undertaken under false pretenses? The Bavli (*Gittin* 46a) records a dispute between R. Yehudah and the Sages on this matter. The Mishnah (*ibid.* 45b) states:

If a man divorces his wife because of ill fame, he must not remarry her. If because she makes a vow, he must not remarry her. R. Yehudah says: [If he divorces her] for vows which she made publicly, he may not remarry her, but if for vows which she did not make publicly, he may remarry her.

The general concern of the Mishnah is that a husband who divorces his wife not be able to claim at a later time that he did so mistakenly because he was unaware of solutions to the problems of the marriage other than divorce, and thereby cast doubt on the validity of the divorce. The *tanna'im* in the Mishnah, as understood by the Bavli, argue as to whether a vow undertaken in public can be annulled under any circumstances. According to the anonymous *tanna kamma*, a public vow may be annulled and hence, one who divorces his wife because of such a vow might claim later that had he known that the vow could be annulled, he would never have divorced her. Hence, a husband who divorces his wife over a vow is categorically prohibited from remarrying her. R. Yehudah, however, is of the opinion that a publicly taken vow may not be annulled, and hence, there would be no concern over the husband claiming, "if only I had known I would have annulled the vow and not divorced her," since a publicly taken vow may not be annulled. (Nonetheless, R. Yehudah prohibits remarrying her as a warning to all women, "*she-lo yehiyu benot Yisrael perutzot be-nedarim*.")

The Bavli then states:

> "R. Yehudah says: [If he divorces her] for vows which she made publicly, he may not remarry her, but if for vows which she did not make publicly, he may remarry her." R. Yehoshua ben Levi says: What is the reason for R. Yehudah? Because Scripture says "But the Israelites did not attack them, since the chieftains of the community had sworn to them" (Joshua 9). And what do the Rabbis [make of this verse]? [They reply:] Did the oath there become binding upon them at all? Since they [the Gibonites] said, "We are come from a far country" whereas they had not come from one, the oath was never binding; and the reason the Israelites did not slay them was because [this would have impaired] the sanctity of God's name.

According to the *sugya*, there is a basic disagreement as to why the Jews did not simply annul the treaty on the grounds of deception: according to R. Yehudah, the oath taken was binding (despite the deception)[36] whereas according to the anonymous *tanna kamma*, the treaty was void, and they refrained from killing the Gibonites only because it would have resulted in a *hillul Hashem*, a desecration of God's name.

The *tanna'im* never relate to the "treaty" itself but rather to the oath, which comprised part of the larger treaty. It follows, *a fortiori*, from the Talmudic discussion that a treaty with an oath (or one implied), when undertaken without deception, is binding. Abrogating a legitimate treaty would entail violating an oath according to all views, and even a technically legitimate legal annulment of the oath, *hattarat nedarim*[37] would constitute a *hillul Hashem* (at least according to the *tanna kamma*).

A more basic question that emerges from the discussion is why the oath should not have been null and void because it contradicted a precept of Torah-law, "*lo tikhrot lahem berit ve-lo tehanem*," i.e., not annihilating the seven Canaanite nations. Mishnaic law (*Shevu'ot* 3:6, 8) assumes that an oath that demands violation of a precept of Halakhah is not binding and must be disregarded. If so, the oath should have been void regardless of the considerations of a publicly taken vow and oath taken under mistaken premises. The *Rishonim* propose a number of answers, all assuming that, for one reason or another, there was nothing that violated Halakhah in concluding a treaty with the Gibonites under the circumstances. Had, however, the oath mandated violating Halakhah, it would not have been binding.

Two important questions, which pertain to a situation where there is a conflict between a treaty and Halakhah remain:

1. Would considerations of *hillul Hashem* prevent the abrogation of a treaty that is deemed invalid because it contravenes Halakhah? The discussion of the *Rishonim* focuses on why R. Yehudah considered the oath itself binding on a fundamental level if its contravening of a precept should have invalidated it. They all solve the problem by explaining how the treaty did not require such a contravention. Yet, they do not raise the same consideration within the position of the Sages who posit that they did not kill the Gibonites only because of *hillul Hashem*, i.e. that if the Torah commands "*lo tihayyeh kol neshamah*," how can considerations of appearances override an explicit precept? This could be because: (a) once they solve the problem for R. Yehudah by explaining that the treaty itself did not contravene Halakhah, the same explanation would apply to the position of the Sages or (b) because it was clear to them that the issue of *hillul Hashem* would have trumped the concern of "they shall not dwell in your land." According to the former, *hillul*

Hashem would play no role if fulfilling the treaty would violate Halakhah. According to the latter, *hillul Hashem* might dictate observing a treaty's commitment even if it requires violating Halakhah. However, one would still have to determine to which cases this would apply. Following the model of the treaty with the Gibonites, one might cogently argue that *hillul Hashem* would only override violations that are passive in nature, i.e., not wiping out the Gibonites. Perhaps only in such a case would we argue that the passive violation would be preferable to *hillul Hashem*, but in cases where the treaty would require us to actively violate Halakhah, *hillul Hashem* of a passive nature would be preferable.

2. Following the argument above that the halakhic foundation of a treaty is the oath, would a treaty be binding in situations that it violates Halakhah only incidentally, not by definition, i.e., a treaty contravenes Halakhah in some but not all situations? We might further divide this scenario by asking if such a treaty would be valid in those situations (a) when it does not contravene Halakhah and those (b) when it does?

The Yerushalmi (*Shevuʾot* 3:4/34:3) writes:

> One who says "I swear that I will not eat *matzah*," is prohibited from eating *matzah* [even] on the nights of Passover. One who says "I swear I will not eat *matzah* on Passover nights," is flogged and [is required] to eat *matzah*. [One who swears,] "I will not sit in the shade," is prohibited from sitting in the shade of a *sukkah*. [One who swears,] "I will not sit in the shade of a *sukkah*," is flogged and [is required] to sit in the shade of a *sukkah*.

According to the Yerushalmi, an oath that contravenes Halakhah in some but not all situations is binding not only in cases where its demands do not conflict with those of Halakhah, but even in those where they do. Thus, if a person swore not to eat *matzah* without any mention of the first night of Passover (when consumption of *matzah* is mandatory), he would be bound by the oath not only during the rest of the year, but even on the first night of Passover. *Rif*[38] and *Rosh*[39] cite this Yerushalmi as normative, as does the *Shulhan Arukh*.[40] The *Rema*[41], however, qualifies this by adding:

> The idea that a generalized oath can supercede a *mitzvah* applies only to positive commandments, but not negative commandements.

The *Taz*[42] understands the *Rema*'s comment as distinguishing between active violation of a prohibition, where his oath would not mandate that he violate the prohibition, and a passive violation of a commandment, where his oath would prevent him from fulfilling the commandment. Thus, according to *Rema* even an oath that occasionally demands active violation of Halakhah (and would not be binding in those circumstances) would be valid in those situations where no violation would be entailed.

Returning to the discussion of treaties, it would follow that if a treaty sometimes, but not by definition, entails passively violating Halakhah it would be binding in all situations. If, however, adherence to the treaty would incidentally demand an active violation of Halakhah, we would, putting aside considerations of *hillul Hashem*, be obligated to ignore its provisions, but only in those circumstances where the conflict exists.

One final issue that merits some consideration in the discussion is the abrogation of treaties. We discussed earlier the question of *neder she-hudar be-rabbim* and *neder she-hudar al da'at rabbim*. Unilaterally annulling a treaty's oath would most likely entail a violation of *hillul Hashem*. Hence, to the extent that the vow might itself be voidable on technical grounds through *she'eilah*, it might still be forbidden to void it. It should also be taken as a given that any explicit or implicit[43] rights to withdraw that are contained within the treaty itself would be recognized by Halakhah as a stipulation (*tenai*) in the oath that would limit its application. The question that remains is what if the other party abrogates the treaty? Clearly again, if it was customarily understood that one party's abrogation

creates an automatic right for the other party to abrogate the treaty as
well, we would argue that the oath of the treaty contains an implicit
stipulation that nullifies it. If there was no clear custom, what would
Halakhah say about our right to nullify the oath?

The *Shulhan Arukh* (*Yoreh Deʾah* 236:6) writes: "When two parties enter into a joint oath and one of the parties violates the terms,
the other party is exempt and does not require *hatarah*." Here the
Halakhah clearly acknowledges an implicit stipulation of either
party to withdraw pursuant to the abrogation of the treaty by the
other party.

Along the same lines, in the context of international relations,
there is a discussion of this on the now-famous *aggadah* of the "three
oaths," which was, for a time, the primary source used to argue
against the Zionistic enterprise. *Ketubot* (111a) posits that there were
three oaths taken between the Jews and nations of the world: (1) That
the Jews would not attempt to return to the Land of Israel using
force. (2) That the Jews would not rebel against their rulers in exile.
(3) That the nations of the world would not abuse the Jews in exile.
If the oaths here are to (a) be regarded as genuine (not aggadic) and
(b) as ordinary oaths (not as a reflection of a divine covenant), one
would have a test case for the last questions. There were those who
argued that the oaths taken by the Jews were not binding because
the gentiles had violated their oath.[44] Thus, as matter of general
rule, Halakhah would treat mutual oaths as conditionally dependent
upon the adherence to the oath by the other party unless explicitly
stipulated otherwise.

III. OTHER CONSIDERATIONS

There are two other major considerations, which, independent of any
theoretical halakhic framework or signed treaty, might mandate the
Jewish state's participation in a system of international law in some
circumstances. First is the consideration of the danger to life that
could potentially arise from the treatment of the Jewish state as a
pariah and its isolation if it were to flout international law. There
was a time when international trade played a considerably smaller

role in the economy of states. Many states were self-sufficient in developing and producing the resources they needed. For better or worse, that world no longer exists. With the explosion of trade, particularly in the area of food, and the proliferation of advanced weapons systems, which are both expensive to produce and require a good deal of natural resources that many countries do not possess, few countries can choose to exist and turn their backs on the world. Israel is by no means an exception to this rule. Absent clear divine communication to ignore pragmatic considerations and display faith in God, the Jewish state must take prudent action to protect the lives of its citizens. Since it depends upon many other members of the international community for various ingredients that aid in its survival, it may be obligated to take into account international law. This does not mean that international law is actually binding, but simply that the Jewish state must sometimes act as if it is, and since the issue of *pikuah nefesh* is involved, the obligation might theoretically apply even in cases where international law conflicts with other Halakhah considerations.

The other "pragmatic" consideration would be the issue of *hillul Hashem*. There is a notion among some halakhists that practices that are permitted in Halakhah may nonetheless be forbidden when the gentiles regard the practice as immoral or, in a generic sense, religiously inappropriate. The Yerushalmi (*Bava Kamma* 4:1/4b) records an incident in which concerns about *hillul Hashem* prompted a change in Halakhah:

> Once the government sent two officials to learn Torah from Rabban Gamliel, and they learned from him Bible, Mishnah, Talmud, *halakhot* and *aggadot*. They said to him, "Your whole Torah is beautiful and praiseworthy except for these two things: (1) That you say, 'a Jewess may not help a non-Jewish woman give birth, but a non-Jewish woman can help a Jewess give birth; and a Jewess may not nurse the child of a non-Jewish woman, but a non-Jewish woman many nurse the child of a Jewish woman, with her permission. (2) Goods stolen from a Jew are

prohibited but from a non-Jew are permitted.'" Immediately, Rabban Gamliel decreed that the stolen goods of a non-Jew are prohibited because of *hillul Hashem*.

Commenting on the theoretical possibility of a synagogue being built on Shabbat by non-Jewish workers who are paid by the job (and not by the hour or day), the *Magen Avraham* states:

> It would seem that it is permissible for non-Jews paid on a per-contract basis to build a synagogue on *Shabbat*, however, I have seen that the *gedolim* did not wish to permit it, for in our time the non-Jews do not permit anyone to do public labor on their holy days, and if we permit such, it would be a *hillul Hashem* (*Orah Hayyim* 244, n. 8).

If the international community were to adopt certain practices because they are regarded as morally proper, such practices may, at times, bind the Jewish state as well. That is only the case, however, if such behavior does not contravene Halakhah and if the Jewish tradition does not consider the practice immoral.

IV. PRELIMINARY CONCLUSIONS

The discussion within traditional sources regarding the interaction between nations in the context of war is limited. There are a number of halakhic models that could provide a theoretical framework for Halakhah recognizing the implementation of international law, although none of them are definite enough to be considered compelling and binding. In the absence of such a system, the Jewish state would still be bound by the strictures of war, which are included within the traditional halakhic system, but not to any customary international law. Of course, treaties to which the state chose to be a signatory would be binding; to the extent that such treaties would sometimes mandate practices that contravene Halakhah, they would be subject to the considerations of "*nishba le-vattel et ha-mitzvah*" and *hillul Hashem*.

NOTES

1. Reisman, W. Michael and Chris T. Antoniou, *The Laws of War*, xvii–xvix (Vintage Books, New York 1994).

2. I should emphasize that the possibilities outlined here should not be taken as advocating that a framework of international law should be created. Rather, they should be seen as approaches that might be taken if one has concluded, from a secular viewpoint, that a system of international law is both morally desirable and practically feasible. The possibilities I outline are just that – possibilities, not clear mandates.

3. See R. Zevin, *Le-Or ha-Halakhah* (*Mossad ha-Rav Kook*, 1946), pp. 9–84 and R. J. David Bleich, "Pre-emptive War in Jewish Law," *Tradition* 21 (1983):3–41.

4. It should be noted, though, that in some sense this is really the rationale advanced by the *Netziv* cited below.

5. *Sotah* 8:7. For a full discussion of these categories, see Rabbi Bleich's "Pre-emptive War in Jewish Law."

6. Presumably, when its survival is threatened, the nation would be permitted to fight embracing whatever tactics necessary, and once its survival is no longer threatened, it would no longer be considered defensive warfare.

   Obviously there is a category of war which, conceptually speaking, falls between blunting the enemy's attacks and destroying or permanently disabling the enemy and whose status would be unclear. But, in principle, there would probably be a point up until which we would treat military action as defensive warfare but beyond which we would define as offensive warfare.

7. One might even argue that if initiating warfare were permitted, there would be rules governing the behavior of the attacked nation. The permissibility of warfare, presumably, would reflect a view that war is part of the human condition – just as one nation may initiate an attack, so too should it expect to be subject to attack, and hence may also be bound by rules in its response.

8. The case of *sikrikon* in *Gittin* 55b may serve as an example of this, especially in wartime. According to the Bavli, at an early stage in the war of the Destruction (when Roman soldiers who refrained from killing Jews were, themselves, to be executed) property "given" by a Jew as ransom to his potential killer was treated as a binding gift, as it was given with genuine intent (out of fear for his life – *agav onseih gamar u-makni*; cf. *Bava Batra* 48b). Even at the first historic stage of *sikrikon*, where the *sikrikon* gained full title to the property, Halakhah still did not regard his acquisition of the property as anything but theft.

9. *Teshuvot Hatam Sofer, Yoreh De'ah* 19, *Devar Avraham* 1:11, R. Zevin, "*Le-Or ha-Halakhah*," pp. 17–8.

10. The term first appears in Nahmanides' discussion of the Talmudic passage in *Bava Batra* 54b.

11. R. Yisraeli, *Amud ha-Yemini* (Moreshet, 1966), 185–6.

12. In the opening part of the *halakhah*, Maimonides speaks of a king who wages war against another nation, suggesting an offensive action; when he speaks of permitting

somebody to kidnap a member of another nation in a raiding action, he writes "a king who is waging war against him," suggesting that his role in the war is primarily a response of self-defense.

13. R. Yisraeli, *Amud ha-Yemini*, 185–6, *Shulhan Arukh ha-Rav* vol. v, *Hilkhot Hefker ve-Hasagat Gevul*, and R. Zevin, *Le-Or ha-Halakhah*, 9–84. I presume here that if war itself is a legitimate enterprise and Halakhah expresses opinions about its aftermath, that the conduct of war itself would also be regulated. One might argue, to borrow the colloquial expression, that "all is fair in love and war" and that the Halakhah is concerned only with the aftermath of war when society resumes its civilian mode of operation. I think this to be unlikely since the Halakhah clearly delineates acceptable and unacceptable behavior in the context of a Jewish war and also concerns itself with the general (i.e., non-military) conduct of Noahides. It seems probable, then, that if the Halakhah permits war among gentile nations it would also regulate its conduct.

14. R. Yisraeli, *Amud ha-Yemini*, p. 186.

15. *Bava Kamma* 113a.

16. *Sanhedrin* 56b.

17. *Hilkhot Melakhim* 9:14. According to Maimonides, the entire thrust of the law is to enforce the other Noahide laws, and, as such, the citizens of Shekhem were liable for capital punishment since they failed to punish Shekhem, the son of their ruler. Nahmanides takes strong exception to the notion that they were liable for passive activity (and to the idea that the townspeople were capable of punishing Shekhem) and limits capital punishment for this precept to active violations, e.g., a judge taking bribes and perverting justice.

18. Commentary to Genesis 34:13. There is some debate among the *Aharonim* as to whether these laws are the same as those found in *Hoshen Mishpat*, or simply that there must be a full system of civil law, *nimmusim*. See *Teshuvat ha-Rema* #10 and the *Netziv* in *Ha-Emek She'alah*, *She'ilta* #2.

19. *Teshuvot ha-Rema* #10.

20. *Netziv, ha-Emek She'alah*, *She'ilta* #2.

21. *Ibid*. However, the *Rema* himself ultimately rejects this approach.

22. *Ran, Nedarim* 28a, s.v. *be-mokhes, ha-omed me-elav*.

23. In some sense, one might argue that this is indeed the current reality. The reason that the Serbs ultimately failed in their ethnic cleansing campaign was that the international community was able (and willing) to use force to prevent it. There is no country, however, that would be capable of stopping China's behavior in Tibet (at least for a price that such a country would be willing to pay), and hence that has, *de facto*, continued to happen.

24. R. Henkin adopts a broader approach to this opinion of the *Ran* and posits that the *Ran* means that since the king provides many useful services of which they partake (allowing them to dwell there is just one), the inhabitants are, by exchange, bound by his laws. In the case of international law, this rationale would, for the most part be absent and, hence, *dina de-malkhuta* once again could not serve as its basis.

25. *Bava Batra* 54b, s.v. *ve-ha-amar Shemuel dina de-malkhuta dina*.

26. The only place in the world that would, in the halakhic system, naturally lend itself to such clear demarcation is the Land of Israel by virtue of *kedushat Eretz Yisrael*, although it is not obvious that the sanctity of the land itself should have an impact on law that is civil, not ritual, in nature.

27. *Amud ha-Yemini*, pp. 196. See also pp. 188–9. The argument of the world as one large subdivided country is my formulation; R. Yisraeli does not explain his extrapolation.

28. R. Yisraeli implies here that this would be the case only if, in fact, the law was observed. A treaty that was signed but not actually implemented would not make war illegal.

29. R. Shlomo Z. Auerbach, *Ma'adanei Eretz*, 20:3. See Shilo, *Dina de-Malkhuta* (Defus Akademi, 1975) 83–4.

30. This type of an argument might have bearing on local environmental issues that have a global impact. This is something for consideration in a discussion about the Kyoto protocols.

31. This is the obvious inference from the Talmud's example of a non-binding tax being *mokhes she-ein lo kitzvah*. For a full collection of the sources, see Shilo, *Dina de-Malkhuta*, pp. 109–14.

32. This point is obviously not merely a theoretical one, but very relevant today, both in the context of Israel's treatment in the international community and in the context of more powerful countries violating international law (e.g., China's behavior in Tibet) and not being censured or certainly punished. While one might argue that enforceability does not indicate that the law is not regarded as law but that the law simply cannot be enforced, it is difficult to understand why, in the context of censure, the international community should remain essentially silent in some cases while extremely vocal in others if the law is anything but the law of the jungle.

    In this context, there is a famous passage in the *Teshuvot* of the *Maharik* (#194) cited by the *Rema* (*Hoshen Mishpat* 369) that a tax only on the Jews is valid since the king's treatment of all his Jewish citizens is consistent. In the modern context, where discrimination among groups based on ethnicity, religion or gender are ostensibly prohibited by international law, the *Maharik*'s approach would not be acceptable.

33. Shilo, *Dina de-Malkhuta*, 99–109.

34. See the views of R. Herzog and R. Uziel cited in Shilo, *ibid.*, 107.

35. See Genesis 21:22–32, 26:26–33 and 31:44, 53 where treaties are accompanied by oaths. No oath is referred to in either the *berit bein ha-betarim* (Gen. 15:7–21) or in the *berit* of manumission of Jeremiah (Jer. 34:8–22). The one obvious distinction between the two scenarios is that those that involve two human parties require an oath, whereas those between God and man do not. This may reflect two different kinds of *berit*: covenants vs. treaties. This distinction, however, does not hold in the *berit* recorded at the end of Deuteronomy (29:11) where it is stated "that thou shouldest enter into the covenant of the Lord your God – and into His oath." (Note that the *berit* at Sinai involved no oath).

36. The *Rishonim* offer a number of suggestions as to why this was so. *Tosafot* (*ibid.*,

s.v. *keivan*) suggests that R. Yehudah believed the oath must have been binding; had it not, there would have been no *hillul Hashem* in its abrogation, and the Jews would have abrogated it. This does not explain substantively why it was binding, but rather why R. Yehudah felt compelled to see the oath in the biblical account as binding. *Rashba* (*ibid.*, s.v. *ve-Rabbanan*) quotes in the name of the *Tosafot* that, in fact, even R. Yehudah agrees that the Gibonite oath itself was not binding. However, he assumed that if a *"neder she-hudar ba-rabbim"* could be annulled, there would have been no *hillul Hashem* in abrogating the treaty and hence, from the fact that they refused to abrogate the treaty (with the emphasis on "since the chieftains of the community *had sworn to them*"), it is clear that such a vow cannot ordinarily be abrogated. Finally, *Ritva* (*ibid.*) suggests an answer on highly technical grounds: he posits that even though the Gibonites presented themselves as strangers initially, no explicit stipulation was included in the oath, rendering it what we term *"devarim she-ba-lev,"* "unspoken stipulations," which are not valid in an agreement.

37. The discussion of this matter would revolve around the question of a vow taken *"al da'at aherim,"* i.e. contingent upon or subservient to the interests of others. In the case of a treaty specifically, the issue would relate to the concept of *"neder she-hudar al da'at rabbim,"* a vow undertaken with the consent and understanding of a larger population. For more on this topic, see *Gittin* 36a and *Yoreh De'ah* 228:21.

38. *Shevu'ot* 12b in the *Rif*.

39. *Ibid.* 3:26.

40. *Orah Hayyim* 485:1, *Yoreh De'ah* 236:5. The *Ba'al ha-Ma'or* differs strongly with the position of the *Rif*, arguing that the *sugya* in the Bavli in *Shevu'ot* 24a disagrees with the Yerushalmi and hence, following the normal rules of *pesak*, the Yerushalmi should be disregarded. See the responses of Nahmanides in his *Milkhemet Hashem* and the *Ran* in his commentary on the *Rif*. The *Ran's* qualification of the Yerushalmi (to harmonize it with the Bavli) is adopted by the *Rema* in *Yoreh De'ah*.

41. *Yoreh De'ah, ibid.*

42. *Ibid.* 236:5, note 12. The *Shakh* as well comments that the *Rema's* distinction between positive and negative commandments is imprecise; it is unclear whether he believes that the *Rema* disagrees, or simply used imprecise language for the purposes of brevity.

43. I assume this with respect to implicit conditions, which would fall under the rubric of *devarim she-be-libbo u-be-lev kol adam*. (See *Tosafot Kiddushin* 49b s.v. *devarim she-ba-lev*).

44. For a collection of these views, see R. Shlomo Avineri, *"Be-Inyan she-Lo Ya'alu ba-Homah,"* *No'am* 20 (5738).

International Law, Israel, and the Use of Force: Historic Perspectives/ Current Perplexities

Michla Pomerance

What war is deemed to be a milhemet mitzvah? *A war against the Seven Nations, or against Amalek, or to deliver Israel from an enemy that is attacking him...For a* milhemet mitzvah, *the king need not obtain the sanction of the* Beit Din.

(Maimonides, Laws of Kings and Their Wars, 5:1–2)

I knew that this Government, at least, would never agree to submit to a tribunal the question of self-defense, and I do not think any of them [the other states parties to the Kellogg-Briand Pact] would.

(U.S. Secretary of State Frank B. Kellogg, in testimony before the Senate Committee on Foreign Relations, December 7, 1928)

America will never seek a permission slip to defend the security of our country.

(U.S. President, George W. Bush, State of
the Union Address, January 20, 2004)

To initiate a war of aggression…is not only an international crime; it is the supreme international crime differing only from other war crimes in that it contains within itself the accumulated evil of the whole.

(Judgment of the International Military
Tribunal, Nuremberg, 1946)

Israel's current war on terrorism is, in its dimensions and many of its aspects, unprecedented. It shares many of the features, dilemmas, and asymmetries of the global war on terrorism, but it is also unique. The asymmetries are sharper, the anomalies greater, and the dilemmas starker. Above all, Israel, rather than the Palestinian Authority that unleashed the terror, has been put in the international political and judicial dock. Alone among the nations, Israel has been called upon repeatedly to justify every measure that it takes to defend its existence and that of its inhabitants. Its efforts – including very prominently those of its judicial arm – to balance its security needs with the maintenance of civil rights in wartime, are often scorned.

It is not the purpose of this article to explain the phenomenon of anti-Israelism; as with classic anti-semitism, there are many explanations, and none. Nor have any of the proposed "cures" to this malady succeeded. (Perhaps, as Anton Chekhov, a medical doctor by profession, once remarked, when numerous remedies are recommended for the same disease, it is a sure indication that none would be effective, and the disease is incurable.)[1] The purpose of this article is to highlight the manner in which Israel's present predicament has been tragically sharpened by some of the more worrisome trends in international law and international organizations; and to indicate briefly how the more blatant attempts to delegitimize Israel's right of self-defense may be, and have been, countered.

I.

The two areas of international law that need to be examined most closely are first, *jus ad bellum,* related to the initiation of war (or in modern terminology, recourse to force); and second, *jus in bello,* the laws of war (or in present-day lingo, the laws of armed conflict or "international humanitarian law"). Theoretically, these are two separate spheres (and it is the second that has the longer history and is more greatly codified in international, and also in Jewish, law). They are, in fact, integrally related. In just war theory, for example, a war launched for a just cause may become unjust if cruelly or unjustly waged. On the other hand, in the UN and other international forums, there is a current propensity (particularly strong in relation to Israel) to condone the most heinous war crimes committed by a belligerent deemed to have "justice" on its side, and to condemn the self-defensive acts of the "unjust" party – even if these conform to all the requirements of international law.

That the norms of international law are often vague and undefined is a truism obvious to all but the uninitiated or over-committed. The existing uncertainties are especially conspicuous in relation to the rules regarding permissible recourse to force; and they are more greatly magnified still when a state is called upon to defend itself against terrorist, rather than conventional state-to-state, threats.[2] The unrelenting Arab campaign to prevent Israel's birth and later to extinguish its sovereignty has entailed both types of threat. Understandably, Israel has embraced principles, such as that of anticipatory self-defense (the equivalent of the tenet *ha-ba le-hargekha hashkem le-horgo*) in order to thwart the politicidal – indeed genocidal – plots of its enemies. For their part, even friendly states, such as the United States, as long as they felt immune from terrorist threats themselves, freely condemned Israel and ostensibly rejected her operative legal doctrines.[3] Nevertheless, a broad interpretation of the right to self-defense was sustainable as a matter of law, and it began to be openly espoused in some quarters as the terrorist threat became palpable for other countries as well. The post-9/11 Bush Doctrine on the preemptive use of force is the most obvious recent example. It is neither as novel in theory nor as unprecedented in state practice as is popularly assumed; but Israel has not benefited as greatly as might have been expected from such renewed awareness. In this matter, as in so many others, politics and expediency tend to trump law and principle.

As codified in international legal texts, the modern laws and principles designed to restrain the unfettered recourse to war are of relatively recent origin. The first modest step was taken at the Hague Conference of 1907, with the adoption of the Porter Convention, which restricted the right to use force for collecting contract debts. More significant attempts followed World War I, in the form, most prominently, of the League of Nations Covenant and the 1928 Kellogg-Briand Pact for the Renunciation of War. The League Covenant established mainly a procedural framework for distinguishing legal from illegal (rather than "just" from "unjust") resorts to "war."[4] There were famous "gaps" in the Covenant, which allowed member states to initiate war without thereby violating any legal obligation;[5] and throughout much of the interwar period, statesmen and international lawyers, tormented by the existence of these "gaps," strove mightily to plug them, primarily by defining more precisely the concept of "aggression."[6] The definitional enterprise did not succeed, and many doubted whether the goal was achievable or worth pursuing. Sir Austen Chamberlain, for one, considered that such definitions would be "traps for the innocent and signposts for the guilty."[7] World War II and its preludes occurred not because of any unplugged "gaps" but because the whole League structure was spurned and jettisoned. The same fate, of course, greeted the Kellogg-Briand Pact, which, in terms of its implementation, turned out to be the international equivalent of the Eighteenth Amendment of the U.S. Constitution (the Prohibition amendment). Noteworthy, too, are some of the reservations attached to the Pact by leading powers, including the United States, whose reservation included an absolute claim of self-judgment with respect to the right of self-defense. "There is nothing in the treaty," the reservation stated, "which restricts or impairs in any way the right of self-defense." Such a right "is inherent in every sovereign state." Each "is free at all times and regardless of treaty provisions to defend its territory from attack or invasion and it alone is competent to decide whether circumstances require recourse to war in self-defense." [8]

Following the Second World War, the Nuremberg Charter (in Article 6) conferred jurisdiction on the Nuremberg Tribunal to try major war criminals for, *inter alia*, "*Crimes against peace*: namely, planning, preparation, initiation or waging of a war of aggression, or a war in violation of international treaties, agreements or assurances, or participation in a common plan or conspiracy for the accomplishment of any of the foregoing." The Charter for the Tokyo Tribunal contained a similar mandate, with the addition that the war might be declared or undeclared. But neither document defined the term "war of aggression"; nor did the tribunals feel the need to do so. [9] They were, after all, confronted with clear-cut core cases of aggression. For the judges – who, significantly, were all from states that were victims of the just-concluded "wars of aggression" – there was no question of who were the aggressors, and who the victims exercising the right of legitimate self-defense. The issue of subjective assessment was thus not seriously contemplated – and not only because the trials predated the era of post-modernism and moral relativism. In a later era, where these elements would be lacking, elaboration of the "Nuremberg principles" would become much more problematic.

The framers of the UN Charter did not employ the term "war of aggression." In their attempt to regulate more rigorously the ability of states to use armed force against other states, they replaced the word "war" with terms such as "threat or use of force," "threat to the peace," and "breach of the peace." Though they used the term "aggression" (in Article 1, on the Purposes of the Organization, and in Article 39, relating to the Security Council's powers of determination), they too, like their predecessors, did not include any definition. The application of the term in concrete cases was left to the discretion of the Council, which was expected to act in accordance with the Purposes and Principles of the Organization and not arbitrarily.[10] Only some of the Council's decisions were to be binding on member states – the prevalent erroneous contrary assumption notwithstanding. Decisions under Chapter 6 (Pacific Settlement of Disputes) were recommendatory only;[11] nor did all Chapter 7 decisions necessarily have binding force. As the late British Judge of the International Court of Justice (ICJ), Sir Gerald Fitzmaurice, convincingly argued, the Council may not, for example, "in the guise of peace-keeping order transfers or cessions of territory"; and *even when acting under Chapter VII of the Charter itself*, the Security Council has no power to abrogate or alter territorial rights, whether of sovereignty or administration." After all, "it was to keep the peace, not to change the world order, that the Security Council was set up."[12]

When the UN was established, it was expected that the Council would act effectively to deal with the threat or use of force and, if necessary, adopt even military sanctions. Such sanctions would be undertaken only following the conclusion of special agreements between the Council and member states, as contemplated by Article 43. But the original plan never came to fruition, even after the end of the Cold War. No such agreements were adopted. (Peacekeeping forces, which are not mentioned in the Charter, have different legal bases, and are premised on the consent rather than the coercion of the host state.) Against this background, the two main UN Charter provisions dealing with the use of force and self-defense – Article 2(4), which states the general prohibition on the use of force, and Article 51, which permits individual and collective self-defensive actions – assumed greater significance.

The two provisions, however, raise more problems than they solve. "All members" according to Article 2(4), "shall refrain in their international relations from the threat or use of force against the territorial integrity or political independence of any state, or in any other manner inconsistent with the Purposes of the United Nations." What if the force used or threatened does *not* affect the territorial integrity or political independence of a state? What if, in fact, it *enhances* them, for example by ridding the populace of an oppressive regime? Does the provision connote a guarantee of territorial inviolability and a total ban on the use of force in international relations? If so, why did the period not appear after the word "force"? Are a state's intentions relevant or not? Would an Entebbe-style operation to protect one's nationals be permitted? Or an attack like the one Israel executed on the Iraqi nuclear reactor, which did not in any way affect Iraq's territorial integrity or political independence? Is force that is used to advance one of the UN Purposes – strengthening universal peace, promoting respect for human rights, for example – included in the prohibition? Above all, is not the ban, in any case, premised on a bargain – namely, that the *Organization* will guarantee peace by means of "effective collective measures," its primary purpose? (This was the view of such eminent international law experts as Julius Stone and A.L. Goodhart.) And surely the proscription was meant to apply to "international" rather than "internal" uses of force, the latter remaining, in principle, unregulated (unless they entail the kind of threat to international peace that would call into play enforcement action under Chapter 7).[13]

As for Article 51, it is no less riddled with unresolved conundrums, some of which the terrorist threat has served to heighten. Its interpretation has been hotly debated by scholars over the years, most famously regarding the permissibility of anticipatory self-defense. "Nothing in the present Charter," the provision states, "shall impair the inherent right of individual or collective self-defense if an armed attack occurs against a Member of the United Nations, until the Security Council has taken the measures necessary to maintain international peace and security." Measures so taken are to be immediately reported to the Security Council and are not to affect that organ's responsibility "to take at any time such action as it deems necessary in order to maintain or restore international peace and security."

On the basis of the drafting history of the provision and considerations of logic, renowned international law experts such as James Brierly, Sir Humphrey Waldock, Julius Stone, A.L. Goodhart, Georg Schwarzenberger, Derek Bowett, and Myres McDougal concluded that anticipatory self-defense was included.[14] Several alternative and complementary arguments have been put forward to justify this view. First, Article 51 was a "saving clause," designed merely to clarify the fact that there was no intention to impair the pre-existing and "inherent" right of self-defense, which encompassed preventive as well as reactive steps. And in the phrase "if an armed attack occurs," the word "if" was used in a descriptive, rather than conditional, sense. It clearly does not mean "if and only if" an armed attack occurs. Second, the decision to include a reference to self-defense in the Charter was dictated by the need to provide for *collective*, rather than individual, self-defense; had the latter alone been at issue, it would have remained an unstated, self-understood, reservation of rights (as in the League Covenant). (Guaranteeing the right of collective self-defense was a way of resolving the "Latin-American crisis" at San Francisco. By means of Article 51, the Charter régime was to be harmonized with the system of inter-American regional security, launched early in 1945 with the adoption of the Act of Chapultepec.) Third, even assuming that the "if" was conditional, the term "armed attack" need not be so restrictively interpreted as to require that the armed attack will have actually begun; it is sufficient if the "armed attack" is imminently threatened. And finally, in any event, the provision had to be interpreted in the context of changed realities (the *rebus sic stantibus* principle). A state faced either with a nuclear threat, on the one hand, or guerrilla and terrorist threats, on the other, could not reasonably be expected to adhere to the standards set in an earlier, less menacing, international environment.

State practice, too, accords with the view that there is no need to wait for an attack to occur and that an "imminent" attack may be preempted. The famous *Caroline* formula regarding self-defense, enunciated in 1842 by U.S. Secretary of State Daniel Webster in correspondence with Britain, is often quoted in this regard, since it clearly encompassed the concept of preemption.[15] At the same time, the formula – which required that a "necessity of self-defense" be shown to be "instant, overwhelming, leaving no choice of means and no moment for deliberation" – may be too rigid for application in a modern nuclearized and terrorized world. (It may also be narrower than the definition of anticipatory self-defense incorporated by implication in the U.S. Constitution.)[16] Certainly when dealing with rogue states that support, harbor, and encourage terrorism, it has been plausibly suggested, the test of "imminence" and "necessity" requires reassessment and revision.

Moreover, while "necessity" and "proportionality" are standardly deemed to be essential concomitants of the right of self-defense, both have always entailed generous doses of subjective appreciation along with some fundamental theoretical questions. Is the "necessity" to be limited to *repelling* the immediate danger or does it include the *removal* of the danger? Must actions be proportionate to measures *taken* or also to those *threatened*? Both American and British legal spokesmen have in recent years come out forcefully (in cases in which they have been involved) in favor of assessing proportionality by reference to the overall threat to the victim state.[17] In an ongoing armed conflict (whether labeled "war" or not) involving a series of attacks (some of them deemed, in isolation, to be "pin-prick"), must the response be proportionate to *each attack*, or is the entire context of continuous conflict to be the referent?[18] The former position, if combined with the assumption that Article 51 requires that an armed attack will have actually occurred *and* that reprisals are no longer permitted,[19] would mean that the hands of the victim of a non-conventional guerrilla war would be tied. Such a stance is not only unreasonable; it finds no support in state practice (except when directed *against* disfavored states, especially Israel.)

These issues were perceptively discussed by Robert W. Tucker, in his edition of Hans Kelsen's *Principles of International Law.*[20] And in an article justifying Israel's war in Lebanon in 1982, he reverted (in words that ring, sadly, no less true today than when they were penned) to the question of how "necessity" and "proportionality" should be measured. After chiding critics of Israel for demanding that it abide by "a very rigid standard – one that no government would seriously consider holding to in practice," since none would dare to jeopardize its national security in this manner, he noted:

> Even according to the prevailing standard, it has never been altogether clear whether acts of legitimate self-defense must be limited to repelling the immediate danger or may be directed toward removing the danger. A license to remove the danger obviously may be abused, yet an action limited to repelling a danger may lose its purpose if circumstances permit the danger to reappear.[21]

In some instances, too, "necessity" might include action taken to induce régime change. As Judge Stephen Schwebel (the American judge on the ICJ bench) observed in the *Nicaragua* case, government overthrow can be a defensive measure – as it was in anti-Axis acts in World War II.[22] (Even before the latest Gulf War, similar arguments were put forward at various times regarding the need to remove the Saddam regime in Iraq. Iran, for example, openly but vainly strove to accomplish this goal during the Iran-Iraq war.)

II.

The attempts of the interwar statesmen and jurists to "plug" the troublesome "gaps" of the League Covenant have been paralleled during the UN period by a series of endeavors to plug the gaps that the bare UN provisions have exposed. The results of these, still continuing, endeavors have been no more felicitous, in legal terms, than those in the earlier world organization. Indeed, instead of closing existing gaps, they have widened them, obfuscating still further issues about which there had previously been some consensus. Politically, they have been even more damaging. Not only have they created "traps for the innocent and signposts for the guilty"[23]; they have, arguably, *reversed* the roles of "innocent" and "guilty." This has been accomplished insidiously, through the adoption of a new "just war" doctrine, whose roots go back to the 1960–1961 period and whose pernicious offshoots have continued to spread uncontrollably ever since. The doctrine affects, most obviously, the sphere of *jus ad bellum*; but its effects may be felt no less poignantly in the realm of *jus in bello*. What occurred in the halls of the Peace Palace at The Hague in 2004 is but a further reflection of processes long operative in the various organs and sub-organs of the World Organization.

At the end of 1960, following the influx of new African states into the UN, the General Assembly adopted the famous Declaration on the Granting of Independence to Colonial Countries and Peoples (Resolution 1514). Viewed by the Third World as its Magna Carta, it heralded a new direction in the halls of the UN, one that places "self-determination" at the pinnacle of UN values, above the prohibition of the use of force. The Charter, of course, had never done so. Nor had it ever referred to "self-determination" as a "right"; and the Assembly is not competent to amend the Charter. Moreover, the proposition that "all peoples have the right to self-determination" was intrinsically unrealizable, if the right was understood (as increasingly it was in UN halls) as synonymous with the right to full independence. Self-determination claims do not, as a rule, clash with *anti*-self-determination claims, but rather with conflicting claims to self-determination; thus, the very act of fulfilling one claimant's right will generally constitute the denial of the claim of another contender to the right.[24] The Declaration was also internally inconsistent since in the one paragraph most firmly premised on Charter tenets (paragraph 6), it was stated that "any attempt aimed at the partial or total disruption of the national unity and the territorial integrity of a country is incompatible with the purposes and principles of the Charter of the United Nations." But which claimant is entitled to its "national unity and territorial integrity" and which to separate self-determination? What is the territorial unit within which such separate self-determination is to be implemented, and who are the people who belong to it and are thus entitled to exercise the right?

To answer these questions the UN adopted assorted formulas that merely shifted the semantic ground and gave no real guidance, but that could be conveniently exploited against target states. The beneficiaries of the "right" of self-determination were "peoples under colonial and alien domination"; "peoples subject to colonial exploitation"; and those under "alien occupation" or "racist régimes." All of these terms, as the West German representative at the 1977 Geneva Conference on Humanitarian Law, observed, "are not objective criteria, but lend themselves to arbitrary subjective and politically motivated interpretation and application."[25] They raise further issues such as: which is the "indigenous" population that "belongs" to the territory (once it has been delimited) and which, the "alien," "colonial," or "settler" population? What is the "critical date" to determine such "belonging"? How is one to define régimes that are "racist" rather than simply "nationalist"? And how does one do so in a world in which so many régimes are undemocratic?

Untroubled by these issues, the majority of the UN proceeded to expand on some of the propositions that were not yet spelled out in 1960 but came to be part of the "collective wisdom" soon thereafter. In December 1961, India invaded and annexed Goa and two other Portuguese enclaves in India (for good measure, without consulting the local inhabitants), and enunciated what was later termed the "Goa Doctrine."[26] To justify their use of force, the Indians presented several arguments, among them that Portugal's conquests of 1510 could not confer good title; that its continued presence in the Indian enclaves constituted "permanent aggression," giving rise to an Indian right of self-defense; and that the Declaration on Colonialism legitimated India's liberation of this colonial vestige by force. These assumptions were rejected by the majority of the Security Council at the time; but when a Soviet veto prevented adoption of a resolution deploring India's actions and calling for its withdrawal from the conquered territory, the matter was not transferred to the General Assembly (as it might have been under the Uniting for Peace resolution). It was obvious already then that for the reigning Third World-Soviet coalition in the Assembly, the culprit was Portugal, not India, and that the latter's actions were subjects of commendation rather than condemnation.

Elaborated further before very long, the new doctrine became a full-blown modern version of the medieval doctrine of the "just war." In place of the medieval church, there was the Assembly, with its automatic majority purporting now to determine whose struggles were "*legitimate*" because they were *for* "self-determination" or "national liberation" and *against* "colonial, alien or racist domination." For those thus blessed, Article 2(4) was effectively deemed to be overridden, while for those who would *suppress* such "legitimate" struggles, the prohibition was considered absolute. Colonialism was not only "permanent aggression"; it was a "crime."[27] Resisting it was thus a right, and assisting the resisters, an obligation. But the "colonial," "racist" and "occupying" states forfeited any inherent right to self-defense. For them, Article 51 was, in this new perspective, annulled.

Just how disturbing the corollaries of this new "just war" doctrine could be, both for *jus ad bellum* and *jus in bello*, started becoming more apparent from the mid-1960s onward. Moreover, as the decade of the 1970s wore on, Western resistance to Soviet-Third World perspectives began to weaken discernibly. It is sufficient to examine, in this respect, three major oft-cited documents produced from 1970 to 1977, each of which was preceded by "grand debates." The first was the Declaration on Friendly Relations, adopted by the General Assembly in October 1970, and intended to elucidate key UN principles, including those relating to self-determination and the use of force.[28] Several years later the Assembly adopted a so-called "Definition of Aggression," ostensibly ending the half-century quest begun during the League period. Both of these were adopted by consensus. And in 1977, a long process, fueled by General Assembly initiatives, culminated in the adoption of Additional Protocols to the 1949 Geneva Conventions. (The First Additional Protocol was and remains controversial, and unratified by either the United States or Israel.)

What happened, in brief, was that the Third World-Soviet coalition steadily pushed to give special exemptions from use-of-force prohibitions to "national liberation movements" and their supporters and correspondingly to restrict the rights of those who would suppress the "legitimate struggles" of such movements. Thereby, they aimed to replace long-established customary international law with a new "UN Law." For example, in traditional international law a state was culpable if it knowingly permitted its territory to be used as a base for hostile activities against a neighboring state. In the Declaration on Friendly Relations, the traditional rule was still fairly accurately stated. "Every State," it said, "has the duty to refrain from organizing or encouraging the organization of irregular forces or armed bands, including mercenaries, for incursion into the territory of another State." Additionally, "every State has the duty to refrain from organizing, instigating, assisting or participating in acts of civil strife or terrorist acts in another State *or acquiescing in organized activities within its territory directed towards the commission of such acts*, when the acts referred to in the present paragraph involve a threat or use of force" [italics added]. Elsewhere, ambiguous formulations served to bridge differences between the various blocs.

By cross-reference to the Charter régime (which, of course, was not amendable by a mere Assembly resolution, whether labeled "Declaration" or not), the debate and uncertainty were perpetuated. Thus, on the role of third states in support of self-determination struggles, the Declaration asserted first, most unhelpfully, that "every State has the duty to refrain from any forcible action which deprives *peoples referred to in the elaboration of the present principle* of the right to self-determination and freedom and independence" [italics added]. (One searches in vain in the cited section for a list or a definition of the "peoples" entitled to self-determination as opposed to those who were not to be beneficiaries. The "right" of self-determination is simply ascribed to "*all peoples*" – a formulation that does not in any way limit the universe of potential claimants to the right. Nor are later references to peoples under "alien subjugation, domination and exploitation" any more illuminating; they merely shift the semantic ground.) "In pursuit of the exercise of their right to self-determination," the Declaration adds, these – unspecified – peoples "*are entitled to receive support in accordance with the purposes and principles of the Charter*" [italics added].

In the Consensus Definition of Aggression, the traditional rule regarding the culpability of sanctuary states was considerably enfeebled. Among the "acts of aggression" enumerated in Article 3 we find: "The sending by or on behalf of a State of armed bands, groups, irregulars or mercenaries, which carry out acts of armed force against another State of such gravity as to amount to the acts listed above [i.e., invasion, bombardment, etc.], or its substantial involvement therein." Still later, in the *Nicaragua* case, the International Court of Justice assumed that this watered down provision reflected customary law, and it then proceeded to misread it and water it down still further. The provision of weapons or logistical or other support was not, in its view, sufficient to trigger any right to collective self-defense.[29] Even more disturbing was the Court's clear implication, in an apparent aside, that intervention in a decolonization context would have a privileged status – a hypothesis vigorously objected to by Judge Schwebel in his dissenting opinion.[30] It is not lawful, he said, "for a foreign State or movement to intervene in that struggle [of peoples seeking self-determination] with force or to provide arms, supplies and other logistical support in the prosecution of armed rebellion;" and this was true whether or not "the struggle is or is proclaimed to be…against colonial domination." Moreover, he observed, in many cases, the identity of the "colony" and the "colonizer" was "a matter of sharp dispute." Perceptions differed, and "the lack of beauty," in this context, "is in the eye of the beholder."[31]

The Court's implied willingness, in its aside, to grant a privileged status to decolonization struggles contrasted starkly with its adoption of an otherwise extremely restrictive interpretation of Article 51 of the UN Charter. Evidently, the Court was opting for the Third World's interpretation of the "self-determination" saving clause in the Consensus Definition of Aggression. That provision had been purposely worded ambiguously, to read:

> Nothing in this Definition, and in particular article 3, could in any way prejudice the right to self-determination, freedom and independence, as derived from the Charter, of peoples forcibly deprived of that right…, particularly peoples under colonial and racist régimes or other forms of alien domination; nor the right of these peoples to struggle to that end and to seek and receive support, *in accordance with the principles of the Charter*…. [italics added.][32]

Despite the multiple ambiguities in the clause,[33] the Third World perceived it as an absolute entitlement of peoples struggling for self-determination to use force and for third states to assist them in their armed struggle. Legally, their argument was controversial, to say the least. But, as noted by Julius Stone, "the fact that the Consensual Definition makes the point seem even arguable gives for the future a certain spurious *political* legitimacy to devices of indirect armed aggression, which the preexisting rule of international law condemned as unlawful."[34]

The purpose of the Definition, in truth, was not to state the law unambiguously – something which, in any event, the consensus procedure precluded. "Defining aggression," as Stone aptly observed, was a way of "conducting political warfare by other means."[35] And for that purpose, imprecision, omissions, and ambiguous formulations could be very convenient. The various loopholes could always be plugged later, in specific cases, by means of automatic majorities in the General Assembly and other international forums. But for those who would be disfavored by those majorities, the situation was fraught with dangers that Stone presciently described at the time. "By its very gaps and equivocations," he noted, the Definition had produced "a new armoury of weapons of political warfare, which may well herald a new level of confrontation and tension." The results would be very negative for the cause of peace, since negotiating positions would be hardened rather than tempered; states that were "particular targets of manipulated majorities in the General Assembly" would be subjected to "grave political and military wrongs to which they are unlikely to submit," leaving them with "military alternatives" only.[36]

　　To such long-debated questions as the legality of anticipatory self-defense, the standards of "proportionality," and the relationship between Articles 2(4) and 51 of the Charter no answers were furnished or attempted. Interestingly though, perhaps the main disputed matter that was decided least ambiguously was that of the acquisition and occupation of territory entered into by *lawful* force. Article 5(3) provides that "no territorial acquisition or special advantage resulting from aggression is or shall be recognized as lawful." The Egyptians had led an unsuccessful bid to substitute for "aggression" the term "the threat or use of force." Similarly, in the Preamble, the Assembly reaffirmed that the territory of a state shall not be "the object, even temporarily, of military occupation or of other measures of force taken by another State *in contravention of the Charter*, and that it shall not be the object of acquisition by another State resulting from such measures or the threat thereof" [italics added]. An attempt to delete the words "in contravention of the Charter" was rebuffed. What all this signified, as Stone correctly observes, was an unwillingness, at least at that point, to go beyond the accepted legal principle *ex iniuria non oritur ius*, that one is not permitted to benefit from one's own wrong-doing. And though, given the political realities, reaffirmation of this principle was unusual, it was not, he thought, "a substantive achievement" since "the principle was clear" in any case.[37] But where Assembly majorities are involved, even the reaffirmation of accepted and logical principles is to be reckoned a minor miracle. It would have been much more in character for the Assembly to grant to favored aggressors the immunity from punishment desired by Egypt, and to convey to them the message: if at first you don't succeed, try, try again![38] Hints, some more and some less transparent, of this message were sadly not so rare in later years.[39]

The new UN perspective on self-determination, which became so dominant in the 1970s in the sphere of *jus ad bellum*, spilled over simultaneously and progressively into the sphere of *jus in bello* as well.[40] Pursuing, in main outline, the guidelines that the General Assembly had been urging since the late 1960s, the 1977 Diplomatic Conference on the International Humanitarian Law Applicable to Armed Conflicts, adopted a controversial Additional Protocol (No. 1), which, among other things, conferred special international standing on "self-determination" struggles, eased immeasurably the conditions for granting combatant status to those engaged in such struggles, and relaxed even more the conditions for receiving prisoner-of-war "treatment."[41] Many objections were voiced to these provisions, including the inescapable subjectivity entailed in interpreting such terms as "colonial domination," "alien occupation," and "racist régimes"; [42] and – a matter referred to innumerable times in the conference debates – the attenuation of the distinction between combatants and civilians, which would likely result in a net loss, rather than a gain, for human rights in armed conflicts. "The consequence," the Swiss representative warned, "would be that the adverse party could take draconian measures against civilians suspected of being combatants."[43] "Military necessity," the Italian representative feared, might be invoked "in justification of an attack on the civilian population as a whole."[44] The problem was perhaps explained most cogently by Professor Richard Baxter of Harvard University (and later judge of the International Court of Justice). "If combatants disguise themselves as civilians," he warned, then civilians become suspect. "Military considerations will demand that more forceful measures be taken against them – that they be interned" and that they be "more widely attacked on the ground that disguised combatants are intermingled with those who take no active part in the hostilities." The maintenance of "strict standards for irregulars and guerrillas," he concluded, was "conducive to the amelioration of the condition of warfare and to the immunity of the civilian population" and the safeguarding of its rights.[45]

Israel, understandably, is not a party to this Protocol; nor is the United States. Yet, many of its controversial elements have been incorporated in the 1998 Rome Statute establishing the International Criminal Court. Its drafters viewed the Protocol as embodying customary law regulating armed conflicts, thereby affirming for this new tribunal, too, a tilt toward privileging "national liberation movements."[46] Such privilege, in effect, knocks out the crucial prop holding up the entire law-of-war edifice: the assumption of reciprocity and of a mutual distinction between combatants and non-combatants. A law in which one side has all the rights and the other, only obligations, is not apt to be obeyed. Nor will it be very helpful in the battle to overcome the scourge of terrorism.[47] Revival of the just war idea, in its present UN-led reincarnation, can only lead to greater, and unrestrained, violence. And in this environment, the Organization's principal judicial organ, no less than its political organs, has regrettably become part of the problem, rather than of its solution.

III.

"O My people, remember now what Balak king of Moab devised, and what Bil'am the son of Be'or answered him; from Shittim unto Gilgal, that you may know the righteous acts of the Lord."
                    (From the *Haftarah* to *Parashat Balak*, Micah 6:5)

There is much in *Parashat Balak* that seems particularly pertinent to the situation that Israel has been facing in the various UN forums, including that of the International Court of Justice at The Hague. Unable to expel the Jews in regular battle, the Arabs have turned to other means: delegitimizing Israel's existence, by delegitimizing all steps that Israel might take in defense of its citizens' security. Confident, on the basis of previous precedents (relating to South Africa's presence in its former mandate, South West Africa/Namibia) in which the Court was called in, that here, too, it will be a matter of "he whom you bless is blessed, and he whom you curse is cursed" (Num. 22:6) – that judicial delegitimation will bring in its train stronger steps, such as anti-Israel sanctions – the Palestinians and their Arab allies have viewed the present stage as merely the opening salvo in a longer battle. Their not unreasonable expectation was that the Court would share their perspective and that of the UN generally, that *"libbo ke-libbam shaveh."* Ultimately, their hope is to expel Israel, first, from the territories that were conquered in the Six-Day War (as the analogue of South West Africa) and later, from pre-1967 Israel as well (even as the white minority was defeated in South Africa). (In their statements before the Court, some of the Arabs stated candidly that the pre-1967 borders were also illegitimate, and it was necessary to return to those of the 1947 partition resolution – a resolution which, of course, was decisively rejected by the Arabs at the time. And the Egyptian judge, Nabil Elaraby, in his separate opinion, similarly reverted to the partition resolution.) Diplomatic isolation of Israel, as a pariah state, "a people that shall dwell alone, and shall not be reckoned among the nations" (Num. 23:9), is part and parcel of the strategy. So too is the idea that if, at present, "they are too mighty for me," Israel may nevertheless be diminished incrementally – *"Ulay ukhal nakkeh bo,"*[48] and ultimately, through a process of joint political-judicial delegitimation and internal demoralization, expulsion might ensue, *"va-agarashennu min ha-aretz"* (Num. 22:6).

Indeed, the current campaign comports very well with the "plan of stages," adopted by the Palestine National Council on June 9, 1974 (parts of which seem to have been inspired by developments then underway in southern Africa). The plan's stated goal was "the liberation of all Palestinian territory" – to be achieved by "all means, and first and foremost armed struggle." That struggle, in turn, was to be pursued by "an independent combatant national authority ...over every part of Palestinian territory that is liberated"; and after its establishment, "the Palestinian national authority" was to continue its struggle, with help from the surrounding confrontation states. (Much of the terminology is reminiscent of the battle to rid South West Africa/Namibia of the South African presence.)

By turning to the Court, the Arabs reverted to a strategy that they attempted unsuccessfully to employ during the 1947–1952 period.[49] They had then sought to have the Court rule on such matters as the Assembly's competence to adopt the partition plan, the Security Council's right to implement it, the validity of the Assembly's vote to admit Israel despite Britain's abstention in the Security Council, and the rights of Arab refugees. Although in two instances the Assembly came close to adopting the proposed requests for an opinion, a majority of the UN members had considered such moves unhelpful, at best, and positively damaging, at worst. The problem, as was stated at one stage of the proceedings, was "the most uniquely political problem of all questions in international history," and if submitted to the Court, that tribunal would become embroiled "in one of the most intractable problems of political relations."[50]

Judicial embroilment in the problem was precisely what was now eagerly sought by the Arab states, convinced as they were that the Court would be a willing accomplice. Earlier judicial proclivities were reassuring from their perspective – and correspondingly worrisome from the vantage point of Israel and those in the West not blinded by "judicial romanticism."[51] Nevertheless, the extent to which previous tendencies converged in a poisonous brew could not be foretold, despite the troubling omens evident from the start of the consultation process.

In deciding to solicit the Court's opinion, the Assembly circumvented in a most blatant manner the requirement that states not be subjected to adjudication of their disputes without their consent. Objections based on lack of consent of an interested state had been raised in previous cases, and they had been dismissed by the Court, in line with a philosophy that seeks to cooperate maximally with fellow UN organs barring compelling countervailing reasons.[52] But none of the cases involved existential matters bearing so closely on the security of the non-consenting state and on its citizens' right to life. None entailed the kind of daily terrorist threat confronting

Israel. To allow "back-door" compulsory jurisdiction in this context was unconscionable.

Moreover, the wording of the request was objectionable on several counts. The question posed by the General Assembly's "Tenth Emergency Special Session" on December 8, 2003,[53] in a resolution whose constitutionality was justifiably challenged by Israel[54] – was:

> What are the legal consequences arising from the construction of the wall being built by Israel, the occupying Power, in the Occupied Palestinian Territory, including in and around East Jerusalem, as described in the report of the Secretary-General, considering the rules and principles of international law, including the Fourth Geneva Convention of 1949, and relevant Security Council and General Assembly resolutions?

Quite obviously, the Court was not being asked a legal question; it was being *told* what it is that the Assembly wished to hear. Both the factual and legal issues involved were to be *assumed* by the Court, rather than examined by it; and any examination of the underlying premises was to be *pro forma* or, preferably, it would furnish *additional* elaboration and reinforcement of the existing assumptions. There was a "wall" being built, not a security fence; that wall was being erected not only in "occupied" territory, but in "Occupied *Palestinian* Territory [with the capitalization intended to underscore the existence of a separate, recognized, and sanctified legal status]; Israel was the "occupying Power"; the 1949 Fourth Geneva Convention applies to the territories where the wall was being erected, including East Jerusalem [capitalized, again, to denote a status separate from that of West Jerusalem]; the legal obligations of Israel were defined not only by treaties but also by Security Council resolutions [whose binding nature is assumed, and this, regardless of the rubric under which they were adopted, and the absence of a Council competence, even under Chapter 7, "to abrogate or alter territorial rights, whether of sovereignty or administration"];[55] and General Assembly resolutions too are binding on Israel. The references in

the requesting resolution to the report of the Secretary-General
and to the Assembly's earlier resolution (adopted on October 21,
2003)[56] were also significant. In that resolution, the Assembly had
deemed the wall constructed inside the "occupied Palestinian territories including in and around East Jerusalem" to be illegal and
had demanded that its construction cease and that parts of it be
dismantled. In the Secretary-General's report, the factual and legal
issues, as seen through the typical UN lenses, are detailed.

Clearly, the answers to many very controversial questions
were contained within the question posed to the Court. And other
resolutions and actions taken by the Assembly on the identical
subject manifested the absence of any genuine legal doubts. Such
practices are not unknown in advisory cases. They were evident in
the *Namibia* request (the only one ever to be sent to the Court by
the Security Council, and some of whose wording was borrowed by
the Assembly in the present case); and they had aroused misgivings
among some of the judges. The Court there was asked: "What are
the legal consequences for States of the continued presence of South
Africa in Namibia, notwithstanding Security Council resolution 276
(1970)"? Yet in another resolution, adopted simultaneously with
the requesting resolution, the Council had itself spelled out, and
in great detail, what were "the legal consequences for States of the
continued presence of South Africa in Namibia." Judge Petrén, for
one, felt that "the natural distribution of roles as between the principal judicial organ and the political organs of the United Nations
was thereby reversed. Instead of asking the Court its opinion on a
legal question in order to deduce the political consequences flowing
from it, the Security Council did the opposite."[57] Several judges also
objected to the fact that the legal premises had been asserted rather
than questioned.[58]

In the PLO *Mission* case, the Assembly twice adopted resolutions stating its conclusions on the very question sent to the Court
for its determination. This was, in Judge Schwebel's view, unacceptable behavior.[59] "An answer to a legal question normally should
not be sought by an organ that purports to know it," Schwebel later
wrote. "The appearance of telling the Court what the answer is to

the question put to the Court is not consonant with the judicial character and independence of the Court."[60]

In the present case, the problem was far more acute, primarily because of the terrorist context – unmentioned both in the requesting resolution and in the cited Secretary-General's report. As noted by Anne Bayefsky, the question before the court had "been carefully crafted to elicit a list of negative human rights consequences for Palestinians." There was, from the start of the ICJ proceedings, "a glaring omission: consideration of the human rights of Israelis." But this was not so surprising when one considered that "the same 2003 General Assembly that decried the fence was also marked by its refusal to adopt a resolution on the rights of Israeli children – after passing one on Palestinian children." "The UN message," she concluded was clear in both cases. "The human rights of Israelis are not part of the equation."[61]

It is, even as Balak said to Bil'am, "Come with me now into another place from which you will not be able to see them all, but only the outskirts of them; and you will send curses on them from there" (Num. 23:13). It is far easier to condemn Israel if you are shown only the edge, the fence, the partial picture detached from the general context of barbaric acts of slaughter of innocents that Israel's defensive measures are intended to forestall. (This, too, has sadly been a general pattern in the UN, practiced whenever Israeli issues arise. After the March 2002 Pesach massacre at the Park Hotel and the ensuing Operation Defensive Shield, an investigative committee appointed by the UN Secretary-General was set to visit Jenin to examine the extent of Israeli "war crimes" committed there – not the context in which the Israeli operation was launched. Nor would the terms of reference have included the care that Israel displayed to avoid civilian casualties – which translated into many Israeli casualties in house-to-house combat.)

Turning from the forum that asked for the opinion to the one that gave it, it is important to understand certain aspects related to the Court's current composition and philosophy that may not be generally known.

By the mid-1960s, the composition of the Court was beginning to change, reflecting the altered membership of the General Assembly and Security Council and the attitudes of the most powerful blocs in the UN. Since the judges are elected by the Assembly and the Security Council to renewable nine-year terms, and since these elections are not subject to veto, the influence of the five permanent members is weakened and that of the most numerous blocs in the UN enhanced. Additionally, after the Court refused in 1966 to hand down a judgment on the merits in the *South West Africa Cases*, the Assembly, its ire aroused, set about to bring the Court into closer alignment with the philosophy of the reigning majority in the political organs. During the protracted pleadings on the merits of that case, counsel for Ethiopia and Liberia had put forward certain propositions regarding law-formation that even the "liberal" contingent of a deeply divided bench found difficult to embrace. In particular, the Court had been urged to attribute quasi-legislative powers to the General Assembly, and to replace insistence on state consent to legal rules with a recognition that such rules could be formed by a "consensus" of states comprising the "organized international community."[62] By 1971, when the Court rendered its opinion in the *Namibia* case, it was clear that the composition and philosophy of the Court were more in conformity with the prevailing trends in the UN. Indeed, the Court, which had been turned to more than anything in order "to redeem its impaired image,"[63] had not disappointed. As noted earlier, the Court was expected, and did, legitimate the Council's previously stated firm opinions.

U.S. awareness of the effect of the Court's new composition and philosophy did not come until the *Nicaragua* case, which sounded some alarm bells among many American international lawyers.[64] The more expansive view that the Court always tended to take of its advisory competence[65] now seemed to affect the contentious jurisdiction as well. The case involved use-of-force issues (but not ones that impinged on the daily lives of American citizens); the United States presented a strong case, on multiple grounds, against the Court's accepting jurisdiction; and when the Court decided, in 1984, to reject all the American arguments, the Reagan administration became convinced that it would be pointless to continue to participate in the proceedings and argue to the merits. The State Department issued a statement, in which it warned of the perils of an aggrandizing court. "The right of a state to defend itself or to participate in collective self-defense against aggression," it asserted, "is an inherent sovereign right that cannot be compromised by an inappropriate proceeding before the World Court." Regrettably, the Court had departed from its "tradition of judicial restraint" and had ventured into "treacherous political waters," with "long-term implications for the Court itself." It would be a "tragedy," the statement continued, if the trends, rampant in international organizations, to "become more and more politicized against the interests of the Western democracies" were to "infect" the Court as well.[66]

Many in the American international legal community were inclined to agree with the Administration's assessment once the Court gave its judgment on the merits in 1986. The fact that the decision favored Nicaragua was perhaps less important than the legal reasoning employed – especially the attribution of binding force to mere resolutions of the General Assembly (particularly those termed "declarations"), and the implicit willingness to condone force employed for the purpose of decolonization. As noted earlier, Judge Schwebel had strongly objected to the Court's endorsement of such a pernicious double standard.

Additionally, as Davis R. Robinson, former Legal Adviser to the U.S. Department of State recently revealed, suspicions that one of the judges of the Court actively assisted Nicaragua in filing the suit against the United States were confirmed within the last few years. Other unsavory and unethical actions also tainted the actions of some of the Court's members in that case.[67] Since its experience in the *Nicaragua* case, the United States withdrew its Optional Clause Declaration of 1946, and it has, wherever possible, shunned the use of the plenary Court and opted for chambers, in whose composition it could have a say. That "arbitralization" option, of course, is not available in advisory proceedings.

For Israel in 2004, all the standing concerns of the United States were multiplied severalfold. The two Arab judges on the bench – Elaraby of Egypt, and Al-Khasawneh, of Jordan – had been outspokenly anti-Israel in their official and unofficial capacities, and had expressed strong opinions on the issues that formed the legal premises in dispute. Both had been representatives of their states at the UN for lengthy periods. Al Khasawneh had served in that capacity for 19 Assembly sessions until the mid-1990s. As a special rapporteur for the UN Human Rights Commission, he had (unsurprisingly) concluded that Israel's settlements were illegal. Elaraby had been Egypt's representative to the UN in Geneva from 1987 to 1991, and at the UN headquarters in New York from 1991 until 1999. (It might also be noted that as legal adviser to the Egyptian delegation at the 1978 Camp David conference, Elaraby had reportedly opposed the Israeli-Egyptian framework agreement and the ensuing bilateral peace process.) Significantly, Elaraby had been a leading figure in the continuing Tenth Assembly Emergency Session (first convened in 1997 and reconvened, by December 2003, a further eleven times) regarding "illegal Israeli actions in occupied East Jerusalem and the rest of the Occupied Palestinian Territory" – and it was this forum from which the request for an advisory opinion emerged. In an interview that he gave in his personal capacity (and not as representative of his state) before joining the bench, Elaraby was reportedly "concerned about a tendency to play into Israel's hands, and thus to marginalise the crux of the Arab Israeli conflict, which is the illegitimate occupation of territory." "I hate to say it," he was quoted as saying, "but you do not see the Palestinians, or any other Arab country today, presenting the issue thus when addressing the international community: Israel is occupying Palestinian territory, and the occupation itself is against international law."[68] Furthermore, Elaraby asserted (incorrectly) that the Sharon government had "very recently" and unlike earlier Israeli governments, described the territories as "disputed" rather than "occupied," thus "wreaking confusion and gaining time." All of this, he said amounted to "attempts to confuse the issues and complicate any serious attempt to get Israel out of the occupied territories. You can negotiate security, which will be mutual for both parties, but you cannot negotiate whether to leave or not."[69] Israel's request that he be disqualified in the judicial proceedings was rejected by all of the judges, with the sole exception of the American judge, Thomas Buergenthal, who based his dissent on the dictum that justice must not only be done, but must also be seen to be done.[70]

Other decisions on preliminary matters, too, did not reflect an unbiased approach to the case at hand. These included the decision to allow "Palestine," which has only the status of an observer mission at the UN, to appear before the Court as if it were a state; the rejection of Israel's request to extend the unprecedentedly draconian time limits for filing written statements; and the adoption of a title flagrantly tilted against the Israeli position.[71] Nor was the composition of the Court, even apart from its Arab contingent, apt to quash Israel's fears regarding the outcome of the judicial consultation. Among those not known to harbor pro-Israel sentiments were the Court's president, Shi Jiuyong (who had been the legal adviser to the Chinese Foreign Ministry during the Tiananmen Square massacre), Abdul Koroma of Sierra Leone (who had been a delegate to the General Assembly from 1977 to 1994), and even such a Western judge as Gilbert Guillaume of France (who, according to some reports, may have been the principal author of the opinion). Several judges (such as Kooijmans of the Netherlands, Owada of Japan, and Tomka of Slovakia) had been intimately associated with various UN organs, including those dealing with human rights and international humanitarian law, and may well have absorbed (wittingly or not) the condemnatory attitudes to Israel so ubiquitous in those bodies. (Thus, for example, Owada came to refer, in his separate opinion, to "the *so-called* terrorist attacks by Palestinian suicide bombers against the Israeli civilian population."[72]) Many of the judges, too, might naturally be expected to reflect the biases of the states whose nationals they were and to whom they owed their nomination and the lobbying efforts that ensured their election.

Even with such inauspicious signs of what to anticipate from the Court, the "unevenhandedness"[73] of the opinion was startling in its dimensions.[74] To overcome objections based on Israel's nonconsent to the rendering of the opinion, the Court minimized Israel's status as a quasi-litigant and correspondingly, and unjustifiably, magnified the role and rights of the General Assembly, by attributing to that body highly questionable continuing authority over a former League of Nations mandate and implicitly endorsing the Assembly's continuing stark double standard vis-à-vis Israel.[75] The essential historical background was presented in a totally skewed and sanitized fashion – it was, as Judge Rosalyn Higgins noted in typical British understatement, "neither balanced nor satisfactory."[76] Events and wars just "broke out" – like natural disasters. There were no responsible parties, no culprits. One searches in vain for references to the incessant Arab threats to Israel's existence from pre-State days through major wars, wars of attrition, and the still-continuing terrorist onslaughts. The background to the Six-Day War is ignored, and those unaware of the dire Arab threats that preceded it might readily conclude that Israel launched an aggressive war in order to conquer territories that it has been illegally occupying ever since. The "Green Line" – a temporary and precarious Armistice line, whose vulnerability became most manifest in 1967 – is endowed (but, as will be seen, only for certain purposes) with a status it did not legally possess. And nowhere is there any acknowledgment of the rejection of offers of statehood extended to the Arab population of Palestine at critical junctures, nor any hint that that rejection might have been motivated by an unwillingness to co-exist with Israel and accept a Jewish right to self-determination.

The Court's obliviousness to the terrorist context in which the security fence was being constructed – the term "terrorism" does not even appear – is noteworthy. Relying almost exclusively on the inadequate and one-sided reports of the UN Secretary-General and of John Dugard, a special rapporteur whose lack of balance has long been the subject of displeasure in Israel, the Court proceeds to compose a laundry list of all the provisions of the Fourth Geneva Convention that might have been violated by Israel, and to make short shrift of Israel's security concerns. No mention is made of provisions of the cited convention that could justify Israel's actions (even if one accepts the Court's assumption that the territories are "occupied" rather than disputed). Article 27, most prominently, permits the occupying power to "take such measures of control and security in regard to protected persons as may be necessary as a result of the war." And according to Jean Pictet's semi-official *Commentary* on the provision, the measures taken may include "prohibition of access to certain areas" and "restrictions of movement."[77] There is no discernible attempt to clarify the facts, even on the basis of material readily available in the public domain. The impression that emerges is of a tribunal that did not wish to be confused by any facts that might clash with its preconceived conclusions.

This nonchalant and non-judicial approach to the factual nexus was sharply criticized by Judge Buergenthal, the lone dissenter on the propriety of giving an opinion. "The absence in this case of the requisite information and evidence," he felt, "vitiates the Court's findings on the merits." The Court had pronounced itself on "the wall as a whole" and had done so "without having before it or seeking to ascertain all relevant facts bearing directly on issues of Israel's legitimate right of self-defence, military necessity and security needs." It had "never really seriously examined" the nature of the "cross-Green Line attacks and their impact on Israel and its population"; and it had relied on the UN Secretary-General's dossier, which was insufficient, since it barely touched on the "repeated deadly terrorist attacks" on Israel. Moreover, even the summaries of Israel's position that were appended to the Secretary-General's report were barely addressed by the Court.

Instead, the Court merely describes "the harm the wall is causing," discusses "various provisions of international humanitarian law and human rights instruments," and then concludes that "this law has been violated." There was no "examination of the facts that might show why the alleged defences of military exigencies, national security or public order are not applicable to the wall as a whole or to the individual segments of its route." The Court asserted many times that "it is not convinced," but "it fails to demonstrate why it is not convinced, and that is why...[its] conclusions are not convincing."[78]

Among the matters the Court was "not convinced" of were: "that the destructions carried out contrary to the prohibition in Article 53 of the Fourth Geneva Convention were rendered absolutely necessary by military operations"; "that the specific course Israel has chosen for the wall was necessary to attain its security objectives;" and "that the construction of the wall along the route chosen was the only means to safeguard the interests of Israel against the peril which it has invoked as justification for that construction."[79] Indeed, the Court's reasoning throughout is inadequate, inconsistent, and replete with mere *ipse dixits* – assertions that never rise above the level of political discourse in the United Nations. Some of these assertions are deeply disturbing not only to Israel but to all of those concerned with counter-terrorism.[80] Thus, Article 51 of the UN Charter is interpreted as permitting self-defense only if the attack originates from a "state." This interpretation is not sustainable on the basis of the text, the drafting history, or state practice.[81] It is also, of course, illogical in an era in which the worldwide terrorist threats stem primarily from non-state actors. Its logic, however, is neither that of international law, in the sense of consensual law based on state practice; nor is it UN Charter law. It is rather that of the "New UN Law of Self-Determination." Under this law, as noted earlier, favored groups have rights without obligations, and their protagonists have only obligations and no rights, whether in relation to *jus ad bellum* or *jus in bello*.

In its inconsistent attitude to the status and international personality of "Palestine," the Court presents a particularly egregious example of the application of this perspective. "Palestine" is granted the procedural rights of a state (and indeed, it is given the privileges, in the oral proceedings, of a principal quasi-litigant, being placed first among those appearing before the Court). Its violations of its commitments, of the prohibition against using force, and of the most basic of the laws of war – non-targeting of innocent civilians – are not, for the Court, part of the legal equation. "Palestine" possesses no responsibility for acts originating in its territory. The "uneven-handedness" of the Court's approach was criticized by Judge Higgins. Palestine, she wrote, "cannot be sufficiently an international entity to be invited to these proceedings and to benefit from humanitarian law, but not sufficiently an international entity for the prohibition of armed attack on others to be applicable.... The question is surely where responsibility lies for the sending of groups and persons who act against Israeli civilians and the cumulative severity of such action."[82]

Similarly, as noted by Judge Buergenthal, the "Green Line" is viewed inconsistently by the Court. For if it delimits "the dividing line between Israel and the Occupied Palestinian Territory," then according to the Court's own interpretation of Article 51, cross-Green Line attacks should endow Israel with the right of self-defense. (Moreover, how much actual control Israel possessed in the territories from which the anti-Israel terrorism originated was not free of doubt.)[83] So anxious, however, is the Court to deny Israel the protection of that UN Charter provision, and also that of the Security Council's post-9/11 resolutions against terrorism, that it makes a sharp differentiation between national and international terrorism and proceeds to place Palestinian terrorism in the former category. Yet, it has been convincingly argued, the 9/11 terrorism was no less "national" than that to which Israel has been exposed, and the Palestinian terrorism has been no less "international." For example, the perpetrators of the 9/11 atrocities were all residents of the United States and used American planes to crash them into American sites. And Palestinian terrorism certainly has a strong *international* component, if only because it has received financial and other support from Syria, Lebanon, Iran, and Saddam's Iraq.[84] In any event, there was no justification for excluding terrorism against Israel from the terms of the relevant Security Council resolutions.[85]

What emerges is an approach to terrorism that mirrors that of the General Assembly members who voted to request the opinion, and is closer to that of the 1998 Arab League Convention on Terrorism than to the definition of terrorism recently proposed by the UN Secretary-General's High-Level Panel on Threats, Challenges and Change. In the former, "all cases of struggle by whatever means, including armed struggle, against foreign occupation and aggression for liberation and self-determination, in accordance with principles of international law, shall not be regarded as an offense." But, significantly, it was added, "this provision shall not apply to any act prejudicing the territorial integrity of any Arab State."[86] The Secretary-General's panel, on the other hand, stated that the deliberate use of force against civilians, even by peoples resisting foreign occupation, constitutes terrorism.[87] For the Court, as for the UN political organs, "self-determination" for favored "selves" is a supernorm,[88] displacing the linchpin of the UN Charter – the prohibition of the use of force – and permitting exemption from the strictures of the laws of war as well.

In sum, the opinion was one in which the Court rubber-stamped questionable General Assembly practices; adopted, across the board, the Assembly's perspective on the Arab-Israeli dispute; and went so far as to urge – transparently and inappropriately – that the opinion be implemented by the UN political organs. "The United Nations," the Court declared in the opinion's *dispositif*, "and especially the General Assembly and the Security Council, *should consider what further action is required* to bring to an end the illegal situation resulting from the construction of the wall and the associated régime, *taking due account of the present Advisory Opinion*."[89] (In seeking thus to operationalize its opinion and galvanize the UN organs into taking further action, the Court, besides departing from its role, also evinced, yet again, internal inconsistency. In order to overcome objections to the propriety of rendering an opinion in the face of Israeli non-consent, the Court had cited an earlier opinion in which the *non-binding nature* of advisory opinions had been emphasized.)[90]

The attitude of the ICJ to Israel's self-defense is reminiscent of UN Secretary-General U. Thant's decision in 1967 to remove the UN peacekeeping force in the Sinai (UNEF), in the face of dire Egyptian threats. Abba Eban, in his inimitable style, compared that to closing an umbrella once the rain starts. Today, for protection against the rain of rockets and guided human bombs, Israel can clearly not look to the Court, any more than to the UN's avowedly political organs, to acknowledge its right to an umbrella of self-defense (even in the passive form of a security fence).

The tribunal's opinion, it should be emphasized, is not legally binding; nor, in light of its patent bias and unpersuasive reasoning, does it possess any moral authority. It effectively aids and abets the Amalekite acts to which Israel has been exposed without surcease.

Surely terrorism is conceptually well defined by the following verse regarding Amalek:

> Who met you on your way, and attacked you when you were tired and without strength, and cut down all the feeble ones in your rear (Deut. 25:18).

Terrorism has greeted Israelis innocently on their way, pursuing their daily routines – on buses, in cafés, in *Batei Midrash*, at the Seder, in their homes. It targets the weak and defenseless – men, women and children, and babes in arms and in their cribs.

It may be difficult to overcome the tendency of Westerners, including Israelis, to grant automatic deference to judicial institutions. But there are times when it is appropriate to recall the wisdom of Ecclesiastes, and to shout out the truth that "*makom ha-mishpat, shammah ha-resha*" (Eccl. 3:16). It is sometimes necessary to delegitimize the delegitimizers, and to conclude, as did some American scholars of international law post-*Nicaragua*, that "there is no necessary connection between world law and the particular institution that is housed in the Peace Palace in The Hague."[91]

IV.

Israel's decision not to argue to the merits and to boycott the Court's oral proceedings should not be misconstrued. It was not based on any doubts regarding the defensibility of Israel's case. It was premised on the conviction that no state – least of all, one in Israel's present position – was legally obligated to have such matters decided without its consent; that The Hague tribunal, as presently constituted, was manifestly not one to which Israel would, in any event, have referred its disputes; and that presenting arguments on the merits would have been inconsistent with the challenge to the jurisdiction. Significantly, in 1985, Israel, following the U.S. lead, had withdrawn from the general compulsory jurisdiction of the Court. And even when its 1956 Optional Clause Declaration *had* been in effect, Israel had excluded from its application, *inter alia*, disputes arising out of the War of Independence and those "arising out of, or having reference to, any hostilities, war, state of war, breach of the peace, breach of armistice agreement or belligerent or military occupation (whether such war shall have been declared or not, and whether any state of belligerency shall have been recognized or not) in which the Government of Israel are or have been [sic] or may be involved at any time."[92]

In general, it should be noted, even democracies have not viewed with favor even domestic judicialization of measures that they have felt it necessary to take in self-defense. And their judiciaries, in turn, have tended to be deferential during ongoing conflict. As Justice Hugo Black wrote, even while dissenting in the *Eisentrager* case at the end of World War II: "It has always been recognized that actual warfare can be conducted successfully only if those in command are left the most ample independence in the theatre of operations." And while hostilities are in progress, it would be unrealistic "to suggest that alien enemies could hail our military leaders into judicial tribunals to account for their day-to-day activities on the battlefront."[93] (More recent Supreme Court decisions, especially *Hamdi v. Rumsfeld*, adopt a somewhat different tone, but do not go as far as some assume in shackling the administration. Moreover, the sense of an ongoing conflict threatening Americans in their daily lives was not as acute in 2004 as it was in the immediate aftermath of 9/11.)

Israel, of course, has been called upon repeatedly to defend – in domestic and international forums – every step that it takes in its current war on terrorism (a war that it attempted vainly to avert by peaceful means). And within Israel the matter has been unprecedentedly judicialized. This is not surprising, given the Israeli Supreme Court's liberal approach to standing, combined with a judicial philosophy that deems all matters to be inherently justiciable (as opposed to the "political question" doctrine of U.S. courts).

Among the issues that the Israeli courts have had to address over the years, and most keenly since September 2000, are which body of law to apply and to which territories and how to assess whether the measures adopted were necessary and proportionate to the threat. The answers given have often aroused internal dissatisfaction, from both parts of the political spectrum. The complexity of the issues is apparent to anyone even mildly familiar with the web of interconnected questions that present themselves for determination.

A primary question, naturally, and one that arose shortly after the Six-Day War, was whether the Fourth Geneva Convention applies to the areas conquered in the course of those hostilities. The official Israeli position has always been that formally it does not – that the territories are not "occupied" since they were not taken from a previous legitimate sovereign. Israel had not crossed an international boundary; the so-called "Green Line" (of late so ostensibly sanctified by the Arab states and so much of the world community, including the ICJ) had never been accepted as anything other than a temporary armistice line. In Judea and Samaria (the West Bank), Jordan was itself, at most, only a "belligerent occupant," its sovereignty over the areas having been recognized only by Britain and Pakistan (and over eastern Jerusalem, by Pakistan alone). Moreover, it was often noted, Israel, as the only state to emerge from the previous mandate in Palestine, and as the state that waged a defensive war (unlike Jordan), had the better title to the territories, had it wished to annex them.[94] Nevertheless, while denying that the principles of the Fourth Geneva Convention were applicable *de jure*, Israel was prepared, voluntarily, to apply the treaty's humanitarian principles *de facto* and to have the courts judge its actions on that basis.[95] (In contrast, other nations – including, prominently, the United States – have been reluctant to apply the Fourth Geneva Convention strictly, or even to acknowledge its applicability to their occupations, though there have arguably been several clear-cut instances in which they should have done so – as, for example, in relation to Panama, Afghanistan, and Iraq in the two Gulf Wars.) Israeli legislation with respect to the eastern sections of Jerusalem and to the Golan Heights put those two areas in a different category domestically, and correspondingly before the Israeli courts.

The anomalies became compounded with the institution of the "Oslo process" between 1993 and September 2000, after which the terrorist war unleashed by Arafat brought it to a complete halt. While the process was still operative, Israel redeployed its forces

and surrendered to the Palestinian Authority a goodly measure of
autonomy in significant areas of Judea, Samaria, and the Gaza district. In those areas, the PA was to apply its own laws and undertake
a security role in cooperation with Israel, in preparation for final
status negotiations over the future of the territories. Palestinian
violations of critical obligations – including control of terrorism
and non-incitement – are too well known to require repetition. But
successive Israeli governments, anxious to continue the "process"
at all costs and maintain its "momentum," opted to overlook these
breaches (and sometimes to conceal their extent from a peace-hun-
gry public).

Mislabeled by the PA as the "Al Aksa intifada" (a term taken
up by much of the media), the newest intensified terrorist war necessitated some readjustment by the Israeli Supreme Court of its
view regarding the applicable law. Israel was forced to reenter areas
from which it had previously redeployed; the circumstances of that
reentry showed that the law of belligerent occupation could not be
applied as before. The complexity of the new legal-factual nexus
was described by Supreme Court president, Justice Aharon Barak,
in the *Ajuri* judgment of September 3, 2002. The "fierce fighting…in
Judaea, Samaria and the Gaza Strip" since the end of September
2000 could not be characterized as "police activity"; it was rather
"an armed struggle" – one in which "bereavement and pain over-
whelm us." Israel was not faced with a regular army, but rather with
non-uniformed terrorists who "hide among the civilian Palestinian
population in the territories, including in holy sites." The terrorists
"are supported by part of the civilian population, and by their families
and relatives." The Court recognized that Israel's "special military
operations," which was aimed at destroying the infrastructure of
the terrorists and preventing further attacks, were taken by virtue
of Israel's right of self-defense. Nevertheless, despite its recognition
of the unusual nature of the situation, the Court decided to apply
the law of belligerent occupation, while adopting what Justice Barak
termed a "dynamic interpretive approach" to the provisions of the
Fourth Geneva Convention. In this way it could "deal with the new
reality"– one that could hardly have been anticipated by the framers

of that Convention.[96] In the *Ajuri* case, it was decided to permit the transfer to Gaza for two years of two of the three petitioners; the third was not considered to be sufficiently dangerous to warrant such a step. Barak quoted, in support, the verse in Deuteronomy 24:6, "Fathers shall not be put to death for their children or children for their fathers; every man shall be put to death for his own sin."

Commenting on the case, Detlev Vagts wrote admiringly in the *American Journal of International Law*, of "the meticulous and courageous way in which the Israeli Supreme Court, acting as it did in the immediate vicinity of violence, approached the task of distinguishing between appropriate and inappropriate uses of the executive's security powers." And he wondered aloud whether, "if security problems in the United States were to reach the same level of intensity, American courts would do as well.[97]

In the United States, the Geneva Conventions have unsurprisingly also come up for reassessment, as part of a general reappraisal of former failed approaches to the plague of terrorism. Some have considered that those conventions are archaic, and require overhaul (but, of course, in a direction diametrically opposed to that of Additional Protocol I and its unjustified grant of privileged status to irregular combatants having a so-called "just cause"). Since the laws of war are naturally formulated in reaction to the war just ended, they reason that the post-World War II rules must be revised in the light of the post-9/11 political, military, and technological developments that underscored the inadequacy of the present legal régime. Other commentators have focused more on an issue (perhaps insufficiently emphasized in Israel): non-implementation of the existing law by irregular combatants. Thus, Jane Dalton, Legal Counsel to the Chairman of the U.S. Joint Chiefs of Staff, felt that the problem faced by the United States in Iraq was not the unsatisfactory nature of the law but rather "noncompliance with even the most basic principles of the law, such as immunity for noncombatants from intentional attack." She expressed great concern regarding the tendency to focus on what armed forces should *not* do and on searching "for ways to constrain the legitimate use of force, while largely ignoring the fact that terrorists...exhibit an utter disregard for the law." Such an approach "limits those who most diligently seek to follow the law." Were the protections of the Third Geneva Convention extended to those who deliberately target civilians, there would be "no incentive in the world for nations to adhere to the Geneva Conventions or for armies to honor the laws of armed conflict."[98]

For Israel, the problem of non-compliance by its enemies with the most basic laws of war is central, of course – and the inability or unwillingness of so many to acknowledge this fact, tragic. That unwillingness, in turn, stems from a perspective that condemns Israel, rather than those bent on its destruction, as the aggressor in the present conflict. It is Israel's right to life, collective and individual, that is challenged. In this context, it should be added, current efforts by a Special Working Group on the Crime of Aggression to define the crime (which the Rome Statute on the International Criminal Court left for future determination) arouse concern. Among the suggestions being seriously considered are: having the Security Council adjudge, in a veto-proof manner, who the aggressor is; handing that task, essentially, to the General Assembly if the Security Council has failed to act within twelve months; and endowing an advisory opinion of the International Court of Justice with binding force in the matter. Given the UN majority's proclivity to perceive a "cycle of violence" at best, and more usually, Israeli aggression, and given the advisory opinion of the ICJ on Israel's security fence, clearly none of these suggestions would be designed to calm Israeli sensibilities.

V.

"And Jacob was greatly afraid and was distressed." Rashi: "'Afraid' – lest he kill; 'distressed' – that he might have to kill others."

(Gen. 32:7)

"Hear, O Israel! You are about to join battle with your enemies. Let not your hearts falter. Do not be in fear, or in panic, or in dread of them." Rashi: "'With your enemies' – these are not your brethren, and if you fall into their hands they will have no pity on you."

(Deut. 20:3)

"Yet, when they were ill, my dress was sackcloth."

(Ps. 35:13)

The terrorist war against Israel is widely acknowledged to be an asymmetric war. But the more important asymmetries are not the ones upon which most commentators focus, and the implications of the ones that are noticed are not always properly grasped. The fact that Israel's F-16s, tanks, and missiles, are arrayed against the lesser and more primitive missiles of the Palestinians carries with it vulnerability as well as power. In fact, Israel suffers both from the weakness of the powerful and the weakness of the weak. It is unable, practically, and does not wish, morally, to employ the full force of its weaponry against the enemy. It will not and does not desire to embrace the norms of its enemies, and to weaken thereby basic principles of the laws of war and humanity and of deep-rooted Jewish ethical principles. Like *Yaakov Avinu*, it wishes neither to kill nor be killed. And its diplomatic isolation is a source of weakness – compounded, aided, and abetted by elements within Israel and the Jewish Diaspora, some of whom perhaps feel more comfortable with the idea of Jewish powerlessness and victimhood than with Jewish power, even when used in self-defense. Peacemaking efforts by outside powers, even when well-intentioned, tend to expose Israeli vulnerabilities – if only because ostensible "success" is more easily attained when pressure is applied against the more malleable and less intransigent party in the equation. Appeasement of terror tends to be dangerously overlooked.

Conversely, the Palestinians benefit from the power of the weak, and the power of the powerful. The local David combating the Israeli Goliath is a useful self-portrayal, especially for the purpose of summoning worldwide sympathy for the Palestinian cause, and thereby augmenting the support received from regional allies, an increasingly menacing worldwide Muslim and Islamist Diaspora, and the inroads made among Jews in Israel and abroad. Among our enemies there are no readily discernible doubts about the legitimacy of their rights (and to the entire area of mandatory Palestine); no significant

Opposition parties, except those that espouse even greater and more barbarous anti-Israel tactics; and no legal system worthy of its name. *Leit din ve-leit dayyan.* Israeli civilian casualties are reveled in and their perpetrators held up as heroes for emulation by the Palestinian youth. Both killing and being killed for the cause are glorified.

Perhaps the most baneful of the forces arrayed against Israel in its current war are those that come dressed in the false garb of self-determination, human rights, and humanitarianism. Those causes have been hijacked by a so-called "human rights community," for whose members, as Irwin Cotler has observed, "human rights" has become a new secular religion, with Israel as the antichrist.[99] The extent to which this has occurred in the diverse UN and UN-sponsored forums has been well documented by Anne Bayefsky over the past years (and even during the supposed heyday of the Oslo process). Her conclusion that "a human rights cover for a contrary political agenda has become something of a UN art form"[100] is inescapable.

The words of Rabbi Dr. Joseph B. Soloveitchik *ztz"l* in 1945, in his article "The Sacred and the Profane," have unfortunately lost none of their relevance:

> We have witnessed how the corruption of great ideals gave birth to evil forces in religious and ethical impregnation, more dangerous than evil fathered by evil.[101]

Noble paternity should serve to highlight, rather than mask, the waywardness of the progeny.

NOTES

1. Cited in George F. Kennan, *American Diplomacy 1900–1950* (1951), p. 20.
2. Even in the most developed domestic systems of law, the war on terrorism has generated the need for new balancing acts regarding such matters as the rights of the accused, trial by military commissions, and racial profiling. *See*, e.g., the U.S. Supreme Court case, *Hamdi v. Rumsfeld*, 542 U.S. 507 (2004); *Rasul v. Bush*, 542 U.S. 466 (2004); and *Rumsfeld v. Padilla*, 542 U.S. 426 (2004).
3. On U.S. formal justification of its actions in the Cuban missile crisis, its avoidance of the logical Article 51 basis, and reliance instead on a more legally questionable "OAS rationale" coupled with an untenable reading of Article 53 of the UN Charter,

see Hans Kelsen, *Principles of International Law*, 2nd rev. ed. (ed. Robert W. Tucker) (1967), pp. 76–79 n. 69. For explanation of the U.S desire to avoid opening the "Pandora's box" of Article 51 (for states unprotected by a Security Council veto), *see* Richard Gardner, "Neither Bush nor the 'Jurisprudes'," *American Journal of International Law*, Vol. 97 (2003), pp. 587–588; and Abram Chayes, *The Cuban Missile Crisis* (1974), p. 65.

4. *See* Josef L. Kunz, "Bellum Justum and Bellum Legale," *American Journal of International Law*, Vol. 40 (1946), pp. 383–390.

5. *See* Julius Stone, *Legal Controls of International Conflict* (1954), p. 154; Michla Pomerance, *The Advisory Function of the International Court in the League and UN Eras* (1973), pp. 201–207.

6. For an analytic review of the protracted League efforts to define the concept, *see* Julius Stone, *Aggression and World Order: A Critique of United Nations Theories of Aggression* (1958), Chap. 2; and *see* ibid., p. 35, on the continuing relevance of the 1933 Soviet draft definition and its inclusion of state support for, or toleration of, armed bands as constituting aggression.

7. Comment in House of Commons, November 24, 1927; cited ibid., p. 36.

8. Note of June 23, 1928, by U.S. Secretary of State Frank B. Kellogg to the Signatories of the Kellogg-Briand Pact; cited in Ian Brownlie, "The Use of Force in Self-Defence," *British Year Book of International Law*, vol. 37 (1961), p. 206.

9. *See* the explanation of the UN International Law Commission of the UN, in General Assembly, *Official Records*, Fifth Session, Supp. 12 (Doc. A/1316), pp. 11–14, under Principle VI; cited in Stone, *Aggression*, p. 136 n. 15. *And see* the illuminating comments of Supreme Court Justice Robert H. Jackson (who had been the chief U.S. prosecutor at Nuremberg), in his Foreword to Sheldon Glueck, *The Nuremberg Trial and Aggressive War* (1946), pp. viii–ix.

10. *See* Leland M. Goodrich and Edvard Hambro, *Charter of the United Nations: Commentary and Documents*, rev. ed. (1949), pp. 94, 104, 207, 263–264, 300.

11. For a discussion of the effect of the pronouncement of the International Court of Justice in the *Namibia* opinion of 1971 on the question of the binding force of Security Council resolutions adopted outside the framework of Chapter 7 of the UN Charter, *see* Pomerance, *Advisory Function*, pp. 352–354.

12. ICJ *Reports 1971*, pp. 292, 294 (emphasis in original).

13. *See* Article 2(7) according to which the Organization is not, in principle, authorized "to intervene in matters which are essentially within the domestic jurisdiction of any state."

14. *See*, e.g., J.L. Brierly, *The Law of Nations*, 6th ed. (ed. Sir Humphrey Waldock) (1963), pp. 416–421; Julius Stone, *Conflict through Consensus: United Nations Approaches to Aggression* (1977), p. 48; Derek Bowett, *Self-Defense in International Law* (1958), pp. 182–192; Bowett, *The Search for Peace* (1972), pp. 124–125; Sir Humphrey Waldock, "The Regulation of the Use of Force by Individual States in International Law," Hague Academy, *Recueil des Cours*, Vol. 81 (1952-II), pp. 496–498; Georg Schwarzenberger, "The Fundamental Principles of International Law," ibid., Vol. 87 (1955-I), pp. 327 ff.;

Arthur L. Goodhart, "The North Atlantic Treaty of 1949," ibid., Vol. 79 (1951–II),
p. 202; Myres S. McDougal and Florentino P. Feliciano, *Law and Minimum World
Public Order* (1961), pp. 232–241. *See also* Dissenting Opinion of Judge Schwebel
in the *Nicaragua* case, ICJ *Reports 1986*, pp. 347–348, paras. 172–173. On the Latin-
American crisis at San Francisco, *see* Josef L. Kunz, "Individual and Collective
Self-Defense in Article 51 of the Charter of the United Nations," *American Journal
of International Law*, vol. 41 (1947), p. 872.

15. For a good discussion of the context in which the *Caroline* formula was enunciated
   and its aftermath, *see* R.Y. Jennings, "The *Caroline* and McLeod Cases," *American
   Journal of International Law*, vol. 32 (1938), pp. 82–99.

16. For a discussion of a little-noticed Constitutional provision that implicitly incorporates the idea of anticipatory self-defense, *see* S. Slonim, "The U.S. Constitution and
   Anticipatory Self-Defense under Article 51 of the U.N. Charter," *International Lawyer*,
   vol. 9 (1975), pp. 117–120; reproduced in S. Slonim, *Framers' Construction/Beardian
   Deconstruction: Essays on the Constitutional Design of 1787* (2001), pp. 165–170; and
   for a comparison with the *Caroline* formula, *see* ibid., n. 13.

17. *See* the statement of the British Attorney-General, in his argument before the
   International Court of Justice in the *Nuclear Weapons* advisory opinion, cited by
   Judge Stephen M. Schwebel, ICJ *Reports 1996*, p. 321; and the response of William
   H. Taft IV, Legal Adviser to the U.S. State Department, to the ICJ judgment in the
   Oil Platforms case, *American Journal of International Law*, vol. 98 (2004), p. 601.

18. *See* Yehuda Z. Blum, "State Response to Acts of Terrorism," *German Yearbook of
   International Law*, vol. 19 (1976), pp. 223–237.

19. The assumption that reprisals are no longer permissible in international law appears in the Declaration on Friendly Relations of October 24, 1970, which, as will
   be noted below (Section II), was intended to be a kind of "gloss" on the relevant
   UN Charter principles. But *see*, for example, the incisive criticism of this position,
   by Tucker, cited below, note 20.

20. *Principles of International Law*, pp. 82–83. *See also* Robert W. Tucker, "Reprisals and
   Self-Defense: The Customary Law," *American Journal of International Law*, Vol. 66
   (1972), pp. 586–596.

21. "A Reply to Critics: Morality and the War," *New York Times*, July 15, 1982. *See also*
   the British and American statements, cited in note 17, above.

22. Dissenting Opinion of Judge Schwebel, ICJ *Reports 1986*, p. 299, para. 85.

23. *See* Austin Chamberlain comment, at note 7, above.

24. *See*, in general, Michla Pomerance, *Self-Determination in Law and Practice: The
   New Doctrine in the United Nations* (1982), Chaps. 2 and 3; Pomerance, "Self-
   Determination Today: The Metamorphosis of an Ideal," *Israel Law Review*, Vol. 19
   (1984), pp. 310–339.

25. *Official Records*, Humanitarian Law Conference, 1977, vol. 6, p. 61. On the futile
   UN attempts to define the questionable terms so as to rule out any implication that
   "secession" (basically a synonym for self-determination) was permissible, and the
   question-begging definitions that were proffered, *see* Pomerance, *Self-Determination
   in Law and Practice*, pp. 14–15.

26. For a fuller discussion of the Goa incident and doctrine, *see* Quincy Wright, "The Goa Incident," *American Journal of International Law*, vol. 56 (1962), pp. 617–632; Rupert Emerson, *Self-Determination Revisited in the Era of Decolonization* (Occasional Papers in International Affairs no. 9; Harvard University, Center for International Affairs, December 1964), pp. 19–24; and Pomerance, *Self-Determination in Law and Practice*, pp. 49–51.

27. The assertion that colonialism is a "crime" was first made by the General Assembly in Resolution 2621 (xxv), October 12, 1970.

28. Declaration on Principles of International Law Concerning Friendly Relations and Co-operation Among States in Accordance with the Charter of the United Nations, General Assembly Resolution 2625 (xxv), October 24, 1970. For background and analysis, *see* Robert Rosenstock, "The Declaration of Principles of International Law Concerning Friendly Relations: A Survey," *American Journal of International Law*, vol. 65 (1971), pp. 713–735; Gaetano Arangio-Ruiz, "The Normative Role of the General Assembly of the United Nations and the Declaration of Principles of Friendly Relations," Hague Academy, *Recueil des Cours*, vol. 137 (1972-III), pp. 419–742.

29. ICJ *Reports 1986*, pp. 103–104, para. 195. For the view that Article 3(g) of the Consensus Definition enfeebled the customary law, *see* Stone, *Conflict through Consensus*, pp. 73–76. And *see*, for criticism of the Court's handling of this provision, John Lawrence Hargrove, "The *Nicaragua* Judgment and the Future of the Law of Force and Self-Defense," *American Journal of International Law*, vol. 81 (1987), pp. 139–140, n. 15; and the dissenting opinion of Judge Schwebel, ICJ *Reports 1986*, pp. 341–347, paras. 162–171.

30. *See* ICJ *Reports 1986*, p. 108, para. 206; and the Dissenting Opinion of Judge Schwebel, ibid., pp. 350–352, paras. 178–181.

31. Ibid., p. 351, para. 180.

32. Article 7 of Definition of Aggression, annexed to General Assembly Resolution 3314 (xxix), December 14, 1974.

33. *See* Stone, *Conflict through Consensus*, pp. 131–133; Michla Pomerance, "The Consensus Definition of Aggression: The Anatomy of a Failure," *Israel Law Review*, vol. 17 (1982), pp. 116–117; Pomerance, *Self-Determination in Law and Practice*, p. 58.

34. Stone, *Conflict through Consensus*, pp. 138–139.

35. Ibid., p. 57.

36. Ibid., pp. 142, 175.

37. Ibid., p. 126. On the difference between occupation of land by defensive as against aggressive force, *see* Stephen M. Schwebel, "What Weight to Conquest?" *American Journal of International Law*, vol. 64 (1970), pp. 344–347. On reconciling the *ex iniuria* principle with the much-cited and much-misunderstood Security Council Resolution 242, of November 22, 1967, *see* Stone, *Conflict through Consensus*, p. 126. *And see*, regarding the legislative history of the resolution and the deliberate omission of the definite article in the paragraph on withdrawal from territories, ibid. pp. 57–60, 63 (citing, inter alia, the attitude of Lord Caradon, United Kingdom

representative and sponsor of the resolution); and Eugene v. Rostow (a prominent participant in the formulation of the resolution), "Legal Aspects in the Search for Peace in the Middle East," *Proceedings of the American Society of International Law*, vol. 64 (1970), pp. 64, 68–69.

38. *And see,* for the proposition that this kind of approach would be tantamount to replacing a legal principle with an "aggressor's charter," Elihu Lauterpacht, *Jerusalem and the Holy Places* (1968), p. 52.

39. *See,* for example, discussion of the selective manner in which the ICJ cited Security Council Resolution 242 in its advisory opinion on Israel's security fence, in Michla Pomerance, "The ICJ's Advisory Jurisdiction and the Crumbling Wall between the Political and the Judicial," *American Journal of International Law*, vol. 99 (2005), p. 38; and Michla Pomerance, "A Court of 'UN Law'," *Israel Law Review*, vol. 38 (2005), pp. 148–149, 155.

40. *See,* in general, Pomerance, *Self-Determination in Law and Practice,* pp. 51–57.

41. *See* Article 44, paragraphs 3 and 4 of *Protocol I Additional to the Geneva Conventions of 12 August 1949, and relating to the protection of victims of international armed conflicts.* For an analysis of the purport of these provisions and of the difference between the gloss placed on them by the Western states as against that of the Arab states and the PLO, *see* Ruth Lapidoth, "*Qui a Droit au Statut de Prisonnier de Guerre,*" *Révue Générale de Droit International Public,* vol. 82 (1978), pp. 170–210.

42. *See,* for example, the comments of the West German representative, cited in text at note 25, above.

43. *Official Records,* Humanitarian Law Conference, vol. 6, p. 131.

44. Ibid., vol. 15, p. 177. *See also,* e.g., ibid., pp. 156–157, 166, 172–173, 180–182, 185–186; vol. 6, pp. 121–123, 130–134, 137, 143–144.

45. Richard R. Baxter, "The Geneva Conventions of 1949 and Wars of National Liberation," *Rivista di Diritto Internazionale,* vol. 57 (1974), p. 202.

46. On the objectionable nature, from the U.S. standpoint, of some of the provisions of the Rome Statute of July 17, 1998, establishing the International Criminal Court (including Article 8 on war crimes and Article 21 on the "applicable law"), *see* Guy Roberts, "Assault on Sovereignty: The Clear and Present Danger of the New International Criminal Court," *American University International Law Review,* vol. 17 (2001), (and especially text accompanying nn. 80–81). And for Israel's objections, relating also to the attempt to criminalize Israel's settlement activity, *see* Alan Baker, "The International Criminal Court: Israel's Unique Dilemma," in *Justice,* No. 18 (Autumn 1998), pp. 19–25. It may be noted that the current assault against Israel's security fence as an "*apartheid* fence" is connected with the Rome Statute's listing (in Article 7[1][J]) of "the crime of apartheid" among "crimes against humanity."

47. For fears expressed by delegates at the 1977 Geneva Conference regarding the possibility that some of the provisions of the Additional Protocol I might be interpreted as sanctioning terrorism, including urban terrorism: *see,* e.g., *Official Records,* Humanitarian Law Conference, Vol. 6, pp. 122, 138; vol. 14, p. 536; vol. 15, p. 178.

48. *See* the alternative explanation of Rashi to the words "*nakkeh bo*" in Num. 22:6.

49. *See*, in general, Pomerance, *Advisory Function*, pp. 248–259.
50. Ibid., p. 254.
51. The term used by W. Michael Reisman, "The Constitutional Crisis in the United Nations," *American Journal of International Law*, vol. 87 (1993), p. 94.
52. On the issue of consent, *see* Pomerance, *Advisory Function*, pp. 287–296; and Michla Pomerance, "The Advisory Role of the International Court of Justice and its `Judicial' Character: Past and Future Prisms," in A.S. Muller *et al.* (eds.), *The International Court of Justice* (1997), pp. 298–307.
53. General Assemby Resolution ES-10/14.
54. On Israel's challenge to the Court's competence (based, inter alia, on Article 12[1] of the UN Charter, the Security Council's consideration of the issues and its adoption of the "road map," and the "rolling" nature of the General Assembly's "emergency session"), *see Israel's Written Statement to the Court* (available in the ICJ website: www.icj-cij.org); and the unofficial summary of the statement in *Justice*, No. 38 (Spring 2004), pp. 7–9.
55. See *the views of Judge Sir Gerald Fitzmaurice*, quoted at text accompanying note 12, above.
56. General Assembly Resolution ES/10–13.
57. ICJ *Reports 1971*, pp. 127–128; cited by Judge Kooijmans in his separate opinion on Israel's security fence ("Wall"), para. 23.
58. See ICJ *Reports 1971*, Separate Opinions of Judges Onyeama, Petrén, and Dillard, pp. 144–145, 131, 151; and Dissenting Opinions of Judges Fitzmaurice and Gros, ibid., pp. 301–304, 331.
59. ICJ *Reports 1988*, Separate Opinion of Judge Schwebel, p. 42.
60. Stephen M. Schwebel, *Justice in International Law* (1994), p. 20.
61. Anne Bayefsky, "Human Rights the Court Missed," *Jerusalem Post*, February 25, 2004, p. 1.
62. For an analysis of the thesis of counsel for Ethiopia and Liberia, and the judicial reaction to it, *see* Solomon Slonim, *South West Africa and the United Nations: An International Mandate in Dispute* (1973), Chaps. 10 and 11. *See also* the criticism of the concept of the "organized international community" by Arangio-Ruiz, "Normative Role of the General Assembly," pp. 460–469, 629–742.
63. *See* statement of the representative of Nepal, UN Doc. S/PV.1550, July 29, 1970, pp. 38–40.
64. *See*, e.g., some of the critical comments in the *American Journal of International Law*, Vol. 81 (1987), and especially those of John Lawrence Hargrove, Anthony D'Amato, and John Norton Moore, ibid., pp. 135–143, 101–105, 151–159. *See also* some of the articles in Lori F. Damrosch (ed.), *The International Court of Justice at a Crossroads* (1987), and, in particular, Eugene V. Rostow, "Disputes Involving the Inherent Right of Self-Defense," ibid., pp. 264–287.
65. See, in general, Pomerance, *Advisory Function*, Chap. 5; Pomerance, "Advisory Role of the ICJ."
66. U.S. Department of State, U.S. Withdrawal from the Proceedings Initiated by

Nicaragua in the International Court of Justice, January 18, 1985, 24 ILM 246, 248
(1985); excerpted in *American Journal of International Law*, vol. 79 (1985), pp. 438,
441.

67. Davis R. Robinson, "The Role of Politics in the Election and the Work of Judges
of the International Court of Justice," *Proceedings of the American Society of
International Law*, 2003, pp. 280–282. *See also* Judge Schwebel's criticism of the
Court's failure to accede to a U.S. request to substitute a less prejudicial, more
neutral title for the case than the one that was adopted ("Military and Paramilitary
Activities in and against Nicaragua"), ICJ *Reports 1986*, Dissenting Opinion of Judge
Schwebel, pp. 320–321, paras. 128–131.

68. Cited in Judge Buergenthal's Dissenting Opinion to the Court's Order of January
30, 2004 (in which the Court refused Israel's request that Elaraby be disqualified
from sitting in the case), para. 8.

69. Cited ibid.

70. Ibid., paras. 11, 13.

71. On the importance of selecting a neutral title, *see* the comments of Judge Schwebel
in the *Nicaragua* case (cited in note 67, above).

72. Separate Opinion of Judge Owada, para. 31; emphasis added.

73. The term used by the British member of the bench, Rosalyn Higgins, to characterize
some of the Court's reasoning. See text accompanying note 82 below.

74. For detailed critiques, *see* Michla Pomerance, "The ICJ's Advisory Jurisdiction and
the Crumbling Wall between the Political and the Judicial," *American Journal of
International Law*, vol. 99 (2005), pp. 26–42; Ruth Wedgwood, "The ICJ Advisory
Opinion on the Israeli Security Fence and the Limits of Self-Defense," ibid.,
pp. 52–61 [hereinafter: Wedgwood]; Sean D. Murphy, "*Self-Defense and the Israeli
Wall Advisory Opinion: An Ipse Dixit from the ICJ?*" ibid., pp. 62–76 [hereinafter:
Murphy]; and Michla Pomerance, "A Court of 'UN Law'," *Israel Law Review*, Vol.
38 (2005), pp. 134–164.

75. *See* Pomerance, "The ICJ's Advisory Jurisdiction and the Crumbling Wall,"
pp. 34–35.

76. Separate Opinion of Judge Higgins, para. 16.

77. International Committee of the Red Cross, *Commentary on the Geneva Convention
(IV) Relative to the Protection of Civilian Persons in Time of War* (Jean Pictet gen. ed.)
(1958), p. 207; cited in Murphy, "Self-Defense and the Israeli *Wall* Advisory Opinion,"
p. 71. *See also*, on the rights of states within "occupied territories," Wedgwood, pp.
58–59, and the authorities there cited.

78. Declaration of Judge Buergenthal, paras. 1, 3, and 7. See also, *for trenchant criticism
of the Court's handling of the facts*, Wedgwood, pp. 53–54; Murphy, pp. 70–75.

79. "Wall" Opinion, paras. 135, 137, 140.

80. *On the dismay privately conveyed by an array of foreign ministry legal advisers*, see
Wedgwood, p. 57.

81. Ibid., p. 58; and see, *especially*, Murphy, pp. 63–70. *See also* Declaration of Judge
Buergenthal, para. 6; Separate Opinion of Judge Higgins, para. 33.

82. Separate Opinion of Judge Higgins, para. 34.
83. Declaration of Judge Buergenthal, para. 6.
84. See, *on this point*, Murphy, pp. 68–69; Wedgwood, p. 58.
85. See *Declaration of Judge Buergenthal*, para. 6; Murphy, pp. 67–68; Wedgwood, p. 58.
86. The Arab Convention on the Suppression of Terrorism, adopted by the Arab League at Cairo, April 22, 1998, Article 2(a). For comment on this article, see Ruth Wedgwood, "*Self-Defense Sans Frontières*," *Wall Street Journal*, October 8, 2003. *See also* Anne Bayefsky, "The UN World Conference against Racism: A Racist Anti-Racism Conference," *Proceedings of the American Society of International Law*, 2002, p. 73.
87. United Nations, *A More Secure World: Our Shared Responsibility, Report of the Secretary General's High-Level Panel on Threats, Challenges and Change*, UN doc. A/59/565, para. 160 (2004); cited in Wedgwood, "The ICJ Advisory Opinion on the Israeli Security Fence," p. 57.
88. On the Court's approach to the Palestinians' "right of self-determination," its purportedly "*erga omnes*" character, and of Israel's alleged "breach," see *Pomerance*, "A Court of 'UN Law,'" pp. 157–158.
    "Wal" Opinion, para. 163 (2) (E); emphasis added.
90. Ibid., para. 47.
91. Anthony D'Amato and Mary Ellen O'Connell, "United States Experience at the International Court of Justice," in Damrosch, *The International Court of Justice*, p. 422. *See also* Hargrove's observation, that "no aspect of the political order is transformed just because the Court speaks," in "The *Nicaragua* Judgment and the Future of the Law of Force and Self-Defense," *American Journal of International Law*, vol. 81 (1987), p. 136. *See also* the concluding assessment of Sean D. Murphy regarding the role of the ICJ in the opinion on the fence. Murphy, p. 76.
92. Declaration deposited on October 17, 1956, 253 UNTS 301; reproduced in Shabtai Rosenne, *The Law and Practice of the International Court* (1965), pp. 894–895. Israel remains bound, however, through compromissory clauses in certain treaties (including the Genocide Convention), to acceptance of the compulsory jurisdiction of the Court.
93. *Johnson v. Eisentrager*, 339 U.S. 763 (1950) at 796.
94. *See* Yehuda Z. Blum, "The Missing Reversioner: Reflections on the Status of Judea and Samaria," *Israel Law Review*, vol. 3 (1968), pp. 279–301; Julius Stone, *Israel and Palestine: Assault on the Law of Nations* (1981), pp. 118–121. On the misreading of the reference to "withdrawal" in Security Council Resolution 242 and that resolution's non-sanctification of the 1949 armistice lines, *see* citations in note 37, above.
95. *See* Meir Shamgar, "The Observance of International Law in the Administered Territories," *Israel Yearbook on Human Rights*, vol. 1 (1971), pp. 262–277.
96. *Ajuri and others v. IDF Commander of the Area of Judea and Samaria and others*, Case No. HCJ 7015/02, 7019/02, paras. 1–3, 40. The case is reproduced in English translation in *International Law Reports*, vol. 125 (2004), pp. 537 ff.

97. *American Journal of International Law*, vol. 97 (2003), p. 175.

98. Remarks by Jane Dalton, *Proceedings of the American Society of International Law*, 2003, pp. 193–195.

99. Irwin Cotler, "Human Rights and the New Anti-Jewishness," *Justice*, No. 38 (Spring 2004), p. 27.

100. Anne Bayefsky, "The United Nations vs. the Rights of Children," *Jerusalem Post*, October 15, 2002, p. 7.

101. Rabbi Dr. Joseph B. Soloveitchik, "The Sacred and the Profane," *Ha-Tzedek*, Vol. 2 (May–June 1945), p. 6.

"Dilemmas of Military Service in Israel: The Religious Dimension

Stuart A. Cohen

Ever since its establishment in 1948, the Israel Defense Force (hereafter the IDF) has maintained a system of universal conscription.
Israeli law imposes mandatory military service for periods of between two and three years on women as well as men when they
reach the age of eighteen. It also permits the IDF to summons discharged service personnel (principally males) under the age of 45
for compulsory stints of reserve duty, which can total as much as
thirty days per annum.

For many years, this militia-style service system was said to
have endowed the IDF with the character of "a people's army" and
to have justified the classification of Israeli society as a paradigmatic
"nation in arms." Over the past decade, however, both depictions have
lost much of their force. Driven by the twin furies of severe budgetary

restraints and a burgeoning ethos of "military professionalism," the IDF has adopted a policy of more selective service.[1] Influenced by the I-centered fashions of "post-modernism," increasing numbers of Israelis have at the same time signaled their satisfaction with that policy. Combined, these influences have created a situation in which military service – once popularly considered to be the most widely-shared of all Israeli experiences – is now poised to become the exception rather than the rule.

Such is already the case with regard to reserve duty.[2] Figures recently released by the IDF indicate that the same situation will soon apply in the conscript segment too. Already, the draft is clearly not universal. The vast majority of Arab youngsters are not enlisted, and growing segments of the Jewish population, too, are being excused from duty. Altogether, the proportion of male and female *Jewish* Israeli youngsters enlisted in the IDF declined from 72% in 1980 to roughly 66% in 2002, with some 20% of the latter receiving early discharges.[3]

One primary result of this situation is that, for all intents and purposes, military service in Israel has increasingly come to assume a quasi-voluntary character. Conscripts seriously intent on avoiding the draft, for one reason or another, can now do so with greater ease than in the past, and with less fear of social censure. The other side of the coin, however, is that those enlisting clearly do not serve solely because they are legally obligated to do so. They also attach to military service additional attributes.[4] Some can be categorized as "utilitarian," since they are based on a view of military service as a stepping stone to subsequent career advancement in civilian life, too. Other attributes are "normative," in the sense that they reflect the resilience of the notion that the IDF still constitutes Israel's supreme "melting pot" and that enlistment consequently continues to be the principal *rite de passage* to full citizenship.[5] In yet a third category (not necessarily exclusive of the previous two), the impulses to serve are "altruistic," and grow out of the conviction that military duty in defense of the State and its citizens remains essential for the fulfillment of the Zionist vision.

Studies periodically undertaken by and on behalf of the IDF's

Behavioral Science Unit show that, in varying measures, all three
clusters of factors influence the propensities to service of IDF draftees. Combined, they account for the fact that – notwithstanding the
dire warnings of some Cassandras – neither conscripts nor reservists presently show signs of undergoing a "crisis of motivation." On
the contrary, the IDF's elite combat formations are invariably over-
subscribed, and in some units as many as three conscripts vie for
every available place. This spirit now appears to permeate the entire
complement. Whereas in the mid-1990s only some 75% of all new
recruits expressed themselves ready to serve in combat formations,
in November 2003 the figure stood at 88% – an all-time record.[6]

Affirmative attitudes of that sort are especially pronounced
amongst members of what is commonly termed Israel's "national-
religious" (alternatively "religious-Zionist") community. Altogether,
indeed, where commitment to military duty is concerned, graduates
of religious state high schools seem now to own the mantle of civic
service and idealism to which, in a previous generation, the secular
kibbutz movement claimed virtually sole proprietary rights.[7] The
signs of that transformation are easily observed.[8] Throughout the
secular kibbutz system, rates of voluntary enlistment to combat
units and professional military service have sharply declined over
the past decade. During the same period, however, the sight of a
kippah serugah – the most obtrusive sign of male national-religious
affiliation – on the head of an Israeli soldier on front-line active duty
has become commonplace. This is particularly so in those units to
which enlistment is elective and selection especially rigorous. The
bleak evidence of operational casualties since 1990 indicates that the
number of national-religious recruits in elite combat units (*sayarot*)
far exceeds their proportion in the annual conscript cohort, perhaps
by as much as a factor of two.

Where available, statistics with respect to NCOs and junior
officers tell a similar tale. At a rough estimate, some 30% of all IDF
combat troops at those ranks now wear a *kippah serugah*. Moreover,
as many as 60% of those passing out in the first class of NCO infantry
courses in recent years have been products of the national-religious
high school system, one of whose graduates was in 2002 declared

to be the most outstanding pupil of the prestigious pilots' training school. Furthermore, where the males have led, females seem to be quick to follow. In the past, the majority of female graduates of the national-religious school system elected to perform a year or two of civic service rather than of military duty (and, indeed, repeatedly received rabbinic instructions to that effect). Of late, however, trends have shown signs of change. In 2002, fully a third of female graduates of national-religious high schools elected to serve in the IDF, in one capacity or another.[9]

The present paper does not seek to analyze the possible reasons for such phenomena, a subject that sociologists have debated at some length in recent years, in some case rather venomously so.[10] Instead, our purpose is to explore some of their possible implications. Specifically, the paper aims to examine the impact exerted on traditionally observant soldiers by the experience of military service in the armed forces of an independent Jewish state. To that end, we shall, first, outline some of the conditions of their service in the IDF. Thereafter, we shall examine in greater detail the principal dilemmas that they confront.

1. CONDITIONS OF SERVICE

By any standards, traditionally observant draftees into today's IDF enter a far more congenial institution than was available to those of their grandfathers and great-grandfathers who served in the conscript armies of Europe and the United States. The latter, even if they did come into occasional contact with a Jewish chaplain (a post that was not officially recognized in most western armies until World War II), nevertheless served in an institution whose entire ethos was, if not always avowedly Christian, certainly never in any way Jewish.[11] In the IDF, by contrast, strenuous efforts are made to ensure that the force, precisely because it constitutes the army of a sovereign Jewish state, is indeed endowed with a specifically Jewish ambience.

Much of the credit for that situation belongs to the late Rabbi Shlomo Goren, who was the IDF's very first *rav tzeva'i rashi* (chief chaplain). Altogether a man of perpetual motion and boundless energy, R. Goren was also blessed with considerable organizational talents and resounding erudition. In addition, he possessed a remarkable knack for seemingly always managing to be in the right place at the right time. These were gifts that he exploited to the full during his long and productive military career (he held the office of *rav tzeva'i rashi* from 1948–1971, and by the time he retired was the longest-serving Major-General [*aluf*] in the entire Force). His prolific stream of learned publications helped to craft the practical accommodation of traditional *Halakhah* with army life. By means of a series of arrangements worked out with David Ben-Gurion, R. Goren also ensured that the ambience of the IDF as a whole would respect and reflect orthodox practice. Combined, these achievements made it possible for religiously observant conscripts to enlist on equal terms with their secular comrades.[12]

One obvious expression of R. Goren's achievement is to be found in the authority that IDF General Staff Regulations explicitly invest in the military rabbinate (*ha-rabbanut ha-tzeva'it*). The duties of this body are not limited to maintaining an adequate supply on every base of the materials and artifacts required by religiously observant troops. In such obviously critical areas as *shemirat Shabbat* and *kashrut*, the military rabbinate is also responsible for ensuring that the military framework as a whole observes the requirements of Halakhah.[13]

Just as significant (occasionally, perhaps, even more so) are the steps taken to ensure that, in a more subliminal sense, the Jewish religion becomes an integral component of the overall cultural texture of Israeli military life.[14] Some of the mechanisms employed to that end are organizational: the inclusion of lectures on Jewish topics and festivals at every level of instruction, up to and including senior staff college. Others, however, are essentially ceremonial in form. Thus, all new recruits receive a copy of the *Tanakh* at their induction ceremonies, many of which are held at the Western Wall in Jerusalem. Furthermore, by convention, all troops on active service, regardless of rank or military profession, attend the annual

seder service and the weekly Friday night meal that is preceded
by the recitation of *kiddush*. The rationale behind these and other
intrusions of traditional Jewish practice into the military regimen is
not simply to harmonize the particularistic concerns of the observant minority with the more general interests of the non-observant
majority. Rather, in all such cases, traditional religious themes and
motifs provide sources of inspiration and motivation. Quite apart
from legitimizing the use of force as a last resort, they also serve as
a social coagulant. They constitute vehicles for fostering the feelings of affinity and reciprocity that have always been recognized as
essential criteria for military cohesion, and ultimately for effective
battlefield performance.

The support thus made available to the religiously observant
Jewish soldier by the IDF's own frameworks and practices is further
supplemented by external sources. Here, too, the contrast with the
situation prevailing elsewhere in earlier generations is both stark
and instructive. When confronting a ritual or ethical problem, Orthodox Jewish soldiers serving in non-Jewish armed forces during
the era of mass conscription had very limited access to halakhic
guidance and moral instruction. Military chaplains were few and
far between, communication with civilian rabbinic authorities was
uncertain and far from instantaneous, and written Orthodox sources
of direct relevance almost non-existent.[15] Indeed, to the best of my
knowledge, prior to 1948 only two texts were composed anywhere
in the world with the needs of Orthodox Jewish military personnel
specifically in mind. The first was the Hafetz Hayyim's *Sefer Mahaneh
Yisrael* (1st edition, 1881), a pioneering attempt to provide a detailed
summary of *halakhot* possibly pertinent to military life. The second
was *A Book of Jewish Thoughts* (1st edition, 1918), a thin volume of
aphorisms and devotional passages compiled by Rabbi Dr. Joseph
Hertz (1872–1946), the Chief Rabbi of the United Kingdom and the
British Empire during both World Wars.[16] In recent years, both
works have been very much superceded. So, too, in many respects,
have even R. Goren's pioneering studies. Since the late 1970s, especially, analyses of *dinei tzava ve-milhamah* have grown exponentially.
As a result, a field that for almost two millennia constituted one of

the great lacunae of rabbinic analysis now fills entire shelves in any respectable library of Halakhah.

Three features of this voluminous new corpus warrant particular attention. One is the range of topics covered: it addresses – often in microscopic detail – every conceivable challenge that military service might present to the observance of orthodox ritual and practice, as well as ethical and doctrinal issues of a more philosophical nature. Also noteworthy, secondly, is the nature of the authorship of the literature, much of which is composed by rabbis who – unlike any previous generation of halakhic authorities known to history – often themselves possess protracted first-hand experience of military life, sometimes in combat units. Finally, there is the wide variety of formats in which the literature on *dinei tzava ve-milhamah* appears. Some of the relevant publications consist of comprehensive and integrated presentations of the entire subject, or of one of its aspects, in book-length form.[17] Others, take the form of erudite articles on a more specific issue, published either in one of the specialist journals on contemporary *Halakhah*[18] or (especially of late) in a collection of essays compiled in memory of a fallen soldier.[19] In yet a third category, the preferred vehicle is the traditional genre of *she'elot u-teshuvot* (responsa) – whose epistolary form is being increasingly adapted to the abbreviated and instantaneous style required by electronic mail and internet-based chat groups, several of which now contain dedicated portals on military matters.[20]

Quite apart from making intellectual contributions to halakhic scholarship, such works also frequently fulfill a practical need, in that they provide Orthodox religious soldiers with readily accessible and detailed guides to correct behavior and comportment whilst on service. Combined with the infrastructure of amenities provided by the *rabbanut tzeva'it*, they help to moderate many of the religious and ritual difficulties that military service must inevitably pose. Ideally, Orthodox Jewish personnel, whatever their precise military occupation, should now find it possible to be fully integrated members of the IDF, capable of performing their duties without fear of compromising (let alone contravening) their religious beliefs and traditions.

2. THE CHALLENGES OF MILITARY SERVICE:
CONTACT WITH THE NON-ORTHODOX WORLD

Central to the argument that follows is the contention that such aspirations are not always fulfilled. Beneath the surface appearance of harmony between military service in Israel and an Orthodox Jewish life-style, there frequently lurks a reality that is much more complex. As is indicated by the deliberately hyphenated nature of their social identities, national-religious troops in the IDF frequently live compound lives, during the course of which they often face choices that are conflicting, rather than complementary. As a result, military service imposes on them an especially large range of pressures and tensions. National-religious conscripts are not only subject to the anxieties experienced by all new recruits, secular and Orthodox alike, on being thrust into a deliberately harsh environment in which fear of "losing face" is particularly pronounced.[21] They also confront challenges that are specific to the social segment from which they are drawn. It is to these that we now turn.

Both written and oral evidence leaves no doubt that the most prevalent source of stress amongst national-religious troops (male and female), especially prior to and immediately after their enlistment, is the experience of close contact with conscripts who come from a secular background. That is hardly a surprising finding. After all, the vast majority of national-religious youngsters in Israel are reared in a very closed environment, and one that perhaps deserves to be termed very cosseted too. Most are graduates of high-schools – some of which are still residential – in which they have been doubly "quarantined," since quite apart from being restricted to pupils from religious homes they are also single-sex institutions. Many were also members of one of the youth movements (B'nei Akiva, Ezra, the Religious Scouts), which similarly cater exclusively to Orthodox adolescents. The great advantage of this multi-layered system of cocoons is that it helps to foster noticeably robust ties of association, identification and personal acquaintance amongst the graduates themselves.[22] Its drawback, of course, is that it also creates a very introspective sociological cohort, whose members come to military service with virtually no prior contact whatsoever with non-

Orthodox youngsters of their own age. This is especially so in the case of those brought up in neighborhoods or communities whose demographic composition is predominantly religious – in the case of many of the settlements located in Judea, Samaria, and the Gaza Strip, almost entirely so.

Recent studies of twelfth-grade pupils in religious high-schools indicate that a large minority looks forward to military service precisely because it presents them with an opportunity to abandon their Orthodox life-style. Thus, of those surveyed in a large poll in 1999, only 52% declared an intention of remaining fully observant. As many as 20% admitted that they had already decided not to do so, in the case of boys by taking the symbolic step of "removing their *kippah*."[23] Even for them, however, the experience of sustained and close contact with youngsters who have been brought up in a very different cultural milieu comes as something of a shock. For the majority, which still retains varying degrees of attachment to an Orthodox life-style, the traumatic effects of the meeting are all the greater. As much was indicated with some force in an article that two fresh conscripts originally published a few years ago in the official B'nei Akiva bulletin, *Zera'im*. "The IDF," they warned younger members, "is not at all a religious institution." Only in part did they reach that conclusion because conditions in the unit mess do not always meet Orthodox standards of *kashrut*, especially in isolated front-line postings that are too small to billet a military chaplain. Far more significant, they reported, are the challenges posed by other tests, most of which are all the more trying for being so unexpected:

> "Quite apart from experiencing the shock to which every conscript is submitted on entering the military framework, the religious soldier is estranged and struck dumb by the comportment of his secular comrades. Even their everyday speech contains phrases and terms which his own mouth, accustomed to prayer, is unable to utter and which his ears, attuned to words of wisdom, refuse to absorb."[24]

For many years, the national-religious educational establishment seemed either to be unaware of the existence of this problem or to deny its scope. Of late, however, that situation has very much altered. There now exists a growing awareness, sometimes more intuitive than tangible, of the extent to which religious and secular camps in Israel are drifting apart.[25] As a result, an entire series of programs has been created specifically in order to prepare national-religious school-leavers for the "culture shock" of contact with conscripts from backgrounds that are predominantly non-religious, and in some cases even anti-religious.

Broadly speaking, the programs now available seem to reflect two distinct schools of thought: one might be labeled "segregation," the other "fortification." "Segregation" proceeds from the assumption, albeit one that is usually left unspoken, that religiously observant troops can best cope with the challenge of contact with the secular world when – as much as possible – they do so as a group. The program that probably now goes furthest towards meeting that requirement is the *nahal haredi*, an infantry battalion composed entirely of Orthodox personnel. When first established in January 1999, this program was designed to satisfy the needs of the small minority of *haredi* young men who chose to enlist, and were consequently often ostracized by their own communities. Of late, however, the *nahal haredi* has also attracted the interest of some national-religious circles. It now also accepts senior students from Zionist *yeshivot gevohot*, who have hitherto deferred their enlistment for several years whilst pursuing their studies. Largely as a result, the annual intake of the *nahal haredi* unit has more than tripled over the past three years, from 31 to 110.[26]

A far more widespread articulation of "segregation" is provided by the network of *yeshivot hesder*, which now encompasses 33 institutions of that name, the oldest of which was established at Kerem be-Yavneh in 1964. *Hesder* students, quite apart from being permitted an active conscript term that is considerably shorter than the norm (some 18 months instead of 36), also perform their military service in a social milieu that is often largely their own. Most undergo basic training in their own companies, and many thereafter serve in formations in which they constitute a majority. From the

IDF's viewpoint, this arrangement has clear advantages: it provides the military organization with a ready-made cadre of particularly cohesive units, susceptible to very few of the inter-personal frictions that usually consume so much of a commander's time and energies. Therein, too, lies much of the attraction of the *hesder* for individual recruits. It assures them of a notably supportive social framework, which promises to mitigate many of the psychological strains common to military life. After all, in units predominantly manned (and sometimes commanded) by *hesder* conscripts, religious observance is the norm, not the exception.

At the basis of what is here termed "fortification" lies a different philosophy. Rather than providing recruits with a collective protective framework during the course of their service, fortification seeks to prepare them for that experience before it starts. One example of such an effort is provided by a course of study entitled *Efshar La'asot Zot* ("It Can Be Done"), dedicated to the memory of Capt. Noam Cohen, and prepared for use in religious high schools by the Yaakov Herzog Center at Kibbutz Ein Tzurim. The basic "kit," designed to meet the needs of both instructors and pupils, consists of a video film and three booklets, each of which outlines an analysis of a particular theme.[27] Since its inception in 1999, the course has reportedly been distributed to over 200 institutions, which together cater annually to some 5,000 students. No effort is made to persuade this audience to enlist *en bloc*. On the contrary, basic to the entire ethos of the course is the conviction that religiously observant conscripts, if properly prepared, can – as individuals – pass through the military experience unscathed.

Equally explicitly committed to the same principles of "fortification" are the pre-conscript colleges of Torah instruction (*ha-mekhinot ha-kedam tzeva'iyot ha-toraniyot*), the first of which was established under the name of *Bnei David* in the West Bank settlement of Eli in 1988. Now numbering 12 institutions, with an annual intake of almost 1,000 students, the *mekhinot*, too, insist that prepatory instruction constitutes the key to the conscript's survival (religious and otherwise) in the military setting. National-religious male conscripts, they insist, have to enlist on the same terms as any other: as individuals, not as a group, and for the full three years of mandatory service – at least. However, they will best perform their duties if they postpone their induction into the IDF for a year, during which they enroll for a course that combines heavy and heady doses of both physical training and intellectual fare.

Significantly, comparatively little of the latter consists of Talmudic study, which is the staple diet of the *yeshivot hesder*. Instead, the *mekhinot* place particular emphasis on Jewish philosophy and spiritualism, and especially on the writings of the (elder) Rav Kook. Thus, *Ma'amar ha-Dor* is a favored text, not least because it is interpreted to convey the message that the individual ought to regard contact with the world of secular Israel as a primary benefit of military service, and not one of its challenges.[28] Not surprisingly, this teaching is articulated with even greater emphasis in the half dozen "mixed" *mekhinot* that have been established since 1998, whose annual intake consists of some 300 students from secular as well as religious homes.

It is not easy to assess the overall success of what have here been termed the alternative strategies of "segregation" and "fortification."[29] In their different ways, both certainly do appear to alleviate many of the difficulties that enlistment presents for religiously observant soldiers. This is particularly so with regard to their prospects of integration into the wider military community. Largely thanks to the various programs and schedules outlined above, increasing numbers of youngsters from religiously observant homes now feel capable of shouldering a full share of Israel's defense burdens, without in any way thereby being forced to compromise their commitment to an Orthodox life-style. No longer does enlistment give rise to fears that the youngsters concerned will cease to be observant. Neither, by the same token, is the observance of Orthodox rituals necessarily felt to prejudice the performance of military duties. Indeed, far from being mutually antagonistic, military service and religious observance increasingly seem capable of reinforcing each other.

On the other hand, however, several problems still remain. For one thing, conscription clearly does not provide the panacea to the religious-secular divide that constitutes one of Israel's most significant social fault lines. Much though the shared experience of military service might bridge some of the differences between observant and non-observant personnel in the IDF, it can never entirely eradicate them all. On the contrary, in many cases it seems to exacerbate the religious-secular divide, if only because it provides tangible proof of how very different religious and secular troops can in fact be.[30] But to this must be added, secondly, a more specific consideration, of particular reference to religiously observant troops. Even when most successful, neither the "segregation" or "fortification" programs can obscure the fact that military service compels national-religious troops in the IDF to confront several dilemmas that are distinctively their own.

The remainder of this essay will briefly illustrate what such dilemmas are.

A. *"And your camp shall be holy"* (Deut. 23.15).

As is often pointed out, classic Jewish sources have long been aware of the overriding need to take special care to counter the corrosive effect that the military environment threatens to exert on morals and behavior.[31] Much of the contemporary corpus of teachings in the field of *dinei tzava ve-milhamah* is written with those teachings very much in mind. Hence, its main thrust is to ensure that the spark of holiness is indeed kept alive, even within the military setting. But it also serves the ancillary purpose of helping individual soldiers to thereby overcome the crises of conscience likely to be induced should the performance of military duties seem to conflict with the dictates of traditional Jewish religious observance.

Both formal surveys and informal observation leave no doubt that such conflicts are indeed keenly and widely felt. This is especially the case with regard to the observance of *Shabbat* and *kashrut*. Indeed, how both sets of *mitzvot* might be maintained in a military environment (or, alternatively, the military circumstances that might permit or even make obligatory some modifications of required practice in both areas) have long constituted subjects of contention.[32] A rough count of the recent responsa addressed to serving personnel suggests that, in terms of sheer volume, these topics continue to predominate as matters of national-religious concern.[33] Not very far behind come other questions that have proved to be equally persistent: How might the Orthodox male dress code (*kippah, tzitzit*) be harmonized with requirements for military camouflage? How can the regimen of military training accommodate a personal timetable dominated by the need to pray three times each day and to observe periodic fasts? Of late, moreover, circumstances have generated an even wider range of further halakhic enquiries. Can traditional Jewish attitudes towards inter-gender relations (*tzeni'ut*) at all be squared with the growing determination of the IDF High Command to integrate female soldiers into combat units? Do the rules of *pikuah nefesh* apply to the need to alleviate the hardships of the Palestinian population by operating the gates of the "security fence" on *Shabbat*?[34]

Equally worthy of attention is the evidence indicating the national-religious serviceman's concern with the moral dimensions of some combat missions. Questions in this category have clamored for a growing amount of attention in recent years, especially since the outbreak of the second *intifada* in September 2000. In the main, that development must be attributed to the particularly brutal nature of the present round of violence, which has posed many of the ethical dilemmas associated with conflict in a harshly complex and concrete form. It has also compelled IDF troops and commanders to confront questions that have likewise troubled soldiers of other armies (the British in northern Ireland for several years, and now the Americans in Iraq) placed in similar non-conventional situations. Why should they abide by the standard rules of military engagement if their enemies do not observe the accepted distinctions between formal combatants and civilian bystanders? Military wisdom apart, are there not sound *moral* reasons for adopting less orthodox forms of operational conduct, such as the use of potentially hostile civilians as "human shields" or the resort to "targeted killings" as a form of retaliation for a terror outrage?[35]

Non-religious conscripts and reservists can (and do) debate the pros and cons of such suggestions within a legal and philosophical framework that reflects universal moral considerations as well as specifically Jewish ethical traditions.[36] But religiously observant troops expect the Halakhah to provide an additional, if not alternative, perspective. The pressure thus generated helps to account for the increasing attention currently being paid in modern Orthodox halakhic literature to the very specifics of contemporary *jus in bello* concerns. Operational issues of an ethical nature that were once considered fairly marginal to the discourse on *dinei tzava ve-milhamah* have now moved to center-stage. As much is made evident, for instance, in a recent issue of *Tehumin* (vol. 23, 2003). Of the eight articles in the section devoted to "Army and Security," which on this occasion opens the entire volume, at least five constitute explicit responses to combat situations that had arisen during the course of the second *intifada*. "Theft from a Gentile During war" (R. Yaakov Ariel); "Combat in Regions Containing Civilian Population" (R. Dr. Nerya Gutal); "Harvesting the Olives of Gentiles from Trees Located Within the Boundaries of a Jewish Settlement" (R. Yaakov Ariel); "The Distribution of Booty and Loot in Contemporary Warfare" (R. Shlomo Rosenfeld); "Acquisition (*kinyan*) by means of Conquest" (R. Gad Eldad).[37]

Strict military etiquette might require that the ultimate locus of authority for decision in all such matters rest with the *rabbanut ha-tzeva'it*. Practice, however, is very different. As far as can be seen, the current discourse on the ethical dimensions of military operations (and, for that matter, on many other aspects of *dinei milhamah*, too) is principally being conducted in civilian rabbinic circles. In his official capacity, the recently-retired *rav tzeva'i rashi*, General Rabbi Yisrael Weiss – unlike, for instance, the Judge Advocate-General – passed no public comment whatsoever on whether or not current IDF operational practice accords with traditional Jewish interpretations of the *jus in bello*.[38] Indeed, it is doubtful whether he was specifically asked to do so. R. Weiss openly admitted that his unit wields very little influence over most national-religious servicemen, and has hitherto failed in its attempts to attract to its ranks the best and brightest of that population group.[39] He himself certainly made strenuous efforts to repair that situation. Even so, few Orthodox soldiers turn to the *rabbanut tzeva'it* when seeking halakhic advice.

Invariably, they still approach one of the non-military authorities whom they consider to be better qualified to assess such matters – a respected and approachable municipal *rav* (such as R. Yaakov Ariel, the Chief Rabbi of Ramat Gan) or the principal (*rosh*) or teacher (*ram*) of their high-school *yeshivah*, *yeshivat hesder*, or *mekhinah*. Possibly in recognition of that tendency, the person appointed by the Chief of Staff in 2006 to succeed R. Weiss as *rav tzeva'i rashi* was a head of a *yeshivat hesder*, R. Avi Rontzki, and not a serving member of the military chaplaincy.

B. Whom to obey?

Situations such as this have generated charges that religiously observant troops in the IDF might be susceptible to "divided loyalties." In its simplest version (which is also often the most widespread), the argument runs something like this. Only nominally are secular and religious troops in the IDF subject to the same chain of command. In fact, their allegiances diverge. Whereas secular IDF troops are subordinate solely to their military commanders, Orthodox conscripts are also bound to obey the instructions of their rabbis. Should the two authorities issue mutually contradictory orders, many national-religious soldiers might prefer to follow the dictates of their spiritual mentors.[40]

   Such fears become particularly audible whenever some progress in the Israeli-Palestinian peace process seems feasible. After all, it is argued, many (perhaps most) national-religious teachers speak of the retention of Jewish control over the entire Land of Israel in terms that invest it with the status of a categorical imperative. Indeed, in the wake of the Oslo accords reached by the Rabin government and the PLO in the mid-1990s, some rabbinical figures cited both the Rambam and the Ramban when explicitly calling upon troops to disobey whatever orders they might receive to participate in operations designed dismantle either a Jewish settlement in "the territories" or an IDF military base located there.[41] Such exhortations were repeated during the period immediately preceding Israel's disengagement from the Gaza Strip and northern Samaria in the summer of 2005.[42] This situation generated fears that, in view of

the growing prominence of *kippot serugot* in the officer corps, the
IDF might be torn apart. Even the suspicion that so large a body of
junior commanders might subordinate their professional military
duties to their ideological preferences, it was argued, was bound to
create deep schisms within the Force.

In the end, those fears proved to be entirely unfounded. Testify-
ing orally to the Kenesset's Foreign Affairs and Security Committee
in September 2005, a month after completing disengagement, the
Chief of the IDF General Staff, Lieutenant-General Dan Halutz,
stated that it had been necessary to place just 63 national-religious
soldiers on trial for refusing orders during the operation (50 conscripts – 24 of whom served in the framework of the *yeshivot hesder*;
5 petty officers and 3 other ranks in professional service; and 5 reservists).[43] Possibly, these figures do not tell the entire story, and allow-
ances have to be made for troops who might have come to private
"understandings" with their immediate commanding officers, and
hence managed to detach themselves from units directly involved in
disengagement. Even so, the overall picture remains clear. *En masse*,
the *kippot serugot* neither rebelled nor shirked their duties.

A combination of factors accounts for that outcome. In part, it
reflects the influence exerted by a formidable array of rabbinic figures
in the national-religious community (including several principals
of *hesder yeshivot*), who explicitly counseled their student-soldiers
against conscientious objection.[44] In addition, note must be taken of
the extensive efforts made by the IDF's educational and psychological units, with the specific purpose of preparing national-religious
troops, in particular, to face the challenge that disengagement was
anticipated to present.[45] Combined, these processes certainly produced the desired effect. Painful though many male and female
national-religious troops undoubtedly found disengagement to be,
the overwhelming majority did not react to it in a manner that might
threaten their ties of affiliation to the IDF and all that it represents.

c. Service or Study?
Indications of unease amongst national-religious conscripts become
far more concrete, and convincing, once attention shifts away from

the political dimensions of their service and focuses, instead, on the demands that it makes on their time. At issue here are not the halakhic rights and wrongs of individual military orders and actions, nor even the source of authority claimed by the persons who transmit them. Rather, what generates dilemmas is the conflict caused by simultaneous pressures to follow two very different avocations, both of which make monopolistic demands on the individual's energies and attention. One is the pursuit of traditional scholarship, as facilitated by study in a *yeshivah*; the other is participation in the military defense of Israel and its inhabitants against persistent acts of violence.

Although shot through with various ideological implications, at root the tension between study and military service possesses clear structural features. As such, it lends itself to analysis on the lines long ago suggested by Lewis Coser's study of what he called "greedy institutions." This term, he suggested, applied to all social structures that "seek hegemonic loyalty, and attempt to reduce the claims of competing roles and status positions on those they wish to encompass in their boundaries."[46] The IDF certainly conforms to the typology. Even though its overall ambience is notoriously informal, and characterized by the absence of a rigid insistence on parade-ground discipline, the Israeli army (like all others) nevertheless insists that its personnel adhere to a formal code of military conduct. It also invokes the rule of "unlimited liability" when making demands on their resources of time and attention. But so too, *mutatis mutandis*, do *yeshivot*. Hence, they also warrant description as "omnivorous" institutions, to use another of Coser's terms. After all, enrollment in a *yeshivah* likewise constitutes a personal commitment to a particularly demanding time-table that grants *talmud Torah* a position of absolute primacy over any other activity.

The monopolistic claims of *Torah*-study – especially vis-à-vis military service – have found their most explicit expression in *haredi* circles. It is now calculated that over 80% of *haredi* males of conscript age presently claim – and receive – extensive deferments from enlistment on the grounds that "the [study of] the *Torah* is their profession" (*Toratam umanutam*). Indeed, this particular segment of Orthodox Israeli society now posits as an article of faith the argument that the energies that its members invest in their scholarly vocation contribute as much (if not more) to Israel's ultimate survival than do the exertions of IDF troops.[47]

Mainstream religious Zionist thought has always rejected the implication that it, too, must educate towards non-service. Instead, it has consistently advocated the twinning of "the scroll" (*safra*) with "the sword" (*saifa*), teaching that – in Israel's present security situation – study and military service make up two sides of the same coin of religious imperatives, thereby creating a reciprocal dynamic.[48] But, for all the eloquence and erudition with which they are expressed, such efforts to harmonize the seemingly conflicting demands of two greedy institutions cannot be said to constitute the last word on the subject. On the contrary, they have themselves spawned debates about the way in which the reconciliation might best be attained, and the relative benefits and costs of whichever method is adopted – to the individual, to modern religious society, to the IDF, and to Israel at large.

The ramifications of such debates can be observed at every major way-station along the young national-religious conscripts' journey through military life. At each stage, he (for present purposes, the discussion will here be limited to males) confronts choices that are uniquely his own. Dilemmas first arise as soon as call-up papers arrive through the mail. Unlike his secular or *haredi* counterpart, whose choices of possible legitimate action in this situation are limited and stark, the national-religious conscript possesses a variety of possibilities. For one thing, each individual can decide whether or not to enlist at all, the alternative being to enroll in one of the *haredi yeshivot*, and thereby claim exemption. Even if the first option is chosen, there remains the question of timing. Is he to enlist straight away as a "regular" conscript, and thus forego any immediate opportunity of furthering his studies? Is he to embark, *ab initio*, on an extended program of study in a *yeshivah* which, although "Zionist," nevertheless encourages extended deferment of service, usually for periods of up to eight years? Or is he to opt for one of the multiple programs that defer initial enlistment for just a year or two?[49] If the latter is the case, which program should he chose? And – perhaps even more agonizing – to which particular institution should he apply? After all, not all *yeshivot hesder*, nor even all *mekhinot*, are cut of one cloth. Each possesses its own individual style and atmosphere, not least where attitudes towards military service are concerned.[50]

As much frequently becomes apparent when, towards the end of their first year of conscript service, suitably qualified troops are invited by their military commanders to undertake officer's training – a procedure that requires them to contract for an additional year of army service. The *mekhinot* invariably encourage their graduates to take this first step up the ladder of the military hierarchy. Indeed, a high national-religious profile amongst the IDF's junior officers – at least – has always been integral to the entire ethos that the *mekhinot* espouse. But such is not the case where the *yeshivot hesder* are concerned. As a rule (necessarily, provision must be made for differences of nuance), their institutional views of military service are far less enthusiastic and their emphasis on study as an end in itself far more pronounced.[51] Indeed, in order to attend an officer's training course, registered *hesder* conscripts must attain written permission to do so from their *rosh yeshivah*, whose compliance is by no means automatic. Even then, they have to undertake to add a further year of study to their original time-table. In other words, *hesder* students who decide to become officers incur a set of *initial*, (i.e. pre-reserve) combined obligations that stretch over a period of six years – throughout which time their only income will be the pocket money supplied by the IDF to conscript troops on active service.

It speaks volumes for the commitment of *hesder* students to their dual responsibilities that, undeterred by such costs, each year some three to four dozen do register for the IDF's junior officers' courses, on completion of which they return to their *yeshivot* for another year or two of study.[52] Where available, however, the statistics also tell a more complex tale. The appeal of the *hesder* combination of service and study, they suggest, is far from universal. In recent years, it has become limited almost entirely to graduates of *yeshivah* high-schools, who for the most part tend to come from middle and upper middle-class homes – and even there encompasses less than 30% of the annual cohort. Taken as a whole, almost half of the male graduates of Israel's national-religious high schools (together numbering some 6,000) now declare their intention of enlisting in the IDF in the regular way. Some 20% will enroll in *mekhinot kedam tzeva'iyot* and only 18.2% in *yeshivot hesder* (of whom, to judge by past experience, roughly a quarter will drop out of the yeshiva after their first year of study). The remaining 10%, most of whom also come from middle-class homes, declare their intention of embarking on a more protracted course of studies in a *yeshivah gevohah*, some in avowedly *haredi* institutions.[53]

What these figures suggest is that, subject to pressure both to study and perform military service, most young national-religious conscripts tend to think in "either-or" terms. Hence, tracks that appear to express a clear preference for one or another of the two "greedy institutions," the military and the academy, are preferred to those that, correctly or not, are thought to seek to straddle both. In their different ways, both the *mekhinot* and the *yeshivot gevohot* appear to fall into the former category. The *mekhinot* project the image of institutions whose prime purpose is not study at all, but the development of skills and attributes that will enable its graduates to become better soldiers.[54] The "Zionist" *yeshivot gevohot*, on the other hand, satisfy the tendencies of some elements within the national-religious community to adopt a more *haredi* life-style, in which total devotion to scholarship is *de rigueur*.[55] (In a more latent sense, perhaps, they also respond to a long-standing fear that the demands of military service could ultimately prevent national-religious Orthodoxy from producing scholars of the caliber that it needs and deserves.)[56] Under these circumstances, *hesder* in effect becomes the domain solely of those young men who feel capable of charting a course between these two poles.

CONCLUSIONS

Thus to outline the dilemmas that continue to challenge religiously orthodox troops in the IDF is not, of course, to deny the enormity of their efforts to resolve them. Together with their mentors and teachers, individual servicemen and women are indeed endeavoring in several ways to harmonize their theological beliefs with their patriotic duties. The products of those efforts – both institutional and intellectual – in many respects deserve to be considered some of the most significant developments in the entire world of contemporary modern Orthodoxy.

NOTES

Thanks are due to participants at the 16th Orthodox Forum, held in 2004, for comments on an oral version of this paper. Research was supported by THE ISRAEL SCIENCE FOUNDATION (grant No. 157/04).

1. Stuart A. Cohen, "Israel's Defense Force: From a 'People's Army' to a 'Professional Force,'" *Armed Forces & Society*, 21 (1995): 237–254.

2. It has been estimated that only three of every five potential reservists has since 2000 been summonsed to any service whatsoever, and that 80% of the entire burden of duty is now borne by just 30% of the available reserve complement (itself only 53% of the entire male Jewish population). See: Major-Gen. Gil Regev (CO IDF Personnel Branch), in *A People's Army? Reserve Duty in Israel* (Hebrew: Jerusalem: The Israel Institute for Democracy, 2002), pp. 55–59.

3. *The Contract Between the IDF and Israeli Society: Conscript Service* (Hebrew: Jerusalem; The Israel Institute for Democracy, 2002), pp. 12–13. Amongst males, much of the rise in the number of exemptions reflects the recent exponential growth in the number *haredim* now being excused on the grounds that *Toratam umanutam*. Moreover, the present number in this category (almost 40,000) seems set to grow still further, since the percentage of youngsters attending *haredi* schools rose from 6.6% in 1960 to some 15% in 2000.

4. Reuven Gal, "Motivation to serve in the IDF in the mirror of time," *Strategic Survey*, 2/3 (Dec. 1999): 11–15.

5. This consideration plays an especially important role in the "propensity to service" of new immigrants from Ethiopia and the former USSR, who now comprise 15% of the IDF's conscript intake.

6. *Ha-Aretz*, December 5, 2003, p. A3. Responses to summonses for reserve duty were likewise high, and frequently reached 100%.

7. Yaron Ezrachi and Reuven Gal, *General Perceptions and Attitudes of Israeli High-School Students Regarding the Peace Process, Security and Social Issues* (Hebrew: 2 vols. Zikhron Yaakov, 1995).

8. Yagil Levy, *A Different Army for Israel: Materialistic Militarism in Israel* (Hebrew: Tel Aviv, Yediot Aharonot, 2003).

9. "*Almot*" in a Mine-Field: An Interview with Yifat Sela," *Amudim* (Hebrew), no. 674 (summer 2003): 22–25.

10. As is evident from the tone that pervades Levy (above n.8).

11. Jewish chaplains in non-Jewish armies still await their historian. For one pioneering effort, see Albert Isaac Slomovitz, *The Fighting Rabbis: Jewish Military Chaplains*

and American History (New York: New York University Press, 1998). For a full discussion of the dilemmas that military service in non-Jewish armies posed for Orthodox Jews in the diaspora see Judith Bleich, "Military Service: Ambivalence and Contradiction," paper presented to the 16th Orthodox Forum, New York, March 2004 (in this volume).

12. R. Goren's principal writings on military-related topics are: *Meishiv Milhamah* (3 vols. Jerusalem, 1983–1993) and *Sefer Torat Ha-Medinah* (Jerusalem, 1996). Many of his early halakhic rulings in the IDF were collated in Capt. Mordechai Friedlander (ed.), *Kovetz Piskei Hilkhot Tzava ve-Dinim le-Hayal* (2 vols., IDF Chief Rabbinate, 1961). For an interim appreciation see: Arye Edrei, "Divine Spirit and Physical Power: Rabbi Shlomo Goren and the Military Ethic of the Israel Defense Forces," *Theoretical Inquiries in Law*, 7 (2005), 255–297.

13. Benny Michaelson, "*Ha-Rabbanut ha-Tzeva'it*," in: *The IDF and its Arms*, Vol. 16 (Hebrew: eds. I. Kfir and Y. Erez; Tel Aviv: Revivim, 1982), pp. 83–132. The IDF *Rabbanut* is also responsible for providing religious services to non-Jewish IDF servicemen, whose numbers have very much increased as a result of the large waves of immigration from both Ethiopia and the former USSR during the 1990s. At present some 8–9,000 new immigrant soldiers are registered as non-Jewish. To these must be added the larger complement of Druze troops, and some 5,000 servicemen drawn from Israel's Arab Christian minority.

14. Charles S. Liebman and Eliezer Don-Yehiyeh, *Civil Religion in Israel: Traditional Religion and Political Culture in the Jewish State* (Berkley: Univ. of California Press, 1983).

15. For the situation in the Conservative and Reform movements in the U.S.A. see, respectively: *Proceedings of the Rabbinical Assembly* 8 (1941–1944), pp. 34–35, and *Responsa in War Time* (New York: National Jewish Welfare Board, 1947), most of which was written by Solomon Freehof.

16. *Sefer Mahaneh Yisrael* was re-printed by the Nehardea Publishing Company of Jerusalem in 1941, primarily for the benefit of the *Yishuv*'s servicemen then drafted into in the Jewish Brigade. It also formed the basis for R. Moses M. Yoshor's *Israel in the Ranks: A Religious Guide to Faith and Practice for the Jewish Soldier* (Yeshivat Chofetz Chaim: New York, 1943) – although this work focused on ethical teachings and has nothing to say on practical *halakhah*. Hertz's *A Book of Jewish Thoughts* was reprinted several times during World War II both in Britain and the U.S.A. (e.g., New York: Jewish Welfare Board, 1943).

17. E.g. R. Yitzchak Kaufman, *Ha-Tzava Ka-Halakhah: Hilkhot Milhamah ve-Tzava* (Jerusalem, Kol Mevaser, 1994). Especially popular are the paperback manuals of instruction, conveniently printed in editions that can easily fit into a battledress pocket. See, e.g., R. Shlomo Min-Hahar, *Dinei Tzava u-Milhamah* (1st edition, 1972); and R. Zechariah Ben-Shlomo, *Nohal Ahid* (Sha'alavim, 1997).

18. Particularly noteworthy in this respect is *Tehumin*, published annually since 1980 by the *Tzomet* institute at Alon Shevut, which regularly contains a section of articles on "Security and Army." Considerable material is also to be found in the leaflets,

newsletters and journals produced by individual *yeshivot hesder*, specifically targeted at students on active service.

19. E.g., R. Eliezer Shenwald ed., *Sefer Harel* (sub-titled: Israeli Militarism from a Torah
Perspective; Chispin, 2000); Yehiel Rozensohn & R. Azriah Ariel eds., *Be-Orekha
Nireh Or* (A Collection of Articles on Chanukah in Memory of Lt. Dani Cohen,
2003).

20. E.g., http://www.moreshet.co.il and http://www.kippah.co.il. Amongst the authors
of military-related responsa that retain a more traditional format, R. Shlomo
Aviner has been particularly prolific, publishing: *Am ke-Lavie* (1983); *Shut Tzni'ut*
(1999); *Me-Hayyil le-Hayyil* (2 vols., 1999); and *Al Diglo* (2000). See also R.
Nachum Rabinovitch, *Melumedei Milhamah* (Yeshivat Hesder "Birkat Mosheh,"
Ma'aleh Adumim, 1994); R. Avi Rontski, *Halikhot Tzava* (Yeshivat Ateret Kohanim,
Jerusalem, 1994) and *Ke-Hitzim be-Yad Gibbor* (3 vols. so far, 1996–2003); R. Mishael
Rubin, *Ha-Morim ba-Keshet* (Hebron, the Institute for Settlement Rabbis, 1998);
and R. Eyal Mosheh Krim, *Kishrei Milhamah* (2 vols., Jerusalem, The Institute for
the Study of Israel's Campaigns, 2001).

21. Amiah Lieblich, *Transition to Adulthood during Military Service: The Israeli Case*
(SUNY Press: Albany, NY, 1989).

22. Mordechai Bar-Lev, *Bimshokh ha-Yovel* (Tel Aviv: Mizrahi, 1989).

23. Avraham Laslo and Yisrael Rich, *Survey of 12th grade students in national-religious
high schools – 5759: Research Report* (Bar-Ilan University: School of Education, Feb.
2001), p. 44. Compare with the lower figures in: Avraham Laslo and Mordechai
Bar-Lev, *The religious world of graduates of national-religious schools* (Bar-Ilan
University: School of Education, Nov. 1993).

24. Yaakov Levi and Aaron Furstein, "It's not easy to be a Religious Soldier," *Zera'im*, 8
(July 1995), pp. 8–9. Similar sentiments in: Yehoram Shai, "To Expand and Deepen,"
Amudim, 43/5 (March 1995):142–3.

25. For a full discussion: Asher Cohen and Baruch Susser, *Israel and the Politics of Jewish
Identity: The Secular-Religious Impasse* (Baltimore: Johns Hopkins University Press,
2000).

26. Ze'ev Drori, *Between Faith and Military Service: The Haredi Nahal Battalion*
(Jerusalem: The Floersheimer Institute for Policy Studies, 2005).

27. *Together: Meeting non-religious youth* (by Naham Ilan and Sima Greenbaum); *Going
to the Army – halakhah and military service* (by R. Itamar Chaikin); *Belief in the
Army – Religious Belief and Military Service* (by Yaron Tenah).

28. A new edition of this essay, first published in 1906, has been annotated by R.
Binyamin Elon and was issued by Sifriyat Beit El in 1991.

29. It would be incorrect to exaggerate the binary nature of these alternatives. Thus,
most *hesder yeshivot*, too, provide their students with short prepatory courses ("fortification") prior to their enlistment. Many *mekhinah* graduates tend to gravitate
towards the same units, thereby displaying traces of "segregation."

30. For detailed illustrations see Stuart A. Cohen, "From Integration to Segregation: The
Role of Religion in the IDF," *Armed Forces & Society*, 25 (3), spring 1999: 387–406.

31. E. g., Ramban's commentary to Deut. 23:10, as cited in, for instance, R. Aharon Lichtenstein, "This is the Law of the Hesder" (Hebrew), in *Darkah shel Yeshivah* (Yeshivat Har-Etziyon, 1999), p. 20, and R. Shlomo Rozenfeld, "Distribution of Booty and Loot in Contemporary Wars," *Tehumin*, 23 (2003), p. 57.

32. One of the first military trials in IDF history concerned two religiously observant cooks who refused to prepare a hot meal on *Shabbat*. Zahava Ostfeld, *Tzava Nolad* (Tel Aviv, Ministry of Defense, 1994), vol. 1, p. 748.

33. Mosheh Binyamin & Yair Cohen (eds.), *Index to Army Halakhot* (Hebrew: Atzmona, The Pre-Conscription Mekhinah Otzem, 2000).

34. On the latter two issues see, respectively, *Ha-Aretz* 19 June 2002, A8 and the exchange between rabbis Yisrael Rozen and Yoel Bin-Nun in *Ha-Tzofeh*, 26 March 2004 B11.

35. See, for example, the discussions in: Patrick Mileham, "Military Virtues 1: The Right to be Different?" (on the British army) *Defense Analysis* 14/2 (1998):171–192; and (on U.S. forces) David Kellog, "Guerilla Warfare: When Taking Care of Your Men leads to War Crimes" (1997) http://www.usafa.af.mil.jscope/JSCOPE97/Kellog97.htm and Maj. Michael Carlino, "Ethical Education at the Unit Level" (2000), p. 6, http://www.usafa.af.mil/jscope/JSCOPE00/Carlino00.html.

36. Tamar Liebes and Shoshana Blum-Kulka, "Managing a Moral Dilemma: Israeli Soldiers and the Intifada," *Armed Forces & Society*, 27 (1994):45–68. Significantly, the IDF's own Code of Ethics. (http://www.idf.il/hebrew/doctrine), refers to the "tradition of the Jewish people throughout the ages" as only one amongst its four main sources of inspiration.

37. For earlier discussions of such issues see Yaakov Blidstein, "The Treatment of Hostile Civilian Populations: The Contemporary Halakhic Discussion in Israel," *Israel Studies* 1 (1996):27–44 and idem, "The State and the Legitimate Use of Force and Coercion in Modern Halakhic Thought," *Studies in Contemporary Jewry*, XVII (2002):3–22. Also Yitzchak Blau, "Ploughshares into Swords: Contemporary Religious Zionists and Moral Constraints," *Tradition* 34/4 (winter 2000): 38–60 and Ehud Luz, *Power, Morality and Jewish Identity* (Hebrew: Magnes Press, Jerusalem, 1998), pp. 383–8.

38. E.g. remarks by the former Judge Advocate-General, Major-General Menachem Finkelstein, at the 6th meeting of the Army-Society Project, Jerusalem, 13 January 2003 in *Morals, Ethics and Law in Combat* (Hebrew: Jerusalem: The Israel Democracy Institute, 2003). The example is especially interesting since Finkelstein is himself an Orthodox Jew, who holds a doctorate in Jewish law.

39. Thus, a recent course planned to train 100 IDF rabbis was under-subscribed. Weiss attributes this situation to the fact that neither the *yeshivot hesder* nor the *mekhinot* encourage their pupils to enter the IDF Rabbinate. Interview, *Ha-Tzofeh*, 11 April 2003, 6.

40. Uri Ben-Eliezer, "Do Generals Rule Israel?," (Hebrew) in: Hannah Herzog, ed. *Hevra Bitmurah* (Tel Aviv: Ramot, 2000), pp. 235–269. Dual loyalty is also a motif in the popular Israeli film "The Hesder" (2000).

41. E.g., the manifesto issued by the "Union of Rabbis on behalf of the People of Israel and the Land of Israel," published in *Gilyon Rabanei Yesha*, Tammuz 5795 (summer 1995), p.1. Of the 15 signatories to this document, three were principals of *yeshivot hesder* and two others taught in institutions of that name. Others, however, vigorously opposed the statement. See, e.g., R. Yoel Bin-Nun, "The manifesto and the Law," *Ha-Tzofeh*, 28 July 1995 B:5 and R. Yehudah Amital, "A Political Opinion in Halakhic Camouflage" (Hebrew), *Meimad*, 5 (September 1995):3–8.

42. For the most famous, see the interview with Rabbi Avraham Shapira in *Ba-Sheva* (Hebrew-language right-wing religious daily), 15 October 2004, p.1

43. Report in *Ha-Aretz*, 8 September 2005, A12.

44. E.g., R. Shlomo Aviner, *Be-Ahavah u-ve-Emunah* (Hebrew weekly), 429 (October 2004), p. 12; R. Yuval Sherlow, *Ha-Aretz*, 26 September 2004, p. B1; R. Aharon Lichtenstein, *Ha-Aretz*, 19 July 2005, B3–4; R. Yoel Bin-Nun, *Ha-Tzofeh*, 12 August 2005, B3 and two further letters by R. Lichtenstein (dated September 2005) available at: http://www.etzion.org.il/hitnatkut/hitnatkut.htm.

45. Capt. Hadas Minka-Braun, "To Be an Example," *Bein ha-Zirot* (Hebrew: journal of the IDF Behavioral Science Unit), 4, April 2006, pp. 36–49.

46. Lewis Coser, *Greedy Institutions: Patterns of Undivided Attention* (New York: Free Press, 1974), p. 4.

47. For numerous citations to this effect see: Charles Selengut, "By Torah Alone: Yeshivah Fundamentalism in Jewish Life," in: *Accounting for Fundamentalisms* (eds. M.E. Martin and R. Scott Appleby; Chicago: Chicago University Press, 1994), pp. 236–263. In general, I. Sivan and K. Kaplan (eds), *Haredim Yisraeliyim* (Tel Aviv: Ha-Kibutz Ha-Me'uchad, 2003).

48. E.g., R. Aharon Lichtenstein (above n. 31); R. Eliezer Shenwald, "Hesder le-Khathilah," *Sefer Harel* (above n. 19), pp. 322–369. For the ideological and historical roots, see Elie Holzer, "Attitudes to the Use of Military Force in Ideological Currents of Religious Zionism," paper presented to the 16th Orthodox Forum, New York, March 2004 (in this volume).

49. The *hesder* and *mekhinah* programs, although the most popular, are not the only such options. There also exist alternatives, known as *shiluv* and *gahelet*, which likewise offer combinations of service and study. These have been analyzed by my student Ms. Elisheva Rosman-Stollman in *Iyunim Bitkumat Yisrael*, vol. 10 (Be'er-Sheva, 2000): 259–297.

50. For an interesting (albeit somewhat idiosyncratic) depiction of the increasing variety of *yeshivot* hesder, see: R. Shimon. G. Rozenberg (Shagar), *Kelim Shevurim*: (Efrat: Yeshivat Siach Yitzchak, 2003), esp. pp. 113–120.

51. Note, however, the suggestions for reform in: R. Mordechai Gudman, "Towards a Renewal of the Structure of the *Yeshivot Hesder*" (Hebrew), *Tzohar* 8 (Autumn 1992), pp. 151–170

52. By way of contrast, as many as 30% of *mekhinot* graduates (i.e., some 300 soldiers per year) now register for officers' training. See report by Amos Harel in *Ha-Aretz*, 11 December 2003, A1.

53. Laslo and Ritch, 2001 (above n. 23), p. 80. For earlier years see: Yaakov Hadany, "From Alternative Purposes to Reciprocal Purposes," *Mayim Mi-Dalyo*, 11 (2000): 61–66.

54. And for that reason, are frequently accused of appealing mainly to non-scholastic types. See Hanoch Daum, "Pre-Military Summer Camps," *Nekudah* (monthly journal of settlers in Judea, Samaria and Gaza Strip), 216 (July 1998):48–9 and the inverted compliments in R. Shlomo Aviner, "Hymn to a Mekhinist," *Be-Ahavah u-ve-Emunah*, 424 (Sep. 2003), p. 8.

55. On this tendency, sometimes known as *Hardal* (= *haredi-dati-le'umi*), and more recently still as *Habakuk* (=*Habad+Breslav+Kook* [+ *Carlebach*]), see: Yair Sheleg, *The New Religious Jews: Recent Developments among Observant Jews in Israel* (Hebrew: Jerusalem, Keter, 2000), pp. 249–263.

56. This issue generated some contention in the 1960s and 1970s, and continued to receive attention in the 1980s. See R. Zalman Melamed, "Torah Giants – That is the National Need," *Tehumin*, 7 (1986): 330–334.

Attitudes Towards the Use of Military Force in Ideological Currents of Religious Zionism

Elie Holzer

INTRODUCTION

The very possibility that the Jewish people, as a national-political entity, would fight its own wars was thought for many generations unrealistic and beyond the bounds of history. For religious Jews, fighting wars seemed little more than a remembrance of things past, perhaps also to be associated with a utopian, messianic future. There were two different varieties of this utopian dream: a nationalistic-messianic variety, essentially a reconstruction of ancient times, when God and/or Israel fought the nations; and a universal, eschatological variety, in which "nation shall not take up sword against nation" – the

Jewish people and the site of the Temple would be a destination for pilgrims of all nations.[1]

However, the historical developments of the twentieth century transplanted the idea of a fighting Jewish army from its utopian context into historical reality. How was this new reality internalized by religious ideology?

This question should, I believe, be applied over a wider canvas: Nationalist-Zionist ideology profoundly transformed the ethos of passivity once typical of observant Jews, as solution of the existential problems of the Jewish people demanded a return to political activism. In time, the collective's ability – sometimes also need – to resort to military power became one of the most extreme expressions of this activist ethos. Religious Zionism, by definition, internalized the call for political activism.[2] Its ideology combined several different outlooks, all of which grew out of a commitment both to the new reality (the emergence of the secular Jewish nationalism and the establishment of the State of Israel) and to the normative sources of Judaism as they interpreted them. For a religious outlook that identifies with the Jewish-nationalist movement, what normative imperative is implied by nationalism, and how does it relate to religious norms? How can the normative imperatives of religion be reconciled with the emergence of secular Jewish nationalism, and how do these imperatives relate to physical, military activism and to possible confrontation with other nations? In other words, what happens to a religious outlook – committed to ideas of a religious, ethical mission, a glorious national and military past, a present typified by political and military passivity, a messianic future which seems violent on the one hand but pacifistic and harmonious on the other – when it encounters a nationalism that advocates a return to political and perhaps even military activism? Are these two normative systems seen as contradictory, complementary, identical, or perhaps just neutral? And what were the positions of religious-Zionist thinkers vis-à-vis the *possibility* of a return to military activism and, consequently, vis-à-vis the very phenomenon of the use of military force as a collective?

This article will examine these questions on a theoretical and a typological level.[3] Three ideological models, exemplified by three thinkers whose views were formed in the early days of Zionism, will be described. In addition, the processes that developed in each of the models, in light of the development of a violent political reality and the existence of a Jewish state embroiled in warfare, will be identified.

In the *harmonistic-dialectical* model it will be shown how, by endowing Jewish nationalism with a spiritual, teleological, and messianic meaning, R. Abraham Isaac Kook (1865–1935) sought to absorb Jewish nationalism and the implied activism into his religious thought. It will be seen that this is a pattern of "redemptive interpretation." Thus, for example, this line of thought seeks to ascribe religious significance to expressions of activism such as the return to agricultural labor, which R. Kook considered a harbinger of the "Manifest Redemption." In his vision, the nation of Israel would return to the political and historical stage without need of any military action. Normatively speaking, this vision would have contradicted both the messianic mission entrusted to the Jewish people and the prohibition of the use of force to which it was committed by the so-called "Three Oaths."

My thesis is that the line adopted by R. Kook's ideological heirs expresses, in a paradoxical way, a reversal of positions while maintaining a continuity of ideas. R. Tzvi Yehudah Kook and his pupils viewed the phenomenon of military activism and Israel's wars through the lenses of the redemptive interpretation, whose roots lay in R. Abraham Kook's writings. However, R. Tzvi Yehudah's ideological adherence to his father's thought turned several of its premises on their heads: While for the elder R. Kook the achievement of national revival without force was a hallmark of redemption, his son and the latter's pupils interpreted Israel's renewed involvement in military affairs and wars as yet another sign of ongoing, visible redemption. In their view, military activism had also become an expression of the "Manifest Redemption" (*ha-ketz ha-megulleh*) and the renaissance of the "Uniqueness of Israel" (*segullat Yisrael*; see below). It was no longer the messianic dialectic of the contrast between the nations engaged in war and the Jewish people with its alternative culture; instead, the messianic dialectic existed within the Jewish people itself. It would first have to make war against the opponents of the culture that it represented; only then would it be able harmoniously to fulfill its messianic function. Furthermore, R. Kook senior's perception no longer justified the actions of the secular Jew alone; it also encompassed specific actions that raised ethical questions. Put differently: The harmonistic language had internalized a new element – the use of force.

One can therefore point to a gradual but unmistakable process of radicalization, a progress from the interpretation of military renaissance and wars as having spiritual meaning, to a call for purposeful military activity. In this model, religious thought seeks to blur the distinctions between the normativeness of nationalism and the normativeness of religion, attributing both to the same source. In R. Kook senior's thought, this argument underlies the assumption that there will be no need for military activity. For his successors, however, it made military activity itself an integral part of the overall religious ideal.

The roots of the *realistic-ethical* model lie in the thought of R. Isaac Jacob Reines (1839–1915). Underlying his approach is a concern for the existential, real needs of the Jewish people, combined with the hope for its spiritual renaissance. In R. Reines' view, there are two guiding principles: (a) the need to tackle problems that arise in an unredeemed world conditioned by political interests; (b) the need for adherence to the religious-ethical principles to which Jews are committed, as expressed in the culture of the Book of which they are the bearers, as against the culture of the Sword that characterizes the rest of the world. This conception makes a clear distinction between the need for political activism, on the one hand, and the prohibition of political activity directed into messianic channels, on the other. Inherent in this model is a "Kantian" halakhic approach, according to which reality must be evaluated and judged in accordance with primary ethical principles. Religious thought should not assimilate new phenomena at any cost, but rather examine any new phenomenon and measure it against those basic imperatives.

In light of a changing reality, R. Reines' principles evolved into positions that supported the use of force in self-defense, but voiced sharp religious-ethical criticism of belligerent radicalism or secularization of the use of force. The use of force was seen as permitted only if dictated by circumstances, not as part of the spiritual and national revival of the Jewish people. In that context, the activist ethos of Zionist nationalism cannot be seen as a normative competitor of the Jewish religion, as long as it confines itself, as R. Reines writes, to "safe measures which are legitimate according to the laws of Judaism."[4] R. Reines himself was implying that military action *per se* is forbidden, whereas his successors understood such statements to refer to the use of force for purposes other than self-defense. In other words, in this case, religion would act as a barrier against the possible belligerent tendencies awakened by nationalism, though it would not criticize nationalist-political ideology *per se*.

Our third model is the *antithetical-critical* model, whose roots lie in the thought of R. Aharon Shmuel Tamares (1869–1931). In this model, the concept of "Torah" becomes a critic of nationalist-political ideology when the latter becomes total and radical. Such a position of nationalist-political ideology is liable to lead to moral corruption, the worship of physical force, and an inevitable clash with the religious-ethical mission of the Jewish people. It tramples the status of the individual and in so doing violates the religious-moral imperative (according to R. Tamares and R. Amiel) or the commandment of divine worship (according to Yeshayahu Leibowitz); hence the necessity of criticism.

There is a tension in the thought of R. Tamares and R. Amiel between their desire for the existence of an independent Jewish polity and their awareness that the Jewish people evolved a universal outlook and ethical sensitivity because of its divorce from political life. If so, given the ambitions of political Zionism, religion must become a focus of religious-ethical criticism, and care must be taken lest the new activist ethos dominate the ethical sensitivity and norms that have evolved in the Jewish people.

Both R. Tamares and R. Amiel consider the "Torah" concept first and foremost as a religious-ethical ethos, whereas Leibowitz sees it as a religious law, defining the essence of divine worship.

Nevertheless, Leibowitz may also be counted among the representatives of the antithetical-critical approach, since the concept of "Torah" plays a similar role for all three thinkers, as a transcendental factor seeking to challenge the totality of the nationalist-political imperative. Like R. Tamares and R. Amiel, Leibowitz expresses concern primarily for the dangerous, immoral implications of that imperative. In this model, therefore, religion not only has a restraining effect on the possible belligerent tendencies of the Zionist enterprise, but it also seeks to identify such tendencies, which it deems to be inherent in the ideology of political nationalism, and to warn against them.

1. THE DIALECTIC-HARMONISTIC MODEL: R. ABRAHAM ISAAC KOOK AND HIS IDEOLOGICAL HEIRS

It was R. Abraham Isaac Kook, more than any other thinker, who incorporated political and historical activism into the framework of a comprehensive religious outlook, as an integral component of his messianic philosophy.[5] In most of the subjects that he deals with, R. Kook adopts a dialectical approach that enables him to reconcile contrasts and contradictory phenomena, as for example in his attitude to secular Zionism. That is not the case, however, in regard to the use of force. For R. Kook, national redemption must precede universal redemption. The essence of the messianic goal, in his view, is the Torah state and the social life of the Jewish people, which will become a model for the rest of the world. Such a position necessarily implies the centrality of the *harmonious* influence of the Jewish people on the nations in R. Kook's messianic vision. This is evident from his general descriptions of the messianic goal, which do not provide for a confrontation between Israel and the nations of the world, and from the normative imperatives imposed on the Jewish people in the course of the realization of the messianic goal, as it assembles in its particularistic state. In addition, R. Kook was encouraged in his harmonistic outlook by the events of the First World War and by the great cultural upheavals taking place among the European nations.

As a rule, the Jewish people has an exclusive task to perform in a process aimed at the restitution (*tikkun*) of Creation in general. This ideal is expressed in observance of the precepts of the Torah,[6] on its exoteric and esoteric levels, as a result of which spiritual ideals are realized in human life, individual as well as collective. Thus, political organization is a necessary condition for achievement of that task.[7]

The quest for universal influence is an essential part of the process of national ingathering in the framework of a state. This quest, in fact, possesses metaphysical status within the national idea itself: it is inscribed, as it were, in the essence of the uniqueness of the Jewish people. It is part of the divine presence in the world and the basis for the Jewish nation's desire to achieve its goal: "We must invest the permanence of our position in the Land of Israel with divine, holy, content…[That content] will surely be the pillar and fortress of future *world peace*."[8]

Clearly, then, R. Kook was in favor of a return to political life in order to serve as a moral and spiritual model.[9] The important question here is, what are the attitudes and modes of influence that the Jewish people is supposed to establish, according to R. Kook, while working toward that messianic goal? In other words, are the ideas we have been considering relevant only to a far-off messianic age, or did R. Kook expect – perhaps even demand – that this be the defining principle of the political organization from its beginnings? Can a distinction be made in R. Kook's thought between the harmonious conditions that will reign during the distant messianic era, and the non-harmonious relationships existing at the start of the historical process that will culminate in the messianic goal?

It is clear from the following passage, for example, that the Jewish religion will not be disseminated by the use of force:

> Very different is the spirit of the Lord that rests on Israel, which is destined to be a light unto the world: It does not possess the ability to spread by an encounter of conflict; for we have not been commanded to raise the sword of war and to invoke the Lord's name to nations who know Him not. Only when the name of Israel grows great, and many nations witness the

sacred glory and magnificence and the universal peace that will
emerge from the glory of such sublime ideas, with which the
sanctity of Israel is imbued – [only then,] without an encounter
of conflict, without overpowering, will they hasten to seek the
Lord God of Israel.[10]

In other words: The moral limitation of activism is an inevitable
consequence of the desire to exert influence through harmony.[11] As a
rule, when discussing the messianic era, R. Kook does not explicitly
distinguish between the use of force in self-defense or for any other
purpose. The passage just quoted implies that the use of force cannot
possibly be a means for achievement of the messianic goal.

Furthermore, the age of exile and non-participation in political
and military life has also had a beneficial effect, in that the Jewish
people acquired the quality of moral sensitivity and willingness.[12]
Now, in the messianic age, the Jewish people is called upon to realize this moral principle in practice, in social and political life. It
is not surprising, therefore, that the moral principle received such
prominence in R. Kook's discussion of the harmonious nature of
the messianic vision.

Alongside *descriptive* statements about the harmonious dimension of the messianic age, one also finds statements of a *normative*
nature, in which R. Kook demarcates the return to political activism,
excluding the use of military force. An obvious example of this is
his new interpretation of the Midrash of the "Three Oaths" (a. that
the nation not ascend "on the wall" [*ba-homah:* interpreted by Rashi
to mean ascending to the land of Israel by force]; b. that it not rebel
against the nations of the world; c. that it not attempt to "force the
End" by attempting to bring the Messiah before the proper time).[13]
In his view, the oaths impose a moral restriction on the Jewish
people, forbidding the use of military force even in the messianic
era. R. Kook thus converts the three oaths from a divine decree to
a religious-ethical imperative, thereby also expanding their scope.
They are no longer exclusively a decree of exile, but also a decree of
redemption. The oaths restrict messianic activism, confining it to
non-belligerent modes of operation.

R. Kook also found support for his position in historical events, in particular the First World War. Somewhat paradoxically, he believed that those terrible events corroborated his harmonious thesis, whose realization was imminent. The conflict, for him, became a focus of messianic hopes. The world war represented the eradication of a religiously and morally corrupt culture and the emergence of signs that a cultural alternative would be created by the Jewish people. Since R. Kook's historiosophy is essentially teleological, it proposes its own "theodicy" in relation to such horrendous phenomena as war. If human history is the embodiment of a process of the advance and evolution of Creation, an expression of divine providence, it is not surprising that even in wars "one must accept the sublime content of the Lord's light that reveals itself in marvelous action, in particular in the events of these wars." Therefore, "when there is a great war in the world, a messianic power awakens. The time of pruning has come, the pruning of tyrants, the wicked will be eradicated from the world and the world will become fragrant, and the voice of the turtledove will be heard in our land."[14] In R. Kook's system, historical events on the scale of a world war form part of a process in which the world, and together with it human history, achieve perfection. War plays a role in the evolving dialectic. It heralds the emergence of a religious-cultural alternative replacing the culture that the war has obliterated. The terrible bloodshed, R. Kook believes, demonstrates the failure of secularism, which cultivated the use of force in its cultural and educational system. In contrast, the culture represented by the Jewish people will rise on the ruins of secular culture.

This is a dialectical process, whose actors are the gentile nations, on the one hand, and the Jewish people, on the other. The very fact that the Jewish people did not participate in the war has prepared it and paved the way for its culture, for its return to the historical stage as the bearer of a political-cultural alternative: "a political and social state...at the pinnacle of human culture."[15] This idea confirms my thesis that, in R. Kook's thought, a military confrontation with the participation of the Jewish people is inconsistent with its national and spiritual renaissance as he understood it. It was not merely a question of theory; R. Kook demanded that the Zionist movement prepare itself in practical and diplomatic terms for the day after the war.[16]

To summarize the harmonious nature of R. Kook's messianic vision, let us consider a passage from his writings that clearly expresses my thesis up to this point. The passage in question clearly illustrates the way in which the two dimensions – messianic goal and historical reality – nourish each other and generate a unified perception. As far as one can tell from the context, it was written toward the end of the First World War, in the wake of the Balfour Declaration.

First, R. Kook creates a link between ethical self-perfection in the Diaspora and his harmonious messianic vision: "We abandoned world politics under duress but also out of an inner desire, until that joyous time should come when it will be possible to administer a state without evil and barbarism: that is the time for which we yearn."[17] The Jewish people will return to the historical arena after the world has experienced an ethical and cultural transformation, creating a world in which it will be able to concern itself with politics without bloodshed: "But the delay is a necessary delay, *our soul abhors* the appalling sins of statehood in evil times."

R. Kook is presumably referring here to the qualities in the unique quality (*segullah*) of Israel that make it abhor the use of force. He adds, "It is not fitting for Jacob to engage in statehood when it involves bloodshed, when it demands a talent for evil." Up to this point the author has been describing his vision. He now goes on to evaluate reality as he sees it:

> Lo, the time has come, and very soon the world will become fragrant and we shall be able to prepare ourselves, *for it is now possible for us* to administer our state on foundations of good, wisdom, integrity, and clear divine illumination.

Note the expression "the world will become fragrant' (Hebrew: *yitbassem*), alluding to the beginning of the redemption process, which figures in R. Kook's writings in a variety of contexts. One such context is his description, already quoted above, of the consequences of the First World War and the ensuing destruction of culture: "The wicked will be eradicated from the world and the world will *become fragrant*, and the voice of the turtledove will be heard in our land."[18]

How did R. Kook envisage his harmonious perception as part of the normative system of re-emergent Jewish nationalism? For example, was he not apprehensive that the national ideology might cultivate an ethos of physical force, which would be ethically questionable in light of his own messianic vision? Furthermore, as we know, R. Kook considered the national Jewish awakening as a sign, perhaps even as the first stage, of the realization of the redemptive process. If so, what guarantee did he have that secular Zionism, which had rebelled against the traditional ethos of Torah and *mitzvot*, would not breach the limits of permitted activity and become a violent nationalistic movement?

In the present context, there is no need to repeat what is known of R. Kook's attitude to secular Zionism.[19] On the other hand, in order to understand how his ideological successors developed the idea of the use of force, I think it necessary to describe the hermeneutical elements that informed his attitude to the phenomenon of secular Jewish nationalism.

Basically, R. Kook's approach to these questions has distinct Hegelian elements. This approach does not distinguish between the ideal and the real. Hegel took reality for granted, considering it as the true ethical essence. While not ignoring the phenomenon of evil, he argued that a philosopher should not criticize reality but justify it from the standpoint of speculative thought. All of reality, including the evil within it, is the embodiment of reason, and it is the task of the historiosopher to *reveal* this.[20]

a) Explanation of the phenomenon

For the speculative philosopher of history, writes Isaiah Berlin, the explanation of an event, that is, its description as it "truly is…is to discover its purpose." This is a typical teleological outlook, postulating "a category or framework in terms of which everything is, or should be, conceived and described."[21] Therefore, for any historical process, "the question 'why?' means 'in pursuit of what unalterable goal?'"[22] In other words: the interpretive approach finds expression in the *revealed explanation*. We call this approach "redemptive interpretation": The interpretation, as it were, *illuminates* a phenomenon that was previously shrouded in the darkness of incomprehension by placing it in a purposeful frame. Redemptive interpretation has two properties:

(1) *Totality*: It possesses a dimension of totality, in the sense that it sometimes seeks to explain the most minute details of certain events. It should be noted that R. Kook believed *a priori* that all such details combine to create a single, total meaning, though he never claimed to know how this was done; thus, for example, he considered the First World War as also being part of a comprehensive order.[23]

(2) Redemptive interpretation is *harmonistic*, in the sense that it tries as far as possible to explain all, even seemingly contradictory details, as being different parts of a single, comprehensive whole.[24] One might say that in R. Kook's system the *messianic concept* creates the teleological frame through which the phenomenon of secular Jewish nationalism should be interpreted:

> If the idea of our national renaissance were not so lofty and supreme, so that its content includes a comprehensive world-vision that encompasses the whole of humankind and existence as a whole, we could not connect to it at all with such internality of our soul.[25]

b) The reason for the phenomenon

In addition to the meaning ascribed to a phenomenon as an "explanation," R. Kook's redemptive interpretation also seeks to give it meaning by directing attention to the *reason* for the phenomenon. In other words, given some phenomenon, one can emphasize its invisible origin. In this sense, the concept of the *segullah*, a special property, uniqueness, inherent in the Jewish people, is seen as a reason for the phenomenon of Jewish nationalism.

R. Kook understands the essence of *segullah* in an ontological sense: it sets Israel apart from other nations.[26] He is thus led to a distinction that is highly significant in relation to all aspects of secular Zionism, namely, the distinction between actions that express the *segullah* and actions that derive from *behirah*, choice. The *segullah* is "the power of its inner sanctity, located in the nature of the soul by God's will, like the nature of any thing in reality, which cannot possibly change, for He spoke and it was."[27] That is, the weight of actions that derive from *segullah* does not depend on the awareness and consciousness of the actors, but on the "specific weight" or intrinsic value of those actions. On the other hand, actions that derive from choice depend on a person's intent and consciousness. Through this distinction, R. Kook creates a sacralization of the ethos and the enterprise that the nationalist ideology seeks to achieve: "The part of *segullah* is great, immeasurably so, *much greater and holier* than the part dependent on choice." It is the *segullah* that provides the *reason* for the normative activism inherent in the nationalist ideology. The normative imperatives of religion and nationality thus combine to form a single unit that is completely holy. Hence the realization of activism is also in holiness:

> The spirit of Israel is so linked with the spirit of God that even a person who says he does not need the spirit of the Lord at all, insofar as he says that he desires the spirit of Israel, the divine spirit inspires the innermost core of his desires, even against his will. A single individual may cut himself off from the source of life, but not the entire nation of the collectivity of Israel (*keneset Yisrael*); hence all the achievements of the nation, which it loves by virtue of its national spirit, are all informed by the spirit of God: Its land, its language, its existence in history, its customs...The spirit of the Lord and the spirit of Israel are one.[28]

In other words, the foundation of nationality – identification with it and devotion to it – is directly nourished by sanctity, and there cannot possibly be any theoretical contradiction between nationality and religious imperatives.[29]

The innovative element in this doctrine is R. Kook's espousal of the principle that actions are good when performed by good people; that is to say, by people who by their very essence are linked with the good. In other words, ontology precedes ethics or, at least, it is the principal criterion for the moral judgment of actions when they are performed by the collective or out of devotion to the collective.[30]

The two elements of redemptive interpretation underlying R. Kook's all-embracing conception are linked together in one expression: "In the footsteps of the messiah the power of *segullah* waxes great."[31] That is to say, the two elements nourish one another: The *segullah* will reveal its full force only in the messianic era; in fact, the very essence of the messianic era is its creation of strong expressions of *segullah* – and not necessarily through observance of the Torah and the *mitzvot*. This idea originates in the theory of opposites, which in turn derives from kabbalistic and Hasidic sources and may also be found in R. Kook's thought.[32]

Which field of secular Zionist activity did R. Kook consider as suitable for redemptive interpretation, as being an expression of *segullah* or of the complete realization of the Torah in accordance with the messianic goal? R. Kook applied the expression *ha-ketz ha-megulleh* (literally: "the manifest Redemption") to numerous aspects of Zionist activity. This expression, originating in the Talmud,[33] directs attention to concrete, historical realia, pointing out the signs of imminent redemption. It occurs frequently in R. Kook's writings, and note should be taken of the phenomena to which he applies it – they represent the beginnings of national and spiritual revival. The importance of these phenomena lies in their being an expression of the *internalization* of activism in R. Kook's comprehensive religious outlook. We shall see later that his successors appealed to this term in order to "sanctify" military activity. R. Kook himself uses the expression in several contexts. Thus, for example:

1. He applies it to the renewed settlement and flourishing agriculture of the Land of Israel: "Through *ha-ketz ha-megulleh* of the hills of Israel, which are beginning to yield branch and fruit for the holy nation, the returnees from Exile…"[34]
2. In connection with the Jews' re-entry into public life: "In a

period when the time of *ha-ketz ha-megulleh* has already arrived: To be seen in life, in restoring the content of its general
life to the abode of its life, to the Holy Land and its reconstruction."[35]

3. In relation to activity in all realms of life, in order to achieve
the universal messianic goal.

These examples all illustrate the sanctification of the new ethos.
R. Kook also stresses the connection between the sanctification of
the new ethos and the need to cultivate physical activity; however,
he does so very cautiously, warning that such activity should not
lead to a cult of physical rather than moral strength.[36]

R. Kook was aware of the moral dangers inherent in the modern nationalist ideology, which he feared might degenerate into
narrow ultra-nationalism. If not merged with religion, nationalism
is in danger of becoming distorted:

> Secular nationalism becomes defiled by the filth of hatred for
> one's fellow, which is a cover for many hidden evil spirits; but
> we shall succeed not by ejecting it from the generation's soul,
> but by vigorously striving to bring it to its supreme source, to
> link it with the original sanctity from which it flows.[37]

But while warning against the moral dangers lying in wait for
the Jewish people, R. Kook assumed *a priori* that Israel's *segullah*
would protect it from total moral corruption. In his view, *non-rec-
ognition* of this unique quality of the nation was liable to turn nationalism into hatred and bloodshed. There is an obvious tension in
his thought: On the one hand, he warns against turning nationalism
into ultra-nationalism; on the other, he argues that such a conversion
is not possible thanks to the inherent *segullah* of the Jewish people.
One might say that the metaphysical element creates a conception
that prevents Jewish nationalism from falling into total, anti-ethical
ultra-nationalism:

A covenant has been made with the entire collectivity of Israel that it will not become wholly impure; though impurity will be able to affect it, to create blemishes in it, *it will not be able to cut it off entirely from the sources of divine life.*[38]

In sum, R. Kook's concept of "the *segullah* of Israel" has become, to some extent, a shielding, protective concept. This tension in R. Kook's writings – the danger of moral corruption as against the reliance upon *segullah* to ensure that the corruption would not be absolute – does not seem to be present in the thought of his son, R. Tzvi Yehudah Kook, and his followers.

R. Kook thus envisions a harmonious relationship between the non-use of force by Israel in the messianic era, on the one hand, and awareness of the tension between "protective" and critical elements, on the other. This harmony, as we shall soon see, is no longer present in the doctrines of his son, R. Tzvi Yehudah Kook, and his disciples. They assign nationalism a merely protective role and, more importantly, consider a return to the use of force as one of the harbingers of redemption.[39]

We see, therefore, that the relation between R. Kook, on the one hand, and R. Tzvi Yehudah and his disciples, on the other, may be described as "reversal of positions" while at the same time maintaining continuity of ideas. In other words, while in comparison with the elder R. Kook, one finds his son espousing a different approach to the use of force and the phenomenon of war, the apparent reversal derives, paradoxically, from the son's adoption and application of principles inherent in the father's thought.

R. TZVI YEHUDAH KOOK AND HIS DISCIPLES:[40]
REVERSAL DESPITE IDEOLOGICAL CONTINUITY

Several studies of the thought of R. Tzvi Yehudah Kook and his disciples have argued that it was the victory of the Six-Day War that triggered the specifically religious attitudes to the use of force and the renewed involvement of the Jewish people in military activity.[41] However, a close reading of R. Tzvi Yehudah's book *Li-Netivot Yisrael*, which presents ideas written from the 1940s through 1967, clearly indicates that most of the supposedly late views had been advanced and had matured even before the Six-Day War. The war indeed magnified their impact and intensified their wording, but it did not create them.

Beginning in 1948, various articles by R. Tzvi Yehudah clearly indicate that the idea of military involvement had become part of a comprehensive religious outlook. For example, in 1948, two months *before* the declaration of the State of Israel, R. Tzvi Yehudah writes that Israel's strength at that time was merely an expression of a special divine property, a *segullah*, immanent in the nation. It was this property that formed the basis for the emergence of the new Jewish military organizations:

> Since then, from the "Eretz-Israel Hebrew Regiment" and the "American Jewish Legion" at the end of the previous World War, to "The Jewish Brigade" at the end of the Second World War, we have seen the gradual consolidation of the revealed might of the Lord our God, God of the Hosts of Israel, Who was named "[Lord of] Hosts" only after Israel (*Shavu'ot* 35b), Who gives us the power to succeed (Deut. 8:18) in the mighty deeds of our days, against all the nations who surround us, to appear before Him in Zion. Since then, the path of redemption has gradually been prepared by His awesome deeds and wonderful salvation.[42]

Not only is emphasis laid on the confrontation between Israel and the nations at the time of redemption – the confrontation is attributed to God's will. This is an expression of the immanent conception of the *segullah* of Israel. Through his redemptive interpretation, R. Kook senior had argued that the secular national rebellion embodies a divine revelation. This was a descriptive approach to the new reality, resulting in a comprehensive religious outlook in which what exists is transformed into what should be. The son was now expressing a similar approach in relation to the renewed military involvement of the Jewish people, which should be understood as part of the revival in preparation for the messianic era.

Like his father, R. Tzvi Yehudah also uses the messianic context in order to expand the meaning of the new phenomena. Hence anyone who participates in military action is required to understand the meaning of such actions in light of the great messianic vision:

> Let every person in the army of Israel know and remember his vital membership in the army of the Sovereign of the World, his historical and ideal role in the supreme mission of guiding the understanding of our generations.[43]

It was obvious to R. Tzvi Yehudah that a single thread of thought led from his father's views to his own. Thus, for example, R. Kook senior had been thrilled by the immigration of so many Jews to the Land of Israel, seeing it as a sign of imminent redemption. And now R. Tzvi Yehudah himself thought it quite natural to mention immigration to the Land of Israel in one breath with military activism. Both phenomena, immigration and military activism, represented the revelation of the *Shekhinah* in the era of Redemption.[44] In general, the idea of the *segullah*, the uniqueness of the nation, as a totalizing concept is a familiar element in modern nationalist ideologies as well. Thus, for example, Talmon distinguishes between two democratic ideologies: the liberal democratic school and the totalitarian democratic school. He defines totalitarian ideology as follows:

> It may be called political Messianism in the sense that it postulates a preordained, harmonious and perfect scheme of things, to which men are irresistibly driven, and at which they are bound to arrive. It recognizes ultimately only one plane of existence, the political.... Its political ideas are not a set of pragmatic precepts or a body of devices applicable to a special branch of human endeavour. They are an integral part of an all-embracing and coherent philosophy.[45]

Two central ideas of totalitarian ideology stand out in Talmon's analysis: It is comprehensive, "all-embracing," and it assigns priority to the active, political dimension of life. In the present context, I shall briefly summarize the dimensions of modern Jewish nationalism to which redemptive interpretation attributes a total dimension of sanctity. It will be seen that this position inevitably implies internalization of the idea of the use of military force as a basic value.

R. Tzvi Yehudah indeed demands an understanding of the general picture, without which the religious significance of the period and its events cannot possibly be grasped:

> We must accustom ourselves to see, to look, to encounter the Lord of the Universe in the march of generations. The world is not ownerless, nothing happens by chance. One's view of the world must be comprehensive: the divine history of Creation.[46]

One of the characteristic features of the harmonistic conception is its tendency to modify whatever seems to deviate from the overall picture in order to force it back into the mold. In other words, realities must sometimes be adapted and adjusted:

> ...seeing the unity, perfection, wholeness.... If there at times seems to be a blemish in the nation of Israel, that is because one is seeing only one particular thing or one isolated case, without seeing everything from a complete, all-inclusive, point of view.

In terms of the Aristotelian distinction, a "complete, all-inclusive" point of view is not content without form, but it acquires different dimensions of reality – in particular, as Talmon pointed out, the political dimension. In the "complete" view, the collective dimension, nationality is considered something total and wholly sacred.[47]

Of course, the real polity, the state, also assumes a status of sanctity:

> This is the state that Ben-Gurion declared some years ago before all the nations of the world. Ben-Gurion was an unbeliever, I knew him. In the religious sense he was an unbeliever. Nevertheless, "The Holy One, blessed be He, entrusts His

message to all." There is an order of souls, and he [Ben-Gurion] was merited to be the person who arranged our independence.[48]

We have already seen that in R. Kook senior's thought, any undertaking, any new ethos, any event resulting from the initiative of the nation or of the sovereign state of Israel, will be interpreted as an expression of "sanctity," both because it is undertaken by "the nation," which possesses the *segullah* that embodies God's presence in human history and because it is a meaningful element in the context of the ongoing process of redemption. Now, just as R. Abraham Kook tried to apply redemptive interpretation even to the small details of the First World War, his spiritual heirs seek to do the same for the Jewish state. This total outlook is aptly phrased by two rabbis who were students of R. Tzvi Yehudah, for example:

> The general reality, not of one detail or another but of the entire nation, of the entire state as a state, the state of the Jewish people, is the state most closely associated with the name of heaven. The Holy One, blessed be He, has no other nation, we are His nation, and so, as a matter of course, everything that happens in the state is associated with His name, may He be exalted, and with every advance, the name of heaven is further sanctified.[49]

Here we have a typical expression of redemptive interpretation: The emergence of the state has to be incorporated as a meaningful element in the comprehensive outlook. Even national *glory* is seen as totally sacred, in fact embodying divine glory. Once again, this is a far-reaching expression of the total symbiosis of nationality and religion:

> In the entire Torah, the exoteric as well as the esoteric, it is written that the glory of Israel is the glory of the Lord. Even the Land of Israel and its settlement are a detail in comparison.

The foundation of everything is the divine glory that dwells within us.[50]

Political *sovereignty* itself becomes an expression of God's presence in the world. This point needs special emphasis: The focus of religious discourse is no longer observance of the *mitzvot* and ethics, but political sovereignty. One expression of this idea is the use of the category of defamation of God, *hillul Hashem*: As a rule, this expression refers in our traditional sources to religious/ethical behavior,[51] while in R. Tzvi Yehudah's view *hillul Hashem* is a function of the political situation, the fact that the Jewish people lacks sovereignty:

> When Israel are in a situation of a collective and a state, God's glory appears in the world, encompassing everything. On the other hand, when there is no collective, no kingdom of Israel, that is the most terrible *hillul Hashem*.[52]

Just as the state has a total dimension of sanctity, the institutions necessary for its existence are not mere means toward an end, but also expressions of sanctity. Most salient in this respect is the army:

> The state needs an army, and therefore the army is sacred.... Divine might also reveals itself in the army, and thank God we also have a magnificent army, whose reputation is known and famed throughout the world.

This in turn implies the sanctity of *military power and courage*. Based on the same "interpretive" principle proposed by R. Kook senior, R. Tzvi Yehudah draws a direct line from his father's thought to his own time:

> Everything that the *Rav* predicted one, two or more generations ago is coming true. The Land of Israel in its full extent, producing its fruit, is in Jewish hands. All of Jerusalem is being built. The immigration of the Jews of Russia. The might of the IDF.[53]

Similar thoughts are expressed by one of his disciples, R. Shlomo Aviner:

> Now the manifest redemption of the ingathering of our exiles and the settlement of our land, which appeared about one hundred years ago, has steadily progressed from then to now, is gradually multiplying in its vast dimensions, in the renaissance of the nation and the land, the revival of the language, the re-emergence of valor and the army, the renewal of our independence and our release from gentile enslavement, and the revival of the Torah – the Torah of the Land of Israel.[54]

Thus, this passage combines the same expressions of the "manifest redemption" that were found in R. Kook senior's writings, together with renewed involvement in military matters. Significantly, by attributing military re-involvement to the manifest redemption, the writer is defining it as an expression of the re-emergent _segullah_ of Israel, and as one of the signs – perhaps even proofs – that the age of redemption has begun. Any phenomenon associated with the manifest redemption is _ipso facto_ invested with a transcendent dimension, a dimension of sanctity. This is stated explicitly by R. Dov Leor, who points to God Himself as the source of the renewed strength of the Jewish people: "The Lord God of Israel restored to the Jewish nation the strength and courage to triumph."[55]

Just as sovereignty has become a focus of the religious norm subject to the concepts of _kiddush Hashem_ and _hillul Hashem_, the same is true with regard to the IDF's military victories: "So every one of our successes, successes of the Jewish people, sanctifies the name of heaven; every success of the IDF is _kiddush Hashem_."[56] The normative dimension of military activity is identified with religious observance proper. While we shall not deal here with the halakhic aspect of the subject, it is important to note that the view of military activity as a _mitzvah_ automatically implies that the means for performance of the _mitzvah_ are also sanctified. Indeed, when R. Tzvi Yehudah was asked in 1967 if he did not consider military parades on Israel's Independence Day as a violation of the biblical admonishment against the glorification of physical strength, he replied that, since the conquest of the Land of Israel is a *mitzvah*, military weapons are endowed with sanctity as the instruments of that *mitzvah*: "Everything that is associated with this day of the re-instatement of the kingdom of Israel – everything is holy!"[57]

Ultimately, the all-inclusive conception has been translated into a call for increased military activism, to the extent of deliberate military *aggression*. Up to this point, we have seen that the proponents of redemptive interpretation, responding to a comprehensive religious perception, sought to assimilate a dramatic change – the transition to military activism. But it is now clear that this investment of military matters with renewed sanctity, as restoring the nation's ability to observe the *mitzvah* of conquering the Land, is not limited merely to military action in self-defense. As we have seen, an attempt has been made via interpretation to assimilate the new reality into a comprehensive, binding, religious outlook. This implies approval of military activism *per se*. Nevertheless, I would say that explicit calls for military initiatives, as a necessary measure in the implementation of that comprehensive religious outlook, represents another stage in the gradual internalization of military activism. In other words, redemptive interpretation has become explicitly *prescriptive*. This is perhaps the most extreme manifestation of the internalization of military activism in this school of thought. The first stage was, in a sense, the transition from ethos to Halakhah – the comprehensive perception outlined, analyzed, and illustrated above is expressed in particular in the reinstatement of the *mitzvah* to conquer the Land of Israel by military means. Redemptive interpretation is in action, but now it is capable even of reinstating the *mitzvah*. In the second stage, the trend toward radicalization reaches a peak in explicit appeals for military aggression, which are also rooted in the comprehensive outlook.

In religious movements, including the religious-Zionist movement, the desire to apply religion to all walks of life is considered as a way of internalizing modernity and the idea of man as a creator.[58] R. Tzvi Yehudah and his disciples applied this idea to the renewed possibility of fulfilling the *mitzvah* to conquer the Land

by military means, though of course this was also a direct implication of redemptive interpretation. If the *mitzvah* of conquering the
Land by military means has always existed, but the Jewish people
could not perform it in practice as long as it was in Exile, it follows
that, in a time of redemption, the original status of Halakhah must
be restored:

> It is the King Messiah who will restore the Jewish people to its
> perfect, healthy, and normal state, *to a state in which it will be
> possible to observe Halakhah fully*...Therefore, if when in Exile
> we do not observe half of the *mitzvot* of the Torah because "for
> our sins we were exiled from our Land and removed far away
> from our country, *and we cannot* etc.," that is to say, because *we
> are coerced*, like a person who does not have an *etrog*... – but
> when we are given an opportunity to emerge from the state of
> coercion and approach the possibility of observing the entire
> Torah, surely we shall hasten and make all efforts to do so....
> *The first and simplest messianism* is a basic halakhic imperative,
> *the imperative to observe the Torah*, the imperative to emerge
> from the chains of coercion that were imposed upon us by the
> destroyers of our country...to the holy freedom of realization
> of *Torah and mitzvah life in full*.[59]

The possibility now presenting itself, to perform the *mitzvah* of
conquering the Land by military means, becomes part of the comprehensive outlook through the prism of the renewed observance
of Halakhah *in toto*. We know that according to R. Kook senior, any
person purchasing land in the Land of Israel was thereby performing the *mitzvah* of conquering the Land in our times. This was also
R. Reines' interpretation of Nahmanides.[60] This was so, R. Kook
explained, because the Jews had to be a "righteous nation" in Gentile eyes – a view consistent with his messianic vision of universal
harmony. His ideological heirs clearly abandoned this interpretation
of the commandment, advocating instead conquest by war. Once
again, we find that a position rooted in redemptive interpretation

has been reversed. According to Hanan Porat, for example, historical events play a decisive role in halakhic debate:

> The *mitzvah* of settling the Land of Israel, as explained by…R. Tzvi Yehudah…, must be examined not from the standpoint of the laws of the Torah, but also from that of the vitality of the Torah as revealed through the character and actions of this nation, which is able to discern the will of the Creator in the depths of its soul, even when it is not relying on something written in a book…. The halakhic question, whether the *mitzvah* of the settlement of the Land of Israel is binding in our time, and whether it should be fulfilled with devotion, has long been decided. The law was decided and ruled by the Jewish people, which mined the answer from the depths of its soul, from the vitality of the Torah as revealed in its soul.[61]

Porat's expression "the vitality of the Torah," as against "the laws of the Torah," deserves special emphasis, as does his reference to "the soul" of the nation as against "something written in a book." Here we have an apt expression of a meta-halakhic ideological conception that in this case, as we have stated, is decisive even in a halakhic debate. There is perhaps no better example of the monistic approach of this ideology: There is one ruling principle – the Torah's vitality is manifest in the soul of the nation and determines the laws of the Torah.

R. Tzvi Yehudah, in his halakhic deliberations on the religious obligation to conquer the Land of Israel, frequently cites Nahmanides, who holds that this *mitzvah* is binding in every generation, not only in the messianic age. R. Tzvi Yehudah, for his part, combines Maimonides' conception of the messianic age, as expounded in *Mishneh Torah*, and Nahmanides' interpretation.[62] The Jewish people, he argues, has now been empowered to fulfill this *mitzvah* – and it is able to do so. Nahmanides, indeed, has become a major source and "canonical" figure for R. Tzvi Yehudah and his disciples: "Have we not heard from the mouth of Nahmanides, *'father of Israel,'* of the *mitzvah* of conquest and war? Thank God, we have been – and are even now – merited to fulfill God's command, the glory and might of our army."[63] This is not halakhic discourse in the usual sense. R. Tzvi Yehudah is not arguing merely that an opportunity has arisen to fulfill a *mitzvah* that could not be observed for many generations. His halakhic discourse is deeply – and avowedly – rooted in his messianic conception. Put differently: in this respect, too, redemption has become an "explanation" in exegesis that "redeems" conquest through war. "The fact that today we have, to some degree, a situation in which we rule the land, and that we have achieved this situation through our own powers – that constitutes an important part of redemption. It is more than just the beginning of redemption (*athalta de-geulah*) – it embodies an important aspect of contrast with exile."[64] This position was adopted to such an extreme that the new possibility of fulfilling the *mitzvah* to "blot out" Amalek was greeted with joy.[65]

The special nature of the *mitzvah* to conquer the Land in this school of thought is worthy of note. It is not merely "one more" *mitzvah*, important though it may be; it is considered a kind of "super-*mitzvah*," not subordinate to any other halakhic consideration, even danger to life (*pikuah nefesh*). In R. Tzvi Yehudah's view, the obligation exists and is halakhically binding; no discretion is allowed. On the contrary: Theologically speaking, we are duty-bound to thank God that the *mitzvah* can once again be performed.[66]

Summing up, the Jewish people's return to the use of military force is not to be perceived as a necessary evil, imposed upon it by circumstances. On the contrary, the religious and ideological foundations of Judaism have assimilated the phenomenon and made it an explicit, supreme, religious value. In fact, some of R. Tzvi Yehudah's ideological heirs have taken the process of radicalization one step further. This might perhaps be seen as a process in which Halakhah shapes ethos: The renewed validity of the obligation to conquer the Land of Israel by military means has produced, through redemptive interpretation, a favorable attitude to deliberate military aggression. Thus, for example, Hanan Porat, writing in 1978 about the Litany Campaign, said: "The war should have been declared out of an inner

Jewish rhythm and not merely in response to the wickedness of the world and the other nations. It should have been a response to the End that is forcing us!"⁶⁷

But that is not all. Even halakhic discourse exhibits a quantum leap toward greater activism. It was stated above that the renewed relevance of military matters was seen as part of a halakhic renaissance; it was still possible to argue that this was merely absorption of an idea, not at the outset calling for action. Now, however, it turns out that the halakhic imperative has made of military aggression an *a priori* halakhic obligation. As expressed, for example, by R. Aviner:

> We have to settle the Land even at the cost of war. Moreover, even if there is peace, we must launch a war of independence to conquer it. Without this Land, we are not the Jewish people!⁶⁸

Notably, this rhetoric also alludes to the total, harmonistic outlook. Ruling over the entire Land is part of the national identity. This may be seen as a clear expression of a harmonistic position, whose basic concept is the "nation" or "people" (Heb. *am*), here raised to an explicitly metaphysical level. As we have seen, it is this position that has made the nationalism-religion symbiosis possible. That is to say, one of the consequences of the sanctity of nationality – the principle of sovereignty – has been merged with military involvement, which has also become an absolute "super-*mitzvah*." Porat writes emphatically, citing Nahmanides, of the religious obligation to maintain Jewish sovereignty over all parts of the Land of Israel, and he adds:

> The *mitzvah* of settling the Land, which requires that the Jewish people conquer its land from the foreigners that rule over it, even at the cost of war – how is that consistent with the ethical desire for peace? How does it permit shedding the blood of those Jews who may, God forbid, be killed by Gentiles, or the blood of the Gentiles who may, God forbid, be killed by ourselves?…True, we must restrict what we have said and stress

that it is not our duty *a priori* to declare war and destroy the Gentiles living in the Land.... But at any rate, if the nations ruling the land are not willing to make peace with Israel and recognize its sovereignty over the Land of Israel, then it is universally agreed that the *mitzvah* of conquering the Land is fully binding, even at the heavy cost of war.

There is yet another aspect of this internalization of the activist ethos, to the extent of becoming normative. The human activism born of a secular nationalist ideology sought to contrast responsibility for initiative and human action in the real world with the submissive passivity created by religious and messianic perceptions. Now, however, military activism has blended into religious ideology to such an extent that it is straining to breach the constraints imposed by *Realpolitik*. In other words, if in the past religion was a source of political and military passivity, of inability to cope in practice with problems and dangers entailed by historical reality, it has now created an ideology that seeks, in the name of total "religious" devotion in an age of redemption, to ignore real and historical data. So while religion in pre-Zionist days, as a cause of political passivity, hindered the Jews' ability to deal with the political reality around them, religious (messianic) faith has now engendered extreme activism, refusal to take political constraints into consideration. Thus, for example, R. Aviner contends that "to the extent that we devote ourselves body and soul to the divine enterprise, with all the natural means at our disposal, more and more miracles will appear from heaven and combine with the natural frame of our actions." This is clearly a meta-halakhic position; devotion arouses miraculous intervention by God. Aviner goes on to ask, what about the principle that one should not rely on miracles? His answer: Such scruples have no place at a time when events are set in motion by the redemptive process: "In actions performed in the footsteps of the messiah, all the more so when performed by a community, heavenly assistance is far greater than measure for measure."[69]

These sentiments are expressed with particular force when the new ethos born of Zionism, which centered on human activism, is interpreted at the end of the day as an expression of divine activism. Not only is it true that the limits imposed on political-messianic activism by the "Three Oaths" have disappeared – from now on the activism is primarily divine. Whereas it was once forbidden for human beings to force the issue by their own actions, God Himself is now forcing Israel off the stage of history:

> For they [= the observant Jews who oppose Zionism] have not realized that it is not we, flesh and blood, who are forcing the issue, but the "Owner," the Sovereign of the Universe, Who is forcing us; it is not the voice of flesh and blood but the voice of the living God Who has knocked down the wall that separated us from our homeland, calling to us, "Rise!"[70]

I believe these examples adequately demonstrate the absolute reversal in the attitude to the activist ethos of political Zionism. While the essence of early Zionism was the desire to abandon the passive, spiritual positions of Diaspora life, seeking instead to influence reality and shape it, activism has now been assimilated into the harmonistic ideology to such an extent that realia themselves have given way before a spiritual understanding of reality. One's reference point is determined not by the demands imposed by the empirical, historical world, but by the realization of the divine plan.

At this point we come face to face with an intriguing question: What do R. Abraham Isaac Kook's ideological heirs think of their spiritual father? Is his ethical interpretation of the "Three Oaths," through which he restricted the resumption of activism or the use of force, still valid, or has it disappeared? How do R. Tzvi Yehudah and his disciples relate to R. Kook senior's harmonistic vision? What religious significance could they ascribe to Israel's wars in light of his belief that the Jewish people would not wage war as part of the redemptive process? How could they explain the confrontation between Israel and the nations after he had presented his harmonistic vision as an essential foundation of that process?

It can, in fact, be shown that R. Tzvi Yehudah and his disciples were guided in this connection by the principles of redemptive interpretation, but such a discussion would be beyond the scope of this article. Suffice it to say here that the "Three Oaths," which R. Kook senior interprets as a moral obligation prohibiting the use of military force in the messianic age, are again used by his ideological successors as a divine decree that dictates political and military passivity in the Diaspora – but that decree becomes null and void in the messianic age.[71] Moreover, Israel's wars are now invested with religious meaning. Just as R. Kook senior applied redemptive interpretation to the First World War, considering it as a *Sinnbild*, a symbol of profound internal events in a meta-historical order – his successors did the same with regard to the wars of the modern State of Israel.[72] They understood the reasons and meaning of these wars as expressed in a variety of ways. First, war is an expression of divine *presence*.[73] Second, war serves the divine *plan* in history. Thus, R. Eliezer Waldman has written that the Six-Day War was God's device to bring the Jewish people, almost unwillingly, to sovereignty over the different parts of the Land of Israel.[74] Furthermore, it has also been argued that the goal of war is *educational-messianic*. For example, R. E. Avihayil contends that the repeated wars in Lebanon are not an accident or a consequence of a particular geopolitical constellation. The significance of the Lebanese war, he writes, should be sought in the broad context of the redemption of the Land. He criticizes the agreement to give up the south of Lebanon which, in his view, is part of the Land of Israel. Terrorist attacks are, he claims, part of God's intervention, designed to induce the Jews to seize all parts of the Land of Israel: Until we rectify the cause, until we fulfill God's word in the Torah, to return to all of our country, the whip will continue to be wielded over us. We cannot evade our responsibility.[75]

Some writers even spoke of the wars as having an *evolutionary* meaning. R. Aviner, for example, holds that wars are part of the national renaissance and growth in the age of redemption:

> The War of the Peace of the Galilee [= the Lebanese War], like all previous wars of Israel, constitutes a further stage in the national maturing of the Jewish people. Out of its wars, our nation is

gradually being born, even if the birth pangs are sometimes difficult to bear. Out of its wars, its salvation is also emerging.[76]

R. Kook senior envisaged a cultural, not military, confrontation between Israel and the nations in the messianic age. His spiritual heirs are now explaining the Arab-Israel military conflict as a necessary confrontation between the forces of good and their opponents.[77] The main theoretical step taken by R. Tzvi Yehudah's disciples is the argument that his father's harmonistic vision is a thing of the future; wars and confrontation are a *means* toward its achievement, a component in a kind of dialectical progress. An instructive illustration of such "conversion" of R. Kook's writings may be found in the thought of R. Tzvi Tau. Unlike Aviner, Tau's point of departure is that the use of force cannot possibly be part of the realization of universal redemption; he therefore rejects the idea that wars possess messianic significance. Seeking to anchor his interpretation in the writings of R. Kook himself, he explains them as follows (R. Kook's words italicized):

> The nationhood of Israel in itself, in sense of national courage and our own innermost sanctity, is not the supreme goal. We have another frame of reference that must figure in our lives – our attitude to the whole world as an ancient nation [Heb. *am olam* = (lit.) a nation of the world].... Therefore, *it is otherwise with God's spirit that is upon Israel, which is destined to be a light unto the nations* not only in relation to themselves but in relation to the whole world. *It does not possess the quality of confrontation, to expand through its strength*, to overcome through victory and courage, *for we were not commanded to carry the sword and wage war, to call in the Lord's name upon the nations who know Him not.* Our wars are designed for the establishment of our state, for establishment of our national strength and courage, not in order to force the entire world to accept the religion of Israel.[78]

Now, R. Kook senior made no distinction between national revival, which requires wars, and universal, harmonious, redemption. The very opposite is true; the passage quoted by Tau, in its original context, made no distinction between national revival and the universalistic ideal.

To our mind, this too is a good example of redemptive interpretation of the writings and views of the person who, more than anyone else, developed the principles of redemptive exegesis. That is to say, since wars were part of historical reality, it was necessary to "redeem" not only the phenomenon itself, in order to explain its place in the process of redemption, but also – and in no lesser degree – the views and writings of R. Kook himself!

2. THE REALISTIC-ETHICAL MODEL: R. I.J. REINES AND HIS IDEOLOGICAL SUCCESSORS

The roots of the realistic-ethical model lie in the teachings of R. Reines,[79] who founded the political "Mizrahi" movement in 1903. This model is based on what I call the "realistic" and "ethical" principles. The realistic principle seeks to initiate political and practical solutions to the plight of the Jewish people as part of human, non-messianic, history. It represents a perception committed first and foremost to the idea of *Kelal Yisrael*, that is, responsibility for the Jewish collective as a whole, irrespective of the way of life practiced by its different parts. The term "ethical principle" is self-explanatory: commitment to the religious and ethical principles that are binding for any Jew.

There is, indeed, an important difference between R. Reines' position and that of the figures that we refer to as his ideological successors. While he himself was generally opposed to military activism, his ideological successors formulated a position in favor of military organization and activity for purposes of self-defense. This change, however, was a necessary outcome of historical circumstances. We shall see that, despite the changing conditions, R. Reines' successors' discussions of the question of the use of force were informed by the same two principles, and they adopted assumptions that were similar, sometimes very similar, to his own.[80] However, as we have dealt with this ideological school at length elsewhere,[81] a brief summary will have to satisfy us here.

R. Reines distinguishes between Exile and Redemption as two states of the world, one of the major criteria for the distinction being the presence of wars and bloodshed. In effect, he was speaking of two opposing cultures, the culture of the Sword and the culture of the Book. As long as humankind is steeped in the culture of the Sword, that is, locked in warfare, the world as a whole is in Exile. In this spirit, for example, R. Reines interprets the following statement of R. Eliezer in the Midrash: "Sword and Book came down from heaven intertwined. [God] said to them: If you do what is written in this Book, you will be saved from this Sword, but if not, you will be slain by this Sword."[82] The Midrash, he writes, teaches us that the world may be ruled either by the Sword or by the Book. The two cannot possibly rule in tandem: "For the Sword and the Book will oppose one another, and their dominion and rule are intertwined, as being follows close upon non-being."[83]

The *Beit ha-Midrash* – the study house – is the place where the culture of the Book is cultivated, a radical alternative to the culture of the Sword rampant in the world: "There is no greater blasphemy than to bring instruments of destruction into the house of Torah and wisdom." The transition from Exile to Redemption marks not only a point in time but – and perhaps this is its main significance – a radical shift of world culture; as to the transition between the culture of the Book and the culture of the Sword, there is no middle ground, no possible gradation between the two. This is true both existentially and historically:

> The dominion of the Sword and the spear and the dominion of Torah and wisdom are like non-being and being, as being always follows close upon non-being, and when non-being comes to an end, being and reality always come straight after, separated only by the wink of an eye, one leaves and one arrives.... And when the dominion of the Sword and Destruction disappear from the world, the dominion of Torah and wisdom will take its place.[84]

These distinctions are not so much descriptive of the Gentile nations as they are of the Jewish people. Much has been written of R. Reines as advocating a model of redemption to be found in earlier Jewish sources, which Avi Ravitzky has called a "paradoxical conception."[85] Another manifestation of this is R. Reines' discussion of the significance of the First World War. Citing a saying of R. Eleazar bar Avina: "If you see kingdoms warring with one another, expect the advent of the Messiah,"[86] R. Reines explains this Midrash as a source for the basic idea of a sharp, dichotomic, distinction between Exile and Redemption: The human condition in Exile is an antithetical image of the situation in a redeemed world.[87] Hence, we learn that the messianic idea acts as a kind of regulative-ethical idea, against which one can measure the distance between the world's place in the present and its place when that idea is actually realized. Wars are *scrutinized* in light of the messianic goal, not *internalized* in a philosophical framework, as envisaged by redemptive exegesis. Wars not only do not herald redemption – they in fact imply that it is far off in the future.

How, then, can one explain R. Reines' role as the founder of religious Zionism in a political context? How did he see the rise of Jewish nationalism and the emergence of political Zionism? Would he not have viewed the attempt to revive political activism, even the mere attempt to gather some of the Jewish people in the Land of Israel, as a kind of messianic-political activism? Was he not apprehensive that the resumption of political action might entail adopting the culture of the Sword? Might this not involve a contradiction, an inconsistency in R. Reines' own attitudes, as has indeed been claimed?[88]

Let us now briefly summarize the foundations of R. Reines' teachings, then going on to illustrate how he and his ideological successors shaped their position vis-à-vis the use of military force on the basis of the two principles outlined above.

For R. Reines, the national and religious dimensions of Judaism are intertwined. While he clearly recognizes the element of national affiliation, he considers its content to be defined by the Torah and the *mitzvot*. It was inconceivable to him, normatively speaking, that there could be a secular national-Jewish existence. The ideological and axiological meaning of Jewish nationality is invested in the nation that obeys the *mitzvot* of the Torah and adheres to its ideas.[89] While R. Reines certainly admired self-sacrifice for the collective, the aspiration to immigrate to the Land of Israel, and fulfillment of the *mitzvah* to settle the Land, the fact is that secular Jewish nationalism, as a social and ideological phenomenon, received no standing and significance in his philosophy, whether positive or negative (that is, he did not see it as a deliberate attempt at systematic secularization of the Jewish people). Nevertheless, he believed that the rise of Jewish nationalism was religiously meaningful: It was an act of Divine Providence, expressing a first step toward stemming the tide of assimilation. He did not believe, however, that it would necessarily lead people back to a religious way of life.[90] One cannot, therefore, discern in his teachings any totalization of Jewish nationalism or of Zionism. This "non-total" approach is the key to the attitudes of his ideological successors to Israel's wars and to the use of force. Even at this stage, in fact, one can already point to two distinct hermeneutical approaches.

Underlying R. Abraham Isaac Kook's outlook is a primarily teleological-descriptive approach: Events possess significance by virtue of their being part of the Divine plan, whose goal is known *a priori*. Accordingly, the interpreter can do no more than describe the event, whose occurrence is inevitable. We have seen that this approach, which we have called "redemptive exegesis," is one of the keys to understanding the internalization of the ethos of brute force in the teachings of his spiritual successors. This is to be contrasted with R. Reines' approach, which characteristically measures reality and phenomena on the basis of values. He was not aiming at a system that interprets and "redeems" reality as perceived by the believer; it is the believer's task to analyze any phenomenon on the basis of the possible intentions of those who brought it about, to choose between the desired alternatives based on a system of guiding values and ideas. Thus, what should be is not determined by what is; rather, the data and constraints of reality must be examined in order to permit realization of the desired values as far as possible.

The practical expression of these hermeneutical methods is

relevant to the question of cooperation with the Zionist movement – a question which, as far as the religious public is concerned,
was phrased in terms of cooperation with sinners.[91] It was agreed
that the Jewish people was in dire straits, that Torah study itself
was insufficient to ensure continued physical existence; it was this
realization that persuaded R. Reines and his followers to recognize
the priority of the concept of *Kelal Yisrael*, the Jewish collective. The
concept expresses the value of unity, of a shared fate beyond the
differences between secular and traditionalist circles. R. Reines' non-
total, pragmatic approach produced this conception. That is not to
say that the religious Zionist community never conducted a critical
examination of the nature of the national Jewish movement.[92] The
novelty of R. Reines' position was his attempt to embrace the realistic,
material aims of the Zionist endeavor as a *guiding principle* for his
own approach to Zionism. As long as he believed that the Zionist
goals were subordinate to *Kelal Yisrael* as a value, R. Reines was ready
for practical cooperation with political Zionism.[93] Therefore, even
if Herzl did not envisage a political framework in which the Torah
would actually be realized, it was necessary and important to take a
positive approach to this attempt to find a solution for the difficult
condition of the Jewish people.

As a rule, R. Reines believed that Zionism had nothing to do
with the messianic idea; however, that did not affect one's duty to
take political steps that might better the lot of the Jewish people, for
realistic, non-messianic goals:

> However, there is no doubt that we are not only permitted but
> even actually required to try and improve our very [grave][94]
> situation through safe measures which are legitimate accord-
> ing to the laws of Judaism;[95] for indeed the transfer to which
> the Zionist movement aspires is by no means total, and at
> best one can only hope to transfer a large part of our people
> to Zion – so why should we not take up this task? The hope of
> Redemption will not obstruct the path of search and endeavor
> (Heb. *hishtadlut*), and people who think that wherever there
> is hope there is no room for endeavor show that they do not

understand the meaning of the word "hope" and its inherent concept... Surely, the Torah permits the struggle for existence by legitimate means, and it is a *mitzvah*, even a duty, to engage in it.[96]

We will now illustrate the role of two principles in R. Reines' philosophy, the realistic principle and the religious-ethical principle, and demonstrate the existence of the same two principles in positions taken by religious figures in the 1930s and after the establishment of the State of Israel.

The *realistic* principle draws on the national aspect of Judaism, expressing itself in two ways. First, it ascribes religious, but not messianic, significance to the Jewish national awakening. This is a realistic position in the sense that it eschews totalization of the phenomenon of Jewish nationalism, as expressed in the nature of the debate over cooperation with it. Second, a sense of realism governs the definition of the earthly goals of Zionism and the overriding value behind political decisions – the existence and welfare of the Jewish people in existing geopolitical conditions. R. Reines saw this value as calling for political and historical activism, in a manner fully consistent with the continued existence of the Jewish people in the age of Exile.

The *religious-ethical* principle draws on the religious aspect of Judaism, expressing itself in the present context in the content of the nation's religious-ethical ideals, in the "culture of the Book" exemplified by the Jewish people. The role of this principle is to set the limits of legitimate activity in the framework of political activism.

This concept was to guide Reines in situations that obliged him to reach crucial decisions, as, for example, in the Uganda debate;[97] as he wrote to Herzl after the Sixth Zionist Congress (August 1903), in which the Uganda Scheme was proposed:

Nevertheless, we have acceded to the African proposal, because we are attentive to the needs of the people, which we love more than the land; and the needs of the people, whose situation is deteriorating materially and spiritually, dictate a safe refuge, wherever it may be… If there is no Israel in the world, there is no Zion in the world.[98]

Underlying his approach was the concern for the existential condition of the Jews, and it was this value that guided his actions. He wrote repeatedly in this vein:

> The Mizrahi as a religious party places the existence of the Jewish people above the *mitzvah* and the desire to return to the Land of Israel, but it rejects the territorialist approach, which denies the sanctity and value of the Land of Israel. The hope to return to the Land of Israel and its value in general are among the foundations of the Jewish religion.[99]

This example clearly demonstrates the sharp distinction that R. Reines made between two levels: the level of principle, or religion or ideals, which treats ideas in their pristine purity ("among the foundations of the Jewish religion") but cannot necessarily be realized in an era of Exile; and the level of the realistic, human situation, which is of necessity fragmented – the era of Exile, in which actions must be governed by realistic considerations in order to achieve a well-defined goal, expressive of the fulfillment of an important value. Another example of his realistic attitude to the world is his establishment of a secondary-school and *yeshivah* in Lida. Though the founder and leader of the Mizrahi, he did not see Zionism as the be-all and end-all. Since he believed that Zionism would be able to bring at best only part of the Jewish people to the Land of Israel, he attached much importance to the education of young Jews in the Diaspora, to help them face a very difficult social, economic, and spiritual situation.[100]

The root of the religious-ethical principle in R. Reines' thought is the messianic mission of the Jewish people, expressed, *inter alia*, in the "culture of the Book," as already mentioned. In his view, the Torah, its study, and its fulfillment constitute the exclusive means for the achievement of human ethical perfection. The *tikkun* (restoration, improvement) of humanity is first and foremost *tikkun* of the individual. The laws of the Torah are essentially human laws; it is only by studying and obeying those laws that man becomes "man."[101] Unlike R. Kook senior, however, R. Reines did not advocate the realization of religious and ethical goals by political means. His teachings concentrate, first and foremost, on the *tikkun* of the individual. The objective of the study of Torah and the observance of the *mitzvot* is to educate humanity and prepare it for a situation in which human action will be shaped not by desire but by logic and rational considerations. One of his most prominent criteria for the establishment of the messianic time in history is the abolition of war. According to R. Reines, the Jewish people's existence in Exile has a purpose: to enable the nation to achieve ethical and spiritual perfection and so to prepare it for its messianic mission. One means to that end was isolation from political life and avoidance of the need to wage wars.[102] The Rabbis of old, he believed, knowingly reshaped the national ethos through the spiritualization of sources that they deemed to be problematic in their emphasis on physical force.

While R. Reines embraced political activism as designed to better the desperate condition of the Jewish people, he sought to impose clearly defined constraints on that activism, to ensure that it would not entail the use of military force. This, he believed, would have been inconsistent with the mission of the Jewish people. One of the most extreme expressions of that position was his ethical interpretation of the Three Oaths. The oaths, he wrote, were meant to prevent the Jews from engaging not in political activity *per se*, but in the use of force. Rather than a Divine decree, they were an ethical-religious imperative, which will stay with the Jewish people until the advent of the messiah. As I have shown elsewhere, R. Reines was not content merely to propose a reinterpretation of the Three Oaths; he used the concept itself as an exegetical principle in other contexts, for example, in a sermon about the lessons the Talmud learns from the Hasmonean Revolt, and even in a purely halakhic discussion, of Nahmanides' interpretation of the *mitzvah* of the conquest of the Land of Israel.[103] So what happens to the realistic-ethical perception when reality turns violent?

The year 1936 marks the beginning of the period known as that of "blind terror." While the New Yishuv had already experienced at-tacks in the early 1920s and at the end of that decade,[104] the generally accepted view among historians is that only in 1936 did the leaders of the Yishuv realize that, without proper military preparation and without a military confrontation, the establishment of a Jewish state was highly unlikely. Moreover, since the War of Independence, the State of Israel has been embroiled in a war at least once each decade. Given such development of a violent political reality, it was no longer feasible to continue to advocate the military passivity that R. Reines had postulated as a condition for joining the Zionist enterprise. Since he died in 1915, he could not have formulated a position in relation to the need for military organization. Indeed, his unique standpoint, in its attempt to combine political activism with non-violent modes of operation, was doomed to run aground on the rocks of the new reality.

The new reality emerging in the Land of Israel heightened the tension between the two principles of R. Reines' teachings. On the one hand, *Realpolitik* was necessary to ensure the welfare and safety of the Jewish people, which now required the use of force as well. On the other hand, there was a desire to adhere to the ethical principles of the Torah, perhaps also an even broader ethos, which frowned on the use of force in general. Thus, both in the 1930s and later, certain religious-Zionist figures adopted a position in relation to the use of force representative of what we have called the realistic and ethical-religious principles. As a rule, this position recognizes the need and value of the use of military force in self-defense, but at the same time struggles to continue to cultivate an ethical-religious sensitivity to bloodshed.

The voices heard in the 1930s came both from the Rabbinical establishment and from the ranks of the ha-Po'el ha-Mizrahi move-ment and the religious kibbutz movement. In later years similar sentiments were voiced by members of the Mizrahi and such move-ments as the Movement for Torah Judaism, *Netivot Shalom*, and "Meimad." These views will now be briefly reviewed.

One of the most prominent figures in the public debate among religious-Zionist circles in the 1930s was Yeshayahu Bernstein, a leader of ha-Po'el ha-Mizrahi. Referring to indiscriminate anti-Arab terror, he argues:

> Heaven forfend that the seed of Israel should repudiate the Rock from which they were hewn and the Torah of their God. It was we who heard and accepted the [commandment] "Thou shalt not kill" and for generations it has been absorbed in our blood and our flesh.[105]
>
> We are not commanded by our Torah to leave ourselves unprotected, not to defend ourselves and fight for our lives. The other's blood is no redder than ours. But neither is our blood redder than that of others. Everything that is permitted to us in such situations is for lack of choice, of necessity, that cannot be avoided without suicide.[106]

Accordingly, the objection to bloodshed was based on two principles: it was implanted in the Torah, and had been internalized by the Jewish people as a second nature. Here is a resounding, clear-cut formulation of the principle of self-defense. A similar argument was voiced by the rabbinical establishment of the time. Chief Rabbi Isaac Herzog, for example, wrote in 1938:

> The voice is the voice of Jacob, yet the hands are the hands of Esau. Indeed – the hands, the hands of defense, to defend ourselves, to defend our lives, to fight for our homeland and the cities of our God. Legitimate defense, such is the action of the hands of Jacob. So did our forefathers.[107]

In this passage R. Herzog formulates, first of all, the principle of the self-evident religious moral imperative ("the voice is the voice of Jacob"), and then the principle of self-defense. This might be considered one of the characteristics of the ethical principle in the realistic-ethical perception. Just as it was clear to R. Reines that some modes of action "cannot be admitted to the Congregation of Israel," so, too, there is a meta-halakhic, moral insight establishing the point of departure for any discussion of the use of force. R.

Reines expresses this moral insight in terms of the Three Oaths. In the examples we have just considered, the moral insight is expressed in such general terms as "spirit of the Torah," and "morality of the Torah," which need no further proof from the sources or further clarification.[108]

Remarkably, throughout the 1930s and 1940s we find almost no halakhic discussion in rabbinical debates of the issues involved in the use of force. R. Herzog, for example, called for self-control and restraint in the name of "our holy Torah" or "the honor of our people."[109] Another rabbinical figure in the Mizrahi movement, R. Moshe Ostrovsky, was even more outspoken in this respect. He condemned retaliatory operations not only because "Torah morality, on which we have been reared, decries these repulsive acts," but also because, in the context of self-restraint and refraining from revenge, we must also learn from the civilized nations.[110] He, too, cited sources reflecting meta-halakhic values, such as the Mishnah, "Who is a hero? – he that subdues his evil impulse" (*Avot* 4:1), or Jacob's rebuke of his sons Simeon and Levi (Gen. 49:5–7). A similar observation is valid for other questions that were raised in the 1930s, such as the partition of Palestine.[111] Alongside the religious-moral arguments, there were also arguments purporting to weigh the utility of the use of force in political confrontations. Thus, for example, the chief rabbi, in a manifesto issued in 1947, declared that since the Yishuv was opposed to fighting the British, "any killing of persons, whoever they might be – policemen, officials, soldiers…is the spilling of innocent blood."[112]

After the establishment of the State of Israel, it was almost universally felt that the state was fighting for its very life. Nevertheless, in some cases the issue of the ethical limitations on the use of force came up for discussion, and quite forcibly. In October 1953, for example, after a series of terrorist acts, the Israel government authorized the Israel Defense Forces to carry out a retaliatory raid on the Arab village of Qibya. In the course of the raid, a large number of houses were blown up and sixty-nine villagers, including women and children, were killed. The raid shocked world public opinion and became one of the most traumatic events in the history of the

Israel-Arab conflict. The complete minutes of a government meeting
held three days later, on October 18, 1953, were published in April
1997. Notably, the most passionate ethically motivated reaction to the
operation came from the minister of welfare and religions, Moshe
Shapira of ha-Po'el ha-Mizrahi:

> I do not wish to discuss the matter from a political point of view.
> I want to discuss it from an ethical point of view. We cannot
> accept such a reaction by any means. Throughout the years, we
> have opposed this.... We have never said, Let the innocent be
> swept away with the guilty.... We know what happened at Deir
> Yassin. That happened in the heat of war, but nevertheless, we
> were all so incensed!.... We said that such a path is forbidden
> from a Jewish point of view.... Jews cannot act thus.[113]

Shapira was expressing a view shared by many Israelis who identified
with the Mizrahi movement. Thus, for example, ha-Po'el ha-Mizrahi
addressed its followers before the 1955 elections with an apology,
insisting that "we opposed the operation in Qibya."

Another example of this line of thought was represented by
the Movement for Torah Judaism (*Tenu'ah le-Yahadut shel Torah*),
headed by Professor Ephraim Elimelekh Urbach, which was active
between 1964 and 1968. This small movement, most of whose members belonged to the so-called "religious intelligentsia," proposed,
in its founding assembly, to close two gaps: the gap between the
nation and its Torah, and the gap between Halakhah and political,
economic, and social realities.[114] As to the use of force, Urbach
continued R. Reines' interpretation of the concept of *gevurah*. Pro-
posing to explain the concept on the basis of R. Abraham I. Kook's
teachings, he wrote:

> What is *gevurah*? *Gevurah* is not expressed in extreme phrase-
> ology or saber-rattling. R. Kook, who is frequently quoted,
> explains the blessing, "Who girds Israel with might [*gevurah*]"
> as follows: Israel's might is a special kind of might, a might
> that excels not in conquest of others, but relates mainly to a

person's conquest of himself. That is the might with which Israel is girded, which subordinates itself to the element of pure morality and the elevation of man as superior to beast.

After the Six-Day War, the ideas of R. Tzvi Yehudah Kook and his disciples gained increasing currency. In reaction, several religious-Zionist movements were established in the late 1970s and early 1980s, such as Oz ve-Shalom and Netivot Shalom; later, in 1987, the "Meimad" movement was founded. Despite the differences in nuance between these movements, they all spoke in a religious-ethical voice, advocating a realistic approach in the two senses proposed above. In other words, their supreme value was of the idea of the Jewish people's welfare in the real world. It is striking that the proponents of the realistic-ethical position have aimed their criticism at the elements of the harmonistic-dialectical position as represented by R. Tzvi Yehudah and his followers, seeking to undermine that position and suggest an alternative. Almost all of them are concerned primarily with the practical and ethical implications of the theological conception of the period. They attack the physical and military activism implied by the harmonistic-dialectical position, which they term a "messianic ideology." Moreover, like R. Reines, they stress the ethical-religious obligations of the Jew. They seem to be saying: Both things of which R. Reines warned – political-messianic activism and the ethos of brute strength and militarism – have materialized, of all places, in an important school of religious Zionism, that of R. Tzvi Yehudah Kook and his disciples. They deplore the radical messianic position and its political and ethical influence, expressing a demand to base the policies of the Jewish people on values.

Thus, for example, one of the founders of Netivot Shalom, Aviezer Ravitzky, believes that the root of this military radicalism is the definition of our time as the messianic age:

> No more the absolute messianic model, but the model that emerges in light of the period of the Judges, the kingdom of Judah, and the kingdom of Israel, and not less that emerging in light of the Second Temple and the Hasmonean kingdom.[115]

Similarly, R. Yehudah Amital, referring to the Lebanon War, writes:

> The struggle for the Land of Israel has assumed a militant, total, image. What is the meaning of this militancy?... For every problem there is only one answer: to take an unyielding, hawkish line.[116]

Representatives of this line of thought, recognizing the need to weigh different values against one another, favored a realistic approach. We have already seen that in R. Reines' view, whenever it was necessary to make such choices, it was the welfare and condition of the Jewish people that tipped the scales. Similarly, we find R. Yehudah Amital writing in the 1980s and 1990s, using almost the same phraseology as R. Reines:

> There is a certain scale of values in Judaism, and whoever fails to differentiate between "holy" and "holy" will ultimately not differentiate between "holy" and "profane." The order in the scale of values of which we are speaking is: *Israel, Torah, the Land of Israel.* The interest of the people of Israel takes precedence over the interest of the Land of Israel.[117]

Here is an emphatic representation of the realistic principle as embodied in a scale of values.[118] R. Amital is repeating R. Reines' formulation in his letter to Herzl – and we have come full circle.

3. THE ANTITHETICAL-CRITICAL MODEL: THE THOUGHT OF R. AHARON SHMUEL TAMARES AND ITS OFFSHOOTS

R. Aharon Shmuel Tamares, R. Moshe Avigdor Amiel, and, to a considerable degree, also Yeshayahu Leibowitz, reflect what we have called here the antithetical-critical position. All three figures see in "Torah" the defining concept of Judaism. According to R. Tamares and R. Amiel, the concept includes a clear-cut humanistic-ethical commitment. Leibowitz, on the other hand, considers Torah to be a divine commandment that a person accepts in order to worship God. Despite the differences, a salient element in the thought of all three is the "antithetical," in the sense that they perceive a confrontation between the "Torah" concept, normatively and programmatically speaking, and the values characteristic of political nationalism, and particularly the adoration of physical force. While R. Abraham Kook's position and that of his disciples was typically harmonistic, the "antithetical" thinkers see religion in general, and "Torah" in particular, as transcendental relative to the total demands of political nationalism, as a radical alternative to those demands. I have also called this position "critical": all three considered the emergence of radical Jewish political nationalism – the main target of their criticism – not only as an ideological revolution, but as a religious and ethical danger of the first stamp. Criticism, they believe, is in fact the task of religion, as a barrier against programmatic and normative political nationalism. Nevertheless, clearly expressed in the writings of all three figures is the tension between harsh criticism, on the one hand, and a significant measure of identification with the Zionist enterprise and desire to guarantee the Jewish people an independent political framework, on the other. In this context, one might say that none of the three distinguished to a sufficient degree between the different conceptions of nationalism in the Zionist movement – a fault which at times led them to indiscriminate statements.[119]

Since there is a considerable literature on the thought of Y. Leibowitz,[120] we shall concentrate in what follows on the teachings of R. Tamares[121] and R. Amiel.[122] The two lived in very different environments. Most of R. Amiel's Torah creativity took place during his terms of office first as Chief Rabbi of Antwerp and later as the Chief Rabbi of Tel Aviv-Jaffa. R. Tamares, on the other hand, spent all his life in Eastern Europe. R. Amiel occupied various positions in the rabbinical establishment and was prominent in the conferences of the Mizrahi movement during the 1930s, so that his scathing criticism, which did not even spare the Mizrahi movement, stands out in particular. R. Tamares, in contrast, preferred to remain for the most part the rabbi of a small community, remote from the religious establishment. Despite these differences, and the fact that nowhere in their writings do they explicitly refer to one another (it is highly doubtful whether they were even acquainted with each other's writings), we shall present their formulations side by side, in light of the considerable – and surprising – similarity in their ideas.

The pivot of their outlook is the antithetical-critical connection between the individual, faith and ethics, on the one hand, and between political nationalism, idolatry and wars, on the other.

We shall first set out the principles of their religious thought, which are concerned with the individual, with religious faith, and with ethics, and contrast them with what they call idolatry, that is, total ideologies that assimilate the individual. The prime example of such an ideology is political nationalism when it becomes total.

The second stage will be an analysis of their criticism of political Zionism as a natural outcome of total political nationalism, in particular the ethos of political Zionism that revolves around physical force. Finally, we shall examine the principles that guided their vision of the Zionist enterprise and the role R. Amiel assigned religious Zionism in that context.

Religion and the Individual

Nathan Rotenstreich has written that one of the elements responsible for the religious crisis in the modern era is the perceived antithesis between humanity's sovereign ability to know and "conquer" the world and nature, on the one hand, and religion, according to which man is dependent on the deity, on the other.[123] I believe that R. Tamares' thought may be seen as a radical philosophical attempt to tackle this issue. Like other modern thinkers, R. Tamares consistently adheres to an ethical-anthropocentric approach, both didactically and philosophically speaking. In other words, the point of departure in his analyses is humanity, not God: his interest lies in the human being in relation to the "other," to God, and to the world. The element defining his religious outlook is the individual. The essence of religion lies in the human being's level of self-awareness; similarly, the history of the evolution of religion is the history of humanity's self-awareness. This self-awareness began when humanity emerged from its wild state and discovered itself as an existing entity. The content of religion reflects humanity's general outlook vis-à-vis itself and its position in the real world. The foundation of R. Tamares' thought is the relationship between the cognitive and the connate; the human being's self-recognition entails moral behavior. R. Tamares' outlook essentially expresses a humanistic-individualistic position: "The foundation of the universe is the individual human being."[124]

The opposite of this outlook is idolatry – that is to say, not only the ancient pagan beliefs, but a whole world outlook. In this sense R. Tamares was following Maimonides, who also shifted the focus of the concept of idolatry from religion to erroneous thought.[125] Unlike Maimonides, however, he does not identify idolatry as intellectual error, but as any consciousness and ideology that fails to give precedence to the position of humanity, of the individual as an autonomous being. That is to say, any ideology or world view that rejects the priority of the human being as a value and subjugates it to another, supposedly more important, idea or concept is idolatrous. In R. Tamares' words, idolatry is "the eradication and humiliation of man, enslaving him to the forces of darkness and to the demons that rule the world as envisaged by idolatry." Education, in contrast, is "elevation of man's value, enthroning the human intellect over the world and subjugating all natural forces to him."[126] In essence, there is "a tendency imprinted upon man's soul to yearn for some ideal." Man may strive to realize the ideal by cultivating his own unique position, believing in himself, and realizing his ethical side; alternatively, he may embrace some collectivist ideology that commits the sin of idolatry, that is, he may be drawn into the totality of the collective.[127] The Torah, he writes, is a constitution that cultivates and develops a collective which takes pride in its *individuals*, who possess a religious-moral personality; according to the Torah-Jewish perception, freedom – freeing of the individual – is the heart of the matter and society is secondary.

Like R. Reines and R. Abraham Kook, R. Tamares bases his thought on the dichotomy between the idolatrous outlook common to many national cultures, on the one hand, and the religious mindset transmitted by the Jewish people. The Jewish people's mission is a commitment, first and foremost, to promote the idea of the human being's precedence and of humanity's spiritual and ethical improvement. The Jewish people must embody, through its life, constant protest against the use of force to oppress and kill human beings, as implied by the idolatrous point of view:

> Judaism, throughout its long history, is charged with a single mission: to lift up the spirit of the human race through the image of the Jewish people, which the Supreme Wisdom elected to preach its message to the world."[128]
>
> Because of this goal...Judaism continually preaches two things that are the foundations of the dominion of the spirit;... a) the moral feeling, that is, to do what is good and right, justice and law; b) the religious feeling, that is, to express the longings of man's soul for the "infinite" through various expressions, to be determined by "faith" for that purpose.

Political-nationalist ideology, by contrast, is the embodiment of idolatry. On an ideological plane, it prescribes such supreme ideals as "homeland," "state," "nation," transcending the precedence of the individual as a value; in practical terms, it promotes a culture of wars and international confrontation. Like the idolatrous civilizations of antiquity, the ideology of political nationalism does not direct human desires, through ideals, to the human soul, in order to deepen self-awareness and develop moral sensitivity; instead, it perpetuates personal existential vacuity, it "attracts" the human being to supposedly sublime ideas and values, to the extent that the uniqueness of the human being as an individual is dissipated.[129]

According to R. Tamares, the modern phenomenon of nationalism was a disaster for humanity, for it interrupted the human progress that had begun with the Enlightenment.[130] Repudiation of personal liberty illustrates, more than anything else, the sweeping totality of the nationalist ideology. This totality has ethical implications, embodied in a culture that advocates war and practically treats it as a cult, expressive of the new idolatry. As far as the ethical implications are concerned, the emergence of nationalism is a "sickness,"[131] since the core of its outlook is denial of the worth of the individual. Wars, too, are for the most part a product of the militant nature of nationalist ideology: "But now, the idol that is called 'The Homeland' and its cult that is called 'War,' in which evil plays a greater part than stupidity, have not abandoned even modern man, but have left him in his place."[132] The mission of the Jewish people, in our time more than ever, is to voice a perpetual moral protest against the idolatrous conceptions that bring about so many wars and so much bloodshed:

> We, the nation that has such an ancient tradition of going against all the nations, that for thousands of years has refused to kneel or bow down to the idol of the nations – we now have a sublime task, namely: to rise up against the idol of war that has so grown and flourished in recent generations and has become the senior of all idols…. [E]verything that has been created in our world should be free of the poison of the primeval serpent.[133]

We may well ask how such a radical viewpoint, based on the spiritual world of the individual, can be conveyed by a whole nation. R. Tamares had a unique historiosophical perception of the Jewish people, based on the idea of gradual improvement and perfection of religious life to ensure the personal religious experience of the subject. It should be noted that he considered that waging even optional war, which the Talmud and later halakhic authorities consider to be permitted in appropriate circumstances and under certain conditions, as a product of cultural assimilation, tantamount to acceptance of a political viewpoint inherent to the Gentile nations, diametrically opposed to the basic objective of the Torah.[134] As a rule, even past manifestations of Jewish statehood, such as Solomon's kingdom, did not escape R. Tamares' barbed tongue.[135] Only in the Second Temple period and later, after the cessation of its political independence, did the Jewish people achieve ethical and religious perfection. In R. Tamares' words: "We have explained that Exile was useful in converting the *official deity* that dominated Israel when they were living a political life into an *intimate deity*."[136] Nevertheless, one should stress that R. Tamares distinguished between the Torah objective, which seeks to educate a person whose attitude to bloodshed is one of profound disgust, and pacifist protest movements, which he regarded as general declarations of intent.[137]

R. Amiel, like R. Tamares, saw in the rise of modern political nationalism a re-emergence of ancient idolatry. There were several reasons for this attitude. First, the two phenomena had a similar psychological motive: The fear of natural catastrophe that brought ancient humans to deify nature is very similar to the fear of human violence that induced human beings to group themselves into "nations." Second, both phenomena accord absolute priority to a certain concept or idea that enslaves the individual. R. Amiel, like R. Tamares, argues that in political regimes "the entire right of the individual to exist is only for the collective.... Compared with the collective, the individual is like mere clay in the potter's hand."[138] One expression of the priority of the idea over the individual is the intolerable ease with which people are sent out to war, to kill and to be killed:

> They entirely forget about the private domain, as if it did not exist, and for that reason they have so many swords and spears, and for that reason they are busy evening, morning, and noon with waging war only.[139]
> ...to take individuals out, against their will, to the battlefield, to kill and to be killed in a holy war or an optional war, a defensive war or an aggressive war, and whoever refuses to do so is condemned to die.[140]

Third, the world outlook of political nationalism becomes idolatrous because of its limited, particularistic, and territorial viewpoint. Ancient idolatry commonly postulated the existence of the particular god of a nation, a deity whose mission was confined exclusively to the territory of the nation living there and who would protect that nation. The same element, R. Amiel claims, may be identified in modern political nationalism:

The form of the old idolatry is the new, modern nationalism, for buried deep within it are those idols of the nations, each nation believing in its particular god, that would save it from its enemies – who had other gods.[141]

Here, too, R. Amiel sees a direct link between the theological position, on the one hand, and on the other, ethical behavior that is inclined to collective egoism and therefore considers the nation to be the be-all and end-all, so that the use of force against other human groups is legitimate and even preferable:

> Nationalism, with a capital "N," is based on the materialistic view of the world, which sees in everything only the triumph of brute force, and justice belongs to the strongest…. Therefore, the core of this nationalism relies on material toughness, on physical might, and on an "iron fist." This nationalism derives its nourishment first and foremost not from "God's Image" that is in man, but from the corruptive devil that dwells within, that is, from the hatred harbored toward anyone of a different race or nationality. Nationalism of this kind derives from the ancient idolatry in which "every nation had its particular idol, there was a god of Assyria and a god of Aram."[142]

Opposing this nationalist-idolatrous world view is the humanistic Torah of Israel, which is founded on a monotheistic-universal theological outlook and centers on the priority of the individual as a supreme value:

> Our nationalism derives its nourishment from one God, Who exists from eternity to eternity, and His house is "called a House of prayer for all the nations." …Its most basic foundation and deepest root is the image of God that is in humanity and the absolute spirituality that reigns over everything.[143]

In other words, the monotheistic belief in a single Creator implies a universalistic perception of the world, a moral obligation toward all people, wherever they may be. Only such a religious faith can guarantee a humanistic conception of the world, since it necessarily implies a universal view of humanity. That is why, for example, the Torah was given in the wilderness: "For we have neither the idols of nature nor the idols of the nation, all of which are artificial things invented by human beings; but there is the God of the universe, who exists from eternity to eternity."

Like R. Tamares, R. Amiel is convinced that such distaste for the deification of brute force and for bloodshed is a product of profound cultural internalization throughout history; it is important for the ethical-religious mission of the Jewish people, and it can express the significance of its religious-moral goal:

> If you wish, you can say that the new nationalism as well, as understood today by the modern nations, is also a kind of idolatry in a new guise…and the sacrifices that are offered up to idols we indeed saw in the last war, the world war, their numbers reach tens of thousands…. We still have to stand guard to fulfill *our mission, which is to reject this idolatry in the world.*[144]

Criticism of Jewish Political Nationalism

The ideas we have outlined up to this point are the basis for R. Tamares' position that political Zionism, as taught by Herzl and Jabotinsky, is tantamount to importing an idolatrous nationalistic ideology into the Jewish world. In R. Tamares' view, political Zionism seeks to replace the defining Torah concept of Judaism:

> From the outside, from imitation of the cultures of the children of Ham and the Edomites, together with all the filth, all the clamor of tyranny and emptiness devoid of a holy and pure spirit that imbue their hymns of "nationalism" – from these have such elements been drawn into our own camp.[145]

Political Zionism seeks to recreate in the Jewish people an externalized perception of political life as the exclusive focus of human identity, to make them internalize a predatory, force-centered ethos in favor of warfare. The similarity of such ideas with R. Amiel's views in the 1930s is self-evident:

> All in all, Zionism has brought about a kind of *Copernican revolution* in the world of Judaism, that is to say, if in the past God and the Torah were central to all thoughts of Judaism, and we ourselves, the people of Israel, and all the more so the Land of Israel, danced around that center – Zionism has reversed the situation: The Land, the Land of Israel, has become the center of all centers, and on the other hand even the Torah and God, as it were, have been demoted to the periphery.[146]

In R. Amiel's view, adoption of a nationalist political ideology by the Jewish nation "derives from the origins of nationalism in the Gentile spirit, for which Bismarck laid the foundation-stone and Hitler celebrated the dedication of its house – a nationalism that is wholly idolatry. How could this resemble the Jewish religion, which is wholly sanctity and wholly purity?"[147]

The emergence of nationalism is not an expression of "renaissance of the holy," as believed by the proponents of the harmonistic view; rather it expresses the internalization of an idolatrous, power-centered, philosophy. So we see that, like R. Tamares, R. Amiel's principal criticism was aimed at the adoption of a philosophy whose offense was its force-based rather than moral ethos. The first signs to that effect may be discerned, for example, in a rhetoric that reflects a world view founded on a negative dimension:

> The nationalism of secular Zionism derives its vitality from hatred, the hatred of the Gentiles for the Jews, and it is no accident that it points to all the actions of the anti-Semites as proof of its validity; whereas our nationalism derives its vitality, on the contrary, from love, the love of Israel for God and for all those born in the image of God.

According to R. Amiel, only religious nationalism ("our nationalism"), which derives from a monotheistic-humanistic perception, can guarantee that secular political nationalism will not degenerate into ultra-nationalism. This is the strength inherent in the Torah, because

> Was not all Judaism's war against idolatry directed primarily against disdain for "the special moral sense pervading our hearts, which was seen as God's voice within man, that is, the image of God that is in man"?[148]

Strikingly, neither R. Tamares nor R. Amiel focuses on the realistic, political goals of political Zionism. In this respect, their approach is radically different from that of R. Reines. Moreover, in contrast to R. Reines and, to some degree, R. Abraham Kook, they make no attempt to analyze the geopolitical features of the Middle East[149] in order to determine the relationship between the ideology of political nationalism, the use of force, and moral decline. Their interest lies in uncovering the world view inherent in the nationalist ideology; they hold that it embodies an ethos, ideas, and values diametrically opposed to the religious-humanistic ethos of the Torah.[150] Their criticism is penetrating and biting: nationalism has become a defining value, while Torah or religion has become a merely tolerated option within the political-national identity. A distinction should be made, they argue, between two definitions of nationality, on the basis of which the nature of the Jewish national awakening must be judged. The first definition derives from the unique cultural content of Judaism and its values, whereas the second seeks to base the definition on a particular race.[151] The nationality of the Jewish people is defined through the very fact that it is alive and cultivates the Torah and Torah values: "[Nationality] is founded on spiritual distinction, with the purpose of combining actions and concepts." Unlike the perception of "nation" as a biological given or a primary fact, R. Tamares embraces the concept of "spiritual nation," which is defined almost exclusively by the spiritual values according to which a human group shapes its life.

What R. Abraham Kook considered a harbinger of comprehensive spiritual and national revival, R. Tamares saw as an illusion, leading inevitably to moral corruption. In his thought, the concept of "Torah" denotes first and foremost a set of ideas and values, not merely observance of the precepts that govern the relations between God and man. Thus R. Tamares is able to consider the proponents of humanistic liberalism as partners in the religious-ethical mission of the Jewish people:

> [The Torah] knows only the individual man of the Creator, who was created *ex nihilo* in His very image, the image of God, to live and to exist, to rule nature, but not to rule his fellow man and conquer him. This is also *the culture of the first liberals*, disciples of the visionaries who, at the beginning of the last century, looked to the Bible as their guide.[152]

For R. Tamares, the Torah and liberal humanism, which holds up the individual as an exclusive ontic entity, are practically identical; for R. Kook, however, and even more for his disciples, the individual derives his position from the collective of Israel.

At first sight, there is some similarity between R. Tamares' critique and that of the *haredi* opponents of Zionism, whose world view is also rooted in the "Torah" concept. However, the reason for R. Tamares' opposition to political Zionism is utterly different. He by no means takes a theological position that demands political and historical passivity until the advent of the Messiah.[153] Moreover, his opposition is based not on the secular way of life, in which there is no observance of the *mitzvot*, but on rejection of the nationalist ideology that leads to moral corruption and to essential conflict with the religious and ethical aims of the Torah. Witness, for example, his sharply worded letter to Shlomo Zalman Shragai, in which he tries to explain the meaning of his objection to political Zionism:

> However, I fear that the enslaved preaching of the priests of Zionism, which constantly declares, "There is no free man other than one who rules a state and wears a sword," has already succeeded in confusing the thoughts of our young people entirely,

to obliterate from their hearts the motto, "There is no free man
other than one who occupies himself with the Torah," and to
invest them with a frenetic spirit according to which they can
no longer perceive spiritual life without the "blue and white"
flag, and without it they are considered as spiritually dead.[154]

In order to differentiate his stand from the critique of the ultra-Orthodox camp, he adds:

> Nevertheless, I have not come here to accuse [the secular
> Zionists] of "religious violations," like the complaint that is
> current today in *haredi* circles[155]...First, I am no partner to the
> "heavenly Cossacks"...that they have taken upon themselves
> to build a "state" for me, to award me with a "homeland,"[156]
> with "camp battalions," "divisions,"...and all the rest of those
> excellent things upon which the "*goyim*," those lovely grand-
> children of Esau, pride themselves.... *It is not the fact that the
> Zionists are undermining Torah Judaism*, threatening to burn
> its spiritual treasures (something that is entirely foreign to me),
> that angers me, but that they are striving to give me another
> Judaism, a Judaism of "Homeland." It is not, for example, that
> they slaughter swine like the *goyim* and eat them on the Day
> of Atonement that enrages me, but that they wish to favor us
> with *the abominable idol*, the desired goal of the slaughterers of
> swine, with *the idol of the "Homeland"* with all the *contaminat-
> ing* things that appertain to the worship of that idol.[157]

As we have pointed out, he was criticizing political Zionism
for its adoption of political nationalism and the identity thereby
established, with all the moral implications of such ideologies.

Criticism of the Mizrahi

Even the Mizrahi movement, which aimed to create a synthesis of
nationalism and the Torah, represented for both R. Tamares and
R. Amiel a problematic, dangerous attempt to befog the ongoing
revolution of ideas and values. R. Tamares was voicing his criticism

as a bystander; R. Amiel, however, was speaking from the heart of
the establishment, in the context of the conferences of the Mizrahi
movement in the 1930s. Thus, R. Tamares writes in 1905:

> You Mizrahyites have chosen for yourselves a new God for
> Israel and set up the idol of "nationalism" to lead the life of
> the Congregation of Israel. Whereas hitherto the Matron of
> Israel was the Torah, and after it the Hebrew nation was called
> "people of the Torah," "people of the God of Israel,"...the nation
> has now been renamed for "nationalism," that is, the founda-
> tion of the Israelite nation is "nationalism," just as there is a
> nation of those known as "Frenchmen."... It follows that the
> idol of "nationalism," that poisoning idol invented by the worst
> nations of the world, is today the God of Israel, *while the "Torah"*
> *is tolerated [by nationalism] with patience.* Lord of Abraham!
> How terrible and strange is this situation!

Indeed, based on the accumulated experience of modern history since the emergence of the ideology of political nationalism, R.
Tamares believes that the philosophy of political Zionism will sooner
or later give birth to a cult of military force and war:

> So we must know that the attempt to introduce little Jacob to
> *the market of nationalist politics is like preparing Israel for war*
> *and teaching the sons of Judah the bow.* For war is at any rate
> implicit in political machinations, or war in the literal sense,
> blood and fire, shooting real bullets – if there were a possibility
> that foreign thoughts would enter our mind, to obtain a terri-
> tory for ourselves by brute force.[158]

R. Amiel, too, in the 1930s and in an entirely different historical and
political context, criticizes the prevalent ideology of the Mizrahi
movement. Briefly, one might say that R. Amiel believed that the
Mizrahi had the task of standing guard, of preventing the transformation of secular political nationalism into ultra-nationalism. This
task required ideological alertness, a clear distinction between these

movements, and critical activity. First and foremost, therefore, R. Amiel attacked attempts to synthesize the concepts of "nationalism" and "religion:"

> We are deceiving ourselves if we think that we have already achieved real peace between the Torah and Zionism, *between religion and nationalism*, for in truth we have hereby achieved only a state of duality, in which each ideology derives its vitality *from a different source*, and if we do not sense and feel the mutual contradiction, that is only because as the days go by, one of them gradually contracts and retreats more and more into a corner, until it will not be sensed at all. And that "one" is of course the Torah and religion.[159]

In other words, the problem lies in the failure to recognize the difference between two normative sets of values. This blurring of differences in the religious Zionist camp has launched a process in which nationalism is supplanting the normative precepts of religion. R. Amiel's vision of a situation in which the "Torah" concept would determine one's world view is very typical of the antithetical-critical position. Like R. Tamares, he believes that the significance assigned to nationalism and the independent political framework would be determined entirely by the "Torah" concept:

> The Mizrahi is not a party based on two foundations, Zionism and Orthodoxy, or religiosity and nationalism, for these terms too came from Babylon and not from the Land of Israel.... Whoever says that he has in Judaism these two things [= religion and nationalism] together, understanding thereby two separate things – in the end he has nothing together.[160]

The Mizrahi's offense, at the level of principles, was not only in its faulty definition of its terms, but also in the principles governing education in the religious-Zionist camp. Here, too, instead of more sharply delineating problems and differences, the religious Zionists tend to create confusing syntheses:

Our education is based on a superficial program, on the small-
ness of our thought: "The Land of Israel for the nation of Israel
according to the Torah of Israel," as if the only difference between us and the secular Zionists were those last three words,
whereas in the first two things, "the Land of Israel for the nation
of Israel," we have no argument at all, as if there is no difference between our understanding and theirs in the meaning of
"Land of Israel" and "nation of Israel," and as if we too agree,
like them, to understanding the Land of Israel and the nation
of Israel in a completely secular sense.[161]

On what basis did R. Tamares decide, unhesitatingly, that
the Jewish political-nationalist ideology implied a power-centered,
militaristic, anti-ethical ethos? Several reasons and phenomena seem
to have shaped his conviction that Zionism would not lead to the
spiritual and ethical revival of Judaism that he had envisaged, but
to imitations of the ultra-nationalist culture of certain European nations. For example, he complains that representatives of the Zionist
movement expressed admiration for the First World War and for
political exploitation, and advocated the use of force.[162] Certain
Zionists praised the war for the new spirit it had created, with such
expressions as "these are great days,"[163] refusing to recognize that
tens of thousands of people had lost their lives in the war.[164]

He was convinced that this power-centered ethos had also
taken over culture and education.[165] One sign to that effect was the
type of hero that was promoted among Zionists. Around Trumpeldor, for example, there was a veritable cult of personality. According
to R. Tamares, Trumpeldor was the embodiment of brute force and
ultra-nationalism, an obvious product of pagan culture.[166]

At the same time, our picture will not be complete without
mentioning R. Tamares' explicit advocacy of self-defense as an
ethical and religious duty. He did not discuss this subject frequently,
preferring mostly to aim his criticism at the cult of physical force.
Nevertheless, it should not be thought that he was in favor of extreme
pacifism, excluding the right of self-defense:

Even when we proceed to seek improvement of our unstable situation, we seek only a remedy for our oppression, not for our humility, wishing to straighten our backs but not to raise our pride; in simple words, our desire or ambition is not to be subjugated, a desire for equality and enjoyment of "human" rights, but not to subjugate others, as implied by "political" ambitions.[167]

R. Tamares' perception of the ideal political structure for the Jewish people in the Land of Israel revolved around the idea of a spiritual center, *à la* Ahad Ha-Am.[168] The emphasis would then be placed on renewal of Judaism, on spiritual and ethical renaissance rather than on the political dimension. It was clear to him that not all Jews in the world would wish to live in such a frame, so that the goal of the spiritual center in the Land of Israel would be to exert influence "throughout the Jewish Diaspora, for the sake of the Torah that would issue from Zion and water the flocks of the Children of Israel wherever they landed in the Diaspora." This would, he believed, include an independent political entity that would guarantee the physical welfare of the nation of the Torah, but in which the state would be seen at most as a means toward an end.[169]

As to R. Amiel, despite his vehement objections to the use of force, he was not in favor of a pacifistic position. One might say that ideas implicit in R. Tamares' writings received explicit expression in R. Amiel's thought, which makes a sharp distinction between the use of force for political or ideological purposes and its use in self-defense. The sole justification for the use of arms, he writes, is in unambiguous circumstances requiring self-defense – and even then weapons should be used most reluctantly, for lack of choice:

For the Israelite nation harbors the utmost hate for war, even defensive war, and if it at times has no choice but to apply the undisputed *Halakhah* as ruled, that "if a person comes to kill you, kill him first," he does so with sorrow and regret, for they are the descendants of Jacob, who was more fearful of killing than of being killed.[170]

Unlike R. Tamares, R. Amiel also found himself reacting to a practical reality that had become violent. In response to attacks on the Jewish population, various avenging actions were undertaken against Arab civilians. In 1938 there were several terror attacks against the Arab population; some innocent Arabs were killed and the perpetrators were not found. Rumors that Jews had been responsible aroused passionate arguments in the Jewish population in general, and among religious Jews in particular. R. Amiel was one of the important figures who reacted, participating in the public debate *inter alia* in articles published in the press. He focused mainly on two issues: 1) Indiscriminate revenge was forbidden; 2) there could be absolutely no distinction between murder committed for the sake of revenge and murder committed for utilitarian purposes. To his mind, both these phenomena, acts of vengeance aimed at innocent people and condemnation of murders for merely utilitarian reasons, were expressions of the same underlying ideas, which he deplored.

It was absolutely forbidden to kill innocent people, even when Jews were victims of terrorist attacks, "even in the case of the murder of murderers, if there is the slightest doubt, even one chance out of a thousand that there is one person among these murderers who has not committed murder." This was not a question of political or personal restraint, but a fully ethical question involving personal courage: "Self-restraint, for which one indeed requires special courage, unsurpassed heroism."

As stated, there were some who deplored the murder of innocents even when committed for purely utilitarian reasons; even worse: there were some who expressed understanding, if not agreement, for murder motivated by ideological reasons, for the common good:

> After all, we are not talking here about material benefit, or about the benefit of individuals, but about the benefit of the collective, *of the entire nation....* "Thou shalt not kill" is one of

the Ten Commandments, but the life and redemption of Israel is, after all, the whole Torah.

In other words: The justification of people who advocated killing for ideological motives was the benefit of the people, which was a supreme value, dominating any other ethical consideration. In such an argument the nation becomes a supreme, absolute value. For R. Amiel, such arguments exemplified the danger inherent in the nationalist-political ideology. In such times of indiscriminate terror and lukewarm responses, R. Amiel applied the ideological distinctions of his own teachings to deplore the phenomenon:

> Such morals are the morals not of Judaism, but of the Gentile nations. Each nation, each people, says that its existence is the supreme value, and that "Thou shalt not kill" is merely one of the Ten Commandments. And wherever it believes that by abandoning "Thou shalt not kill" it will gain something for its own common good, it harbors no doubts and violates the commandment. These, indeed, are the morals of the nationalism of *Bismarck and Hitler*, morals based on the rule that the ends justifies the means, and that for the good of *their* collective it is permitted to use any deplorable means. But the ethics of Judaism teaches us the very opposite: It is not the end that justifies the means, but the shameful means that violate even the sacred end.

R. Amiel is clearly assuming that an ethical approach is the result of a basic ideological outlook: If the concept of "nation" is absolute and supreme, any action that serves the nation will suppress one's moral obligation toward the other. On the other hand, the "ethics of Judaism," a defining, axiomatic concept, dictates above all an ethical attitude to issues on the public agenda. He expressed his view in particularly sharp terms when questioned as to what he would say if it turned out that the killers of innocent Arabs were indeed Jews:

If there are such people, the guilty persons are those who, for more than fifty years, have based Judaism entirely on "Let us, the House of Israel, be like all the nations," who have falsified not only our Torah but all our history; for all our history is entirely contrary to "nationalism" of this kind. If our nationalism is the nationalism of the Gentiles, then our ethics is also not the "ethics of Judaism" but "ethics of the Gentiles."

According to R. Amiel, the establishment of the state was conditional on insistence on our ethical-religious uniqueness: "We cannot possibly build our national home by the sword that has been wielded upon innocent people; such a home is violated from the start."[171]

In sum, internalization among religious-Zionist circles of the political activism taught by Zionism, and later experience of a violent reality, produced different, sometimes even widely divergent, positions on the question of the ethical-religious dimension of the Zionist enterprise from a Zionist and religious standpoint.

All one can say at this point is, that the story is hardly over.

NOTES

I wish to thank Mr. David Louvish for translating this article from the Hebrew.

1. Joseph Klausner, *The Messianic Idea in Israel* (Hebrew; Tel Aviv, 1956), 2:215–232.

2. Aviezer Ravitzky, *Messianism, Zionism and Jewish Religious Radicalism*, trans. Michael Swirsky & Jonathan Chipman (Chicago, 1996), 2–3; Eliezer Schweid, *Jewish Thought in the 20th Century: An Introduction* (Atlanta, GA, 1992), 35–36. On the normative imperatives of nationalist ideologies, including the use of force, see Yaakov Talmon, "Unity of the Nation and Revolutionary Brotherhood" (Hebrew), in idem, *Unity and Uniqueness* (Hebrew; Tel Aviv, 1965).

3. This article is a condensed version of a more comprehensive study: Elie Holzer, "Nationalism and Morality: Conceptions on the Use of Force within Ideological Streams of Religious Zionists" (Hebrew), Ph.D. dissertation, Hebrew University (Jerusalem, 1998).

4. R. Isaac Jacob Reines, *Or Hadash al Tziyyon* (Vilna, 1902), 116.

5. See, e.g., Ravitzky, *Messianism, Zionism and Jewish Religious Radicalism*, 86 ff.

6. R. Avraham Isaac Ha-Kohen Kook, *Orot ha-Kodesh* (Jerusalem, 1985), 3:69.

7. R. Avraham Isaac Ha-Kohen Kook *Orot* (Jerusalem, 1963), 102–104.

8. R. Avraham Isaac Ha-Kohen Kook, *Hazon ha-Geulah* (Jerusalem, 1941), 290 [my italics]. These ideas should be treated with some caution, since *Hazon ha-Geulah* was edited by R. Meir Bar-Ilan after R. Kook's death, and the source of the various

parts of this book in the writings of R. Kook is not clear. See *Orot*, 55; cf. ibid., 140, 139, 151, 158.

9. See Eliezer Schweid, *A History of Jewish Thought in Modern Times* (Hebrew; Jerusalem, 1977), 373–385.

10. R. Avraham Isaac Ha-Kohen Kook, *Olat Ra'ayah* (Jerusalem, 1985), 1:233.

11. As to Israel's wars in the time of the Bible, see *Iggerot ha-Ra'ayah* (Jerusalem, 1962), 1:100; *Orot*, 14, #4.

12. R. Avraham Isaac Hacohen Kook, "Nehamat Yisrael," *Ma'amarei ha-Ra'ayah* (Jerusalem, 1988), vols. 1–2, 281.

13. *Ketubot* 111a. See Elie Holzer, "The Evolving Meaning of the Three Oaths within Religious Zionism" (Hebrew), *Da'at* 47 (Summer 2001): 129–145.

14. He plays on the Hebrew words Zamir/Zemir (pruning or song) based on two biblical verses: Song of Songs 2:12 and Isaiah 25:5.

15. *Orot*, 13, 15, 104.

16. R. Avraham Isaac Ha-Kohen Kook, *Iggerot ha-Ra'ayah*, 2:317.

17. *Orot*, 14.

18. Ibid., 13, #1.

19. Tamar Ross, "Rav Kook's Conception of God" (Hebrew), *Da'at* 9 (1982):68–69; Binyamin Ish Shalom, *R. Abraham Isaac Kook – between Rationalism and Mysticism* (Hebrew; Tel Aviv, 1990), 21 ff., 106; Yaakov Katz, "Orthodoxy in Historical Perspective" (Hebrew), *Kivvunim* 33 (1987): 95.

20. Eliezer Schweid, *The Idea of Judaism as a Culture* (Hebrew; Tel Aviv, 1995), 266–270.

21. Isaiah Berlin, "Historical Inevitability," in idem, *Four Essays on Liberty* (London, New York, etc., 1969), 53.

22. Ibid., 57.

23. *Orot*, 27.

24. R. Avraham Isaac Ha-Kohen Kook, *Orot ha-Kodesh*, 2:453–456.

25. R. Avraham Isaac Ha-Kohen Kook, *Ma'amarei ha-Ra'ayah*, vols. 1–2 (Jerusalem, 1988), 417.

26. The real nation of Israel is linked with *Knesset Yisrael* (the collectivity of Israel) and the kabbalistic *sefirah* of *malkhut* (Kingship); see *Iggerot ha-Ra'ayah*, 3:117.

27. R. Avraham Isaac Hacohen Kook, *Iggerot ha-Ra'ayah*, 2:186.

28. *Orot*, 63.

29. See, e.g., R. Avraham Isaac Hacohen Kook, *Sefer Eder ha-Yakar* (Jerusalem, 1906), 111.

30. *Hazon ha-Geulah*, 3 [emphasis in the original].

31. *Iggerot ha-Ra'ayah*, 2:186 (written in 1913).

32. For the theory of opposites in this context, see Yehudah Gellman, "Zion and Jerusalem: The Jewish State according to R. Abraham Isaac Kook" (Hebrew), *Iyunim Bitkumat Israel* 4 (1994):505–514.

33. "There can be no more manifest [sign of] redemption than this.... O mountains of Israel, you shall shoot forth your branches and yield your fruit" (*Sanhedrin* 98a).

34. *Iggerot ha-Ra'ayah*, 1:244.

35. R. Avraham Isaac Ha-Kohen Kook, "Mi-Ma'amakkei ha-Kodesh," *Ha-Hed* (1931).

36. *Iggerot ha-Ra'ayah*, 1:56–57; "Kodesh va-hol be-Tehiyyat Yisrael," *Ha-Hed* (1931);
    R. Avraham Isaac Ha-Kohen Kook, *Otzerot ha-Ra'ayah*, 888; Letter to R. Zerihan,
    Peri ha-Aretz [a journal for matters of Halakhah and faith] (1986):25.

37. R. Avraham Isaac Ha-Kohen Kook, *Arfillei Tohar* (Jerusalem, 1983), 104.

38. *Orot*, 63.

39. In this respect, I disagree to some extent with the view that the transition from R.
    Kook's thought to that of his heirs was a transition from a doctrine of vision versus
    society as a critical pattern, to the idea of a "protective enclosure," as argued by
    Ravitzky, *Messianism, Zionism and Jewish Religious Radicalism*, 143; there are ad-
    ditional expressions of the "protective" motive in R. Kook's writings; see, e.g., *Orot*,
    65, 20–21; *Hazon ha-Geulah*, 103.

40. The ideas represented by those generally known as R. Tzvi Yehudah's "disciples" –
    particularly those who consider themselves his disciples though not seen as such by
    their peers – cover a fairly wide spectrum. This account does not claim to discuss
    all of them, but only those whose thought was shaped to some degree or another by
    the harmonistic-dialectical doctrines of R. Kook senior and who applied redemp-
    tive exegesis to the new violent realities.

41. See Uriel Tal, "Foundations of a Political Messianic Trend in Israel" (Hebrew), in
    Myth and Reason in Contemporary Jewry (Hebrew; Tel Aviv, 1987), 115; Eliezer
    Don-Yehiya, "The Book and the Sword: The Nationalist Yeshivot and Political
    Radicalism in Israel," in Martin E. Marty & Scott Appleby (eds.), *Accounting for
    Fundamentalisms: The Dynamic Character of Movements* (Chicago, 1994), 273.

42. R. Tzvi Yehudah Kook, "El mishmar ha-Am ha-Yisraeli," *Li-Netivot Yisrael*
    (Jerusalem, 1989), 106, 108.

43. R. Tzvi Yehudah Kook, "Va-Hare'otem ve-Nosha'tem," ibid., 153 (undated article).

44. R. Tzvi Yehudah Kook, "Le-Mitzvat ha-Aretz," ibid., 119.

45. Jacob L. Talmon, *The Origins of Totalitarian Democracy* (London, 1955),
    Introduction.

46. R. Tzvi Yehudah Kook, "Orot ha-Geulah u-Netivoteha," in H.A. Schwartz (ed.),
    Mi-tokh ha-Torah ha-Go'elet 4 (Jerusalem, 1991), 55. The comprehensive view
    may be expressed even in extreme cases, as for example in incidents in the War
    of Independence in which Jews were mistakenly killed by other Jews; see "Mi-
    Ma'amakkim," *Li-Netivot Yisrael*, 125.

47. R. Tzvi Yehudah Kook, "Shelihuto shel ha-Ra'ayah," in Jacob Bramson (ed.), *Ba-
    Ma'arakhah ha-Tzibburit* (Jerusalem, 1986), 84.

48. R. Tzvi Yehudah Kook, *Mi-tokh ha-Torah ha-Go'elet*, 54.

49. Editorial, "Malkhut u-Memshalah," *Yesha Yemino*, no. 35, ed. Yehudah Veitzen &
    Jacob Shahor (Pesagot, 1993), 4.

50. Ibid., 77. On the concept of national honor in nationalist ideologies see W.R.
    Garret, "Religion and the Legitimation of Violence," in J.K. Hadden & A. Shupe
    eds., *Prophetic Religions and Politics* (New York, 1986), 1:105.

51. See, e.g., Maimonides, *Mishneh Torah, Hilkhot Yesodei ha-Torah*, chap. 5.

52. *Eretz ha-Tzevi: Rabbenu ba-Maʿarakhah al Shelemut ha-Aretz* (Bet El, 1995), 73.

53. R. Tzvi Yehudah Kook, *Ba-Maʿarakhah ha-Tzibburit*, 120, 86.

54. R. Shlomo Aviner, "Ha-Reʾalizm ha-Meshihi," *Artzi* 3 (1983): 63; He adds there in a note: "The manifest redemption of the settlement of our land was perceived as an unmistakable sign of our redemption by the great scholars of Israel and decisors of Halakhah, the Gaon of Vilna…our Master the *Rav*, etc."

55. R. Dov Leor, "Ger Toshav ve-Hagdarato be-Dorenu," *Tzefiyyah* 2 (1985): 80; S. Aviner, *Itturei Kohanim* 57 (Jerusalem, 1990), 7.

56. "Malkhut u-Memshalah" (above, n. 49), 4.

57. *Eretz ha-Tzvi*, 4. See further: "Every Jew who returns to the Land brings back to Zion part of the *Shekhinah* that stayed with the people in Exile. Every Jew who comes to the Land of Israel, every tree planted in the soil of Israel, every rifle added to the army of Israel – these are one further really spiritual stage, another step in the Redemption, like the glorification and increase of the Torah in the proliferation of yeshivot;" *Maʿariv* (Eve of Passover, 1962); quoted in R. Tzvi Yehudah Kook, "Li-hyot [to be] Yehudi Tov – Kodem Kol li-hyot [to live] be-Eretz Yisrael," in *Ha-Medinah be-Hagut ha-Yehudit: Mekorot u-Maʿamarim*, ed. Arieh Strikovsky (Jerusalem, 1982), 212.

58. This approach is known in the scholarly literature as "expansionism"; see Don-Yehiya, "The Book and the Sword," 267.

59. Yitzhak Sheilat, "*Mi Mefahed mi-Meshiah Tzidkenu*," *Artzi* 3 (1983): 57–58 (emphasis in the original).

60. R. J.I. Reines, *Or Hadash al Tziyyon* (Vilna, 1902), 36.

61. Hanan Porat, "Ha-Pulmus im ha-Rav Amital al Eretz Yisrael," *Nekudah* 56 (1982): 36.

62. Maimonides, *Mishneh Torah, Hilkhot Melakhim*, chap. 11 and Nahmanides in his *Commentary on Maimonides' Sefer ha-Mitzvot*, in the list of Positive Commandments that Maimonides has forgotten according to Nahmanides, Commandment #4.

63. *Eretz ha-Tzvi*, 5. This statement dates from 1967; R. Tzvi Yehudah first refers to Nahmanides as "father of Israel," in "Ha-Torah ve-ha-Geulah," *Li-Netivot Yisrael*, 90.

64. *Ba-Maʿarakhah ha-Tzibburit*, 23.

65. R. Yehoshua, *Bat Kol* 9 (26.2.1980); at the time of writing, R. Hess was the Campus Rabbi of Bar-Ilan University.

66. *Mi-Tokh ha-Torah ha-Goʾelet*, 31.

67. Quoted by Ravitzky, *Messianism, Zionism and Jewish Religious Radicalism*, 130.

68. Shlomo Aviner, "Yerushat ha-Aretz ve-ha-Baʾayah ha-Musarit," *Artzi* 2 (Iyyar–Sivan 1982): 111.

69. Idem, "Ha-Reʾalizm ha-Meshihi," *Arzi* 3 (1983): 64.

70. R. Tzvi Yehudah Kook, "Li-hyot [to be] Yehudi Tov – Kodem Kol li-hyot [to live] be-Eretz Yisrael," *Ba-Maʿarakhah ha-Tzibburit*, 24.

71. See Elie Holzer, "The Evolving Meaning of the Three Oaths within Religious Zionism."

72. For the concept of *Sinnbild*, see Paul Mendes-Flohr, "Buber between Nationalism and Mysticism" (Hebrew), *Iyyun* 29 (1990): 75.
73. *Eretz ha-Tzvi*, 13.
74. R. Eliezer Waldman, "Li-khbosh et ha-Har," *Nekudah* 20 (1980): 21.
75. R. Eliyahu Avihayil, "Ha-Hashgahah ha-Elokit Doheket Banu," *Tzefiyyah* 2 (Spring 1985): 82. On this assumption, the terrorists are actually God's emissaries, a divine tool in the ongoing process of redemption.
76. R. Shlomo Aviner, "Le-Romem et ha-Ruah," *Nekudah* 48 (1982): 4.
77. R. Eliezer Waldman, "Ha-Ma'avak ba-Derekh la-Shalom," *Artzi* 3 (1983): 18.
78. R. Tzvi Tau, *Le-Emunat Ittenu: Kavvim la-Havanat ha-Tekufah* (Jerusalem, 1994), 139.
79. For a biography of R. Reines, see J.L. Fishman (Maimon), *Zekhor zot le-Yaakov: Toledot ha-Rav I.J. Reines* (Jerusalem, 1932). For a partial summary of his views see Joseph Wanefsky, *R. Jacob Reines: His Life and Thought* (New York, 1970).
80. In contradistinction to the previous section of this paper, we cannot claim here to be dealing with a self-conscious philosophical "school." Moreover, the writers we call "R. Reines' ideological successors" cannot all be considered thinkers who developed a comprehensive, systematic ideology.
81. Elie Holzer, "The Use of Military Force in the Religious-Zionist Ideology of R. Jacob Reines and His Successors," *Studies in Contemporary Jewry* 18 (2002): 74–94.
82. *Deut. Rabbah* 4:2.
83. R. Isaac Jacob Reines, *Sha'arei Orah ve-Simhah* (Vilna, 1899), 42.
84. Ibid. See also similarly note 44.
85. Aviezer Ravitzky, "Ha-Tzafuy ve-ha-Reshut Netunah: Messianism, Zionism and the Future of Israel in the Different Religious Outlooks in Israel" (Hebrew), in: *Towards the 21st Century: Targets for Israel*, ed. Aluf Hareven (Hebrew; Jerusalem, 1984), 135–198, esp. 178–179. On comparisons between R. Kook and R. Reines see idem, 146–158; Michael Tzvi Nehorai, "R. Reines and R. Kook – Two Approaches to Zionism" (Hebrew), in: *Yovel Orot: Haguto shel ha-Rav Avraham Yitzhak ha-Kohen Kook*, ed. Benjamin Ish Shalom & Shalom Rosenberg (Jerusalem, 1988), 25–34; idem, "On the Essence of Religious Zionism" (Hebrew), *Bi-Shvilei ha-Tehiyyah* 3, ed. M. Eliav (Ramat-Gan, 1988), 25–38.
86. *Gen. Rabbah* 42.
87. *Sha'arei Orah ve-Simhah*, 44.
88. Ehud Luz has argued that R. Reines' thought is self-contradictory and philosophically obscure: E. Luz, *Parallels Meet: Religion and Nationalism in Early Zionist Movement (1882–1904)* (Hebrew; Tel Aviv, 1985), 310.
89. The uniqueness of the Jewish people lies in its Torah. Only through the Torah is the Jew able to realize himself as an *adam*, "a person." See R. Reines' interpretation of the Midrash "You are called *adam*, but the nations of the world are not called *adam*," *Sha'arei Orah ve-Simhah*, (Vilna, 1899), 30.
90. These ideas are based on a complex theory of Divine Providence; see Eliezer Schweid, "The Beginnings of a Zionistic-National Theology: The Philosophy

of R. Isaac Jacob Reines" (Hebrew), in: *Studies in Jewish Mysticism, Philosophy and Ethical Literature (Presented to Isaiah Tishby on his 75ᵗʰ Birthday)*, (Hebrew; Jerusalem, 1986), 700–707.

91. Yosef Salmon, "Hibbat Zion's Struggle for *Haredi* Support during the 1890s," in idem, *Religion and Zionism: First Encounters* (Jerusalem, 2002), 235–278.

92. R. Reines writes of being undecided for as long as two years as to whether to cooperate with political Zionism; see *Nod Shel Demigod* (Vilna, 1904), 16.

93. R. Reines, *Or Hadash al Ziyyon*, 128.

94. Reading *he-hamur* for an apparent misprint.

95. That is, without the use of military force; see Holzer, "Nationalism and Morality," 192.

96. *Or Hadash al Tziyyon*, 116. R. Reines was critical of those who saw in Zionism a harbinger of redemption: "If there are any sermonizers or preachers who, while seeking the welfare of Zion, also speak of Redemption and the advent of the messiah, giving the impression of the corrupt thought of this idea as if encroaching on the limits of true Redemption – whose fault is that? They are expressing only their own conceit" (Manifesto by R. Reines, R. Aharon Dov-Baer Ha-Kohen Lapp, R. Nahum Greenhaus, and R. Pinchas Rozavsky, *Ha-melitz* 78 [1900]). At the same time, however, R. Reines sees Zionism as seeking to release the Jewish people from its passive ethos. See his letter to Herzl, December 9, 1903: "Because thereby [by agreeing to the Uganda resolution, E.H.] we hope to rescue one sizable *part* of our people and restore its physical and spiritual wholeness" (in Moshe Heiman, ed., *Minutes of the Zionist General Council. The Uganda Controversy*, vol. ı [Jerusalem, 1970], 180; my italics, I am indebted to Dr. Yaakov Tzur for referring me to this source).

97. Personally, however, R. Reines abstained in the final vote; Ge'ulah Bat Yehudah, *Ish ha-Me'orot* (Jerusalem, 1985), 214.

98. Letter to Theodor Herzl, see note 96.

99. From "Lifnei ha-Kongress," *Ha-Zeman* (1905), no. 119.

100. Introduction to *Or Hadash al Tziyyon*; Eliezer Don Yehiya, "Ideology and Policy in Religious Zionism–R. Yitzhak Yaakov Reines' Conception of Zionism and the Policy of the Mizrahi under His Leadership" (Hebrew), *Ha-Tziyyonut* 8 (1983): 127.

101. *Sha'arei Orah ve-Simhah*, 17, 58.

102. R. Isaac Jacob, *Sefer ha-Arakhim* (New York, 1926), 1:283–285, 132–133.

103. *Or Hadash al Ziyyon*, 36, 238; see also in general ibid., *Sha'ar* 7, chap. 3. See Elie Holzer, "The Evolving Meaning of the Three Oaths within Religious Zionism."

104. Anita Shapira, *Land and Power* (Hebrew; Tel Aviv, 1992), 156 ff.

105. Yeshayahu Bernstein, "*Ha-Dibbera ha-Shishit*," *Ha-Tzofeh* (June 19, 1939), 37.

106. Ibid. On the "*havlagah*" period in general see further H. Genizi ed., *Religion and Resistance in Mandatory Palestine* (Hebrew; Tel Aviv, n.d. [1995]); N. Gal-Or, *The Jewish Underground: Our Terrorism* (Hebrew; Merhaviah, 1990), 23–30.

107. R. Isaac Herzog, "Nahpesah Derakhenu," in: *Neged ha-Teror. Ma'amarim, Reshimot,*

Ne'ummim ve-Gilluyei Da'at, ed. Binyamin & Yaakov Peterseil (Ramat-Gan & Jerusalem, 1939), 42; see also his colleague, R. Ben-Zion Hai Uziel, the Sephardic Chief Rabbi in the 1930s, in his article, *"Lo Yishafekh dam be-Kerev Artzekha,"* ibid., 69.

108. As stated by R. Uziel, quoted in Jacob Shavit ed., *"Self-Restraint" or "Reaction": The Debate in the Jewish Community 1936–1939* (Hebrew; Ramat-Gan, 1983), 149.

109. *Ha'aretz* (November 19, 1937). The reason for *"havlagah"* was given as "Her ways are pleasant ways, and all her paths, peaceful" (Prov. 3:17).

110. R. Moshe Ostrovsky, "Kiddush Hashem," *Ha-Tzofeh* (July 18, 1939) (quoted by Don-Yehiya, "Religion and Political Terror: Orthodox Jews and Retaliation during the 1936–1939 'Arab Revolt'" [Hebrew], *Ha-Tziyyonut* 17 [1993]:172–173).

111. Shmuel Dothan, *The Partition of Eretz-Israel in the Mandatory Period* (Hebrew; Jerusalem, 1980), 174; see also Hilda Schatzberger, *Resistance and Tradition in Mandatory Palestine* (Hebrew; Ramat-Gan, 1985), 95, who argues that early signs of halakhic debate over the question of religiously obligated war (*milhemet mitzvah*) first appeared in the 1930s. However, she is dubious as to the significance of these early stages.

112. *"Kol koreh shel ha-Rabanim ha-Rashiyim,"* 15 Shevat 5707 [= February 5, 1947] (quoted by Hilda Schatzberger, *Resistance and Tradition*, 104).

113. Quoted by Yosi Melman, "Ha-Sheker ha-Muskam shel Qibya," *Ha'aretz* (April 18, 1997), 6b.

114. Ephraim Elimelekh Urbach, *"Le-Shorsham shel Devarim"* (Movement for Torah Judaism, 1966), 10.

115. Aviezer Ravitzky, "Ha-Geulah ve-ha-Berit," *Netivoteha Shalom* (Jerusalem, 1987), 21; R. Yehudah Amital, the founder of the movement, has criticized the concept of *athalta de-geulah* (beginnings of Redemption), on the grounds that "the only certain thing is the end of the process; the duration of the process, whether it will be long or short, depends on our actions and our behavior" (R. Y. Amital, "Hitmodedut ve-Etgar ba-metzi'ut ha-Hadashah," *Meimad* [1994], 7).

116. R. Y. Amital, "Meser Politi o Meser Hinnukhi," *Alon Shevut* (1983): 37, 49; *Netivot Shalom* has published several meta-halakhic sources expressing a primary ethical position similar to that of many personalities and Rabbis in the 1930s.

117. R. Y. Amital, "Be-Milkud ha-Shelemut," *Nekudah* 26 (1982): 10.

118. Another expression of the realistic principle has been represented by Uriel Simon, who distinguishes between the ideal plane and historical realization, between the Divine right to the Land of Israel and the obligation to confine that right within the limits of political and historical reality: U. Simon, "The Biblical Destinies – Conditional Promises," *Tradition* 17/2 (Spring 1978): 88.

119. For a classification of nationalist ideologies see, e.g., Carlton J.H. Hayes, "The Major Types of Nationalism," in Louis L. Snyder ed., *The Dynamics of Nationalism: Readings in Its Meaning and Development* (Princeton, 1964), 51–52.

120. See for example Avi Sagi ed., *Yeshayahu Leibowitz: His World and Philosophy* (Jerusalem, 1995).

121. R. Aaron Samuel Tamares (1839–1931) studied *inter alia* at the Kovno *"Kolel*

Perushim" and the Volozhin Yeshiva. He studied together with Hayyim Nahman Bialik and was a member of the "*Netzah Yisrael"* society of adherents of *Hibbat Tziyyon.* Invited by Bialik and *Rav Tza'ir* [Hayyim Tschernowitz] to teach at the yeshivah in Odessa, he refused to move to the big city, preferring to officiate as rabbi of the small town of Milejczyce, near Bialystok. He published numerous books and articles in the Hebrew press and in literary anthologies. For further biographical details, see Aharon Shmuel Tamares, *Pacifism in Light of the Torah*, ed. Ehud Luz (Hebrew; Jerusalem, 1992), editor's introduction. See also *Encyclopedia of Religious Zionism* (Hebrew), ed. Y. Raphael, 5:847–851; Zalman Rejzen, *Leksikon fun der Yidisher Literatur*, vol. IV (Vilna, 1929), 897–902.

122. R. Moshe Avigdor Amiel was one of the most prominent rabbinical figures in religious Zionism. Chief Rabbi of Tel Aviv in the 1930s, he became one of the central figures out Mizrahi conferences. His Zionist activities in the Mizrahi movement essentially date back many years before, in Eastern Europe and Belgium, his two homes before immigrating to the Land of Israel in the early 1930s. For a bibliography of his writings see Yitzhak Raphael, *Kitvei ha-Rav M.A. Amiel* (Jerusalem, 1943). For a biography see *Encyclopaedia Judaica*, 2:846–847.

123. Nathan Rotenstreich, *Iyyunim ba-Mahashavah ha-Yehudit ba-Zeman ha-Zeh* (Tel Aviv, 1978), 30.

124. R. Aharon Shmuel Tamares, *Sefer ha-Yahadut ve-ha-Herut* (Odessa, 1905), 85.

125. See, e.g., Moshe Halberthal & Avishai Margalit, *Idolatry* (Cambridge, 1992), 42–45; see R. Aharon Shmuel Tamares, *Musar ha-Torah ve-ha-Yahadut* (Vilna, 1912), 14, and cf. Maimonides, *Mishneh Torah, Hilkhot Avodah Zarah*, chap. 1.

126. *Musar ha-Torah ve-ha-Yahadut*, 76.

127. R. Aharon Shmuel Tamares, *Keneset Yisrael u-Milhamot ha-Goyim* (Warsaw, 1920), 16.

128. R. Aharon Shmuel Tamares, "Li-she'elot ha-Yahadut," in *He-Atid*, ed. S. Horowitz (Berlin, 1913), 149.

129. See *Keneset Yisrael*, 16–17.

130. *Sefer ha-Yahadut ve-ha-Herut*, 82, 85. Specifically, the First World War made it impossible to speak of – or to believe in – human progress; see R. Aharon Shmuel Tamares, "Hishtahrerut ha-Mahashavah ha-Ivrit," *Kolot* 6–8, ed. E. Steinman (Warsaw, 1922–1923), 176. War makes a mockery of the culture that views nation and state as the be-all and end-all; see *Keneset Yisrael*, 64.

131. R. Aharon Shmuel Tamares, "Hashbatat ha-Milhamot im ha-She'elot ha-Kalkaliyot," in: *Sheloshah Zivvugim Bilti Hagunim* (Pietrkow, 1930), 86.

132. *Keneset Yisrael*, 16.

133. *Kolot* 6–8 (1922–1923), 224.

134. *Keneset Yisrael*, 29 ff. See *Sanhedrin* 20b; Maimonides, *Mishneh Torah, Hilkhot Sanhedrin* 5:1; *Hilkhot Melakhim* 5:2; *Sefer Mitzvot Gadol*, Pos. Comm. 117. R. Tamares does *not* reject the halakhic category of *milhemet mitzvah*, which he defines as a defensive war, "aid to Israel in distress;" see Maimonides, *Mishneh Torah, Hilkhot Melakhim* 5:1.

135. *Keneset Yisrael*, 31; he considers even the construction of the Temple as a regres-

sion from the inward-directed nature of religion. Relying on a Midrash in *Shabbat* 30a, he concludes that it would have been better to devote attention to spiritual life by studying Torah than to build the Temple and offer sacrifices; see *Keneset Yisrael*, 30; the sacrificial rites, he believes, were merely lip service that the Jews were obliged to pay King Cyrus.

136. *Keneset Yisrael*, 41 (my italics) Cf. R. Amiel: "During the First Temple period, when the Jews lived in the land of Israel, they also knew about the God of Israel, just as they knew that the Assyrians had the god of Assyria and the Babylonians, the god of Babylonia, etc.; but only later, when they had left the land and been scattered to the four corners of the world, did they achieve the correct apprehension of the God of Israel as the God of the universe, Whose Glory fills the whole world; more precisely, the God of the universe is their God of Israel" (*Ha-Mizrahi* 49, 6).

137. *Kolot* 6–8 (1922–1923), 224.

138. R. M.A. Amiel, *Derashot el-Ami* (Tel Aviv, 1964), 2:37.

139. Ibid.

140. *Ha-Mizrahi* (May 14, 1919), 190; the contradiction between nationalism and faith, in R. Amiel's view, is that nationalism is based on the egotistical behavior of animals (R. M.A. Amiel, *Ha-Yesodot ha-Ide'ologiyim shel ha-Mizrahi* [Warsaw, 1934], 18); R. Amiel stresses that the Torah begins with Adam, a single person, not with a special land or nation. This expresses the inherent universalism of the Torah (idem, *Am Segulah, ha-Le'ummiyyut ve-ha-Enoshiyyut be-Hashkafat Olamah shel ha-Yahadut* [Tel Aviv, 1943], 10).

141. *Derashot el-Ami*, 2:39.

142. *Ha-Yesodot ha-Ide'ologiyim*, 18–19.

143. *Derashot el-Ami*, 2:19.

144. R. M.A., *Ha-Galut ve-ha-Geulah, Ha-Mizrahi* 49 (1920): 6 (my italics).

145. *Sefer ha-Yahadut ve-ha-Herut*, 90.

146. *Ha-Yesodot ha-Ide'ologiyim*, 11. Zionism has "turned everything upside-down and is telling us that not only may the Jews live without Torah, but even that Judaism can be complete without Torah."

147. *Ha-Yesodot ha-Ide'ologiyim*, 41.

148. R. M.A. Amiel, *Ha-Be'ayot ha-Ruhaniyyot she-ba-Tziyyonut: Le-Verur ha-Matzav ha-Ruhani ba-Aretz* (Tel Aviv, 1937), 11.

149. R. Reines believed that it would possible to establish a Jewish state in the Land of Israel without using force. R. Kook also believed, in the aftermath of the First World War, that in light of the situation, it would be possible to establish and maintain a state without wars.

150. *Sefer ha-Yahadut ve-ha-Herut*, 33–34.

151. On the cultural definition of nationalism see, e.g., Benedict Anderson, *Imagined Communities* (London, 1993); Yael Tamir, *Liberal Nationalism* (Princeton, NJ, 1993), 68.

152. *Sefer ha-Yahadut ve-ha-Herut*, 85, 90; R. Tamares' arguments were also concerned with present-day confrontations, see ibid., 92.

153. See Ravitzky, "Ha-Tzafuy ve-ha-Reshut Netunah."
154. S.Z. Shragai, "Iggerot ha-Rav A.S. Tamares (Ehad ha-Rabbanim ha-Margishim)," *Shragai* (Journal for research into religious Zionism and immigration to the land of Israel) 2 (1985): 55.
155. E.g., violation of the Sabbath or of dietary regulations.
156. He was writing in 1927; Anita Shapira has pointed out that the term *moledet* ("homeland") was not common in Zionist writing until the Tel Hai incident; see Shapira, *Land and Power*, 144.
157. "Iggerot ha-Rav A.S. Tamares," 56–57 (my italics).
158. *Sefer ha-Yahadut ve-ha-Herut*, 24–25, 60 (my italics).
159. *Ha-Yesodot ha-Ide'ologiyim*, 23 (my italics).
160. R. M.A. Amiel, *Ha-Mizrahi* (May 14, 1919), nos. 19–21, 35.
161. *Ha-Be'ayot ha-Ruhaniyyot she-ba-Tziyyonut*, 37.
162. *Keneset Yisrael*, 6–7.
163. *Pacifism in Light of the Torah*, 18.
164. Ibid., 38. See also his position regarding the establishment of the "Jewish Legion" toward the end of the First World War: *Sheloshah Zivvugim*, 40.
165. For example, in *Sefer ha-Yahadut ve-ha-Herut*, 37.
166. See *Sheloshah Zivvugim*, 60–61, note. Elsewhere in the same book (9), he writes of Trumpeldor "who drew his last breath, according to the Zionist narrative, with a smile on his lips and the declaration, 'It is good to die for our land.'" He also attacks the use of Hanukkah as a means to cultivate the hero concept.
167. *Sefer ha-Yahadut ve-ha-Herut*, 99.
168. *Keneset Yisrael*, 79; in some of his letters, nevertheless, he criticizes the idea of the spiritual center. See, e.g., *Sheloshah Zivvugim*, 70; *Shragai* 1985, 60. However, I do not think this contradicts my arguments up to this point; whenever he criticizes the "spiritual center," his complaint relates to its territorial exclusivity and centralizing tendency.
169. *Keneset Yisrael*, 80.
170. *Derashot el-Ami*, 3:137–138.
171. R. Amiel, *Ha-Tzofeh* (July 27, 1938).

Military Service: Ambivalence and Contradiction

Judith Bleich

There are many fighters in the midst of my nation.
> (Hakham Isaac Aboab Da Fonseca, *Zekher Asiti Le-nifla'ot E-l*, Recife, Brazil, 1646.[1])

The profession of a soldier is the profession of an assassin.
> (Chmoul To His Son, in Leon Cahun, *La Vie Juive*.[2])

There upon the battlefield of honor...there also will the barriers of prejudice come tumbling down.
> (Eduard Kley and Carl Siegfried Günsburg, *Zuruf An Die Jünglinge*, 1813.[3])

Rabbis and schoolteachers in their teaching must present military service as a sacred duty....
> (Instructions to the Westphalian Consistory, 1808.[4])

[W]ar is an unmitigated evil, and...we should abstain from all participation in it.

(Proposed Resolution before the Central
Conference of American Rabbis, 1935.[5])

I. INTRODUCTION

Is the role of a soldier that of a hero or of an assassin, a fate to be embraced or to be dreaded, a source of pride or of anguish? Living, as they did during the medieval period, a separate existence in the lands of their dispersion in which they constituted an *imperium in imperio,* Jews for a large part of their history were spurned as soldiers and spared the dilemma. But there came a time when the question was placed squarely before them.

In an attempt to force the members of the Jewish community to define their relationship to the state from the vantage point of Jewish law, Napoleon, by a decree of July 10, 1806, convened the Assembly of Notables and, subsequently, on September 24, 1806, announced his decision to summon a Great Sanhedrin to convert the decisions of the Assembly of Notables into definitive and authoritative religious pronouncements. Indicative of Napoleon's desire to assure that those synods issue unequivocal declarations regarding the primacy of the responsibilities of Jews as citizens of the state is the sixth of the twelve questions placed before those august bodies: Do Jews born in France, and treated by the law as French citizens, acknowledge France as their country? Are they bound to defend it? Are they bound to obey its laws and to conform to every provision of the Civil Code?

By the time that the Paris Sanhedrin was convened, Jews had already served in the French revolutionary armies, in the National Guard, and in Napoleon's forces. When the sixth question was read before the Assembly and the question of whether Jews were duty-bound to protect France was articulated, the deputies spontaneously exclaimed, "To the Death!"[6] In the course of the ensuing proceedings of the Assembly, an affirmative response to the question was formally adopted by unanimous vote. Moreover, during the subsequent deliberations of the Sanhedrin, the only matter regarding which the Sanhedrin formulated a position that went beyond the previous resolutions adopted by the Assembly was with regard to this sixth question. The Sanhedrin went so far as to declare that Jews were exempt from religious obligations and strictures that might interfere with performance of military duties.

The resounding declaration of the Sanhedrin found an echo in numerous public statements in the years that followed. Yet, as Jewish nationals were called upon with increasing frequency to serve in the armed forces of their host countries, that emerging phenomenon evoked contradictory responses.

Consistent with its clear and unambivalent regard for the sanctity and preservation of human life, Judaism manifests a distinctly negative attitude toward warfare and idealizes peace as the goal of human society. Although Scripture is replete with accounts of military conquests, the taking of human life in warfare was consistently viewed as, at best, a necessary evil. Despite King David's distinction, both temporal and spiritual, he was informed, "You shall not build a house in My name, because you have shed much blood upon the earth in My sight" (1 Chronicles 22:8). The ultimate utopian society was envisioned as one in which "Nation shall not lift up sword against nation, neither shall they learn war any more" (Isaiah 2:4 and Micah 4:3).

Subsequent to the biblical period there are few instances of Jews voluntarily engaging in armed warfare. Although Jews can hardly be described as a militaristic people, beginning with the garrison of the Jews of Elephantine five centuries before the common era[7] and extending to the soldiers of the quasi-autonomous Jewish community of Joden Savane, Surinam, in the New World,[8] there have been situations in which Jews served as mercenaries or as volunteers in peacetime army units.[9] Those forces constituted the exception rather than the rule. Over the centuries there have also been occasions when Jews took up arms in self-defense or in order to achieve political objectives, including military uprisings in the Roman Diaspora (115–17 C.E.), the rebellion of Mar Zutra (513 C.E.) and an eighth century rebellion in Iraq led by Abu Isa. In Europe there is ample evidence of Jews having borne arms until

they lost that right sometime in the thirteenth century. A Spanish
Jewish military figure who headed the armies of Grenada in the early
eleventh century was the renowned Samuel Ha-Nagid. There are
scattered references to Jews rendering military service in Italy and
Sicily in the fifteenth and sixteenth centuries. From the sixteenth to
the eighteenth centuries there were also occasional instances of Jews
using weapons in self-defense in Polish cities and of Jews serving, at
times, in civil defense units and even in the national army.[10]

However, it is only after the Emancipation that large numbers
of Jews were conscripted into non-Jewish armies. In the global wars
of the twentieth century the numbers increased significantly. Thus,
for example, a quarter of a million Jews served in the U.S. army in
World War I and over a half million in World War II; over a half
million Jews were conscripted into the Soviet army in World War
II; over 50,000 Jews fought in the British army in World War I and
over 60,000 in World War II.[11]

When Jews first began to be conscripted into European armies
in the late eighteenth and early nineteenth centuries, two sharply divergent attitudes found expression in the broader Jewish community.
For observant, traditional Jews, aside from the quite cogent fear for
life and limb, the terrors of the military experience were magnified
by the difficulties army service posed in terms of ritual observance
of Sabbath and festivals, dietary laws, Torah study, prayer, and the
wearing of beards and sidelocks. Little wonder that, for such persons,
army service was perceived as a calamity to be avoided at all cost.
In stark contrast, to liberal elements within the Jewish population
service in the army represented a tangible means of demonstrating
patriotic zeal and was welcomed as the key to emancipation, enfranchisement, and achievement of political equality. Sadly, although
much heroism was displayed and much Jewish blood was shed, nevertheless, prejudice persisted without mitigation, and in far too many
jurisdictions political and social equality remained a chimera.

In responsa and writings of the next century and a half, both
of these contradictory reactions were articulated. Most – but not
all – traditionalist halakhic authorities were far more negative
toward army service than might be assumed on the basis of the

published record. Within the liberal sector, which initially uniformly acclaimed army service as a sacred duty, one finds striking shifts and permutations. In the changed *Zeitgeist* of the twentieth century, when pacifism became the vogue and the ideal of *dulce et decorum est pro patria mori* lost its luster, liberal ideologues sought to discover a mandate for pacifism and conscientious objection in Jewish law and tradition. Ironically, in seeking to espouse what they believed to be a non-normative halakhic stance those writers did, in fact, draw close to the normative, but seldom candidly expressed, halakhic perspective.

II. THE TRADITIONALIST APPROACH

1. Published Responsa

Although the published corpus of halakhic responsa devoted to the topic of military service is not unduly sparse, it provides but a veiled and hazy portrait of the traditionalist perspective. Perusal of the responsa reveals that the respondents were fully conscious of the need for utmost caution in dealing with so sensitive a subject. They grasped far too well the implications of expressing opinions inconsistent with, or even not fully supportive of, policies espoused by the governing authority. Thus, the respondents were extremely circumspect and wrote with an eye constantly over their collective shoulder. Such vigilance is evident in the cryptic nature of some comments, in the explicit expressions of concern frequently incorporated in their responsa, but most of all in what is not written.

Of the early responsa discussing the compulsory draft in the modern era, the two most significant are those of R. Samuel Landau, son of R. Ezekiel Landau, included in his father's posthumously published responsa volume, *Noda bi-Yehudah, Mahadura Tinyana, Yoreh De'ah*, no. 74 and of R. Moses Sofer, *Teshuvot Hatam Sofer*, VI, *Likkutim*, no. 29. Perhaps the most remarkable aspect of both responsa is the fact that discussion of the most fundamental issue is conspicuous in its absence. There is no reference whatsoever to the basic problem of complicity in an unjust or halakhically illicit war. Another responsum of R. Moses Sofer, *Teshuvot Hatam Sofer*, *Yoreh De'ah*, no. 19, is the classic source for the ruling that non-Jews are enjoined from engaging in any form of warfare other than for purposes of self-defense.[12] Yet, in his discussion of problems associated with conscription, *Likkutim*, no. 29, *Hatam Sofer* makes no mention of the problem of Jewish complicity in a war of aggression. Virtually all subsequent discussions of the subject similarly avoid this sensitive issue. It is not surprising that, a century later, in addressing the vexing problem of Jews fighting other Jews in opposing enemy forces, Rabbi Ze'ev Wolf Leiter wrote that he was unable to find this question clarified in the literature of rabbinic decisors.[13]

Moreover, the one clear reference in the writings of early-day authorities to Jews fighting in non-Jewish wars is entirely ignored by later rabbinic scholars who discuss participation in military campaigns. *Tosafot, Avodah Zarah* 18b, cites a certain Rabbenu Elhanan who comments cryptically that it is forbidden for a Jew "to be of the number of members of the army." The omission of this source is far too glaring to have been a simple oversight. Rabbinic writers dealing with questions pertaining to military service appear to have adopted the policy of Rabbi David Sintzheim, a member of the Paris Sanhedrin, as extolled by *Hatam Sofer*, who said of him: "He…knew how to answer his questioners…. After he had revealed one handbreadth, he concealed two handbreadths."[14]

The reason for such reticence is obvious. As a result, these responsa demand careful examination by the reader with close attention to what is hinted at only between the lines. That such scrutiny is required is apparent from explicit cues embedded in the text designed to serve as red flags indicating the delicacy of the topic and underscoring the fact that some matters must remain unsaid.

In discussing cooperation or non-cooperation with the military draft, R. Samuel Landau prefaces his ruling by stressing that "It is difficult to issue a ruling in a matter that primarily entails a question of life and death. Who shall raise his head [to render a decision] in these matters?" In his concluding remarks he adds, "I know that it is difficult to rule with regard to this [question] and with regard to this our Sages, of blessed memory, said, 'Just as it is a *mitzvah* to say that which will be accepted, so it is a *mitzvah* not to say that which will not be accepted'[15] and at this time a sagacious person will be silent."[16]

Hatam Sofer, also addressing the question of the conscription of Jews in non-Jewish armies, states that, "Regarding this, silence is better than our speech." Referring to unspecified reprehensible actions of Jewish communal officials, *Hatam Sofer* resignedly comments, "Great Jewish authorities perforce looked aside and permitted those appointed by the community to do as was fitting in their eyes according to the times. And it is a time to be silent." Presumably, silence was the best response since protest would have proven unproductive. Rabbis did not have the power to reverse or rescind communal policies without creating a situation in which government authorities would become aware of Jewish reluctance to serve in the military. There was a strong probability that overt intervention on their part would give rise to serious punitive reprisals against the entire Jewish community. In such an era, the only course of action open to responsible rabbinical leadership is one involving "the choice of the lesser evil." Accordingly, *Hatam Sofer* concludes, "Lo, I have been exceedingly brief for it is not fitting to expand upon this subject, as is understood."[17] In a similar vein, R. Meir Eisenstadt writes of the situation facing the rabbis: "And if perhaps they looked aside because it is not in their power to find another solution, we, what can we answer in their place?"[18]

The issues addressed in these early responsa are the right of the state to conscript soldiers and the halakhic questions posed by the manner in which the draft was initially conducted. Government authorities demanded that the community produce a given number of recruits and, frequently, Jewish communal officials were placed in charge of filling the quota. Usually the selection was carried out by means of a lottery. In some locales it was also possible for a recruit to hire a substitute. The fundamental halakhic issue raised is the dilemma posed by the classical problem of *tenu lanu ehad mi-kem* (Palestinian Talmud, *Terumot* 8:4), i.e., the question of delivering a single individual in order to save the entire community. Generally speaking, one is prohibited from delivering an individual Jew for execution even in order to save the lives of many (*Mishneh Torah, Hilkhot Yesodei ha-Torah* 5:5). The case discussed in the Palestinian Talmud serves as a paradigm prohibiting the singling out of a Jew for exposure to danger or harm in order to spare others from a similar fate. Assuming that cooperation in conscription is legitimate, a second and closely related question involves the issue of how the lottery is to be conducted and whether deferments or exemptions may be granted to some individuals when such a policy would entail substituting others in their stead.

The earliest rabbinic respondent to the question of communal conscription, Rabbi Samuel Landau rules unequivocally that, "It is forbidden to hand anyone over to them" and that "There is no room to be lenient in this matter." Individuals may do all in their power to avoid the draft, provided that they have not yet been designated by name. Moreover, the community may also strive to assist such individuals in securing an exemption prior to their actual designation. However, once an individual has been identified for conscription, the community may no longer seek his exemption if such exemption would be obtained only at the expense of another person who would be taken in his stead. Such substitution is forbidden on the basis of the Talmudic argument "Who says your blood is redder than his?" (*Pesahim* 25b). However, faced with a situation in which such efforts were made, R. Samuel Landau counsels, "At this time the wise should be silent." In contradistinction, R. Samuel Landau is adamant that even non-observant youths or those who mock the law may not be handed over for military service. Although such individuals may be deserving of punishment, it is nevertheless absolutely forbidden to turn them over to civil authorities in order to fill the draft quota imposed upon the community.[19] R. Samuel Landau is cognizant of the difficulty of ruling in matters of this nature. Nevertheless, while fully aware of the delicacy of the situation in negotiating both with lay communal officials and with government authorities, he does not shrink from declaring categorically that if, in fact, individuals were to be handed over to the civil authorities, it would become obligatory to engage in preventive action and in public protest ("*mehuyav limhot be-yad*").[20]

In a responsum, dated Sivan 1830, *Hatam Sofer*, the preeminent halakhic authority of the time, affirms the obligation of conscripted Jews to perform the services required of them. His position is based upon the premise that the power to conscript is encompassed within the ambit of the halakhic principle *dina de-malkhuta dina* (the law of the land is the law) and flows from the power of the ruler to levy "taxes" in the form of personal service. *Hatam Sofer* affirms the right of the state to require military service from its nationals ("*Dina din u-mimeila muttal akarkafta de-kol mi she-ra'uy la-tzet u-she-ein lo ishah u-banim kefi nimus ve-hok malkhuto*"). The only members of the community who must be excused by communal leaders from the obligation imposed upon the community as a whole are students of Torah who, argues *Hatam Sofer*, on the basis of Jewish law (*Bava Batra* 8a), are free from the obligation regarding military service. *Hatam Sofer* notes that rabbinical students and occupants of rabbinical positions were usually exempted by the government[21] and adds that he himself had frequently given testimonials to such students to assist them in obtaining exemptions.

Hatam Sofer recommends utilization of a lottery system for filling the quota imposed upon the Jewish community but emphasizes that it must be equitable and that all persons suitable for military service, observant and nonobservant, be included in the lottery ("*me-ha-ra'uy she-ya'amdu kulam be-shaveh lifnei ha-eidah va-yatilu goral*"). He stresses that it is absolutely forbidden to compel any person to serve in the stead of an already drafted individual, even if the replacement is a Sabbath desecrator or an immoral person. *Hatam Sofer* regarded such coercion as tantamount to biblically proscribed kidnapping and sale of an innocent victim. Nonetheless, he rules that it is entirely permissible – and indeed advisable – for individuals to seek exemptions or deferments and to devise ways of avoiding military service even by means of hiring a substitute or by paying a sum of money in order to secure a reprieve. Moreover, *Hatam Sofer* regards it as praiseworthy for fellow Jews to render every assistance to their coreligionists in order to obtain such exemptions ("*ve-kol Yisrael mehuyavim le-sayyo ve-yekar pidyon nafsho*").[22]

In concluding his comments, *Hatam Sofer* notes that it was

common practice for nonobservant individuals to volunteer to serve
as substitutes for conscripts in exchange for a sum of money. He
rules that it is permissible to avail oneself of such an arrangement
since those volunteers were unconcerned with regard to violation
of religious law at home as well as in the army and, moreover, in any
event, would likely make their services available to others. Using
such replacements had become common practice and, given the
realities of the overall situation, *Hatam Sofer* asserts that availing
oneself of the services of these substitutes constitutes choosing the
lesser of two evils ("*livhor ha-ra be-mi'uto*"). [23]

It is quite evident that *Hatam Sofer* urges that military service
be avoided if at all possible. Although his language is restrained, a
decidedly negative view of military service and the necessity for
ritual infractions inevitably attendant thereupon is manifestly evident. It should be noted that his comments appear to be directed
entirely to peacetime service since the issue of subjecting oneself to
endangerment is not raised.

Similar views regarding the draft are articulated by a contemporary of *Hatam Sofer*, R. Moshe Leib Tsilts of Nikolsburg, *She'elot
u-Teshuvot Milei de-Avot*, 1, *Hoshen Mishpat*, no. 4, who stresses the
need to abjure preferential treatment in administering the lottery.[24]
Writing in 1841, R. Meir Eisenstadt, *She'elot u-Teshuvot Imrei Esh*, 1,
Yoreh De'ah, no. 74, goes beyond *Hatam Sofer* in declaring that not
only is the hiring of substitutes permissible but, from the perspective
of the draftee, may be described as a "*mitzvah.*" *Imrei Esh* declares,
"It is absolutely permissible and a *mitzvah* to do so" ("*hetter gamur
u-mitzvah la'asot ken*") and in the conclusion of his discussion he re-
iterates his view with the emphatic exclamation, "It is permitted and
a *mitzvah*" ("*muttar u-mitzvah*"). In explaining why this practice is
the best available solution to the dilemma, *Imrei Esh*, perhaps naively,
asserts that: (a) no one compels the substitutes to transgress Torah
law; (b) dietary observances need not be violated by a conscript
who is willing to accept inconvenience; and (c) problems involving
Sabbath observance can be resolved since Jewish law permits arms
to be carried on the Sabbath under specified conditions. *Imrei Esh*
also addresses the issues posed by the danger inherent in military

service but concludes that volunteering for army service is not to be forbidden on the grounds that it is tantamount to suicide.[25] Nonetheless, *Imrei Esh* rules that it is forbidden to obtain substitutes by means of coercion simply because a person may not "deliver" another individual to harm, loss, or inconvenience in order to be spared the burden he seeks to shift to another.

Many later respondents assert that it is commendable to avoid army service at all costs. As noted, *Imrei Esh*, 1, *Yoreh Deah*, no. 74, asserts that it is a *mitzvah* to hire a substitute. Others point to the physical danger associated with military service in ruling that it is preferable to accept employment involving desecration of the Sabbath rather than to serve in a battle zone. Thus, R. Eliezer David Greenwald of Satmar, *Keren le-David*, *Orah Hayyim*, no. 100, rules that when there is no threat to life, one should not seek exemption from army service by accepting a post in which Sabbath desecration is a certainty. However, one should do everything possible to avoid being sent to the battlefront, including accepting a position that will definitely entail ongoing Sabbath desecration, because "there is nothing that stands in the way of saving life." R. Mordecai Leib Winkler, *Sheelot u-Teshuvot Levushei Mordekhai*, *Mahadura Tinyana*, *Orah Hayyim*, no. 174, maintains that one must assume that any wartime service will entail battlefront conditions, i.e., military service represents at least possible danger to life. Consistent with that view, he rules that unless an individual has already been selected by a draft board he should not accept a position involving Sabbath desecration in order to avoid being called up because prior to being selected there is no imminent danger.[26] However, if a person has already been selected by a draft board he may accept employment involving Sabbath desecration in order to obtain a deferment from military service since "in our day, in the awesome battle at this time, with multiple instruments of destruction and catapult stones," such service entails danger to life.[27]

Perhaps because hiring a substitute was no longer a viable option, unlike respondents of an earlier period, Rabbi David Zevi Hoffmann, *Melammed le-Ho'il*, *Orah Hayyim*, no. 42, was forced to confront the issue of outright evasion of the draft. Writing after the

first World War, Rabbi Hoffmann rules that one should not seek to
evade army service on account of fear of Sabbath desecration for
more "than a question of a *mitzvah*" is involved. Evasion of army service may give rise to the profanation of God's name (*hillul Hashem*),
Rabbi Hoffmann warns, "because the enemies of the Jews say that
the Jews do not obey the laws of the kingdom."

Although, in application, Rabbi Hoffmann's ruling is unequivocal, his views regarding military service upon which it is based are
somewhat more complex. A careful reading of this responsum indicates that Rabbi Hoffmann does not deem army service *per se* to be
a religious duty since he speaks of actions that might be performed
by a soldier that would constitute a *mitzvah* "such as to save the lives
of Israelites or other *mitzvah*" with the implication that army service
in itself does not constitute a *mitzvah*. It is the negative outcome in
the form of profanation of the Divine Name and possible attendant
danger to Jews that is the focus of his concern. Rabbi Hoffmann observes that, if rabbinic decisors ruled that an individual was obligated
to evade army service to avoid Sabbath desecration, the result would
be widespread evasion of the draft. This would be counterproductive "for assuredly the majority would not achieve their desire and
it would cause a great profanation of the Name, God forbid, for no
purpose." Again, the implication appears to be that his ruling is
based on a pragmatic assessment of the situation at the time and
realistic considerations as distinct from an idealistic position. Were
it possible for Jews successfully to avoid army service the conclusion
might have been entirely different. Rabbi Hoffmann's own introductory comment in delineating the problem, namely, that the question
requires an answer based "not on the inclination of our heart alone"
also implies that the instinctive Jewish reaction is to avoid military
duty. It is noteworthy that Rabbi Hoffmann's responsum focusing
on avoidance of *hillul Hashem* was penned at a time when there
was an upsurge of anti-Semitism in Germany and accusations were
widespread that Jews had evaded the draft in large numbers or had
shirked frontline service.[28]

A further query addressed by Rabbi Hoffmann in the very next
responsum, *Melammed le-Ho'il, Orah Hayyim*, no. 43, is whether it is

obligatory for an individual to take advantage of a student deferment in order to delay military service and possible attendant Sabbath infractions or whether one might accept immediate army duty in order, upon completion of the tour of duty, to be able to enter into a marriage. In the case submitted to him, Rabbi Hoffmann, for a variety of reasons, rules that it is permissible not to accept the deferment.[29] Again, from the context of the discussion, it is evident that Rabbi Hoffmann is far from enthusiastic about military service. He writes to the interlocutor, who had written on behalf of his son, that delay may be unadvisable because it might result in a longer tour of duty since "it is possible that your son is not so strong at the present time and may prove inept in army service and will soon be discharged which may not be the case three years later when he will be stronger and assuredly will be taken and will be forced to remain there the entire year."[30]

R. Israel Meir ha-Kohen, *Mishnah Berurah* 329:17, rules that Jews must allow themselves to be conscripted and implies that failure of Jews to participate in the military when foreign forces attack may enrage the populace and result in loss of life. His comments certainly do not constitute a blanket endorsement of military service and a dispensation to engage in warfare under any and all circumstances; they urge acquiescence to conscription simply as a matter of *pikuah nefesh* or preservation of life.[31]

There are, however, two halakhic respondents whose views differ significantly from the majority. Writing in Germany in the nineteenth century, R. Samson Raphael Hirsch extols the positive religious duty of serving in the army in defense of one's fatherland. R. Hirsch contends that loyalty to one's country is a "religious duty, a duty imposed by God and no less holy than all the others."[32] In *Horeb*, a work devoted to the discussion of *mitzvot*, R. Hirsch includes this obligation in the fifth section, the section devoted to what he terms "commandments of love." Encompassed in the religious duty of a subject and citizen, he maintains, is the obligation "to sacrifice even life itself when the Fatherland calls its sons to its defense." R. Hirsch goes far beyond most rabbinic writers in positing that this obligation must be fulfilled "with love and pride." In a most remarkable statement, he declares, "But this outward obedience to the laws must be joined by the inner obedience: i.e., to be loyal to the State with heart and mind…to guard the honor of the State with love and pride."[33] One can but wonder to what extent R. Hirsch was carried away by the rhetoric of the time and to what extent he internalized these sentiments.[34] R. Hirsch does not address the substantive question of participation in a war of aggression. However, he does conclude his remarks on patriotism with the observation that loyal citizenship is an "unconditional duty and not dependent upon whether the State is kindly intentioned toward you or is harsh."[35] The comment seems to suggest that R. Hirsch assumed that one is duty-bound to serve in the army even in an unjust war of aggression when such is the mandate of the state.

The strongest rabbinic endorsement of army service as a positive religious obligation and the sharpest rabbinic criticism of army evasion was penned by Rabbi Moshe Shmuel Glasner of Klausenberg, the author of *Dor Revi'i*, who is known as an independent-minded and unconventional scholar. Rabbi Glasner maintains that "According to the law of the holy Torah we are obligated to heed the king's command." In a play on words, Rabbi Glasner declares that Jews are obligated to pay the burden of *damim*. *Damim*, he notes, is a homonym having a double meaning, namely, "money" and "blood." Thus the word implies both a financial tax and a "blood" tax. Rabbi Glasner concludes that, although it is unlikely that soldiers will be able to avoid infraction of dietary and Sabbath regulations, "This *mitzvah* of observing the decree of the king supersedes all."[36]

The position of Rabbis Hirsch and Glasner is the exception to the rule. In contrast, Rabbi Ze'ev Wolf Leiter, *She'elot u-Teshuvot Beit David*, I, no. 71, is much closer to the halakhic consensus in writing negatively with regard to all forms of army service. Rabbi Leiter questions the propriety of a Jew fighting a fellow Jew in opposing enemy forces and is explicit and forthright in ruling that voluntary army service on the part of an individual who has not been conscripted or compelled to enlist[37] is an unequivocally forbidden form of self-endangerment. Giving voice to what in rabbinic writing is a rare approach,[38] Rabbi Leiter calls for resolving the dilemma by obviating the need for army service and advocates a proactive response in declaring: "The obligation devolves upon every God-fearing individual (*haredi*) to labor on behalf of world peace in order that innocent blood not be spilled...and that warfare cease."

Jewish participation in World War II may well have been regarded in an entirely different light by rabbinic authorities. That war was waged by the Allies against a power that had targeted Jews for annihilation. Although there is scant published material devoted to the question, the military campaign to defeat the Nazis may readily be considered as an undertaking in the nature of "*ezrat Yisrael mi-yad tzar*–rescue of Jews from the hand of the oppressor." Such a war is categorized by *Rambam, Mishneh Torah, Hilkhot Melakhim,* 5:1, as a *milhemet mitzvah,* i.e., an obligatory war. In a previously unpublished private letter to his son,[39] the late Rabbi Yosef Eliyahu Henkin discusses volunteering for service in the United States Army in 1942. Rabbi Henkin writes that in the period prior to institution of the draft, volunteerism was to be encouraged. With establishment of the draft, those who receive exemptions need not volunteer since others will be available to fight in their stead. In particular, educators who are exempt and contribute to the needs of society render vital assistance to the war effort. Rabbi Henkin does, however, recommend that those who are suited to do so should volunteer to serve as air-raid wardens. The letter lends itself to being read as a blanket endorsement of voluntary army service. In light of the consensus of rabbinic opinion that regards participation in wars of aggression to be impermissible, it may be the case that Rabbi Henkin's comments were limited to the context in which they were written, i.e., war against the Nazis who were recognized as posing a threat to Jewish survival.

2. Rulings Reported in Biographical Sources

A number of biographical studies of Eastern European authorities contain reports of emphatically negative oral pronouncements regarding army service but, understandably, those statements are not to be found in the formal halakhic literary record. Rulings that are not committed to writing, even when transmitted by persons of unquestionable probity, lack the authoritativeness of published decisions. Oral reports often lack contextual clarity as well as nuances of meaning and expression, not to speak of their inherent unreliability because of possible misunderstanding on the part of the transmitter. Nevertheless, in this instance the oral reports must be given a high degree of credence both because they are congruent with the circumspection evident in the published material and because of the unanimity of opinion reflected in those reports.

Even the members of the liberal sector of the Jewish community did not view military service in Russia in the same positive light as did their counterparts in Western Europe for the simple reason that, in Russia, conscription was clearly neither a harbinger of civil emancipation nor a duty shared equally by all citizens; instead, it was a burden selectively imposed by the government. In the case of Jews, conscription was an integral element of a policy of Russification and forced apostasy. Until 1874, each nationality and ethnic group within Russia was governed by its own set of military regulations. In 1827, shortly after Nicholas I ascended to the throne, obligatory military service was imposed upon Jews. Under the provisions of the new regulations, a specified number of Jews were to be drafted for a twenty-five year period. Conscription began at the age of eighteen but the regulations contained a provision allowing for the taking of youths from the ages of twelve to eighteen for preparatory training. The units in which youths under eighteen served were known as Cantonist battalions. Exemptions were available for some categories of individuals and substitutes might be employed, but only other Jews were acceptable as substitutes.

Sociologically, the worst aspect of the decree was the fact that administration of the draft was placed in the hands of the Jewish communities. Jews guilty of non-payment of communal taxes or of vagrancy, or their children, were often designated for military service by the community in order to meet its quota. Individuals drafted by the community in excess of the quota for a given year might be credited to the following year's quota. Pressured to fill the heavy quota, communities often hired kidnappers (*khappers*), whose ruthless methods, including seizing children under twelve, became legendary. As has been well documented, Tsar Nicholas was driven by a missionary zeal that strongly influenced the policies of his government; tales of forced conversion and torture abound. From 1827 through 1854 some 70,000 Jews were conscripted into the Russian army; of that number, approximately 50,000 were minors.[40]

Rabbinic authorities bemoaned the conduct of the communal officials in implementing the decree and, in isolated instances, strove to forestall acts of injustice. They were, however, powerless to defy the system. The complicity of communal officials and Jewish kidnappers in the oppressive government policies led to an unprecedented breakdown of Jewish society.[41] As might be anticipated, given the fear of reprisal and an atmosphere of terror, there is a dearth of published material in rabbinic writings regarding the plight of the Cantonists.[42]

It is well known that R. Joseph Ber Soloveichik, renowned as the author of *Bet ha-Levi*, was a vociferous opponent of the kidnappers who, with the complicity of communal officials, sought to satisfy the demands of the Russian authorities. In his fierce opposition to this abhorrent social evil, Rabbi Soloveichik is reported to have advocated the total dismemberment of the official *kehillot*, or communal governing structures, throughout Russia so that the Russian government would find itself with no Jewish communal body capable of executing its decrees.[43]

Since he did not succeed in implementing this radical solution, Rabbi Soloveichik undertook the task of providing refuge and securing exemptions in individual cases. In particular, he was moved by the plight of the poor who bore the brunt of the edict. On one occasion, while Rabbi Soloveichik was yet rabbi of Slutsk, he is said to have requested the local commandant to draft only youngsters who were members of wealthy families. He later explained to the distressed and angry lay leaders of Slutsk that justice demanded such a policy. The rich, Rabbi Soloveichik pointed out, invariably succeeded in obtaining exemptions for their children by one means or another, whereas the poor were helpless and forced to endure army service with attendant exposure to persecution and often enforced baptism.[44]

The accuracy of Rabbi Soloveichik's assessment of the situation is dramatically illustrated in the words of a popular folksong of the time:

> Rich Mr. Rockover has seven sons,
> Not a one a uniform dons;
> But poor widow Leah has an only child,
> And they hunt him down as if he were wild…
> But the children of the idle rich,
> Must carry on without a hitch.[45]

On the basis of oral reports of his disciple, R. Naftali Amsterdam, biographers of R. Israel Salanter, founder of the Mussar movement, detail Rabbi Salanter's fruitless efforts to persuade government officials to abolish the harsh decree. They recount how Rabbi Salanter rescued an orphan from his abductors and the manner in which he publicly castigated those in Salant and Kovno who turned a deaf ear to the pleas of indigent women whose sons were among the victims. The day that the decree was finally rescinded, Rabbi Salanter proclaimed a day of thanksgiving and was incensed at those of his disciples who did not on that occasion pronounce the full blessing "*ha-tov ve-ha-metiv*" with the inclusion of the Divine Name.[46]

The hasidic leader, Rabbi Menachen Mendel Schneerson, known as *Tzemah Tzedek*, sought to organize communal strategies to thwart the kidnappers. There is evidence that *Tzemah Tzedek* asserted that the *khappers* were morally and halakhically culpable for violation of the biblical admonition, "And he that steals a man and sells him, or if he be found in his hand, he shall surely be put to death" (Exodus 21:16) and hence, in the struggle against them, even extreme measures might be countenanced.[47]

It is quite apparent that in Poland and Russia, long after mitigation of earlier harsh decrees, avoidance of army service continued to be advocated by rabbinic figures. It is common knowledge that R. Hayyim Soloveichik of Brisk rarely issued halakhic rulings himself, preferring instead to submit the questions that were referred to him to the *dayyanim* of Brisk or other authorities. However, with regard to questions that involved possible danger of loss of life, R. Hayyim customarily departed from that practice and did not hesitate personally to issue rulings in such matters. Those rulings were invariably lenient in nature. R. Hayyim was wont to say that it was his policy to be *mahmir* (stringent) in matters involving preservation of life, i.e., that his apparent leniencies in permitting matters that might otherwise be regarded as forbidden were not at all reflective of a posture of leniency but of a policy of stringency with regard to preservation of life. For example, he was lenient with regard to questions of fasting on *Yom Kippur* because of his conviction that it is necessary to be stringent in avoiding even remote danger to life.[48]

Army service and its attendant perils was viewed by R. Hayyim with great trepidation. It is related that on one occasion an individual approached R. Hayyim on a Friday with the following dilemma: His son, who was undergoing medical treatment in a nearby town, was scheduled to appear before the draft board the next day for a medical examination to determine his fitness for army duty. The father questioned whether he might desecrate the Sabbath and travel to the neighboring city in an attempt to secure an exemption for his son. R. Hayyim permitted the man to travel on the Sabbath and explained his reasoning as follows: If the young man were to be taken to the army and his service were to extend over a period of years it was probable that, in the course of time, war would break out and he might be sent to the front and killed. Even a "double doubt" (*sfek sfeika*) of danger to life warranted suspension of Sabbath regulations.[49]

A similar ruling of R. Hayyim Soloveichik, as attested to by R. Hayyim Ozer Grodzinski, is recorded by R. Barukh Ber Leibowitz.[50] When asked whether he might accept a position in an office that would involve desecration of the Sabbath in order to obtain an exemption from army service, R. Hayyim ruled permissively. However, in a situation in which an individual was able to secure an exemption only by attending a *gymnasium*, R. Hayyim ruled restrictively, declaring that, in his opinion, the latter case involved the grave transgression of the study of heretical works and hence could not be condoned even for the purpose of avoidance of danger.

Another report regarding R. Hayyim Soloveichik's attitude toward some of the complex problems posed by army deferments is recorded in two disparate versions. During World War I, the Russian authorities granted rabbinical exemptions. Consequently, many synagogues provided letters of appointment to young men eligible for the draft. R. Hayyim was opposed to the granting of spurious letters of appointment indiscriminately lest the fraudulent nature of these appointments be discovered and the government revoke all rabbinical exemptions, thereby endangering the lives of those who actually occupied rabbinical posts. Despite the fact that his own son Ze'ev and his son-in-law, R. Hirsch Glicksman, were of draft age, R. Hayyim refused to allow them to accept the offer of several congregations in Minsk, where they at the time resided, to "appoint" them as rabbis.[51]

According to another, probably more reliable, version of the narrative, R. Hayyim's motivation in refusing the letters of appointment reflected an entirely different consideration. R. Hayyim harbored a deep and abiding distrust of Tsarist officialdom. He was convinced that any official record would eventually be used by the authorities to compromise the interests of persons whose names appeared in such records. He feared that recording the names and addresses of potential conscripts in conjunction with issuance of exemptions would result in that information being entered in an official file that in all likelihood would later be used to their detriment. In dealing with Tsarist authorities, R. Hayyim believed that the prudent course of action was to avoid formal documentation in any guise whatsoever. The soundest protection was to remain "invisible."[52]

The extent to which army service was dreaded is also reflected in accounts of the Novardok yeshivah. In accordance with the policy espoused by Rabbi Joseph Yozel Hurwitz, the *Alter* of Novardok, students at the Novardok yeshiva disregarded all government induction orders and simply failed to report to the recruitment stations. For a period of time during World War I, the tactic succeeded and most of the students avoided detection. In 1919, the young R. Yaakov Yisrael Kanievski, later renowned as the *Steipler*, was appointed *mashgiah* in a branch of the Novardok yeshivah established in Rogachov. There, agents of the Yevsektsia arrested Rabbi Kanievski and he was inducted into the Red Army and stationed at a military camp in Moscow. A considerable sum of money was raised but efforts to secure his release by means of bribery failed.[53]

A similar aversion to military service prevailed among hasidic leaders as well. The counsel and assistance of R. Yehudah Leib Alter of Gur, better known as the author of *Sefat Emet*, and R. Yerachmiel Yisrael Yitzchak Danziger, *Rebbe* of Alexander, in avoidance of the draft became legendary. Reports of their subornation of draft regulations reached the ears of government officials, whose wrath, as might have been anticipated, was aroused. In an endeavor to put an end to these activities and probably to punish the rabbinic figures involved, they contrived a stratagem designed to trick the rabbis into revealing their antagonism to the draft. Agents were sent who pretended to seek advice and aid in evading military duty. The rabbinic figures in question are reported to have astutely recognized that those agents were not *bona fide* supplicants and avoided the trap that had been set for them.[54]

It is related of Rabbi Kalonymus Kalman Shapira of Piaseczno (known later as the *Rebbe* of the Warsaw Ghetto) that he exerted great effort to obtain army exemptions for his followers. He would not hesitate to expend large sums of money in bribing draft authorities in order to secure a reprieve for a conscript. Failing that, he would employ all manner of other tactics, including the use of amulets or performance of particular mystical acts, in order to spare his disciples the fate of army duty.[55]

3. Ritual Observance

For the observant, as noted, the difficulties involved in fulfilling religious obligations and observing dietary proscriptions were most worrisome aspects of army service. Away from the battlefield such problems were much easier to resolve. The very first Jewish soldiers in the Western Hemisphere concerning whom a contemporaneous record is extant were Jews who served as mercenaries in the Dutch expeditionary force that arrived in Brazil in 1630. For the privilege of exemption from guard duty on the Sabbath, the Jews who settled in Dutch Brazil and served in the local militia were willing to pay a fee but, nonetheless, on several occasions, the exemption was not honored.[56] In North America, the environment was more tolerant. Thus, when Hart Jacobs petitioned the authorities in Philadelphia in January 1776 to be exempt "from doing military duty on the city watch on Friday nights which is part of his Sabbath" the request was granted provided that he perform "his full tour of duty on other nights."[57]

In Western Europe when recruitment of Jews for military service began in earnest, there are reports in community after community in France, Austria, and Italy that provide tangible evidence that ritual observance was a grave issue. In France the problem of Sabbath observance was a crucial factor in reluctance on the part of Jews to serve in the army. During the period of 1790–93, the petitions of Jews in a number of different communities for Sabbath exemptions were rejected, and ultimately all Jews were forced to perform military duties on the Sabbath. Municipal authorities frequently made arrangements for provision of kosher food to Jewish soldiers but that practice was curtailed during the Reign of Terror.[58] Service in the army aroused concern among those who wore beards and sidelocks, which then were popular targets of ridicule and anti-Semitic acts.[59]

Although a number of Jewish communal leaders in Alsace-Lorraine encouraged army service as proof of patriotic fervor, among ordinary Alsatian Jews who were traditional in observance a lingering aversion to military service prevailed. In the Judeo-Alsatian dialect the term reik (empty or devoid of value) was used as a derogatory cognomen for "soldier."[60] Draft avoidance was extremely difficult since, under the provisions of Napoleon's "Infamous Decree" of March 17, 1808, unlike other Frenchmen, Jews could not hire substitutes.[61] A mystical ceremony designed to evoke divine mercy in the form of drawing a high number in the lottery and thereby escaping service gained currency. At midnight, the young man of draft age would light a lamp with oil, make a pledge to charity, and utter a prayer for exemption from the draft invoking the sage Rabbi Meir

Ba'al ha-Nes and the angels Michael, Gabriel, Uriel and Raphael. Quite obviously, aspirations for equality and civil rights had not quenched the deeply-rooted distrust and fear of military service harbored by the populace.[62]

With tears in his eyes, Rabbi Ezekiel Landau is reported to have addressed the first group of Jewish recruits conscripted in Prague in May 1789. Encouraging them to remain steadfast in their fealty to *mitzvot*, he suggested that they exchange tours of duty with Christian comrades so that the latter would be on duty on the Sabbath and the Jews, in turn, would perform their duty on Sunday. He also urged the Jewish conscripts to observe dietary regulations for as long as possible, i.e., until malnutrition became life-threatening. He urged that, even in the event of sickness, they endeavor to subsist on tea for warm liquid nourishment unless it became absolutely necessary to partake of non-kosher soup.[63] However, at the same time, Rabbi Landau expressed his awareness that their comportment as soldiers would bring honor and respect to their people and that their actions would demonstrate to the monarch the sacrificial loyalty of his Jewish subjects.[64]

Subsequent to the conquest of Mantua by Napoleon's forces in February 1797, the walls of the ghetto were razed and the Jews of Mantua were granted civil rights. Rights entailed duties and with the privileges they received the Jews became subject to civic obligations, including army service. Members of the community turned to R. Ishmael ha-Kohen of Modena with a query regarding performance of guard duty and bearing arms on the Sabbath. R. Ishmael, *Zera Emet*, part 3, *Orah Hayyim, Hilkhot Shabbat*, no. 32, responded permissively, noting that refusal might endanger Jewish lives and that the city had an *eruv*. From the details of the reply, it is clearly evident that R. Ishmael condones violation of religious law only when absolutely necessary.[65]

In the heat of conflict, matters became far more complicated and it required a great measure of self-sacrifice to remain meticulous in religious observance. It is particularly moving to read accounts of the lengths to which some Jewish soldiers went in order to observe *mitzvot* under trying circumstances. Especially noteworthy are reports of the efforts of soldiers in what was commonly considered to be the godless United States to observe religious precepts even in battle situations. Private Isaac Gleitzman, who received the Cross of Honor for "conspicuous gallantry in the field" during the Civil War, remarked that he was "prouder of never having eaten any nonkosher food or 'trefa.'"[66] Similarly, according to the diarist Emma Mordecai, the Levy brothers, Ezekiel J., who attained the rank of captain in the Richmond Light Infantry Blues, and the younger twenty-one year old Isaac J., who was killed by an exploding shell in August 1864, "had observed their religion faithfully, ever since they have been in the army, never eating forbidden food."[67] A few months before he died, Isaac wrote to his sister telling how the brothers had purchased sufficient *matzot* to last the Passover week and that "We are observing the festival in a truly orthodox style."[68]

Although responsible halakhic authorities certainly did not maintain that mere service in the army automatically entailed exemption from religious observances, there was a marked concern to find ways and means within the Halakhah to ease the hardships experienced by the conscripts. Thus, R. Israel Meir ha-Kohen, *Hafetz Hayyim*, in the manual he prepared for Jewish soldiers, *Mahaneh Yisrael* (first published in 1881),[69] states his avowed intention to ascertain whether "There may possibly be found, in accordance with the law, a remedy or expedient to make matters less burdensome for them [the soldiers] in any regard because, assuredly, we perceive individuals such as these as being subject to difficult circumstances."[70] Presenting a précis of Sabbath regulations and other laws, *Hafetz Hayyim* endeavors to explain to the unlearned how to conduct themselves under duress in a manner that would diminish the seriousness and minimize the number of infractions of Jewish law. Intricate halakhic complexities are unraveled by *Hafetz Hayyim* in uncomplicated language in this remarkable work, the pages of which are suffused with *ahavat Yisrael*, love and compassionate empathy for fellow Jews.

Mahaneh Yisrael is singularly important in its focus not only on matters of ritual but on ethical and moral issues as well. *Hafetz Hayyim* identifies those issues as constituting the most serious challenges associated with army service. It is noteworthy that *Hafetz Hayyim* strongly recommends early marriage for recruits both in order to enable them to fulfill the *mitzvah* of siring children and because he believed that marital bonds would strengthen a soldier's ability to withstand the lax morals common in an army milieu.[71] Above all, *Hafetz Hayyim* seeks to raise the recruits' spirits and to bolster their self-esteem. Cognizant of the supreme effort required in order to maintain an observant lifestyle in the army, *Hafetz Hayyim* adds words of encouragement:

> If he [the soldier] will become valiant…and shall see to observe the Torah in all its details at that time (*in that which is not contrary to the laws of the government*), in the future these days will be the most cherished of all the days of his life. Not as they appear to the soldier [now] in his thoughts that these times are the lowliest of his days. He will be of God's holy ones on account of this and no man free [of military obligation] will be able to stand in his precincts…. When a person withstands a trial he becomes most exalted in stature.[72]

III. THE POSTURE OF THE LIBERALS

1. Early Reform –
Rendering Jews Suitable for Army Service

Israel Jacobson, commonly regarded as the founder of the Reform movement, was president of the Westphalian Consistory, a principal aim of which was to institute a coherent program of religious reform. It is of more than passing interest that the most controversial of the consistorial innovations was a matter relating to military service. The relationship between participation in the armed forces and religious reform merits analysis.

In the pre-Emancipation era, Jews did not regard themselves as potential participants in active warfare. In a sermon delivered in London during the Seven Years' War on the occasion of a national day of prayer ordered by the King (in 1757 or 1758), Rabbi Hirschel Levin (Hart Lyon), Rabbi of the Great Synagogue, declared that Jews could best serve their country through prayer rather than through

military service. Although, in England, the Militia Bill enacted in
June 1757 subjected all citizens to military service with the quota to
be filled by lottery, attempts to enforce the law were not successful.
The question of whether Jews would also be subject to conscription
had not yet been raised. In his remarks, Rabbi Levin discounted
the possibility of benefit accruing to a country by virtue of Jewish
participation in the armed forces:

> Now it is obvious that we are always obliged to pray for the
> welfare and prosperity of our kings.... For how else can we
> serve the king under whose protection we live? If we were to
> suggest that we serve him by fighting in his armies, "What are
> we, how significant is our power?....
>
> How then indeed shall we serve our king? Our only
> strength is in our speech. The Sages expressed this in com-
> menting upon Isaiah 41:14, "*Fear not, O worm Jacob*; just as the
> worm's power lies only in its mouth, so the power of Israel is
> only in its prayer." (*Mekhilta, Be-Shallah* on Exodus 14:10). It
> is incumbent upon us to pray for the welfare of the sovereign
> under whose protection we live, and for the welfare of the land
> in which we reside, for our welfare is bound up with theirs.[73]

In the years that followed, however, a different attitude soon
came to the fore. In 1773, Rabbi Levin was appointed chief rabbi of
Berlin, a post he occupied until the year 1800. It is doubtful that he
would then have delivered a similar public address in Berlin because
during the period of his incumbency it had become fashionable for
Jews to argue that, as would-be citizens of the state, they should assume both the privileges and the duties of citizenship, including the
honor of defending the fatherland by means of military service.

When, in 1655, Asser Levy petitioned for the right to serve in
the militia in New Amsterdam and won this right in 1657, he did so
simply because he had difficulty paying a tax in lieu of home guard
service.[74] At a later time, in many European lands where Jews had
lived for centuries in relative social isolation, this right was, however,
welcomed as tangible evidence of political equality. In 1806, when

Düsseldorf came under Napoleonic rule and the French civil code was adopted, Heinrich Heine's father gained a commission in the local civil guard. In all likelihood, he was the first Jew to hold such office in Germany since the early Middle Ages. The first day he wore the distinctive colorful uniform he celebrated the event by treating his fellow officers to a barrel of good wine.[75]

Following promulgation of the "Edict Against the Civil Status of the Jews in Prussia" (March 11, 1812), Prussian Jews were accorded the prerogatives and duties of citizenship, including the right to serve in the army.[76] In a burst of enthusiasm, hundreds of Jews volunteered for military service.[77] Jews of that period believed that demonstration of willingness to sacrifice life and limb would serve as proof positive of Jewish devotion to the state and the worthiness of Jews for citizenship. As stated eloquently and unabashedly by Eduard Kley and Carl Siegfried Günsburg in the stirring call to arms they addressed to their coreligionists:

> O what a heavenly feeling to possess a fatherland! O what a rapturous idea to be able to call a spot, a place, a nook one's own upon this lovely earth…There upon the battlefield of honor where all hearts are animated by one spirit, where all work for a single goal: for their fatherland; there where he is best who submits most loyally to his king – there also will the barriers of prejudice come tumbling down. Hand in hand with your fellow soldiers you will complete the great work; they will not deny you the name of brother, for you will have *earned* it.[78]

Gabriel Reisser, the passionate advocate of Emancipation, later voiced a similar sentiment: "There is only one baptism that can initiate one into a nationality, and that is the baptism of blood in the common struggle for a fatherland and for freedom."[79]

Paradoxically, Jews who were eager to serve in the military faced a unique problem: They were ready and willing to fight alongside their non-Jewish compatriots but not all their fellow citizens were prepared to welcome them with open arms. They were ardent suitors fearful of rejection by their beloved both because of ethnic and religious prejudice and because of a perception that their religious practices would perforce interfere with proper discharge of military duties. It is for that latter reason a desire to demonstrate their suitability for military service became a motivating factor in the efforts of Jewish liberals to affect religious reforms.

The liberal view that, in order to be accepted as citizens, Jews must first adapt to the non-Jewish environment merely echoed statements openly expressed by non-Jewish writers. Jewish integration, it was believed, necessitated a reconceptualization of the Jewish religion. Judaism was portrayed as primitive and backward and it was widely assumed that Jews would have to undergo a process of *"Verbesserung"* or "improvement" in their religious observance and social mores if they were to participate fully in the social and intellectual life of non-Jews, but that interaction and the granting of civil rights would hasten their transformation. In France in 1787, Abbé Grégoire had explicitly stated that Jews should be subject to the direction of rabbis in ritual matters and to the authority of government in civil matters but that they would assimilate and modify their religions observances when accepted into French society. "We have reason to believe," he declared, "that the Rabbis will relax upon that head when their decisions come to be authorized by necessity, and the Jew will give up his scruples when he is warranted by the infallibility of his doctors."[80] Campaigners for Jewish rights such as Wilhelm von Dohm affirmed the view that, with integration into the secular state, Jews "will then reform their religious laws and regulations according to the demands of society. They will go back to the freer and nobler ancient Mosaic Law, will explain and adapt it according to the changed times and conditions, and will find authorizations to do so alone in the Talmud." [81]

Less sympathetic was the attitude of Abbot F.M. Thiebault, who had opposed Jewish emancipation when that proposal was brought before the National Assembly with the forthright argument that dietary restrictions and Sabbath laws would interfere with proper military service on the part of Jews.[82] Indeed, the charge that Jews were not suited to serve as soldiers was a common anti-Semitic slur. As expressed by Johann Michaelis, "For the power of a state does not depend on gold alone, but rather, in large part, on the strength of its soldiers. And the Jews will not contribute soldiers to the state as long as they do not change their religious views…. As long as they observe the laws about kosher and non-kosher food it will be almost impossible to integrate them into our ranks."[83]

It is probable that it was a perceived need to negate these and similar allegations that motivated the Jewish Consistory in Westphalia to institute a controversial religious innovation. In a directive to the rabbinate dated January 17, 1810, the Consistory ruled that, contrary to accepted Ashkenazi practice, the rabbis were to declare rice and legumes to be permissible for consumption on Passover. The Consistory stated that Jewish soldiers had bemoaned the scarcity of permissible food available to them on Passover and the scant supply of *matzot* and, accordingly, requested dispensation to use peas, beans, lentils, rice and millet for their sustenance during the holiday. The Consistory noted that those foods are not leaven and that the ban on those foods dating from the post-Talmudic era had been opposed by some authorities. Motivated by concern for the welfare of their brethren and by the desire that they be enabled to fulfill their civic duties with ease, the Consistory proceeded to rule that such foodstuffs were to be permitted not only to soldiers but "to every Israelite…in good conscience."[84]

In order to understand why, even when bitter controversy ensued, the Consistory persisted in advocating this innovation – as well as their decision to urge an innovation in respect to the laws of *halitzah*[85] – one must recognize the extreme sensitivity of the members of the Consistory to the issue of military service. In his initial formal audience with King Jerome on February 9, 1808, the President of the Consistory, Israel Jacobson, hastened to assure the ruler of the patriotism of his Jewish subjects and their eagerness to serve as soldiers. "It will be a pleasure for me," responded Jerome, "if, as good citizens, they furnish me with brave soldiers for my army, true servants of the state."[86] The very first royal edict of March 31, 1808 establishing the Westphalian Consistory directed the rabbis and teachers to stress that military service is a sacred duty and that one is absolved from any religious observances that are incompatible with such service.[87] Accordingly, in the consistorial order of March 15, 1809, enumerating rabbinic responsibilities, the rabbis were specifically so instructed (*"Der Rabbiner muss...den Militärdienst als eine heilige Pflicht darstellen"*).[88] It is quite likely that a need to provide further assurance to the authorities in this regard prompted the Consistory to issue the dispensation regarding consumption of legumes on Passover.[89]

It is significant that, in instituting changes, the Westphalian Consistory chose to issue a broad ruling extending to all Jews rather than a narrower ruling providing only for dispensation on grounds of hardship to soldiers.[90] In contrast, in drafting its response to the sixth of Napoleon's questions concerning the duties of Jews in defense of their country, the Paris Sanhedrin formulated a position that went beyond the decisions of the Assembly of Notables and declared that soldiers are released from obligations and strictures that might interfere with military service. The Sanhedrin's mitigation of religious obligations was, in that case, expressly restricted to soldiers.[91] Moreover, the dispensation itself was circumscribed. The decisions of the Sanhedrin were recorded in both French and Hebrew texts. While the French text states that the exemption applies during the time of military service, *"pendant la durée de ce service,"* the Hebrew text limited the exemption to time of war and only to the extent that such religious obligations might interfere with performance of soldiers'military duties. Thus the Hebrew text provided for exemption "as long as they are obligated to stand on their post and to do their service in war" (*kol zeman she-hem hayyavim la'amod al mishmartam ve-la'avod avodatam be-milhamah*).[92]

The concern for halakhic integrity evidenced in the decisions of the Paris Sanhedrin was, to a great extent, a reflection of the influence of Rabbi David Sintzheim, who apparently personally drafted many of the answers of the Assembly of Notables and who later served as President of the Sanhedrin.[93] At the Sanhedrin's final meeting, Rabbi Sintzheim forcefully asserted that the Sanhedrin's consent to an exemption from religious duties under certain conditions applied only when the sovereign and the state were in danger. Rabbi Sintzheim was unequivocal in his concluding declaration that the laws of Israel are perfect and that "whoever betrays divine laws will soon trample underfoot human laws."[94] Rabbi Sintzheim's remarks validate the accolade accorded to him by *Hatam Sofer*:

> During his lifetime he was honored and was very close to the monarchy in Paris; he was asked a number of questions and knew how to answer his questioners…he did not allow others to rule over him, and was not seduced into following them, God forbid! After he had revealed one handbreadth, he concealed two handbreadths. His integrity stood by him…. [95]

With the fall of Napoleon a wave of reaction swept over Western Europe. Throughout Prussia there was a move to pare down or entirely to rescind the civil rights that had been granted to the Jewish populace. Reactionaries such as Friedrich Rühs and Jacob Fries, who sought to reverse the emancipatory trend, asserted that Jews constituted a distinct nation rather than a mere religious denomination and that, as such, they were unassimilable in the body politic. In vain did Jewish apologists remonstrate that Judaism was but a religious confession, that Jews did not constitute a nation, and that customs and folkways might be modified. As the national-Christian reaction reached a peak in the summer of 1819, anti-Jewish riots took place throughout Germany accompanied with cries of "Hep! Hep! Down with the Jews!"[96] During the ensuing years the pendulum swung back and forth. In the ongoing debate regarding whether Jews were fit to be citizens, the issue of military service often come to the fore. It is noteworthy that, as late as 1844, when Frederick William IV adopted reactionary policies and proposed recognition of Jews as a national minority, he sought to release them from the obligation of military service.[97]

2. Persistence of Anti-Semitism in the Army

The tragic fate of assimilationists, particularly in Germany, unfolded most dramatically in the army experience. Those individuals who wished to embrace their fatherland and render it service shoulder-to-shoulder with their fellow citizens were crudely rebuffed. The desire to demonstrate loyalty and to achieve political equality were motivating factors for Jews who welcomed army service as a privilege. Yet, the military itself all too often remained an arena in which anti-Semitism flourished. In country after country, Jews served in the army but were accused of slacking and draft-dodging. Their defenders compiled list upon list detailing the Jewish contribution to military endeavors[98] and excelled in composing apologetic literature, but the stigma persisted.

Even in the comparatively tolerant United States, the canard that Jews did not pull their weight in the armed forces surfaced again and again. In the late eighteenth century, responding to aspersions cast on Jews, Haym Solomon insisted that Jews had served in the Revolutionary armies in numbers beyond their proportion to the total population.[99] Almost a century later, anti-Semitism, almost nonexistent in the United States, was aroused by the turmoil of war and was why Jews were singled out in Grant's Order No. 11. More serious than economic anti-Semitism was the charge, repeated frequently until the end of the 1800s, that Jews had not fought in the Civil War. That charge gained credibility because, in the North, a conscript could buy an exemption upon payment of three hundred dollars; in the South one needed simply to provide a substitute in order to avoid service. To counter the charge that Jews had been slackers, the prominent Washington lobbyist Simon Wolf published a work entitled *The American Jew as Soldier, Patriot and Citizen* (1895) in which he listed the names of 8,000 Jewish men who had served in the Union and Confederate forces, a list that was far from comprehensive.[100]

In the United States, some Jews rose to high rank in the armed forces, but religious bias was not totally absent. Uriah Phillips Levy, who ran away to sea at the age of ten and was commissioned a lieutenant of the Navy in 1817 at the age of twenty-five, was made a commodore in 1857. George Bancroft, who had been Secretary of the Navy in 1845–1846, testified that at the time he had refused to give Levy a command because of "a strong prejudice in the service against Captain Levy, which seemed to me, in a considerable part attributable to his being of the Jewish persuasion" and, as Secretary of the Navy, Bancroft stated, he had felt obliged to take into consideration "the need for harmonious cooperation which is essential to the highest effectiveness" of the armed forces.[101]

In France, as well, Jews attained positions of prominence in the army throughout the course of the nineteenth century. During the Third Republic, as many as twenty-three Jews rose to the rank of general.[102] Nonetheless, anti-Semitism was prevalent in the army, as is best exemplified by the notorious case of Captain Alfred Dreyfus, in which the superficial veneer of acceptance was rudely torn away to reveal a morass of bias and hostility simmering beneath the surface.

Prejudice against Jews in the army was even more blatant in Germany. False accusations and canards about Jewish cowardice prompted Ludwig Philippson, editor of the *Allgemeine Zeitung des Judentum*, to collect and publish the names of all German Jews who had served on the front lines during the 1870 Franco-Prussian War.[103] Despite the fact that thousands of Jews had participated and hundreds had suffered casualties, the slurs persisted. Even subsequent to promulgation of the new emancipation law of 1871 effective for the entire Reich, German Jews continued to be excluded from the officer corps. In Prussia, they were refused commissions even in the reserves. This was a serious disadvantage in German society, in which military status played an all-important role and in which an army commission was a prerequisite for a serious career in government. None of the close to 30,000 Jews who had served in the army since 1880 and who had appropriate educational qualifications was promoted to the rank of officer, although several hundred Jews who had converted were given commissions.[104] "For every German Jew there is a painful moment that he remembers his entire life: the moment he is first made fully conscious that he was born a second-class citizen. No ability and no achievement can free him from this."[105] These are the words of Walther Rathenau, later to become a German foreign minister, who was humiliated by his inability to receive an officer's commission and by the fact that upon his discharge from his mandatory year of military service he had only attained the rank of a mere lance corporal.

The situation in the German military did not substantially improve with the passage of time. Emblematic of the status of the Jews at the time is the case of Max Rothmann, a Berlin neurologist whose father and grandfather had been decorated in the Wars of 1815 and 1870, respectively, and whose elder son fell on the Western Front in 1914. Nonetheless, Rothmann's younger son's application to the Prussian cadet academy was rejected because, as the deputy war minister wrote, "Since your son adheres to the Jewish faith, the War Ministry regrets that it must reject your application."[106]

In World War I, 12,000 German Jewish soldiers died on the battlefield. Yet, the extent to which prejudice persisted is most strikingly apparent in the infamous *Judenzählung* (census of the Jews) ordered by War Minister Wild von Hohenborn in 1916 to determine the number of Jews who served on the frontlines as opposed to those who served in the rearguard. The census disproved the calumnies and demonstrated that eighty percent had served on the frontlines. Not only did the War Ministry fail to make the results public, but the findings were also distorted by anti-Semitic agitators.[107]

Anti-Semitic propaganda dating from the early 1900s in Germany focused upon alleged Jewish ineptitude and unsuitability for military service. Popular postcards abounded presenting caricatures of Jews exhibiting exaggerated stereotypical Jewish features, hooked noses and dark curly hair, and portrayed those individuals being turned away at recruitment centers because of their pronounced physical weakness, extreme shortness of stature, etc. A typically nasty cartoon postcard depicts "Der kleine Cohn," a tiny naked Jewish specimen measuring barely half the minimum height required for induction. The purpose of those hateful caricatures was to defame Jews and to foster a climate of opinion in which a military career, and perhaps also the subsequent possibility of high government office, would remain off bounds to Jews.[108]

3. Jew Against Jew
Challenged with regard to their preparedness to defend their country, the Assembly of Notables, in reply to Napoleon's sixth question, intimated that Judaism created no national bond and was but a

religious confession. The love of French Jews for their fatherland is so powerful, they stated, that a French Jew feels himself a foreigner even among English Jews: "To such a pitch is this sentiment carried among them that…French Jews have been seen fighting desperately against other Jews, the subjects of countries then at war with France" – and, impliedly, this gave rise to no special problem.[109]

This statement in itself is highly significant. In the first place, it reflects egregious servility. In offering unnecessary and gratuitous assurance of their allegiance, the delegates to the Assembly were quite willing to compromise Jewish self-respect. Secondly, and more importantly, their response represents a fundamental shift in Jewish self-identification and anticipates the philosophical stance of later assimilationists who renounced Jewish peoplehood, utterly denying the existence of the ethnic and national dimension of Judaism.

Perhaps even more so than any other statement of the Assembly, this assertion fails to reflect truthfully the sentiments of most Jews. For many a Jewish soldier, the very thought of engaging in combat against a fellow Jew was unsettling. While the quite serious halakhic question was seldom raised in public, on occasion, ethical and emotional qualms were expressed at the prospect of Jews going to battle against their coreligionists.[110] In the United States during the Civil War, Jews faced the dilemma not only of fighting fellow Jews but of fighting fellow Jews of their own country and possibly even of their own immediate family. Thus, for example, John Proskauer served in the Union Army, but his son, Major Adolph Proskauer, joined the Confederate forces. During the Battle of the Wilderness in May, 1864, Major Proskauer was close enough to his father, who was in charge of the commissary of the opposing force, to ask him for food.[111] With Jews arrayed on both sides of the conflict, a number of both Orthodox and Reform spokesmen passionately affirmed allegiance to opposing forces. Isaac M. Wise chose the path of neutrality and silence motivated in part, he claimed, because beloved kinsmen were to be found in both camps.[112]

Some 200 Jews bore arms in the Greco-Turkish War of 1897. In the wake of the hostilities, Saul Tschernichowsky composed a poem, "*Bein Ha-Metzarim*," depicting two brothers, one fighting for the

Turks, the other for the Greeks, who meet in the dead of night and shoot one another and only "In the light of the lightening shot did each one his brother recognize – *Le-or berak ha-yiriyah ish et ahiv hikkiru.*" Whether or not there is a historical basis for the poem has not been ascertained but it is highly plausible that Tschernichowsky was moved to portray the drama of such a tragic confrontation by a story that reached Odessa during the war.[113] In any event, several years thereafter, in the Balkan Wars of 1912–1913, Jews did face coreligionists in battle. There is a record of a meeting between King Constantine and Rabbi Jacob Meir, Chief Rabbi of Salonika, in the course of which the King praised the contributions of his Jewish soldiers and specifically pointed to the fact that they had fought against fellow Jews in the enemy camp as compelling evidence of their genuine loyalty.[114]

During World War I, patriotism bordering on chauvinism found expression in the writings of liberals on both sides of the conflict. One may contrast the remarks of Hermann Cohen in Germany regarding "Jews who can battle for our Fatherland...the land of intellectual freedom and ethics"[115] with those of Theodore Reinach in France concerning French Jews who "risk health, youth, life in order to liberate a freedom-loving France."[116] The halakhic and ethical problems involved in fighting against coreligionists were suppressed by those nationalists. On the other hand, although Simon Dubnow found himself supporting the Russian war effort, he gave voice to his abiding sorrow over the prospect of Jews battling other Jews.[117]

The devastation caused by the First World War was incalculable. More soldiers were killed in World War I than in any previous war and countless civilians died from starvation and resultant disease. Millions continued to suffer from physical and psychological wounds. Exposure to massive casualties and overwhelming feelings of despair shattered the emotional wellbeing of soldiers who had fought in trenches and, for many, lasting mental illness was a legacy of the war.[118]

The veterans continued to be haunted by their experiences. One veteran expressed the melancholy reality:

> The older I get, the sadder I feel about the uselessness of it all,
> but in particular the deaths of my comrades…. I thought I had
> managed all right, kept the awful things out of my mind. But
> now I'm an old man and they come back out from where I hid
> them. Every night.[119]

Those who had killed others in battle were unable to shake the memory. Not atypical is the account of one shell-shocked soldier being
treated with hypnosis who wept and made trigger movements with
his right forefinger while at the same time crying out: "Do you see,
do you see the enemy there? Has he a father and a mother? Has he
a wife? I'll not kill him."[120] If those who had taken the lives of other
soldiers were haunted by the recollection, how much more poignant
and painful was the experience of the Jew who may inadvertently
have slain a coreligionist.

One such episode is detailed in a recent film, "Shanghai Ghetto,"
that depicts the experiences of German refugees in Shanghai. In one
scene, a woman named Evelyn Rubin reminisces regarding her experiences in the ghetto and presents a vivid portrayal of her late father,
Benno Popielarz. A World War I veteran who had been decorated for
valor and suffered the remaining years of his life from the effects of
a war wound, even when transported to Buchenwald, her father had
simply been unable to believe that despite his loyalty and patriotism
he would be subject to the anti-Jewish Nazi decrees. Pointing to a
picture of her father in his uniform, Evelyn Rubin relates one terrible
event that occurred during the war of which her father often spoke.
One day, during face-to-face combat, he and the soldier opposite
him raised their rifles and took aim simultaneously. Her father fell
to the ground wounded but, at the same time, his opponent was hit
as well. As the other soldier fell, her father distinctly heard him call
out, "*Shema Yisrael.*" The knowledge that he might have killed a fellow Jew left her father with a pain that could not be assuaged.[121]

It was following the First World War, at a time when some
individuals began to confront the enormity of the atrocities of war,
that Rabbi Ze'ev Wolf Leiter forthrightly addressed the emotion-
laden topic of Jew fighting against Jew. Rabbi Leiter cites a narrative

recorded by Josephus describing how Jews were coerced into doing battle against fellow Jews which, writes Josephus, is "against our religion." Rabbi Leiter also refers to *Or Zaru'a, Avodah Zarah*, chap. 1, no. 132, which addresses halakhic problems attendant upon fighting against enemies among whom Jews reside. Probably because he was writing subsequent to the conclusion of World War I, after hostilities had come to an end, Rabbi Leiter could permit himself to address a topic others had avoided and regarding which, as noted, he writes, "I have not seen this law clarified in the writings of rabbinic decisors."[122] Rabbi Leiter's responsum prefigures the changing attitude to warfare that was to be expressed widely in the coming decades.

4. Pacifism and Twentieth Century Reform Writers

A pronounced shift in the attitude of exponents of Reform Judaism toward warfare and military service becomes apparent in the twentieth century.[123] That shift constituted nothing less than a one hundred and eighty degree reversal of policy from advocating military service as a sacred duty to endorsement of absolute pacifism.

During World War I, the Central Conference of American Rabbis (CCAR) overrode a passionate minority of its members in refusing to endorse the position that acceptance of the tenets of Judaism constitutes valid grounds for conscientious objection. The Conference stated that an individual who asserts that Jewish religious teaching is the basis for his claim to exemption from military service "does so only as an individual, inasmuch as historic Judaism emphasizes patriotism as a duty as well as the ideal of Peace."[124] At the time, several rabbis went on the record as disagreeing with that proposition. One of these, Martin Zielonka, argued that, while he himself was not a pacifist, he believed that Jews were obliged to "protect the honest and sincere conscientious objector who places his objections upon a religious ground" and maintained that the biblical verse "What man is there that is fearful and faint-hearted; let him go and return unto his house, lest his brethren's heart faint as well as his heart" (Deuteronomy 20:8) should be interpreted as grounds for excusing conscientious objectors.[125]

In the wake of World War I, sentiment in America in general

and among many Christian groups in particular became increasingly anti-war. A similar attitudinal progression was reflected in the gatherings of the Reform leadership. While a stance of absolute pacifism was not adopted, the proceedings of the Conference reflect unrelenting opposition to war. A 1924 CCAR resolution stated, "Because we love America…for this reason we urge upon our fellow citizens…that…they adopt an uncompromising opposition to war. We believe that war is morally indefensible."[126] During that period the Conference established a Standing Committee on Peace which functioned from 1925 until 1942, when it was incorporated in the Commission on Justice and Peace.[127] In practical terms, the CCAR lent its support to a series of measures designed to lead to cessation of warfare and proclaimed: "We believe in the outlawry of war by the nations of the earth. We support all movements which conscientiously and honestly strive to that end."[128] Accordingly, the Conference advocated America's participation in the Permanent Court of International Justice, endorsed Senator Borah's program to ban war, and endorsed international conferences leading to disarmament.[129] Compulsory military training programs in schools and colleges were strongly condemned:

> We reaffirm our opposition to the militarization of our schools and colleges by compulsory military training. We advocate in all educational systems an increasing emphasis on the comity and partnership of nations and, rather than the extollation of military prowess, the glorification of the heroes who have made for peace and progress.[130]

In 1932, the prominent Reform spokesman Stephen Wise expressed "everlasting regret" for his pro-war stance during World War I and pledged "without reservation or equivocation" never to bless or support any war whatsoever again.[131] Another influential Reform ideologue, Abraham Cronbach, was an uncompromising pacifist[132] who crusaded for the total renunciation of warfare. An ever greater proportion of Reform clergy became convinced that religious imperatives mandated a policy of refusal to bear arms under all circumstances since "war is a denial of all for which religion stands."[133] In 1935, the issue of pacifism was placed squarely before the Conference. The Committee on International Peace asked the Conference to declare that "henceforth it stands opposed to all war and that it recommends to all Jews that, for the sake of conscience, and in the name of God, they refuse to participate in the bearing of arms."[134] After prolonged debate this recommendation was, however, tabled for further study. While espousing pacifism in general, a majority of Reform rabbis insisted on the right to self-defense in the event of invasion.[135] They continued to oppose compulsory military training and any educational policies designed to promote warfare. A majority now claimed that conscientious objection by Jews on religious grounds was valid.[136]

With the rise of the Hitlerian forces, the pacifist position of many of those rabbis was modified. In 1939, the Conference officially noted the distinction between innocent and aggressor nations.[137] Subsequently, when the United States entered the war, the CCAR, with few dissenting votes, expressed "complete support for our country in its present war" and declared, "We believe that God is on the side of Justice and that it is His will to see a tyrant-free world."[138]

Anti-war sentiment again rose to the forefront in the Reform movement in the mid-1960s as opposition mounted to American involvement in Vietnam. The Reform movement soon became the most outspoken Jewish organization decrying United States military activity in Southeast Asia. A 1965 resolution of the Union of American Hebrew Congregations urging a cease-fire and negotiated peace settlement represented what was at the time a minority position in the United States among Jews and the general public. After the Six-Day War, some Reform clergy found difficulty in opposing American policy in Vietnam while at the same time urging support for Israel. However, Reform clergy and laity remained in the forefront of demonstrations and protests against the Vietnam conflict.[139]

The emphasis in Reform ideology in favor of pacifism in the 1930s and later the opposition to the Vietnam conflict in the 1960s prompted an attempt on the part of Reform thinkers to find precedents and sources in Jewish law and teaching that would serve as a mandate for conscientious objection to military service and pacifism.

In the intense debate on pacifism before the annual convention of the CCAR in 1935, a tentative resolution placed before the assembly proclaimed:

> ...the time has come to change the traditional attitude of our faith toward war. We realize to the full the seriousness of this change we propose, and we adopt it because of our belief that the spirit of Israel, the first faith and people to love peace and pursue it, necessitates such a vital change in the text and letter of our historic attitude. In the past Israel has made the distinction between righteous and unrighteous wars. In the light of the foregoing, we believe that this distinction has no reality for our day. And we are now compelled to adopt as our belief, and as the basis for action of our religious followers and ourselves, the principle that war is an unmitigated evil, and that we should abstain from all participation in it.[140]

Several discussants at the Conference questioned these sweeping generalizations regarding historical Jewish attitudes to war and urged further scholarly study of the subject.[141] The following year, Abraham Cronbach presented the Conference with a paper, "War and Peace in Jewish Tradition," in which he had assembled a vast array of sources regarding this topic in biblical and talmudic literature.[142] Cronbach wished to demonstrate that Jewish tradition encompasses teachings which can be applied at various points "on a modernistic scale" ranging from extreme militarism to extreme pacifism. He claimed, incorrectly, that the moral differentiation between wars of aggression and wars of defense is a distinction of which the tradition is not conscious.[143]

Vigorous Reform opposition to the Vietnam conflict in the 1960's spurred renewed interest in this subject and a number of studies appeared emphasizing the teachings of Judaism that lend themselves to pacifist interpretation.[144] Some writers sought to demonstrate that alongside the normative halakhic position there was a position that refused to condone violence even in extreme situations.[145] One writer posited "an undercurrent of non-violence which grew alongside the Halakhah (and even in it at one point)…. At times this position was at the forefront…at others, it remained the view of small groups."[146]

The view that it was necessary to abandon the traditional attitude of Judaism toward war as expressed by the CCAR in 1935 persisted. Only now the position was stated more baldly:

> We have faced the tradition and have found its normative halakhic position wanting…. [147] We cannot accept its normative patterns as the only meaningful expression of God's demands on us as Jews. As liberal Jews, we cannot accept the notion that the *memrah* and the *mitzvah* are always heard in the *din* given by the *g'dolei ha-dor*.[148]

Yet in order to anchor the emerging liberal position in Jewish tradition, Reform writers argued that the longstanding non-normative halakhic view must now be affirmed.

Ironically, the position a number of these writers espoused was hardly one that differed from what is, in reality, the normative halakhic position. Sheldon Zimmerman wrote:

> Thus, although we find ourselves not to be pacifists (and there is a pacifist trend in Judaism as seen by the non-violent tradition), we cannot countenance any military forms of violence in this country or by this country where no *clear* issue of self-defense of *home* and *family* can be established…. Thus, some of us find ourselves differing with the normative halakhic position.[149]

Zimmerman found himself conflicted because of his own misunderstanding of the halakhic sources. The position he himself articulated is much closer to the normative halakhic view than to the non-normative. Zimmerman and other liberal writers who addressed this issue were attacking a straw man and disputing a tradition that they misconstrued.

Certainly, as Isaiah Leibowitz wrote, while there is no enthusiasm for military prowess *per se* in Judaism, Halakhah recognizes that, when war is necessary, "legitimate value is attached to one who fulfills his responsibilities in this area of human reality...."[150] Yet, in most instances, warfare is not legitimate and is not condoned by Halakhah. The normative halakhic view of the Vietnam conflict does not differ significantly from the view espoused by Zimmerman. Indeed, as aptly expressed by Rabbi Joseph Grunblatt:

> If a Viet Cong takeover of South Vietnam cannot be considered a clear and present military danger to the United States[151] it would make this war a *milchemet reshut* for America, which is not permissible for a *Ben Noach*. One may question whether the Halakhah and *Daat Torah* have been considered by those supporting our government's policies in Vietnam.[152]

In the final analysis, one comes back full circle. Neither patriotic enthusiasm that extols warfare nor absolute pacifism that precludes self-defense is reflective of the Jewish tradition. The view that for Jews in our day, and for Noahides at any time, there is no legitimate discretionary war appears to be the normative halakhic position as accepted by the majority of halakhic authorities.[153] Perhaps in the contemporary historical epoch, in which the horrors perpetrated by the ravages of warfare have shocked our society to its foundation and the ethical dilemmas of political aggression in the name of patriotism are confronted more forthrightly, articulation of the halakhic view need not be hampered by apologetic obfuscation and halakhic objections to complicity in participating in a war of aggression need no longer be relegated to the sphere of *Torah she-be-al peh*.

IV. A POLITICAL ASIDE – ALL-JEWISH BATTALIONS IN NON-JEWISH ARMIES

During an age in which civic and social equality were the anticipated goals prompting participation in military endeavors, promotion of all-Jewish army units would have been counterproductive. Such units would have served to affirm difference precisely when the desire was to assert commonality. However, from time to time, efforts were made to establish all-Jewish battalions in order to achieve entirely different objectives.

Whether or not one's personal value system, in consonance with that of the Sages, regards weapons in a negative light ("They are but a disgrace," Mishnah, *Shabbat* 63a), it would be naïve not to recognize that in society in general an undeniable mystique surrounds the accoutrements of war, such as uniforms, arms, and medals. Similarly, an aura of power and authority is associated with military personages. The phenomenon of former generals rising to positions of civilian prominence even in peace-loving democracies is familiar to all. An acute awareness of those factors and the recognition that military exploits bestow a measure of political and social influence on participants served as motivating considerations for those who sought to promote the establishment of all-Jewish battalions in both World Wars.

During World War I, two diametrically opposite perspectives regarding Jewish participation in the conflict emerged among Zionist leaders. In Palestine, Ben-Gurion and Ben-Tzvi proposed the formation of a Jewish Legion attached to the Turks on the side of the Central Powers. Initially approved by the Turkish authorities, who rapidly rescinded their approval, the project ended in the imprisonment and deportation of the Jewish volunteers. In contrast, Jabotinsky and others proposed the formation of a Jewish Legion to fight on the side of the Allies in order to free Palestine from the Turks.

The Zion Mule Corps, organized in 1915 and composed in part of Russian Jewish immigrants to Britain, fought under a battalion flag of their own. Later, two battalions attached to the Royal Fusiliers, consisting mainly of Jewish volunteers from America, were sent to Egypt and fought under their own flag in the campaign to conquer Palestine. It was hoped that, if Jews fought as a national unit, as cobelligerents, they would later gain the right to advance claims at the peace table. The presence of such a Jewish military unit fighting for Palestine, hailed as "the first Jewish army since Bar Kochba," had great emotional resonance to Jews throughout the world.[154] Those sentiments are captured in a poem published just before a large contingent of American volunteers left to join the Legion:

> The swords of many nations
> Have made of thee a prey,
> The feet of many strangers
> Have worn thy stones away;
> But harken, O Jerusalem,
> And hear a joyful sound –
> The tread of Jewish warriors
> On their ancestral ground!
>
> Arise and sing, Jerusalem,
> Who art no longer dumb;
> O citadel of David,
> The sons of David come![155]

During the Second World War, a Jewish Brigade Group was formed to serve alongside the Allied forces as an independent Jewish national military unit. From 1940 on, many Jews served in the British East Kent Regiment in Jewish companies primarily involved in guard duty and not fully equipped. In 1944, those units together with new volunteers and a number of Jews serving in other sections of the British army were incorporated into an independent Jewish Brigade of approximately 5,000 soldiers. The Brigade took part in assaults against the Germans and later played an important role in caring for Jewish survivors of the concentration camps and ghettos.

Winston Churchill, no stranger to political nuance and keenly attuned to the import of propaganda and symbol in boosting morale, had his own agenda in favoring the organization of the Jewish Brigade as a distinct and recognizable body. In a telegram sent to President Roosevelt, Churchill demonstrated sympathetic understanding of the unique nature of Jewish involvement in the struggle against the Nazis and that "surely…of all other races" Jews qua Jews had the right to strike at the Germans. Therefore, he concluded, the assembling of a Jewish regimental combat team with its own flag "will give great satisfaction to the Jews when it is published…[and] would be a message to go all over the world."[156]

As was the case with regard to the Jewish Legion, the formation of the Jewish Brigade was the culmination of efforts on the part of Zionist leaders to enhance the status of the *yishuv* and to promote the political aims of Zionism. The Zionist leadership well understood the powerful psychological and political impact that would result from the existence of Jewish fighting units. In forming the Jewish Legion and the Jewish Brigade, deeply-rooted ambivalences toward warfare and the military were overcome by the desire of ardent Zionists to achieve overriding aims, viz., realization of nationalist aspirations and, with regard to the Brigade, also elimination of a threat to the very existence of the Jewish people.

V. AFTERWORD

Plato, in the *Republic* (v, 466), suggests that in the ideal state men and women who go out to the battlefield should take children along as spectators in order to enable them to observe and to learn "this trade like any other" and to familiarize themselves with their future duties. Men who are destined to become warriors, Plato argues, should see something of warfare in childhood.[157]

Plato articulates the very antithesis of a Jewish educational perspective. The extent to which his model differs from a Jewish one is exemplified by a *bon mot* current among European Jews. When the German Emperor William I passed away, an elderly officer was given the honor of carrying the deceased Kaiser's sword on a cushion in the funeral procession. Berlin Jews characterized that distinction as "*goyishe naches*" (satisfactions of the gentiles).[158]

In point of fact, the Jewish educational ideal represents a reinterpretation and transformation of the notion of the military hero. Thus a characteristic aggadic commentary on Song of Songs 3:7–8 states:

> "Behold his bed, which is Solomon's; threescore valiant men are about it, of the valiant of Israel. They all hold swords, being expert (schooled) in war – *melumadei milhamah*":

Melumadei – Schooled, *she-melamdim et beneihem, ve-limade-tem et beneikhem* – that they teach their children, and you shall teach them unto your children; *milhamah* – war, *milhamtah shel Torah* – the war of Torah.[159]

The sole instruction in battle commended by rabbinic teachers is to hone the minds of students so that they become expert in intellectual struggle and strive for the truth and knowledge necessary to triumph in the "war" of Torah.

NOTES

1. Manuscript in the possession of the Livraria Ets Haim-D. Montezinos in Amsterdam cited by Arnold Wiznitzer, "Jewish Soldiers in Dutch Brazil (1630–1654)," *Publication of the American Jewish Historical Society (PAJHS)*, 46:1 (1956):47.
2. Paris, 1886, p. 53.
3. *Zuruf an die Jünglinge, welche den Fahnen des Vaterlandes folgen*, (Berlin, 1813), p. 10.
4. *Sulamith*, II:1 (1808):6.
5. *Central Conference of American Rabbis Yearbook (CCARY)*, 45 (1935): 66–67.
6. Simon Schwarzfuchs, *Napoleon, the Jews and the Sanhedrin* (London: Routledge and Kegan Paul, 1979), p. 62.
7. See A.E. Cowley, *Aramaic Papyri of the Fifth Century B.C.* (Oxford: Clarendon Press, 1923; Rep. Osnabrück: Zeller, 1967), pp. xv, xvi and 12.
8. See Jacob Beller, *Jews in Latin America* (New York: Jonathan David, 1969), pp. 107–108 and *Historical Essay on the Colony of Surinam 1788*, trans. S. Cohen, Jacob R. Marcus and Stanley S. Chyet, eds. (New York: American Jewish Archives and Ktav Publishing House, 1974), pp. 42–48 and 65–72.
9. Note should be taken of R. Judah Halevi's incisive statement, *Kuzari*, Part V, sec. 23, categorizing the behavior of those who endanger their lives by volunteering for army service "in order to gain fame and spoil by courage and bravery" as morally reprehensible and "even inferior to that of those who march into war for hire." Halevi's distinction between frivolous self-endangerment and self-endangerment for purposes of earning a livelihood prefigures the thesis later developed in the classic responsum of Rabbi Ezekiel Landau, *Noda bi-Yehudah, Mahadura Tinyana* (Prague, 1811), *Yoreh De'ah*, no. 10.
10. See the intriguing summary of Jewish military activity in the Middle Ages in David Biale, *Power and Powerlessness in Jewish History* (New York: Schocken Books, 1986), pp. 72–77 and sources cited in Yitzhak Ze'ev Kahane, "Sherut ha-Tzava be-Sifrut ha-Teshuvot," *Sinai* 23 (1948): 129–134.
11. See "Military Service," *Encyclopedia Judaica*, XI, 1550.
12. Cf. R. Abraham Dov Ber Kahane, *Dvar Avraham*, I, no. 11 and R. Menachem

Ziemba, *Zera Avraham*, no. 24, sec. 10, and the discussion in R. J. David Bleich, *Contemporary Halakhic Problems*, II (New York: Ktav Publishing House, 1983), 164–166.

13. *Sheelot u-Teshuvot Bet David*, 2nd ed. (Vienna, 1932), I, no. 71.

14. Eulogy published in "*Sefer Hatam Sofer*," *Derashot*, I (Cluj, 1929), pp. 80b–82a and republished in Rabbi Joseph David Sintzheim, *Minhat Ani* (Jerusalem: Machon Yerushalayim, 1974), p. 30. English translation in Schwarzfuchs, *Napoleon*, p. 116.

15. *Yevamot* 65b.

16. *Noda bi-Yehudah, Mahadura Tinyana, Yoreh Deah*, no. 74.

17. *Sheelot u-Teshuvot Hatam Sofer*, VI (Pressberg, 1864), *Likkutim*, no. 29.

18. *Imrei Esh, Yoreh Deah* (Lemberg, 1852), no. 52.

19. Cf. the complex and rather strained argument presented by R. Abraham Teumim, *Hesed le-Avraham, Mahadura Kamma* (Lemberg, 1857), *Yoreh Deah*, no. 45, in favor of compelling such persons to accept induction in order to preserve observant individuals from transgression.

20. *Noda bi-Yehudah, Mahadura Tinyana, Yoreh Deah*, no. 74. For a discussion of why Rabbi Samuel Landau demands protest against delivery of prospective soldiers to the authorities but does not demand similar protest against communal intervention to secure the release of designated individuals when substitution of others is a certainty, see R. J. David Bleich, *Be-Netivot Ha-Halakhah* (New York: Ktav Publishing House, 1996), I, 120–124.

21. Policy with regard to clergymen and rabbinical student exemptions differed from country to country. In France, after 1808, Jewish youths preparing to enter the rabbinate were not granted a clergy exemption. See S. Posener, "The Immediate Economic and Social Effect of the Emancipation of the Jews in France," *Jewish Social Studies*, 1 (1939):317. However, in Russia, under a decree issued in 1827, rabbis and students in rabbinical seminaries were exempt from military service. See Michael Stanislawski, *Tsar Nicholas I and the Jews: The Transformation of Jewish Society in Russia, 1825–1855* (Philadelphia: Jewish Publication Society, 1983), p. 19. Cf., also, the comments of R. Baruch ha-Levi Epstein, *Mekor Barukh* (New York, 1954), II, 1060–1061.

22. *Hatam Sofer*'s ruling was by no means unique. Thus, for example, R. Zevi Hirsch Chajes reports that he had occasion to advise a synagogue to pawn the synagogue lamps in order to raise funds necessary to enable prospective conscripts to avoid military service. See *Minhat Kenaot*, in *Kol Sifrei Maharatz Hayes* (Jerusalem: Divrei Hakhamim, 1958), II, 991.

23. *Sheelot u-Teshuvot Hatam Sofer*, VI, *Likkutim*, no. 29. Sheldon Zimmerman, "Confronting the Halakhah on Military Service," *Judaism* 20:2 (Spring, 1971): 207 and 210, errs in positing a fundamental disagreement between *Hatam Sofer* and Rabbi Samuel Landau and in asserting that Rabbi Landau represented a minority view in censuring the methods used by the Jewish community in filling their quotas. Both respondents categorically forbid substitution of nonobservant youths for draftees who have been designated by name. The stronger language of Rabbi

Landau, "*mehuyavim limhot be-yad*," in contrast to *Hatam Sofer's* "*ha-shetikah yafah me-dibbureinu ba-zeh ve-et la-hashot*," may simply reflect the difference between an earlier theoretical stance and a later deterioration in communal practice at which time protest might have proven more harmful to the welfare of the greater community. While *Hatam Sofer* affirms that the conscripted individual has an obligation to serve if he cannot avoid induction, Rabbi Landau states only that once an individual has been designated the community must desist from efforts to secure a reprieve at another's expense, but is silent regarding the individual's own obligation. However, there is no explicit contradiction between the two responsa. Nor does *Hatam Sofer* express "the majority view" (Zimmerman, p. 207) with regard to the legitimacy of the draft as flowing from the power of the ruler to levy "taxes." Whether or not the prerogatives of the king ascribed by 1 Samuel 8 to the Jewish king (*mishpetei ha-melekh*) apply to non-Jewish rulers as well is the subject of considerable controversy among halakhic scholars. See Shmuel Shilo, *Dina de-Malkhuta Dina* (Jerusalem: Jerusalem Academic Press, 1974), pp. 62, 64–67, 71–73 and 101.

24. Again Zimmerman errs (p. 207) in deeming this a stronger position than that of *Hatam Sofer*. Exemptions are simply not discussed by *Hatam Sofer*; they are not necessarily forbidden.

25. See infra, note 37.

26. Cf., however, infra, note 49.

27. R. Moshe Joshua Judah Leib Diskin, *She'elot u-Teshuvot Maharil Diskin* (Jerusalem, 1911), *Pesakim*, no. 4, forbids a soldier to reveal an infirmity to the authorities in order to avoid army duty lest he be coerced instead to work on the Sabbath. This responsum should not be viewed as contradicting the views of *Keren le-David* or *Levushei Mordekhai* since the responsum does not appear to apply to army service during wartime. The conclusion drawn by Zimmerman (p. 209) that Maharil Diskin deems profanation of the Sabbath a greater evil than danger to one's life is without basis.

28. See infra, notes 106 and 107 and accompanying text.

29. It must be emphasized that this responsum addresses the situation of a peacetime army and involves no discussion of danger to life. In wartime an additional factor would have had to be taken into consideration, namely, preservation of life for as long as possible.

30. *Melammed le-Ho'il, Orah Hayyim*, no. 43. The comments of Rabbi Alfred Cohen, "In this century, R. David Hoffmann (*Orach Chaim* 42–43) considered it the obligation of every citizen, including Jews, to participate in the army like all citizens. Even if one can get a deferment for 2 or 3 years, R. Hoffmann opposes it and says one should enlist right away," are not an accurate representation of Rabbi Hoffmann's views. See R. Alfred Cohen, "On Yeshiva Men Serving in the Army," *Journal of Halacha and Contemporary Society*, No. 23 (Spring, 1992), p. 30, note 65.

31. The note below the text marked with an asterisk, "And it has already been ruled in the Gemara 'the law of the land is the law,'" may constitute a somewhat enigmatic

reference to the legitimacy of conscription. However, the form in which it appears, i.e., outside the annotations on *Shulhan Arukh* and without the usual marginal signal makes it possible that this comment was intended for the benefit of the authorities rather than the reader.

32. *Horeb: A Philosophy of Jewish Laws and Observances*, trans. Dayan I. Grunfeld (New York: Soncino Press, 1962), sec. 609, p. 462.

33. *Loc. cit.*

34. The unquestioning patriotism of Rabbi Hirsch is subjected to a pointed critique in Rabbi Howard I. Levine, "Enduring and Transitory Elements in the Philosophy of Samson Raphael Hirsch," *Tradition* 5:2 (Spring, 1963): 290–293. Cf. the response of Rabbi Shelomoh Eliezer Danziger, "Clarification of R. Hirsch's Concepts – A Rejoinder," *Tradition* 6:2 (Spring-Summer, 1964): 155–156.

35. *Horeb*, p. 462.

36. *Tel Talpiyot* (Moetzin, 1916), no. 104.

37. Surprisingly, *Imrei Esh*, *Yoreh De'ah*, no. 52, permits voluntary enlistment despite the danger to life involved. For a recent discussion of that issue, see R. Yitzchak Zilberstein, *Kol ha-Torah*, No. 55 (Tishri, 2003): 153–154.

38. Another orthodox rabbinic figure of the time who wrote eloquently on pacifism was R. Aaron Saul Tamaret (1869–1931). See infra, note 144 regarding an English translation of one of his sermons on non-violence.

39. This letter has recently been published by his grandson, Rabbi Yehudah H. Henkin, in his article, "Ha-Ga'on Rabbi Yosef Eliyahu Henkin Zatzal, Shloshim Shanah le-Motto," *Ha-Ma'ayan*, 44:1 (Tishri, 2003): 75–76.

40. See Stanislawski, *Tsar Nicholas*, pp. 13–34 and Salo W. Baron, *The Russian Jew under Tsars and Soviets*, 2nd rev. ed. (New York: Macmillan, 1976), pp 29–32. For a discussion of Cantonists' memoirs and literary works devoted to the Cantonist theme see Adina Ofek, "Cantonists: Jewish Children as Soldiers in Tsar Nicholas's Army," *Modern Judaism*, 13 (1993): 277–308.

41. See R. Baruch ha-Levi Epstein's description of the "era of the sin of the community," *Mekor Barukh*, II, 962–969 and 999–1003 and III, 1191–1192; cf., Stanislawski, *Tsar Nicholas*, pp 26–34. Cf. also Kahane, "Sherut ha-Tzava," p. 147.

42. Indicative of the wariness of rabbinic scholars to address these matters in print is material on the Cantonists that has only now been published. In a recent article, "'Gezeirah Hi Mi-Lefanai': Derashot be-Inyan ha-Kantonistim," *Yeshurun*, XII (Nisan 2003): 695–726, Rabbi Yisrael Meir Mendelowitz incorporates the text of a number of discourses devoted to the Cantonists as they appear in an unpublished manuscript of Rabbi David of Novardok (1769–1836), author of the celebrated rabbinic work, *Galy'a Massekhet*. In *Galy'a Massekhet*, posthumously published (Vilna, 1844) by the author's son-in-law and grandson, portions of these discourses appear but with the glaring omission of explicit references to the Cantonist decree. Thus, for example, in one discourse that is published in *Galy'a Massekhet*, R. David of Novardok mentions a prayer assembly called in response to the troubles that had beset the community "which cannot be recorded in writing" (*Galy'a Massekhet*, p. 13a). The identical prayer assembly is described in the now published manuscript

as having been called "in order to stir the populace because of the occurrence of the decree and edict" (*Yeshurun*, p. 717). In particular, in the discourse delivered on the *Rosh ha-Shanah* immediately following the conscription edict of August 26, 1827, Rabbi David of Novardok reflects the somber and anguished mood of a stricken community of whom he writes that it is "difficult for us to recite on these holidays the [blessing] *she-heheyanu*" (p. 726) and whose feelings he can best depict (p. 718) in the words of Ezekiel 21:12, "And it shall be when they say unto you: Wherefore do you sigh, that you shall answer: Because of tidings that are coming and every heart shall melt and all hands shall be feeble and every spirit shall grow faint and all knees shall be weak as water. Behold it is come and shall happen...." Rabbis could express such sentiments in the privacy of their congregations but, at that time, were loath to disclose them to alien eyes that might alight upon a published work.

43. Aharon Soraski, *Marbitzei Torah u-Mussar*, I (Brooklyn, NY: Sentry Press, 1977), 80.

44. For a description of various other incidents in which Rabbi Soloveichik intervened in such matters, see ibid., pp 80–81.

45. Cited in translation in Baron, *Under Tsars*, pp. 30–31; for a slightly different Yiddish version see Epstein, *Mekor Barukh*, II, 964. See also ibid., pp. 965–967 and p. 967, note 2, for the exploits of R. Eliyahu Shik and for a description of efforts of other rabbinic figures to oppose the tyranny of the communal officials who surrendered children to army authorities. Regarding R. Eliyahu Shik cf. Stanislawski, *Tsar Nicholas*, p. 129 and the popularized account of Larry Domnitch, *The Cantonists: The Jewish Children's Army of the Tsar* (Jerusalem and New York: Devora Publishing, 2003), pp. 55–56.

46. See Dov Katz, *Tenu'at ha-Mussar*, I (Tel Aviv: Avraham Zioni, 1958), 204–206.

47. See Mendelowitz, *Yeshurun*, XII, 443, note 18. Cf. Domnitch, *The Cantonists*, pp. 57–60. The hasidic leaders, R. Yitzhak of Worki and R. Israel of Rizhin, prevailed upon Moses Montefiore to travel to Peterburg in order to intercede with Tsar Nicholas and urge mitigation of the harsh draft decree but Montefiore's intervention was unsuccessful. See Aaron Marcus, *Ha-Hasidut*, trans. into Hebrew from German by M. Schonfeld (Tel Aviv: Nezah, 1954), pp. 213–214. For the application of the conscription decree in the areas of Poland under Russian rule and Polish Jews' fruitless efforts to mitigate provisions of the law, see also Jacob Shatzky, *Die Geshikhte fun Yidn in Varshe* (New York: Yiddish Scientific Institute-Yivo, 1948), II, 74–81.

48. R. Shlomoh Yosef Zevin, *Ishim ve-Shittot* (Tel Aviv: Avraham Zioni, 1958), pp. 63–64 and Soraski, I, 112.

49. Zevin, *Ishim*, p. 65; Soraski, *Marbitzei*, p. 112. For a discussion of how that ruling involves an expansion of the *holeh le-fanenu* ("a patient before us") principle necessary to justify suspending biblical strictures, see R. J. David Bleich, *Bioethical Dilemmas: A Jewish Perspective* (Hoboken: Ktav Publishing House, 1998), pp. 154–156. Cf., however, *Hazon Ish, Oholot* 22:32 and *Yoreh De'ah* 208:7.

50. *Birkat Shmu'el*, I (New York, 1947), *Kiddushin* 27:6, p. 41.

51. Zevin, *Ishim*, pp. 73–74, as related to him by R. Iser Zalman Meltzer.
52. Ibid., p. 74, note, as related to Rabbi Zevin "by a reliable source." Rabbi Zevin suggests that R. Hayyim's attitude may have been formed by his personal experience in the Volozhin Yeshiva. So long as the Yeshiva did not come to the attention of the authorities, its operation was unimpeded. Once the Yeshiva was formally recognized by government bureaus, harassment and attempts at regulation began. The lesson to be learned was that safety was to be found in obscurity.

   R. Hayyim's aversion to army service was shared by other members of his family. His grandson, the late Rabbi Joseph B. Soloveitchik of Boston and New York, was not eager to serve in the army. In 1924 he enrolled in the Free Polish University in Warsaw and in 1926 left for Berlin to continue his studies in the philosophy department of the University of Berlin. A factor influencing his decision to leave for Berlin was the possibility of being drafted into the Polish army. See Aaron Rakefet-Rothkoff, *The Rav: The World of Rabbi Joseph B. Soloveitchik* (Ktav Publishing House, 1999) I, 26 and 68, note 11 and Bertram Leff, "Letter to the Editor," *Torah u-Madda Journal*, IX (2000):268–269. Another grandson, the late Rabbi Moshe Soloveitchik of Switzerland (together with Rabbi Aaron Leib Steinman, currently Rosh Yeshiva of Yeshiva Ga'on Ya'akov in Bnei Brak), fled Poland in 1937 after receiving draft notices from the Polish army and thus survived the war. See Moshe Musman, "A Reiner Mentsch, A Reiner Torah: HaRav Moshe Soloveitchik zt'l," *Yated Ne'eman* (May 3, 1996), 19.
53. M. Sofer, *Homat Esh* (Israel, 1985), I, 114–115 and 126–130.
54. A number of incidents are recorded by the popular historian Abraham I. Bromberg in his *Admorei Aleksander* (Jerusalem: Ha-Machon le-Hasidut, 1954), pp. 93–94 and *Ha-Admor R. Yehudah Leib Alter mi-Gur, Ba'al "Sefat Emet"* (Jerusalem: Ha-Machon le-Hasidut, 1956), pp. 114–117. Cf. Yisroel Friedman, *The Rebbes Of Chortkov* (Brooklyn: Mesorah Publications, 2003), pp. 221–222, for a similar unsuccessful attempt on the part of the authorities to apprehend R. Yisrael Friedman, the *Rebbe* of Chortkov, in the act of advising his followers to evade conscription.
55. Aharon Soraski, "Foreword: Kalonymus Kalman Shapiro, Rebbe of the Warsaw Ghetto," in R. Kalonymus Kalman Shapiro, *A Student's Obligation: Advice from the Rebbe of the Warsaw Ghetto*, trans. by Micha Odenheimer (Northvale, NJ: Jason Aronson, 1991), pp. xxv and xxxiii–xxxiv. On the use of amulets and other mystical practices for avoidance of conscription cf. infra, note 62 and accompanying text. See also Epstein, *Mekor Barukh*, II, 1061, note 1.
56. Wiznitzer, "Jewish Soldiers in Dutch Brazil," *PAJHS*, 46:1 (1956):40–50.
57. Arthur Hertzberg, *The Jews in America: Four Centuries of an Uneasy Encounter: A History* (New York: Simon and Schuster, 1989), p. 52
58. Zosa Szajkowski, *Jews in the French Revolutions of 1789, 1830 and 1848* (New York: Ktav Publishing House, 1970), pp. 557–558, 786 and 794.
59. Ibid., p. 792. In some instances Jews were forced to have their beards and sidelocks publicly cut off and were forced to pay the barbers for this service. A surprising exception is the case of the head of the yeshiva in Metz, Rabbi Aaron Worms, who

reportedly voluntarily shaved off his beard and enlisted in the National Guard, and, upon being given a lance, proclaimed in Hebrew, "This is the day that we awaited" (*loc. cit.*). Rabbi Aaron Worms, the author of novellae entitled *Me'orei Or,* later, in 1815, became Chief Rabbi of Metz.

It is noteworthy that during the Polish uprising of 1831, at a time when several hundred Jews bore arms in the national army, there were several Jewish units comprised of observant individuals in the Warsaw militia who received specific dispensation not to cut their beards and sidelocks. See N.M. Gelber, "Yehudim bi-Tzva Polin," in *Hayyalim Yehudim be-Tzeva'ot Europah,* Yehudah Slutzky and Mordecai Kaplan, eds. (Israel: Ma'arkhot, 1967), pp. 94–95 and Shatzky, *Geshikhte,* I, 322–323.

60. Paula E. Hyman, *The Emancipation of the Jews of Alsace: Acculturation and Tradition in the Nineteenth Century* (New Haven & London: Yale University Press, 1991), p. 74 and p. 174, note 29.

61. Hyman, ibid., p. 17, observes that, since many other departments were exempt from the decree, the burden of this provision fell heavily on the Jews of Alsace-Lorraine. Regarding the question of substitutes in the French army and Jewish agents active in recruiting and pressuring individuals to serve as substitutes, see Szajkowski, *French Revolutions,* pp. 564–565.

62. Hyman, *Jews of Alsace,* pp. 69–70, and p. 174, notes 26.

63. For the text of the address see Solomon Wind, *Rabbi Yehezkel Landau: Toldot Hayyav u-Pe'ulotav* (Jerusalem: Da'at Torah, 1961), Appendix 3, pp. 115–116.

64. Ibid., p. 116. Yekutiel Aryeh Kamelhar, *Mofet ha-Dor: Toldot Rabbenu Yehezkel ha-Levi Landau Ba'al ha-Noda bi-Yehudah ve-ha-Tzlah* (Pietrkow, 1934), p. 82, note 6, cites a communication regarding a letter from R. Shlomo Kluger of Brody in which Rabbi Kluger delivers a report concerning Rabbi Landau's reaction to the conscription edict. According to this account, Rabbi Landau was told that the king had announced that the Jews would be accorded great honor in that they would henceforth be able to serve in the army. Of this honor, Rabbi Landau is said to have remarked that it constituted the curse alluded to in Leviticus 27:44: "And yet for all that, when they be in the land of their enemies, I will not cast them away, neither will I abhor them to destroy them utterly and to break My covenant with them for I am the Lord their God." Rabbi Landau allegedly declared that, because in the army Jews will be susceptible to violating all the dietary laws, to give Jews the honor of military service and no longer to "abhor them" and "cast them away" is "to destroy them utterly and to break My covenant with them."

65. The text of the question is included in Baruch Mevorach, *Napoleon u-Tekufato* (Jerusalem: Mossad Bialik, 1968), Part 1, p. 37.

66. Robert N. Rosen, *The Jewish Confederates* (Columbia, SC: University of South Carolina Press, 2000), p. 173. His family still has in its possession his two mess kits – one for meat and one for milk. See ibid., p. 421 note 39.

67. Myron Berman, *Richmond's Jewry, 1769–1976: Shabbat in Shockoe* (Charlottesville: University Press of Virginia, 1979), p. 175; Rosen, *Jewish Confederates,* p. 199.

Knowledge of the rudiments of Jewish dietary law was common among the non-Jewish populace, as is evident from the following charming vignette: Major Alexander Hart of New Orleans, one of the highest ranking Jewish Confederate infantry officers, was seriously wounded in his thigh by grapeshot early in the war. The surgeon wished to amputate the leg but was restrained by the mistress of the house to which Hart had been taken after the battle. She implored the doctor to delay the amputation and permit her to try to nurse Hart back to health because, she argued, so young and handsome a man should not lose a leg. After the war, Hart visited his benefactress annually. Once, when her daughter-in-law complained that there was no ham on the table, the elderly lady responded, "No, there shall be no ham on my table when my 'Jewish son' is here." See Herbert T. Ezekiel and Gaston Lichtenstein, *The History of the Jews of Richmond from 1769 to 1917* (Richmond, Virginia: Herbert T. Ezekiel, 1917), p. 157.

68. Rosen, *Jewish Confederates*, p. 200. See also ibid., p. 115, Edward Kursheedt's letter in which he communicates, "I have not been able to see the Chanucka lights this year." For further details regarding observance of Passover and the Day of Atonement and informal Sabbath services see Bertram W. Korn, *American Jewry and the Civil War* (Philadelphia: Jewish Publication Society, 1961), pp. 88–94.

69. I am indebted to Rabbi Samuel N. Hoenig for drawing my attention to the fact that a slim English-language manual for Jewish soldiers was distributed in the United States during World War II. That work by Moses M. Yosher, based on *Hafetz Hayyim*'s *Mahaneh Yisrael*, is titled *Israel in the Ranks* (New York: Yeshiva Chofetz Chaim Publication, 1943).

70. R. Israel Meir ha-Kohen, *Mahaneh Yisrael* (New York: Shulsinger Bros., 1943), Introduction, p. 8. *Hafetz Hayyim*'s concern for Jewish soldiers expressed itself in other practical endeavors as well. An open letter, "Regarding Kosher Food for Soldiers," signed by him dated 5683 (1923) emphatically underscores the interdependence and mutual responsibility of each Jew for his fellow and calls on Jewish communities to establish kosher soup kitchens for the benefit of soldiers stationed in their environs. The letter is published in *Hafetz Hayyim al ha-Torah*, ed. S. Greiniman (New York: Shulsinger Bros., 1943), p. 237.

71. *Mahane Yisra'el, "Davar be-Itto,"* pp. 175–187.

72. Ibid., pp. 19–20.

73. See "Sermon on Be-Ha'aloteka" in *Jewish Preaching 1200–1800: An Anthology*, ed. Marc Saperstein (New Haven and London: Yale University Press, 1989), pp. 351–353, and the very informative notes, ibid., p. 351, notes 3 and 4. Although he stressed the obligation of Jews to obey their kings and pray for their welfare, victory and prosperity, Rabbi Levin did not hesitate to comment upon the ethical and philosophical problems posed by military excursions. He stressed the fact that warfare engendered deplorable economic and political disruption. Nonetheless, he expressed assurance that rulers, in their wisdom, had their own compelling reasons for leading their nations into battle. Even though thousands might perish in a particular war, the monarch might feel compelled to engage in battle in order to forestall even greater

bloodshed in the future. Thus, in addressing the morality of war, this traditional preacher expressed confidence in the royal leader, even while echoing the age-old messianic aspiration for universal peace. See ibid., pp. 355 and 358.

74. Hertzberg, *Jews in America*, pp. 28–29; Jacob Rader Marcus, *Early American Jewry*, I (Philadelphia: Jewish Publication Society, 1951), 30–31.

75. Amos Elon, *The Pity of It All: A History of Jews in Germany, 1743–1933* (New York: Henry Holt & Co., 2002), p. 91; cf. Hans Brandenburg, ed., *Das Denkmal. Heinrich Heine: Denkwürdigkeiten, Briefe, Reisebilder, Aufsätze und Gedichte* (Munich: W. Langewiesche-Brandt, 1912), p. 62.

76. Ironically, even conservative elements in Prussia favored army service for Jews. If Jews would not participate in the struggle, they argued, Jews would benefit financially from the war while Christians were killing one another. See H.D. Schmidt, "The Terms of Emancipation, 1781–1812," *Leo Baeck Institute Yearbook*, I (1956), 33.

77. See Martin Phillippson, "Der Anteil der jüdischen Freiwilligen an dem Befreiungskriege 1813 und 1814," *Monatsschrift für Geschichte und Wissenschaft des Judentums* (MGWJ), 50:1–2 (1906): 1–21 and 220–247, for lists of Jewish volunteers who served in the military campaigns against Napoleon. Phillippson refers to the intriguing narrative of a Jewish woman, Esther Manuel (1785–1852), later known as Luise Grafemus, purportedly of Hanau, who fought against the Napoleonic forces in 1813–1814. According to her own account, confirmed in an official Russian military gazette, her husband had abandoned her and their two children and enlisted in the Russian army. In an attempt to trace him, she traveled to Berlin and then, disguised as a man, enlisted in an East Prussian cavalry regiment. Allegedly, she took part in several battles, advanced to the rank of *Wachmeister* (sergeant-major), was twice wounded, and was awarded the iron cross by General Graf Bülow von Dennewitz. She succeeded in finding her husband in Montmartre, Paris on March 29, 1814 but he was killed by a cannonball the next day. Eventually, she returned to Hanau with great honor. See the journalistic accounts reported in Comité zur Abwehr antisemitischer Angriffe in Berlin, *Die Juden als Soldaten* (Berlin: Sigfried Cronbach, 1896), p. 4. In his account, written in 1906, Martin Phillippson, MGWJ, 50 (1906): 9, commented that whether Esther Manuel did indeed receive the iron cross as she claimed "remains unsubstantiated but is not improbable." In the course of time, because of the numerous discrepancies in her account, later writers have questioned the veracity of the facts as reported by her. There also appears to be no record of Esther Manuel's residence in Hanau at any time. Nonetheless, whether or not Esther Manuel actually served in the army, she did succeed in receiving a veteran's pension. See Moritz Stern, *Aus der Zeit der deutschen Befreiungskriege, 1813–1815*. Vol. II, *Luise Grafemus* (Berlin: Verlag Hausfreund, 1935) and Sabina Hermes, "Eine Tasse mit grosser Geschichte – oder: Kennen Sie Luise Grafemus?" *Der Bote aus dem Wehrgeschichtlichen Museum*, 37 (1999):29–33. If indeed she did not take part in the military campaigns, such recognition on the part of German authorities well known for their bureaucratic punctiliousness may perhaps be viewed as an even more astonishing exploit.

78. *Zuruf an die Jünglinge, welche den Fahnen des Vaterlandes folgen,* (Berlin, 1813), pp. 5 and 10. Cited in Michael A. Meyer, *The Origins of the Modern Jew: Jewish Identity and European Culture in Germany, 1749–1824* (Detroit: Wayne University Press, 1979), p. 139.

79. Cited in "The Paulus-Riesser Debate," *The Jew in the Modern World: A Documentary History,* Paul R. Mendes-Flohr and Jehuda Reinharz, eds. (New York and Oxford: Oxford University Press, 1980), p. 131.

    To these integrationists, persistence of virulent anti-Semitism in face of full participation in the burden of military service was not only unanticipated but unimaginable. The faulty nature of their thesis is perhaps best illustrated by an incident that occurred in 1896. When Jewish war veterans protested the continued discrimination against them, the Rumanian War Ministry responded bluntly, "The tax of blood bears no relation to the question of citizenship." Zalman Filip "Yehudim Bi-Tzva ha-Romani," *Hayyalim Yehudim,* p. 169.

80. Abbé Henri Grégoire, "An Essay on the Physical, Moral and Political Reformation of the Jews" (London, 1791), p. 150 cited by Gil Graff, *Separation of Church and State: Dina de-Malkhuta Dina in Jewish Law, 1750–1848* (University, Alabama: University of Alabama Press, 1985), p. 59.

81. Christian Wilhelm von Dohm, *Concerning the Amelioration of the Civil Status of the Jews,* trans. Helen Lederer (Cincinnati: Hebrew Union College–Jewish Institute of Religion, 1957), p. 80.

82. Szajkowski, *French Revolutions,* p. 794.

83. "Arguments Against Dohm," text included in *The Jew in The Modern World,* p. 38. On an ironic note, Moses Mendelssohn responded to Michaelis that if "Christians have neglected the doctrines of their founders and have become conquerors, oppressors and slave-traders…Jews too could be made fit for military service." See "Remarks Concerning Michaelis' Response to Dohm," ibid., p. 43. Later apologists countered these anti-Semitic arguments by predicting that with attainment of emancipation the Jewish personality itself would become transformed. In David Friedlander's opinion, if Jews achieved equality, they would become like everyone else, "physically stronger and more stupid." Cited in Meyer, *Origins,* p. 68.

84. The text of the directive may be found in *Sulamith,* III:1 (1810); 15–17 as well as in B.H. Auerbach, *Geschichte der Israelitischen Gemeinde Halberstadt* (Halberstadt, 1866), pp. 215–216. The Consistory had leaned heavily on the view of *Hakham Zevi* in issuing the dispensation. The opinion of *Hakham Zevi* is cited by his son R. Jacob Emden, *Mor U-Ketzi'ah, Orah Hayyim* 453 and *She'ilat Ya'avetz,* II, no. 147. In a lengthy discussion of this topic in *Minhat Kena'ot* written in 1849, R. Zevi Hirsch Chajes analyzes the view of *Hakham Zevi* and explains why the conclusions drawn by the Consistory are not applicable. See *Kol Sifrei Maharatz Hayes,* vol. 2 (Jerusalem: Divrei Hakhamim, 1958), 1027–1030. For a discussion of a number of additional reasons advanced for the prohibition of legumes on Passover see *Encyclopedia Talmudit,* XVII, 101–102.

85. See *Sulamith,* III:1 (1810): 145–148. To avoid difficulties in cases in which the groom's

brothers were of military age, the Consistory proposed that a conditional clause be incorporated in the marriage ceremony that would serve to circumvent the laws of *halitzah* enabling the widow to remarry freely. The proposed conditional marriage was an innovation for which there was significant halakhic precedent, but such precedent was fraught with controversy. See A.H. Freimann, *Seder Kiddushin ve-Nisu'in: Me-Aharei Hatimat ha-Talmud ve-ad Yameinu* (Jerusalem: Mossad Harav Kook, 1964), pp. 386–388 and Aaron Dov Alter Waranawski, *Ein Tenai be-Nisu'in* (Vilna, 1930).

86. Ludwig Horwitz, *Die Israeliten under dem Königreich Westfalen* (Berlin: S. Calvary, 1900), pp. 10–11.

87. *Sulamith*, II:1 (1808):6.

88. Ibid., II:2 (1809):301.

89. The permissive ruling of the Consistory was defended by the junior rabbinical member of the Consistory, Menahem Mendel Steinhandt, *Divrei Iggeret* (Rödelheim, 1812). See my "Menahem Mendel Steinhandt's *Divrei Iggeret*: Harbinger of Reform," *Proceedings of the Tenth World Congress of Jewish Studies* (Jerusalem: World Union of Jewish Studies, 1990), pp. 207–214, in which I argue that the "hidden reasons" to which Steinhandt alludes as motivation for the dispensation were in all likelihood the need to reassure the government with regard to the suitability of Jews for service in the military.

90. Graff, *Separation*, p. 100.

91. Schwarzfuchs, *Napoleon*, p. 93.

92. Graff, *Separation*, p. 93. The full Hebrew text is included in Mevorach, *Napoleon u-Tekufato*, Part 2, p. 97. Cf. ibid., p. 115, the response to this question of the aged Rabbi Ishmael of Modena who formulated answers to the questions although he did not attend the proceedings in Paris. Rabbi Ishmael acknowledged the obligation of a Jew to serve in the army but added the caveat that the principle "the law of the land is the law" does not encompass ritual matters for which the king surely extends dispensation to inhabitants of the state. By contrast Napoleon's own instructions dated February, 1807, stated: "When some of their youth are requested to join the army, they will stop having Jewish interests and sentiments: they will acquire French interests and sentiments." See Schwarzfuchs, *Napoleon*, p. 100. With regard to the distinction between actual battle and peacetime maneuvers, it is instructive to note an address to Jewish draftees into the Austrian army, "Toldot ha-Zeman," *Ha-Me'assaf* (Berlin, 1788), p. 334 (cited by Graff, *Separation*, p. 162, note 67), exhorting them "to serve the Lord through His commandments in the days of respite and to serve the Kaiser at the time of war and battle."

93. Regarding Rabbi Sintzheim's role and influence see Schwarzfuchs, *Napoleon*, pp. 66–67, p. 202, note 6 and p. 206, note 9.

94. Ibid., pp. 95–96.

95. Translation cited ibid., p. 116. Graff, *Separation*, p. 176, note 44, cites Simon Dubnow's condemnation of the Sanhedrin's response to the questions regarding civic patriotism in which "servility passed beyond all bounds." *Hatam Sofer*, with a

perhaps more realistic appraisal of the harm that might have ensued to the Jewish
nation had the Sanhedrin been more forthright, expressed his admiration of Rabbi
Sintzheim's combination of cautiousness and halakhic integrity.

96. Meyer, *Origins*, pp. 139–142.

97. Ismar Schorsch, "Ideology and History in the Age of Emancipation," in *The
Structure of Jewish History and Other Essays by Heinrich Graetz*, trans. and ed. I.
Schorsch (New York: Jewish Theological Seminary, 1975), pp. 19–20.

98. Brief but intriguing accounts of Jewish soldiers in the armies of various European
countries and a useful bibliography are included in the collection of essays
Hayyalim Yehudim be-Tzeva'ot Europah edited by Slutzky and Kaplan.

99. Hertzberg, *Jews in America*, p. 136. In actuality (see ibid., p. 62), of the 2000 Jews
in America at that time, almost one hundred have been identified as soldiers in
the revolutionary armies. In Charleston, South Carolina, Captain Lushington's
company was half Jewish and became known as the "Jew Company." See also ibid.,
p. 178.

100. Ibid., pp. 132–136. See the extensive discussion of Grant's Order No. 11 and of
"American Judaeophobia" in Korn, *American Jewry*, pp. 121–188.

A telling example of how widespread the stereotypical image of the Jew as
non-fighter had become is Mark Twain's spirited essay – part praise, part prejudice – "Concerning the Jews," published in *Harper's Monthly*, vol. 99 (September,
1899). As Mark Twain himself predicted, that essay aroused a storm of protest and
pleased almost no one. Jewish critics acknowledged Twain's respect for Jewish
accomplishments but berated his many factual errors and were incensed because of the credence he lent to the common reproach that Jews are willing "to
feed on a country but don't like to fight for it" (*Harper's Monthly*, p. 534). Twain
subsequently conceded that he had erred and, before including the essay in *The
Man That Corrupted Hadleyburg and Other Stories and Essays* (New York and
London: Harper & Brothers, 1900), added a postscript to his essay titled "The Jew
as Soldier," in which he admitted his and others' ignorance of the facts, attempted
to correct the record of the Jew's "gallant soldiership in the field" and concluded
that "the Jew's patriotism was not merely level with the Christian's but overpassed
it" (*Hadleyburg*, p. 282).

101. Hertzberg, *Jews in America*, p. 100. It is noteworthy that Levy remained loyal to
his religious heritage. The Spanish-Portuguese congregation, of which he was a
member, thanked him for transporting to New York on his ship a wagonload of
earth from the Holy Land for use in burials.

102. "Military Service," *Encyclopedia Judaica*, XI, 1561.

103. *Die Juden als Soldaten*, Introduction, i.

104. Elon, *Pity of It All*, pp. 219, 223 and 248.

105. Walther Rathenau, *Zur Kritik der Zeit* (Berlin: S. Fischer, 1912), p. 189.

106. Elon, *Pity of It All*, p. 337. See the detailed account in R. Vogel, *Ein Stück von Uns:
Deutsche Juden in deutschen Armeen, 1813–1976. Eine Dokumentation* (Mainz: v.
Hase & Koehler, 1977), pp. 65–70. The officer corps' policy appeared to change

because of the exigencies of war in 1914, but by 1916 there was a recrudescence of anti-Semitism. See Ruth Pierson, "Embattled Veterans: The Reichsbund Jüdischer Frontsoldaten," *Leo Baeck Institute Yearbook*, 19 (1974): 141, note 9.

107. Vogel, *Ein Stück von Uns*, p. 148 ff; Pierson, "Embattled Veterans," pp. 142–143. The calumny of seeking rearguard service dogged Jewish soldiers everywhere. Instances of similar allegations in the United States Army were much rarer but did occur. A chronicle of Richmond's Jewish soldiers during the Civil War notes the following incident with regard to Marx Mitteldorfer of the First Virginia Cavalry: During one battle a member of the company jeered that Jewish soldiers were wont to fire and then fall back. Mitteldorfer challenged the accuser to follow him and proceeded to ride so far to the front that the captain had to recall him lest he mistakenly be shot by his own comrades. Thereafter he was known by the sobriquet "The Fighting Jew." See Ezekiel and Lichtenstein, *Jews of Richmond*, p. 183.

108. Cristoph Glorius, "'Unbrauchbare Isidore, Manasse und Abrahams': Juden in deutschen Militärkarikaturen," *Abgestempelt: judenfeindliche Postkarten; auf der Grundlage der Sammlung Wolfgang Haney*, eds. Helmut Gold and Georg Heuberger (Frankfurt am Main: Umschau/Braus, 1999), pp. 222–226.

109. M. Diogene Tama, *Transactions of the Parisian Sanhedrin*, trans. F.D. Kirwan (London, 1807; rep. [Cincinnati]: Hebrew Union College–Jewish Institute of Religion, 1956), p. 24.

110. According to the many authorities who regard the taking of the life of a non-Jew as encompassed within the prohibition against homicide, the issue is one of sentiment rather than of Halakhah. See *Ra'avan, Bava Kamma* 111b and *Kesef Mishneh, Hilkhot Rozeah* 2:11. See also *Mekhilta, Mishpatim* 4:58. For a discussion of the severity of the transgression, see *Meshekh Hokhmah, Parashat Mishpatim*, s.v. *ve-yitakhen*. Cf., however, *Taz, Yoreh De'ah* 158:1 as well as *Bet Me'ir, Evan ha-Ezer* 17:2.

111. Berman, *Richmond's Jewry*, p. 175.

112. See Korn, *American Jewry*, pp. 32–55 and James G. Heller, *Isaac M. Wise: His Life, Work and Thought* (New York: Union of American Hebrew Congregations, 1965), p. 335.

113. A. Moaisis, "*Yehudim bi-Tzva Yavan*," in *Hayyalim Yehudim*, p. 182.

114. Ibid., p. 183.

115. Cited in Gunther W. Plaut, *The Growth of Reform Judaism* (New York: World Union for Progressive Judaism, 1965), p. 78.

116. Ibid., p. 80.

117. See Koppel S. Pinson, "Simon Dubnow: Historian and Political Philosopher," in Simon Dubnow, *Nationalism and History: Essays on Old and New Judaism*, ed. Koppel S. Pinson (Philadelphia: Jewish Publication Society, 1958), p. 24.

The phenomenon of Jews facing other Jews on the opposing side in the trench warfare of World War I was sufficiently common for the following apocryphal story to circulate: A puny Jewish soldier was successful in taking several enemy soldiers prisoner. When the occurrence repeated itself, his superior officer became suspicious. The soldier explained that Jewish practice requires a quorum for recitation of memorial prayers on the anniversary of the death of a loved one. He added that, when there was a lull in the fighting, he had simply called out, "I have *yahrzeit*; I need a *minyan*" and forthwith a number of Jewish soldiers came over to his side.

118. Louis Breger, *Freud: Darkness in the Midst of Vision* (New York: John Wiley and Sons, 2000), pp. 243 and 250–253.

119. Quoted in Richard A. Gabriel, *No More Heroes: Madness and Psychiatry in War* (New York: Hill and Wang, 1987), frontispiece.

120. Cited in Eric J. Leed, *No Man's Land: Combat and Identity in World War I* (Cambridge U.K.: Cambridge University Press, 1979), p. 107. For decades Freud and many other psychoanalysts failed to appreciate the long-term effect of these adult traumas. See the discussion in Breger, *Freud*, pp. 252–268. Breger portrays the manner in which actions and thoughts associated with armies and war permeated the consciousness of Europeans in the years before the First World War. Interestingly, elsewhere (pp. 192–193), Breger incisively comments upon the repeated occurrences of militaristic terminology in Freud's own writings regarding himself and his colleagues and questions the appropriateness of battle imagery in Freud's version of the history of the psychoanalytic movement.

121. In a personal communication (November 19, 2003), Evelyn Rubin informed me that the incident occurred at the Battle of Verdun. The story left a profound impression on her because her father spoke of it frequently when she was a young child and, after his death, her mother continued to retell the narrative and to speak wistfully of her husband's deep anguish and remorse at having shot a fellow Jew.

122. *She'elot u-Teshuvot Bet David*, I, no. 71. Although the responsum published in *Bet David* is undated, a handwritten earlier draft of the responsum in the possession of his son, Rabbi Abba Leiter, is dated 9 Tevet 5684 (December 17, 1923). I am indebted to Rabbi Abba Leiter for providing me with a copy of the handwritten responsum.

123. For a detailed discussion of social policies advocated by the Reform movement at this time, see Leonard J. Mervis, "The Social Justice Movement and the American Reform Rabbi," Part I, "The Central Conference of American Rabbis," *American Jewish Archives*, 7 (1955): 171–230. On pacifism in the Reform movement, cf. also Michael A. Meyer, *Response to Modernity: A History of the Reform Movement in Judaism* (New York and Oxford: Oxford University Press, 1988), p. 313.

124. *CCARY*, 27 (1917): 174–75.

125. Ibid., p.176.

126. Ibid., 34 (1924): 91.

127. Ibid., p. 93 and Mervis, "Social Justice," p. 189.

128. *CCARY*, 38 (1928): 85.

129. Mervis, "Social Justice," pp. 189–90.

130. *CCARY*, 38 (1928): 86.

131. Cited in Mervis, "Social Justice," p. 189.

132. See Meyer, *Response*, p. 302 and Mervis, "Social Justice," p. 216. Maurice Eisendrath, also an outspoken pacifist, became executive director of the Union of American Hebrew Congregations in 1943. See Meyer, *Response*, p. 355.

133. *CCARY*, 45 (1935): 60.

134. Ibid., p. 67.

135. Ibid., p. 76.

136. Ibid., 46 (1936): 67.

137. Ibid., 49 (1939): 147–48.

138. Ibid., 52 (1942): 106. Cf., the remarks of Judah Magnes, an ardent pacifist who supported the allies in World War II, cited in Plaut, *Growth*, p. 160.

139. See Meyer, *Response*, pp. 366–367; *CCARY*, 76 (1966): 19 and ibid., 82 (1972): 21–24.

140. *CCARY*, 45 (1935): 66–67.

141. Ibid., pp. 71, 73 and 76.

142. Ibid., 46 (1936): 198–221. See also Cronbach, *The Quest for Peace* (Cincinnati: Sinai Press, 1937).

143. *CCARY*, 46 (1936): 206 and 221. For halakhic sources demonstrating distinctions between defensive and offensive wars, see the discussion of the legitimacy of warfare in R. Shlomoh Yosef Zevin, *Le-Or ha-Halakhah: Ba'ayot u-Berurim* (Tel Aviv: Avraham Zioni, 1957), pp. 1–18.

144. See, for example, Reuven Kimelman, "Non-Violence in the Talmud," *Judaism* 17:3 (Summer, 1968); 316–334; Everett E. Gendler's translation of Aaron Samuel Tamaret, "Passover and Non-Violence," ibid., 17:2 (Spring, 1968): 203–210; and Sheldon Zimmerman, "Confronting the Halakhah on Millitary Service," ibid., 20:2 (Spring, 1971): 204–212. Preoccupation with the question of the morality of the Vietnam conflict characterized intellectual discourse among the Orthodox as well, as is evidenced in the exchange of opinion in Michael Wyschograd, "The Jewish Interest in Vietnam," *Tradition*, 8:4 (Winter, 1966): 5–18 and Charles S. Liebman, "Judaism and Vietnam: A Reply to Dr. Wyschograd," ibid., 9:1–2 (Spring-Summer, 1967): 155–160; the survey of Charles S. Liebman, "The Orthodox Rabbi and Vietnam," ibid., 9:4 (Spring, 1968): 28–32; and more general studies including, Solomon Simonson "Violence from the Perspective of the Ethics of the Fathers," ibid., 10:2 (Winter, 1968): 35–41; Joseph Grunblatt, "Violence and Some Aspects of the Judaic Tradition," ibid., pp. 42–47; and Leo Landman, "Civil Disobedience: The Jewish View," ibid., 10:4 (Fall, 1969): 5–14. See also Isaiah Leibowitz, "The Spiritual and Religious Meaning of Victory and Might," ibid., 10:3 (Spring, 1969): 5–11, for a pertinent discussion prompted by the Israeli Six-Day War.

145. Kimelman, "Non-Violence," *Judaism* 17: 3:323 (1960).

146. Zimmerman, "Military Service," ibid., 20 (1971): 211. As noted earlier, misunderstanding the view of R. Samuel Landau, *Noda bi-Yehudah, Mahadura Tinyana, Yoreh De'ah*, no. 74, Zimmerman (p. 210) assumed there was a contradiction between the ruling of Rabbi Landau and that of his contemporaries.

147. Ibid., p. 212.

148. Ibid., p. 211.

149. Ibid., p. 212.

150. "Religious Meaning," *Tradition*, 10:3 (Spring, 1967): 7.

151. In point of fact, absent considerations of self-endangerment, Jews are required to

intervene in order to rescue Jewish victims of aggression. Insofar as the Noahide obligation is concerned, there is disagreement with regard to whether intervention on behalf of a third party is mandatory or merely discretionary. See Zevin, *Le-Or ha-Halakhah*, p. 17.

152. "Violence," ibid., 10:2 (Winter, 1968):46.
153. Zevin, *Le-Or ha-Halakhah*, p. 17. Cf. Bleich, *Contemporary Halakhic Problems*, 11, 159–165 and 111 (New York: Ktav Publishing House, 1989), 4–10. It must, however, be noted that *Hazon Ish, Orah Hayyim, Mo'ed* 114: 2, astutely observes that a hal-akhically objectionable war may rapidly be transformed into a legitimate war, at least insofar as conscripts are concerned. War, by its very nature, creates danger to human life. Thus, even a war of aggression is a source of danger to the aggressor. Therefore, argues *Hazon Ish*, once hostilities have commenced any combatant who does not have the power to call for a cease fire is, in effect, engaging in an act of self-defense.
154. Hertzberg, *Jews in America*, pp. 231–232.
155. Cited in the fascinating, albeit partisan and subjective, account of Elias Gilner, *War and Hope: A History of the Jewish Legion* (New York: Herzl Press, 1969), p. 177.
156. Martin Gilbert, *The Second World War: A Complete History*, Rev. ed. (New York: Henry Holt & Co., 1991), p. 576. The story of the exploits of the Brigade is recounted in Bernard M. Casper, *With the Jewish Brigade* (London: E. Goldston, 1947).
157. The notion of a warrior profession was taken to an extreme in the morally twisted writings of the Nazi ideologue Alfred Rosenberg, who foretold that a new German church would replace the crucifix with the symbols of the warrior-hero: "Reverence for the soldier fighting for the honor of his people is the new, recently developed living sentiment of our time…the new religion of national honor…the man and the hero in the field-gray under his helmet shall become one and the same person. Then the road shall be opened for the German national religion of the future…." See Alfred Rosenberg, *Myth of the Twentieth Century*, cited in Salo W. Baron, *Modern Nationalism and Religion* (New York and Philadelphia: Meridian Press and Jewish Publication Society, 1960), p. 83.
158. Theodor Reik, *Jewish Wit* (New York: Gamut Press, 1962), p.61. The currency of this expression is reflected in its use as the opening gambit in S.N. Behrman's depiction of 1937 Europe, *The Burning Glass* (Boston and Toronto: Little Brown & Co., 1968), pp. 3–5. Militarism was a favorite target of Jewish folk humor. See Reik, pp. 60–63. Reik (p. 60) cites a line of Heine's poetry, "Lebenbleiben wie das Sterben für das Vaterland is süss" (To remain alive as well as to die for the Fatherland is sweet) that demonstrates Heine's vestigial Jewish response in underscoring a reverence for life in contradistinction to the ideal of military honor extolled in German society.
159. *Yalkut Shim'oni, Shir ha-Shirim* 986. For rabbinic teachings interpreting the might of the hero (*gibbor*) in a spiritual rather than material sense, see Eliezer Berkovits, *With God in Hell: Judaism in the Ghettos and Death Camps* (New York and London: Sanhedrin Press, 1979), pp. 142–154.

War in Jewish Apocalyptic Thought

Lawrence H. Schiffman

Numerous Jewish texts speak of great battles that will inaugurate the messianic age. In general terms, we will see that these texts draw their inspiration from the biblical background of the Holy War, but they develop into full-fledged apocalypses[1] in the Second Temple period. Hints of such concepts can be found in Talmudic literature, and they emerge again in post-Talmudic apocalyptic texts that are connected with the transition from Byzantine, to Persian, to Moslem rule. In general, these texts are associated with the catastrophic form of Jewish messianism, but we will also see that the great rationalist Maimonides likewise expected that his naturalistic messianic era would only dawn after the final defeat of the enemies of Israel personified as Gog and Magog.

THE BACKGROUND IN HOLY WAR

To understand the role of war in Jewish apocalyptic thought, it is necessary to understand the concept that modern scholars have termed "Holy War."[2] This concept overlaps to some extent with the Talmudic notion of *milhemet mitzvah* ("war of obligation"), but the term "Holy War" emphasizes certain concepts of messianic war as well. "Holy War" denotes a war declared, led, and won by God Himself, modeled after the war of conquest of the Promised Land in the time of Joshua. Later we find this concept in terms of prophetic oracles of divine judgment against His own people for their transgressions or against the nations who have tormented Israel. These concepts are intimately linked to the notion of the Day of the Lord, and in a variety of ways these ideas influenced later Jewish apocalyptic literature. In the Bible, God Himself is a warrior (Ex. 15:3) and has the power to be victorious (1 Sam. 17:47).[3] God must be consulted as a prelude to the battles, or the war can even be declared by God Himself (Ex. 17:16, Num. 31:3), often sanctioned by the Urim and Thummim. The commander is inspired by prophetic powers, and if God's spirit leaves him, he will be defeated. Priestly support for the war is a necessity (Deut. 20:2, 1 Sam. 10:1). Soldiers must be ritually pure in battle (1 Sam. 21:14, Isa. 13:3), as they are God's soldiers, and the camps must be ritually pure (Deut. 23:12–14). War becomes a fulfillment of the covenant with God and is essentially a sacrificial or ritual performance.

Most importantly, in a Holy War, God fights along with His armies (Deut. 20:4, cf. Ex. 14:14, Deut. 9:3, Jud. 4:14) and the war can be called the War of the Lord (1 Sam. 18:17, 25:28). This may be the origin of the term Lord of Hosts, referring to God at the head of His army.[4] After we hear of His cosmic powers to defeat the enemy (Jud. 5:4, 20–21; 2 Kings 6:15–19), God's power overcomes the enemy, and the usually smaller forces of Israel destroy them in what is pictured as a mop-up operation (Josh. 10:10, Jud. 4:15, 2 Sam. 5:24, 7:10). Battle can be seen as warfare between gods in which the God of Israel is victorious.

In theory, Holy War for conquest of the Land of Israel was supposed to result in destruction of the enemy and a full ban on his erstwhile property. Outside of Israel, enemy citizens are enslaved and their property is taken as booty. The Holy War is intended to lead to peace for Israel in its land, and assumes the covenant of God with His people whom He delivers and preserves.

After the conquest of the Land of Israel from the Canaanites, these concepts were deemphasized as kings struggled to protect the kingdoms of Judah and Israel from foreign attackers. Holy War gave way to war as an instrument of diplomacy and foreign affairs, or as a means of national defense, and after the destruction of the First Temple, war would shift to an instrument of rebellion against foreign conquerors.

APOCALYPTIC CONCEPTS OF WAR

The concepts we have just described constitute the biblical heritage bequeathed to Second Temple Judaism. But the Second Temple period brought with it, through internal development or through foreign influence, an intensification of some of these ideas. To a great extent, these changes may be described as the creation of a full-blown apocalyptic tradition.

There are basically three elements in the concept of apocalyptic Holy War: (1) It assumes the present world order to be under the control of demonic powers that have to be overturned, (2) the eschatological war is a sign that the world order is soon to come to its end and, therefore, (3) a great Holy War will soon occur to usher in the messianic era of world peace and the kingdom of God.

The people of God are favorite objects of the demonic powers (Dan. 7:24–25, 8:23, 1 En. 91:5–19), and, hence, war and persecution test their faith. 1 En. 69:6–7 traces the very origins of war to Gader'el, one of the fallen angels (Nephilim), who showed human beings all the "blows of death," that is, how to kill other human beings. According to Jubilees, war originated when the rebellious sons of Noah began to fight one another and to teach their sons warfare (Jub. 11:2). Since history is in decline according to the outlook of these books, wars will not only multiply but will also increase in brutality. Uncontrolled warfare is an eschatological sign for the end of the period of history and the coming end time (Dan 8:23–26; 4 Ezra 9:1–3). The demonic powers, whether human or heavenly, take great pleasure in attacking the nation of God (Dan. 7:21–25; 8:23; I En. 91:5–19).

When the dawn of the messianic era approaches, the great battle between the forces of good and evil will cause the destruction of all the demonic forces ruling the world. God will initiate Holy War, reassert Himself as ruler over the cosmos, and subdue the powers of evil. His forces will march under the messiah (of David) against the pagan world and their demonic rulers.

This concept is first seen in the post-exilic prophets who expect a divine punishment of the nations as well as of Israel. It is fully expressed in Ezekiel's prophecy of the destruction of Gog (Ezekiel 38–39). Gog and his armies invade the Land of Israel, and God's anger burns against them. The divine call to war, the victory won by His power, and the sacrificial-ritual nature of the war are all elements that are combined with the apocalyptic imagery in which human forces play a minimal role. Such a picture shows how aspects of a Holy War are combined with prophetic and apocalyptic elements.[5]

In Daniel 7–12 we find that earthly powers and their struggles are mirrored by heavenly powers locked in struggle on high (cf. 10:13, 20–21). Princes of empires oppose angels (cf. Rev. 12:1–9). Such texts illustrate an important element in apocalyptic concepts of warfare. While battles may rage on the earth, God and his angels also fight on the side of Israel in heaven, and it is the heavenly forces that truly secure victory.

THE GENTILES AND THE ESCHATOLOGICAL WAR

At the end of the First Temple Period, a great change occurred with respect to the relationship of Israelite prophecy toward the nations of the world. Biblical literature includes prophecies against the Gentiles that are parallel in their specific contents to forms of curses (execration texts) known to us from Egyptian literature. At the beginning of the Second Temple Period, and perhaps before this, a new type of prophecy against the Gentiles developed in which the framework was eschatological – we might even say apocalyptic. In this type of prophecy, which was defined by an eschatological relationship between Israel and the nations of the world, these ideas were supposed to apply not only to the nations actually neighboring the Land of Israel, namely, those who actually came into contact with the Jews, but rather, they also applied (perhaps at the very outset) to the great nations, Egypt and Mesopotamia. The platform for this type of prophecy was the known world at that particular time. In addition to the geographical broadening of the eschatological world, it is also possible to point to a chronological broadening since these texts flow easily from the historical framework to the meta-historical – the apocalyptic. The vengeance of Israel against its enemies is transformed into a trans-historical event in which the warrior God, already known from pre-Israelite literature and from the Bible as well, participates. God is the one who fights for Israel, with or without its help, and vanquishes its enemies in a final victory that brings about the utopian end of days.

In certain texts, these developments include the destruction of all the nations in the eschatological war. However, in contrast, we encounter many texts with a realistic and rational messianic outlook, which expect that the Gentiles ultimately will recognize the God of Israel and participate in the service in the Temple of Jerusalem, just as advocated by the prophet Isaiah (Isa. 2:1–4; cf. 56:7). For our purposes, it is fitting to emphasize that this motif is also used in apocalyptic literature in texts in which vengeance is taken against the wicked among the nations at the beginning of the eschatological war. Afterwards, however, the non-Jews who recognize God and His Temple remain. Likewise, the motif of the Holy War may appear both in texts assuming the complete destruction of the Gentiles as well as in those texts in which both Jews and non-Jews who recognize the kingdom of God enjoy the messianic era. There is no doubt that the relationship of the apocalyptic literature to the Gentiles, to a certain extent, grew out of the historical experience of the compilers and reflects the historical realities of their lives.

The adherents of the apocalyptic viewpoint thought that the world was under the dominion of demonic powers that utilized the idol-worshipping rulers of the world as their instruments. These, in turn, led the world toward massive destruction. The wars of these rulers, therefore, were evil and arose from the abuse of political power and wealth.

War and persecution are tests of faith for the covenantal community. When God acts to take control of the world, once and for all, the nation of God will march after the messiah from the house of David against the powers of the pagan world and the demonic princes (2 Ezra 12:31–39; 13:5–50; 2 Bar. 72; Pss. Sol. 17:23–24; T. Levi 18:11–12; T. Dan 5:10–12; T. Reuben 6:12; CD 9:10–10).[6]

ANCIENT APOCALYPTIC LITERATURE

A good example of the mixture of the elements that we have summarized until now is Sib. Oracle 3, which was composed in Egypt between 160–50 B.C.E. For the most part, this text brings concepts from biblical literature and weaves them together into a unified picture.[7] This work speaks about wars between countries led by their kings (635–651). After God sends the savior, the nations will attack the Temple (652–668). All of them will be destroyed by God except for the chosen ones – the children of the great God, Who will fight for them and save them (669–731). There will be peace after the war and one law for the entire world (741–761). In this text, it is implicit that among those that survive there will also be Gentiles. Despite the fact that the text does not state this explicitly, only the evil ones from among the nations will die in the eschatological war.

According to Jubilees, which was composed in Hebrew around the period of the Hellenistic reform (or perhaps before or after) in the Land of Israel,[8] there is an expectation of a messiah from the tribe of Judah (31:18–19). Isaac's blessing to Jacob predicts that the Gentiles would fear him. The sins of the generation will be sufficiently severe to bring about natural catastrophes and conflicts between men until God punishes them (23:13–22). It appears that Jews who violate the laws of the Torah are intended here. After these troubles there is said to be an invasion by the "sinners of the Gentiles" (23:23–24). In these wars, many Jews will be killed. Afterwards, Israel will repent fully (23:27–29).

In Jubilees, the Gentiles are used as a goad to bring the Israelites to repentance. However, there is no trace of the destruction of the Gentiles. It is possible that the nations of the world will cooperate in the end of days during the period of peace (18:16; 20:16; 27:23).

According to this text, the war is a harbinger for the coming of the messianic era in which both the Jews and Gentiles will live in peace.[9] It is possible that 1 En. 90:9–18, 30 speaks not only of those Gentiles who repent and are redeemed but also about the destruction of the sinning Gentiles in the eschatological war.[10]

In 2 Bar. (Syriac), which was composed, so it seems, at the beginning of the first century C.E., apparently in Hebrew in the Land of Israel, Baruch receives a prophecy concerning the end of days. Great troubles will befall the Land – hatred and strife – and then the world war will begin (70:8–10). However, the Land of Israel will protect its inhabitants. At that time, the messiah will summon all the nations, sparing some and slaying others (72:4). He will not kill those who did not know or oppress Israel; however, all the enemies of Israel will be killed (72:6–73:4). Only after the destruction of the Gentile enemies of Israel will the end of days begin. In this text we also find that the Gentiles who do not fight against Israel will participate in the blessing of the messianic era together with the Jews.[11]

In the Syriac Baruch, as it is preserved today, sources outside of the principal body of the work are included. In one of them, there is no hope for the Gentiles, since it appears that they will be destroyed completely and that they will disappear from history (82:3–7).[12] In spite of the fact that in the majority of the works that arose in the period prior to the destruction of the Temple only the sinning nations – the enemies of Israel – perish in the eschatological war (2 Bar. 50:1–2; 72:4–6), in later works all the Gentiles stand to be destroyed with the exception of the converts to Judaism. In 4 Ezra, which is dated to the first century C.E., there is a hint (3:36) to the destruction of all the Gentiles. This notion is completely clear in Sib. Oracle 4:166–179. There it speaks about the destruction by God, in the beginning of the end of days, of all the Gentiles that do not return to God (apparently by converting). This text is also dated to the end of the first century C.E., after the destruction of the Temple.[13]

On the basis of all the material that we have summarized to this point, it is clear that attitudes like those that appear in the Dead Sea Scrolls, to which we turn presently, do not result from their sectarian character alone. Rather, they represent part of the general theological-religious thought of the Second Temple period that was substantially widespread in Israel.

THE WAR SCROLL

The Dead Sea Scrolls embody an eschatological, apocalyptic outlook. The Qumran sect held an extreme dualism in which the demonic powers continuously fight for control of the world in opposition to the people of God. These sectarians further believed that they lived on the edge of the eschatological era that would end in a great war ushering in the messianic age.

Their dualism is expressed in the "Treatise of the Two Spirits," a section of the Rule of the Community (1QS).[14] The world is divided into two forces, truth and falsehood or light and darkness. Both heaven and earth are divided into these two camps. Supernatural beings representing good and evil, respectively, direct human forces. The righteous are eternally harassed by the Angel of Darkness and suffer sin and guilt. They may be tempted to vice by the forces of darkness. At the end of days, God will finally vanquish the Angel of Darkness, banish deceit forever, and reward the righteous and punish the guilty.

The dualism in the scrolls assumes that God built this structure into the world when He planned and created it. He purposely created the supernatural leaders of the forces of good and evil, and he planted in each person's heart a certain degree of each of these forces so that they vie with one another in a person's lifetime as well as on a cosmic scale. The forces of good, wisdom, proper conduct, and God's law are often led by the angel Michael or the heavenly priest Melchizedek. Names for their evil counterparts are Belial, Melchiresha, and Mastemah. The sect is led by the Teacher of Righteousness, while his opponent is the Wicked Priest or the Man of Lies.

In the present age, the Qumran texts acknowledge that the world is dominated by Belial. The Dead Sea sect awaited the end of days that, according to its own reckoning, was expected to begin immanently, in its own time.[15] Its apocalyptic messianic tendencies generated a literary corpus that portrays the eschatological war that was expected to bring about the end of days.[16] From an investigation of the manuscripts of the Scroll of the War of the Sons of Light and the Sons of Darkness from caves 1 and 4 at Qumran (1QM, 4QM[a-f]), we discover that this text existed in a few recensions and related texts.[17] The apocalyptic tendency of the sect finds further evidence in other texts related to this subject matter. In truth, it appears that the War Scroll itself was gathered together and edited from disparate pre-existing sources by its compiler.[18] There is no doubt that this composition was in existence by 50 B.C.E. but that some of its sources date to before the Roman conquest in 63 B.C.E.[19]

Often, apocalyptic schemes assume definite, preordained time schedules for the unfolding of the end time, most of which are based on the book of Daniel and its exegesis. The War Scroll presents a schematized, ritualized war expected between the members of the Qumran sect and the nations. The Sons of Light are the men of the sect who will be victorious in the end of days. The Gentiles – the nations of the world – are included among the Sons of Darkness, or the Sons of Belial, together with those Jews who by means of their behavior demonstrate that they have been predestined to be among the Sons of Darkness. The place of the sect's exile is called "the wilderness of the nations" (*midbar ha-ammim*) because it is there that the Sons of Light dwell prior to this war. No remnant of these nations will remain in the end of days according to this perspective (1QM 1:1–7; 14:5; 4QM[a] frag. 8 8 9:3; cf. 1QpHab 4:3–5).

The war is to last forty years, with six cycles of battles, followed by God's intervention in the seventh. The battles are conducted in a planned, ritualized manner. Special prayers and sacrificial rituals based on biblical legislation accompany the war. The enemies are denoted with biblical-period names, including Kittim for the Romans (cf. Dan. 11:30).[20] The sect witnesses the destruction of the nations and the defeat of the sinful Israelites, after which the sect takes control of the Temple. Central to the vision of this apocalyptic war is the dualistic division between the Sons of Light and their opponents, the Sons of Darkness.

The compiler refers to the nations of the world by means of the names used in the Table of Nations that appears in Genesis 10.[21]

The most prominent among them are Assyria (Seleucid Syria) and the Kittim (Rome) because their destruction was among the most pressing exigencies of the compiler (1QM 1:4–6; 2:9–12; 11:11; 4QM^a frag. 2 11). The battles are said to take place in "all the lands of the Gentiles" (1QM 2:7; cf. 11:12–13). Indeed, as one of their standards proclaims, the sect anticipated the destruction of "every nation of vanity" by God (1QM 4:12). The final battle will wreak vengeance on these nations because of their wickedness (1QM 6:6; cf. 9:8–9) and all of them will be killed (1QM 19:10–11).

The songs scattered throughout the text, for the most part, belong to the liturgical-cultic raw material available to the compiler of the scroll. One song, which appears twice in the scroll, seems to contradict the assumption made by the complete scroll in its portrayal of the war that all the Gentiles will be destroyed in the end of days (1QM 12:9–15; 19:2–8; 4QM^b frag. 1 2–8). The song is directed toward God, requesting Him to fight the Gentiles, His enemies. The song then turns to the city of Jerusalem and says: "Open your gates forever in order that the spoils of the Gentiles may be brought to you and that their kings will come to serve you…and you will rule over the kingdom of the Kittim." There is no doubt that this section, which is based almost entirely on Isa. 60:10–14, expects that the Gentiles, including the Romans, will be present in the messianic era since then they will be subservient to Israel. That the Gentiles will continue to exist, but under the rule of the messiah, the son of David, is also the position of Pesher Isaiah (4QpIs 7 25). This outlook is perhaps to be understood as in accordance with the expression "to subdue the Gentiles" in the Rule of the Congregation (1:21); however, it is also possible that this expression points to their destruction. A similar idea appears in the reconstruction of the Rule of Blessings (3:18). It is possible that this phenomenon appears again in the same text, this time written as a blessing to the Prince of the Congregation – an eschatological figure: "All the nations will bow before you and all the Gentiles will serve you" (5:28–29).

However, the prevailing perspective in the War Scroll is that it has been decreed from Creation that the nations would be destroyed completely in the great war that is expected to take place in the beginning of the end of days. The sectarians, with the help of heavenly powers, angels, will defeat and kill all the Gentiles. Similarly, all the Jews who do not belong to the sect will be destroyed. In the end of days, the world will only be populated by the members of the sect.[22]

It is worthwhile to reiterate here that these attitudes in the scrolls find their parallels in the writings of other apocalyptic Jewish groups in the same time period. They spring from the general eschatological tradition, not only from the sectarian outlook of the Qumran sect.

GOG AND MAGOG

For a variety of reasons, is clear that sometime in the amoraic period, apocalyptic traditions were the subject of renewed interest and discussion in rabbinic circles. No doubt, the same was the case among the common people in both the land of Israel and in Babylonia. But for some reason, the emphasis changed in the manner in which such apocalyptic traditions were represented. In some rabbinic texts and in the later apocalyptic material that developed within the Jewish community, great emphasis was given to the war of Gog and Magog as prophesied by Ezekiel,[23] and to other apocalyptic traditions from Second Temple times that were in various ways used to expand this prophecy.

These expansions on Ezekiel's prophecy of Gog of the Land of Magog came to the fore in Talmudic and medieval times in the form of the expectation of a great war, an Armageddon,[24] between the forces of Gog and Magog, now described as two separate kings, and the messiah.[25] Gog and Magog first appear as separate eschatological entities in the Sibylline Oracles (3:319, 512). Sib. Oracle 3 most probably dates to between 163–45 B.C.E.[26] Thereafter, this notion is found in the New Testament (Rev. 20:8–9) where the two, Gog and Magog, will ally themselves with Satan against the righteous.[27] These battles, to be fought at the end of days, carried on the tradition of apocalyptic war from the Second Temple period, and also involve the destruction of the Gentile enemies of Israel. The forces of the messiah are almost defeated by the forces of Gog and Magog, joined by all the nations of the world, but God's miraculous, direct intervention brings about the victory of the messiah and the forces of good. These warlike ideas have been seen as simply the outlet for an oppressed population yearning for revenge,[28] but we need to remember that they are a direct continuation of trends formed in Second Temple times in a period in which the Hasmonean House was at its height of independent Jewish power. Later circumstances may have nourished these notions but do not account for their origins.

A number of sources indicate that the expectation of a great war of Gog and Magog was carried over into early Rabbinic Judaism. *M. Ed.* 2:10 speaks of the punishment of Gog and Magog as lasting for twelve months. *Sifrei* Deut. 357[29] speaks of God's showing Moses the Plain of Jericho where Gog and his armies will fall. Targum Yerushalmi to Num. 11:26 attributes a prophecy to Eldad and Medad to the effect that in the end of days Gog and Magog and their armies will fall to the King Messiah.[30] Targum to Song of Songs 8:8–9 speaks of Israel's victory as resulting not from superior force but from the merit of Torah study.

This theme is also taken up in the Babylonian Talmud. According to *Berakhot* 12b–13a, the war of Gog and Magog is hinted at in Isa. 43:19 and will be a greater tribulation than any Israel has experienced.[31] Similar is the theme of *Ex. Rab.* 12:2[32] that there will be a war such as that associated with the ten plagues (Ex. 9:18) in the days of Gog and Magog. *Lev. Rab.* 27:11[33] tells us that Gog and Magog will attempt to defeat God Himself even before they attack Israel.

All the notions we see here are in consonance with the general reentry of apocalyptic ideas into rabbinic tradition in amoraic times.[34] Post amoraic texts, most from late Byzantine or early Moslem times, lay out the future eschatological war in much more complex terms.

WAR IN MEDIEVAL ESCHATOLOGY

A variety of post-Talmudic texts expanded greatly on these ideas and converted them into full-scale apocalypses. These texts, or their sources, were composed in the years during which the Persian Empire was battling Byzantium in the early seventh century or in the years immediately before and after the conquest of the Byzantine Empire by the Arabs. These events greatly stimulated apocalyptic messianism in the Jewish community.[35]

An important early example of this genre is Sefer Zerubbabel.[36] An angel, Michael or Metatron, reveals the eschatological secrets to Zerubbabel, including the expected war of Gog and Magog in which the messiah, son of Joseph (Cf. *Sukkah* 52a and Targum Ps. Jon. Exod. 40:11), is killed and the Davidic messiah, with the help of his mother Hephzi-Bah, eventually defeats the forces of evil headed by Armilus. This victory is essentially that of the Jewish people over the Christian Roman (Byzantine) Empire. This text, because of its early date, seems to have influenced many of the later medieval Jewish apocalypses, but the absence of some of its specific details in the other accounts argues against direct dependence.[37] The revelation of secrets by a heavenly being is typical of Second Temple apocalyptic literature. [38]

Aggadat Bereshit[39] pictures Gog as deciding that his only hope is to directly and initially attack the Holy One, blessed be He, but, of course, God defeated him easily. Midrash Tehillim[40] pictures a more systemic type of battle. Here, Gog and Magog are expected to attack Israel three times, and in the fourth battle to attack Jerusalem and Judah, but God will help the men of Judah to defeat them.

A full apocalyptic account appears in a small text entitled *Sefer Eliyahu u-Firqe Mashiah*.[41] This is truly an apocalyptic text involving the divulging of secrets of the future by a heavenly being, Michael, to the prophet Elijah. It also has the familiar ingredient of the heavenly guided tour, which typifies what scholars now call the apocalyptic genre.[42]

Here the last king of Persia will go up to Rome for three years and then rebel against Rome for an additional twelve months. He will defeat mighty warriors from the sea, and then another king will arise from the sea and shake the world. He will then come to the Temple Mount and burn it, leading to suffering and war in Israel.

A certain Demetrus, son of Poriphus, and Anphilipus, son of Panapos, will wage a second war, each with 100,000 cavalry and 100,000 infantry. 300,000 soldiers will be hidden in ships. Then the messiah, named Yinnon,[43] will come. Gabriel will descend, slay 92,000 men, and devastate the world. A third war will then take place, and many will be killed in the land of Israel. Then the messiah will come with the angels of destruction and later with 30,000 righteous men, destroying all Israel's enemies. This will bring an end to the rule of the four kingdoms and usher in a period of prosperity and rejoicing. Then God will bring Gog and Magog and their legions, and they and all the peoples will surround and attack Jerusalem, but the messiah, with God's help, will fight them and defeat them.

The notion of the 70 nations, that is, all the nations of the world, making war against Jerusalem is also found in Zohar 2:58b. But here God uproots them from the world. The text even suggests that in order to reveal His greatness, God will reassemble all the enemies of Israel and defeat them at the coming of the messiah.

A final, extensive example is Midrash Alpha Betot.[44] After the messiah gathers the exiles to Jerusalem and rebuilds the Temple, and all the nations recognize his rule, peace and security will reign for 40 years. Then, in order to destroy the forces of evil, God will bring Gog and Magog to attack the land of Israel and launch three wars against Israel, having spent seven years assembling a mighty, well-armed force. The invasion will be massive, entering the land from the north. Israel will soon be conquered, all cities and towns taken, and their riches despoiled.

Then the messiah and the pious will make war against them and a great slaughter will ensue. God will enter the battle bringing plagues like those of Egypt and heavenly fires will burn the forces of Gog and Magog. Along the way we learn that the messiah is called Ephraim, and so it appears that we deal with a messiah, son of Joseph, who appears to be victorious.[45] Then the inhabitants of Jerusalem will despoil their attackers and fill Jerusalem with the weapons and riches of Gog and Magog. The weapons will be burnt as fuel and the bodies of Gog and Magog and their armies will be eaten by animals, and their blood drunk. Then Israel will bury them and cleanse the entire land.

In various medieval texts, the evil king Armilus leads the forces of the nations against Israel and the messiah in the great battle of the end of days.[46] His name seems to derive from Romulus, the legendary founder of ancient Rome.[47] He is mentioned in the Targum to Isa. 11:4, where "*rasha*" is defined as "the wicked Armilus." He appears also in Tg. Pseudo-Jonathan to Deut. 34:3, which also refers to the troops of Gog and to their battles with Michael.[48] In some texts, Armilus kills the messiah, son of Joseph, but is himself killed by the Davidic messiah. Tefillat R. Shimon ben Yohai[49] assumes that Nehemiah is equivalent to the messiah, son of Joseph, and that there will be a big battle occasioned by Armilus' messianic claims. A number of texts stress his ugly, deformed physical appearance.[50]

In this context, it is usual to assume that the notion of wars taking place at the onset of the end of days is consistent with the apocalyptic, catastrophic form of Jewish messianism and not with the naturalistic approach.[51] Yet this apocalyptic notion seems to have made its way into mainstream medieval Rabbinic thought. Sa'adya Gaon (*Emunot ve-De'ot* 8:5–6)[52] sets out the entire messiah, son of Joseph/Armilus battle myth[53] as an option that would take place if Israel did not repent on its own. If it did, however, the messiah son of David would destroy Armilus directly and then fight the battle of Gog and Magog. In any case, Sa'adya seems to assume a messianic battle.[54]

Even Maimonides, a member of the rationalistic, naturalistic school of Jewish messianism, fully expects wars to take place at the onset of the end of days. In describing the nature of the messianic era and of the process that will usher it in, Maimonides, *Hilkhot Melakhim* 11:4, after making clear that he espouses the gradualistic, natural form of Jewish messianism (11:3, 12:1–2), tells us that to attain the state of "presumptive messiah" (*hezkat mashiah*), the messiah will have to fight "the wars of the Lord."[55] Such wars clearly refer to the defeat of the enemies of Israel who oppose the fulfillment of God's will in the world. In 12:2, Maimonides tells us that the messianic era will be inaugurated with the battle of Gog and Magog, in accord with the prophecies in Ezekiel.[56] But clearly, for Maimonides these prophecies are understood to refer to the messiah's role as the deliverer of Israel from foreign domination. So we can expect that this is a reference to wars of a very different sort from the apocalyptic battles that we have seen described in other texts. Here God is not a soldier, even if His help is hoped for and expected. It seems, therefore, that the expectation of war in the end of days in which the evildoers would be destroyed and in which the enemies of Israel would be defeated was actually common to both the apocalyptic and naturalistic forms of medieval Jewish messianism.[57]

CONCLUSION

The material we have studied here indicates a widespread notion, building on the biblical notion of Holy War, to the effect that the onset of the end of days would be accompanied by a war in which the enemies of Israel would be destroyed. In many of the more apocalyptic traditions, those stemming from the Second Temple period and those coming from the post-Talmudic period, these battles are described in an extremely apocalyptic way. These texts recall all the imagery of the Biblical battle (Ezekiel 38–39) of Gog, King of Magog (Gog and Magog), and include all kinds of additional elements based on other texts. An extremely important feature regarding these wars is combat against some or all the nations of the world who oppose God, his messiah and the people of Israel.

Regarding the Gentiles, in the material that we have summarized here we have found two tendencies. One expects the destruction of those Gentiles who do not accept the kingdom of God in the eschatological war. The second anticipates the destruction of *all* the Gentiles. Both of these perspectives are based upon the apocalyptic-catastrophic-utopian messianic idea that the end of days will usher in a completely new world that never existed in the past – a world of perfection without sinners and without sins.

For all the Jewish traditions that we have studied, there is no question that some form of war in which the enemies of God, Israel, and the messiah are destroyed is either necessary or, at the very least, justified, as part of the process that will lead to the ultimate redemption. War, therefore, in apocalyptic Jewish thought, was considered an instrument by which God would bring about the redemption of His people.

NOTES

1. See the separate and overlapping definitions of "apocalypse" in the multi-authored article "Apocalypses and Apocalypticism," ABD 1:279–92 by P.D. Hanson (p. 279) and J.J. Collins (p. 283). For our purposes, an apocalypse is a text devoted to revealing and setting out the details of the eschatological future. We use the adjective "apocalyptic" to refer to immediate forms of Jewish messianism, usually those assuming a catastrophic onset of the end of days leading to a time of utopian perfection.

2. L.E. Toombs, "War, Ideas of," IDB 4:796–800; cf. N. Gottwald, "War, Holy," IDB Suppl. Vol., 942–44.

3. F.M. Cross, "The Divine Warrior in Israel's Early Cult," in *Biblical Motifs*, ed. Alexander Altmann (Cambridge: Harvard University Press, 1966), 11–30.

4. See C.L. Seow, "Hosts, Lord of," ABD 3:304–7.

5. L.L. Grabbe, "Warfare, Eschatological Warfare," EDSS 2:963–65.

6. See D. Christenson, "Nations," ABD 4:1044–6. However, the continuation of the article points to the Christian perspective of the author.

7. See R.H. Charles, *Eschatology: The Doctrine of a Future Life in Israel, Judaism and Christianity* (New York: Schocken, 1963) 207–8; J.J. Collins in J.H. Charlesworth, ed., *The Old Testament Pseudepigrapha* (2 vols. Garden City, NY: Doubleday, 1983–85) 1:354–61.

8. Cf. O.S. Wintermute in Charlesworth, OTP, 1:43–44; J.C. VanderKam, *The Book of Jubilees* (Sheffield: Sheffield Academic Press, 2001) 17–22.

9. Charles, *Eschatology*, 236–40.

10. See also Dan. 2:44; 7:11–12, 14; Charles, *Eschatology*, 246; see also Charles, idem., 296–97 concerning the Gentiles in Similitudes of Enoch and the Psalms of Solomon.

11. Charles, *Eschatology*, 324–32.

12. Charles, *Eschatology*, 331–2.

13. Charles, *Eschatology*, 361.

14. J. Duhaime, "Dualism," EDSS 1:215–20. Cf. J. Licht, "An Analysis of the Treatise of the Two Spirits in DSD," in *Aspects of the Dead Sea Scrolls* ScrHier, 4, ed. C. Rabin and Y. Yadin; Jerusalem (Magnes Press, the Hebrew University, 1958), 88–100.

15. See L.H. Schiffman, *Reclaiming the Dead Sea Scrolls: The History of Judaism, the Background of Christianity, the Lost Library of Qumran* (Philadelphia and Jerusalem: Jewish Publication Society, 1994), 317–50.

16. Cf. J.J. Collins, *The Apocalyptic Imagination* (New York: Crossroad, 1984), 126–33; Schiffman, *Reclaiming*, 330–3.

17. J. Duhaime, *The War Texts: 1QM and Related Manuscripts* (London; New York: T & T Clark International, 2004), 12–24.

18. P.R. Davies, *1QM, the War Scroll from Qumran: Its Structure and History*, BibOr 32; Rome (Biblical Institute Press, 1977), esp. 121–4; Duhaime, *War Texts*, 45–63.

19. Y. Yadin, *The Scroll of the War of the Sons of Light Against the Sons of Darkness*, trans. B. and C. Rabin; Oxford (Oxford University Press, 1962), 244–6; cf. Duhaime, *War Texts*, 64–102.

20. Cf. Yadin, *War Scroll*, 22–26; T.H. Lim, "Kittim," EDSS 1:469–71.

21. Yadin, *War Scroll*, 26–33.
22. Also relevant here is the Aramaic Apocalypse 4Q246, G.J. Brooke, et al., eds., *Qumran Cave 4. XVII: Parabiblical Texts, Part 3* (DJD 22. Oxford: Clarendon Press, 1996), 165–84, which seems to foretell that the messianic era will be preceded by international warfare.
23. For the biblical data, see B. Otzen, "Gog, Magog," TDOT 2:419–25. Note that in the Bible Gog is the king of Magog.
24. A term occurring in Rev. 16:16 meaning "the location of the final cosmic battle of the forces of good and of evil, according to the apocalyptic view of the writer" (R.S. Boraas, "Armageddon," *The HarperCollins Bible Dictionary*, ed. P.J. Achtemeier, New York (HarperSanFrancisco, 1996], 71).
25. R. Patai, *The Messiah Texts* (Detroit: Wayne State University, 1979), 145–55. For a survey of Rabbinic sources, see "Gog and Magog," EJ 7:691–3.
26. Collins, OTP 1:355.
27. Cf. K.G. Kuhn, "Gog kai Magog," TDNT 1:789–91.
28. Patai, *Messiah Texts*, 146.
29. To Deut. 34:3, ed. L. Finkelstein, *Sifrei on Deuteronomy* (New York: Jewish Theological Seminary, 1969), 427.
30. Cf. *Aggadat Bereshit*, ed. S. Buber (Jerusalem, 1973), 5.
31. Cf. *b. Abod. Zar.* 3b.
32. *Midrash Shemot Rabbah: Parashot 1–14*, ed. A. Shinan (Tel Aviv; Jerusalem: Dvir, 1984), p. 246.
33. This is the text in ed. Vilna and in four MSS. Cited by M. Margaliot, ed., *Midrash Va-Yikra Rabbah* (Jerusalem: Wahrmann, 1972), v. 3–4:646, to line 3. Other texts only mention Gog.
34. See L.H. Schiffman, "Messianism and Apocalypticism in Rabbinic Texts," in *Cambridge History of Judaism*, v. 4, forthcoming.
35. Y. Even-Shmuel (Kaufman), *Midreshei Geulah* (Jerusalem and Tel Aviv: Mosad Bialik; 19542), 50–54.
36. The text was composed, most probably, c. 629 C.E. after the Byzantine victory over Persia and before the Arab conquests (Y. Dan, "Zerubbabel, Sefer," EJ 16:1002).
37. Cf. D. Biale, "Counter-History and Jewish Polemics against Christianity: The *Sefer Toldot Yeshu* and the *Sefer Zerubavel*," JSS 6 (1999): 137–42; Even-Shmuel, *Midreshei Geulah*, 56–89, 379–89.
38. Sefer Zerubbabel appears in A. Jellinek, *Beit ha-Midrash* (6 pts. in 2 vols.; Jerusalem: Wahrmann, 19673), 3:65–7; Even-Shmuel, *Midreshei Geulah*, 41–48. On the dating and background of this text, see Even-Shmuel, *Midreshei Geulah*, 31–40. We favor the 7–10th century dating suggested by Patai, *Messiah Texts*, 358.
39. Ed. Buber (Cracow: J. Fisher, 1902/3), 5–7. This text probably dates to c. 10th century (Patai, *Messiah Texts*, 348).
40. Ed. Buber (Vilna: Widow and Brothers Romm, 1890/91), 488–89, to Ps. 119:2.
41. Jellinek, *Beit ha-Midrash*, 3:65–7; Patai, *Messiah Texts*, 150–52.
42. Collins, *Apocalyptic Imagination*, 2–8.
43. Cf. Ps. 72:17 (*kerei*).

44. *Batei Midrashot*, ed. S.A. Wertheimer, 2nd ed. enlarged and amended by A.J. Wertheimer (2 vols.; Jerusalem: Ketav va-Sefer, 1967/8), 2:438–42. The text should be dated to c. 8–9th century (Patai, *Messiah Texts*, 354).

45. On the messiah son of Joseph, see Patai, *Messiah Texts*, 165–70; D. Berger, "Three Typological Themes in Early Jewish Messianism: Messiah Son of Joseph, Rabbinic Calculations and the Figure of Armilus," *AJS Rev* 10 (1985): 143–8; J. Heinemann, "The Messiah of Ephraim and the Premature Exodus of the Tribe of Ephraim," *HTR* 68 (1975): 1–16, although we cannot accept his thesis. The messiah son of Joseph is not found in Second Temple texts and may be a creation of the Talmudic period (Patai, *Messiah Texts*, 166), perhaps created in the image of the antichrist (Biale, "Counter-History," 141).

46. L. Ginzberg, "Armilus," *JE* 2:118–20; Patai, *Messiah Texts*, 156–64; Berger, "Three Typological Themes," 155–62.

47. On this and other etymologies, see Berger, "Three Typological Themes," 157–9. For the "Romulus" derivation see 157 n. 59. Berger gives serious consideration to the derivation from Greek *eremolaos*, "destroyer of a nation."

48. *Pseudo-Jonathan (Thargum Jonathan ben Usiel zum Pentateuh) nach der Londoner Handschrift (Brit. Mus. Add. 27031)*, ed. M. Ginsburger, (Berlin: S. Calvary, 1903), 365 (Armilgos) where n. 2 indicates that he was identified in the MS. as the antichrist, but these references may be later additions (Berger, "Three Typological Themes," 156; cf. Kohut, *Arukh ha-Shallem* 1.291–2).

49. Patai, *Messiah Texts*, 158–59; Jellinek, *Beit ha-Midrash*, 4:124–6.

50. Cf. also *Midrash va-Yosha'*; Jellinek, *Beit ha-Midrash*, 1:56.

51. Cf. G. Scholem, "Toward an Understanding of the Messianic Idea in Judaism," *The Messianic Idea in Judaism and Other Essays on Jewish Spirituality* (New York: Schocken, 1971) and L.H. Schiffman, *The Eschatological Community of the Dead Sea Scrolls* (SBLMS 38; Atlanta, Ga.: Scholars Press, 1989), 1–8 for the application of this approach to the Dead Sea Scrolls.

52. Ed. Y. Kafah (Jerusalem: Sura, and New York: Yeshiva University, 1969/70), 245–52; trans. G.W. Buchanan, *Revelation and Redemption* (Dillsboro, NC: Western North Carolina Press, 1978), 45–54.

53. Cf. Sa'adya's discussion in a *teshuvah* in B.M. Lewin, *Otzar ha-Geonim* (Jerusalem: 1934), 70–72 (to B. Suk. 52a, sec. 193), trans. Buchanan, 131–3 and the similar account of Hai Gaon (E. Ashkenazi, *T a'am Zekenim* [Frankfurt am M., 1854], 59a–61a), trans. Buchanan, 120–31.

54. Cf. J. Sarachek, *The Doctrine of the Messiah in Medieval Jewish Literature* (New York: Jewish Theological Seminary of America, 1932), 41–50.

55. Cf. Num. 21:14, 1 Sam. 18:17, 25:28.

56. Cf. *"Iggeret Teman"* in *Iggerot ha-Rambam*, ed. Y. Shelat; 2 vols.; Jerusalem: Ma'aliyot, 1986/87), 1:108 (Gog and Magog) and his trans. which only mentions Gog, p. 159, following some MSS. Cf. *Iggerot ha-Rambam*, ed. M.D. Rabinowitz; Jerusalem: Mosad ha-Rav Kook, 1980/81), 182 which mentions Gog and Magog.

57. See the discussion of Isaac Abravanel in Sarachek, *Doctrine of the Messiah*, 280–3.

Models of Reconciliation and Coexistence in Jewish Sources

Dov S. Zakheim

The concepts of "peace," "reconciliation," and "coexistence" have elicited far less discussion in halakhic literature than that of "war." The Talmud and subsequent rabbinic sources are replete with discussions regarding the various types of war Israel may conduct, the commandments relating to war and its participants, and the role of the king and others in carrying out military campaigns. Peace, on the other hand, tends to be discussed mostly in terms of relations between individuals, and, insofar as it relates to a Jewish state in its interactions with other nations, is seen more as a condition to be attained than as a practical policy objective. Peace as an ideal is best conveyed by the well-known dictum of Rabbi Elazar in the name of Rabbi Hanina that "[Torah] scholars foster peace in the world."[1]

Similarly, reconciliation and coexistence command relatively little discussion in Jewish sources. In general, these concepts apply to relations between and among Jews. They are best exemplified by the reconciliation between Joseph and his brothers and the midrashic portrayal of Aaron, who reconciled estranged couples and feuding friends. "Peaceful co-existence," in the sense made famous by the Soviet leader Nikita Khrushchev, or international reconciliation as exemplified by the European Union, which has bound such historic enemies as the United Kingdom, France and Germany into an integrated partnership, is discussed only tangentially in Jewish literature. In general, coexistence with non-Jews is framed in terms of dealing with the unpleasant reality that such people must be accommodated, particularly if they represent more powerful host nations. Reconciliation with non-Jews seems almost beside the point.

Yitzhak Rabin's observation regarding the 1993 Oslo agreement that "one makes peace with enemies, not with friends" likewise seems beside the point. Indeed, as an argument for compromise with non-Jewish claimants of historic Jewish patrimony, it appears to run counter to the norms of halakhic Judaism. This paper will nevertheless attempt to demonstrate that the assumptions that underlay Rabin's policy – peace, reconciliation, and coexistence with an erstwhile enemy – are not necessarily inconsistent with those norms, even as the details of his policy, which Rabin never fully fleshed out before his untimely passing, remain open to considerable interpretation and debate.

PEACE, HALAKHAH AND INTERNATIONAL RELATIONS

The notion of "peace" has itself become a highly charged political term in Jewish circles. Although it is nominally the objective of all Israelis, and of Jews everywhere, "peace" as it applies to the Middle East conflict in particular – the major preoccupation of world Jewry – tends to be associated with the political Left in Israel. "Peace" stands in contrast to "land," when discussed in the context of the formula known as "land for peace." In turn, "land" has become increasingly identified with the political Right, most notably the religious political Right, which stridently argues against the cession of as much as a millimeter of *Eretz Yisrael*.

It should be noted that halakhic discourses relating to peace often do so under the rubric of *darkei shalom*, literally "the ways of peace." With respect to intra-Jewish relations, the principle is applied to varied contexts ranging from *aliyot* for Kohanim on *Shabbat* and *Yom Tov*, to laws relating to *Eruvin*, public works, and neighbors.[2] When applied to Jewish relations with non-Jews, *darkei shalom* mandates, among other things, that non-Jews benefit equally from various Jewish charitable activities and that non-Jews be treated with the same basic courtesy as Jews.[3]

Decisors and scholars are divided over whether the principle of *darkei shalom* has been expanded to non-Jews for reasons of Jewish self-protection, or at least self-interest, or as a result of more universal ethical considerations. Some, like Gerald Blidstein, argue that *darkei shalom* must be understood in terms of "human mutuality. It is unfair, ugly and eventually impossible to make claims on society without feeling part of it and making one's contribution." In his view, understanding "the ways of peace" as a reflection of mutual commitments stands in contrast to what he terms the "cynical explanation" that focuses on Jewish self-interest.[4]

On the other hand, cynical or not, the explanation of "ways of peace" based on Jewish self-interest is one that continues to resonate in contemporary halakhic literature. For example, in discussing whether a Jewish taxi driver must compensate his non-Jewish counterpart for damages caused in an accident, Rabbi Moshe Sternbuch, when still residing in Johannesburg,[5] argued that the primary criterion is whether the non-Jewish taxi driver is aware that his vehicle was damaged by a Jew. If he knows this was the case, the Jew must pay damages, so as to avoid creating a *hillul Hashem*, desecration of G-d's name. If the non-Jew is unaware that the Jew was the actual cause of the accident, however, Rabbi Sternbuch ruled that there is no need for the Jew to pay anything, since there is no "desecration of *Hashem*."[6]

Throughout his discussion, Rabbi Sternbuch makes no mention

of *darkei shalom*. Moreover, he evidently sees no parallel between the case he addressed and the opinion expressed by the Ran, Semag, Bah, Shakh, Gra and Taz among others that, for reasons of *darkei shalom*, one visits the non-Jewish sick even if they are not in the same sick bay as Jews who are ill.[7] Rabbi Sternbuch's reasoning clearly implies that if the non-Jew was not aware that Jews were paying sick visits, there would be no need to visit him. In both cases, the inherent obligation to society at large is not what matters; in his view, different values are at play with respect to either *hillul Hashem* or *darkei shalom*. This approach is consistent with perspectives on coexistence that fundamentally view non-Jewish neighbors as a necessary evil to be endured and to be mollified by acts that foster *darkei shalom*, until the coming of the Messiah.

Whatever its underlying rationale, *darkei shalom* does not appear to address "peace" in terms that relate to contemporary international affairs. Despite its implications for wider communal relations, its dictates focus primarily on interactions between individuals. In contrast, national policy in a democratically elected government (and, studies have shown, even in totalitarian regimes) must harmonize, and often adjudicate, among conflicting group interests and objectives. Halakhah itself recognizes the difference between individual and state action – even if the actions are seemingly identical – and legislates accordingly. For example, "private" conquest of territory, such as King David's conquest of Syria, does not sanctify that territory; communal conquest does.[8]

Halakhah is not without guidelines for the pursuit of peace between Jewry and non-Jewish nations, however, nor does it ignore issues arising from Biblical mandates for peaceful coexistence with other nations. Laws affecting a fully sovereign Jewish state are grounded in Biblical pronouncements about the initial conquest of Canaan and the establishment of a monarchy. *Samuel*, *Kings* and *Chronicles* outline additional precedents. In addition, *Tanakh* offers both a few cases of apparent reconciliation and coexistence with individuals whom the Talmud sees as representatives of other enemy nations, as well as laws regarding the immunity of certain nations from attack by a Jewish state.

A second set of guidelines reflected the minority status of Jews both in their own land and elsewhere. These guidelines, initially propagated in the Talmud and expanded upon over the centuries, were designed to protect the community in an alien, and usually hostile, environment. For the majority of Jewry, it was just such an environment that they encountered wherever they happened to reside.

Throughout their history, Jews were either a sovereign or subject people. For the most part, certainly for the past two millenia, it was the latter condition that defined their existence. Thus, halakhic pronouncements about sovereign Jewish policy and international relations, including those relating to war and peace, were fundamentally hypothetical. On the other hand, halakhic principles relating to Jewish communal relations with non-Jews were grounded in reality.

Since 1948, an ever-increasing number of Jews have lived in a sovereign state of their own. As a result, for the first time in two millennia, Halakhah is providing practical guidance on inter-communal relations to Jews who now constitute a majority in their own land. In particular, rulings regarding the religious status of Christians and Muslims have a direct impact on questions not only regarding rights of residency, but also on "their eligibility for social welfare and health benefits, educational assistance and the like."[9]

Nevertheless, it is arguable that the State of Israel's sovereignty is not absolute. While Israeli Jews are a free, majority people, Israel itself is not an independent international actor. To the extent that it is not, halakhic pronouncements that continue to govern Jewish relations with non-Jews, particularly those outside Israel, may have more to offer contemporary Israeli national security and foreign policy.

In theory, many of the norms that condition Israel's pursuit of "peace" and of peaceful coexistence should apply to the international policies of other states. "Peace" is an absolute value; it represents one of G-d's names. As will be shown, however, the Biblical approach to peace, and subsequent Talmudic and rabbinic elaboration of that approach, has many features that are unique to Israel. Only insofar as "peace" can be understood beyond those features might the halakhic context provide guidelines for the pursuit of peace on the part of non-Jewish states.

SOVEREIGN ISRAEL AND THE PURSUIT OF PEACE

There is relatively little Biblical discussion regarding peaceful state-to-state relations with non-Jews. The Torah discusses individual arrangements with non-Jews, notably Abraham's treaty with Avimelekh, the king of Gerar, which the midrash criticizes in harsh terms.[10] The Torah outlines Jacob's treaty with Laban,[11] which committed both parties to peace as long as they did not violate their common territorial border. Finally, it recounts Jacob's reconciliation with Esau,[12] for which Jacob applied the same non-interaction policy that appeared to have worked so well for him with Laban. In legislating for the nation as a whole, however, the Torah focuses primarily on a different set of considerations. These comprise the extermination of certain nations – Amalek[13] and the Seven Nations;[14] a permanent state of war against Ammon and Moab;[15] military operations against Midian;[16] or the ability of members of certain nationalities to join the Jewish community.[17]

When the Torah does discuss peace, it does so in terms rather different from those commonly understood today. In the course of laying down military rules of engagement, the Torah tells Israel that when approaching a city to besiege it, "proclaim peace unto it."[18] The conditions for peace involve an agreement on the part of the inhabitants to provide both tribute (*mas*) and involuntary labor. The definition of tribute is self-evident. Ramban defines involuntary labor as hewing wood and drawing water – the role Joshua assigned to the Gibeonites – for any Jew that requires these services at any time of his choosing as long as he is prepared to pay for them.[19]

In addition, the Rabbis also require that non-Jews, including the Seven Nations, who are under threat of attack inside territorial Israel also accept upon themselves the Seven Noahide laws.[20] Indeed, the Rabbis identify this latter provision as the basis for the continued existence of Canaanite residents in Israel long after it was conquered by Joshua. According to the strict reading of the same chapter of

Deuteronomy, such a situation could not have obtained, since the offer of peace could only be made available to "distant" cities, as opposed to members of the Seven Nations, for whom extermination was the only option.

"Peace," as the term is used in Deuteronomy, is thus more akin to the Treaty of Versailles, a harsh peace to which difficult conditions are attached. It is not even a peace that emerges from negotiations subsequent to a conflict, as that of Versailles, but rather one that actually precedes it.[21] This was the peace that Joshua offered the Canaanite nations, all of whom refused it, apart from the Gibeonites. Indeed, Abravanel argues that even the Gibeonites rejected this form of peace. It was precisely to avoid the conditions that attached to Joshua's offer that the Gibeonites resorted to trickery, eliciting from Joshua a *berit shalom*, a peace treaty between equals, or as Abravanel puts it, a treaty reflecting "deep love...unburdened by taxes or any other obligations."[22]

Tanakh offers few, if any, instances, of the kind of *berit shalom* in the sense that Abravanel would describe it.[23] Peace among equals, without a hint of deep affection, does appear to describe both Abraham's treaty with Avimelekh and Jacob's treaty with Laban. It likewise characterizes Jepthah's interaction with the Ammonites as outlined in Judges; Jepthah is prepared to live in peaceful co-existence with the Ammonites, but the Ammonites reject Jepthah's offer, much to their subsequent regret.[24]

Kings and Chronicles describe the peace between Solomon and Hiram, who is credited with providing the materials for construction of the Temple. There is no indication of any deep affection between the two, however, and they did have a dispute over some territory that Solomon ceded to Hiram that was not of the quality the latter had expected.[25] Moreover, Hiram is not universally admired in later Jewish writings.[26] In particular, the Talmud describes him in rather unflattering terms, while also devising rather tortuous explanations for Solomon's willingness to cede what seems to have been consecrated territory to his erstwhile ally.[27] Nevertheless, Hiram and Solomon's kingdom clearly coexisted in peace for a number of years.

While some historians point to later peace treaties between the Davidic line and other nations, *Tanakh* refers to none explicitly[28]. There were treaties between Judah and the Northern kingdom, most of which brought on prophetic scorn, and others between the Northern Kingdom and the likes of Aram, which similarly won no plaudits from the prophets. Indeed, other than the generally positive references to benevolent Persian rule in the books of Ezra and Nehemiah, there is no further record of peace, as it is commonly understood, between a Jewish political entity and its non-Jewish neighbors.[29]

In any event, such agreements fit neither of Abravanel's models. They were not Versailles-like imposed treaties, nor did they constitute reflections of deep amity between the Jews and another nation.

Biblical "peace" therefore generally reflects a concept that is markedly different from that which has come to be understood in modern times. It is harsher than "unconditional surrender," which is a condition for the termination of war. It is harsher than a negotiated post-war treaty, since it is a precondition for the avoidance of combat operations and allows for no negotiation, as the Gibeonites learned to their regret. It allows for no meaningful post-war arrangements. It is not *berit shalom*.

TALMUDIC DISCUSSIONS OF WAR
AND PEACEFUL COEXISTENCE

The Talmud does not fundamentally change the Biblical notion of peace. Instead, its primary focus is to elucidate the nature of war. *Sotah*[30] and *Sanhedrin*[31] discuss two categories of war – mandatory wars (*milhemet mitzvah*) and permitted or discretionary wars (*milhemet reshut*). *Sanhedrin* states that a discretionary war requires the leadership of a king, the priest who serves as *mashuah milhamah* (the spiritual commissar, literally "anointed for war"), the direction of the *urim ve-tumim*, and the Sanhedrin as representatives of the people.[32]

The Talmud also speaks of a third type of war, one of self-defense, which does not call for the prerequisites that pertain to the other forms of warfare.[33] It is as wars of self-defense that the operations Israel has undertaken have been justified, even the launching of the 1982 Lebanon War, which most secular observers considered to be a preemptive attack. The Lebanon War was launched to achieve more than just self-defense, however; it was to establish a peace treaty with that country's Maronite leaders that would ensure a permanent settlement on Israel's northern border.[34] In that regard, it is somewhat different from wars of self-defense discussed in the Talmud. Such wars are discussed in the narrow context of a potential enemy attack, and the need for an appropriate response. The nature of peace in the aftermath of such a conflict, much less its role as an objective of a preemptive military operation, does not command much attention from either the Talmud or its commentaries.

The Talmud says little that is positive about peaceful coexistence with other nations. There are the documented relations between Rabbi Judah ha-Nasi and "Antoninus," most likely the Emperor Caracalla.[35] Rabbi Joshua ben Hanania is reported to have met with the Emperor Trajan.[36] The Talmud also notes the interaction between the *amora* Mar Samuel, head of the yeshiva at Nahardea, and *Shevor Malka*, identified as the Sassanid king Shapur I.[37]

While these rabbis, particularly R. Judah ha-Nasi and Mar Samuel, were communal leaders, the fact that they met and spoke with non-Jewish royalty is no indication of any formal arrangements between the Jews and their hosts, although Mar Samuel's dictum of *dina de-malkhuta dina* did reflect his efforts to promote harmony between the Jewish community and its Sassanid rulers.[38] In general, the Talmud demonizes those with whom such arrangements were adopted. Laban is invariably described as evil.[39] So, too, is Esau,[40] the historic proxy for Rome and Christianity. Coexistence is represented as a harsh necessity; reconciliation is unthinkable. "Esau hates Jacob"[41] has long been the watchword of those opposed to Jewish interaction with the outside world.

The Commandment to Show No Mercy: Lo Tehanem. When enjoining the Children of Israel to exterminate the Seven Nations, the Torah underscored the absolute nature of this commandment with the injunction to show them no mercy.[42] Both the Babylonian

Talmud and the Jerusalem Talmud highlighted views that expanded the Biblical prohibition on showing mercy to the Seven Nations in two critical ways. First, it was argued that *lo tehanem* could also incorporate a prohibition on the sale of property inside consecrated Israel.[43] Second, the case was made that this prohibition applied to the sale of property to all idolators, not just the Seven Nations.[44]

While the Biblical context in no way explicitly supported either argument,[45] subsequent halakhic decisors have generally adopted both interpretations. Indeed, most decisors have further expanded the prohibition to all non-Jews, even if they are not manifestly idolators.[46] Some have even attempted to apply the prohibition outside the land of Israel as well.[47]

It would appear that these rulings mandated a permanent state of tension with non-Jews, and effectively obviated meaningful coexistence with their non-Jewish neighbors. In fact, they did not necessarily rule out coexistence *per se*. Their practical effect was to apply a brake to the expansion of non-Jews into Jewish territory in the years that followed the Destruction of the Temple and again after the Bar Kokhba revolt.[48] They likewise were applied in the Diaspora to preserve the integrity of Jewish neighborhoods. As long as Jewish areas were preserved intact, however, it need not have been inevitable that there be tension with surrounding non-Jewish towns or neighborhoods. Nevertheless, the application of *lo tehanem* to post-Biblical circumstances could only have reinforced prejudices that colored the views that Jews and non-Jews had of each other.

The Three Vows. In contrast to the laws deriving from *lo tehanem*, the Talmudic statement regarding three vows that God imposed upon the Jews and the other nations appears to promote coexistence. The Jews were enjoined both from going to war to recapture Israel and from rebelling against the nations of the world. The latter, for their part, were ordered to vow not to treat Israel with excessive harshness.[49]

The rationale behind the oaths imposed upon the Jews was straightforward: it was a matter of their self-preservation. Rabbi Jose bar Hanina, and those of his generation living under the Antonine Caesars, recognized that another rebellion could lead to the extermination of the Jewish people. Some Jews were leaving the fold in despair. In addition, and crucially, "the reduced circumstances of the Jews after the [Bar Kochba] war made it necessary for them to work more closely with the non-Jewish element in the country. Out of this need arose a doctrine favoring coexistence and cooperation with gentiles in social and economic spheres."[50]

There were limits to coexistence, however, as the laws derived from *lo tehanem* made clear. Moreover, the oaths were very much a concession to an unpleasant, indeed, harsh reality. It is difficult to argue that they pointed to an ideal norm. Indeed, the third oath, addressed to the non-Jews, underscored the subservient status of the Jewish people; it was hoped that the Romans, and in later centuries, so many others, would show some moderation in their behavior toward the Jews.[51]

Special Status of Certain Nationalities. A third line of Talmudic discussions of peaceful coexistence relates to the permissibility of various nationalities to intermarry with the Jewish people. The Talmud rules that the biblical ban on Moabites and Ammonites applies only to males. It also concludes that once Sannecherib of Assyria dislocated the world's nations (*bilbel et ha-umot*)[52] these nationalities, and possibly Egyptians and Edomites, no longer can be identified. Intermarriage with any of these nations is therefore no longer is an issue.

RAMBAM ON PEACE BETWEEN A SOVEREIGN JEWISH STATE AND NON-JEWISH NATIONS

Maimonides' *Yad Ha-Hazakah* affords the major post-Biblical source for discussion of peace between a Jewish entity and its non-Jewish counterpart or counterparts. In the most frequently reproduced version of the *Yad*, the text states that it is forbidden to sign a peace treaty with the Seven Nations, unless they accept the Seven Noahide laws and accept the obligation of paying tribute to the Jewish state.[53] Rambam's statement elaborates upon what he had already posited in his earlier *Sefer ha-Mitzvot*.[54]

Although he does not say so explicitly, it is clear that Maimonides is referring to peace agreements not only with nations outside the Land of Israel, but those within it, since that is where the Seven Nations resided. In addition, he appears to be referring to military operations within territory that is either consecrated, or eligible for consecration. As he notes elsewhere, both obligatory and discretionary wars can only be fought in circumstances where the land is subject to consecration.[55] Moreover, it is arguable that Maimonides is referring to circumstances that can only obtain during the Messianic era, since his rules of military conduct, and of peacemaking concomitant with that conduct, are addressed in the first instance to a Jewish king.[56]

It is noteworthy that while most decisors and commentators adopt the version of the *Yad* that restricts the ban on peacemaking to the Seven Nations, and adhere to that view, there is an alternate reading that extends the ban to all nations. While conceding that Maimonides explicitly limited the ban in his *Sefer ha-Mitzvot*, and that indeed many of his *nos'ei kelim* likewise adopt a narrow reading of the Rambam in the *Yad*, R. Eliezer Waldenberg is not prepared to accept that the more expansive reading is, in effect, merely a scribal error.[57] Instead, perhaps because he is unwilling to rule out a ban on all peace agreements with non-Jews, he simply speculates that the alternate, broader reading of the Rambam could reflect a change of heart after he had completed *Sefer ha-Mitzvot*.

Adopting the reading of Maimonides that does not restrict the ban solely to the Seven Nations would also call in question whether Maimonides limited himself to conflicts on consecrated territory in the Land of Israel. Wars with other nations need not be mandatory; if they are indeed discretionary, which Maimonides defines as wars of territorial conquest, they invariably will be fought outside the Land of Israel. Under such circumstances, extension of a ban on peacemaking with non-Jewish nations would effectively obviate peace with non-Jews anywhere.

R. Waldenberg had every opportunity to reject such an expansive ruling, since he cites numerous decisors who do just that.[58] What troubles him is a passage in *Tanna de-Bei Eliyahu* that takes a very harsh position against any sort of intercourse with idolators. R.

Waldenberg points out that the midrash criticizes Abraham for his business partnership with Avimelekh. It notes that Abraham then went on to sign a treaty with the king, sparking protests from the angels that led to his being tested with the command to sacrifice Isaac. Moreover, the midrash adds, as a result of Abraham's signing a treaty with an idolator, "there is no nation that has not subjugated Israel for at least several hundred years."[59] Drawing explicitly upon this midrash, and in the face of the contrary views of the other halakhic decisors that he cites, R. Waldenberg therefore explicitly concludes that there is a case for the variant reading of the Rambam, and implicitly does not constrain that reading to the territory of the Land of Israel.

R. Waldenberg's conclusion appears to be unrestricted in terms of time as well as territory, so that it would apply today as well as in the Messianic era. Despite its cogency, his case is not easily sustained, at least within the context of Maimonides' ruling. For in addition to his other citations of decisors who take the more restrictive view, R. Waldenberg also quotes a ruling in *Yoreh De'ah* that not only explicitly limits the ban to the Seven Nations, but actually is a direct quote from Chapter 9 of the *Yad* itself. Specifically it states that "if Jews were living among idolators and concluded a treaty with them, they are permitted to provide weapons to the king's servants and his forces."[60] It is somewhat curious that R. Waldenberg cited this passage in the context of his discussion, since it refers to a rather different set of circumstances involving Jewish minority status. It is equally surprising that he did not identify that difference in the course of justifying his position. Most difficult of all, however, is why he did not acknowledge the Rambam as the original source of the statement. Whatever the reason, his case in support of the alternative reading of the Rambam becomes exceedingly difficult to defend. While it might have been plausible to argue that the Rambam reversed his position after completing *Sefer ha-Mitzvot*, it is virtually incredible that Maimonides would have expanded the ban in Chapter 10 after having restricted it in the previous chapter. R. Waldenberg's thesis therefore stands or falls primarily, if not solely, on a *midrash aggadah*.

Whether a midrash is a viable source of *pesak halakhah* has been the subject of debate since the Geonic period, and is an issue well beyond the scope of this paper.

OTHER DECISORS ON PEACE AND PEACEFUL COEXISTENCE BETWEEN SOVEREIGN ISRAEL AND NON-JEWISH STATES

As noted above, most other decisors adopt the common reading in the Rambam that limits the ban on peace with non-Jews to the Seven Nations. Yet some adopt a more nuanced approach to treaties with non-Jews than the Rambam, who argues that all such agreements must be predicated on the harsh terms laid out in Deuteronomy. The *Hinnukh* appears prepared to validate peace treaties with non-Jewish idolaters without any particular preconditions, as long as they do not live in Jewish territory. Should they choose to live in Israel, however, they must renounce idolatry (*elah she-lo yeshvu be-artzenu ad she-ya'azvu advodah zarah*).[61]

Like the *Hinnukh*, the *Semag* also adopts the more restrictive reading of the *Yad* regarding treaties with idolaters. He explicitly states that "with other nations, peace is permitted," citing both the Gibeonites and Solomon's treaty with Hiram. Since the *Semag* attaches no conditions whatsoever to such treaties, it appears that his position is even more lenient than that of the *Hinnukh*. To be sure, Joshua amended the terms of the Gibeonite treaty and thereby subjected them to helotry. Nevertheless, the *Semag* makes no mention of this fact, and simply treats Hiram, an independent king outside Israel, and the indigenous Gibeonites in equivalent terms.[62]

On the other hand, R. Moshe Mitrany takes an unequivocal hard line, akin to the variant reading of Maimonides. He states bluntly that "it is forbidden to sign a treaty with idolaters so that we can make peace with them and permit them to continue their idolatry." He does not appear to differentiate between nations living within Israel and outside it, except insofar as it affects those who would be killed if a peace offer is rejected. All are killed within Israel; only men are killed outside it.[63]

War (and Peace) in R. Kook's World View

R. Abraham Isaac Kook's writings about the nature and consequences of war were highly original, and deserve special mention in light of their impact on contemporary Israeli politics. R. Kook wrote his seminal *Orot* during the First World War. Despite the wreckage that the war had caused, which he witnessed from his vantage point in London, R. Kook saw war as a harbinger of the Messiah, which he termed the Messiah's "footsteps."[64] He felt that war served a number of functions toward that end: in particular, it revealed the folly of Western culture and it dislocated international structures and society, thereby enabling new forces, such as that for the creation of Jewish state, to emerge.[65]

R. Kook's view of peace was not as grounded in current affairs. It was an objective, an ideal, that could only be achieved when an independent, Torah-abiding Jewish state came into existence. Such a state would serve as a guidepost for other nations, bringing them into harmony with one another.[66]

R. Kook's religious nationalism has left an ambiguous legacy with respect to his views on the relationship between Jews and other nationalities. On the one hand, while he never blurred the "qualitative" distinction that existed between "the soul of Israel" and that of other nations, he nevertheless adopted a humanistic and universalistic approach to the nations. Their nationalism, which spurred that of the Jewish secular Zionists, was an unwitting contributing factor toward universal spiritual redemption.[67]

In contrast, some of R. Kook's disciples, following and expanding upon the lead of his son, R. Tzvi Yehudah Kook, have transmuted the elder R. Kook's legacy into a strident Jewish ultra-nationalism and glorification of war that allows for neither peace nor reconciliation with Israel's neighbors.[68] Arguing from an essentially racial perspective that individual nations represent particular character traits,[69] some of Rabbi Kook's disciples have nothing but scorn for non-Jews. "Peace," in this construct, would simply hark back to the original Biblical concept: it would essentially be a precondition for avoiding conflict, entailing full and unconditional submission to

Jewish authority and custom. Peaceful coexistence does not appear to be an acceptable option, if another choice is available; on the other hand, even cruelty in support of the higher objective of redeeming the Jewish people is to be condoned.[70]

Conditions for Peacemaking: The Nature of Sovereign Israel

All commentators agree that the Biblical description of "peace" as a precondition to the onset of warfare can only be realized in a sovereign Israel that fulfills a special set of requirements. First, the Jewish nation must be led by a king, specifically, a scion of the Davidic line. To be sure, *Tanakh* recounts other kings, namely Saul, a Benjaminite, and the various kings of the Ten Tribes. Yet those kings were specifically designated by prophets.[71] The Hasmoneans, and certainly later dynasties, did not merit any such official recognition, which is why they did not survive.[72]

Second, to initiate military operations a king must rule over all the land of Israel. It is not enough to rule a truncated kingdom, as was the case under Hasmoneans. Thus, only a duly authorized king of the Davidic family, who is sovereign over that entire territory, can undertake either mandatory or discretionary wars as they are defined in the Talmud.[73]

Even a king as halakhically defined cannot launch an operation on his own. He must have the assent of a duly constituted Sanhedrin.[74] He must have the sanction of the *urim ve-tumim*. Moreover, some commentators argue that he must also be ruling over virtually all Jews, as opposed to the kings of the Second Commonwealth, who ruled over only a portion of the worldwide Jewish population.[75]

There is one case whereby it is possible for Jews to undertake mandatory or permissive wars without being led by a king. Were a prophet to lead Israel, and were the entire population fully supportive, such wars might be permitted. Even in such circumstances, however, a duly constituted Sanhedrin would still have to function. Needless to say, neither king, nor prophet, nor Sanhedrin, exists today. Nor do all Jews live in Israel, nor are the *urim ve-tumim* at hand.

Launching a war as it is Biblically defined, whether it is a mandatory or discretionary war, is therefore moot.[76]

Peaceful Coexistence and Immunity From Jewish Attack

Most decisors agree that a sovereign Jewish state would no longer be bound by the Biblical restrictions on attacking Ammon, Moab and Edom.[77] Egypt presents a somewhat different case, since the ban on returning to Egypt may be a function of the land itself, not necessarily its people.[78] Some decisors nevertheless are of the opinion that a Jewish sovereign could invade Egypt as well, since in so doing he would consecrate the land and remove it of its impurities.[79] All other states appear to be fair game, insofar as they have not accepted the Seven Noahide laws.

On the other hand, given the absence of the requisite actors for carrying out a discretionary war, it would appear that there is no compulsion on the part of Israel to launch an attack against any of its neighbors, if there is no credible threat that they are planning a preemptive attack of their own. Determining the existence, credibility, urgency and magnitude of such a threat is a matter for military and intelligence specialists. Only then would a political leadership grapple with the various factors that might permit, or constrain, a preemptive, but nevertheless defensive, military operation such as the Sinai Campaign and the Six Day War. In all other circumstances, peaceful coexistence is at a minimum a viable option, if not the preferred one, except, perhaps, for those who would offer an extreme interpretation of R. Kook's writings.

Making Peace with Other Nations when Jews are a Minority

At first blush it appears counterintuitive that Jews could make treaties with other nations when they themselves enjoy at best minority status in foreign lands. Such treaties would go beyond mere peaceful coexistence with majority non-Jewish populations, a necessary condition for Jewish self-preservation. Yet both Maimonides and, following him, the *Mehaber*, rule specifically on the validity of such treaties. As noted above, they assert in identical language that Jews can reach formal agreements to serve as armaments suppliers to the governing non-Jewish authorities. This ruling, when repeated in *Yoreh De'ah*, is not modified by the Rema, and evokes minimal comment from the most frequently reproduced *nos'ei kelim* to the *Shulhan Arukh*. Its basis is R. Ashi's dictum in *Avodah Zarah*[80] that Jews may sell military provisions, including equipment and weaponry, to their Persian overlords because they will then be protected in the event of a conflict. Of course, implicit in R. Ashi's statement is that if Jews did *not* sell military provisions to the Persians, the latter might not be as willing to protect them in the event of an enemy attack.

It is noteworthy that R. Ashi did not actually discuss the sale of military materiel in the context of a peace agreement. It is Maimonides who does so. Indeed, the *Tur*, when recording R. Ashi's ruling, likewise is silent on the issue of peace. He simply updates Rav Ashi's view by lifting any restrictions that might have applied to particular weapons: "nowadays, it is customary to sell all forms of weaponry to non-Jews, because through them we are saved from enemies who attack the city."[81] It is the *Mehaber* who, by citing Maimonides verbatim, reinserts "peace" into the discussion of weapons sales to non-Jews.

Given the circumstances in which both Maimonides and R. Yosef Karo lived, however, it would appear that they actually are referring to an inter-communal agreement, rather than an actual treaty between equals. The Spain, Morocco, and Egypt of Maimonides' time, or the Ottoman province of southern Syria that was home to Rabbi Karo, did not accord to Jews a state of equality with their Muslim masters. As *dhimmi*, therefore, Jews might conclude communal arrangements with their non-Jewish neighbors; it essentially represented a codification of the peaceful coexistence that defined their unequal relationship. A treaty between equals, in its currently understood sense, or in the sense of *berit shalom*, as Abravanel would interpret it, was out of the question. So too, of course, was the kind of unequal peace that favored the Jews, such as that which Deuteronomy and Maimonides describe.

It should be noted that there is a difference between the "peace"

that relates to the sale of weapons, and laws relating to *"eivah."* In
order to prevent *eivah*, literally "enmity," the Rabbis enacted a series
of laws to address issues that might arise between Jews and non-Jews.
The laws of *eivah* do not only address interaction with non-Jews,
however. They also encompass many other relationships, including
those between husband and wife, parents and children, the ignorant
and the learned, and potential rivalries among *Kohanim.*[82] What all
of these laws have in common is that they address *individual* relationships. As noted above, laws governing individual circumstances
cannot automatically be extrapolated into regulations governing the
community or the nation. The ruling regarding the sale of weapons,
however, appears to derive from a *communal* relationship with the
governing power, since Maimonides' language, and thus that of the
Mehaber, employs the plural verb form (*hayu Yisrael shokhnim bein
ha-akum ve-kartu lahem berit…*).[83]

Co-Existence in Alien Societies

Although the years of exile were often marked by Jewish suffering
and dislocation, there were periods when Jews did coexist peacefully with their non-Jewish host communities. Indeed, Jews often
flourished in such circumstances. The "golden age" of Spanish Jewry
has been widely recognized as the prime exemplar of this phenomenon.[84] Less well known are the instances of Jewish communal
prominence in medieval Christian Europe; a number of these cases
were described in the recorded travels of Benjamin of Tudela.[85] What
is notable about these instances is that entire communities coexisted
with their neighbors, in contrast to the cases of individual Jews who,
due to a variety of circumstances, rose to prominence in Christian
or Muslim society.[86]

Some scholars also assert that the many instances over the
centuries in which non-Jewish authorities intervened to resolve
internal Jewish disputes "demonstrates how far the Jews were part
of the societies, cultures and polities in which they lived…Jews accepted the fundamental moral legitimacy of non-Jewish governing
institutions and, in many cases, were willing to trust their fairness."
Moreover, "the willingness of the non-Jewish authorities to intervene

shows that they viewed the Jewish community as an integral part
of the polity and Jewish institutions as no more than an arm of
their administration which happened to be designated to deal with
Jewish matters" [italics in original].[87] It is not at all clear that either
side really perceived the relationship in such positive terms, however. Certainly the interventions by Russian or German authorities
in various communal disputes in no way signified a sense of real
coexistence on the part of those authorities. They simply wanted
to maintain order – or influence outcomes. As for the Jews, their
contempt for those authorities was matched only by their inability to
resist them. Nevertheless, there is little doubt that in some cases, for
example, when Ottoman authorities intervened in Jewish disputes
during the reign of Sultans who were more friendly to the Jews, the
spirit of communal coexistence was very real.

Meiri's Attitude to Communal Co-Existence

Unlike the vast majority of decisors who preceded – and followed –
him, R. Menahem Ha-Meiri adopted an exceedingly tolerant attitude toward the majority Christian society within which he lived.
Ruling that Christianity was not idolatry, he articulated a series of
lenient positions regarding not only commerce with Christians, but
also their juridical status and, indeed, social standing vis-a-vis Jews.
Indeed, his definition of idolatry as being an absence of religious
restriction and his distinction between "idolaters and worshippers
of the Divine" meant that polytheism did not in itself translate into
idolatry.[88] As long as nations "were restricted by the ways of religion," as Christianity certainly was, they would not be considered
idolatrous.[89]

Meiri's view clearly fostered harmonious inter-communal relations. For example, his ruling permitting Jews to visit and warmly
greet Christians on their festival days not only represented a sharp
break with previous rulings,[90] but could only have had the effect of
engendering comity between the two often hostile communities.
Indeed, by ruling that one could prepare food for Christians on
Yom Tov, thereby seemingly including Christians within the class
subsumed within the Torah's term "for you," he went even further

toward regarding Christianity as a sister religion, much as Muslims regard Judaism and Christianity.[91]

Despite the consistency of his views throughout his commentary, and the power of his reputation, the fact that Meiri was, and remained, virtually a lone voice is testimony to the widespread lack of harmony between the two religious communities. Jewish hostility toward Christians was a mechanism for self-preservation. It was also the reciprocal of the maltreatment that Jews suffered at the hands of Christians. Nevertheless, Meiri's rulings do point to a strand in Judaism that could anticipate better communal – and perhaps inter-state – relations under circumstances different from those that prevailed in most of Europe until quite recently (and, unfortunately, continues to prevail in many parts of that continent).

Peace, Sovereignty, and the State of Israel

It is self-evident that the concept of Jewish communal "peace" arrangements with a non-Jewish majority outlined above cannot serve as a model for potential peace treaties between Israel and other states. The Jews are not a minority in Israel, but rather a powerful majority. They have their own military force that is the envy of the entire world.

Israel is widely believed to have nuclear weaponry, putting it in a class with a very small number of powerful states, and, if its command and control expertise is taken into account, probably ranking it no lower than the major European nuclear powers, Britain and France. Thus, the argument that *yad ha-goyim tekifah alenu*, which often accompanies discussions of Jewish arrangements with non-Jews, simply does not apply in the same sense to the State of Israel's relations with other states.

It is similarly obvious that the Biblical model, as encoded by Maimonides and others, likewise is not an appropriate one for modern day Israel. The Biblical model is essentially one of a Jewish state with untrammeled sovereignty, able to impose onerous conditions upon its enemies without reference to any exogenous factors or influences. Certainly, the State of Israel cannot force any non-Jews in territories that it conquers to choose between conversion and permanent vassalage on the one hand, or death on the other. But Israel's inability to do so derives not only from factors of *realpolitik* peculiar to a small Jewish state. It also results from the fact that it in no way could qualify for eligibility to carry out Biblical injunctions regarding peace with non-Jews even if it were a Jewish version of the Islamic Republic of Iran, ruled by religious leaders and, at least nominally, if not in fact, governed by religious law.

As outlined above, in order to impose its will upon non-Jewish nations without any constraints whatsoever, Israel would have to meet a number of conditions that will remain beyond its capability to fulfill for the foreseeable future. It has neither a king, nor a prophet, nor a Sanhedrin, nor the *urim ve-tumim*. All of these are conditions are only expected to be realized in the Messianic era.

To be sure, some conditions that attach to the commandment to exterminate one particular nation, Amalek, might be met in the pre-Messianic era, in particular that which requires that Jews live in peace in their land.[92] Yet leaving aside the highly charged halakhic issue of whether one can identify Amalek as a contemporary nation,[93] the injunction to exterminate that nation likewise requires that a king rule over Israel. Therefore, even if one were to set aside international norms on the one hand and questions of Amalek's identity on the other, it would nevertheless be impossible to fulfill this *mitzvah* at this time.

If the Biblical model is inappropriate and the communal model is inappropriate, what kind of guidance can Halakhah provide for the formulation of Israel's national security policy as it might relate to the conduct of peace negotiations with other states? Are such negotiations within the bounds of Halakhah, and if so, what principles should guide them?

Is Reconciliation an Acceptable Policy Outcome, and Peaceful Coexistence a Viable Objective?

To come to grips with these questions, it is first necessary to evaluate the nature of sovereignty as it affects all states, not only Israel, within the international community. Israel is not alone in having to meet international norms. The international system simply does not permit any state, however powerful or however isolated, to enjoy unimpeded sovereignty.

It is widely acknowledged that the United States is the single most powerful nation on earth, a "hyperpower" as then-French foreign minister Hubert Vedrine put it. Some would go further, and argue that the United States is the greatest military power in history. Nevertheless, despite assertions to the contrary, America would not be able to implement a unilateral international security policy even if it sought to do so, which it has not. Its membership in international organizations, such as the United Nations, the World Trade Organization, the International Monetary Fund, and the World Bank, as well as the multinational alliances – NATO and the Rio Treaty – and bilateral alliances to which it adheres, all constrain its freedom of action to a greater or lesser degree.

America's current experience in both Iraq and Afghanistan testify to the constraints that the world's greatest power has voluntarily accepted upon itself when conducting military operations. Prior to launching operations against either country, Washington sought UN support in the form of Security Council Resolutions. Subsequent to undertaking Operations Enduring Freedom and Iraqi Freedom, the United States argued (even if others disagreed) that it was indeed operating consistent with the will of the UN.

In both cases, as indeed in the case of the first Gulf War, the United States did not fight alone, but rather as part of a "Coalition of the Willing." Dozens of countries supported one or the other of the operations, providing combat forces, materiel, financial support, or transit rights. In fact, there were far fewer countries that opposed the war than those that provided support toward its success.

Subsequent to the successful end of major combat operations in Iraq, the United States organized a Coalition Provisional Authority to govern that country. Again, Washington sought and received support from UN Security Council Resolutions and contributions from other states, both in terms of manning the Authority and in terms of financial wherewithal to sustain it. At the same time, the United States sought, and received, active military participation on the ground for post-conflict operations. Countries as diverse as

Britain, Italy, Poland, Ukraine, Japan, and Mongolia are all part of the coalition whose forces are deployed in Iraq today.

In theory, the United States military, the most powerful the world has ever seen, could have launched operations without the support of any other state. But geography and logistics, as well as international politics, rendered such a unilateral operation moot. Similarly, the United States could have undertaken to govern Iraq on its own, without seeking any form of UN blessing, or any troops and or resources from other states. But the United States has chosen not to stretch its resources or isolate itself politically. Israel, far less powerful, and with fewer friends internationally, could not be expected to function any differently. This is not just a matter of *realpolitik*[94] but of reality.

Does Israel therefore lack real independence or sovereignty? By no means is that the case. It certainly is an independent, sovereign state, able to make decisions affecting its citizens without the need for approval from another capital. But, like all other states, Israel's sovereignty is delimited by international arrangements, to most of which it voluntarily adheres. In that sense, it represents a more robust version of both the independent, but short-lived, Maccabean state and the Jewish state that functioned even more briefly under Agrippa I, who was appointed by the Roman Emperor but was then able to conduct his country's affairs with some degree of independence, and who even intervened on behalf of his Jewish brethren in the Diaspora.[95]

Modern-day Israel has significantly more freedom to conduct its internal affairs than Agrippa ever did, and its ability to exert its influence abroad exceeds by far that of the Hasmoneans, who spent most of their time trying to establish their own authority within their rump kingdom. International constraints upon it certainly exist, but it is not at all clear that they are greater than for most other states. In theory, Israel could attempt to function as a kind of hermit state, a Jewish North Korea, operating on its own without regard to the views of others. It would not need to be as strong as any state, much less the United States, only strong enough to fend off enemies, a sort of international porcupine. In such circumstances, it could be argued, pursuing a "peace" policy that in some way derives from aspects of the "peace" outlined in Deuteronomy might at least seem feasible.

There are no true hermit states in today's world, however. Even those that are thought of as rogue states both seek international support and are subject to pressure from friends and enemies alike. It was such pressure that recently led Libya to terminate its nuclear weapons program, much as South Africa and Argentina did in years past. North Korea, perhaps the most hermetically sealed of all states, has to appeal to China, and even the United States, for economic, especially agricultural, assistance. It cannot function alone and has never closed the door entirely on an accommodation with South Korea and the Free World.

It might nevertheless be argued that Israel should seek to ghettoize itself to the maximum extent possible, creating a kind of *Meah Shearim* within the international community. It could rely upon its arms to coexist with others, and avoid reconciling itself with any other state or nation. In this regard, the laws of both *eivah* and *darkei shalom*, although they are geared to individual behavior, may have particular relevance for national Jewish behavior as well.

Relating to the "Other:"
A Key Principle Underlying *Eivah* and *Darkei Shalom*

It will be recalled that the laws of *eivah* are essentially intended to forestall resentment between interacting parties. Resentments are not restricted to individuals; history is full of resentments that have been magnified on a national scale. The Treaty of Versailles led to German resentment that unleashed the Nazi monster. Great Russian dominance of the Soviet Union nurtured national resentments that led to a break-up of that country, while Soviet subjugation of Eastern Europe bred resentment that drove the nations of that region into the hands of the West as soon as they had the freedom to choose their own destinies.

The laws of *eivah*, like those of *darkei shalom*, recognize that it is counterproductive to demonize the "other," that doing so will aggravate tensions that may already exist, or breed new ones that heretofore were non-existent. Understanding the feelings, goals and aspirations of the "other" is a central tenet of modern day practitioners of conflict resolution, a discipline that has not been without its successes (Macedonia is a recent example). In Jewish terms, recognition of the other, as reflected in laws of *eivah* and *darkei shalom*, can involve, among others, the "*am ha-aretz*," the *kohen* who is temporary *kohen gadol*, or the non-Jew.

The guiding principle of recognizing the humanity of those who are different is made easier by the fact that none of the ancient nations that are demonized in the Torah are identifiable today. As noted above, the Talmud tells us that Sennacherib *bilbel ha-umot*, thereby destroying the identities of the Seven Nations, and of many others besides. Even those who appear to be direct descendents of identifiable nations in the Bible, such as the Ishmaelites, really are not considered as such by Halakhah.[96] The State of Israel thus has no recognizable ancient enemies, just as it would have no way of recreating the ancient means of dealing with them even if they could have been identified.[97] There is therefore no Biblical barrier relating to the ethnic nature of its current enemies that might prevent Israel from seeking to understand and subsequently engage them in peaceful enterprise.

Conclusion:
Peace for a Jewish State is a Halakhically Viable Objective

This paper has thus far attempted to demonstrate that the conditional "peace" discussed in the Torah and subsequently in the Talmud and in halakhic rulings and responsa is one that is not applicable or attainable in current international affairs. Both the halakhic conditions and the unadulterated sovereignty necessary for its realization simply do not apply. Equally inapplicable is the "peace" that a Jewish community, whether in Israel or the Diaspora, might arrange with its more powerful overlords. Nevertheless, Halakhah does not rule out peace as it is commonly understood in the context of international relations.

To begin with, there is no ban on Israel's reaching agreements with neighboring non-Jewish states. Indeed, such agreements have been anticipated in the responsa literature.[98] Even an agreement with Syria, which clearly would involve the return of territory, is not beyond the realm of halakhic acceptability, although there are rabbis who argue that it is part of historic Israel.[99] Moreover, such agreements could involve, beyond peaceful coexistence, at least some degree of reconciliation.

The central issue, of course, is whether Israel could reach an agreement with the Palestinians that does involve the cession of territory that is part of the ancient Jewish patrimony. Many extra-halakhic factors would enter into such a decision, beginning with the limitations on Israeli sovereignty noted above, and its vulnerability to international pressures as a result of those limitations. Indeed, in addition to pressures that might to brought to bear upon Israel as a result of its active participation – and desire to become even more entwined – in the international community, Israel remains vulnerable to special pressures from the United States, which, while remaining committed to Israel's security, constantly retains the option of conditioning its massive monetary assistance upon the achievement of a settlement with the Palestinians.

Yet Halakhah itself offers considerable room for maneuver on this issue. There is no ethnic bar to reaching peace with the Palestinians. The Biblical conditions for launching a war of conquest against them to resolve their status once and for all simply do not exist. Nor does there exist a requirement to convert them to the Seven Noahide laws.[100] Indeed, Palestinian Muslims, and according to the Meiri, even Palestinian Christians, may well qualify as *geirei toshav*.[101]

In addition, the laws of *lo tehanem* do not apply when life is at stake, and it is the threat to life that ultimately would have to justify the yielding of any territory to non-Jews.[102] And the principles of *eivah* in particular, and *darkei shalom* to a lesser extent, mandate that consideration must be given to the legitimate hopes of ordinary Palestinians who simply wish to go about living their own lives in peace and prosperity. In fact, it is these very principles that can be applied, and – perhaps unconsciously – have been applied, to the resolution of conflicts between non-Jewish states and Jewish sub-state units elsewhere in the world.

To say that Halakhah permits the search for a peace agreement

with the Palestinians does not automatically lead to particular conclusions about how much territory to cede to a Palestinian government and whether or not to uproot Jewish towns, villages, or
settlements. Nor does it imply that Jews and Palestinians will become any more reconciled than Jacob and Laban. But neither does
it forestall the possibility they might live peacefully alongside each
other, as Jacob and Laban did, while the bonds of the international
community, and those of time, might possibly result in a dissipation
of long-standing hostility.

In any event, halakhic decisors are unlikely to have the final
word on the nature and scope of a peace agreement between Israel
and any of its neighbors, Palestinians included. These matters will
inevitably be the purview of political, economic, and especially
military experts. The latter in particular will determine the degree
to which an agreement can best enhance Israeli national security,
in other words, whether such an agreement truly achieves *pikuah
nefesh* for the Jewish people in Israel.[103] Nevertheless, peace, as it
is understood in its modern, secular sense, is a religious, halakhic
value that can, and should, color Israeli policy as its addresses its
geopolitical predicament. And it should also be central to any perspective that committed Jews everywhere might bring to debates
over contemporary international security policy.

NOTES

1. *Berakhot* 64a.
2. For a thorough discussion, see the entry *Darkei Shalom*, in the *Encyclopedia Talmudit*, vol. vii, Columns 716 ff.
3. Ibid.
4. Gerald J. Blidstein, "*Tikkun Olam*," in David Shatz, Hayyim I. Waxman, and Nathan J. Diament, eds., *Tikkun Olam: Social Responsibility in Jewish Thought and Law* (Northvale, nj and London: Jason Aaronson, 1997), pp. 56 ff. Walter Wurzberger is somewhat more tentative, stating that "at least for Maimonides, and possibly for many other Jewish authorities, the ways of peace are treated as the ethical reli- gious norm and not merely as a pragmatic device to safeguard Jewish self-interest." See Walter S. Wurzburger, "*Darkei Shalom*," in *Gesher: Bridging the Spectrum of Orthodox Jewish Scholarship*, p. 86. I am grateful to Rabbi Jack Bieler for drawing my attention to this article.
5. He is now *Dayan* and leader of the *Edah Haredit* in Jerusalem.
6. *Teshuvot ve-Hanhagot*, vol. i, no. 824. This is not a universal view. See for example

Hiddushei Rabbi Ephraim Mordekhai (Ginsburg) *al ha-Rambam: Hilkhot Melakhim*, ch. 10, who argues that even in private there is a reality *(ita le-metzi'ut)* of *kiddush* and *hillul Hashem.*

7. Ran on *Gittin* 61a, who takes issue with Rashi's dictum that one buries non-Jews only when their bodies are found with those of Jews. See also *Yam Shel Shelomoh's* citation of the Ran on that passage. See also *Bah, Yoreh De'ah* 151: "*asur*" and *Shakh*, op. cit., 151:12, n. 19; *Taz*, n. 9; *Gra*, n. 20; *Semag, Hilkhot Tzedakah*, no. 162.

8. The Talmud describes King David's attack on Syria as a discretionary war (*Sotah* 44b). The question of whether halakhic dictates regarding individual behavior can necessarily be transferred to the behavior of a Jewish nation-state is one that is so complex that it can evoke seemingly conflicting views on the part of the same author. J. David Bleich cites numerous sources that outline the criteria for distinguishing between what he terms "communal" and "private" conquests, offering the case of King David's conquest of Syria as a prime example; see *Contemporary Halakhic Problems* vol. II (New York: Ktav, 1983), pp. 175 ff. On the other hand, he states unequivocally in vol. III of that work (New York: Ktav, 1989), p. 304, that "what is true for the individual is true for a community or a nation as an aggregate of individuals." Any senior official serving in a democratically elected government would confirm that R. Bleich's earlier distinction between individual and communal or national interests is a more accurate portrayal of contemporary political reality. (Since identifying the apparent contradiction in R. Bleich's writings, I have been told by Professor Judith Bleich that Rabbi Bleich did not intend that his assertion in Volume III of *Contemporary Halakhic Problems* should be interpreted as somehow conflating individual and community interests.)

9. R. Yehuda Gershuni, "Minority Rights in Israel," in Ezra Rosenfeld, ed. *Crossroads: Halakhah and the Modern World*, vol. I (Alon Shvut/Gush Etzion, Israel: Zomet Institute, 1987), p. 19.

10. *Gen. Rabbah*, 54:5; *Seder Eliyahu Rabbah*, ch. 7.

11. Gen. 31:44–54, 32:1.

12. Ibid. 33:1–16.

13. Ex. 17:16, Deut. 26:19.

14. Deut. 20:16–18.

15. "Thou shalt not seek their peace nor their prosperity all thy days forever" (Deut. 23:7). R. Yitzhak Zev Soloveitchik points out that these nations are not eligible to be offered even the harsh preconditions for peace that are made available to others (see below), nor are they to be encouraged to accept the Noahide laws. If they do so of their own volition, however, they can be accepted as resident aliens (*gerei toshav*). See *Hiddushei Maran Ri'z Ha-Levi: Hilkhot Melakhim* 6:6.

16. Num. 26:16–18, 31:1 ff.

17. These laws address who can marry into the Jewish nation – Ammonites and Moabites are permanently banned; Edomites and Egyptians are permitted after three generations (Ibid. 23:4, 8–9). As is well-known, these bans applied only to males; that is one of the primary themes of the book of Ruth.

18. Ibid. 20:10. There is a disagreement between Rashi and Nahmanides regarding the

nature of a conflict (actually a "city" under siege) referred to in the text. Rashi, citing *Sifrei*, is of the view that the conflict is permissible, but in such circumstances, even if the inhabitants are of the Seven Nations, their lives can be spared. Nahmanides argues that the Biblical ruling regarding an offer of "peace" applies even to a mandatory war against the Seven Nations – for indeed Sihon was king of one such nation (the Amorites) – yet Moses offered Sihon peace before attacking him.

19. Ramban, Deuteronomy 20:11. Maimonides defines servitude as a lowly, reviled status, akin to the Athenian Helots (*Yad ha-Hazakah: Hilkhot Melakhim* 6:1). See also R. Yehudah H. Henkin, *Benei Banim*, vol. II, excursus 3.

20. *Sifrei*, ch. 202.

21. David Hazony writes that "there is no discounting the fact that…the call to 'peace' refers to a peaceful *surrender* [author's italics] to invading Jewish forces. Not only are conflict and force preserved as legitimate ideas, but it is through their threat that peace is obtained." David Hazony, "Plowshares Into Swords: The Lost Biblical Ideal of Peace," *Azure* no. 3 (Winter 5758/1998), p. 95.

22. Abravanel's commentary, Joshua 9:15.

23. There is the case of the *berit shalom* with Pinhas, and there are also references in the prophets to the *berit shalom* with Israel. In both cases, G-d is a party to the arrangement, rendering it a rather different type of peace covenant.

24. Judges, 11:12, 32–33.

25. I Kings, 9:11–13.

26. *Midrash Tanhuma, Va-Era*, 9.

27. See Abravanel on I Kings, 9:10.

28. See, for example, John Bright, *A History of Israel*, 3rd ed. (Philadelphia: Westminster, 1981), p. 285. Basing himself on passages in Isaiah 30:1–7 and 31:1–3, Bright argues that Hezekiah sent envoys to Egypt and negotiated an anti-Assyrian treaty. The passages are ambiguous, however. Rashi attributes them to Hoshea ben Elah. Radak speculates that they might indeed refer to Hezekiah, but points out that there is no clear guidance from the verses themselves (ibid. 30:1).

29. Despite their cordial relations with the Persians, the books of Ezra and Nehemiah stress the degree to which their eponymous protagonists, and especially Nehemiah, went to great lengths to distance the Jewish community from its non-Jewish neighbors.

30. 44b.

31. 2a and 16a.

32. Meiri, cited in R. Zvi H. Zakheim, *Tzvi ha-Sanhedrin*, Vol. I, p. 257. For an excellent overview, see *Contemporary Halakhic Problems*, Vol. III, R. J. David Bleich, 251 ff.

33. There is an extensive literature that discusses the nature of these wars. Some scholars, e.g. Meiri, loc. cit., include wars of self-defense as mandatory wars. According to Maimonides, the disagreement between the *tanna kamma* and R. Yehudah in the Mishnah *Sotah* 44b focuses on a war of self-defense. The first *tanna* considers it a discretionary war, R. Yehudah, a mandatory war, thereby freeing Jewish troops from the burden of other commandments. Maimonides rules according to the first

tanna (*Peirush Hamishnayot*: "*be-milhemet reshut*)." For a discussion see R. J. David Bleich *Contemporary Halakhic Problems*, Vol. III, pp. 271–78, 289–91.

34. Recent halakhic decisors have argued that the Lebanon War was a defensive war; see for example Bleich, ibid., especially pp. 289–91 and R. Henkin, *Benei Banim*, Vol. II, excursus 3. See however, Ze'ev Schiff and Ehud Ya'ari, *Israel's Lebanon War*, trans. Ina Friedman (New York: Simon and Schuster, 1984), pp. 39–43. Israel's defensive operation ended when its forces penetrated more than forty kilometers into Lebanon, that distance being its announced objective. Ya'ari and Schiff (the latter is internationally acknowledged as one of Israel's foremost military analysts) argue persuasively that defense minister Ariel Sharon misled his own cabinet and prime minister as he ordered the Israeli Defense Forces to march to Beirut (see pp. 301–306).

35. See Gedalia Alon, *The Jews in their Land: in the Talmudic Age* ed. and trans. Gershon Levi (Cambridge, MA: Harvard, 1984), p. 682.

36. *Berakhot* 9a.

37. *Berakhot* 8b–9a; *Sukkah* 33a; *Sanhedrin* 98a.

38. Menachem Elon, ed., *The Principles of Jewish Law* (Jerusalem: Encyclopedia Judaica, n.d.), Columns 710–11.

39. *Sanhedrin* 105a identifies Laban with Cushan Rishatayim (the doubly evil), who makes a brief appearance in Judges 3:8–11, and with Be'or, Balaam's father. The Passover Haggadah describes Laban as seeking to deracinate (*la-akor*) the Jewish people. *Avot of Rabbi Nathan* speaks of the idolatry in his household (Ch. 8). Other equally negative characterizations appear in Yerushalmi *Nazir* 9:1; *Gen. Rabbah*, 57:4; and *Gen. Rabbati*, 35:15.

40. *Yoma* 38b; *Bava Batra* 17b; *Pesikta de-Rav Kahana*, 3:34, 47 and other later midrashic works.

41. *Sifrei, Be-Ha'alotkha*, 69.

42. Deut. 7:2.

43. Dictum of R. Jose bar Hanina, *Avodah Zarah* 19b–20a. R. Zeira in the name of R. Jose Bar Hanina and R. Abba and R. Hiyya in the name of R. Yohanan, *Yerushalmi Avodah Zarah* 1:9.

44. Mishnah, ibid.

45. See *Torah Temimah*, Deuteronomy 7:2, note 1.

46. See *Minhat Hinnukh, mitzvah* 426.

47. *Tur* (*Yoreh De'ah* 151), *Beit Yosef* (loc. cit.) and *Shakh* (loc. cit., sub-section 15) prohibit selling to non-Jews three or more residences in a Jewish neighborhood. *Semag* (negative commandment no. 48) prohibits the sale of three adjacent houses to non-Jews when Jews would be living alongside them, but does not mention a Jewish neighborhood per se. See also the discussion under the heading *Hutz la-Aretz* in *Encyclopedia Talmudit*, Vol. XIII, column 363.

48. Alon, *Jews*, pp. 285–87.

49. *Ketubot* 111a. The version of R. Jose bar Hanina's dictum as it appears in *Shir Hashirim Rabbah* lists only two oaths. In addition, R. Levi cites six oaths, including

the three of R. Jose bar Hanina (*Ketubot* 111a) and the midrash quotes R. Helbo, who lists four oaths. *Midrash Tanhuma* (Deut. 4) lists three oaths, but none are attributed to non-Jews.

50. Alon, *Jews*, p. 642.

51. For a discussion of the contemporary application of the three vows, see R. Hershel Schachter, "*Yishuv Eretz Yisrael*," *Journal of Halacha and Contemporary Society* VIII (Fall 1984), pp. 27–29. See also R. Shaul Yisraeli, "Ceding Territory Because of Mortal Danger," in Ezra Rosenfeld, ed. *Crossroads: Halakhah and the Modern World*, vol. III (Alon Shvut/Gush Etzion, Israel: Zomet Institute, 1990), pp. 31–35 passim.

52. *Yadayyim*, 4:4. A variant reading is *bilbel ha-olam* (R. Eliezer Menachem Man Shach, *Avi ha-Eezri*, 3rd ed., *Hilkhot Melakhim*, 5:8.)

53. *Yad Ha-Hazakah: Hilkhot Avodat Kokhavim*, 10:1

54. *Sefer ha-Mitzvot, mitzvot* 48–51. Ramban lists "conquering the land" among those *mitzvot* that Rambam overlooked (positive commandment no. 4). Embedded in this commandment is the injunction against permitting other nations to maintain sovereignty over Eretz Yisrael. It is unclear, however, whether Ramban would advocate going to war to carry out the commandment. For differing views on this issue, see R. Nahum E. Rabinovitch, "The Conquest of *Eretz Yisrael* – The View of the Ramban," in Rosenfeld, ed. *Crossroads*, vol. II (Alon Shvut/Gush Etzion, Israel: Zomet Institute, 1988), pp. 186–87, and Rav Yaakov Ariel, "Conquest of the Land According to the Ramban," ibid., pp. 192–95.

55. For a discussion, see R. Israel Meir Lau, *Yahel Yisrael*, I, no. 26.

56. *Yad ha-Hazakah: Hilkhot Melakhim* 5:1 ff., 6:1–4.

57. *Tzitz Eliezer*, Vol. 15, no. 48.

58. Among those he cites are the *Hinnukh* and the *Semag*; their views are discussed more extensively below.

59. *Seder Eliyahu Rabbah*, loc. cit.

60. *Yoreh Deʾah* 151:6. This citation, which also appears in *Tzitz Eliezer*, would also appear to support a narrower reading of the Rambam, and R. Waldenberg acknowledges as much.

61. *Hinnukh, mitzvah* 93 and *Minhat Hinnukh*, loc. cit. See also the distinction that the latter draws between the position of the Rambam and that of the *Hinnukh*.

62. *Semag*, negative commandment no. 47. Alter Pinhas Farber notes that there are variant readings in the *Semag*'s introduction to this *mitzvah*: some include the term "in our land" in the opening statement of the prohibition on treaties with the Seven Nations. Other versions do not include the phrase, and would therefore restrict treaties with these nations wherever they resided. See Alter Pinhas Farber, ed. *Sefer Mitzvot Gadol: Semag* (n.p. 1992), Vol. II, p. 15. The language of the *Semag* discomfited a number of later commentators, because of its seemingly unconditional nature (see for example, the comments of R. Isaac Stein on this passage). It is nevertheless difficult to explain away the *Semag*'s treatment of Hiram and the Gibeonites on identical terms.

63. *Kiryat Sefer: Hilhot Avodat Kokhavim ve-Hukkot ha-Goyim*, ch. 10, *azhara* 41.

64. R. Avraham Yitzchak Ha-Kohen Kook, *War and Peace*, commentary by R. David Samson and Tzvi Fishman, Vol. II (Jerusalem: Torat Eretz Yisrael, 5757 [1997], p. 34.

65. Ibid., pp. 130, 152.

66. See his *Ein Aya, Berakhot* 64a, reproduced in *War and Peace*, pp. 358–59.

67. See Ella Belfer, *Be-Tzipiat ha-Yeshua ha-Shelemah:* The Messianic Politics of Rav Avraham Yitzchak Kook and Rav Tzvi Yehudah Kook," in Moshe Sokol, ed., *Tolerance, Dissent and Democracy: Philosophical, Historical and Halakhic Perspectives* (Jerusalem and Northvale, NJ: Jason Aaronson, 2002), especially pp. 355–61.

68. Kook, *War and Peace*, pp. 69 ff., 167 ff. It is important to emphasize that this interpretation of R. Kook's work is by no means universally shared by his followers. For a detailed discussion, see Belfer, *Be-Tzipiat ha-Yeshua ha-Shelemah*, pp. 311–61. See also, Eliezer Don-Yehiya, "Two Movements of Messianic Awakening and Their Attitude to Halakhah, Nationalism and Democracy: The Cases of Habad and Gush Emunim," Ibid., 284–85.

69. Ibid., Newton, Churchill and Shakespeare, among others, would no doubt be surprised to learn that the definition of the English character is to "stand politely in line" (p. 161). See also p. 158.

70. Ibid., p. 77.

71. *Yad ha-Hazakah: Hilkhot Melakhim* 1:8.

72. Ramban, Gen. 49:10. R. Abraham Isaac Kook argues that if, in the absence of a prophet, the Sanhedrin nevertheless appoints a king (*be-di'avad*), he is legally sovereign. See *Mishpat Kohen: Hilkhot Melakhim*, no. 144:15a.

73. *Teshuvot ve-Hanhagot* III, no. 222.

74. *Yahel Yisrael*, loc. cit.

75. *Teshuvot ve-Hanhagot*, loc. cit.

76. R. Yehudah Henkin argues that operations ordered by duly constituted military authorities do have the status of either mandatory or discretionary war, at least in certain circumstances, such as the rescue of hostages (he writes specifically about the 1976 Entebbe operation). He does not clearly indicate whether full-scale wars that Israel might initiate would have a similar status. See *Benei Banim*, vol. I no. 43.

77. While the identities of these nations are not certain, Ramban argues that their territories are included among those promised to Abraham. For a discussion see *Avi ha-Ezri*, 3rd ed., loc. cit.

78. *Minhat Hinnukh, mitzvah* 600; *Avi ha-Ezri*, loc. cit; *Hayyim Sha'al* 1:91.

79. *Mishpat Kohen: Hilkhot Melakhim*, no. 145.

80. 15a.

81. *Yoreh De'ah*, 151.

82. A good summary discussion may be found under the heading *Eivah* in the *Encyclopedia Talmudit*, vol. I, columns 488 ff.

83. *Yad ha-Hazakah: Hilkhot Avodat Kokhavim* 9:1.

84. There is a vast literature on the history of Spanish Jewry. The Government of Spain recently released its own contribution, a traveling exhibit of Sephardi culture. See Isidro G. Bango, *Remembering Sepharad: Jewish Culture in Medieval Spain* (Madrid: State Corporation for Spanish Cultural Action Abroad, 2003), see especially pp. 21–27.

85. For example, Benjamin wrote of the Jews of Rome: they "occupy an honorable position and pay no tribute and amongst them are officials of the Pope Alexander." *The Itinerary of Benjamin of Tudela*, trans. with commentary by Marcus Nathan Adler (London: Oxford University Press, 1909), p. 8.

86. While Jews, and their leaders, often invited non-Jewish authorities to mediate their disputes, such interventions did not necessarily reflect any real degree of peaceful coexistence between the Jews and their neighbors. For a discussion, see Moshe Rosman, "The Role of Non-Jewish Authorities in Resolving Jewish Conflicts in the Early Modern Period," *Jewish Political Studies Review XII* (Fall 5761/2000): 53–65.

87. Ibid., 62.

88. Moshe Halbertal, "'Ones Possessed of Religion': Religious Tolerance in the Teachings of The Meiri" trans. Joel Linsider, *Edah Journal* I (*Marcheshvan* 5761/2000) p. 8.

89. See, for example, Meiri's discussion in his commentaries on *Bava Kamma* and *Avodah Zara*: Kalman Schlesinger, ed. *Rabbi Menahem Hameiri's Commentary* BETH HABEHIRA *on the Talmud Treatise Baba Kamma* (Jerusalem, 1963), p. 330 (111b) and Abraham Schreiber, ed. *Beis Habechira al Maseches Avodah Zara* (Jerusalem: Kedem, 1964), pp. 4 (*hakdama*) and 9 (6b).

90. Halbertal, "Ones Possessed," p. 11. See Kalman Schlesinger, ed. *Rabbi Menahem Hameiri's Commentary* BETH HABEHIRA *on the Talmud Treatise Gittin*, (Jerusalem, 1965), pp. 257–58.

91. Kalman Schlesinger and Y.S. Lange, eds. *Rabbi Menahem Hameiri's Commentary* BETH HABEHIRA *on the Talmud Treatise Beitsah* (Jerusalem, n.p. 1959), pp.117–18; Halbertal, "Ones Possessed," p. 12.

92. For a discussion see the communication of R. Ezra Batzri in R. Yitzhak Nissim, *Yayn Hatov*, Vol. II, no. 4.

93. See ibid., which offers the views of R. Nissim (no. 2), Rabbi Shelomoh Karelitz (no. 3), R. Batzri (loc. cit.) and R. Hayyim Ozer Katz (no. 5).

94. See J. David Bleich, in "*Tikkun Olam*: Jewish Obligations," in Shatz, *et al.*, *Tikkun Olam*, p. 72.

95. Josephus, *Antiquities*, XVIII: 237, 252, 257 ff.; XIX 274–304 passim. Philo, *Flaccus*, 103. See also Alon, *The Jews in their Land*, p. 345, f.n. 1.

96. They are in fact seen as an admixture both of the sons of Keturah, about whom specific legislation relating to *milah* pertains, and the sons of Ishmael.

97. There is considerable dispute regarding the nature of Amalek, as noted above, n. 80.

98. See the comments of R. Batzri, loc. cit.

99. R. Eliezer Menachem M. Shach was well-known for his indifference to the return of the Golan if that was the price of peace; see Don-Yehiya, "Two Movements of Messianic Awakening," p. 287. For contrary views, see Bleich, *Contemporary Halakhic Problems*, vol. II, pp. 181–82.

100. Some would go so far as to forbid conversion, see *Halakhot u-Minhagot* Vol. III, no. 317. On the other hand, others are of the opinion that modern, enlightened nations do in fact come under the category of those who keep the Noahide laws. See *Torah Temimah*, Deut. 22:3, note 22; and *Benei Banim*, Vol. II, no. 45:3, who also quotes Meiri, *Bava Kamma* 113b.

101. Gershuni, "Minority Rights," pp. 32–33. As noted above, Meiri's rulings regarding Christians are a minority view; most decisors have followed Maimonides in considering them idolaters. Nevertheless, the fact that Meiri unambiguously argues that they are not idolaters, coupled with practical political considerations, not the least of which involves *darkei shalom*, render it difficult to distinguish between Palestinians of different creeds.

102. R. J. David Bleich, "Withdrawal from Liberated Territories as a Viable Halachic Option," *Journal of Halacha and Contemporary Society* XVIII (Fall 1989), p. 104; *Benei Banim*, Vol. II, No. 52; R. Ovadiah Yosef, "Ceding Territory of the Land of Israel in Order to Save Lives," in Rosenfeld, ed. *Crossroads*, Vol. III, pp. 17 ff. For an opposing view, see R. Shaul Yisraeli, "Ceding Territory because of Mortal Danger," pp. 29–46. R. Yisraeli appears to argue that any agreement will increase the threat to Jewish lives, hence the principle of *pikuah nefesh* overrides all other considerations. Moreover, R. Yisraeli argues that military advice is irrelevant, since the West Bank must be treated as a *sefar*, for which defenses can be mobilized on the Sabbath even against the mere threat of robbery (ibid., pp. 41–42). There is a significant difference between the West Bank and a *sefar*, however, no matter how liberally that term is defined (for varying interpretations, see Rashi and Rabbenu Yehonatan, *Eruvin* 45a, and the discussion in *Benei Banim*, Vol. III, no. 45). A *sefar* must be defended at all costs because its collapse in the face of an enemy renders neighboring Jewish towns vulnerable. The loss of a portion of the West Bank, on the other hand, would not necessarily render the rest of Israel vulnerable, since the State's powerful land forces, with close air support can be deployed to Israel's borders to prevent, and defend against, invading forces (R. Yisraeli's comment that long distance air attacks would be ineffective appears to confuse long range strike against terrorist incursions with close air support against massed forces). Only the military can determine whether the loss of a particular portion of the West Bank endangers the security and defensibility of remaining Israeli territory.

103. *Pikuah nefesh* remains the ultimate determinant, from both a halakhic and secular national security perspective, of the viability of any particular settlement regarding the future of the West Bank. For a discussion, see R. Ovadiah Yosef, "Ceding Territory of the Land of Israel," pp. 27–28.

ORTHODOX FORUM
Sixteenth Conference

Sunday & Monday, March 14 & 15, 2004
4–6 Adar 5763
Park East Synagogue
164 East 68th Street
New York City

LIST OF PARTICIPANTS

Rabbi Elchanan Adler	Mazer Yeshiva Program/Yeshiva University, New York, NY
Dr. Norman Adler	Yeshiva University, New York, NY
Prof. David Berger	Brooklyn College/Yeshiva University, New York, NY
Dr. Ditza Berger	Hebrew Academy of the Five Towns and Rockaway, NY
Rabbi Gedalyah Berger	Fleetwood Synagogue, Mount Vernon, NY & Yeshiva University, New York, NY
Rabbi Yitzhak Berger	Hunter College, New York, NY
Dr. Rivkah Blau	Author & Lecturer, New York, NY
Rabbi Yosef Blau	RIETS/Yeshiva University, New York, NY
Dr. Judith Bleich	Touro College, New York, NY
Prof. Alan Brill	Yeshiva University, New York, NY
Rabbi Michael Broyde	Emory University School of Law, Atlanta, GA

Rabbi Shalom Carmy	Yeshiva University, New York, NY
Prof. Jerome A. Chanes	Barnard College, New York, NY
Rabbi Zevulun Charlop	RIETS/Yeshiva University, New York, NY
Prof. Stuart Cohen	Bar-Ilan University, Ramat Gan, Israel
Mr. Nathan Diament	Orthodox Union, Washington, DC
Rabbi Mark Dratch	The Jewish Institute Supporting an Abuse-Free Environment, West Hempstead, NY
Ms. Betty Ehrenberg	Orthodox Union, New York, NY
Prof. Roberta Farber	Yeshiva University, New York, NY
Rabbi Daniel Feldman	Yeshiva University, New York, NY
Rabbi Ozer Glickman	RIETS/Yeshiva University, New York, NY
Dr. Martin Golding	Duke University, Durham, NC
Rabbi Jay Goldmintz	The Rabbi Joseph H. Lookstein Upper School of Ramaz, New York, NY
Rabbi Mark Gottlieb	Yeshiva University High Schools, New York, NY
Mr. Ira Green	Ranana, Israel
Rabbi Shmuel Hain	The Jewish Center, New York, NY
Prof. Malvina Halberstam	Benjamin N. Cardozo School of Law, New York, NY
Prof. Jonathan Helfand	Brooklyn College, Brooklyn, NY
Rabbi Nathaniel Helfgot	Yeshiva Chovevei Torah, New York, NY
Rabbi Basil Herring	Rabbinical Council of America, New York, NY
Rabbi Robert S. Hirt	RIETS/Yeshiva University, New York, NY
Dr. Elie Holzer	Bar Ilan University, Israel
Dr. Arthur Hyman	Bernard Revel Graduate School, Yeshiva University, New York, NY
Rabbi David A. Israel	RIETS/Yeshiva University, New York, NY
President Richard Joel	Yeshiva University, New York, NY

Rabbi Joshua Joseph	Yeshiva University, New York, NY
Prof. Zvi Kaplan	Yeshiva University, New York, NY
Rabbi Yaakov Kermaier	Fifth Avenue Synagogue, New York, NY
Dr. Eugene Korn	American Jewish Congress, New York, NY
Dr. Norman Lamm	Yeshiva University, New York, NY
Mr. Shalom Lamm	West Hempstead, NY
Dr. Herbert Leventer	Yeshiva University, New York, NY
Mr. Nathan Lewin	Attorney, Washington, DC
Rabbi Dov Linzer	Yeshiva Chovevei Torah, New York, NY
Rabbi Eitan Mayer	Menahel Hinukhi, Midreshet Moriah, Bayit v'Gan Israel
Mrs. Sally Mayer	Midreshet Lindenbaum/Noga High School, Beit Shemesh, Israel
Rabbi Adam Mintz	Visiting Lecturer: Judaic Studies Brooklyn College, Brooklyn, NY
Dr. Moses Pava	Yeshiva University, New York, NY
Prof. Michla Pomerance	Hebrew University, Mount Scopus, Israel
Mr. Yossi Prager	Avi Chai Foundation, New York, NY
Rabbi Yona Reiss	Beth Din of America, New York, NY
Ms. Jennie Rosenfeld	Tzelem at CJF/Yeshiva University, New York, NY
Prof. Smadar Rosensweig	Touro College, New York, NY
Rabbi Sol Roth	Yeshiva University, New York, NY
Rabbi Gidon Rothstein	Hebrew Academy of the Five Towns & Rockaway (HAFTR) Community Kollel, Cedarhurst, NY
Dr. Lawrence Schiffman	New York University, New York, NY
Dr. David Schnall	Azrieli Graduate School of Jewish Education and Administration, Yeshiva University, New York, NY
Mr. Carmi Schwartz	New York, NY
Rabbi Ezra Schwartz	Yeshiva University, New York, NY

Capt. Yosefi Seltzer	U.S. Army Legal Services Agency, Arlington, VA
Prof. Charles Selengut	Drew University, Madison, NJ
Dr. David Shatz	Yeshiva University, New York, NY
Rabbi Charles Sheer	Columbia University, New York, NY
Dr. Michael A. Shmidman	Touro College, New York, NY
Dr. Michael D. Shmidman	Yeshiva University, New York, NY
Dr. Moshe Sokolow	Azrieli Graduate School of Jewish Education and Administration, Yeshiva University, New York, NY
Mr. Marc D. Stern	American Jewish Congress, New York, NY
Prof. Suzanne Last Stone	Cardozo School of Law/Yeshiva University New York, NY
Prof. Moshe D. Tendler	RIETS/Yeshiva University, New York, NY
Dr. Chaim I. Waxman	Jewish People Policy Planning Institute, Jerusalem, Israel
Rabbi Jeremy Wieder Mazer	Yeshiva Program/Yeshiva University, New York, NY
Dr. Joel B. Wolowelsky	Yeshivah of Flatbush High School, Brooklyn, NY
Dr. Dov Zakheim	Consultant, McLean, VA
Prof. Noam Zohar	Bar Ilan University, Ramat Gan, Israel

Index

hillul Hashem (desecration of God's
name), xxv–xxvi, xxx,
5, 255–257, 259–260, 361,
362, 499
Holocaust, 206, 219
Holy War
apocalyptic, 477, 479–480
Biblical support for, xxxiv
defined, 478
homicide, condemnation of, 192
horaat shaah, xvii, 4, 234, 238
hostages, 106
hostile act, defined, 104
hostile force, defined, 104
hostile intent
in anticipatory self-defense, 97
defined, 104
hovah, 241
hubris, 144
humane treatment, of enemy
combatants, 11–12, 114
humanitarian interventions, 58, 68,
82, 86, 102
humanity, recognition of, 56
human rights, violations of, 58,
68, 96
human sacrifice, 82, 191
human shields
complicit, 106–107
use of, 73–74, 106, 326
Hundred Years War, 53
hyperpower, 519

I

idolatry, 176, 177, 191, 223–224, 388,
508, 516
illegitimate offspring, treatment of,
210, 224
indigenous populations, humane
treatment of, 275
innocent aggressors, 72–75
intermarriage, prohibitions against,
xxxvi, 213, 525

International Committee of the Red
Cross (ICRC), 113
International Court of Justice,
xxvii, 311
International Criminal Court, 103,
282, 308
international law, xviii,
xxiv–xxvii, 11
actions that legitimately fall
within, 96
applicability of to the
Jewish state, 249–251,
258–259, 267
binding nature of, 61–62
customary, concept of, 87–88
dina de-malkhuta dina (law of the
kingdom is law) model,
xxiv, xxv, 242–243
dinim (court systems) model,
xxiv–xv, 6–7, 244–246
enforceability of, 263
in Halakah, 241–251
mandatory nature of, 248–249
origins of, 54
rule of duty in, 84
twentieth-century, sources of, 61
international trade, 258
international tribunals, 102–103, 126
International Tribunal to Adjudicate
War Crimes Committed
in the Former
Yugoslavia, 103
interrogation, by private
contractors, 118
Iraq, xiii, 12
ir naddahat (punishment of a
subverted city), 135,
139–140
Israel
Ajuri judgment, 300
Arab attempts to delegitimize,
282–283
Biblical record of relations with